Performance culture and Athe

These new and specially commissioned ...ways in which performance is central to the practice and ideology of democracy in classical Athens. From theatre to law-court to gymnasium to symposium, performance is a basic part of Athenian society; how do these different areas interrelate and inform the politics and culture of the democratic city? Drama, rhetoric, philosophy, literature and art are all discussed by leading scholars in this interdisciplinary volume.

SIMON GOLDHILL is Reader in Greek Literature and Culture in the University of Cambridge and Fellow of King's College. He has published widely in Greek literature and culture. His books include *Reading Greek Tragedy* (1986), *The Poet's Voice: Essays on Poetics and Greek Literature* (1991) and *Foucault's Virginity: Ancient Erotic Fiction and the History of Sexuality* (1995).

ROBIN OSBORNE is Professor of Ancient History in the University of Oxford and Fellow and Tutor of Corpus Christi College. He has published widely in Greek history and archaeology. His books include *Demos: The Discovery of Classical Attika* (1985), *Classical Landscape with Figures: the Ancient Greek City and its Countryside* (1987), *Greece in the Making 1200–479* (1996) and *Archaic and Classical Greek Art* (1998).

Together Simon Goldhill and Robin Osborne edited *Art and Text in Ancient Greek Culture* (1994).

Performance culture and Athenian democracy

edited by
Simon Goldhill and Robin Osborne

PUBLISHED BY THE PRESS SYNDICATE OF THE UNIVERSITY OF CAMBRIDGE
The Pitt Building, Trumpington Street, Cambridge, United Kingdom

CAMBRIDGE UNIVERSITY PRESS
The Edinburgh Building, Cambridge CB2 2RU, UK
40 West 20th Street, New York NY 10011–4211, USA
477 Williamstown Road, Port Melbourne, VIC 3207, Australia
Ruiz de Alarcón 13, 28014 Madrid, Spain
Dock House, The Waterfront, Cape Town 8001, South Africa

http://www.cambridge.org

© Cambridge University Press 1999

This book is in copyright. Subject to statutory exception
and to the provisions of relevant collective licensing agreements,
no reproduction of any part may take place without
the written permission of Cambridge University Press.

First published 1999
First paperback edition 2004

Typeset in Plantin   [AO]

A catalogue record for this book is available from the British Library

Library of Congress cataloguing in publication data

Performance culture and Athenian democracy / edited by Simon Goldhill
and Robin Osborne.
    p.   cm.
Includes bibliographical references and index.
ISBN 0 521 64247 7 (hardback)
1. Athens (Greece) – Civilization. 2. Greece – Civilization – To 146
BCE. 3. Performance – Social aspects – Greece – Athens. I. Goldhill,
Simon. II. Osborne, Robin.
DF275.P47   1999
938′.5 – dc21   98-38083 CIP

ISBN 0 521 64247 7 hardback
ISBN 0 521 60431 1 paperback

Contents

	List of figures	*page* vii
	List of contributors	viii
	Preface	ix
	List of abbreviations	xi
1	Programme notes SIMON GOLDHILL	1

I The performance of drama

2	Spreading the word through performance OLIVER TAPLIN	33
3	The *aulos* in Athens PETER WILSON	58
4	Actor's song in tragedy EDITH HALL	96

II The drama of performance

5	Performative aspects of the choral voice in Greek tragedy: civic identity in performance CLAUDE CALAME	125
6	Actors and voices: reading between the lines in Aeschines and Demosthenes PAT EASTERLING	154
7	Aristophanes: the performance of utopia in the *Ecclesiazousae* FROMA ZEITLIN	167

III Rhetoric and performance

8 The rhetoric of anti-rhetoric in Athenian oratory 201
   JON HESK

9 Reading Homer from the rostrum: poems and laws in
   Aeschines' *Against Timarchus* 231
   ANDREW FORD

10 Plato and the performance of dialogue 257
   SITTA VON REDEN AND SIMON GOLDHILL

IV Ritual and state: visuality and the performance of citizenship

11 Processional performance and the democratic polis 293
   ATHENA KAVOULAKI

12 The spectacular and the obscure in Athenian religion 321
   MICHAEL H. JAMESON

13 Inscribing performance 341
   ROBIN OSBORNE

14 Publicity and performance: *kalos* inscriptions in Attic
   vase-painting 359
   FRANÇOIS LISSARRAGUE

   List of works cited 374
   Index 410

Figures

1. Krater, red-figure, Paris (Louvre inv. CA 1947), *ARV* 240 no. 44, *c*. 480. (Paquette (1984) A54) — 71
2. Plate, red-figure, Paris (Cliché Bibliothèque nationale de France, Paris. Cabinet des Medailles no. 509), *ARV* 77 no. 91, *c*. 520–510. (Paquette (1984) A28) — 73
3. Hydria from Athens, red-figure, Boston (Museum of Fine Arts 03.788), *ARV* 57 no. 75, *c*. 470. Francis Bartlett Donation of 1974. Courtesy, Museum of Fine Arts. — 74
4. Pelike, red-figure, Berlin (3223), *ARV* 586 no. 47. Photo: Johannes Laurentius. — 77
5. Amphora, red-figure, Berlin (1966.19), *Para.* 323/3, *c*. 510. Photo: Johannes Laurentius. — 83
6. Cup, red-figure, Paris (Louvre G82), *ARV* 98.18 and 103.6. — 364
7. Cup, red-figure, New York 09.221.47, *ARV* 91.52. — 366
8. Amphora, red-figure, London E270, *ARV* 183.15. — 368
9. Cup, red-figure, Berlin F2314, *ARV* 336.14. — 370
10. Oinochoe, Munich 2447, *ARV* 425. — 371
11. Lekythos, Berlin F2252, *ARV* 263.54. — 372

Contributors

CLAUDE CALAME, Professor of Greek, University of Lausanne.

PAT EASTERLING, Regius Professor of Greek, University of Cambridge, and Fellow of Newnham College.

ANDREW FORD, Associate Professor of Classics, Princeton University.

SIMON GOLDHILL, Reader in Greek Literature and Culture, University of Cambridge, and Fellow of King's College.

EDITH HALL, Lecturer in Classical Languages and Literature, University of Oxford, and Fellow of Somerville College.

JON HESK, Lecturer in Greek Literature, University of St Andrew's.

MICHAEL JAMESON, Crossett Professor Emeritus of Humanistic Studies, Stanford University.

ATHENA KAVOULAKI teaches at the Peripheral Centre of Continuing Education in Crete.

FRANÇOIS LISSARRAGUE, Professor at the Ecole des Hautes Etudes en Sciences Sociales, Paris.

ROBIN OSBORNE, Professor of Ancient History, University of Oxford, and Fellow of Corpus Christi College.

SITTA VON REDEN, Lecturer in Ancient History, University of Bristol.

OLIVER TAPLIN, Professor of Classical Languages and Literature, University of Oxford and Fellow of Magdalen College.

PETER WILSON, Research Fellow in Classics, University of Warwick.

FROMA ZEITLIN, Charles Ewing Professor of Greek Language and Literature, Princeton University.

Preface

This book is the intended product of an intense conference held in King's College, Cambridge in July 1996. Thirty invited scholars participated in lengthy and often heated discussions over four days, focused on sixteen pre-circulated papers. Participants were invited to contribute to discussion rather than to present material, and did so with remarkable verve. It is right to list them here, because their critical influence is felt on every page: as well as the contributors to this volume (of whom Michael Jameson and Athena Kavoulaki were prevented at the last moment from attending), there were Leslie Kurke, Carole Dougherty, Helene Foley, Richard Seaford, Eric Csapo, David Wiles, Rosanna Omitowoju, Danielle Allen, John Henderson, Johannes Haubold, Paul Cartledge, Katerina Zacharia, Ewen Bowie, Rosalind Thomas, Ian Ruffell and Tim Whitmarsh. This book is the product of dialogue, and we all hope it will produce more.

Thanks are due to King's College Research Centre, the Cambridge University Classics Faculty, and the Craven Fund at Oxford for financial backing. Thanks are due to King's College Research Centre for administrative assistance and their enthusiastic support for a project in the ancient world.

Rather than imposing a standard form, contributors' preferred spellings of Greek names have been retained throughout.

March 1998

Abbreviations

Abbreviations of the names of Greek authors generally follows the practice of LSJ except that some of the more minimal abbreviations are filled out.

AC	*L'antiquité classique*
AJP	*American Journal of Philology*
Ann.Nap	*Annali del' Istituto Orientale Napoli*
ABL	C. H. E. Haspels, *Attic Black-Figured Lekythoi* (Paris, 1936)
ABV	J. D. Beazley, *Attic Black-Figure Vases* (Oxford, 1956)
ARV	J. D. Beazley, *Attic Red-Figure Vases*, 2nd edn (Oxford 1963)
Beazley Addenda	T. H. Carpenter with T. Mannack and M. Mendonca, *Beazley Addenda*, 2nd edn (Oxford, 1990)
BICS	*Bulletin of the Institute of Classical Studies*
C&M	*Classica et Medievalia*
CP	*Classical Philology*
CVA	*Corpus Vasorum Antiquorum* (Paris and elsewhere, 1922–)
FGrH	F. Jacoby ed., *Die Fragmente der griechischer Historiker* (1923–)
Fornara	C. W. Fornara ed., *Archaic Times to the End of the Peloponnesian War*, 2nd edn: *Translated Documents of Greece and Rome* I (Cambridge, 1983)
GRBS	*Greek, Roman and Byzantine Studies*
HSCP	*Harvard Studies in Classical Philology*
HThR	*Harvard Theological Revue*
IG	*Inscriptiones Graecae* (Berlin, 1913–)
JHS	*Journal of Hellenic Studies*
L–P	E. Lobel and D. Page, *Poetarum Lesbiorum Fragmenta* (Oxford, 1963^2)
LIMC	*Lexicon Iconographicum Mythologiae Classicae* (7 vols. in 14 pts., Zurich, 1974–)

LSJ	H. G. Liddell and R. Scott, *A Greek-English Lexicon*, 9th edn, rev. H. Stuart-Jones (Oxford, 1940). Suppl. 1968
ML	R. Meiggs and D. M. Lewis, *A Selection of Greek Historical Inscriptions*, rev. edn (Oxford, 1988)
M–W	R. Merkelbach and M. L. West, *Fragmenta Hesiodea* (Oxford, 1967)
MDAI(R)	*Mitteilungen des deutsches Archäologisches Instituts, Rome*
Para	J. D. Beazley, *Paralipomena*
PCPS	*Proceedings of the Cambridge Philological Society*
RA	*Revue Archéologique*
RE	Pauly's *Real-Encyclopädie der klassischen Altertumswissenschaft* (Stuttgart, 1894–1963)
REG	*Revue des Etudes Grecques*
RhM	*Rheinisches Museum*
RPh	*Revue de Philologie*
SIG³	W. Dittenberger, *Sylloge Inscriptionum Graecarum* (Leipzig, 1915–24³)
TAPA	*Transactions of the American Philological Association*
Tod	M. N. Tod, *Greek Historical Inscriptions* vols. I² and II (Oxford 1946, 1948)
TrGF	*Tragicorum Graecorum Fragmenta*, I: ed. B. Snell, *Tragici Minores*; III: ed. S. Radt, *Aeschylus*; IV: ed. S. Radt, *Sophocles* (Göttingen 1971, 1985, 1977)
TRI	*Theatre Research International*
W	M. L. West, *Iambi et Elegi Graeci* (Oxford, 1971)

1 Programme notes

Simon Goldhill

Why 'performance'? It is not a word from a Greek root, nor is it easy to see how an adequate case could be made for regarding 'performance' as an ancient Greek conceptual category. The hazard of this volume, however, is that the notion of performance will not merely appropriate ancient materials to a distorting modern framework, but will bring into significant focus a series of related terms, institutions, attitudes and practices integral to the society of classical Athens in a way which will be especially illuminating for the culture of democracy. A politician's speech, a footballer's game, a musician's concert, a lover's antics, can be linked directly enough in contemporary English discourse through the category of 'performance': the persuasiveness of the connection depends on a set of barely concealed, if rarely articulated, assumptions about the subject and the subject's relation to social norms and agendas. When the Athenian citizen speaks in the Assembly, exercises in the gymnasium, sings at the symposium, or courts a boy, each activity has its own regime of display and regulation; each activity forms an integral part of the exercise of citizenship. This volume suggests that 'performance' will provide a useful heuristic category to explore the connections and overlaps between these different areas of activity, and, moreover, that these connections and overlaps are significant for understanding the culture of Athenian democracy.

The temporal and spatial scope of this volume is largely, though not totally, restricted to Athens of the fifth and fourth centuries BCE. In part, this is because there is so much more evidence from Athens in comparison with any other classical Greek city; in part it is because of a desire to explore how Athens and its democracy might depend on performance in specific and special ways, for all that gymnasia, symposia, political assemblies, festivals (for example) are seen throughout Greek culture. The intellectual space of this project needs more careful articulation. Let me first try to map some boundaries in Greek. The space we are hoping to explore could be outlined – as a first and non-exhaustive gesture – by four crucial Greek terms: *agōn, epideixis, schēma,* and *theōria* (with their relevant cognates). *Agōn* is normally translated 'contest', but it has a wide range of application. It is the normal, general term used to refer to the grand events of the international athletic circuit, such as the Olympic games: in this sense, it is used both of the whole festival and of particular competitions within it. It can denote the space of the contest itself, a competitive arena. Although the Homeric and Hesiodic instances of the term may imply a restricted sense of a 'gathering' of people,[1] in the classical period it almost inevitably implies a competitive framework, and often a space for the contests of manhood. It is thus the standard expression for the debates of the law-court and Assembly (where men compete both for public status and for victory in particular issues), but it is also a privileged term for the conflict of war (where masculinity is also paradigmatically tested). Thus, as Greek faces Persian in war – a clash not merely of military forces but of ideology, culture, way of life – Aeschylus famously has the troops shout out (*Pers.* 405), 'Now the *agōn* is for everything!.' It also remains the usual expression for any rhetorical conflict, especially the central, formal argumentative scenes of tragedy or the extended clashes of comedy. That this cursory account has already listed the major public institutions of the democratic polis – Assembly, law-court, games, theatre, war – is not by chance. Greek culture in the classical era, and Athens in particular, as has often been noted, is an intensely competitive culture, a culture where authority and status are contested, struggled over and maintained by men, families, states, in a series of hierarchical and oppositional institutions and behavioural practices. The *agōn* as form and expectation links the different areas of public display for Greek males. Indeed, that Athenian culture is so profoundly agonistic informs not merely the rhetoric and organization of institutions, but also the construction of the social self. The hierarchical pursuit of *timē* ('personal honour'), the concomitant elaborate discourse of outrage (*hubris*), the interactions of *philoi* ('friends') and *ekhthroi* ('enemies') around the injunction to do good/ harm in an economics of carefully observed reciprocal treatment, all play an integral role in the social exchanges in which the Athenian

---

[1] See e.g. *Iliad* 18. 376, and its use in *Iliad* 23 both for the audience of Patroclus' funeral games (e.g. 258, 617) and for the space of competition (e.g. 685, 799); *Theogony* 91, with West's note *ad loc*; for its shift in the fifth century see Fraenkel's notes to *Agamemnon* 513 and 845, where he comments that Aeschylus' apparent use of the term to mean agora 'was presumably felt as a Homerism by Aeschylus and his audience'.

citizen's self is enacted.² For all of this, the *agōn* is a fundamental cultural context.

Epideixis, 'display', is more markedly a term of the intellectual enlightenment of the classical polis.³ The new intellectuals of the fifth century (and the more established intellectual teachers of the fourth) drew on the agonistic nature of public life in the city, along with the institutional emphasis on verbal activity, to privilege rhetorical display as a major sign and symptom not merely of the pursuit of success in democracy but also of what Geoffrey Lloyd has called 'the revolutions of wisdom' – that is, the turn towards the self-conscious reflection on the processes of the city of words, or what might be called the elaboration of meta-discursive systems. *Epideixis* becomes, at least by the fourth century, fully established as the name of one branch of rhetoric as a formal study – the set, display speech – but it is also linked to the ideas of argumentative proof and demonstration – showing as well as showing off.⁴ For Herodotus, however – who called his whole history an *apode[i]xis*, 'demonstrative display' – the display of a naked woman by her doting husband is also an *epideixis* (Her. 1.11); as is the display of troops (Xen. *An.* 1.2.14). Display can be physical as much as verbal, an act of embodying forth authority, glamour, position. So military display is part of the parade of power and is described in the language of *epideixis* by historians and orators in their analysis of political behaviour. Persian displays of wealth are countered by Athenian demonstrations of austere manhood. In democracy, the conspicuous parading of wealth by the polis is set in contrast with personal gain or kingly grandeur, as the spectacle of consumption becomes fully imbricated in a politicized discourse of material prosperity.⁵ The institutions of democracy from the gymnasium to the Assembly required display, and with it comes elaborate protocols and self-aware discussion, of which the rhetorical theories (and practice) of *epideixis* are only one albeit most evident and developed aspect. *Epideixis* requires an audience; when competitive, as *epideixis* almost inevitably is, it necessarily triangulates competition through an audience. It establishes a dynamic of

---

[2] See on honour Cairns (1993); Adkins (1960); *timai*, 'honours', is a term used of public office in democracy; on *hubris*, Fisher (1992); Cohen (1991); Herman (1993), (1994), (1996); on *philia*, Herman (1987); Konstan (1997); Blundell (1989); reciprocity, von Reden (1995), Millett (1991), all with extensive further bibliography.
[3] See Lloyd (1987).
[4] See e.g. Aristotle *Rh.* 1.3.3ff., and on demonstration, II.22; III.17.
[5] See Hall (1989); Miller (1997); the promised books on money by Kurke, Seaford, and von Reden are all eagerly awaited. See now von Reden (1997).

4   Simon Goldhill

self-representation where self-promotion is restricted by the fears and limitations of the group constituted as an audience. *Epideixis* becomes the site where the self-advancement of the citizen is negotiated in the city of words.

Schēma is a complex term whose history has not yet been adequately researched in contemporary scholarship. I shall trace here some aspects of its range of sense. Demosthenes in his attack on Stephanos describes (45. 68–9) how his opponent walks around town with a grim expression, which a spectator might reasonably think is a 'sign of his propriety' (*sophrosunēs* ... *sēmeia*), but which is really a sign of his misanthropy, since, according to the orator, his gait and expression are an attempt to avoid any demands or social contacts by being standoffish. 'This *schēma*', concludes Demosthenes, 'is nothing but a screen (*problēma*) of his character (*tropou*)'. *Schēma* is the physical appearance presented to the gaze of the citizens – appearance which may be simply what is seen, a 'form', but which also may be a mere appearance, a semblance or concealment of true nature. The connection of gait (*badisma*), expression and attitude repeatedly epitomizes a man's *schēma*.[6] So Demosthenes, describing what it is like to be hit in public, explains that it is hard for a victim to express to someone else his attacker's '*schēma*, his expression, his voice' (21.72). Xenophon describes Socrates' grand exit from the courtroom as (*Ap.* 27) 'he departed radiant in his eyes, his *schēma*, and his gait'. Indeed, Xenophon's Socrates generalizes this physiognomics for the painter Parrhasius by claiming that (*Mem.* 3.10.5) 'the dignified and free, the humble and slavish, the controlled and the wise, the outrageous and vulgar, are distinctly visible in still and moving humans through the face (*prosōpon*) and the *schēmata*'. The gaze of the citizens, in which honour and status are contested, constructs the citizen's bodily appearance as a *schēma* open to evaluation, regulation and scrutiny. It is the gap between *schēma* as form and *schēma* as appearance that allows for the performance of self – that is, the self-presentation, self-regulation, self-concealment which construct or stage the citizen in the public eye.

Schēma, then, is a fundamental expression for the embodiment of *epideixis* in the agonistic world of the polis. But its range of sense goes much further. It can be used more generally for the 'form' or 'structure' of a government (so, for example, the '*schēma* of democracy' (Thuc. 6.89) or, more generally, the '*schēma* of a constitution' (Plat.

---

[6] For a very brief introduction to this, see Bremmer (1991).

Plt. 291d), although even such expressions can easily become tinged with a negative tone, as when the Great King's rule is described as 'no small *schēma* of power' – the 'pomp' of regal government (Plato *Laws* 685c)). It can refer, in Euripides' memorable phrase, even to a 'manner of living', a 'form of life' – as Medea preparing to kill her children regrets (1038–9) 'you will no more look upon your mother with your dear eyes, when you have departed to another manner of life (*schēma biou*)'. It is not by chance that the deceptive, rhetorical Medea, a barbarian outraged by Greeks, should turn to the language of *schēma*, of (misleading) form. Perhaps more strikingly, however, *schēma* develops a range of technical senses. It standardly and commonly refers to a dancer's moves or gestures or 'positions'. Indeed, Isocrates also describes the aim of athletic trainers as 'teaching the *schēmata* devised for contesting (*agōnia*)' (*Antid.* 183). A *schēma* is a posture which can be learnt, studied, prepared – composed: a model or exemplary form, to be enacted or embodied. Furthermore, *schēma* also refers to the technical 'forms' of composition itself, not merely in such phraseology as Aristotle's description of prose as 'not a metrical *schēma* of expression' (*Rh.* III.8.1), but also in music theory's idea of a 'figure' of musical composition, and rhetoric's use of *schēma* for what Roman writers called 'figura', a figure of speech.[7] *Schēma* thus expresses the composed form of an observed phenomenon. Both the fact that *schēma* thus stresses a regular and regulated form, and that it also emphasizes something which is composed, modelled, learnt, made up, make the language of *schēma* fundamental to the performance of the citizen.

I have already referred several times to 'the gaze of the citizens'. The establishment of democratic institutions made public debate, collective decision making, and the shared ideals of participatory citizenship central elements of political practice. To be in an audience was not just a thread in the city's social fabric, it was a fundamental political act. To sit as an evaluating, judging spectator was to participate as a political subject.[8] *Theōria* is a convenient term under which to discuss this changing politics of spectacle.

As with the previous terms, the range of meaning for *theōria* is extensive, covering indeed each aspect of the dynamic of spectating. At one level, it can mean the act of watching itself. This can be an

---

[7] The use of *schēma* in rhetoric becomes increasingly technical and increasingly common from the fourth century onwards, see Kennedy (1963) and for a convenient collection of sample passages, Russell and Winterbottom (1972) index *sub* 'figures'.

[8] See Goldhill (1995); (1997) specifically on the theatrical audience; and Lanni (1997) on types of audience; more generally, Sinclair (1988); Ober (1989).

explorer's sight-seeing:[9] the speaker of Isocrates' *Trapezeticus* explains (4) that since he had conceived a desire to find out about the world, his father had sent him off 'to trade and to see the world', *kata theōrian* (as, indeed, according to Herodotus (1.29), Solon left Athens for the same reason). Particularly under Plato's influence, this expression of the act of viewing is applied to the act of the philospher's intellectual contemplation of the world (and hence arises the English word 'theory': the connection between 'viewing' and 'theory' has been a commonplace of contemporary theoretical writing). More commonly, however, *theōria* has an institutional frame (a sense less often noted by modern theorists). To be a *theōros* or to *theōrein*, is the normal expression for attendance at the games or at religious festivals. Thus in a telling phrase, where Demosthenes is disparaging Aeschines' political life in comparison with his own, he exclaims scornfully, 'You were a secretary, but I attended the Assembly; you were an actor, but I was a spectator' (*etheōroun*). Both the active political status of spectating, and its institutional frame are neatly marked by Demosthenes' rhetoric, which makes watching plays in the theatre analogous to political participation in the Assembly, and – as the orator would have it – being an actor parallel to taking notes as a scribe. So, the orator marks himself as a figure defined by this judging audience when he describes himself in a significant juxtaposition as 'the object of judgement, the object of gaze' (*krinōmai kai theōrōmai* 18.315).

Indeed, there is a further more formal sense to *theōros* which distinguishes it from the closely related word *theatēs*, 'spectator'.[10] For to be a *theōros* is to be a state official appointed and paid to attend games or festivals in an official representative capacity – consequently it is often translated 'state ambassador'. This was funded by liturgy, the system of raising money from wealthy individuals which was the mainstay of democratic economics, and the *theōros* often performed a specific religious duty, and was often splendidly dressed, escorted and crowned – thus creating a spectacle (*theōrēma*) in himself. In a sense, however, every citizen performed such a role: the theoric fund (*to theōrikon*) was established to enable every citizen to attend the theatre (and for other similar purposes), and it was a fund carefully buttressed by law against any challenge. To be a *theōros* is a right and duty of the

---

[9] For the historical specificity of 'tourism' as a term, which I have thus avoided, see e.g. Buzard (1993); and on earlier models of travel, Campbell (1988); Greenblatt (1991); Pratt (1992). On Herodotus, see Redfield (1985). On the development of pilgrimage and artistic viewing, see Hunt (1982); Sivan (1988); Ousterhout (1990); Elsner (1992). On 'world pictures' and travel in general for the Greek material, see Romm (1992).

[10] Whether there is an etymological connection between the two terms is debated.

Athenian citizen, performed in the institutions of the state and institutionally supported by financial and legal means.

As the act of viewing defines the political subject of democracy, so it becomes a source of discussion and debate. Thucydides' Cleon (3.38) accuses the Athenians of being merely '*theatai* of speech making' – as opposed to being willing to act, to provide *erga*, 'deeds', in response to *logoi*. Typically for Thucydides' sophisticated and cynical narrative technique, Cleon addresses these remarks to the people as he fails to persuade them to keep to an earlier resolution to destroy the city of Mytilene. From a different perspective, the role of *theōros* becomes material for Aristophanic comedy, ever swift to debunk the claims of class and privilege. When Bdelycleon is trying to teach Philocleon how to behave like a rich man ('look at – *theō* – my *schēma*', he says, 'and see which rich man I look like'), he advises him to tell 'impressive stories' of 'how he was a fellow *theōros* of Androcles and Cleisthenes' (both men are regular butts of comedy for social and sexual improprieties). 'I've never been on state delegation (*tetheōrēka*) anywhere', replies Philocleon, 'except to Paros, and that was for two obols'. The two obol payment suggests that Philocleon was a rower in a state ship, rather than a delegate, as Aristophanes typically sets his 'common man' against elite expectations. Xenophon's *Hiero* (10–13) – to turn to political theory – makes the first distinction between a tyrant and a private citizen (*idiōtēs*) the fact that a citizen can exercise the duties and pleasures of *theōria*, whereas a tyrant because of his inability to appear in public or travel cannot enjoy 'spectacles through vision' (τὰ διὰ τῆς ὄψεως θεάματα[11]). For Xenophon, no democrat, it is pleasure as much as political positioning that is at stake in the ideology of viewing. In a similar vein, though with far more complex ramifications, Plato distinguishes (*Resp.* 475d1ff.) between the *philotheamon* ('lover of spectacles/sights') who is motivated by pleasure to engage in the arts (where they delight in 'fine voices, colours and *schēmata*'), and the *philosophos*, who is, as it were, 'a *philotheamon* of truth' (*Resp.* 475c4). The development of optics as a new science in this period,[12] tragedy's discourse of vision and knowledge (especially in plays like the *Oedipus Tyrannus* or the *Bacchae*),[13] the attack by the new intellectuals on the assumption

---

[11] The pursuit of what is 'worth seeing' stretches from Herodotus through Xenophon to Pausanias and the Greek novel: see Elsner (1992); Bartsch (1989); Goldhill (1996a).

[12] See Simon (1988).

[13] Tragedy 'extended the practical problems of vision and visibility that belong to the conventions of its *mis en scène* into an epistemological concern with insight, knowledge, revelation and truth', Zeitlin (1955a) 176. See for discussion and bibliography Goldhill (1986) chs. 8 & 11.

of the necessary connection between perception and knowledge, all contribute to the extensive discussion of the viewing audience as an integral social and political element of democracy. As *epideixis* highlights the function of speech-making in democracy (which is, as Demosthenes put it (19.184), a *politeia* of *logoi*) and in the construction of the political subject of democracy, so *theōria* emphasizes the role of the evaluating, judging spectator as a key factor in the construction of democratic culture. Both terms show how visual and verbal display become the topic of self-reflexive concern in Athenian democratic discourse.

These four terms, then, *agōn*, *epideixis*, *schēma* and *theōria*, with their cognates and related language, show something of the complexity with which the public discourse of democracy is constructed, articulated and reflected on in Athens. Some evident connections between these vocabularies have already emerged in, say, the agonistic context of *epideixis*, or the focus on the judgemental viewing of a citizen's *schēma*. I wish briefly to stress, however, four particular notions which run throughout the preceding discussion, and which together go some way towards explaining the instructive power of the idea of 'performance culture' for the society of classical Athens.

First, spectacle. Both in the most general sense that, as Xenophon's Hiero (*Hier.* 1. 11) puts it, 'different countries certainly have different things worth going to view (*axiotheata*)',[14] and in the more institutional and political sense that the Assembly, law-court, and theatre (not to mention the processions and rituals of religion) depend on staging a scene to be watched, evaluated and enjoyed, Athenian democratic culture constantly parades its politics of spectacle. According to the Old Oligarch (3.8), Athens had more festivals than any other state; according to Aristophanes, more law suits.[15] Demosthenes and Aeschines imagine their speeches to be delivered 'before all Greece'. Plato attacks Athens as a theatocracy, a society ruled by the dangers of a crowd's pleasure in spectacle. There is a public awareness of the specialness of Athens' culture and its concomitant requirements on its citizens. Thus, it can be instituted that the tribute of the allies should be paraded, ingot by ingot, in the theatre before the plays were performed at the Great Dionysia,[16] a grand statement of the power and

---

[14] Cf. *Hiero* 11 for a theoretical discussion of the politics of competitive display.
[15] On Athenian festival calendar, see Mikalson (1975); for other states, see Nilsson (1957); for general introductions, Cartledge (1985), Bruit Zaidman and Schmitt Pantel (1992); and the general case of Seaford (1995). For detailed work on festivals, see for bibliography below nn. 21, 64, 69, 71.
[16] For discussion and testimonia, see Goldhill (1990).

prestige of the polis, but, in turn, Isocrates (*de pace* 82) can see this ritual as a way of the democratic state becoming more hated by its allies. Similarly, Pericles' funeral speech in Thucydides – an *epideixis* central to a major state ritual, instituted by democracy[17] – also reflects (2.38) on Athenians' attitudes to contests and religious rites as part of a culture of festival which is essentially Athenian and quite unlike the Spartans'. Democracy repeatedly makes a spectacle of itself.

Second, audience (or spectators). A spectacle needs its audience, its spectators. And as much as the different types and forms of spectacle can be analysed (as I shall continue below), so too different constructions of the audience are an essential dynamic of the functioning of spectacle and of democracy. Considering the role of the spectator will involve questions of the boundaries of the collective (fundamental to democratic polity), questions of how insiders and outsiders are defined (included and excluded). It will involve issues of how power is circulated in the public events of democracy, which, beyond the interplay of mass and elite, requires a consideration of the activity and passivity of spectators, the role of public knowledge, the (self)-awareness and manipulation of such defining categories. Iconically, Dicaeopolis in Aristophanes' *Acharnians* starts the play sitting in the audience of the Assembly, commenting on his role, and eventually separating himself from the collective by a private peace treaty with the Spartans (after he has invaded the political stage and stripped the masks off returning ambassadors, revealing their corruption). The politics of this comedy articulate at all levels a tension between individual desires and collective procedure, as it stages a series of festival activities (processions, feasts, dressing up), enjoyed by one man at the expense of the community. Enacted before the collective of the city, this comedy makes a joke out of joining in.[18] Democracy privileges 'individual participation in collective processes', and that sense of a dynamic between the collective and the personal makes the formation of an audience an integral and contested aspect of its culture.

Third, the construction of the self. It is important that each of the Greek terms I began by considering plays a fundamental role in the construction of the political subject of democracy. One of the objections that might be raised against utilizing the category of 'performance' for ancient culture is that the modern term may imply and impose anachronistic and distorting ideas of the self as a political and social entity with notions of inwardness, privacy and individual personality

---

[17] See Loraux (1981); Clairmont (1983).
[18] I have discussed this, with extensive bibliography in Goldhill (1991).

which might be out of place in ancient Athens.[19] What this volume hopes to show, however, is that the notion of a performance culture can enable the development of a historically specific and nuanced account of the constitution of the citizen as a political subject across and through a range of particular social practices and discourses. This in turn may prove instructive for contemporary performance studies, which have not always faced up to the historicity of the category of performance.[20]

Fourth, self-consciousness. By this I mean that each discourse I have considered integrally involves reflection on its processes as they are enacted. The theory of rhetorical epideixis as informing the rhetoric of epideictic oratory; the extensive discussions of how vision functions; or of the philosophy of justice and reciprocity in the most litigious of cities; or of the ethical theory underlying a citizen's behaviour; all these mark the fifth century's turn to self-conscious theorization. Democratic culture proceeds in a symbiotic relation with (democratic) theorizing (a theorizing that goes beyond the narrowly defined political theory of constitutional matters). The citizen's self-representation and self-regulation are formulated within this self-reflective critical discursive system.

'Performance culture', this volume suggests, is a valuable heuristic category to explore the interconnections of these areas of Athenian society. It is intended that thinking thus generally about a cultural system and its connections with the performative will encourage a comprehension of the interplay between aspects of the polis which are often treated as bounded fields but which are integral and interrelated elements of the developing democratic city.

II

It would be easy to produce a diachronic account of the development of Athenian democracy which focused on performative elements. Starting, say, from the tyrant Peisistratus, and the story of his rise to power by the drama of being led into the city by a statuesque woman, dressed as Athena; or, say, from Solon's performance of his political and revolutionary poems in the agora; following through the invention of democratic institutions of public performance, the growth of civic

---

[19] For discussion of these issues, see Pelling (1990); Gill (1996).
[20] See, for example, the muddled approaches to universality in Turner (1990), Schechner (1990), Blau (1990), or the collections edited by Diamond (1996a) and Parker and Sedgwick (1995) whose admirable pursuit of interdisciplinarity has a far from adequate historical frame.

festivals, to the rhetorical control of the city and his policy of its material glorification through an imperial building programme.[21] And so forth. But before turning to fill in some of the context of the sites and narratives of performance in classical Athens, I want to outline some of the contemporary thinking that has informed the conceptualization of this volume. For 'performance' has certainly come to hold a central place in the modern academy's analysis of culture, and it will be helpful to locate the contributions of this book in and against contemporary theoretical approaches to performance.

Now 'performance studies' as a discipline in itself is a very recent phenomenon.[22] If it began with theatre, music and dance departments broadening their scope to include anthropological study of ritual on the one hand, and sociological analyses of the performance of everyday life on the other, the further addition of psychoanalytic vocabulary of 'scenes' (primal and other), or 'acting out', has meant that 'performance studies' now often aims to cover a huge range of social interaction (to the degree that, when performance becomes such an all-embracing term, it becomes difficult to maintain it as a useful and specific analytic category).[23] There is no single 'founding text' or 'school' for this heterogeneous field, and, as with rhetoric departments in the U.S.A. in particular, there remain substantive and considerable differences between various practitioners within departments and between various departments. Nonetheless, it would be useful to suggest some common theoretical starting points. One figure, whose late absorption into Western academic work has been especially influential, is Mikhail Bakhtin. His analysis of 'carnival' as an institution (and the notion of the 'carnivalesque' as its 'aesthetic') regards a particular ritual and social phenomenon as a type of performance.[24] It is a performance with a strong political agenda, in Bakhtin's eyes, and, equally important, a performance that necessarily implicates a view of the social functioning of language, and a view of the political subject. Bakhtin's sense of how social occasions are the location of the con-

---

[21] For such diachronic moments, see on Phye, Peisistratus and Herodotus, see Sinos (1993); on civic festivals, see e.g. Connor (1987); Osborne (1993); Sourvinou-Inwood (1994), and, more generally, Osborne (1996); on imperial building, see Castriota (1992); Rhodes (1995).
[22] See e.g. Schechner (1977); Zarilli (1986); Dolan (1993); Case (1990) 1–13; Diamond (1996).
[23] For an attempt to see 'performance' as a universal, see Turner (1990); Schechner (1990); Blau (1990). For a typically wide collection, see Diamond (1996a).
[24] See Bakhtin (1968); (1981); with the commentaries of Todorov (1984); Hirschkop and Shepherd (1986); Stallybrass and White (1986); Holquist (1990) and for a brilliant placement of Bakhtin in his Russian setting, Emerson (1997).

testation of social norms and transgressions, a site for staging and acting out tensions of cultural order, has stimulated some extraordinary accounts of the location and narratives of such performances. Whether it be 'the pig and the fair', the eighteenth-century masked ball in London, or, indeed, the festival of Aristophanic comedy, Bakhtin's argument about the construction of special spaces for the viewing, articulation and participation in social power has proved remarkably productive.[25]

Bakhtin's work is repeatedly concerned with clashes of power, when social systems seem to be most at risk, and working hardest to maintain order. Victor Turner, who took his exemplary material primarily from his field work among the Ndembu in Africa, focuses more on rituals which inform and ground social cohesion and order. Nonetheless, performance is for him an absolutely basic category (which was treated, in his final writing, as a cultural universal).[26] He regards ritual as a 'social drama' and sees the acting out or performance of ritual as the staging of a culture's values and (thus) a fundamental means for the construction of the social subject. The performance of ritual communicates a culture's values to its citizens. In particular, the constitution of social norms requires the articulation of boundaries, which makes 'liminality' for Turner (as for Mary Douglas[27]) a key to the staging of order. Repeatedly, Turner sees ritual as enacting a pattern of separation and integration, linked and divided by a liminal time of transition – a pattern which draws closely on van Gennep's groundbreaking study of initiation and *rites de passages*, and a broadly Durkheimian agenda[28] – and he regards the performance of this pattern as basic to society's self-regulation and self-expression. Turner's work has been utilized to investigate far more than ritual in traditional societies.[29] That a society's and a subject's conceptual space is represented in performances marked as special by ritualization, and that participation in such performances is integral to the formulation of a social subject is the starting point of much recent performance studies. Central to Bakhtin, Turner, and the scholars who follow them, then, is the essential insight that social action, especially ritualized social action, is a form of com-

---

[25] See e.g. Castle (1986); Stallybrass and White (1986); Davis (1987); Bristol (1989); and, on Aristophanes, von Möllendorf (1995); Carrière (1979); Rösler (1986); Goldhill (1991) 176–88.
[26] Turner (1967); (1969); (1990).
[27] Douglas (1966).
[28] Van Gennep (1960).
[29] See e.g. MacAloon (1984); Castle (1986); Schechner and Appel (1990); Schechner (1993), and, for theatre itself, Burns (1972).

munication. This insight has been widely adopted into classical studies, especially the studies of ritual and of theatre itself.[30]

Erving Goffman, however, who worked closely with Turner, took the sense in which action is to be understood as communication a step further, when he challenged the definitional boundaries of ritual space by constructing a sociological model for ordinary behaviour that depended on ideas of theatricality and role-playing.[31] 'All the world is not of course a stage, but the crucial ways in which it isn't are not easy to specify', he wrote paradigmatically.[32] For Goffman, perception of and participation in the world depend on 'framing', constructions of roles and masks, and 'collaboration' – a complicit agreement on the definition of situations as, say, social (as opposed to 'natural'). This attempt to locate 'performance' in everyday life, rather than in a specialized institutional context (or foreign country), or, perhaps better, this attempt to construct a continuum rather than an opposition between everyday life and markedly institutional events, offers a formalist model of social interaction where social subjects are committed to the convention and enactment of social roles – to the script of culture.

Both Bakhtin's comprehension of the dangers and controls of language, specifically language exchange (through his influential ideas of heteroglossia and dialogism), and also Goffman's dissection of the scripted encounter, place socio-linguistics at the heart of performance. The discipline of linguistics has become increasingly important for 'performance studies' since the foundational work of J. L. Austin. Austin in a celebrated move attempted to distinguish between constative and performative utterances, between utterances which report, describe, propose, and utterances which 'do', which enact by virtue of being uttered.[33] If for Turner, action is communication, for Austin, communication is action. His elegant propositions were extended and formalized by Searle,[34] and have become the source of a heated and powerful debate,[35] not least because of the way that Austin allowed his own distinctions to slip and slide. (Typically, he begins: 'the only merit I would like to claim for [what I am about to say] is that of being true, at least in parts', where the politesse of qualification becomes an

---

[30] See e.g. Osborne (1985); Goldhill (1990); Dougherty and Kurke (1993); Connor (1989); Henrichs (1978); (1984); Burkert (1983).
[31] Goffman (1969); (1975).
[32] (1969) 78.
[33] Austin (1962).
[34] Searle (1969).
[35] Especially, of course, around Derrida's critique. See Derrida (1988); Searle (1977); (1983). See also Petrey (1990); Felman (1980); Fish (1980); Pratt (1977). I have had my go in Goldhill (1994).

epistemological risk.[36]) Although the theoretical debates continue, the notion of the linguistic performative, where 'doing things with words ... can make and unmake our world',[37] has been rapidly appropriated into literary studies to uncover how 'the poem is the cry of its occasion', as Wallace Stevens wrote.[38] What is more, in linguistics itself both 'pragmatics' and 'relevance theory' have further explored the conditions of socio-linguistic performance with special focus on the complicity and framing of dialogue as an event.[39] Interestingly, some of the most passionately argued debates in this area have focused on the the possible distinctions between the performative in everyday life and the ritualized and institutional performance – between saying 'I do' on stage in a play, in a wedding, or in reply to a question whether you like ice-cream; between 'the peculiar hollowness' of literature (as Austin put it), and the power of literature as an (un)acknowledged legislator. As with the study of ritual itself, the category of performance seems to lead inevitably to a question about the boundaries of the performative. Thus, social analysis that begins either from language or from ritual, makes performance a central and contested category.

This applies also when the focus shifts to the internal life of agents. For although Goffman's actors, like Turner's, are figures largely without internal life, or at least without an internal life of the sort recognized and validated by psychoanalysis, in recent years performance studies have also adopted a marked psychoanalytic strain. At one level, this draws out a fascinating aspect of Freud's language which has perhaps not been adequately traced, namely, his use of theatrical terminology (as opposed to the theatrical models of Oedipus or Electra).[40] There is for Freud a theatre of the mind, where 'scenes' are staged and observed, screens are erected and images flow through them, enactment occurs, and acting out may lead to a form of catharsis. This sense of a 'performance of the self' has been greatly extended by the dependence of film theory (ever part of performance studies) on a Lacanian model of the gaze, and its centrality in his model of the construction of the self.[41] At another level, Judith Butler's careful and sophisticated claims for viewing gender as a performative – 'gender is always a doing,

[36] Austin (1962) 1.
[37] Petrey (1990) 21.
[38] See Petrey (1990); Pratt (1977); Fish (1980); Felman (1980).
[39] See Grice (1975), the contributors to Cole and Morgan (1975); Sperber and Wilson (1986); Levinson (1983) with further bibliography.
[40] See the very mixed bag of essays on at least a 'French Freud' and theatricality collected in Murray (1997).
[41] See e.g. Doane (1987); Silverman (1988); Penley (1988); Mulvey (1989); Copjec (1994).

though not a doing by a subject who might be said to pre-exist the deed'[42] – has set an agenda for much recent feminist writing (and inevitably much of performance studies). Butler's analysis of gendering is not simply psychoanalytic, however. It is deeply indebted to – and engaged with – linguistic philosophy, anthropological theory, and political sociology. This is paradigmatic of the way in which 'performance' has become an interdisciplinary linking term – and a most productive one – for the contemporary academy.

Thus, partly in response to so-called 'performance art', art history and performance studies have together approached not merely the turn of artistic display into a performance (Cristo's wrapping of the Reichstag, Tilda Swinton's sleep in a glass box[43]), but also what might be called the performativity of material culture. Thus on the one hand the question of how images (as well as words) do things – the performativity of representation – has evoked a passionate interaction between academic work and social policy, particularly with regard to pornography, politics, and advertising.[44] On the other hand, topography has been opened to analysis through the category of performance. The museum as a site of engagement designed to produce a privileged image of culture – and of the citizen in it;[45] the memorial as constructing an observer's relation to the past;[46] architecture's direction and regulation of its users;[47] these have led to claims to recognize a dynamic of performance – most broadly conceived – within material culture.

This bricolage of intellectual material could clearly be extended in scope and depth, and different routes could be plotted through it. Indeed, for all the claims of 'performance studies' to be a discipline, it remains a bricolage, loosely collected around a central term. Enough, however, has been traced to show that – in sum – 'performance studies' and its analysis of culture has made performance a central explanatory term for the articulation of the subject in relation to social norms and practices.

At the same time as 'performance studies' has been trying to establish itself as a discipline, 'performance' has increasingly become a

---

[42] Butler (1990) 25. See also Butler (1993); (1997).
[43] For a useful introduction to performance art, see Goldberg (1988). Christo wrapped the Reichstag in 1995, see Christo and Jean-Claude (1996); Tilda Swinton was displayed asleep in a glass box in the Serpentine Gallery for a week in the fine show, 'The Maybe'.
[44] See e.g. Kappeler (1986); Itzin 1990; MacKinnon (1993); Hunter, Saunders and Williamson (1993); Hunt (1993); Gibson and Gibson (1993); Steiner (1995).
[45] See e.g. Karp and Lavine (1991); Bal (1996), with further bibliography.
[46] See e.g. Young (1993) with further bibliography.
[47] As a starting point, see Bachelard (1964); or on Paris (e.g.) Clark (1984) 23–78.

clarion call in the study of drama itself, a call to view plays not merely as texts but as events. This implies a focus on the staging of plays, on the one hand, with the technical and interpretative problems thus raised. On the other hand, it promotes a view of the importance of the socio-political occasion of drama. Renaissance theatre has been particularly well explored along these lines, and in work such as Stephen Orgel's *The Illusion of Power*, it is precisely the combination of the details of staging practice and the implication of the politics of display that is so illuminating for the culture of Renaissance performance.[48] It is within such a light that, say, recent discussions of the role of the female voice in the performance of opera (and film)[49] should be viewed.

'Performance studies' and the contemporary study of theatre, opera, film, have thus constructed an extremely broad notion of performance, which this volume reflects. Nonetheless, there is a further range of scholarly work which, while not strictly part of 'performance studies' or of the study of the performing arts, has been important in the conceptualization of this volume. This is a series of analyses of the elements of performance I outlined in the previous section of this introduction with regard to Greek culture. In particular, I want to trace briefly here some ways in which 'the spectacle' and the construction of the viewer have become open to acute historical analysis. For the business of seeing others act, and seeing oneself being seen – observing and participating, participating by observing – makes 'performance' a dynamic category in comprehending culture.

Now, Michel Foucault, with his characteristic blend of insightful generalization and worrying lack of nuance, writes: 'We are much less Greeks than we believe. We are neither in the amphitheatre, nor on the stage, but in the panoptic machine': 'our society is not one of spectacle, but of surveillance.'[50] On the one hand, Foucault points towards an important difference between the framing of modern power and ancient institutions and discourses. One of the prospects of studying classical Athens is the comparison of modern and ancient idea(l)s of participation and their implications for the construction of citizenship. Foucault's own juxtaposition of the brutal public punishment of the regicide, Damiens, and Bentham's Panopticon, a machine for the perfect and complete observation of prisoners, has proved extremely

---

[48] See also Tennenhouse (1986); Berry (1989); Greenblatt (1980).
[49] See on opera Clément (1988); Abbate (1991); and from a different perspective Poizat (1992); on film, Silverman (1988); Lawrence (1991); Barthes' essay 'The Grain of the Voice' has been influential here (Barthes (1977)); more generally, on female 'vocality', Dunn and Jones (1994).
[50] Foucault (1977) 217.

productive for other scholars exploring the changing relations between the exercise of power and the systems of knowledge.[51] (The connection between *theōria* and theory is strongly marked here.) On the other hand, the continuing commitment of democracy to spectacle in at least the manipulation of public images of power, say, or the worlds of sport or entertainment (that form a basis of influential analyses of culture such as that of Debord from French left wing circles[52]), suggest that the opposition of spectacle and surveillance can scarcely be exclusive or totalizing. What is more, not only have detailed studies in nineteenth-century culture shown how clearly connected are modern science, observation and the spectacular (as I shall note further below) in developing modern notions of the body, of the self, and of political subjectivity; but also cultural critics studying the ancient world have emphasized how the ancient self is repeatedly open to the scrutinization of an invasive surveillance.[53]

What Foucault has underlined tellingly, however, is the need to bring together discursive, intellectual developments and social history. This has been seen in a series of brilliant studies of nineteenth-century cultural shifts around the notion of the spectacle and the observer. Jonathan Crary, for example, has explored in great detail how changing models of vision developed by scientists, philosophers and psychologists in the years between 1810 and 1840 not only had impact on the developments of those disciplines, but also fundamentally altered a conceptualization of the observer and his or her place in the order of society:[54]

Even before the actual invention of cinema ... it is clear that the conditions of human perception were being reassembled into new components. Vision, in a wide range of locations, was refigured as dynamic, temporal and synthetic – the demise of the punctual or anchored classical observer began in the early nineteenth century, increasingly displaced by the unstable attentive subject ... it is a subject competent both to be a consumer of and to be an agent in the synthesis of a proliferating diversity of 'reality effects', and a subject who will become the object of all the industries of the image and the spectacle in the twentieth century.[55]

Crary moves thus from a detailed historical account of the sciences of vision, to a comprehension of a changing notion of spectacle, and its

---

[51] Convenient starting points to what has become a large bibliography can be found in Hoy (1986); Dreyfus and Rabinow (1983); and, more recently, Rouse (1994).
[52] Debord (1967).
[53] See especially Hunter (1994); Gleason (1995).
[54] Crary (1990).
[55] Crary (1994) 44.

implications for a social subject in the twentieth century. Looking at the role of the observer, and how it is influenced by epistemological constructions, leads through an analysis of 'spectacle' to a socio-political account of the 'industries of the image' central to modern Western culture. 'Performance' suggests that events are constructed, composed: Crary shows how important it is to offer a culturally and historically specific account of the construction of the notion of performance itself.

This analysis inevitably has considerable implications for, say, the production, display, and effect of high art in this period. In the course of the article from which I quoted above, Crary takes Manet's picture 'A Bar at the Folies Bergères' as an iconic example of a new representation of (in)attentiveness as a sign of subjectivity. Tim Clark's *The Painting of Modern Life*, which also discusses that picture at length, develops an account both of its display and of its politics of representation which focuses more on elements of class identity (and of fashion – in the strong sense of a *schēma* of self-representation). Clark shows well both how a painting can be 'a complaisant spectator of this spectacle' of the leisure world of the modern city, but also on occasion can 'suggest the unease and duplicity' involved in such representation.[56] Clark quotes the nineteenth-century theorist Veblen that leisure was 'a performance', and he adds 'and the thing performed was class'[57] – and he indicates how published responses to the painting when it was displayed enacted such class positioning. The picture's now famous depiction of a world of looking (and of mirrors) thus participates in the articulation of the spectacle of modern life, as it becomes a significant object of display and criticism through its public exhibition.

So, too, the Victorian London street as a staging of class and gender has been fascinatingly explored particularly through the representation of prostitutes in the art gallery, popular press, legal system, theatre.[58] The show of the street (that so fixated the flâneurs of Paris) thus through the street-walker becomes fully imbricated in a politics of display and representation. Street theatre's social drama...

The need to explore 'spectacle' and 'the observer' as historically and culturally specific notions has been similarly well demonstrated for earlier periods. The Enlightenment's commitment to a model of vision is conjoined with a self-conscious set of regulations for the body of the spectator, with classed and gendered models of participation in society,

---

[56] Clark (1984) 204. See also Cohen and Prendergast (1995), especially the chapters of Matlock, Schwartz, and Garelick.
[57] Clark (1984) 205.
[58] See e.g. Nochlin (1989); Walkowitz (1980); Nead (1988); Davidoff (1983); and for Parisian equivalents Bernheimer (1989) and Corbin (1990).

and with a view of nature – to construct both a set of locations for the spectacle in eighteenth-century culture (that joins the art gallery, the pleasure garden and the stately home) and a discourse of viewing that can be traced through a wide range of texts.[59] Thus for Michael Fried, 'theatricality' is a key term for comprehending artistic production in eighteenth-century France;[60] or, for Terry Castle, in the riotous spectacle of participation that is the English Masquerade, 'the spirit of theatricality, though reigning everywhere, followed no explicit programme' in its transgressive costuming and role-playing.[61] In short, 'The period' was 'obsessed with questions concerning spectatorial comportment and behaviour. This was a culture in which one of the most significant publications was entitled *The Spectator*, and in [which] all manner of public events, from hangings to masked balls, were deeply implicated in the conceptual folds of the spectacle.'[62]

Perhaps predictably, some of the implications of this type of analysis are given a fully post-modern (or perhaps just cynical) ethnographical twist by, say, James Clifford, who questions not merely the position of the anthropologist as observer of the spectacle of society – a position adopted by Turner and his followers without quite such self-consciousness – but also the cultural integrity of that spectacle itself: 'Twentieth-century identities no longer presuppose continuous cultures or traditions. Everywhere individuals or groups improvise local performances from (re)collected pasts, drawing on foreign media, symbols, language.'[63] For Clifford, in a paradigmatic late twentieth-century strategy, to observe is both to affect and to be affected by the phenomenon. Reconsidering 'spectacle' thus provokes critical exposure both of the performance of the observer/analyst and of the performance of the participants in culture itself.

In short, recent cultural history and its focus on 'the spectacle' has repeatedly explored the interface of the practices of representation with social and intellectual forces, and has found in the notion of performance a fundamental analytical category for the constructedness of social experience. This volume's detailed analyses of different elements of performance in the classical Athenian polis draw on the injunction of this theoretical work to consider in depth the interconnected

---

[59] For bibliography and discussion see de Bolla (1989); de Bolla (1996); de Bolla (forthcoming).
[60] Fried (1980).
[61] Castle (1986): the quotation is from p. 20.
[62] De Bolla (1996) 74.
[63] Clifford (1986) 19. This position has been widely discussed in subsequent anthropological work.

intellectual, social and institutional conditions that constitute the spectacle and the act of viewing as historically and culturally specific.

I have offered these cursory signposts to a complex field in part to help situate the following (and preceding) discussion against current theoretical debates; in part, to offer some assistance to readers who wish to follow up some of these general theoretical issues. In part, however, it is to mark a decision of the editors. We have chosen not to follow in the organization of this volume one common and often justifiable strategy, namely, to explore the issue of performance through a comparativist lens. (From the Ndembu to Annie Sprinkle, as it were...) This is not because there is not a great deal to be learnt from such a perspective, and indeed the influence of the theoretical debates I have alluded to will be evident in much of what follows. Rather, it is because we hope and expect that an extended, detailed look at one particularly involved, important and wide-ranging case over a restricted time period will allow to emerge a deeper and more nuanced comprehension of the complexity of what may be entailed by a 'performance culture'.

III

The specific studies that follow need some general contextualization in Athenian culture. In this section of the introduction, I offer some brief indications of the elements of Athenian democracy that have led us to turn to the notion of 'performance culture'. Although there may be few surprises for students of classical culture here, the weight of potential material and the complexity of the different locations and forms of performance remain quite remarkable.

I have already cited the Old Oligarch's comment that Athens had more festivals than any other Greek city. I wish to begin by looking at Athenian festival culture. Although all these festivals fall nominally under the aegis of the gods, and nearly all involve some obvious appurtenances of what could be called religion (sacrifice, prayer, temple or sacred site ceremonial), the separation of 'religion' as a discrete aspect of polis life is quite misleading (until Christianity's different demands on its adherents). All aspects of polis life engage with the divine (in different ways), and all aspects of religious activity were open to the scrutiny of the polis and its officials. Indeed, if one were to try to list the festival events included in the calendar (of the more than a hundred and twenty festivals), it would make an impressive catalogue that combined – by way of brief example – horse, boat and soldier racing, competitive wine drinking, acting in tragedy, parading orphans in full military equipment, poetry performance, carrying umbrellas, large model phalluses, boxes, and sacred objects in procession, ritual marriage with a god, dressing up in costume as satyrs, processing as maenads, singing and dancing in choruses, and the full gamut of mystery religion's hidden activities. Despite this extraordinary profusion of events, some more general characteristics can nonetheless be outlined.

Many festivals involve processions (*pompai*), which usually open the occasion (or dominate it), and thus provide a frame by means of spectacle and the articulation of a spectator/performer dynamic. *Pompai* articulate space as well as community,[64] most notably in the Panathenaia, whose procession followed what became known as the Panathenaic Way. It is not by chance that the Parthenon, that icon of Athenian democracy, has a frieze which represents a procession. In the heated debates about what the figures of this frieze represent, it is sometimes forgotten that the choice of a procession is extremely uncommon on monumental architecture (though not on votive reliefs) and signifies in itself: it represents the performance of the construction of a representative community in a socio-religious context, sited significantly on a temple designed to give a set of normative messages about Athenian culture from the heights of the Acropolis.[65] Processions are (ritual) performances of the ideological articulation of community links and divisions.

Many festivals involve competition.[66] Even where there is no formal aspect of competition, display inevitably involves competition and status. The speaker at the public burial of the war dead, for example – an institution and ritual practice introduced under the democratic regime[67] – was chosen because he was outstanding, and his public distinction not only thus increased his *timē* over and against other citizens, but also set his *epideixis* in (competitive) contrast with the roll-call of other chosen orators. ('The majority of former speakers from this spot ...', as Thucydides' Pericles begins.[68]) Many festivals combine different forms of competition in an intricate programme. The *Panathenaia*, which has been very well described and analysed of late,[69] combined a particularly extensive number and variety of events over an

---

[64] See for a strong model, de Polignac (1995). Also Cole (1993); Sourvinou-Inwood (1995). A typology of *pompai* can be found in Nilsson (1957) 166–214.
[65] See Osborne (1987); Connelly (1996).
[66] See Osborne (1993).
[67] Loraux (1981); Clairmont (1983).
[68] Thuc. 2. 35.1.
[69] See especially the articles collected in Neils (1992); also the less interesting, Neils (1996).

eight-day period. It began with the great procession to the Acropolis, which represented the city to the city (with each socio-political group of the citizen and non-citizen body, distinguished spatially and ritually by costume or position) and which culminated in a huge sacrifice (and thus feast). The following days included poetry and music competitions, including a competitive recitation between bards of both of the Homeric epics. There were boat races, organized on a tribal basis (the tribes are the socio-political divisions of the democratic state), male trials of strength and bodily excellence (also organized tribally), athletic competitions for boys, youths and men (these were open international events as were the music competitions), horse racing, a torch race connected to a night-time celebration, dancing and racing in hoplite equipment. Prizes included the famous Panathenaic amphorae of Athenian oil (as well as money and crowns). The Panathenaia, as Jennifer Neils writes, 'was a remarkable spectacle, even in ancient Greece where elaborate religious ceremonies were frequent occurrences'.[70] Both the Lenaia and the Great Dionysia (both festivals of Dionysus) lasted over a week, and both had similarly complex and varied types of performance, including the production of tragedy and comedy which rapidly became an internationally attended demonstration of Athenian culture.[71] Such festivals mapped the city, formed a calendar, and were integral in the construction of community – in the performance of citizenship.

Funding for the festivals was raised in part by liturgy – the selection of citizens by the state to make extensive financial donations.[72] This duty played a major role in the self-presentation of the elite citizen in the law-court. Participation in festivals was evaluated and discussed at different levels, however. Officials who organized events, as with all democratic officials, were publicly and formally evaluated at the end of their office. Playwrights, actors, and choruses were selected by the state and judged in competition by publicly appointed judges (and public opinion). Aeschines mocks Timarchus in court for getting drunk in an inn with some foreigners when he was meant to be part of the Panathenaic procession.[73] He also mocks Demosthenes for the sycophantic way he treated foreign ambassadors present at the Great Dionysia.[74]

---

[70] Neils (1992) 23.
[71] On the Great Dionysia see Goldhill (1990); on the other Dionysiac festivals, see Pickard-Cambridge (1968) and, less empirically, Daraki (1985). Csapo and Slater (1995) is a most useful collection of material.
[72] See Wilson (forthcoming).
[73] Aeschin. 1.43.
[74] Aeschin. 3.76.

Demosthenes, for his part, recalls the audience's hostile response to the appearance of his opponent, Meidias.[75] As festivals were a stage for the performance of citizenship, so that performance becomes restaged as a factor in the contestation of status and the politics of self-representation that constitutes public life in democracy.

Festivals provided one privileged site for what could be called artistic performance. Tragedy and comedy were staged primarily at the Great Dionysia and the Lenaia, and the festival context is fundamental for understanding the role of drama in the polis. Actors were as a rule citizens (rather than a dodgy demi-monde as in so many cultures), but throughout the fifth and fourth centuries they became increasingly professionalized and celebrated;[76] some foreign actors are also attested, who were sometimes awarded citizenship.[77] There were also choral competitions at the same festivals and elsewhere that were often (at the Great Dionysia, for example) tribally organized, and involved a great many citizens in performance and preparation. Homer too, as I have mentioned, was presented by rhapsodes at the Panathenaia (but could also be heard throughout the year in a range of more or less formal surroundings from schoolroom, to dinner party, to street, to private house). Along with the formal contexts for performance, the agora provided a public but less formal space where sophists, jugglers, actors, magicians competed with the gossip of the perfume stalls, the spectacle of the fish stall, and the other business of the city in action. A training in singing, music, and movement, however, was regarded as a normal and basic part of a citizen's education, and singing at symposia, both collectively and individually, maintained such performance as an aspect of the social performance of masculinity.[78] Although there were slaves and metics (resident aliens) involved in some aspects of musical production (which were by definition 'less honourable', although some became celebrated), a citizen's engagement with *mousikē* was a sign of *paideia* – being cultured, educated – in citizenship.

Theatre became a defining indicator of Greekness, as Alexander's imperial campaign spread Hellenized culture throughout the Eastern Mediterranean. Two other key institutional signs of this culture were the gymnasium and the symposium, both of which were inevitably important in Athens also (though, as noted above, neither can be called especially 'democratic' institutions). Despite the democratic claims of political equality between citizens and the concomitant complexities of

---

[75] Dem. 21.226. See Wilson (1991).
[76] See e.g. Ghiron-Bistagne (1976); Sutton (1987); Csapo and Slater (1995) 221ff.
[77] See Csapo and Slater (1995); Taplin in this volume.
[78] See Robb (1994) index *s.v. mousikē*; Marrou (1956).

social performance, both the symposium and the gymnasium were often associated with the social elite and with a certain social exclusiveness. The symposium's ritualized space and costume provided a space for the performance of song, but also, and more importantly, for the displays of erotic courtship and other aspects of male bonding from political pressure groups to philosophical circles.[79] The symposium parades the protocols typical of a central cultural institution. Interestingly, it was also the subject of much regulatory writing, not merely by moralists in prose works, but also by poets, in poems to be performed at the symposium. This self-reflexive normative voice is part of the performance as it comments on (the) performance (just as so many images that decorated the implements used at the symposia depicted sympotic activity[80]). The adoption of a voice at the symposium is especially marked in the performance of the first-person, highly sophisticated and elegant lyrics of sympotic poetry. What did it mean for a citizen to sing of Sappho's burning passion or Anacreon's ironic self-humiliation in the first person?[81] Erotic courtship (and erotic expression) is mediated through the narrative fiction of an other. Poetry teaches the citizen in part by providing exemplary models to be enacted. Such enactments inform the self-consciousnes of the lover's performance.

The gymnasium was a prime site for the contests of masculinity, both through competitive exercise and through erotic and other status pursuits and displays.[82] The exhibition, evaluation and cultivation of bodies in the public gaze was conjoined with the regulatory discourse of the *diaitai*, or books on regimen, studied well by Foucault (amongst others).[83] The gymnasium was where the 'care of the self' and 'discourse of the body' were performed in a privileged, regular and regulated fashion. This reached a pinnacle in the great festivals of athletics (such as the Olympics, and, to a lesser degree, the Panathenaia and other occasions) where a panhellenic reputation could be won. Yet the gymnasium was also perceived explicitly as a preparation for military excellence. A citizen was expected to play a full role in military activity, a role which was likely to be regular and severe, especially in the fifth century.[84] How one performed in such military activity was a defining

---

[79] See Murray (1990); Slater (1991); Levine (1985).
[80] See Lissarrague (1990).
[81] See Stehle (1997).
[82] See for testimonia Miller (1991), and for a more interpretative account Sansone (1988) (with further bibliography).
[83] See Foucault (1987); (1988).
[84] See Vernant (1980) 19–70. Finley (1983) 60–1 notes that there were 'few years in the history of most Greek city-states (of Sparta and Athens in particular), and hardly any years in succession, without some military engagements. We must also bear in mind

characteristic of masculine adult evaluation. As Plato's dialogues dramatize especially well, the gymnasium as a scene for news, argument, exercise, and above all, for men looking at men agonistically, makes it a key location for performance in the construction of public discourse of Athens as much as in the construction of the male body.[85]

The law-court and the Assembly were specifically democratic institutions, at least in their Athenian form. The mass audience of citizens (and only citizens) moving towards a decision, based on competitive performance before them, created the paradigmatic agonistic arena especially for elite competition. Recent scholarship has explored how elite speakers dramatize and manipulate their positions before mass audiences, and how both institutions were perceived as analogous to the theatre in their performative elements (and took up dramatic vocabulary to express their drama).[86] Rhetoric as a discipline theorized the persuasive performance (persuasively), and the bodies, voices, behaviour and gestures of orators was the subject of scrutiny and contest in the law-courts and Assembly themselves, as well as in historians and other theorists. Above all, both institutions were means of gaining status and authority within the political realm of the city, and thus such performances became key instruments of power. The political subject is constituted in and by performance; and citizens require self-conscious manipulation of performance in the pursuit of power.

Finally, with regard to the concerns of art history and performance, specifically with reference to material culture, Pericles' building programme is only one of the most prominent examples of the glorification of empire through stone – the creation of the imperial city (and its citizen). The Stoa Poikile, along one side of the agora, constructed a programme of images of military success, military memorials, and political statues, which faced the citizen with a normative repertoire of expressions of military duty.[87] The war-dead *stēlai* (with their politics of naming);[88] the long walls with their shrines and dedications, as well as their political and military construction of a link with the Piraeus, and their consequent expression of autonomous power; and, above all, the Acropolis as a site itself and in relation to the agora;[89] all created

that the brunt of the fighting was borne by citizen militias ... and the men who made the decisions to fight were largely those who went straight into battle themselves.' See also Davies (1978) 31ff.

[85] See Lewis (1996) and von Reden and Goldhill in this volume.
[86] See e.g. Eden (1986); Ober (1989); Hall (1995); Todd and Millett (1990); Foxhall and Lewis (1996).
[87] See Castriota (1992).
[88] See Loraux (1981) 31ff.; and for description see Clairmont (1983) 46–59; Bradeen (1969).
[89] See e.g. Rhodes (1995); Pollitt (1974); Loraux (1993) 148–236.

monuments and spaces which were meant to do things to the citizen. Athens indeed was a city of images (as it was a city of words), and the role of such exemplary representation in the formation of the ideals of citizenship cannot be ignored.

It would take many pages to review more fully the performances of the Panathenaia, say, or the Great Dionysia, let alone provide a synoptic account of ritual in religious contexts, display in political life, or the construction of the social self through the gymnasium, symposium and other institutions of cultural life. What I have tried to do here is merely to lay out a bare framework necessary for the detailed studies that follow, and to indicate some of the fine work upon which this volume sees itself as building.[90] What needs particular emphasis, however, is the different levels and sites of performance in Athenian culture – a complexity and range which make the example of classical Athens so stimulating, and so much more dynamic than many of the cases that have been used in performance studies.

IV

What we had originally hoped to do in the following chapters was twofold: first, to look within particular areas of performance at specific aspects, strategies, technical problems or historical concerns. So, for example, Oliver Taplin considers how drama spreads to different cities and becomes an international genre. Edith Hall in turn investigates when and why actors sing (as opposed to speak) in tragedy. Second, to look at the interfaces between different arenas, genres, or sites of performance. So, Andrew Ford investigates what happens when Homer is cited in the law-court; Sitta von Reden and Simon Goldhill look at what happens when the scene of the gymnasium is depicted in philosophical dialogue. It is, however, a noticeable and most welcome development of this intention that even in the examples I have offered the initial distinction could not hold. What might have appeared to be bounded questions rapidly implicate other issues and institutional frames. Thus, Pat Easterling begins by investigating the focus in orators on the orator's voice, but finds it immediately related to ideas of acting and performance (as well as the ideals of a citizen's body). Peter Wilson's project of characterizing the *aulos* (a kind of double oboe) is, it finally appears, not just a question of musicology, but requires a broad political framework concerning freedom, education, and the

---

[90] It should be probably stated explicitly that the bibliography provided above is intended to be selective and representative only.

regulation of the male body. Froma Zeitlin's interest in the performance of comedy requires comprehension of mythic models on the one hand, and ideas of the *schēma* of dress and identity on the other. The complexity of these projects reflects the complexity of the performance culture of Athens.

The structure of the book is simple enough, however. There are four sections. In the first, The Performance of Drama, we focus on one of the most important centres of performance in the polis, and the one which has been most discussed, namely, the festivals of drama. Oliver Taplin takes a broad look at what makes Athenian tragedy exportable, and how it became an international genre. How did the specifics of a performance context interact with the generality of the drama's themes to produce a performance which could be spread and be repeated? Peter Wilson looks at the musical instrument *par excellence* of tragedy, the *aulos*, a reed instrument often translated wrongly as 'flute'. He finds that to explore the place of this instrument in Athenian culture involves a wide range of cultural ideas – from the body to education to mythology – and he shows how deeply inscribed the technical aspects of performance are in the very widest ideological delineations of culture. Finally, Edith Hall considers the class and gender elements that inform the production of singing (as a representation and as a practice) as opposed to declaiming, with regard to the actor's voice.

Hall's paper acts as a bridge also to the second section, The Drama Of Performance, where the subject turns to how elements of performance on stage engage with – and become inscribed in – the social. Claude Calame explores first what a collective singing performance means for the authority and self-positioning of a group of figures. Collective performance, and individual authority, it need hardly be emphasized, are a central tension in democracy – for which the *choros* of collective singing becomes a privileged expression. Both Hall and Calame thus from different directions look at the politics of singing. This is juxtaposed to Pat Easterling's account of the 'voice' of the orator (and actor as orator), which investigates how this crucial tool of performance becomes the subject of self-conscious reflection, as well as training, in the polis. Finally, Froma Zeitlin in a characteristically broad-ranging piece, investigates how comic performance engages with ideal images of society and of the body. Performance studies has often claimed that performance 'reflects', 'encodes' cultural models. Aristophanic comedy offers a ludic, but also intellectually charged and self-conscious analysis of the relation between performance and such models, which Zeitlin draws out instructively.

The third section, Rhetoric and Performance, turns to different frames of performance and specifically rhetoric and philosophy. Jon Hesk looks at how rhetoric becomes increasingly obsessed with articulating, self-consciously, the limits and practices of deception. Once rhetoric recognizes that persuasion and deceit are integral to the public life of democracy, how is the scene of language exchange to be controlled, viewed, feared? The orator's performance becomes the means and matter of intense debate. Andrew Ford looks at how the elite and privileged genre of epic poetry enters the world of political debate. Who cites Homer and for what purposes or effects? What is it to perform poetry in court? The interface between genres of performance becomes the site of a contest in power and prestige. Finally, Sitta von Reden and Simon Goldhill investigate Plato's dialogues as a performance and as a representation of a performance. Plato's type of dialogue is not only articulated against other forms of political expression (thus marking the oblique position of the philosopher within democracy), but also raises questions in itself for the ability of philosophy to deal with the topics it raises. The philosopher's performance is thus placed under question.

In the fourth and final section, Ritual and State: Visuality and the Performance of Citizenship, spectacle comes to the fore. Athena Kavoulaki constructs an account of the processions which form so important a part in the civic world of democracy; Michael Jameson considers further how the ritual world of Athens also involves questions of what sorts of messages were available to audiences and participants and how ritual should be analysed as a 'spectacular' event. Robin Osborne and François Lissarrague focus on material culture. Both the State and private individuals in Athenian democracy decorated the city with a display of inscriptions recording decisions, honours, votes, victories. What did this epigraphic habit mean? What sort of a performance is this display of a memorial? François Lissarrague by contrast looks primarily at cups and pots which are inscribed with the word *kalos*. What did it mean in this culture of publicity to display someone as beautiful and noble – or merely to display that 'beauty and nobility' were to be predicated of an unnamed figure – in this way? The symposium's group culture, with its special protocols of play and status, provides one special context for thinking about how the values of a society are formed and circulated.

Despite this structure, there are many significant connections across sections: Taplin's arguments about the spread of tragedy relate to Lissarrague's about the spread of images; Easterling's account of the orator's voice finds strong echoes, of course, with Hall and Calame on the actor's and chorus's voices – but also with Hesk and Ford on the self-positioning of the orator; Osborne on civic inscriptions looks back to von Reden and Goldhill on civic spaces and philosophy's position in them; Kavoulaki and Jameson's accounts of ritual are usefully juxtaposed to Wilson's account of a key instrument of ritual. And so forth. Nor is this a chance set of connections (nor, we hope, a product of arbitrary organization). Rather, it is telling testimony of the necessary interconnections between what might appear disparate areas of study. It is this pattern of interconnections that has led us to term the object of our study 'performance culture and democracy'.

Part I

The performance of drama

2 Spreading the word through performance

Oliver Taplin

Performance studies has become a 'bricolage of intellectual material... loosely collected around a central term', as Simon Goldhill's Introduction has admirably adumbrated. That central 'core' might be defined as something like 'an occasion on which appropriate individuals enact events, in accordance with certain recognized conventions, in the sight and hearing of a larger social group, and in some sense for their benefit' (though it is not difficult to think of examples that infringe the borders of this rough delineation). And the closer one sticks to this central notion of 'performance', the more evident it is that ancient Greek societies were extraordinarily performanceful – and much more so than our own. Cultic rites, processions, athletic contests, musical contests, intellectual *epideixeis*, political and forensic oratory, gymnastic activities, military parades, battle exhortations, funeral *thrēnoi* and choral dance-songs of many kinds – given how widespread most of these were, it might even be contested whether fifth- and fourth-century democratic Athens was so exceptionally a performance culture as the Introduction maintains.[1] On the other hand, it is incontestable that drama is a key paradigm of performance, and that it was effectively Athens that added theatre to the repertoire for ancient Greece, and thence to a significant extent for Europe and for the whole world. Theatre has proved to be one of the most resilient and widespread of the achievements of ancient Athens – even the jewel in her violet crown – and implicitly an ornament for the form of government under which tragedy and comedy first flourished. Throughout ancient times Athens was give due credit as the motherland and metropolis of drama, even if with limited acknowledgement of the colour of the political seedbed.

A question which has not been much explored, however, is how far this potential to spread beyond Athens, and beyond the special Athenian

---

[1] And it was contested at the Cambridge conference in July 1996. I would like to thank all those at the conference for their constructive and challenging interaction, especially Peter Wilson, Eric Csapo and Robin Osborne. Martin Revermann and Roger Brock have also contributed helpful comments.

brand of democracy, was built into theatre, and tragedy in particular, already from the early days.[2] How *exclusively* Athenian was tragedy in the first place? How does tragedy's 'claim to universalizing value ... proven by its eventual status as an exportable product to be performed far and wide' relate to 'its original fusion with the city of Athens and its self-representation', to quote Froma Zeitlin's formulation of the issue?[3] Edith Hall, one of the few to recognize the non-Athenian element in tragedy's original public, speaks of 'the inherent contradiction' implied by it being both an opportunity to promote Athenian hegemonic propaganda and to celebrate the panhellenic ideal.[4] But what kind of 'contradiction' is this?

I shall pose, first, the 'factual' historical questions: what can we say about the chronology and mechanisms and extent of the spread of tragedy from Athens? I hope to make the case that it spread earlier, more readily and more widely than has usually been supposed. This then becomes an opportunity to explore the indivisibility of such 'merely antiquarian' questions from ideas, readings and ideologies. If tragedy appealed beyond Athens, why was this? Why did other cities so enthusiastically adopt the 'national poetry' of another far from universally popular megalopolis? Perhaps our scholarship of post-authoritarian disillusion has overemphasized the exclusive and hegemonic image of Athens, and has underrated the ways that cultural achievements were able to permeate through political and military barriers?

I

I shall approach the early spread of tragedy by working back through time towards the primary era. To begin from undeniably firm ground: tragedy was thoroughly panhellenic by the third century BCE – 'panhellenic', that is, in the weak sense of popular and shared throughout the Hellenic world.[5] It was as essential for a city to have a theatre as

---

[2] I am generally steering clear of comedy in this paper, in order to explore the case of tragedy in its own right. In Taplin (1993) I have made a case for the spread of Athenian Old Comedy to Megale Hellas within the lifetime of Aristophanes. If true, this is far more surprising than the contemporary spread of tragedy, since comedy was so much more overtly local and topical.

[3] Zeitlin (1993) 147 n. 2. Her own insistence is that the eventual spread 'should not obscure' the original fusion: my aim here is not to obscure it, but to qualify and variegate it.

[4] Hall (1989) 162 n. 8, pointing out that the Loraux/Goldhill account of Athens is in danger of being over-simply chauvinist. The whole section 'A theatre of Panhellenic ideas' (pp. 160–5) is particularly thought-provoking.

[5] This period of theatre is explored, along with its political implications, in the generally excellent article by le Guen (1995).

Spreading the word through performance 35

it was to have an agora and a gymnasium. Theatre-related art and artefacts are found from all over; texts are found in rubbish-tips and mummy-cartonage from Egypt. The substantial body of epigraphic evidence for the guilds of performers, the *Technitai*, begins in the 280s, indicating how widespread and well rewarded their activities were.[6] One of their guilds was based at Athens, but only one of the five most prestigious.

Less formalized troupes of travelling players, like that which included Aischines, must have been already active well back in the fourth century. Furthermore, some of the most famous names in the acting profession in the fourth century are non-Athenian, including Archeas of Thourioi, Neoptolemos of Skyros and Polos of Aigina. The great Aristodemos of Metapontion seems to have won his first victory as early as the 370s.[7] The only significant non-Athenian actor of the fifth century, however, seems to have been Mynniskos of Chalkis, whose career began in the time of Aischylos and continued down into the 420s. It is likely that the fourth-century thespians, at least, first encountered tragedy at performances in their own home-cities, though they evidently gravitated to the 'mother-city' to establish their careers.

The evidence for non-Athenian playwrights is, if anything, even more striking. Of the first ninety-four tragedians in volume 1 of *TrGF*, which takes us down towards the end of the fourth century, well over 10 per cent are 'foreign'. Even putting on one side the very early, and possibly problematic, Pratinas of Phlious (no. 4) and his son Aristeas (9), and discarding some dubiously attested names,[8] we still have such celebrated figures as Ion of Chios (19) and Achaios of Eretria (20) from the fifth century and Theodektas from Phaselis in Lykia (72) from the fourth. Other cities producing tragic playwrights included Tegea, Thourioi, Syracuse, Sinope, Aigina and Halikarnassos. The obsession of Dionysios of Syracuse, eventually crowned at the Lenaia of 368, is notorious. All of these poets evidently composed their tragedies in Attic Greek (though they may well have also composed other genres in other dialects). Nearly all, if not all, competed at Athens during their careers; but it is hardly plausible to suppose that they all first encountered tragedy at Athens.

---

[6] On this and related matters the chief works are Pickard-Cambridge (1988) ch. 7, Sifakis (1967) *passim*, Ghiron-Bistagne (1976) 154ff., Stephanis (1988); selected sources are translated in Csapo and Slater (1995) IV A ii (pp. 239–55). Stephanis 530–56 gives a catalogue of the 'ethnic origins' of performers in the theatre and related art-forms, which reveals that, after Athens, the places with the largest entries are Argos, Boiotia, Ephesos, Thespiai, Thebes, and Sikyon and (reflecting our sources) Oxyrhynchos.
[7] For evidence see Ghiron-Bistagne (1976) 174–9, Stephanis (1988) *sub nominibus*.
[8] Such as Neophron of Sikyon (15) or Sphinther of Herakleia (40).

In the second half of the fourth century tragedy is also associated with big spending on big occasions, evidence both of its panhellenic prestige and of its increasing detachment from Athenian predominance and from Athenian politics. Extravagant stories cluster round Jason of Pherai, Mausolos of Karia, and, above all, Philip and Alexander of Macedon. Quite often these occasions gathered actors, playwrights and other performers from far and wide: they presuppose the mobility and internationalism of the practitioners.[9]

As we trace the story of the spread of tragedy back into the earlier fourth century, and even into the fifth, it becomes less definite. The evidence is bitty, or in one way or another questionable – indeed the main reason why this chapter of theatre history has not been written before is that the evidence has been generally dismissed as inadequate. I shall maintain, nonetheless, that the main categories of evidence, taken together, do begin to form a coherent and convincing picture – fragmentary of course, in places speculative, but adding up to a probable rather than only possible scenario.

Theatre buildings beyond Athens supply one way in. Nearly all major cities and sanctuaries had built their first monumental theatre well before 300 BCE. There has been, so far as I know, no recent survey or reassessment of the archaeological evidence,[10] but it is agreed that some go back to early in the fourth century, or even before that. Besides Syracuse, where theatrical structures have been traced well back into the fifth, the best candidates seem to be Isthmia, site of the panhellenic *agōn* nearest to Athens (and later base of one of the troupes of Artists), and Eretria, a good ally of Athens, and only a short trip from the northern coastal demes of Attica.[11] Megalopolis also makes a particularly interesting case since it was founded as a new federal city in the 360s.[12] The huge theatre there looks to have been part of the original civic design and was architecturally of a piece with the council-chamber.

Whatever the exact dates of these 'foreign' theatres, tragedies were definitely being performed at the Rural Dionysia around Attica in the fifth century. Epigraphic and other archaeological evidence vouches for

---

[9] The main material is in Pickard-Cambridge (1988) 279–81, cf. Csapo and Slater (1995) 231–8. Plutarch's account (*Alexander* 29) of the dithyrambic and tragic contests in Phoenicia in 331, with the kings of Cyprus acting as rival *chorēgoi*, is a nice illustration.

[10] Any such survey would be helped by the series of bibliographies by Moretti (1991, 1992, 1993). The lavish 3-volume Possetto and Sartoro (1995) is weak throughout on chronology; and the diachronic survey by H. P. Isler (ibid. I pp. 86–125) fails to address this question.

[11] For Syracuse see Polacco (1981, 1990); for Isthmia see Gebhard (1973); for Eretria see Auberson and Schefold (1972).

[12] Immediately after 370 according to Hornblower (1990); cf. Wiles (1997) 36–8.

Ikarion, Thorikos, Euonymos (Trachones), Anagyros and Eleusis; early fourth-century evidence adds Aixone, Acharnai, Kollytos and Rhamnous.[13] Thucydides 8.93 is evidence for the Piraieus theatre close to Mounychia by 411.

We do not know whether the usual programme at the deme theatres was supplied by new plays by local playwrights, or re-plays of the big hits from the City Dionysia, or – perhaps most plausible – a mixture of the two. Re-performances would help to explain how the audiences of comedy could be expected to know some old tragedies quite well. And there is an important item of evidence which has usually been overlooked. Herodotos' famous anecdote (6.21) about Phrynichos' *Sack of Miletos* tells not only how Phrynichos was fined a thousand drachmas, but adds καὶ ἐπέταξαν μηκέτι μηδένα χρᾶσθαι τούτωι τῶι δράματι ('and they ordained that no one was ever again to exploit this play'). It is hard to see the point of this additional clause unless there were means and opportunities for further performances. And even if the story is not in fact true (the size of the fine is suspicious), it is still good evidence for the practice in the time of Herodotos.

Similarly we do not know whether the rural performances in the fifth century were always performed by locals, or always by travelling troupes, or, as is again most likely perhaps, by both, varying from time to time and place to place. We do know, however, from Demosthenes' *On the Crown* and related speeches that by mid-fourth-century, even perhaps the 360s, Aischines played the circuit of the rural Dionysia, acting in the repertoire that had become established by then. It may well be that aspiring actors, and aspiring playwrights likewise, first had to attract attention on the rural scene. On the other hand, to counteract the analogy of village-hall amateur dramatics, we know that Aristodemos himself sometimes acted in the same troupe as Aischines.

Once good quality productions with quasi-professional performers are going round the Attic demes, we have a plausible scenario for a rapid and easy spread to other parts of the Greek world. There is plenty of evidence for non-Athenians at the Great Dionysia in the later fifth century,[14] and by the time of Plato *Symposium* 175e Agathon's audience is thought of as 'Greeks' rather than 'Athenians'. How long would it be before these visitors thought of arranging for performances to be put on back in their home-cities? At first this may have been at places with close relations with Athens, or even with cleruchies, but, as we shall

---

[13] Helpful material in Whitehead (1986) 215–20; Csapo and Slater (1995) 121–32; Wiles (1997) 23–33.
[14] See, e.g., Pickard-Cambridge (1988) 58–9, Taplin (1993) 4–6.

see, political alliance was not a prerequisite for taking to tragedy. We lack direct evidence for this sequence of events, but it makes good sense and we have nothing to contradict it.

We also do not know whether the travelling troupes normally included a choros. Given that a choros is normally an expression of local order and collaboration, it may well be that they were usually provided from local talent. This prompts a new answer to an old problem. It might have become the practice for a locally rehearsed choros to sing 'interlude songs' rather than to attempt the dramatist's original (sometimes difficult?) lyrics. And this might have led in scripts to the replacement of the lyrics with the simple indication χόρου (μέλος) ('lyric by the choros').[15] In other words, the conventional marker χόρου might not, at least not at first, have meant that the playwright had not composed any song at all for that slot, but that for the purposes of re-performance it was left for a local choros to supply one of their own.

To return to rather more solid ground, Plato bears clear witness to the spread of theatre in the first half of the fourth century. First, in the *Laws*, where there are several complaints about 'modern theatrocracy', there is a reference (659c) to the degenerate practice 'these days in Sicily and Italy', by which the whole audience, and not select judges, award the dramatic prizes – a system, we may note, rather more 'democratic' than the Athenian. Then, later in *Laws* (817b–c) 'the Athenian' sets up the legislators in direct rivalry with purveyors of drama, warning them not to expect that they will be granted the licence 'to fix up stages (σκηνάς τε πήξαντας) in the agora, nor that mellifluous actors will be allowed to sway the children and women and the whole mass of the people (ὄχλον)'. It is also worth noting here the bricolage of temporary stages, which are shown by the comedy-related vase-paintings to have been common practice in fourth-century Megale Hellas.[16] So this passage fits well with the picture reconstructed above of the widespread activities of travelling troupes already in Plato's day.

There are also two interesting Platonic passages which have usually

---

[15] I owe this idea to Martin Revermann. 'χόρου' occurs, of course, in our texts of Aristophanes' last two surviving comedies, in New Comedy, and in several tragic papyri. If 60 T1h in *TrGF* 1 does come from Astydamas II *Hektor*, that would be mid-fourth century.

[16] Hughes (1996) has argued that the stages shown on the vases were permanent rather than portable and temporary. His case is better for the vases which are later than for those earlier in date. Another possible indication that Plato was thinking of performance outside Athens is his inclusion of women in the audience. If they were admitted to shows outside Athens, but were debarred from the Great Dionysia, then this would explain those passages of Plato, above all *Gorgias* 502d, which seem to contradict the main flow of the evidence against their presence at Athens.

been taken to refer only to Attic festivals, but which include a plurality of 'cities' that points beyond. At *Republic* 475d theatre-lovers and music-lovers are regarded by Glaukon as hardly suitable to be counted among wisdom-lovers (φιλοθεάμονες ... φιλήκοοι ... φιλόσοφοις ...): they go rushing round to every possible Dionysia οὔτε τῶν κατὰ πόλεις οὔτε τῶν κατὰ κώμας ἀπολειπόμενοι ('not missing any, neither in the cities nor in the villages'). This has always been taken to refer to *the* City Dionysia and the Rural Dionysia. But as Albert Henrichs observes, κατὰ πόλεις is 'a difficult plural, unless he was looking beyond Athens'.[17] In that case, it is evidence that some dedicated theatre-goers would even travel to 'away matches', let alone doing the rounds of the Attic demes. And at *Laches* 183a–b it is claimed, as an analogy to the main argument, that a talented tragedian brings his goods straight to Athens, the metropolis, and οὐκ ἔξωθεν κύκλωι περὶ τὴν Ἀττικὴν κατὰ τὰς ἄλλας πόλεις ἐπιδεικνύμενος περιέρχεται ('does not go around on a circuit around Attica putting on shows in the other cities'). The phrase κατὰ τὰς ἄλλας πόλεις has been usually taken to refer to the deme theatres of Attica; but the usage of πόλεις and the whole context both point to places beyond the sphere of Athens (cf. τὰς ἄλλας περιιόντες πόλεις at *Resp.* 568c). It looks, then, as though the Greek should mean 'on a circuit outside Attica'.[18] So by the time of *Laches*, which may be as early as the 390s, it was possible for a tragic poet to try to make a living outside Athens, though anyone with ambition would still hope to make his name there.

The next category of evidence is better known but more disputable: the reflection of Athenian tragedy in non-Athenian vase-painting. First, however, it is worth registering that some Athenian ceramics with theatrical subject-matter were exported. The hydria fragments, dating from before the middle of the fifth century, which show an oriental pyre scene, were found at Corinth. The Pronomos vase was found at Ruvo in northern Apulia, and the fragmentary choros of women in Würzburg came from Taras in southern Apulia.[19] Such pieces might mean a public with an interest in theatre, though there are other no less likely explanations.

---

[17] Henrichs (1990) 272 n. 8.
[18] Or if that cannot be squeezed out of περί, then a καί needs to be added either before or instead of κατά. Emlyn-Jones (1996) *ad loc.* glosses as 'cities outside (bordering on) Attica'.
[19] Details of the fragmentary pieces are in Taplin (1993) 119–20 at 7.*119*A and 7.*120*A. Details of Pronomos are accessible as no. 5 on pp. 111–12 of Handley and Green (1995). For Corinth, Macdonald (1982) 113–23 traces the substantial import of Athenian pottery during the fifth century; and he observes that, while it diminishes, it by no means ceases during the hostilities of the last third of the century.

The question of how far (if at all) the viewers of fourth-century south-Italian vase-painting brought to bear an interest in tragedy for the appreciation of mythical scenes is hotly debated. It is too big a complex of issues to be adequately discussed here, and I hope to explore it properly in the future.[20] At the very least, however, it is undeniable that from very early in the century there are paintings of tragic masks, held by actors or by Dionysos.[21]

For now, it is relevant to counteract two arguments that have been given too much weight in some recent discussions which go *against* any significant presence of tragedy. One is the notion that drama was an exclusive, elitist preserve, inaccessible to the public of these ordinary popular ceramics. This is contradicted by the huge theatre buildings and by the complaints of Plato and Aristotle against tragedy's vulgar reception – I shall return to this towards the end. The other is that the vase painters are 'simply telling the story' without recherché literary allusions. But tragedy was neither literary nor recherché, it was popular performed story-telling. Thus, when Giuliani (1996) concludes an interesting discussion by insisting that 'what the image tries to represent is not epic and not tragedy, but quite simply *the story of Rhesus' death*' (his italics), I would question the phrase 'quite simply'.

And some of the iconographies must have originally been inspired by the theatre, however independent they became, because that version of the story was invented by a dramatist. Thus the highly popular scene of Orestes at Delphi (over forty known examples) must have been first drawn from Aischylos' *Eumenides*. Even more directly, the story of Iphigeneia as a priestess among the Taurians and handing over the letter to Pylades originated with Euripides' *IT*. There are now six Apulian paintings of this scene. When Green (1994) 52 insists that 'none ... shows any evidence of direct inspiration from stage performance, but simply the historico-mythical event', he is drawing a false distinction: Euripides' play *was* the 'event', and that is most likely how the audience would have known it. There is no need to thrash out disputed cases, however, to observe that, in so far as there is some degree of interaction between the theatre and some of the vase-painting, Euripides is the playwright most reflected; and that *Telephos*, *Andromeda* and *IT* are the most reflected plays. This fits well with other evidence for the popularity of Euripides in the fourth century.

It is worth dwelling on one particular group of pots, since there is

---

[20] This is a mere beginning in Taplin (1993) ch. 3. Two significant discussions since then: Green (1994) 51–62 and Giuliani (1996).

[21] See Trendall (1988), and note especially nos. I. 1 and 2 on p. 140, dated to *c*. 400, cf. Taplin (1993) 92. There is also an early painting of three actors costumed for satyr-play – see III. 1 on p. 152.

good reason to date them close to 400 BCE. These were excavated in 1963 from a tomb at Policoro, the ancient Herakleia, a city with links with Thourioi, though even stronger with Taras.[22] Of the seventeen vases buried there, twelve have mythological scenes, and at least three of these can be plausibly related to tragedies of Euripides. The 'Policoro Medeia', which shows Medeia triumphant over Jason, seems to be strongly informed by the spatial dynamics of the end of Euripides' play of 431, as does the contemporary 'Cleveland Medeia'.[23] Secondly, the scene of Iolaos at the altar with young descendants of Herakles, which also has a close contemporary parallel, seems to need Euripides' *Herakleidai* of the early 420s in order to be interpreted: that is the 'mythico-historical event' in question.[24] Third, and perhaps most suggestive, is the punishment of Dirke, tied to a bull by the sons of Antiope. There is nothing in this picture to suggest any theatrical connection, yet the story had been very likely told for the first time in Euripides' play *Antiope* of c. 409; and we have two further versions of the same iconography from later in the century which have strong indications that they *are* informed by Euripides' well-known tragedy.[25] The striking inference from this is that the Policoro painting was inspired by a play which had been first performed at Athens less than twenty years earlier, possibly much less. This all fits with a scenario according to which, by the end of the fifth century, a new play might spread from Athens very soon – and it is hard to explain any other way.

The last, and most raked over, category of evidence is that for activity outside Athens by the great fifth-century playwrights in person. Much of this anecdotal material has to be well salted with scepticism, but that does not mean that it is entirely without foundation.[26] Thus, it is beyond reasonable doubt that Aischylos travelled to Sicily, and that he died at Gela; and that he put on a play, *Aitnai* or *Aitnaiai*, to celebrate Hieron's new foundation of Aitne during the 470s 'auguring the good life for the city's settlers' (ὑπεδείξατο τὰς Αἴτνας οἰωνιζόμενος βίον ἀγαθὸν τοῖς συνοικίζουσι τὴν πόλιν).[27] Did he train a troupe of Sicilians, or did he take Athenian performers with him, it would be very interesting to know.

---

[22] Published by Degrassi (1967), dated by Trendall (1967) 51–2; cf. Taplin (1993) 16–17.
[23] Cf. Taplin (1993) 16–17, 22–3.
[24] Cf. Taplin (1993) 16–17, Wiles (1997) 191–4. Wilkins (1993) xxxi–ii has no doubts that the paintings and the tragedy are closely related.
[25] I discuss these three related vases in Taplin (1998). The Dirke Painter's krater in Berlin (c. 380) is well discussed by Csapo and Slater (1995) 60–2 with plate 3A. The later krater by the Underworld Painter was first published by Trendall (1986); cf. Green (1994) 57 with fig. 3.4a–b.
[26] Lefkowitz (1981) comes close to this over-reaction at times, e.g. on pp. 96, 103 where she is inclined to doubt whether Euripides really had *any* dealings with Macedon.
[27] *Life* §9 = p. 34 in *TrGF* III. For *Aitnai* or *Aitnaiai* see Radt *op.cit.* pp. 126–30.

It would also be interesting to know how early the kings of Macedon came to perceive tragedy as a prestigious art-form, whose promotion would give them respectability in the mainstream of Hellenic culture. It is firm ground that Agathon had left Athens before 405, as is shown by *Frogs* 85 (and scholia).[28] Stories of Euripides in Macedon were already circulating by the time of Aristotle *Pol.* 1311b30 (= T61K)[29], which tells a silly anecdote. But far more substantial than this and other such tales, for example about Euripides' death, is the evidence for the play *Archelaos*, which he composed χαριζόμενος αὐτῶι ('to gratify him', viz. King Archelaos), as the *Life* puts it (= T.1.11 on p. 2K). As Annette Harder (1985) has painstakingly established, the play told how the Temenid Archelaos, Argive ancestor of his late fifth-century namesake (king from 413 to 399), suffered various adventures in exile in Thrace, where the play was set. Finally, Apollo *apo mechanes* told him to follow a goat (αἶγα) which would show him where to found his new capital.[30] If this reconstruction is right, then the aetiology has to be of Aigai; and that then has to be the likely setting for the original performance.[31] So the play was quite possibly created for the very theatrical space where the assassination of Philip was 'staged' some seventy years later. But, wherever in Macedon the first production was mounted, it is clear from the quite numerous fragments that *Archelaos* was in Attic Greek and observed the conventions of Athenian tragedy.

So the testimony of the *Life* (T1.10 on p. 2K) that Euripides spent time in Magnesia (in Thessaly) and was granted privileges there, is not necessarily fiction.[32] Similarly the reference in Aristotle *Rh.* 1384b15 (= T94K) to 'Euripides' reply to the Syracusans' (to the effect that the first moves of friendship are welcome) is not incredible enough to justify the various attempts to emend the name of Euripides right out of the passage. It does, after all, tally with the anecdotes about Athenian prisoners in 413 gaining release from the stone-quarries by means of their memorization of Euripides. The similarities and differences between the version in Satyros (Alexandria, third century BCE; T4.21 on

---

[28] Other evidence in Plato *Symp.* 172c; cf. also *TrGF* I 39T9, 11, 22a, 22b, 25.
[29] Testimonia for Euripides are cited from Kovaks (1994).
[30] Harder (1985) 174–5, mainly based on 'Hyginus' 219: *inde profugit ex responso Apollonis in Macedoniam capra duce, oppidumque ex nomine caprae Aegeas constituit.*
[31] Harder (1985) 126–7 seems over-guarded on this. According to Diod. Sic. 17.16 Archelaos established theatrical events at Dion in honour of Zeus and the Muses (lavishly celebrated by Alexander in 335–4). Even if Bosworth (1980) *ad loc.* is right that Arrian 1.11.1 is mistaken to set these festivities at Aigai, that is no reason to displace Euripides' production from the place it celebrates. Wiles (1997) 38–9 discusses the theatre at Aigai, but without reference to *Archelaos*.
[32] Cf. Easterling (1994) 76 'looks like one of the few possibly authentic scraps of information among the fictional constructions identified by scholars'.

p. 24K) and in Plutarch's *Nikias* (T92 on p. 122K) might suggest an earlier common source. The whole story may be a fiction, but there is still nothing unbelievable about it. The detail in Satyros that they taught their captors' sons, and in Plutarch that they performed Euripides' songs are both positively plausible. The Syracusans were Doric-speaking, and never on good terms with Athens even before the bloody conflict of 415–413: nonetheless tragedy had evidently taken root there from early days, indeed since the time of Hieron. To judge from the vase-paintings, Athenian tragedy had also become just as popular – or even more so – at Taras, *apoikia* of the Laconians, and no friend of Athens.

II

My aim so far has been to have made a case on *external* evidence that tragedy was already performed outside Athens on quite a significant scale during the fifth century, especially during, say, its last forty years. If this is accepted as probable, or even as possible, then we can hardly avoid asking whether this exportation has left any *internal* traces within the surviving plays. The primary audience was nearly always, of course, the Athenians – though *Aitnaiai* and *Archelaos* have already been established as exceptions. But is it possible that the surviving plays include traces of an awareness of potential audiences beyond Attica? I should perhaps sound a preliminary health-warning that this section inevitably contains a relatively high level of speculation, or at least of unverifiable reconstruction, but the issue should still be worth exploring. The argument of this paper as a whole is, in any case, in no way dependent on this local speculation.

The most likely internal indicator would surely be matter which more or less explicitly glorifies the audience of a particular polis, or some other place-defined socio-political grouping. I shall call this phenomenon 'localization'. Clearly there was already a strong tradition of localization in certain kinds of poetry, especially choral lyric. Among the fragments of Alkman, Simonides, Bakchylides and others there are unmistakable traces of locally directed praise-motifs in partheneia, paians, hymns, prosodia and, not least, dithyrambs. In fully surviving poetry, it is to be seen – though less blatantly perhaps – in Pindar's epinikia, through the treatment of the site of the games, of the poet's own city and of the victor's city.

At the most basic level, to tell a myth which is set in a certain locality reflects *some* glory on that place; and the story need not be a happy one. Thus, at *Pythian* 3.86ff. Pindar tells of the wedding of Kadmos and

Harmonia and of the divine guests there (strong parallel with the Peleus of *Iliad* 24 throughout). But, he adds, Kadmos' good fortune was destroyed by three of his daughters – though the fourth did, it is true, go to bed with Zeus. Although bad is mixed with the good, this mythology is still to the glory of Thebes. At *Olympian* 13.49–54 Pindar praises Corinth by alluding to stories which in Athenian drama are far from favourably treated: Sisyphos and Medeia show, he sings, that Corinth is remarkable ἐν ἡρωϊαῖς ἀρεταίσιν ('for heroic achievements').

More explicitly, there can be poetry referring to the local topography, especially nurturing rivers; to the fertility of agriculture and livestock; to fine buildings or great city walls; to temples, altars, cults and festivals. And, above all, there are local aetiologies, which may be attached to any of these features or to local dynasties.

Clearly there *are* localizations of this sort in tragedy, relating both to Athens and to a variety of other places. So it seems at least worth exploring the possibility that part of their purpose was to appeal to local sensibilities. It is encouraging that Pat Easterling (1994) has been thinking along the same lines, and has pointed to some passages in Euripides that might plausibly be supposed to have been framed, at least secondarily, for the ears of certain non-Athenian audiences. She bases her case on two rather similar lyrics at *Hekabe* 444–83 and *Troades* 197–234, where the Trojan slave-women go through some of the places they might end up at, adding eulogistic and negative comments. In *Hek.* their praise is for Thessaly (and the river Apidanos), for Delos and for Athens. There is a more elaborate sequence in *Tro.*: first Athens (but not, they add, Sparta), then next best Thessaly with the river Peneios and its fertile prosperity (214–19), or Aitnaian Sicily, famed for its victors in the panhellenic games (220–3). Lastly, they think of the prosperous country which is irrigated by the river Krathis (224–9): this is the non-Homeric Thourioi, founded some thirty years before this play, and very likely to have been one of the first places to have hosted performances of Athenian tragedy.[33]

Apart from these, Easterling's attention gravitates to Macedon, especially the archetypal localization at *Bakchai* 565–75.[34] What strikes me more, however, is that the passages of *Hek.* and *Tro.* both praise Thessaly. These are far from the only tragic localizations of Thessaly.

---

[33] The early fourth-century minor tragedian Patrokles came from Thourioi; so, of course, did the major comedian Alexis. It is worth noting that Eur. *Melanippe Desmotis* was set at Metapontion.

[34] Easterling (1994) 77–9. I would, however, deploy this same methodology to argue that Athenians, not Macedonians, were the primary recipients of *Bakchai*. This is because of the play's localization of Kithairon.

In *Alkestis*, for example, the initial setting is vaguely at the city of Pherai (e.g. 235); but when the Servant tells Herakles about the burial-place of Alkestis the site is specific: ὀρθὴν παρ' οἶμον, ἥ 'πὶ Λάρισσαν φέρει, | τύμβον κατόψει ξεστὸν ἐκ προάστιου (835–6, 'by the high-way which leads to Larissa, you will see the tomb of new-cut stone as you leave the outskirts'). This is where Herakles fights Thanatos. It has not been registered, so far as I know, that this instruction precisely locates the major northern cemetery of ancient Pherai (modern Velestina), which has been partially excavated over the last sixty years, and which seems to have been an important cult-centre for this whole part of Thessaly.[35] At the end of the play Admetos establishes celebratory rituals in memory of Herakles' feat, announcing this ἀστοῖς ... πάσηι τε ... τετραρχίαι (1153–6, 'to the citizens and to the whole province (tetrarchy)'). There may also be a hinted aetiology for a hero-cult of Alkestis once she is finally entombed there.[36]

Another play with heavy Thessalian localization is *Andromache*. This is established in the prologue, where Andromache sets her story in Phthia, near the city of Pharsalos (historically the capital of the tetrarchy of Phthiotis), and more precisely at Thetideion (16–20, note esp. Φθίας δὲ τῆσδε καὶ πόλεως Φαρσαλίας | ξύγχορτα ναίω πεδία – 'I live in the borderland plain between Phthia on this side and the city of Pharsalos'); and there are further references to the cult of Thetis (43–4, 115).[37] In his lament at the end of the play Peleus emphasizes that the death of Neoptolemos at the hands of aliens is a disaster for the whole πόλις Θεσσαλία ('land [or city] of Thessaly', 1176 cf. 1187, 1211). Finally, Thetis gives a clear aetiology for the hero-cult of Peleus at Cape Sepias (1263–9).[38] There is, of course, the scholion (on line 445) which says that *Andromache* did not figure in the Athenian *didaskaliai*. Without that incitement I would not even whisper the possibility that the *primary* audience might not have been Athenian; but, even if there were no such scholion, one might suggest a secondary Thessalian audience.[39]

---

[35] See A. Dhoulgeri-Indzessiloglou in Midhrahi-Kapon (1994) II, 71–92, esp. 79, with reference to earlier publications. I am indebted here to Maria Stamatopoulou (Somerville College) who is completing a doctorate on Thessalian funerary practices.

[36] Larson (1995) 147 includes Alkestis for 'possible cult'.

[37] There is a good discussion in Lloyd (1994) 9–10. His details correct Easterling (1994) 79 who says that 'the Thessalian setting is not given any specially detailed attention'.

[38] This is the coast where the Persian fleet suffered such damage: see Hdt. 7.188–91, where the Magi eventually sacrifice to Thetis.

[39] The Thessalian localization is far stronger than the Molossian material in lines 1243–9, though that might suggest a yet further audience (Easterling (1994) 79). For more Thessalian material in Eur. see, e.g., *HF* 364–74; *Bacch*. 410, 565ff.; *IA* 234, 808, 954 and 1031ff.

Before indulging in the picture of a troupe of Athenian players traipsing with their *skēnai* round the plains of Thessaly, I should bring to bear the southern Thessalian localizations in two surviving plays of Sophokles. In *Philoktetes* the pyre of Herakles on Mount Oita and the whole surrounding area are important,[40] especially at lines 490-2 and 721-9, where Malis, Oita and the river Spercheios are all worked in; and finally at 1428-33 there is a reinforcing aetiology of Herakles' hero-cult at the pyre. The area is more strikingly immediate in *Trachiniai*, as in lines 200, 436-7, 1191ff. and other passages. It is the choral lyric at 633-9, however, which stands out because it begins with language so typical of eulogistic localization: ὦ ναύλοχα καὶ πετραῖα θερμὰ λουτρὰ καὶ πάγους | Οἴτας περιναιετάοντες, οἵ τε μέσσαν | Μηλίδα πὰρ λίμναν | χρυσαλακάτου τ' ἀκτὰν κόρας, | ἔνθ' Ἑλλάνων ἀγοραὶ Πυλάτιδες κλέονται ... ('O you who inhabit the harbour by the rocky hot springs, and the spurs of Oita, and you by the inner Malian gulf, and the shore of the maiden-goddess of the golden shuttle, where the celebrated gatherings of the Hellenes at the Pylai are held ...'). The reference here is to the regular meetings of the Amphiktyones or *Pylagorai* at the sanctuary by Thermopylai. The site of the pyre on Oita was close enough to here for locals to pick posies of the rare White Hellebore which grows there and sell them at the gatherings.[41] The Pylaia is cited as a major panhellenic union at Ar. *Lysistrata* 1131 and elsewhere; but membership was in fact predominantly local, especially south Thessalian, though it also included representatives of Athens and Sikyon. Before tragedies came to be played eventually all round Thessaly, it seems plausible that they should have been put on at this festival, and that this should be the audience (if any) to be pleased by Thessalian localizations. There is, however, so far as I know, no external evidence for any theatrical performances at the Pylai. Nor has any archaeological trace been found, though this is not a fatal objection – the theatrical space could well have been natural, and the *skēnai* temporary.[42]

The question is bound to arise whether there was a political or diplomatic dimension to all this material that may have been there in part to please Thessalians, whether at the Pylaia or, less speculatively, at the

---

[40] The pyre was not at the summit (2116m.), as is often supposed, but at *c*. 1800 m. near the present village of Pavliani. See Béquignon (1937) 204-30 (with photo in pl. VII.2), P. Pantos in Midhrahi-Kapon (1994) II, 227.

[41] See Theophrastos, *Hist. pl.* 9.10.2. For a view of Oita from Thermopylai see the photo in Müller (1987) 347.

[42] The area is eroded and very little archaeological work has been done, but there was a substantial stadium. See Béquignon (1937) 181-204, Müller (1987) 303, Pantos in Midhrahi-Kapon (1994) II, 227, and esp. Thalmann (1980), who has an aerial photograph.

Athenian Dionysia. There is, as it happens, a clear case for possible power politics; but it should not be presupposed that there has to be. We have already encountered the high popularity of tragedy at Syracuse, and at Taras, which was very aware of being a Laconian *apoikia*. And before latching onto 'ulterior' motives, it should be registered how there was generally a degree of panhellenism in the appreciation of poets and poetry in ancient Greece – and indeed in many other spheres of artistic and intellectual achievement. The appreciation, and even the performance, of a Pindar poem was not necessarily restricted to the honorand's home-city or to Thebes.[43]

Homer is, in some sense, the archetypal precedent for this cultural supra-nationalism. The epics were performed everywhere, whether or not the locality in question figured in the poems – indeed, many major centres, including Athens and Chios, had to swallow their pride in this matter. Cleisthenes of Sikyon (Hdt. 5.67) with his objection to the epic celebration of Argives and Argos – to a large extent a superficial misinterpretation, in fact – seems to be the exception who proves the rule. There is remarkably little localization of any evident kind in Homer, especially when compared with some later lyric genres; and this may well have been an element in the rapid and universal spread of the epics. If the scattered low-key aetiologies and occasional local allusions that *are* there were slipped in to please any particular local audiences, then they do so in a very sparse and discreet way.[44] Homer seems, then, to be a paradigm of poetry that spreads throughout Greece, becomes to some extent panhellenic,[45] for what might be roughly called 'aesthetic' reasons rather than what might be roughly called 'political' reasons (not that I would wish to press that distinction hard, let alone suggest that it is mutually exclusive). Homer *seemed* at least to be exploring universal human concerns, rather than confined within the particular mind-set of a particular audience.

To return to tragedy; however much the Thessalians themselves may have appreciated the plays for 'aesthetic' qualities, there can be no

---

[43] See Nagy (1990), esp. 113–15.
[44] Janko (1992) interestingly emphasizes Iliadic material with a potential local appeal. But, while I agree with him that 'the idea of the *aition* is already latent in Homer' (396), the claim that 'genealogy formed the basis of the whole epic genre, which Homer knew well' (184) seems far-fetched, seeing that, if it is true, this 'basis' has been systematically submerged.
[45] It has become a commonplace to say, following the influential Nagy (1979), that Homer always was 'panhellenic'. It is still not clear, however, what this actually meant in terms of audiences and reception in the formative period. Is this 'panhellenic' in the weak sense of 'shared by all Hellenes', or in the strong sense of 'promoting the amicable collaboration of all Hellenes'?

doubt that the Athenians had pragmatic reasons for courting their goodwill. Their alliance was of strategic and military importance (see e.g. Thuc. 1.102.4, 2.22); there was the important road which led over from Amphissa (and Delphi) to emerge between Thermopylai and Oita; and the Amphyktiones were of use for their influence on Delphi. During the early Peloponnesian War there was a lot of diplomatic and military activity in this area, most obviously marked by the Spartan attempt to set up a new *apoikia* in the region. Thucydides 3.92.3 tells of the foundation and failure of Trachinian Herakleia, a mere forty stades from the site of Leonidas' historic last stand.[46]

It seems more than possible, then, that the Thessalian localizations in Sophokles and Euripides are there, at least on some level, to promote the Athenian cause in that area. They may be seen, that is, as a kind of 'cultural propaganda', suggesting to Malians, Trachinians, Phthiotians, Pheraians and the rest that they should wish to be closely affiliated with the city which has created such a superb new art-form, and which has celebrated their localities within it. A weaker alternative – which would be the more conventional view – would say that the Thessalian material is there at least partly to please Athenians who were in one way or another well disposed towards Thessaly, and perhaps any few Thessalians who might happen to be in the audience at Athens. But if it is once accepted that tragedy had been re-performed in the fifth century at Isthmia or Aigai, then why not at the Pylaia, or even in Thessalian Magnesia (see p. 42)?

III

I have taken care to signal any potential non-Athenian audiences as 'secondary'; with very few exceptions the citizens of Athens were without doubt the primary audience and the primary assessors in every sense. So how prominent is this primacy *within the plays*, and in particular to what extent is there Athenian localization? This might throw some light on the question of how *exclusively* Athenian tragedy was. Just as there is plenty to please Thebans in the poems of Pindar, even in many with non-Theban patrons, so one might, at first glance, expect Athenian tragedy to be infused through and through with material which is directly or indirectly patriotic or nationalistic. And much recent scholarship does give that impression. On closer inspection, however, the case becomes interestingly much less simple.

---

[46] See Hornblower (1991) 501–8, who argues that at least one of the Spartans' motives was to get a say on the Amphyktionic Council.

About one third, I calculate, of the plays in the surviving corpus have a conspicuous element of Athenian matter in them. There is even one tragedy which is set in the heart of the city – an Athens with a proto-democratic constitution, furthermore – and which is suffused with patriotic aetiologies and aspirations. But, as in many other ways, *Eumenides* proves to be the model for what did *not* become the norm: pouring out blessings on the future citizens of Athens was not the standard way to win the prize. We know about one other play set in the city, Euripides' *Erechtheus*, and that also ended with multiple aetiologies, although all of them were cultic. It was clearly a very different play from *Eumenides*, however, and until the consolations of the aetiologies was evidently deeply distressing for Athens.[47]

Three of the surviving plays are set in Attica, Eur. *Herakl.* and *Supp.* and Soph. *OK*; and all have quite a lot of patriotic localization and aetiology, including Theseus' praise of democracy at *Supp.* 426ff., and the 'Kolonos Ode' in *OK*.[48] Some plays which are set elsewhere still have a strong and explicit Athenian element: *Ion* most obviously, but also *Hipp.* and *Aias*, especially if the aetiology of Aias' Rhoitean cult is to be related to the Aiantis tribe.[49] The most blatant localized eulogy outside *Eum.* is at *Medeia* 824ff. But this lyric, quite apart from the way that it is undercut by Medea's going to this paradise despite her infanticide, brings home the point that this kind of thing is a rarity in our tragedies, and is not the commonplace one might have expected. Then there are Attic aetiologies in plays that are otherwise concerned with other places, for example in *Herakles* (1324ff.) and *IT* (1449ff.). And some tragedies include the odd 'gratuitous' passing reference, such as those already seen in *Hek.* and *Tro.* (see p. 44 above), or the secondary aetiology at *Helen* 1670–5. But there are still four plays of Aischylos and four of Sophokles and seven of Euripides (an interestingly lower proportion) and two anonymous tragedies, where there is (so far as I can recall) either minimal allusion to Athens or no direct allusion at all.

It would clearly not have been beyond the skills of the playwrights to work various sorts of Athenian eulogistic reinforcement and comfort

---

[47] The new edition by Cropp (1995) is very helpful. (I should perhaps take this opportunity to correct a half-error in Taplin (1996) 202 n. 37 where I imply that we know less about the end of *Erechtheus* than we do.)

[48] For some interesting observations on significant Attic localities see Krummen (1993). It might seem particularly surprising to find *Herakl.* reflected in south-Italian pottery painting – see p. 41 above – but it may have had special appeal at Herakleia?

[49] The one tribe whose eponymous hero was not Athenian: Hdt. 5.66. The interpretation of the end of *Aias* has been greatly advanced by Henrichs (1993). In *Hipp.* there is, it is worth noting, an Althenian cult-aetiology in the prologue at lines 28–30 – see Halleran (1995) 22.

into *every* play: on the contrary, there seems to have been, as a rule, a degree of reticence. I don't think that it can be the whole answer simply to retreat behind the fact that there was a relative paucity of suitable Athenian myths, though there may be some substance to this excuse. Given the degree of mythopoeic freedom and ingenuity that was countenanced, or even encouraged, it would surely have been possible to bring any number of myths within the ambit of Athens (as with Soph. *OK*). Nor is it enough to plead that tragedy 'just wasn't like that', or that patriotic localization was somehow against the traditions of the genre, because there are the counter-examples which I have just been briefly cataloguing.

It was quite possible, then, to aspire to win the prize at Athens with plays that alluded little or not at all to the city herself. Moreover, most tragedies were set elsewhere, something which arguably reflects credit on the local setting of the myth, regardless of its treatment – it is better for a city to be the locale of painful stories than not to be immortalized in poetic narrative at all (cf. pp. 43–4 above). But more positively than this, it clearly did not alienate the Athenian public if other places were localized, eulogized, favoured with aetiologies and so forth. It is sometimes maintained that these merely reflect the Athenian political affiliations of the day, but that can hardly be invariably the case. There is no (other) reason to think, for instance, that there were good relations with Thebes in 467 at the time of *Seven against Thebes*. There might, indeed, be a germ of truth beneath Dionysos' over-literal application of the concept of *didaskein* at *Frogs* 1023–4, when he complains that *Seven* is objectionable because it might have inspired bravery in the Thebans!

A mere illustrative sample of other localizations (apart from Thessaly) might include Argos in Aisch. *Supp.* especially the long hymn of praise at 625–709, and in Eur. *Orestes* over fifty years later.[50] Then there is the Troad in *Aias*, Corinth in *Medeia*, Troizen in *Hippolytos*, Delphi in *Ion*, and so on. There is even a notable amount of favourable Spartan material in *Helen*, including the aetiology at 1666–9 (though there are, of course, some virulent anti-Spartan sentiments scattered in other plays, especially *Andromache*).

But far the most striking, and controversial, case is Thebes. There certainly are places where Thebes as a whole is vilified, especially in Euripides' *Supp.* (though note how in Soph. *OK* 919ff. Theseus dissociates the Thebans as a whole from the villainy of Kreon). There is also, however, plenty of favourable localization in *Seven*, and in Euri-

---

[50] On Argos see Saïd (1993).

pides' *Phoinissai*, and in *Herakles*.[51] This is enough, it seems to me, to refute any simple formulation of Athens-positive/Thebes-negative polarity, of the kind now frequently derived from the more nuanced account put forward by Froma Zeitlin in her highly influential article, Zeitlin (1990), further developed in Zeitlin (1993). A proper response to this would open up a large and very interesting nexus of subjects, requiring study of Boiotian cults, of the myths of Mount Kithairon, and of Euripides' intriguing play *Antiope*, set at Eleutherai. This will all here have to be set aside for another essay.

Even putting off the day for confronting the question of how far Thebes was or was not set up as a kind of 'anti-Athens', the point has, I hope, been sufficiently established for now that by no means all tragedies make room for Athens, and that quite a few reflect favour on other localities. This holds good whether the plays were, as a matter of fact, produced only for audiences in Athens (and Attica), or whether there was already an awareness of further audiences beyond. Either way, there should be some attempt to explain why there is this degree of 'reticence' over Athenian eulogy and of 'generosity' towards other places. And the best explanation would seem to be that it is part of an attempt to establish tragedy as a panhellenic (in the weak sense) art-form rather than a local art-form. In other words tragedy is trying to have a scope more like Homeric epic than like, say, dithyramb or paian. This feature of tragedy surely encouraged its export to the rest of the Greek world. (And it was ironically those very panhellenic aspirations which led Hieron and Archelaos to commission heavily localized tragedies for their topical purposes.)

It would be naively simplistic to suppose that the motive for this degree of panhellenism was purely the desire to create a transcendent art-form for all places and all times. On the other hand, there is also a reductionism in the attribution of any form of 'cultural export' purely to the drive for exploitative power.[52] Tragedy did evidently reach places which were habitually hostile, as well as those which were well-disposed, or potentially well-disposed. In ancient Greece as a whole the mobility and communication of artistic, cultural and intellectual 'goods' did not straightforwardly observe politico-military lines. At the same time, there can be little doubt that the Athenians regarded

---

[51] Note Bond (1981) on *Herakles* 784: 'we have here the encomiastic use of geography, of which there is so much in Pindar'. Mastronarde (1994) documents the care that has gone into Theban details in *Phoen.*, see esp. 647–50.

[52] Hall (1989), for example, can tend this way, e.g. (162–3) 'an opportunity to vaunt Athenian ascendancy over the other Hellenic states ... this show of Athenian hegemony was designed with its Panhellenic audience in mind'.

tragedy as one of their greatest achievements, to be witnessed and admired by the other Greeks as well as themselves. It not only 'showed the city to herself', but to others as well. It is worth registering, then, that overt eulogy of Athens was evidently not, on the whole, regarded as a good way of promoting Athens elsewhere. It seems to have been sufficient as a 'trademark' that the whole business of tragedy was known to be an Athenian achievement.

IV

Assuming that tragedy was on some level a kind of implicit 'advertisement' for Athens (but not simply that), what was there to remind non-Athenians that what they were watching was a product of Athens, especially when there was little or no explicit Athenian allusion within the play? The most important and constant, if subliminal, reminder of Attic creativity must have been, I think, the *dialect* of the spoken iambics. This would no doubt have been reinforced if the actors were Athenian, wherever the performance was being mounted; but, as has been seen, the profession early recruited from elsewhere. A good reminder of the significance of dialect is Nikias' exhortation to the Athenian allies at Syracuse (Thuc. 7.63.3): they have the benefit of being admired throughout Greece for their imitation of the Athenian ways of life and of speech (τῆς τε φωνῆς τῆι ἐπιστήμηι) – ironically confirmed by the story of the value of Euripides for those taken prisoner (see pp. 42–3 above). Tragedy (and comedy) are, in fact, more specifically associable through dialect with one particular place than are epic or choral lyric (as composed by, for example, Simonides or Pindar).

How far, then, does tragedy promote Athenian *democracy* and the cause of democratic politics, the constitutional organization which was most likely to dispose cities well towards Athens? In so far as it does so, it is again – but even more so – *not* through explicit praise of the Athenian constitutional system. As with *Eum.* and lavish localization, this time it is Theseus' speech in Eur. *Supp.* (426ff.) which is the exception that proves the rule. There are implicit democratic tendencies in plays as various as Aisch. *Persai*, *Supp.*, *Eum.*, Soph. *OK*; Eur. *Andr.* and *Herakles*, but it cannot be claimed that they are at all prominent.[53] The constitutional 'propaganda' is, rather, through the very existence of tragedy. This astonishing art-form is the achievement of Athens; and

---

[53] On the other hand, I am far from persuaded that tragedy somehow supported aristocratic causes, as is argued, with excellent discussions along the way, by Griffith (1995).

it has been the radical democracy which has nurtured and encouraged its development.

But there might be other ways that tragedy (and comedy) promoted democracy, and more subtle ways than direct political advocacy. The programmatic collocation of our title, *Performance Culture and Athenian Democracy*, leads me to explore a way that tragedy, whenever it was *performed*, might have been inherently democratic, both within Athens and beyond.

In so far as genres of *poiēsis* in ancient Greece were defined by their *occasion*, among other factors, the occasion necessarily included the audience. The attendance at an exclusive symposium was very different from that at a wedding, and that was very different from the participation at a local cult-occasion, and that was very different from a huge panhellenic festival, and so on. The poetry made for these occasions may have been (and may still be) re-performed on other occasions for quite different audiences, but that does not diminish the validity and historicity of the primary genre-appropriate audience.[54] The tragedies at Athens, and indeed the comedies, were open to attendance by all male citizens (the issue of the admission of women and slaves is not of immediate concern here). No citizen was excluded: on the contrary a very large proportion of those qualified to attend a dramatic festival, urban or rural, were, it seems, likely to be there. It is a striking fact that the capacity of the theatral area at the Theatre of Dionysos was at least double that of the fifth-century Pnyx.[55] I am suggesting, then, that it was part and parcel of the basic generic definition of tragedy that it should be played in a very large space, big enough to contain a large proportion of the local citizenry. And that attendance should be open, as opposed to restricted. This was the case at Athens, and it seems likely that it was the case everywhere else as well. It may be, admittedly, that Hieron and Archelaos restricted access to a small elite circle; but it is also possible that even they turned their specially commissioned plays into big public occasions.

This notion of the 'generic requirement' of a non-exclusive audience is supported by the way that, when other cities constructed their own theatres, they built them on a scale big enough to hold a large

---

[54] I would take issue in several ways with Barbara Goff's confident assertion in Goff (1995) 19–20: 'of course this notion of a necessary relation to history as an adjunct of performance is thoroughly flawed ...'

[55] This is by itself a significant point against the thesis of Alan Sommerstein (1997: 63–73) that the audience was significantly restricted in favour of the wealthy. On the entrance-charge I favour the alternative account by Wilson (1997: 97–100) that the purpose of the *theōrikon* was precisely to ensure that poor citizens were *not* excluded.

proportion of the citizen-body. The theatre at the new city of Megalopolis (see p. 36 above) is reckoned to have a capacity of over 20,000, and is the most striking confirmation. Furthermore, the theatre-related ceramics from Megale Hellas were clearly not made exclusively for a wealthy elite – rather the contrary. This all connects with Plato's opposition to the theatre, part of which is precisely on the ground that it reaches such a huge audience, and that no one (not even women and slaves, according to him) is shut out from it or protected from it.

It was also, I suggest, in some sense generically inherent that the *experience* of theatre reached and affected all members of the audience *alike*. The architecture of the Greek theatre aspires to equality for all those in the *theatron*; and the experience of watching gives the spectators a sense of an equally shared experience. It is true that both at Athens and elsewhere there was the *prohedria*, but that was a token of honour: it did not give those sitting in the prohedric places a privileged or enhanced access to the play itself. Tragedy was, then, by genre and not just by convention, an event for the many and not for the few. If this train of argument is right, then it will by its very nature have promoted democracy. Even in later times, under such different constitutional conditions as the Hellenistic monarchies or the Roman Empire, the mounting of plays, both old and new, was, as B. le Guen has well argued, a matter of civic pride which encouraged the sense of communal independence.[56]

To draw now towards some conclusion to what has been, in effect, an attempt to open out Chapter Two of the many-chaptered reception-history of fifth-century Athenian tragedy, the question has to be posed at least: what was it that appealed so strongly and so immediately to the Greeks beyond Athens? There would have to be many layers to a complete answer; and if a complete answer were possible – which of course it is not – it would no doubt also tell us a great deal about what tragedy meant in Athens itself. For now, I shall attempt to draw out just two strands, though important ones I think, one of them (to employ a simplistic distinction) primarily scenic or physical, the other more poetic or perceptual.

First, then, theatre in performance was a thrillingly *novel* form of narrative. It is easy to forget how new it all was. Tragedy told the old stories in a way that was exciting, absorbing and vivid, bringing together many of the qualities of epic and narrative lyric, but adding the crucial new dimension of physical enactment. John Herington, while valuably bringing out the way that tragedy was rooted in pre-existent

[56] Le Guen (1995) *passim*, esp. 74–80, 82–7.

genres, did not register what a vital revolution it was to do away with any narratorial frame and to have the performers directly impersonate their characters.[57] When characters depart, they physically disappear from sight; when they die, they lie motionless on the ground; when they draw their swords, they hold a real sword (or an imitation) in their hand, and so forth. All this is so familiar to us that we forget how fresh and how vivid it must have been in the era of drama's first development.

What is more, tragedy enacted terrifically exciting and horrifying scenes – enacted them palpably, visibly, audibly: supplications, captures, conspiracies, rescues, reunions of long-lost relatives, scenes of murderous violence, intense joy, passionate grief. And all of this was presented with fascinating solidity and splendour. There is plenty of evidence, above all but not exclusively from the vase-paintings, of the trouble and expense which was lavished on the costumes and footwear, on the props and stage objects. Swords, sceptres, altars, letters, finery, statues, wreaths, corpses... The sensational narratives were given a newly persuasive, enthralling, moving, *psychagogic* enactment. While this whole kind of performance inevitably became less novel in itself for the Athenians as time went on, it would still have been an artistic revolution for every part of the Greek world, near and far, to which it spread so irresistibly during the fifth and fourth centuries.

Second, something about what it was in the matter of Athenian tragedy that so appealed to all the other Greeks. The chief answer, among the many, must be, I think – to cram it in a nutshell – that they believed that tragedy was somehow offering them insights into the human condition. Looking at the fourth-century evidence, most of the anecdotes which cite tragedy have to do with tragedy as some sort of source of wisdom. Plato regards tragedy as a serious enough rival to *philosophia* in popular perception for him to devote considerable energy to discrediting it. The Greeks in Apulia, who commissioned or acquired the vase-paintings, especially by the monumental craftsmen of the third quarter of the fourth century like the Darius and Underworld Painters, regarded allusion to tragedy as particularly suitable for funerary contexts. So far as we can infer, tragedy seemed to them to give some meaning to mortality, to offer some consolation, and to lend dignity and even beauty to human suffering.

The temporal preoccupations of the Athenians at the first performance are not going to have loomed large in the interests of these

---

[57] This would be my main criticism of Herington (1985), an important book, which has not received the recognition it deserved. Herington's neglect of the *mask* epitomizes my reservation: the essential function of the mask is (in my view) to signal the act of total impersonation without narratorial frame.

fourth-century non-Athenians. The current historicist and 'culturally specificist' movement in scholarship, represented in the Introduction and throughout this book, is a movement with which I am personally largely in sympathy: but we should not pretend that it was all the rage in the fourth-century BCE Hellenophone world. The political topicalities of the fifth-century creative moment, and even the Athenian mental systems and ideology, will have been of limited interest. The Athenians themselves in the fourth century, to judge from the orators, looked to the great tragedies for universal and timeless insights, rather than for the temporary and local preoccupations of their predecessors.[58] Tragedy was believed to have, like Homer, universalizing value.

We now regard these apparently cross-cultural and cross-temporal insights as constructs of the same order as 'human nature' or 'timeless truths' or 'the human condition'. These imagined 'universals' are all culturally relative, and some may even be regarded as no better than hegemonic hoodwinking. But however much *we* may see through such claims, and however much we may denounce them, the fact remains that in most receptions of Athenian tragedy, in most eras and in most places, it has been *believed* to possess universal profundity. And that goes back to Chapter Two in its reception, if not Chapter One. What spread tragedy and kept it fresh was not, in the last analysis, the mentality and ideology of its primary production, but its gripping and thought-provoking dramatizations of the deepest problems, fears and sufferings of men and women. These *seem* to speak to everyone, not only to fifth-century Athenian free-born males. It was not for The Tragic Moment nor for the 'original fusion' that non-Athenians took the performances into the hearts of their cities, and gave them a stature that rivalled Homer's.

I am certainly not denying the importance of the particular, time-bound cultural context, nor the value of studying it. On the contrary I am convinced that historical contextualization is a key to our understanding this inbuilt potential for value across time and across place. But I am saying that the unique productive context needs to be held in mind alongside the sense of the universal potential. 'The shift of perspective could be liberating.'[59] 'We' after all – in all our multiplicity – can still be moved and fascinated and made to think by these products of a particular society distant in both time and place. The potential to reach out was already there, I am suggesting, from the very start.

Thucydides, in contrasting his own aspirations with those of sophistic *epideixis* struck on some memorable phrasing when he claimed

---

[58] See Wilson (1996).   [59] Easterling (1994) 80.

that his work was to be a κτῆμά [τε] ἐς αἰεὶ μᾶλλον ἢ ἀγώνισμα ἐς τὸ παραχρῆμα ἀκούειν. Recent scholarship has tended to concentrate on tragedy as a 'prize composition to be heard on a single topical occasion'. But tragedy has also turned out to be 'a heritage for all time'. The whole point is that it was, and is, both.

3 The *aulos* in Athens[1]

Peter Wilson

The acoustics of Athens are lost to us. This was a city which depended on the spoken word for its daily operation and – just as significantly – for its manifest self-image as a democracy: a city of speakers and listeners. But alongside the sounds of 'rational' Athens, the sound of word and argument circulating within the institutions of civic logos, there was another world of less articulate sound. Music, virtually omnipresent in all Greek life, occupied an especially privileged place in the 'city of words', which was also the city where the arts of the Muses were developed to the highest degree. And one instrument in particular was to be found in almost every corner of the city's activities: in its numerous festivals; at the central act of religion, sacrifice; on board every trireme; in the symposium; at weddings and funerals. The penetrating sound of the *aulos* was at the heart of most of the important collective activities of Athenian life.

The *aulos* was everywhere in Athens. And yet, when one turns to Athenian reflection on the *aulos*, a paradox appears. For the *aulos* was an object of rejection in Athens. Authorities, from the city's patron goddess to the leading intellectuals of the age, prohibited the Athenian from having it in his mouth. The *aulos* was a danger: it threatened self-control; it marred the aesthetics of the body; it introduced the allure of the alien. So often troped as the enemy and antithesis of logos, the *aulos* blocked the mouth, that most idealized of all the features of the citizen's comportment, corporeal and political. And the socio-political resonances of such a pragmatics were not lost on the Athenians.

And so this instrument 'of alien tongue' that was central to Athenian life occupied an extremely ambivalent position within it, as did its practitioners. Players were routinely foreigners, often slaves. Athens as a polis managed the perceived value derived from this contact with

---

[1] Warmest thanks for helpful contributions to Pat Easterling, Simon Goldhill, Robin Osborne, Oliver Taplin and all who participated in the discussion at the Cambridge colloquium.

others, turning it to its own ends. The fact that Thebes, a neighbour ever on uneasy terms with classical Athens, was the centre of this expertise that was both prized and despised, only added to (and probably helped create) the complexities of the Athenian response to the *aulos*.

This study is organized into three parts. The first looks at a basic template of the Athenian discourse on the *aulos*, the myth of Athena and Marsyas. The *aulos* is incorporated into the world of the city's mythic–religious imaginary, but that incorporation is presented as an act of transgression.

The second section is largely devoted to *Realien*: to the instrument's physical nature and the conditions of the player; to a survey of its performance-contexts and an examination of the status of *aulētai*. No account of cultural practice is entirely free from elements of evaluation, whether they be the society's explicit commentary or indications implicit in the place accorded the activity in question in relation to the centres of value and relations of power within the society. And this account of the 'functional' role of the *aulos* in Athens will not attempt to divorce practice from such evaluations. For the Athenians themselves did not do so.

The more explicitly critical discourse on the *aulos* is reserved for the third part, where Athenian public speech and the reflection of the philosophers are the key areas.[2] From the former, the status of the *aulos* as anti-logos emerges most clearly. Here it surfaces as metaphor for deceptive speech, political immorality, and ignorance – themes that the philosophers resume with insistence. A powerful link between the fifth-century problematic and later more fully theorized critique is Alkibiades. A number of representations, revealing as much in their inconsistencies as in their continuity, fix themselves around him. One tradition depicts the *enfant terrible* of Athenian democracy as the mortal rejector of the *aulos par excellence*, refusing to 'play the satyr' himself, and setting a trend for the youth of his age. Another associates him with the great Pronomos himself as his master on the *aulos*. The contradictory figure of Alkibiades is the perfect mannequin on which to examine complex and conflicting models of civic behaviour in relation to the *aulos*. It is no surprise to find that he should become the testing-point of Athenian anxieties over the instrument; for he is the one Athenian of all whose self-control – or rather, its lack – was most famously a matter for widespread concern.

---

[2] A future study will include consideration of the important role of tragic and comic representation of the *aulos*.

1. An Athenian myth: Athena and Marsyas

In the middle of the fifth century, an Athenian myth of the civic goddess herself attained a high degree of popularity in Athens – or, to put that another way, it spoke in a voice that the city wanted to hear. It is a familiar story of simple outlines, and perfectly indicative of the *parthenos*' constant care for good comportment, her own and that of her citizens. Athena invents the *aulos*, or at least she 'discovers' it (the difference not always being very clear in such myths).[3] She tries it out, thereby inventing *aulētikē*, the art of *aulos*-playing, as well; and subsequently she sees in a reflective surface the image of her own face as she plays. Horrified at the distortions the practice works upon her, she casts the object away in disgust. And what the civic goddess banishes from the realm of appropriate decorum, the satyr Marsyas adopts as his own.[4] It thus becomes the possession, through a transgression of the goddess' wish for its abandonment, of that race in mythology most lacking in decorum and self-control, and characterized, in the words of François Lissarrague, by 'perpetual movement, as though they were incapable of controlling their bodies'.[5]

The first place to go in an investigation of this Athenian story of rejection is the Akropolis, a place saturated with religious and mythic significance. The appearance of the *aulos* here testifies powerfully to its great importance in Athenian collective representations of the time, and there is no doubting the firmness of the position adopted on the matter of the *aulos* by the goddess in her own sacred home in the very middle of the classical century. Among the works known to antiquity by the early classical sculptor Myron was an *Athena and Marsyas* – a monumental group generally considered by modern scholars to be the same as that mentioned by Pausanias: 'In this place [on the Akropolis, near the Panathenaic Way] has been made an Athena striking the Silenos Marsyas for taking up the *auloi* when the goddess wanted them to be cast away for good.'[6]

It is unnecessary to enter into the debate over the reconstruction of this group from contemporary vase-iconography and later, fragmentary copies.[7] It is agreed that the *auloi* were the organizing focal-point of attention and *contention* between the two figures in this group. On the

---

[3] Kleingünther (1933); Huchzermeyer (1931) 14–15; Leclercq-Neveu (1989) 255.
[4] In addition to the sources discussed throughout see Hyginus *Fab.* 165; Apollod. *Bibl.* 1.4.2; Diod. Sic. 3.58–9; Ovid *Ars Am.* 3.505ff., *Fasti* 6.699ff. Weis (1992) for visual evidence. *ARV*[2] has no Marsyas before the classical period, and some thirteen in it.
[5] Lissarrague (1993) 212; cf. Lissarrague (1990a), (1990b).
[6] Paus. 1.24. Pliny *HN* 34.57–8. Arias (1940) dates the work to *c.* 457–447.
[7] Metzger (1951) 163–4; Arias (1940); Schauenberg (1958); (1972); Daltrop (1980); Daltrop and Bol (1983); Demargne (1984); M.-Klein (1988). Whether or not directly

The *aulos* in Athens

one side, a youthful Athena moves away from the instrument that has just left her hand, haughtily vertical, contemptuous but poised and self-possessed, her gaze directed behind her and *down* towards the *auloi*. While Marsyas, in Stewart's words, 'his face a bestial mask, is in three-quarter view, a picture of hesitant curiosity as he tiptoes toward them – yet simultaneously draws back under Athena's withering gaze'.[8] He recoils, yet the agitation of his body, with one foot edging toward the forbidden object, also speaks his overpowering, curious desire... One's comportment in response to the *aulos* is everything: Athena, after the moment of unconscious distortion, quickly recovers her dignity; Marsyas gives himself over to wild contortions of excitement.

The purpose and meaning of this group are often reduced to one or another specific order of reference: it has, for example, been seen as a rather maladroit attempt to reconcile two contradictory versions of the invention of the *aulos* – a Theban one, which placed it in Thebes and by Athena; the other seeing it as a non-Greek creation, coming from Phrygia.[9] Others see it as a partisan statement by proponents of the *kithara* as against the *aulos*, in terms of their relative musical and, more broadly, ethical and 'educational' value.[10] Or as anti-Theban propaganda in which the musical instrument is little more than a metaphor for national identity;[11] or again, as a commemorative monument for a dithyramb by Melanippides called *Marsyas*, a victory-dedication commissioned by poet or *chorēgos*.[12]

All of these explanations may contain some truth, but we ought perhaps to begin with the eloquent gestures of the image. Words or actions of negation, denial, repression, rejection, even abjection (and such, in literal terms at least, is the action of Athena), are often most revealing on the matter of the very thing which they would banish – and this no more so than in the narratives of myth. What can be said with certainty is that the group fixed in the permanency of bronze the

---

influenced by the Myronian version, the popularity of the myth in contemporary vase-images further testifies to its high profile.

[8] Stewart (1990) 147.
[9] This 'contradiction' is of course perceived as such only on a non-mythical view of myth: Leclercq-Neveu (1989) 253, 256. Precisely the same 'contradiction' exists, significantly, for Dionysos himself, the god who came from the east, but is a native-born son of Thebes. Linguists and archaeologists concur with the widespread tradition that makes the *aulos* an outsider in Greece, but as the modern history of the worship of Dionysos shows, we must pay as much attention to the semi-autonomous dynamic and logic of myth as to the facts uncovered by archaeology and historical linguistics. Frontisi-Ducroux (1994) 242 stresses the importance of the foreign origins of the *aulos* in Greek representations.
[10] Huchzermeyer (1931) 60–1; Lasserre (1954).
[11] Kasper-Butz (1990) 184.
[12] Metzger (1951) 163; Boardman (1956); Webster (1970) 132–3.

explosive moment of the goddess' rejection, her discarding of the double pipes of the instrument. And it continued to repeat the gesture of the expulsion of the *aulos* from its position on the most illustrious of all civic and sacred spaces in Athens, *even as* it at the same time fixed it there with equal permanency. There seems to be a double process at work in this myth in its civic environment, a process which at the same time 'officially' – through the unambiguous ordinance of the goddess – sites the *aulos* as the rejected, that which threatens identity and control. Those who take up the *aulos* in Athens are thereafter aligned implicitly on the side of the satyr. Yet this process also, and in the same gesture, incorporates it, with all its disruptive and useful powers, into the heart of civic life, in a realm (that of the Dionysiac) where it can indeed find its 'proper' place.[13]

One final point concerning Myron's *Athena and Marsyas*: the ascription of the Akropolis group to Myron, if not ultimately demonstrable or even true, is certainly *ben trovato*. For Myron was a native of Eleutherai,[14] the region just inside Attike on the Boiotian border from which the cult of Dionysos Eleuthereus was transported each year in the opening rituals of the Great Dionysia. Myron's origin in this 'frontier zone'[15] is altogether appropriate for the creator of a work which pivots around an object of huge cultural importance and conflict, whose meanings were contested across that very border.

Athena and Marsyas were the subject of poetic as well as plastic myth. The most significant remains of these treatments are preserved by Athenaios, where they form part of a continuous dinner-discussion on the subject of *auloi*.[16] Athenaios raids these works of some seven

---

[13] A comparison with the psychological notion of abjection is illuminating: see Kristeva (1982(1980)).

[14] Pliny *HN* 34.57–8. His son was from Eleutherai: *IG* I³ 511. Others (Paus. 6.2.2) make him Athenian. The evidence need not be contradictory, given the degree of incorporation of Eleutherai into Attike.

[15] Zeitlin (1993) 173. The opposition, in the matter of the *aulos*, across the borders by which Dionysos passed from Thebes to Attike, adds another element to the symbolic opposition between Athens and Thebes within tragic discourse so well studied by Zeitlin (cf. (1990)). It also sharpens the conceptual focus of that analysis by introducing, at the level of the practical instantiation of tragedy itself, an opposition between the 'noble' Athenian citizens in their *choroi* and in the *theatron* and the outsiders at the centre of the *orchēstra* who 'introduced' the alterity of Dionysos through the medium of the *aulos*. Many of these had also come across that border on the north-west of Attike.

[16] I omit discussion of the important and difficult fragment of Pratinas (*PMG* 708) because, although he is said to have been active in Athens in the early fifth century, the date, performance context and genre of the fragment are matters of great controversy. Whatever is happening within this frantic scene, the fragment throws up a number of recurrent *aulos*-motifs. We have rejection as the primary response to the *aulos*; we see its alleged encroachment on the sphere of others; and we find it to be a natural slave or machine.

hundred years' antiquity, and shapes his dialogue using a 'debate' he found already there.

The first poet is Melanippides, from the small Cycladic island of Melos, best known as a composer of dithyramb, and associated with the early days of the so-called 'New Music'. Martin West puts his poetic activity from about 440 to 415, and so this fragment, which probably derives from a dithyramb, could be very close in date to Myron's work.[17] As I have already mentioned, some have even argued that the sculpture was a dedication made following a victory with the poem in Athens, perhaps at the Panathenaia.[18] If it was in fact performed at the Panathenaia, it is fascinating that its theme should have been, at least in part, Athena's relation to the world of Dionysian *mousikē*. PMG 758, from *Marsyas*:

ἁ μὲν Ἀθάνα
τὤργαν' ἔρριψεν θ' ἱερᾶς ἀπὸ χειρὸς
εἶπέ τ'· "Ἔρρετ' αἴσχεα, σώματι λύμα·
ὕμμε δ' ἐγὼ κακότατι δίδωμι.

Athena cast the instruments from her holy hand
and said: 'Be gone, you shameful objects,
outrage to my body! I consign you to baseness:'
[or – 'I do not give myself to baseness.']

4 Wilamowitz. ἐμὲ δ' ἐγώ codd., ἐμὲ δ' ἐγώ ⟨οὐ⟩ Maas.

It is indeed an extraordinary coincidence that this fragment captures the very moment that Myron's group made permanent. Perhaps this was the moment which any classical *poiētēs*, plastic or poetic, (or an excerptor closer in time to Melanippides), would have deemed essential to the telling of the story. The action of physical rejection is narrated, and in addition we hear Athena's rationale.

Athenaios' learned diner cites this fragment as evidence of Melanippides' contempt for the *aulos*, but we should avoid an over-hasty conflation of the poet's views with those of the goddess. Any interpretation which sees Melanippides taking an 'anti-*aulos*' stand here must come to terms with the fact that this poem was almost certainly itself accompanied by the *aulos*.[19] One wonders whether any sense of paradox might have been felt by an audience hearing these words sung to the *aulos*. Presumably conflict between Athena and aspects of the Dionysian

[17] West (1992) 356–72, 399.
[18] Boardman (1956). Froning (1971) 40ff. on possible relations between other vase-images of Athena and Marsyas and dithyramb.
[19] The argument that the myth reflects a controversy over the instrumentation of dithyramb, to which, it is said, some were introducing the lyre (cf. Boardman (1956) 19) lacks any firm support.

world was familiar enough. Advancing further into the realm of the imagination, one wonders what the *aulētēs* who served this choros made of this consignment of the tools of his craft to *kakotas*. It is a curious fact about the genre of dithyramb in Athens that, while in some ways it was clearly the most civically-oriented and 'democratic' of poetic performances, requiring at the Great Dionysia alone some 1,000 Athenian men and boys drawn from the ten Kleisthenic *phylai* to compete in its choroi,[20] it produced a *very* small number of native *Athenian* practitioners,[21] and probably the most famous of these, Kinesias, was constantly reviled – and not only by Aristophanes.[22] As a rule then, dithyramb brought these Athenian citizen choroi into close contact with foreign (meaning non-Athenian Greek, not non-Greek) poets, and led them into the *orchēstra* to foreign tunes played by foreign *aulētai* on an instrument 'of alien tongue'.[23] On this wide-angle view of dithyramb in Athens, with its cultural appropriation, on a grand scale, of foreign poetic and musical talent, we can almost see the imprint of the Athenian myth of the *aulos* at work, or a large-scale analogy to its operation: making good use, for the greater glory of Athens and Athenian civic identity, of that which is constructed as alien and excluded. The *aulos* performs culturally useful roles in Athens, but does so through the mechanical agency of others.

The language of this fragment is highly suggestive in its strategies of representation. The noun αἶσχος used of the instruments plays in both a moral and a physical register, appropriately for this myth in which aesthetic, corporeal and socio-political comportment are so intimately bound up. For αἶσχος can mean a deformity or ugliness of mind, behaviour or body. Here the *aulos* is abused by Athena as the object *and* agent of such deformity, of distortion from 'proper' comportment – in physical, aesthetic, moral and social terms. κακότας, 'baseness', has a similarly wide breadth of reference: in it overlap aesthetic, social and physical deficiency. It is to this world of inferiority that the *aulos* belongs in the goddess' eyes. The importance of corporeal integrity

---

[20] There were also performances at the Greater and Lesser Panathenaia, the Thargelia, perhaps the Hephaestia and Promethia; and, perhaps irregularly, at some rural festivals. Zimmermann (1992) 37.

[21] The following are certain or probable: Lamprokles, Telesias, Lysiades, Speuseades: Sutton (1989). Diophon should be added: *SEG* 41 no. 141. Kinesias is called 'that accursed Attic' in Pherekrates 155 KA; but the ΣΣ on Aristophanes *Frogs* 152 and 1437 impugn his Athenian origins, claiming (Σ 152) he was Theban.

[22] See previous note and Ar. *Birds* 1372ff. and Σ, *Frogs* 152f., 366 and ΣΣ; 404ff. Σ mentions a comedy by Strattis called *Kinesias* (cf. Athenaios 12.551a–552b) with the fascinating fragment: 'This is the booth(?) (σκηνή) of Kinesias, the choros-killer'.

[23] Philostratos *Vit. Soph.* 1.16.

The *aulos* in Athens 65

and self-control to an ideal of Athenian civic behaviour are by now well known.[24] The emphasis placed by Athena on the deviation worked on her body by this activity stands as a lesson of sorts for her men, and it is altogether likely that it was precisely a choros of her men (a χορὸς ἀνδρῶν in the language of the festival) who were singing and dancing to these lines in good order. σώματι λύμα, 'defilement to my [– or perhaps more generally to *the* –] body' has connotations of maltreatment by maiming that suggest an assault on physical integrity and 'beauty'.[25]

Control of the body is at the heart of this myth, and is a prime concern of the goddess. It was in her honour, after all, that Athenian men further competed every year before the city for prizes in beauty and control of physique.[26] And the *aulos*, as this fragment suggests, is an enemy of such control.[27] Yet at the same time it provides precisely the delimited, controlled, musical ordering for the special space of a civic performance: in Athenian performance culture, the instrument that so threatens control is also regularly used to maintain it.

Another fragment focuses yet again on the moment of rejection, or its immediate antecedent. Here we find the *satyr* advising Athena, as she tries out the *auloi*, that she should abandon them, because:

οὔτοι πρέπει τὸ σχῆμα· τοὺς αὐλοὺς υέθες
καὶ θὦπλα λάζευ καὶ γνάθους εὐθημόνει

This bearing doesn't suit you – put aside the *auloi*
and take up the arms and put your jaws in order[28]

Only in satyr-play could *Athena* be schooled in appropriate demeanour, in keeping within her proper sphere of activity – warfare – by a *satyr*.[29] The satyr has effectively taken on the role of the reflective surface in the myth, for in looking at his face, Athena sees the kind of contortions unnaturally worked on her own by *auloi*.[30] Plutarch, to whom we owe the citation, goes on to give the usual sequel. Seeing the

---

[24] E.g. Foucault (1987 (1984)); Winkler (1990); Halperin (1990).
[25] λύμη 'maltreatment', 'outrage' is often contaminated in sense with λῦμα 'impurity'.
[26] I am thinking especially of the *euandria*, a contest in 'manly beauty' at the Panathenaia; and the even more mysterious *euexia*: Crowther (1985), (1991); Boegehold (1997). Most of the phyletic events at the Panathenaia set a premium on a combination of bodily strength, coordination and grace.
[27] By the fourth century professional *aulētai* had maximized the potential of the *aulos* (and attracted further criticism) by (*inter alia*) vigorous and mimetic use of their bodies: Theophr. Fr. 92W; Paus. 9. 12.5–6; Arist. *Pol.* ch. 26; Dio Chrys. *Or.* 78 (2.281 Dind.).
[28] *TrGF* II Adesp. 381.
[29] Seaford (1988 (1984)) 36.
[30] Leclercq-Neveu (1989) 255. Vernant (1985) and Frontisi-Ducroux (1994) pursue the relation between the distorted face of Athena and the *gorgoneion*.

sight of her face in a river, she grew angry and did indeed cast the *auloi* away.

The other important set of fragments on the *aulos* provided by Athenaios are from the *Argo* of Telestes, a native of Dorian Selinous, (*PMG* 1 (a,b,c) (805)):[31]

†ὃν† σοφὸν σοφὰν λαβοῦσαν οὐκ ἐπέλπομαι νόωι
δρυμοῖς ὀρείοις ὄργανον
δίαν Ἀθάναν δυσόφθαλμον αἶσχος ἐκφοβη-
θεῖσαν αὖθις χερῶν ἐκβαλεῖν
νυμφαγενεῖ χειροκτύπωι φηρὶ Μαρσύαι κλέος·
τί γάρ νιν εὐηράτοιο κάλλεος ὀξὺς ἔρως ἔτειρεν,
ἆι παρθενίαν ἄγαμον καὶ ἄπαιδ' ἀπένειμε Κλωθώ;

ἀλλὰ μάταν ἀχόρευτος ἅδε ματαιολόγων
φάμα προσέπταθ' Ἑλλάδα μουσοπόλων
σοφᾶς ἐπίφθονον βροτοῖς τέχνας ὄνειδος.

ἂν συνεριθοτάταν Βρομίωι παρέδωκε σεμνᾶς
δαίμονος ἀερθὲν[32] πνεῦμ' αἰολοπτέρυγον
σὺν ἀγλαᾶν ὠκύτατι χερῶν.

> I do not believe in my heart that the clever one,
> divine Athena, took the clever instrument in the
> mountain thickets and then in fear of eye-offending
> ugliness threw it from her hands to be the glory
> of the nymph-born, hand-clapping beast Marsyas:
> for why should a keen desire for lovely beauty
> distress her, to whom Klotho has assigned a marriageless and
>   childless virginity?
>
> No, this is a tale that flew idly to Greece, told by
> idly-talking Muse-followers, a tale hostile to
> the choral dance, an invidious reproach brought among mortals
>   against a clever skill.
>
> It was handed over as a most helpful servant
> to Bromios by the uplifted wing-flashing breath
> of the august goddess with the swiftness of her glorious hands.

In the debate conducted by the deipnosophists, one diner responds to the passage of Melanippides' *Marsyas* with the rejoinder that Telestes 'took up the cudgels against Melanippides and said in his *Argo*, with reference to Athena' – and there follows the first fragment. It is just feasible that Telestes' response to Melanippides was more than a convenient fiction of this fictional dinner-guest. The *Marmor Parium* (Ep.

---

[31] Translation substantially that of Campbell (1993).
[32] For a defence of ἀερθὲν see Comotti (1980).

The *aulos* in Athens

65) records a victory in Athens in 402, and, depending upon how one imagines one dithyrambic poet might have 'responded' to another, he is perhaps not too far removed from Melanippides' (very approximate) *floruit* to have indeed responded poetically to him. The agonistic dynamic of Greek poetics could of course be very strong across long stretches of time – one thinks of Euripides' 'rewritings' of Aiskhylos – and these passages raise fascinating questions of the work of allusion and poetic competition operating synchronically and diachronically in the elusive genre of dithyramb.[33]

Telestes appears to turn the mythic tradition on its head. His 'reply' is in fact so systematic as to suggest the possible influence of a sophistic milieu, with its adoption of a radical, counter-intuitive position towards 'tradition', claiming it as normative.[34] This recuperation of the instrument's reputation is also in keeping with the tenets of the 'New Music' and its practitioners' far from uncontroversial maximization of the potential of the *aulos*. I would signal just a few points here: the *aulos* is now *sophos*, like its maker, Athena. All the stress of the opening, somewhat contrived, juxtaposition is on the assimilation between the goddess and her discovery, on identity rather than difference. The *aulos* attracts the positive qualities of Athenian *tekhnē* (cf. fr. b.3); elsewhere its 'technological' nature is a slur.[35]

Even more interesting is the fact that the motif of *rejection* has become an act of *bequeathal* and patronage (one thinks of the mythopoetics of the opening of the *Eumenides* with its 'conversion' of the story of Apollo's violent assumption of the Delphic shrine to the peaceful account of his receiving it as a gift from his female chthonic namesake). As the third fragment puts it, she did not cast it[36] from her hands at all, nor was it taken up transgressively by Marsyas, but Athena 'passed it on to Bromios as a most helpful fellow-worker'. The art of the *aulos* is now not simply subservient, but a *fellow*-worker of Dionysos – and the rare word συνέριθος is used in Homer of Athena herself, disguised as a

---

[33] I should stress that the genre of both Melanippides' *Marsyas* and Telestes' *Argo*, as well as the places of their production, are, strictly speaking, unknown. That they were dithyrambs presented at Athens is not too outrageous a pair of assumptions, however. Cf. Webster (1970) 133; Zimmermann (1992) 131.

[34] The relation between 'sophists' and 'musicians' deserves further study. Various sources state that a number of important sophists used music as a 'cover' for their activities, among them Pythokleides the *aulētēs* from Keos, who taught Perikles; as well as Damon and Agathokles. The relation further illuminates Plato's distaste for contemporary *mousikē*.

[35] E.g. Pratinas *PMG* 708.13. Positive also it *Anth. Pal.* 13.20. In the Theban milieu of Pindar *Pyth.* 12, Athena's invention of *aulētikē* is described as an act of *weaving* (8, cf. 19).

[36] The referent of ἄν is, according to Athenaios 617a, ἡ αὐλητική.

companion and helper of Nausikaa in the laundry-scene of *Odyssey* 6 (31–2).[37] It seems in fact to be the *breath* (πνεῦμα) of the goddess which is envisaged as 'handing over' the art of the *aulos* to Dionysos – the breath that is 'uplifted, wing-flashing with the speed of her glorious hands'.[38] This stress on the breath and finger-movements of Athena (and note how closely the two go together – the breath itself is described as 'flashing-winged', suggesting the rapid motions of the fingers over the holes letting in and out the stream of air[39]) goes to make the point that it is the whole art, the whole *tekhnē* of *aulētikē*, that Athena is handing over here, not just a discarded object.

What is now rejected is the tale of rejection itself. The choral voice sings in a manner reminiscent of the recantatory gesture of Pindar's *First Olympian* or Stesikhoros' *Palinode*, and the 'debate' remains centred on Athena's face. This version interprets Athena's horror, in the traditional story, at her facial distortion, as an aesthetic concern that is driven by the erotic. And this is presented as self-evidently absurd for the goddess to whom Klotho had assigned permanent virginity, without marriage and without children: the only reasons, of course, for which a good Greek woman, let alone a goddess, could wish for 'lovely beauty'. The strict ambivalence of δυσόφθαλμον (a.3), having both an 'external' force, 'unpleasant to the eyes (of others)', as well as a 'reflexive' one, 'distorting the (one's own) eye', captures the multiple play of the gaze so important to this story: in Telestes' version, Athena cannot have feared the ugliness *which others see*, and equally she cannot have feared the ugliness *of her own eyes*.[40] The two of course overlap neatly in this story in which sight of herself as others see her plays an important role, and in early Greek culture more generally, the sight of oneself and the sight others have of oneself are intimately bound together.

The second fragment explains that the traditional (now rejected) version was an import to Greece: like the story of Pelops and the feast of Tantalos in Pindar, this rejected story began as a rumour. This was not the idle talk of neighbours, but it 'flew to Hellas,' evidently from outside it. The negative connotations of the alien origins of the *aulos* are transferred to the *false story* of Athena's rejection – another turn in the manipulation of the alien.

That this story should be emphatically described as ἀχόρευτος is in-

---

[37] The word may however evoke the instrument's more turbulent qualities: within it lurks ἔρις. (I owe this observation to Robert Fowler.)
[38] Cf. Kinesias' description of the *tekhnē* of dithyramb at Ar. *Birds* 1387–90.
[39] For the digital dexterity of the *aulos*-player cf. Antiphanes fr. 57.15 (KA); Plato fr. 209 (KA).
[40] Note the use again of αἶσχος, now restricted to an aesthetic register.

structive: it is hostile to *choreia*, choral song-and-dance, because it ascribes to its most important musical instrument a disreputable origin, rejected by Athena; and by the end of the fifth century Athena's city was the most important and proud centre for *choreia* in the Greek world.

II. Instrument and performance

The physical attributes and technical capacities of the *aulos* have been much and well studied by 'organologists' and historians of music.[41] A brief account will suffice here. The *aulos* was by far the most important and widespread of the wind-instruments of all the Greeks. Normally played in pairs,[42] each pipe, of cylindrical bore,[43] was made of bone, reed, cane, wood, ivory or metal, and fitted with a mouthpiece that held the reed, known as the 'tongue' (γλῶσσα).[44] The pipes were usually made up of a number of sections fitted together; a special bulbous piece holding the reed was called the ὅλμος. The number of finger-holes varied over time. Five seems usual on the classical instrument, including one underneath for the thumb.

There is little evidence that classical authors ever described the *aulos* in such 'neutral' terms: their descriptions of its physical attributes often evoke ambiguity, focusing for instance on its combination of the organic and the technological.[45] It is 'the labour of the lathe,' τόρνου κάματον in Aiskhylos (*TrGF* 57); it is tainted with a banausic slur in Pratinas as having a 'body fashioned under the drill';[46] in a Philostratean *Imago*, Olympos is depicted with the iron bore-driller which was used in its construction lying beside the *aulos*, somewhat incongruously in the rural scene described there.[47] These strong associations of the *aulos* with the world of *tekhnē* are in keeping with its invention by Athena, that most technologically advanced of deities; but they form an important strand of its very ambivalent, contested evaluations.[48]

---

[41] West (1992) 80–109 and further bibliography; Anderson (1994) 179–284; Schlesinger (1939) with West (1992) 96; Neubecker (1990) 125–30. The writing of musicological treatises specifically on *auloi* begins at least as early as Aristoxenos; cf. note 52.
[42] West (1992) 103–5 on the relation between the two pipes.
[43] For debate over the bore and its significance West (1992) 83.
[44] Probably a double reed, enclosed in the player's mouth: West (1992) 83. On ancient manufacture of reeds: Theophrastos *Hist. pl.* 4.11.1–7 with Barker (1984) 186–9.
[45] Note the way that an organic material (esp. λωτός) is often used of the *aulos*, the plant standing directly for the instrument: e.g. Eur. *El.* 716, *Tro.* 544, *Hel.* 170, *IA* 1036. Cf. *Anth. Pal.* 13.20.
[46] *PMG* 708.13. This description may also work in a sexual register, troping the *aulos* as phallos: Garrod (1920) 135; Seaford (1977–8) 84–5.
[47] Philostratos *Imagines* 1.20.
[48] Cf. the comic tradition that Isokrates' father Theodoros was an '*aulos*-borer' (αὐλοτρύπης): Plu. *Mor.* 836e-f; Strattis Fr. 3 K.-A. Philostratos *VS* 1.17.4 defends him

There was a wide variety of *auloi*, the main physical variant being the length of the pipes. Ancient authorities tend to refer to *auloi* with names that suggest a system of classification based on performance context:[49] for instance, 'maiden' *auloi* (*parthenioi*) accompanied maidens' choral performance. But the five best-established types (known to go back at least to Aristotle's pupil Aristoxenos of Tarentum) can also be understood to refer to register (the 'maiden' being something like a soprano[50]). In all likelihood the two criteria were largely compatible. An interesting case is the 'wedding *auloi*' which we are told consisted of two pipes of different sizes, a 'male' and a 'female', – 'suggesting a concord, but also the importance of the man being the greater'.[51] The social and sexual meaning of this instrument and the sound it makes are inseparable from its physical form. The *auloi* employed for tragedy[52] were probably the same as or very like those used for dithyramb, the 'choral *auloi*' whose generally high register could be heard above a massed choir of fifty adult male voices.[53]

The *aulos*-player had a number of other accoutrements, and the ancient imaging of these, both verbal and visual, again shows how inseparable all aspects of musical practice were from the broad sociopolitical texture of Greek life. Consider the *phorbeia*: this was a leather strap which went around the head of the player, leaving a hole (or holes) at the mouth for the pipes, and passing across the cheeks. A second strap often passed vertically over the top of the player's head to secure the first more firmly (Fig. 1).[54] The *phorbeia* restrained the cheeks of the player and assisted the maintenance of a secure oral grip on the instrument, especially important in outdoor activities involving considerable bodily movement, such as the theatre. But whatever precisely its practical functions were, 'organologists' have pointed to an oddity. The *phorbeia* effectively *restrained* the full inflation of the cheeks; yet, in terms of strict musical technology, the greater the re-

against the slur: αὐτὸς δὲ οὔτε αὐλοὺς ἐγίγνωσκε οὔτε ἄλλο τι τῶν ἐν βαναυσίοις. It is easy to see how rising in Athens on the back of an *aulos*-factory would expose one to attack.

[49] Pollux 4.81. Cf. Ath. 618c (with Barker (1984) 275–6), a list of performances which may in some cases (e.g. the *gingras*) also imply different kinds of *auloi*. Similarly with those at Ath. 176–7, 182, including the 'maiden', the 'child', the 'masculine', the 'super-masculine', the 'harp-accompaniers', the 'finger-*auloi*', the 'tragic', among many others.
[50] West (1992) 89.
[51] Pollux 4.80; cf. Plut. *Coniug. Praecept.* 139c–d.
[52] Athen. 182c–d, citing Ephoros (*FGrH* 70 F3), and Euphranor the Pythagorean and Alexis in their works *On Auloi*.
[53] Poll. 4.81; Aristid. Quint. p. 85.6–8.
[54] Bélis (1986); West (1992) 118–19.

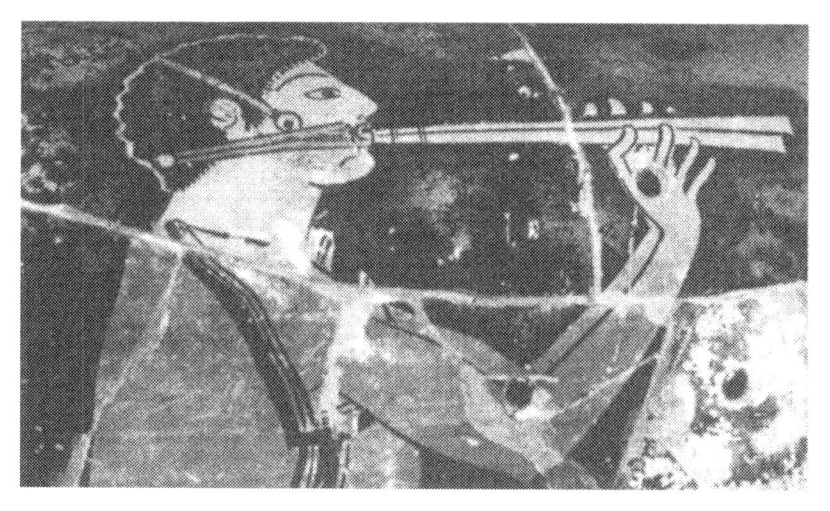

Fig. 1

serve of air available for the player, the better. While I would not hurry to suggest, as some have, that this is a case of pragmatics being sacrificed to aesthetics,[55] nonetheless, this restraining device which reduced or obscured the facial distortions so despised by Athena did effectively go some way to separating the satyr from the star performer.[56] More than technical utility is at stake with the *phorbeia*. A fragment of Sophokles is illuminating (768 Radt):

> φυσᾶι γὰρ οὐ σμικροῖσιν αὐλίσκοις ἔτι,
> ἀλλ' ἀγρίαις φύσαισι φορβειᾶς ἄτερ.
>
> He blusters no longer on his small, delicate *auloi*,
> but with savage blasts and no *phorbeia*.

The *phorbeia* emerges as a form of bridle that helps manage the forces of the wild (ἀγρίαις) within the *aulētēs* that ever threaten to make

---

[55] Paquette (1984) 33; Romer (1983). Others argue that the *phorbeia increased* the air pressure delivered to the reeds.
[56] Players at symposia – a place for the abandonment of control – did not normally wear the *phorbeia*: Bélis (1986) 208–9. A *satyr* might sport the *phorbeia* (ARV^2 p. 585 no. 34 (Pelike *c*. 470) = Paquette (1984) *A* 12) but this seems to be a playful inversion of the norm; cf. the passage of Simonides quoted in the text. Even less frequently do women wear it: *CVA* Geneva 1 (III) pl. 18, no.2 (Oinochoe 470–460) = Paquette (1984) A56 is a unique example of a female *aulos*-player in the dress of a 'competition' performer, with *phorbeia*.

themselves felt.⁵⁷ This is the logic ascribed by Plutarch (*Mor.* 456b–c) to the adoption of the *phorbeia* by Marsyas himself: 'Marsyas, so it seems, controlled the violence of his breath with a *phorbeia* and mouth-bands and so beautified his face and concealed its distortion.' He then cites a passage of Simonides (115 Edmonds) that reproduces this attitude:

> χρυσῶι δ' αἰγλήεντι συνήρμοσεν⁵⁸ ἀμφιδασείας
> κόρσας, καὶ στόμα λάβρον ὀπισθοδέτοισιν ἱμᾶσιν·
>
> He fitted his shaggy cheeks with the dazzling gold,
> and his boisterous mouth with straps that tie behind.

Marsyas controls his 'violent mouth,' his mouth full of the *aulos*, with the *phorbeia*. λάβρος is a word used in Homer only of natural forces, of the wind and the waves, and it is here transferred to the mouth of a creature of the wild, a mouth identified with the *aulos*.

Even the simple *sybēnē*, a carrying-case for the instrument usually made of skin, lent itself to sexual play, both verbal⁵⁹ and visual. Suspended from a satyr's erect penis (Fig. 2), the analogy between the two 'instruments' so difficult to control is inescapable.

Brief mention should also be made concerning the appearance of *aulos*-players on vases engaged at festivals; and this will introduce the all-important issue of status. They wear a special kind of ceremonial dress of great dignity, even magnificence (Fig. 3).⁶⁰ To play for a tragic choros at the Great Dionysia and to traipse around the streets after a group of drunken komasts late in the evening were, no doubt, very different experiences. Sensitivity to different social positionings and statuses in relation to the *aulos* is crucial. But there *is* a certain consistency about the tales of the *aulos* in Athens that seems to represent a colouring of its perception very broadly – at a level perhaps best

---

⁵⁷ Φῦσα/Φυσᾶν are very frequently used for the action of *aulos*-playing. The verb is elsewhere often used of undesirable 'puffing' in pride or arrogance (e.g. Eur. *IA* 125), often with negative socio-political connotations: e.g. Dem. 19.314.

⁵⁸ (συν)αρμόζω is often used of the lyre: LSJ s.v. ἁρμόζω I.5. I suspect that the full context made clear *Apollo's* role in harnessing the satyr. The gleaming gold would be especially appropriate for a *phorbeia* constructed and imposed by Apollo.

⁵⁹ At Ar. *Thesm.* 1215 the joke depends on a word-play between συβήνη, (here used of the Skythian Archer's arrow-case) and βινεῖν: Sommerstein (1994) 235. The Archer 'loses his shaft-case by shafting' (in Sommerstein's phrase) – as it happens, by shafting an *aulētris*.

⁶⁰ Beazley (1955); Taplin (1993) 7, 71, 77–8. The most sumptuously dressed of all *aulētai* is Pronomos of Thebes (Naples H3240), much reproduced (e.g. West (1992) plate 27). See also the solo *auletes* – perhaps Panathenaic – in ceremonial dress on an Attic red-figure amphora (London E270), reproduced in West (1992) plate 25.

Fig. 2

described as ideological. In that case, it might be suggested that the 'dignity' of the *aulētēs*' ceremonial dress might present something of a problem for the structural depriviliging of the activity for which I have been arguing. Yet this dignity is altogether consonant with the Athenian *appropriation* of the *aulos* for the greater glory of the city.[61] It is telling that the two contexts in particular which the evidence suggests saw the employment of this special auletic dress were in the instrumental competitions at the Panathenaia and for the choroi of the Great Dionysia: to honour the goddess who rejected it in myth at her very own festival; and to facilitate the reintroduction of Dionysos as the goddess' special guest, as it were, each year, and, moreover, in the forms of drama that had become one of the city's very greatest glories, within and far beyond Attike. It might indeed be suggested that the

---

[61] Anderson (1994) 56–7 stresses the sacral quality of the clothing and the temporary importance it reflects. Cf. in general Loraux (1990).

Fig. 3

magnificent dress of the professional, public perfomer was *necessary* to mark him off as of very different status from other players.[62]

The evidence of the status of *aulos*-players in Athens shows an overwhelming predominance of foreigners, females, slaves; or a combination of these. The instrumentalists whose services were sought after at Athenian festivals came from the great 'Theban school' of the later fifth and fourth centuries;[63] from Argos, Sikyon, Aigina, Tegea, Epidamnos

---

[62] The fact that, from the late fifth century, *chorēgoi* choose to record the names and ethnics of *aulētai* on their victory-monuments confirms that, under certain circumstances, the foreign *aulētēs* carried a prestige which Athenians sought to contribute to their own cultural achievements. There is no sign that the polis ever kept record of *aulos*-players at festivals, nor indeed of dithyrambic poets. The distinction is significant: the foreign *aulētēs* could become a source of personal glory for his *chorēgos*, but the polis (maintaining, as it were, Athena's 'official' view?) did not recognize him as worthy of permanent record.

[63] Roesch (1982), (1989).

The *aulos* in Athens 75

and elsewhere.⁶⁴ Athenians are virtually invisible.⁶⁵ As Aristophanes' *Akharnians* shows (860ff.), the event to which these experts contributed could involve the *mise-en-scène* of a very Athenian view of the Theban *aulētēs* and of his 'crossing' to Attike. It is from this Lenaian comedy, with its appearance at the market of Dikaiopolis of 'a Theban' surrounded by a swarm of ethnically-stereotyping *aulētai*, that the *aulos*' identification, in Athens, as quintessentially *Theban* is best seen.

At 'lower' levels of performance, identifying status becomes more difficult. But the female 'professional', the *aulētris*, was surely of servile status. And domestic slaves may have been called upon to perform the auletic services for a household's sacrificial needs. The only other Athenians we hear of who take up the instrument are from the very highest tier of the elite: men whose status was beyond doubt; so much so that they could momentarily set it at risk of criticism in the dominant social ideology by taking up the transgressive instrument in the confined space of the symposium.

Contexts

The *aulos* was the instrumental motor driving dozens, if not hundreds, of choral performances in the city and countryside of Attike every year. The twenty annual dithyrambs at the Great Dionysia alone, along with the five comic choroi and three tragic, were sustained by the *aulos*, and the Great Dionysia was only the most high profile of a large number of festivals that included choral performances. The level of our knowledge of Athenian festival practice is so poor that it is safe to assume the existence of a number of performances dependent on the *aulos* at festivals that have left little or no trace.⁶⁶ The *aulos* was the sound of the

---

⁶⁴ Stephanis (1988).
⁶⁵ Democratic institutions required the services of the *aulētēs*: the *boulē*, for the many sacrifices it performed in the name of the city. From *c.* 225 an *aulētēs* appears as a minor officer of the *boulē*, listed last (and irregularly) among those honoured in prytany decrees (*Athenian Agora XV* 127, 128, 130, 132, cf. p. 117). One Dexilaos of Halai served from 223 to *c.* 215, and must have been a citizen. The office is not mentioned in the *Ath. Pol.* (but cf. 62.2) and probably post-dates the classical period. I suspect that in earlier years the task was performed by a public slave.

Other Athenian *aulētai* attested with some security: a Nikarkhos against whom Lysias wrote a speech πρὸς Νίκαρχον τὸν αὐλητήν (Harp. v. ἀκμάζεις, Ἀντιγενίδας); Kleitarkhos, victorious *auletes* at the Great Amphiareia at Oropos in the period 366–338 (*IG* VII.414.6–7). Third century: Diogenes Theodorou (*FD* III.1.477); Timogenes Ath[moneus] (*IG* II²3085); Khariades Khariadou (*SIG* 424); Opis (?)(*Anth. Pal.* 13.20); a lost name (*SIG* 424 col. II.75); another (*IG* II²3086/7). A few more appear in the second century.

⁶⁶ Many of the varieties of *aulēsis* mentioned by Athenaios (above note 49) will have figured in Athenian life. For example, it is tempting to relate the *tetrakomos* (618c) to the

music of tragedy, comedy, dithyramb. And, moreover, it was a matter upon which all three of those performances themselves reflected, made part of their own discourse.

It is all too easy to forget that the *aulos* is the instrument of tragedy, because critics have persisted in speaking for years of 'tragic choral lyric.' However, 'all *baccheia* and all movement of that sort belongs particularly to the *auloi* among the instruments...'[67] If the lyre was ever employed in tragedy, it was only for local and special effect, an effect which depended on the assumed presence of the *aulos* and on a deeply-entrenched polarity – amounting, at times, to a hostility – between lyre and *aulos*.[68] In Attic iconography, the presence of an 'official' *aulētēs* among tragic figures is one of the securest signs of a 'theatrical' context or connection.[69] This testifies to his importance as the mediator between the world of tragedy and the ordinary world, and *visually* establishes him as the 'introducer of alterity' (Fig. 4). The tragedians – their own musical composers – seem to have employed a considerable range among the various modes or *harmoniai*, including the 'noble' Dorian, the 'dithyrambic' Phrygian, the 'soft' or 'relaxed' Ionian and Lydian, and the 'emotional' Mixolydian.

The role of the *aulos* in relation to the institution of tragedy has similarities, but also marked differences from its dithyrambic counterpart: in dithyramb, a group of fifty Athenian citizens, affiliated by their democratic phyletic membership, train in choral song of a largely narrative, often 'patriotic' nature. They wear no masks, but (almost certainly) ivy garlands and lavish robes. However boisterous early dithyramb may have been, that of the classical festivals seems rather a restrained affair[70] and the contact of these citizens with the world beyond the confines of their city is limited, in practical terms at least, to their association with the foreign *aulētēs* in the middle of their circular formation and with the (regularly) foreign poet. In tragedy, on the other hand, a group of twelve or fifteen citizens, chosen it seems by no

---

Tetrakomia of the Phaleron region, a local religious association devoted to Herakles which involved competitive dance: see Parker (1996) 328–9.

[67] Arist. *Pol.* 8, 1342b.
[68] On the musical accompaniment of tragedy: Roos (1951) 216; Pickard-Cambridge (1988 (1968)) 165–7, 257–62, 322; Snyder (1979); West (1992) 351–5; Richter (1983); Anderson (1994) 113–24. It is likely that when employed in tragedy, the lyre was predominantly used to accompany actors, or indeed by actors to accompany themselves in roles which actually required a lyre (but cf. Xen. *Symp.* 6.1). The most famous example is the tradition that Sophokles played Thamyras, accompanying himself on the *kithara*. Lyric monody and exchanges between actor(s) and choros (especially *kommoi*) would surely have employed the *aulos*.
[69] Beazley (1955); Taplin (1993).
[70] Pickard-Cambridge (1962) 77.

Fig. 4

more specific sub-division of the citizen-body, train in choral song of a radically mimetic kind. They regularly take on, with their masks and costumes, identities of groups construed by the coordinates of their culture as alien to their own: those of women, often young women; of foreigners (whether non-Athenian Greeks or non-Greeks); of slaves – or any combination of these; or of old men beyond their political prime; even, rarely, of semi-divine figures.[71] Their entry into the world

[71] Cf. Gould (1996); Goldhill (1996).

of Dionysos, an entry facilitated and to a certain extent 'induced' by the foreign and maskless *aulētēs* who led them on and off, is rather more radical than that of their dithyrambic counterparts. With choral identities consistently alien to their real status as Athenians, and with a frequently-realized potential for dramatizing powerful extremes of collective emotionalism, in performance at least they came closer to the foreigner in their midst, visible as such by the fact that he wore no mask.[72]

The *aulos* was in its own right the centre of competitions at the Panathenaia, though it is evident that the prestige of victory in this *agōn* in Athens was markedly inferior to that for, say, the *kithara*. The prizes were fewer and almost certainly lower in value and there was only one all-inclusive age-category.[73] Perhaps non-Athenians were regular winners.[74] There were agonistic performances on the *aulos* (*aulētikē*), as well as in singing *to* the *aulos* (*auloidia*), and perhaps also in something called *synaulia*, a kind of concert performance of a number of instruments together.[75] Still in the realm of festivals, though in connection with performances which we might classify as gymnastic rather than musical, the *aulos* accompanied the important competitive choral 'dance in armour' or *pyrrhikē*[76] as well as a number of more purely athletic competitions, such as the long jump, discus and other events of the pentathlon. The iconographic evidence also suggests that it was used at least for training in the palaestra and gymnasium.[77] Its im-

---

[72] To judge from iconography, the *phorbeia* did not conceal the face, and *auletai* were remembered for their facial expressiveness.

[73] IG II² 2311.20-2. Shapiro (1992) 58. There is evidence (late 6th to early 5th centuries) of dedications made on the Akropolis by *kitharoidoi* (probably) successful at the Panathenaia (IG I³ 666, 754), while no such thing exists for *aulētai* or *auloidoi*: Kotsidu (1991) 76-80. Vos (1986) on iconography.

[74] One example: Midas of Akragas (Σ Pind. *P.* 12), whom Clay (1992) 519 argues was of low social status.

[75] On *synaulia*: Pollux 4.83; Athenaios 618a-b with Barker (1984) 274-5; Taplin (1993) 109-10. It is a fascinating and little-remarked fact that, at least according to Plutarch (*Per.* 13), part of the Periklean vision of how the performance culture of the democratic city should function included specific stipulations as to what (or how? – καθότι) competitors at the greatest civic festival were to play on the instrument – an implied degree of control over musical culture in one of its most high-profile sites that presents interesting parallels to the prescriptive approach of Plato in the hardly democratic vision of the *Laws*. Cf. Nagy (1992).

[76] Kyle (1992) 94-5.

[77] Attic red-figure cup *c.* 520 (Berlin F2262, *ARV*² p. 46, no. 14 (6), West (1992) plate 10) shows a palaestra scene with practice in javelin, discus and boxing, to the accompaniment of long-robed, *phorbeia*-equipped *aulētai*; *ABV* p. 369 no. 115 (Panathenaic Amphora) (cf. *ABV* p. 365 no. 64) has an *akontist*, *aulētēs* and trainer. Another Attic red-figure cup dated after 505 (Tarquinia RC 2066, *ARV*² p. 101, no. 2) shows a youth with jumping-weights, an *aulētēs*, a spear-thrower, discus-thrower, youths box-

portance in the training for and demonstration of Athenian somatic excellence is thus of the highest order.

The penetrating voice of the *aulos* must most frequently have been heard at that fundamental collective activity of Greek life, sacrifice,[78] and this function more than any other exemplifies its powerful role as a link to the otherness of the divine. In an account of Persian sacrificial practice (1.132.4), Herodotos signals as one of the indices of their defining difference the fact that the Persians do *not* employ the *aulos*.[79] And so the *aulos* takes its place among the standard paraphernalia of Greek sacrifice: raised altars, fire, libations, garlands, barley-grains.[80] And yet it is frustratingly hard to speak with any confidence about such crucial matters as the status of the Athenian sacrificial *aulētēs*; and whether an *aulētēs* would have been required at any sacrifice, even a domestic one, or only on the grander public occasions.[81] Widespread use is probable; as for status, the very marginality of its traces in our records is consistent with a likely servile status for such *aulētai*. The auletic skills of foreign slaves, male and female, may well have been one of the qualities sought after by their citizen purchasers. Whether *aulētai* performing at sacrifices were deemed participants *in* the sacrifice is extremely hard to answer. The topos of the auletic parasite known especially from comedy suggests that at best they were thought to be properly on the margins of sacrifice.[82]

When Dikaiopolis reviles a Theban *aulētēs* called Khairis, he does so both in terms of his lack of musical *sophia* (*Akh.* 15–16[83]) *and* as a figure likely to turn up uninvited to play his *aulos* at a sacrifice and so 'for all his puffing and toiling', demand some return. Rather than assume from this that foreign musicians who performed, and perhaps

---

ing in the palaestra and a trainer with a forked stick in the centre. Cf. Pausanias 5.7.10, 6.14.10; [Plut.] *De mus.* 26 speaks of its use in accompaniment to the pentathlon, but the reference is to the Argives of old at the Stheneia and to his on day; cf. Philodemos 1.26.3–5, p. 14 (Kemke); Pollux 4.55.

[78] Haldane (1966).
[79] Cartledge (1993) 161–2.
[80] Cf. Plut. *Mor.* 16c. Sacrificial procession seems to be the one context in Attic iconography (on vases and in the Parthenon frieze) which shows the *aulos* often in company with the *kithara*: Maas and Snyder (1989) 68–9.
[81] See note 65.
[82] In inscriptions recording honorific distribution of sacrificial meat, skins and special payments, the *auletes* is sometimes among those so honoured, but I know of no Attic example: Sokolowski (1962) no. 38A (fifth-century Andrian theoric mission to Delphoi); Sokolowski (1969) no. 151 A53 (fourth-century Koan cult calendar), cf. 156 A30.
[83] Σ on 866. Stephanis (1988) 455–6 for full testimonia.

lived, in Athens might regularly have served as *aulētai* at sacrifice, these criticisms are better evidence for a fairly strong hierarchy *between* the tasks of sacrificial and festival *aulētai*. For the former are presented in comedy as a magnet for parasites (cf. *Birds* 858ff.), and it is probably the very continuity of instrumentation across a sharp discontinuity of 'real-life' prestige and status that is being played with here to the ends of comic abuse.

The *aulos* was intimately associated with the expression of strong emotions: both joyous emotions, seen for instance in its role in the wedding procession;[84] and with the intensity of grief, in mourning and lament. It appears in funeral processions, and its mythology too is intimately linked with lament.[85] The threnetic qualities of the *aulos* are particularly associated with a Phrygian ambience, and in Athens they surface most prominently in tragedy. Indeed, given the manner in which the Athenian polis exercised control over the public expression of grief, the collective spectatorship of the grief of *others* (performed by men) in *tragedy* may have been the principal context in which the Athenians experienced grief publicly performed to the *aulos*.[86] Iconography fills some of the gaps in this material, but the relative scarcity of references to the part played by the *aulos* in the ritual experience of 'private' grief in Athens, in the context of family funerals, may have something to do with the suppression of emotional 'excess' in such contexts, and the assumption by the classical polis itself of a leading role as carer for the dead, at least of the war-dead, and in a ceremony which conspicuously placed logos in a position of great prominence as the proper form of ritual accompaniment to burial, as opposed to the 'anti-logos' of excessive feminine lament and the wailing of *auloi*.

The *aulos* kept the time for the stroke of the trireme,[87] the backbone of Athenian imperial power which became closely associated with the ideology of democracy; and perhaps too for the advance of the hoplite

---

[84] Already in Homer, *Iliad* 18.491f.; cf. Pollux 4.80. As in symposia and *komoi* in classical Attic iconography, the attendant figures who play the *auloi* in wedding-contexts are usually women; guests more often have a lyre. Maas and Snyder (1989) 86, 114-15.

[85] Pindar *Pyth.* 12; Plut. *Mor.* 394b-c. Reiner (1983) 67-70; Vernant (1985); Frontisi-Ducroux (1994); Segal (1995). Pausanias (10.7.3-5) recounts how both aulodic and auletic competitions were introduced to the Pythia in 586, but the aulodic was dropped at the next festival, because it was felt to be too 'elegiac'. See Bowie (1986) 23-7. The 'problem' of the *aulos*' connection to the world of lament and death is not exclusively an Athenian problem.

[86] A Solonian restriction on the involvement of women in funerary practice forbade the singing of 'set dirges' (Plut. *Solon* 21.4) which were surely accompanied by the *aulos*. Cf. Foley (1993).

[87] Arist. *Akh.* 554; *IG* II² 1951.100-1, 335; Pollux 4.56.

phalanx, though the evidence for the latter is far from unambiguous.[88] In these two last examples in particular, its 'technical' advantages are clear: it is one of the only pieces of equipment available in the ancient world that could make itself heard over the tumult of the advance to war, whether that be dominated by the rattle of bronze and thud of feet or by the loud-echoing waves and plash of hundreds of oars. Its penetrating tone is far better suited to such collective, external activities as proliferated under democracy than that of any stringed instrument. It gave the ordering force of rhythm to these mass operations. The development of the navy and the grand-scale civic festival are two phenomena particularly associated with the growth of democracy and involved, on the one hand, the presence of a mass audience and, on the other, the mobilization of an unprecedented majority of the citizenry. However, it is impossible to say with certainty whether the hundreds of *aulētai* who supplied the penetrating musical tone for the time of the oars were Athenian citizens or slaves owned by the city.[89]

In similar vein, the *aulos* provided a mobilizing rhythm to a variety of other kinds of important labour in the city and countryside, both constructive and destructive: including the bringing in of the harvest, its winnowing, and also, perhaps, women's work at the loom.[90] And, to take one enormously significant historical moment, the very work of demolishing the walls of Athens was driven by the sound of *auloi*. At the end of the Peloponnesian war, the long walls of Athens and the Peiraieus were destroyed 'with great enthusiasm' to the accompaniment of the *aulos*.[91] Here there is a marriage of the technically utilitarian with the culturally meaningful, because as I indicated above, the *aulos* was also the great accompanier of lamentation, and so appropriate for an Athenian view of this moment. But it was also, of course, associated with joyous celebration, especially that deriving from re-

---

[88] Its earliest (mid-seventh century) appearance in this role is on the famous proto-Korinthian Chigi vase. It is unclear however whether the Athenians ever employed the *aulos* on land. The Spartans and Kretans did: Hdt. 1.17.6; Thuc. 5.70; Xen. *Lak. Cons.* 13.8; Plut. *Lyk.* 22.2–3; Theophrastos *Char.* 8.5; Polyb. 4.20.6. Cf. West (1992a) 34.

[89] The current consensus seems to be that the trierarchic *hyperesia* was made up of citizens: Gabrielsen (1994) 106, 248; Morrison (1984). However see Dem. 18.129; and, of the players on *IG* II²1951 one (.100) is a Siphnian, the other (335) looks decidedly un-Athenian. The context from which this derives seems to be one of the exceptional moments late in the Peloponnesian war when slaves also were called upon to row.

[90] West (1992) 28–9.

[91] Xen. *Hell.* 2.2.19–23; Plut. *Lysander* 15, adds that Lysander employed *aulētrides* from Athens itself, and that he burnt the fleet πρὸς τὸν αὐλόν, while the allies wore garlands and celebrated. Elsewhere the walls of cities mythic and/or historical are *constructed* to the sound of *auloi*: e.g. Paus. 4.27.

lease, and this is the dominant tone of the instrument's appearance in Xenophon's account, seen primarily from Spartan – but also, I would stress, from *Theban* eyes – as Day One of Greek freedom.

Last, but hardly least, the *aulos* was an indispensable accompaniment of the symposium.[92] Central to all aspects of symposiastic ritual and entertainment, the *aulos* provided the rhythm for the preparation and distribution of the wine, as for its consumption.[93] The *aulos* was heard too in the prayers sung before the drinking began. And it accompanied the drinking itself, both as the instrumental support for the singing of guests as they entertained, informed and competed with one-another; and in the form of solo performance by professionals.

This elite institution of male social and political bonding was certainly a pre-, and perhaps to some extent, an anti-democratic home of the *aulos* in Athens. An occasion of release from the pressures of civic identity, the symposium provided a frame for momentarily abandoning that control which was at the heart of the civic ethos; for 'playing the other', for a while.[94] The *aulos* appears here in the mouths of players from both poles of the status-spectrum: the super-elite, who prove that playing the *aulos* does not make one an *aulētēs*; and the doubly-excluded female slave *aulētrides*.

The symposium provides one of the very few frames for the playing of the *aulos* by an Athenian citizen. Aristotle (*Politics* 8.1339b9–10) envisages the only situations in which the free man will himself take up the instrument to be 'when drunk or having fun': at a symposium, of course, he is likely to be both. In addition to the tradition concerning Alkibiades' *aulētikē*, we hear of Kritias and Kallias having taken up the instrument.[95] This is a world rather removed from those in which most of the evidence I discuss circulates – the Akropolis and theatre, for instance. Doubtless the 'official' version we find there does not altogether apply in the symposium, or indeed is actively toyed with, in an institution which gives members of the elite a specially demarcated space for 'playing at the outsider'. At the imaginary extreme of this release, the Athenian becomes the satyr, the figure constantly implicated in the use of the *aulos*, its creation and development.[96] Like the satyr, the *aulos* serves as an exploratory device for Athenian male identity. But unlike

---

[92] See e.g. Xen. *Symp.* esp. chs. 2, 3, 6, 7, 9; Plut. *Mor.* 713a–d.
[93] Lissarrague (1990 (1987)); Frontisi-Ducroux (1991) 80, 86–7.
[94] Lissarrague (1990 (1987)) 12.
[95] Athen. 184d = Khamaileon fr. 5 (Giordano); add the evidence in West (1992) 350 concerning Perikles and Damon.
[96] Purely *exempli gratia* see the *aulos*-playing satyr labelled TERPAULOS – 'the one who charms with the *aulos*', and perhaps also 'the one who joys in the *aulos*' – on a red-figure amphora of *c.* 510 (Beazley *Para.* 323/3) (Fig. 5).

Fig. 5

the satyr, it is not forever confined to the realm of the imaginary, of pure representation.

But the symposium is preeminently the home of the *female aulos-*player, the *aulētris*. The connotations of 'professionalism' vary markedly according to the gender of the player. The female professional shows the 'instrumental' functions of the *aulos* for the citizen at their clearest. Doubly removed from the status of the citizen as woman and slave, the *aulētris* appears as another figure marginal to the centre of Athenian society who provides it with the instrumental support and release of the *aulos*. It is, I suppose, just feasible that some *aulētrides* may have been free foreigners, as with their male counterparts who performed at festivals (I know of no clear case).[97] The [Aristotelian]

---

[97] A remark of Alkibiades in Plato's *Symposium* testifies to a marked evaluative difference between male and female players. Alkibiades is speaking of the tunes of Marsyas and Olympos and their effects, which he says are powerful, 'whether a fine *auletes* or a base (φαύλη) *aulētris* plays them' (215c). That the skills should be so distributed across the genders is not accidental, especially given the way a term like φαύλη used of the *aulētris* fuses both a judgement as to technical accomplishment and social worth. The sound-play in φαύλη αὐλητρίς 'confirms' the 'innate' relation.

Ath. Pol. 50.2 shows that it was the duty of the ten civic officials called *astynomoi* to see to it that *aulētrides*, *psaltriai* and *kitharistriai* were not hired out for more than two drachmas. That only female performers are mentioned implies the likely overlap of sexual and musical services, but in any case, slaves are clearly meant. This centralized control of prices may suggest (as Plato *Prot.* 347c3–e1 further implies) that the 'democratization' of symposiastic pleasures forced up the cost of *aulētrides*. But it is fascinating that the Athenian polis assigned control over *aulētrides* to these 'fathers of the city' (Σ Dem. 24.112) whose responsibility it was to keep the most basic order in the streets of Athens, patrolling the rougher edges of the line between public and private: making sure that dung-collectors did their job, and that the streets were not blocked or endangered by overhanging balconies and drainpipes. A link between these areas of concern must lie in the realm of threats to public safety: violent disputes over *aulētrides* were a real danger.[98]

There is a clear continuity here between the musical and the sexual. The *aulētris* is, as it were, pure body, with no logos; or she is the transmitter of voices (*phōnai*[99]) not her own. She is defined by the instrument (with which her body is in a sense continuous) and which has a more than ambivalent relationship to logos, often troped as its enemy or opposite.[100] She serves the pleasure of her male owners or hirers by providing the sound which, as good citizens 'of free mouth', they themselves could never possibly practise with any seriousness; sound to which they may, however, atune their voice in competitive displays of expertise in their culture.

The *aulētris* is synonymous with sexual availability and use. Her sexual use-value is, like her 'musical' value, focused principally on her oral skills. In comedy, a term that plays on this musico-sexual overlap is λεσβιάζειν. Lesbians were known for their skills as musicians – particularly as *kitharōdes*, but also as players of the *aulos*. But *lesbiazein* has a sexual reference in Aristophanes to 'a sexual act performed by a woman upon a man; possibly handling his penis, more probably taking it in her mouth . . .'[101] In the *Frogs*, the appearance of Euripides' Muse, after Aiskhylos has explicitly rejected as inappropriate for Euripides the lyre and associated him instead with the *aulos* and castanets made

---

[98] Dem. 21.36. My thanks to James Davidson for illumination on this point.
[99] Φωνή is repeatedly used of the 'voice' of the *aulos*. It has this in common with animals, possessors of *phōnē* but not logos.
[100] In iconography the *aulos*-player is frequently the 'human machine' facilitating the activities of men. See Lissarrague and Frontisi-Ducroux (1990) 222–3.
[101] Dover (1993) 351.

from potsherds, provokes a question from Dionysos as to her skills in λεσβιάζειν (1308). The musical and sexual degeneracy of Euripides' Muse makes of her, in the imagination of Dionysos, a comic *aulētris* (*vel sim.*) skilled in λεσβιάζειν. It is no surprise that those who supply the pleasurable release of *aulos*-music at symposia should also have – or be imagined as having – supplied the oral pleasuring of λεσβιάζειν. The strong correlation observable in Greek culture between sexual comportment and personal agency and power is nowhere better illustrated than in this instrumental use of the outsider. The *aulētris* perhaps represents the limit case of the Athenian 'instrumental' view of the *aulos* and its practitioners.[102] Though women played the *aulos*, the problems focused by the Athenian discourse on the *aulos* are always 'male' problems, in which the female plays a subsidiary and reflective role. That there is no analogous set of problems with regard to women and the *aulos* is tantamount to saying that female civic identity does not exist.

III. Representation and critique

Athenian logoi on auloi

The discursive place of the *aulos* in Athens outside the realm of heightened poetic language pinpoints some of the basic anxieties which attached themselves to it, and gives us a sense of dominant Athenian attitudes. We have already encountered the comic trope of the *aulētēs* as parasite. The *Suda* (Prov. 4438) glosses a proverb, whose provenance from Attike we can scarcely doubt, – 'You live the life of an *aulētēs*' – as 'referring to those who live off others; inasmuch as *aulētai* keep watch over those who perform sacrifices and live *gratis*'. Once again the parasite motif derives from a particular association with sacrifice. But as a rhetorical reflection of Athenian views, the metaphor, which determines the profile of the *aulētēs* by its lowest common denominator, could hardly encapsulate more forcefully a sense of the marginality of the *aulētēs*.

---

[102] The comic image is not always straightforward, however, and the figure of the *aulētris* can serve a comic critique of notions of male identity. While the scene at the end of *Wasps* shows the objectification of the *aulētris* at its most brutal, it also shows a man pathetically out of control as a result of his sexual urges, and not necessarily getting what he needs to satisfy them. Whether Philokleon actually gets 'Dardanis' or not is unclear; he certainly has to negotiate with not just cash but a promise to ransom her and make her his *pallakē*. And in any case, the point is largely irrelevant, because he 'can't do anything' (1380–1). This impotence undercuts his representation as a potent, rejuvenated male expressed through use of the *aulētris*.

It is no surprise to find that the *aulos* is used to trope an opponent in Athenian courts. Both Aiskhines and Demades compare, respectively, Demosthenes and the Athenians collectively to *auloi* – 'because, if you take away the tongue [and γλῶσσα is used of the instrument's reed as well as the human tongue] what remains is useless'.[103] This critical comparison of Athenians *as such* to *auloi* for the penetrating powers of their tongues reflects Athenian self-definition, even self-admiration, for their skills of speech, while at the same time identifying the dangers of such powers in the political realm – the possibility that the effect of Athenian speech can be that not of rational persuasion but of commandeering and violent, albeit seductive, domination, imitative and infinitely adaptable to expediency and with no necessary relation to rational intelligence or communitarian concern.[104]

A fascinating variation on this theme is preserved in an apophthegm which Philostratos uses to sum up his altogether black portrait of the life of Kritias, the Athenian philosopher, tragedian, elegist and tyrant. I strongly suspect that Philostratos may be employing one of Kritias' own sayings against him:[105]

εἰ γὰρ μὴ ὁμολογήσει ὁ λόγος τῶι ἤθει, ἀλλοτρίαι τῆι γλώττηι δόξομεν φθέγγεσθαι, ὥσπερ οἱ αὐλοί.

If the speech doesn't coincide with the character, we shall appear to be talking with a tongue that belongs to another – just like *auloi*.

The dangerous powers of appearance and imitation, the feared lack of identity between expression and character in the realm of public life, are readily compared to the instrument that speaks directly to the emotions, takes on the voices of many others and does so, what's more, with two tongues (the *aulos* employed in Athens was almost always of the *double* form).[106]

An epigram partly preserved by Athenaios (337e) condenses another strand of the Athenian view very succinctly:

ἀνδρὶ μὲν αὐλητῆρι θεοὶ νόον οὐκ ἐνέφυσαν
ἀλλ' ἅμα τῶι φυσῆν χὠ νόος ἐκπέταται

---

[103] Aeschin. *In Ktes.* 229; Demades: Stobaeus *Flor.* 4.69. Cf. the related metaphor in Ar. *Akh.* 681.
[104] These qualities also lie behind the linguistic development in the word ἔναυλος, which came to be applied in Attic prose to words or the voice of a speaker 'singing in one's ears' (cf. Plato *Menex.* 235b8, *Laws* 678c) as well as to things that were especially 'piercing' of the mind (cf. Aeschin. 3.191).
[105] Philostratos *Vit. Soph.* 1.16 (DK 88).
[106] Frontisi-Ducroux (1994) 250. In the absence of clear evidence for a notion of the double tongue as an image of deceptive speech (cf. Eur. *Rhes.* 394–5, 422–3), one would not wish to push this too far.

The *aulos* in Athens 87

> The gods did not endow the man who plays the *aulos* with
> intelligence, but it flew out of him along with his puffing.

The *aulos* in Athens is an enemy of the rational mind. Then there is the quip of Antisthenes (Plu. *Perikles* 1.5), a Sokratic and cynic much concerned with self-control. When he heard that Ismenias (a Theban) was an excellent *aulētēs*, he replied 'Yes, but he's a base man; for otherwise he wouldn't be a serious *aulos*-player.' Excellence as an *aulētēs* precludes excellence as a man. Moral, social and intellectual inferiority are the mark of the 'Athenian' *aulētēs*.

The *aulos* clearly came to mind very readily in Athens as the vehicle of metaphor, and this fact, and the cases we have, tell us much. It was always regarded by its critics and partisans alike as the most mimetic of all instruments, able to imitate an extraordinary range of sounds and to induce 'ecstatic' dispositions in its hearers, making them other than their normal selves. It was thus in itself a profoundly 'metaphoric' or 'metabolic' instrument.[107]

The aulos *banished: philosophical anxieties*

An anecdote from the childhood of Alkibiades condenses around this *enfant terrible* of the democracy many of the concerns regarding the *aulos* I have been studying. Plutarch recounts it to illustrate Alkibiades' powerful 'love of rivalry and preeminence' (2.1), demonstrated from his earliest years. Alkibiades plays Athena, and by this descent, as it were, from the Akropolis, and entering, however fictively, the wider orbit of the city, some of the social and political ramifications implicit in the myth come to the surface in clear view:

When it came to schooling, he usually paid proper attention to his teachers, but he resiled from playing the *aulos*, holding it to be an ignoble thing unsuited to the free man. The use of the *plektron* and the lyre, he argued, wrought no havoc with the bearing (σχήματος) and appearance (μορφῆς) that were becoming to a free man; but when a man blows at the *auloi* with his mouth, even his own acquaintances can scarcely recognize his face (πρόσωπον). (§5) Moreover, the lyre blended its tones with the voice and song of its user, while the *aulos* blocked up and barricaded the mouth, robbing its master both of voice and speech (τήν τε φωνὴν καὶ τὸν λόγον). 'So let the sons of the Thebans play the

---

[107] In the earliest account of the *aulos* of any length, Pindar's *Pyth*. 12, the art of the *aulos* began life as an *imitation* created by Athena of the lament of the Gorgon for her slain sister – the sister, incidentally, whose power when alive had been to render her viewers, through the gaze, forever and irrevocably the same. This fascinating Theban account of the *aulos* is beyond my concern here: see esp. the excellent discussion of Frontisi-Ducroux (1994); cf. Ahl (1991); Gentili and Luisi (1995).

88   Peter Wilson

aulos', he said, 'for they do not know how to converse. But we Athenians, as our fathers say, have Athena as foundress and Apollo as patron, and the former threw away the *aulos*, while the latter flayed the *aulos*-player.' (§6) In this half-joking, half-serious way, Alkibiades emancipated himself from this discipline, along with the rest of the boys. For word soon made its way to them that Alkibiades was quite rightly disgusted with the art of *aulos*-playing and mocked those who learnt it. As a consequnce the *aulos* became entirely dissociated from the pastimes of free men and was utterly despised. (Plutarch *Alkibiades* 2. 4–6)

The *aulos* becomes a question in the educational formation of Alkibiades, the highly 'performative' figure who became the obsessive and problematic focus of the democracy of late fifth-century Athens. Alkibiades ties his rejection into a whole series of oppositions at work in Athenian self-representations. On the side of the *aulos* and Marsyas are the *aneleutheroi*, the *kakoi*, the youth of Thebes;[108] on the side of the lyre and Athena and Apollo, are the *eleutheroi*, the *kaloi kagathoi*, the youth of Athens. The *aulos* blocks the use of the mouth; the lyre makes possible a pleasing synthesis of logos and music under the physical control of the performer. Logos is here not simply the faculty of speech; it implies the full range of rational powers and their articulate expression so prized by the Athenians.

The Athenian story of the *aulos* is fundamentally and literally a story of self-regard, and in a society like that of ancient Greece, the notion of self-regard is inseparable from that of the regard of one's peers. The point is brought home through the detail of Alkibiades' rationale in rejecting the *aulos* that 'even one's close acquaintances could scarcely recognize one's face' when playing it. This, at the human and social level, is the equivalent of the goddess' edifying vision of herself when playing the *aulos*.[109]

But as I mentioned at the outset, Alkibiades' musical career is not solely and unambiguously under Athena's aegis. It does not bother me – on the contrary – that our sources significantly *conflict* on the matter of his relation to the *aulos*. We have Plutarch's full account to the effect that Alkibiades refused to learn how to play it.[110] But on the other hand, Douris is reported to have written – in a work, interestingly enough, on Euripides and Sophokles – that Alkibiades learnt *auletikē* 'not from just anybody, but from the person who had the greatest rep-

[108] Cf. Pl. *Symp.* 182b.
[109] Proclus (commentary on Plato *Alk.* 1.106) reports the view that the reason Alkibiades avoided the *aulos* was concern for his beauty. He goes on to label this a precipitate condemnation of Alkibiades, since it fails to observe that it is a common practice for all who are nobly born – indeed all 'upright citizens' – to avoid the instrument.
[110] This probably derives in part from Plato's *First Alkibiades* 106e.

utation of all, Pronomos'.[111] The banal solution of making Pronomos the teacher whom the boyish Alkibiades rejects will not do. No doubt it is significant, in terms of the shape of Plutarch's *Life*, that Alkibiades' rejection of the *aulos*, which can be viewed as a kind of *conformity* with a dominant fifth-century Athenian attitude, is emphatically consigned to his *youth*. It is as though the inversions of or transitory divergences *from* conformity that are associated with that age take the form, in the case of Alkibiades, of conformity: a further reversal that one might expect from (antiquity's representations of) Alkibiades. And this account of his boyish rejection of the *aulos* – a rejection which supposedly affected the attitude of his entire peer-group – is also surely to be read in the knowledge of the Alkibiades of Plato's *Symposium*, a fully adult Alkibiades who *reinstates*, rather than rejects, the *aulos* among his peers. It is no surprise to find Alkibiades serving this role as a contradictory, but eminently useful, focalizing figure for the particularly Athenian problems of the *aulos*.

Sokrates joins Alkibiades and Marsyas to form a curious trio around the *aulos*. The group is not of my own fashioning, for Alkibiades seeks to make Sokrates (whom he emphatically terms a *hybristēs*[112]) powerfully intelligible to his audience in the Platonic *Symposium* 'through images ... and the image will be for the sake of the truth' (215a). Alkibiades' images will derive predominantly from the world of the *aulos*.

In this dialogue to whose philosophical 'message' dramatic form, rhetorical texture and representational complexity are so important,[113] the early banishment of the *aulētris* (on the doctor's advice) (176e) 'who has just now come in', is far from an idle stage-direction. It is analogous to the symposiasts' decision not to impose any of the usual regulations for the consumption of wine, overhung as they are from the effects of the Dionysian celebration of the previous day in honour of Agathon's first tragic victory. '... so let her pipe to herself or, if she likes, to the women within, but let us seek our entertainment today in conversation'. The *aulētris* is banished, to a curiously autistic performance for herself, and to the feminine interior space of the house. While, in a precisely gendered polarity, the men will 'be together with one-another through the medium of logoi'. Logos ousts an enemy, as it is agreed that 'we should pass the time satisfactorily in logoi' (177d). The unusual notion of a symposium of pure logos is in part signalled by this (in some ways 'traditional') rejection of the *aulos*; but that theirs are to be logoi of and on *eros* at once sounds a paradoxical note.

[111] Athenaios 184d.
[112] Esp. *Symp.* 215b; cf. 175e.
[113] See e.g. Halperin (1992); Nussbaum (1986) ch. 6; Rutherford (1995) ch. 7.

The irruption of Alkibiades and his *kōmos* at the point where Sokrates' report of Diotima's account of the ascent to 'true' *eros* is concluded also represents the disruptive return of the *aulos* (along with wine, garlands of ivy and violets, and *tainiai*). 'And suddenly there was a knocking at the outer door, which had a noisy sound like that of revellers, and they heard the sound of an *aulētris*.' (212c) With the undifferentiated noise (ψόγος) (as if) of komasts, the 'voice' (φωνή) of an *aulētris* is heard. The significance of these acoustics is clear: there is no logos in this crowd bursting in from the 'outside'. The komasts produce an inarticulate sound; nor is the *aulētris* possessed of (a) logos. But she does have a voice.[114] Yet that voice, there can be no doubt, is not 'her own'. It is the voice of the *aulos*, the voice of others, of the outside and other. And it is *leading* Alkibiades to the symposium (212d), and thus towards his own encomium of Sokrates as master *aulētēs*. There are many models and instances of leadership and pursuit, physical, erotic and intellectual, in the *Symposium*. Only Alkibiades is physically led by an *aulētris*, yet he goes on to give an account of the utterly compelling leadership that Sokrates-the-Silenos exercises over them all with his auletic words.

Sokrates is most like those figures of Silenoi sitting in statue-makers, the ones that hold *syringes* or *auloi*. They open up and reveal images of gods on the inside. 'And what's more, I say he is most like Marsyas' (215b) 'Are you not an *aulētēs*? Yes, and one much more astounding than he.' For Marsyas enchanted his audience by means of his instruments with the power that issued from his mouth, something which even today can be done by an *aulos*-player playing his tunes. But Sokrates achieves the same effect 'without instruments, by unadorned logoi' (215c). Sokrates' words enchant, constrain and lead the hearer on towards a closer relation with the divine, that otherness within the strange, satyr-like body of Sokrates, through which it is possible to gain access to the illumination of the beautiful.

Alkibiades outlines a psychopathology of *aulos* performance in Sokrates' words which a later Sokrates will identify as of a kind incompatible with the strict control of identity within the ideal city. But this most famous and extended of all *aulos*-metaphors establishes a highly paradoxical equation between the prime Athenian cultural item of non-logos and the preeminent individual Athenian embodiment of logos, particularly in its guise of deductive, 'scientific' knowledge. The in-

---

[114] There may be a pun linking the place from which the sound emerges and the auletic element of the sound itself (τὴν αὔλιον θύραν ... αὐλητρίδος), as though both player and sound of the *aulos* were properly 'outside'.

The *aulos* in Athens 91

tensity of the paradox generated in this way should not be resolved by assuming that Alkibiades' imagistic miscegenation of philosophical logos and one of its traditional enemies is so framed by the structure and movement of the work as to condemn it as nothing more than the product of a hopelessly misguided, unregenerate and dangerously uncontrolled individual.

Alkibiades' understanding of the power of Sokratic discourse is as a power that exceeds the limits of its own terms. The rationalist project, the ascent to a purified *eros* that lies at the heart of Sokratic/Diotimean philosophy, works through a medium and a form of relation that is antithetical to a life lived according to reason. Alkibiades – along with any other member of a Sokratic audience, man, woman or child – is dazed and controlled by Sokrates' words (215d), whether they come from his mouth or are in the mouth of another (as with the tunes of Marsyas). His heart leaps more wildly than that of the possessed korybants; he is taken over by tears. All those present at the symposium have been touched by this 'philosophical madness and *baccheia*' (218b). Alkibiades' soul has been thrown into turmoil and reduced to slavery (215e). The loss of control implied by such a pathology, is, paradoxically, the polar opposite of the desired aim of the knowledge being imparted by the words of Sokrates. Only with the return of the excluded *aulos* to the symposium, true to its mythic paradigm, can this difficult other side of the project to produce a powerfully ordered, controlled and passionless world, be fully grasped.

Sokrates as an *aulētēs* would seem at first blush to turn the ambivalence of the civic discourse of the *aulos* against the certainties of philosophical truth. The point is only emphasized by the fact that Alkibiades' account remains unchallenged (although he explicitly tells Sokrates to correct him if he diverges from the truth), and by the fact that it is the general experience of all who hear him.[115] And yet, through another metaphoric turn, the *aulos* might appear to have become a servant of philosophy, the 'as if' of comparison permitting a rhetorical use of its power without too radically implicating the identity of Sokrates or his project. The enchantment and possession of the soul that Sokrates' 'unadorned words' work on his hearers, although represented in threateningly non-rational terms, is an emotional possession perhaps necessary for the aspirant's difficult progress towards τὸ καλόν. The

---

[115] Cf. 215e, 216c. It is important that the effect of Sokratic auletic logos is far from being the unique and idiosyncratic experience of Alkibiades. To this extent the stress laid by Nussbaum (1986) on the particularity of the Sokrates–Alkibiades relationship as the central, corrective piece of 'knowledge' to be derived from Alkibiades' speech needs to be nuanced.

aulos retains a generative, even productive or resolving force in the *Symposium*. A later Plato and Sokrates are less open to its powers.

It should be clear that the philosophers' anxieties have their roots in concerns already articulated in the fifth century. A story is told of Damon coming across an *aulētris* playing in the Phrygian mode to a group of drunken youths who were getting up to some mad behaviour. He ordered her to change to the Dorian mode, 'and they at once ceased from their capricious behaviour'.[116] Criticism of the *aulos* is often nuanced according to the music and the mode in which it is played. The conservative and traditional Dorian was accepted by all; but Aristotle is compelled to criticize his master (or at least the Sokrates of the *Republic*) for admitting the Phrygian to his ideal city:

The Sokrates of the *Republic* is wrong to leave the Phrygian mode beside the Dorian, especially as in the matter of instruments he disapproves of the *aulos*. For of the modes, the Phrygian has the same potential as the *aulos* among instruments: both of them are exciting and emotional. (*Politics* 1342a32–b12)

Sokrates' unusually permissive attitude towards the Phrygian should not be regarded as too worrying a lapse in the philosopher's management of the musical order of the city: for, as we shall see, there will in any case be no *auloi* in the city on which to play in the Phrygian mode.

The anecdote confirms very clearly Damon's theoretical position in relation to music, as the leading proponent of the view of the *harmoniai* as actively formulative of *ethos*; a more consciously articulated development of the very traditional notion that *mousikē* conditions individual and collective social identity. Elsewhere he is reported as having held that 'in singing and playing the lyre a boy ought properly to reveal not only courage but also justice'.[117] It is hardly fortuitous that the lyre and not the *aulos* is the instrument through performance on which the young Athenian will reveal his 'justice'.

Plato's anxieties about *mimēsis* find a particularly strong focus in the *aulos*, whose mimetic powers are repeatedly stressed. The discussions led by Sokrates in *Republic* Book Three, on what and why the Guardians should not imitate in order to become 'expert craftsmen of civic liberty' (315c), reveal that at base the fear evoked by *mimēsis* is a fear for the stability of an ideal civic identity:

'if [the Guardians] practice *mimēsis*, they should from childhood up imitate what is appropriate – men who are brave, restrained, pious, free and all things

---

[116] Galen *de Hipp. et Plat.* 9.5. The same story is told of Pythagoras: Cicero *De Consiliis suis* fr. 3 p. 339 Müller, Sext. Emp. *Math.* 6.8, Iambl. *De Vita Pythagorica* 112.
[117] *Mus.* 3.77.13–17; 37 B4 Diels.

The *aulos* in Athens

of that kind; but things unbecoming the free man they should neither do nor be clever at imitating, nor indeed any other base thing, lest from the *mimēsis* they imbibe of the reality ... We will not then allow our charges, whom we expect to prove good men, being men, to play the parts of women and imitate a woman young or old wrangling with her husband, defying the gods, loudly boasting, fortunate in her own conceit, or involved in misfortune and possessed by grief and lamentation – still less a woman that is sick, in love, or in labour ... Nor may they imitate slaves, female and male, doing the offices of slaves ...' (395b–d)

There are powerful echoes here of Athena, and the parallels become clearer when the mimetic quality of the instrument is explicitly aired. I argued that the Athenian myth of Athena and the *aulos* 'usefully' incorporated its powers into the city under the banner of civic rejection. The Platonic Sokrates is even more stringent. He goes on to show that the need to imitate only the brave, restrained and noble man, means that all pan- or poly-harmonic musical modes should be banished, and with their removal, the presence of the *aulos* becomes a question:

'Well then, will you admit to the city makers of *auloi* and *aulos*-players? Or is this not the most "many-stringed" of instruments and are not the "panharmonics" themselves an imitation of the *aulos*?' 'Clearly so', he said ... 'So we are not innovating in any way, my friend, in preferring Apollo and the instruments of Apollo to Marsyas and his instruments.' (399d–e)

The *aulos* is the model of musical multiplicity, so much so that even the most 'many-stringed'[118] instruments are imitations of the versatile, mimetic *aulos*. It has no place in Plato's Kallipolis. But Sokrates is deploying a certain amount of rhetorical sleight-of-hand when, in appealing to the traditional cultural paradigm that codifies a preference for Apollo's instruments over those of the satyr, he would turn myth into a hard reality.

Aristotle is also intransigent, although, because his discussion in *Politics* 8 of the ideal educational training for the free youth of a polis, in gymnastics and – especially – in *mousikē*, is more detailed and ostensibly more *practical* than Sokrates', he does nuance his discussion with the blurred reality of historical practice. Obsessed by the stigma of professionalism, he worries a good deal about whether the free man should take up any instrument at all, and finally decides in favour of active learning because of a perceived need to cultivate the critical skills of judgement so important for the citizen. The way to avoid the objection of 'some people' that this makes men vulgar is to place tight and

---

[118] For this use of πολυχόρδος of the *aulos* see already Simon. 46 (Bergk); cf. Eur. *Medea* 196, *Rhesos* 548; Plut. *Quaest. conv.* 2.4.3.

careful controls on the rhythms and instruments permitted, and to restrict this form of education to a closely-monitored period of childhood. All forms of the *aulos* are the prime offenders here, since this instrument exercises an exciting (ὀργιαστικόν) influence rather than a moralizing one (ἠθικόν 1341a). The other great drawback of the *aulos* is that it 'prevents the use of logos' (1341a25). From an Athenian point of view, this renders it anathema to the citizen whose 'free mouth' was one of the most idealized features of his entire comportment, corporeal and political.[119]

Aristotle speaks of the adoption, and subsequent rejection, of the instrument by earlier ages, and the historical pattern he outlines significantly reflects the Athenian mythology of the *aulos* – discovered, tested and authoritatively rejected by the city's patron-goddess herself. Indeed, he goes on to praise this piece of 'ancient mythology about the *auloi*' (1341b1ff.) while advancing his own view concerning Athena's rejection that it was more likely to have been motivated by the fact that education in *aulos*-playing 'has no effect on the intelligence' than because of her 'annoyance at the ugly distortion of her face' (1341b4–5).

In those earlier times, however – roughly the period after the Persian wars, when increased leisure and wealth produced a certain 'high-spiritedness directed at excellence' – the Greeks were led to take up all forms of learning without distinction, *even aulētikē*. Aristotle continues:

For in Lakedaimon a certain *chorēgos* played the *aulos* for his choros himself, and at Athens it became such a fad that almost the majority of free men had a go at *aulos*-playing; this is evident from the tablet which Thrasippos set up after being *chorēgos* for Ekphantides. (1341a33–7)

This description of the craze among the Athenian upper-class for *aulos*-playing is highly suggestive. In demonstrating the point by his reference to an Attic choregic inscription in this way, Aristotle surely means his reader to understand that the Thrasippos who was the *chorēgos* (and thus certainly an *eleutheros*) for the comic poet Ekphantides, was *also* his *aulētēs*.[120] If so, this would represent an extraordinary case of a wealthy Athenian citizen serving as comic *chorēgos* in part by piping his choros into the *orchēstra* himself.[121] High-spirited stuff indeed for an Athenian, and the kind of thing that perhaps could only ever have been pulled off with the transgressive genre of comedy, where the natural supremacy of 'the beautiful' is regularly challenged. Where the balance

---

[119] Cf. e.g. Aiskhylos *Hiketides* 948–9.
[120] Csapo and Slater (1995) 151–2.
[121] As he was maskless, Thrasippos' presence would be all the more obvious than if he had taken on a choral role.

lies between myth and history here we cannot say. But it is clear that the historian of the theatre, scandalized by this epigraphic find, finds the Athenian mythology of the *aulos* more edifying when writing with the education of 'free men' in mind.

4   Actor's song in tragedy

Edith Hall

I

Why do choruses in tragedy sing neither in the hypodorian nor in the hypophrygian mode? ... both these modes are inappropriate to the *choros*, and more suitable to the actors on the stage. For those on stage are imitating heroes, and in the old days only the rulers (*hēgemones*) were heroes, while the rest of the people (*hoi de laoi*), to whom the *choros* belong, were ordinary human beings (*anthrōpoi*). [Aristotle], *Problems* 19.48

Two features of this *Problem* have attracted interest. The first is its conception of the contribution made by choruses to tragedy, for the author proceeds to distinguish the active role of the characters on stage from the relative passivity of the *choros*.[1] The other feature, cited by musicologists, is its evidence for the aural effects of the different musical modes.[2] Yet the *Problem* also offers evidence for views of social class in tragedy. It states that 'in the old days' there were social distinctions within tragedy. Moreover, it implicitly acknowledges that those social distinctions were related to musical expression. In tragedy of the old days the *anthrōpoi*, of whom the *choros* were a part, were to be distinguished from the rulers (*hēgemones*), and this distinction explains why different kinds of songs are given to each different type of person. This article takes a hint from this *Problem*, and thinks about actor's song in tragedy from a perspective conditioned by sensitivity to the social identity of the characters represented as singing.

In the earliest surviving tragedy, Aeschylus' *Persians*, Xerxes never speaks a single iambic trimeter. This makes him unique amongst the important characters in extant tragedy. He briefly exchanges lyric anapaests with the *choros* (908–30),[3] before abjectly launching the antiphonal dirge which he shares with them for fifteen increasingly wild lyric stanzas until the end of the play. Yet it seems never to have been

---

[1] See e.g. the comments in Flashar (1967), 625–6; he suggests that this is the original source of A. W. Schlegel's influential notion of the *choros* as the 'ideale Zuschauer', on which see Calame, this volume.
[2] See e.g. West (1992) 183–4.
[3] On the vocal delivery of anapaests, see below section II.

observed that the voice of the great theatrical Persian monarch is only heard performing in a vocal medium distinct from speech.

If we travel forwards perhaps a century to what is probably the last extant Greek tragedy to be written, the *Rhesus*, we find another actor dressed up as an unnamed Muse.[4] She appears in the machine with the corpse of her Thracian son, over whom she sings a monodic lament (895-903, 906-14). The Muse is an immortal practitioner of the art of singing itself, who once competed against the bard Thamyris (917-25). She is also the first character to sing a monody in this particular play, and the earliest known immortal with a tragic monody. That immortals in fifth-century tragedy hardly ever sing lyrics is in itself a suggestive expression of classical Athenian theology and ideology – a performed differentiation between gods and mortals.[5] Yet nobody seems to have been interested in the ramifications of this emotional *singing* theophany of this tragic Muse.[6] Still less thought has been given to its implications for the development of the performative dimension of tragedy in the fourth century.[7]

Ancient Greek music, however, has exerted a fascination. Discussions of music in ancient authors, including the tragedians, have attracted attention.[8] Reconstructed ancient music enjoyed a vogue a century ago,[9] and reconstructions can now be purchased on CD.[10]

---

[4] The text of the play offers no support for the identifications of the Muse made by either the author of the first hypothesis (who calls her Calliope), or by Aristophanes of Byzantium, who in the third hypothesis specifies Terpsichore. In his edition, however, Ebener (1966) 114 follows Aristophanes.

[5] Hera, disguised as a (human) mendicant priestess, may have performed the lyric hexameters, preserved on a papyrus, which have been attributed to both Aeschylus' *Xantriai*, and to his *Semele* or *Hydrophoroi* (Aeschylus fr. 168.16-30). On the possible connection of the disguise with this startling 'monody' entry see Taplin (1977) 427. Dionysos in *Bacchae* (also disguised as a mortal) delivers a few lyric utterances in the 'earthquake' amoibaion with the choros following the second stasimon (between 576 and 603). It is intriguing that Polyphemus and Silenus, who are immortals of a kind, can sing lyric metres in satyr drama (*Cyc.* 503-10, Aeschylus' *Dictyulci* fr. 47a. 799-820).

[6] Ritchie (1964) 340, in his influential book, minimized the extraordinary nature of this scene, because he was arguing that the tragedy was an authentic work of Euripides. But even he conceded that the monody was unique: 'In no other surviving tragedy do we find a monody in the *exodos* and in the mouth of a *deus ex machina*.'

[7] Certainly by the second century BCE the role of the god Dionysos in *Bacchae* could be realised as a sung *aisma*, with *kithara* accompaniment, by the star performer Satyrus of Samos: *SIG*³ 648B. See Gentili (1979) 27-8; Eitrem, Amundsen, and Winnington-Ingram (1955) 27.

[8] See e.g. Moutsopoulos (1962).

[9] For bibliography see e.g. Stumpf (1896) 49 n. 1. Macran (1912) 12 recorded with touching candour the disappointment felt at an experimental comparison of foreign and ancient Greek music organized at Trinity College, Dublin: 'It was the unanimous verdict ... that ... the Greek hymn stood quite alone in its absolute lack of meaning and its unredeemed ugliness.'

[10] A recent book on Greek music optimistically boasts a 'Discography' as well as a 'Bibliography': Anderson (1994) 239.

Friedrich Marx's 1933 article on Greek tragic music argues that a relic of it is to be heard in the *Volga Boat Song*.[11] In the 1951 MGM movie *Quo Vadis*, directed by Mervyn LeRoy, the composer was Miklós Rózsa, an historian of music interested in recreating the authentic melodies of antiquity. He persuaded Peter Ustinov (Nero) to perform the 'Song of Seikilos', a dirge which was inscribed, with musical notation, on a first-century stele in Caria.[12] The *parodos* of Aeschylus' *Persians* was performed (to music by M. L. West) at the Triennial Meeting of the Greek and Roman Societies in Oxford in August 1995, thus definitively proving comedy's ability to subvert tragedy. Yet this perennial curiosity about ancient Greek music has not been accompanied by the level of interest in the aural impact of tragic poetry which, since the publication of Taplin's *The Stagecraft of Aeschylus* (1977), has attended upon the *visual* dimensions of the genre.

Diomedes the grammarian said that we should sing Greek lyric poetry when we read it, even if we do not know or cannot remember the tune.[13] It is not clear how this should be done, beyond raising the pitch of our voice on accented syllables.[14] But Diomedes' recommendation suggests that the difference between sung and spoken verse was so powerfully perceived that even an invented melody would help the reader to recover the experience of a sung lyric poem.

Yet a modern student coming to Greek tragedy would not easily be able to practise the imaginative reading Diomedes prescribes. She probably knows that choral odes were sung. She may also know that some parts of some actors' roles were sung. But unless she takes a course in advanced Greek metre she will not know which parts they are. Even then she will be so confused by the terminology of choriambic anaklasis and the resolved lyric prokeleusmatic that she will lose sight of the performance wood for the forest of metrical trees. Translations rarely indicate which sections were sung, and Greek texts, while engaging in complex colometry, fail to convey the most crucial information from a performative perspective, that is, which bits were sung to musical accompaniment. Thus most individuals coming to

[11] Marx (1933).
[12] See Palmer (1975) 38–40. For a transcription of this surviving four-line example of ancient Greek music, see West (1992) 301–2. It was fortunate for *Ben-Hur* (1959) that Rózsa threatened to resign when instructed to insert the tune of *Oh come, all ye faithful* into the part of this (Oscar-winning) score that accompanied the nativity scene.
[13] *Dei meta melous anagignōskein*: Hilgard (1991) 21, 19–21. Diomedes' advice appears in his commentary on a passage in Dionysius of Thrace's *Ars Grammatica* where it is recommended that lyrics be read *emmelōs*, and laments in an abandoned and dirge-like manner: Uhlig (1983) 6, par. 2.8–11.
[14] So Pearson (1990) xlix.

Greek tragedy are deprived of one of the most important hermeneutic tools in deciphering its expressive logic: it is inconceivable that a similar state of ignorance would be allowed to apply to the texts of, say, William Shakespeare.[15]

Already in the fifth century actor's song was regarded as noteworthy. In Aristophanes' *Wasps* Philocleon leans out of a window to perform a burlesque of a tragic song (316–33), perhaps originally delivered by Danaë in a tragedy where she was shut up in her tower.[16] Euripides' songs, both monodic and choral, made a huge impact.[17] In *Thesmophoriazusae* Euripides' in-law parodies Andromeda's monody in her Euripidean name-play (1015–55), and the instant popularity of *Andromeda* may partly have been caused by brilliant acting in the tragic scene where Echo replicated Andromeda's singing.[18] Moreover, songs are one of the only two features of tragedy (the other is the prologue) to be examined at length in *Frogs*. On Dionysos' invitation Euripides promises to show that Aeschylus was a repetitive song-writer (*melopoion*, 1249–50). Subsequently, in Aeschylus' parody of Euripides' music (see below), the song 'from the stage' (*apo skēnēs*), or 'actor's song', is subjected to thorough analysis.

When a dimension of tragedy has been neglected by scholars, it usually transpires that Aristotle was not interested in it, either. Tragic song is no exception. Aristotle's theoretical writings on both poetry and rhetoric articulate a prejudice against delivery (*hupokrisis*) and the performative dimensions of both theatrical and oratorical texts.[19] Yet even Aristotle regards song-writing as a more important enhancement of tragedy than spectacle (*Poet.* 6.1450b 15–16). Aristotle, furthermore, despite his attempts in the *Poetics* to divest tragedy of its performative and socio-political dimensions,[20] nevertheless drops a clue about the ideological ramifications of song. This clue attests as clearly as the later

---

[15] I am of course not alleging that scholars have dismissed the importance of understanding actor's song in tragedy. But it is unarguable that in the English- and French-speaking scholarly worlds, at least, infinitely more has been published on, say, the *agōn*.

[16] See Rau (1967) 150–2; MacDowell (1971) 176.

[17] Testimony abounds to the popularity of Euripidean songs (see Michaelides (1978) 117–19), although it is often not clear whether choral odes or actors' songs (or both) are indicated. See, for example, Plutarch's report that some Athenians in Sicily saved themselves after the disaster at Syracuse in 413 BCE by singing some songs (*melē*) by this poet (*Vit. Nic.* 29); in Axionicus' comedy *Phileuripides* (fr. 3) a character speaks about people who hated all but Euripidean lyrics. In Strattis fr. 1.1 (from *Anthroporestes*) the speaker seems to say that he doesn't care about the songs (*melē*) of any poets except Euripides, although the point of comparison is not clear.

[18] See Gilula (1996) 163–4.

[19] See Hall (1995) 40–1.

[20] See Taplin (1977) 24–6; Hall (1996) 295–309.

Problem quoted above to a perception that the choice of spoken versus sung self-expression for represented characters in performed *mousikē* was conditioned by perceptions of social roles.

The clue is in chapter 15, which offers two examples of inappropriateness in characterization. The first is Odysseus' lament (*thrēnos*) in the *Scylla*, probably the dithyramb by Timotheus to which Aristotle later refers in connection with *aulos*-playing.[21] We are not told why Odysseus' lament was inappropriate, but the example is paired with that of 'Melanippe's speech' (*rhēsis*). This almost certainly means Melanippe's famous (iambic, spoken) repudiation of misogynist rhetoric in Euripides' *Melanippe Desmōtis* (fr. 499 N²), 'Men's criticism of women is worthless twanging of a bowstring and evil talk', etc.[22] Odysseus' sung lament, and Melanippe's spoken diatribe, are thus 'inappropriate' when judged by a criterion implicated in the discourse of gender and its representations. But was Odysseus' *thrēnos* inappropriate because he was a man, or because he was a high-status hero, or a Greek, or all of these?

Aeschylus' Xerxes is a man who utters nothing but a *thrēnos*, yet the implications of this for the tragic encrypting of Persia through performative mode have not penetrated the scholarly consciousness. *Why* does he not speak? (his words are kept in *oratio obliqua* in the messenger speeches, too).[23] Is it because he is *a* barbarian, or rather because as King of Persia and erstwhile invader of Hellas he is *The* Barbarian? Is it because of the ritual orientation of his scene, which is a funerary *kommos*, albeit with no corpses? Given the ubiquitous association of funerary lamentation with women in Greek thought, is it a formal strategy which effeminizes him through genre, vocal delivery and choice of metre? Is it because he is emotionally disturbed, like Polymestor, another intemperate barbarian male given a wild song in Euripides' *Hecuba*? Could Xerxes have sung if he were a slave? In the *Life of Sophocles* (6) it is said that the tragedian took account of his actors' abilities when composing his tragedies: does Xerxes' unusual role suggest the availability of a performer with a remarkable singing voice,[24] a factor which may have been involved in the creation of the elaborate arias in Euripides' *Orestes*?[25] It has even been suggested that the relative dearth of actors' lyrics in Euripides' *Bacchae* and *IA* is a

---

[21] *Poet.* 15.1454a 29–30 and 26.1461b 29–32 = *PMG* fr. 793.
[22] Translation from Lefkowitz and Fant (1992) 14.
[23] E.g. 365–71, 469–70. See Hall (1996a) 363.
[24] See Pintacuda (1978) 31. On the evidence that actors were selected for the power of their voices see Hunningher (1956).
[25] See West (1987a) 38; Hall (1989) 119, 210; Damen (1990) 141–2.

result of these plays' supposed composition in Macedonia, where there might have been a lack of operatic talent.[26]

Although an important doctoral thesis on Euripidean monody is now being completed by Jane Beverley,[27] such questions have been insufficiently aired. There are several reasons for this. One is the complexity of the terminology: it is rarely possible to distinguish with confidence between a 'kommos', an 'amoibaion' and a 'monody with interruptions', even if we could be sure that the ancients really cared about such definitions.[28] Another problem is the ambiguity of the evidence about actor's song (to be reviewed below), especially concerning so-called 'recitative' performance of metres neither iambic nor lyric. This confusion was already apparent in the Renaissance and was creatively implicated in the birth of European opera: the founding fathers in Italy at the end of the sixteenth century imagined all of Greek tragedy to have been sung.

Yet the most important explanation for the neglect of the socio-aesthetic ramifications of tragic song is to be sought, rather, in the history of classical scholarship itself. In our century there has been an estrangement between formalist analyses of tragedy and anthropologically informed studies promoting the erasure of the distinction between what used to be called 'art' and 'reality'. The German-speaking philological tradition has produced important books about the formal and metrical elements of tragedy; they have titles like *Monolog und Selbstgespräch: Untersuchungen zur Formgeschichte der griechischen Tragödie*, or *Stasimon: Untersuchungen zu Form und Gehalt der griechischen Tragödie*, or (more recently) *Die Bauformen der griechischen Tragödie*.[29] The French and Americans (at least since the 1960s), on the other hand, have written about gender, polis group identity, democracy, myth, and the interpenetration of cultural artefacts such as plays and vase-paintings with the more overtly civic discourses.[30] In Britain until

---

[26] Owen (1936) 153. Owen further develops his theory that musical roles were composed according to an actor's talent at singing: he suggests, for example, that when a role only uses one lyrical metre (e.g. Creon's dochmiacs in *Antigone*), it could be entrusted 'to an actor with only limited musical ability' (150).

[27] I first delivered the contents of this paper as 'Mad, sad, and foreign voices: why characters sing in Greek tragedy' at an interdisciplinary theatre seminar run by Patricia Fann at St Cross College, Oxford, in May 1990. I have recently seen Jane Beverley's excellent chapters on *Ion* and *Phoenissae*, and have heard her discussion of Theseus in *Hippolytus*. I take confidence from the fact that we have quite independently come to similar conclusions.

[28] See Barner (1971) 277-9.

[29] Schadewaldt (1926), Kranz (1933), and Jens (1971) respectively.

[30] Although three of the few discussions of actor's song in tragedy are in nineteenth-century French: Gevaert (1875-81) II 501-62; Décharme (1893) 522-40; Masqueray (1895).

recently scholars at Oxford largely read the analytical Germans, while those at Cambridge preferred the synthetic French.[31] Tragic studies would benefit from a flirtation between the metrical, analytical school and the society-oriented synthetic approach, especially if it resulted in offspring recognizing that both form itself, and the codes by which tragedians selected form, are ideologically conditioned.[32]

II

Attempts to reconstruct the vocal delivery of a classical Greek tragic actor when singing his lyrics are no longer fashionable. Gone are the days when scholars compared Greek tragic anapaests with the recitative in Handel's operas or the overtures to Schumann's *Manfred* and Beethoven's *Egmont*;[33] nobody today would (in print) ask whether Greek tragic song more closely resembled the declamatory 'ranting' of the nineteenth-century actor or the Catholic priest intoning the liturgy;[34] it would be a fruitless diversion to enquire, with Kathleen Schlesinger's book on the *aulos*, 'Would the songs sung by a Greek tragic choros remind us of the choir of St Paul's or of the peasant in the uplands of Andalusia?'[35] There is no way to achieve an 'archaeology of ears' and scrape away the barnacles of our culturally determined emotional and aesthetic responses in order to replace them with those of an ancient audience.[36]

It is, however, certain that the voice of the ancient actor needed to be loud. It has even been suggested that the convention of the mask survived because it allowed the singer to concentrate on sound production at the expense of facial expression.[37] A popular ancient anecdote demonstrated the primitivism of some Spanish natives by reporting their terrified reaction to their first experience of a tragic actor's huge singing voice; in one source the actor, an unnamed itinerant *tragōidos* of Nero's time, is said to have selected a song from Euripides' *Andro-*

---

[31] The book whose approach to tragic song is most nearly consonant with this proposal is actually in Italian (Pintacuda (1978)).
[32] On the ideological implications of the trilogic form see Rose (1992) 185–97; on tragedy and in particular the *agōn* as democratic form see Goldhill (1997a).
[33] Greenwood (1953) 138–9; Stumpf (1896) 73.
[34] Helmholtz (1885) 238.
[35] Schlesinger (1959) xvii.
[36] For a chastening discussion of the ease with which modern Western-centred aesthetic judgements can creep into the study of the music of other cultures see the great ethnomusicologist Alan Merriam's *The Anthropology of Music* (Merriam, 1964), ch. xiii, 259–76.
[37] Hunningher (1956) 326–8.

Actor's song in tragedy

meda.[38] There is also evidence that the training of an actor's voice was severe ([Aristot.], *Probl.* 11.22): Pollux reports that the comic actor Hermon, a contemporary of Aristophanes, once arrived late at the theatre because he had been doing his vocal exercises (*Onomastikon* 4.88).[39] Yet it is now impossible to recover the quality of the noise emitted by ancient tragic actors. Allegations that they used the bass register, rather than the higher pitch of the tenor, are insubstantial.[40] Although Euripides tells his in-law to *speak* in a convincingly feminine way at the Thesmophoria (*tōi phthegmati/gunaikieis eu kai pithanōs, Thesm.* 267–8), we do not even know whether actors sang in a style comparable with what we call 'falsetto' when they performed lyrics in female and juvenile roles,[41] let alone whether they distinguished the voices of virgin girls from those of mature women.[42]

Ancient Greek's clear distinction between long and short syllables even makes it probable that singing and speaking were not separated from one another in the same way as in most modern European languages.[43] Moreover, in later antiquity even iambic speeches could be performed to music. By the third century the performance of drama had changed significantly, and the movement seems to have been inexorably toward increasing the amount of song. Fourth-century sources already attest to the emergence of professional actors like Neoptolemus and Theodorus, who went on tour as distinguished protagonists, stagers of revivals, and virtuoso performers (Theodorus, for example, was a specialist in female roles).[44] Hellenistic theatre practice increasingly focused on the performance of individual tragic speeches, scenes, and arias, often set to new music by specialist *tragōidoi*. Such actors are attested, for example, by the inscription of the Delphic *Soteria* on the constitution of theatrical companies in the first fifty years

---

[38] Eunapius fr. 54, in Dindorf (1880–1) I 246–8. There is another version in Philostratus, *Vita Ap.* 5.9. Lucian, *How to Write History*, 1, locates the story in Abdera. Here the actor Archelaüs's performance of *Andromeda* caused an epidemic whose symptoms included sweats, fever, nosebleeds, and crazed singing of monodies!
[39] See Hunningher (1956) 324, 329.
[40] E.g. Gevaert and Vollgraff (1901–3) II 204–5.
[41] See Pintacuda (1978) 31. The ancients did discuss the phenomenon of the breaking adolescent male voice: the Hippocratic *Coän Prognoses* 1.321 says it happened in a boy's thirteenth year. It was thought standard for boys and men to sing with the voices an octave apart ([Aristot.] *Probl.* 19.39).
[42] Ancient medical texts attest to a belief that women's voices became lower in pitch when they lost their virginity (see Hanson and Armstrong (1986)); much more recently it has sometimes been asserted that larynx size is related to sexual activity, so that prostitutes are supposed to speak in low voices, and promiscuity to endanger the singing careers of sopranos and tenors. See Ellis (1929) 101–2; Baron (1986) 73–4.
[43] See Monro (1894) 113–26; Pearson (1990) xxix.
[44] Dem. 19.246. See Dihle (1981) 29–31; Easterling, this volume.

104   Edith Hall

of the third century BCE. These singing *tragōidoi* offered virtuoso performances (*epideixeis* or *akroaseis*), accompanied by *kithara* or *aulos*, of both lyric and dramatic texts.[45] By the Roman imperial period Lucian complains that tragic actors of his day chant iambic trimeters and sing even messenger speeches (*de Salt.* 27, see also Suetonius, *Nero* 46). But mercifully we can be fairly sure that an iambic trimeter still meant spoken enunciation in democratic Athenian tragedy.[46]

In Aristotle's *Poetics* the philosopher claims that iambics were substituted for trochaic tetrameters in tragedy after dialogue had been introduced, because the iambic is the metre most suited to speech (*malista ... lektikon*); he adds that we easily drop into iambics in conversation, whereas we seldom talk in hexameters (4.1449a 19–28). In the *Rhetoric* the same perception is articulated in a manner which even brings social class into the picture: 'Iambic speech is the very rhythm of the masses (*hē lexis hē tōn pollōn*), which is why, of all metres, people in conversation speak iambics' (3.1408b 24–6). On the other hand, sounding completely natural when speaking iambic trimeters was a skilled accomplishment. Aristotle says that Theodorus' ability to do so distinguished him from other actors, and that it was only possible after Euripides had composed iambics consisting of everyday vocabulary (*Rhet.* 3.1404b 18–25).

Aristoxenus, the musicologist writing in the late fourth century, has a clear criterion for distinguishing speech from song. He held that speech was continuous, whereas song moved in discrete intervals. This theory, according to the arithmetician Nicomachus five hundred years later, was originated by the Pythagoreans (*Encheiridion harmonikēs*, p. 4); Nicomachus adds that if the notes and intervals of the speaking voice are allowed to become separate and distinct, the form of utterance turns into singing.

Aristoxenus' account of the speech/song distinction is suggestive for tragedy because he brings emotion into the equation. Movement between the high and the low positions of the voice happens both when we speak and when we sing, but the movement is not of the same kind:

... continuous motion we call the motion of speech, as in speaking the voice moves without ever seeming to come to a standstill ... Hence in ordinary conversation we avoid bringing the voice to a standstill, unless occasionally forced **by strong feeling** (*dia pathos*) to resort to such a motion; whereas

---

[45] See Sifakis (1967) 75–9, 156–65; Gentili (1979) 22–7.
[46] There is one late piece of evidence that iambic trimeters could be sung already in the classical period. The second sophistic text *On Music* attributed to Plutarch (1140f–1141a) claims that the tragedians 'took over' from Archilochus the practice of accompanying some of their iambics with music, and even singing some of them.

in singing we act in precisely the opposite way, avoiding continuous motion and making the voice become, as far as possible, absolutely stationary. The more we succeed in rendering each of our voice-utterances one, stationary, and identical, the more correct does the singing appear to the ear. (*El. Harm.* 1.9–10)[47]

This distinction may illuminate the testimony that jurors in Athenian courts complained that defendants who delivered speeches poorly were guilty of 'singing' them (*aidein*, Aristophanes fr. 101): perhaps strong feeling made defendants lose the 'continuous motion' of speech and resort to the song-like 'stationary' intonation which we might call 'moaning'.[48]

Besides iambics, lyrics, and anapaests, other types of song occasionally appeared. Sophocles' biographical tradition claims that he sang himself in his *Thamyris*, and was consequently portrayed playing the lyre in the Painted Stoa (*Vita* 5, Sophocles T Ha): a fragment of *Thamyris* consisting of two dactylic lines with heroic content show that hexameters were performed (fr. 242). The mythical lyre-player Amphion began Euripides' *Antiope* in similar vein by accompanying his own hexameter monody (fr. 182 N²),[49] and the numerous other plays where mythical bards took roles suggest that kitharodic hexameter performances were more familiar features in tragedy than our extant remains imply.[50] Another atypical song is constituted by Andromache's threnodic elegiacs in Euripides' *Andromache* (103–16), a metre whose uniqueness to extant tragedy led it to form part of the evidence Page used for his case that the play's first production was in Argos.[51]

Besides tragic portions that were almost certainly spoken (iambic trimeters) and those which were sung (lyric metres), there was probably a distinct third mode of delivery. This is called 'speaking to musical accompaniment', 'chanting', 'intoning', 'reciting', 'recitative' or even

---

[47] Translated by Macran (1912).
[48] This might also explain why, according to the MSS of Aristophanes' *Clouds* (often emended) Strepsiades, who asked his son to speak (*lexai*) some Aeschylus, uses the verb *aidein* of the Euripidean rhesis from *Aeolus* which Pheidippides actually performed (1371). Perhaps Strepsiades wants to characterize his son's (spoken) delivery as whining.
[49] Webster (1970) 168.
[50] Orpheus was a central character in Aeschylus' lost *Bassarids*; Aeschylus as well as Sophocles composed a play named *Thamyris* dramatizing the singing competition between this bard and the muses; Euripides' *Hypsipyle* portrayed the *kitharode* Euneus, who founded an Athenian clan of musicians; his *Antiope* also featured a full-scale debate between lyre-playing Amphion and his brother Zethus about the benefits which poets confer on a community: see Webster (1967) 207–8. On the use of the *kithara* in tragedy see also Koller (1963) 165–73.
[51] See further note 119, below.

'singing', depending on which book you happen to be reading. The metrical unit with which this type of 'recitative' delivery is usually associated is the anapaest (basically, ∪∪–). The anapaest was thought to be a descendant of the Spartan military marching songs (*embatēria*) of poets such as Tyrtaeus (e.g. *PMG* 856.6, 857).[52] It was associated with processions and a synchronized military pace,[53] although Parker has warned against subsuming all 'recitative' anapaests in tragedy under the label 'marching anapaests'.[54] A conventional distinction is drawn between so-called 'marching' or 'recitative' anapaests and 'melic' anapaests, which are more likely to have been fully 'sung'. But in practice this distinction is often wobbly: it is based on the *extent* of Doricism and, more importantly, resolution, so that some passages of allegedly sung anapaests in tragedy are 'scarcely distinguishable rhythmically from recitative'.[55] The distinction certainly needs sociological investigation, since high status is likely to be a prerequisite of more 'lyric' anapaests,[56] but the primary focus of this article is actors' lyrics.

The anapaest was clearly conceived in a different way from lyrics in tragedy, for the significant reason that servants like the nurses in *Medea* and *Hippolytus* are regularly given anapaests, whereas, with two extraordinary exceptions, low-status characters never sing lyrics (see below, section III). On the other hand, there are reasons to believe that all anapaests in tragedy were accompanied by the *aulos* and that their delivery was nearer to song than to speech. A scholion on Aristophanes' *Wasps* 582 states that in tragic *exodoi* the *aulētēs* used to play the *auloi* while leading the members of the choros in procession.[57] Since anapaests (unlike iambics) followed a musical line different from the natural pitch of the tonal Greek language,[58] their delivery cannot have sounded identical to ordinary speech. They were therefore probably performed in a manner which can legitimately be denoted by the verbs 'intone' or 'recite'.

In the classical period the verb *katalegein* designates the type of delivery which should probably be associated with anapaests, although

---

[52] Cole (1988) 169 (see also 117, 118), goes so far as to describe anapaestic systems as 'part of the Doric heritage of tragedy'.
[53] See Raven (1968) 56–61; West (1987) 29, 48–9.
[54] Parker (1997) 56–7.
[55] Parker (1997) 57.
[56] Webster (1970) 117, suggests that 'melic' anapaests were originally processional, like 'marching' anapaests, but that their special features were a result of being performed specifically at funerals.
[57] That in comedy anapaests (at least in parabaseis) were accompanied by the *aulos* is suggested by a scholion on Aristophanes' *Birds* 682.
[58] Pötscher (1959) 79–98.

Actor's song in tragedy 107

the text which supports this view is actually a comment on the effect created by *aulos* accompaniment of tetrameters. In Xenophon's *Symposium* Hermogenes offers to converse with Socrates to *aulos* music, 'just like Nikostratos the actor *katelegen* tetrameters to the *auloi*' (6.3). Thus it is safest to assume that *kataloge*, whether of tetrameters or anapaests, means a form of utterance more marked and less 'smooth' than speech, more estranged from natural conversation, but not necessarily approaching song.[59]

There may have been a far greater range of modes of vocal delivery available to actors than it is possible to reconstruct from the sources.[60] But it is clear that difference – 'unlikeness' – between such modes created an emotional effect. An Aristotelian *Problem* (19.6) asks why the form of delivery called *parakataloge*, when in (or 'inserted into') the songs, is tragic:

Is it because of the contrast involved (*dia tēn anōmalian*)? Contrast is emotive in situations of great misfortune or grief; regularity (*to homales*) is less conducive to lamentation.

The meaning of *parakataloge* here is disputed. Is it 'intoned recitative, to instrumental accompaniment'? Does it refer to the anapaestic introductions which often precede lyrics (e.g. those introducing Xerxes' *kommos*)?[61] Or is it a reference to the insertion of a different kind of metrical form and/or vocal delivery into a song *after* its commencement?[62] But this problematic *Problem* nevertheless shows that the ancients were sensitive to the differences between lyric song and other types of vocal delivery, and that the dissimilarity was perceived to create the emotional impact appropriate to tragedy. 'Unlikeness', fluctuation in noise and/or metre, in itself generated a tragic effect.

To summarize: iambic trimeters were originally spoken and sounded closer to ordinary speech than other metres; lyric song sounded less

---

[59] This was the conclusion reached by Pickard-Cambridge (1988) 156–64. See also Christ's still impressive collation of evidence (1875) 163, 166.
[60] The Byzantine treatise *On Tragedy* dating from around 1300 CE (probably to be attributed to Michael Psellos), but containing information in part deriving from Hellenistic sources, describes a mode of utterance in tragedy different from either song or recitative (par. 9): 'There are some other things classified along with tragic music and metre, such as ... *anaboēma* ('crying aloud'?) ... *anaboēma* is very nearly like singing but something between song and *kataloge*.' And satyr drama apparently allowed more shouting noises (*epiphthegmata*) than tragedy: see Browning (1963) 79.
[61] Other examples in Parker (1997) 57.
[62] A further possibility is that the 'anomaly' signifies the discrepancy between the music of the accompanying *aulos*, which raises the expectation of sung delivery, and the actual recitation or spoken utterance in(serted) into the song (Flashar (1967) 602). It would be good to know more about the musical theorist Damon's principle of 'similarity' (*homoiotēs*), on which see Anderson (1966) 40.

108   *Edith Hall*

smooth and continuous than speech; lyrics sounded emotional; the *contrast* between tragic song and an inexactly understood third type of tragic vocal delivery, different from both lyric song and from unaccompanied speech, was in itself emotionally effective. So without getting bogged down in the recitative controversy, or in the distinctions between species of lyric verse, let us instead focus on the suggestive notion of emotive contrast, and take the 'unlikeness' of lyric song to other types of delivery as the benchmark for a sociological review of tragic actors' song.

III

The metrician Paul Maas once formulated a principle in relation to Greek tragedy:

Characters of lower status (except the Phrygian in *Orestes*) have no sung verses, but they do have anapaests, like the nurse in *Hippolytus*, or hexameters, like the old man in the *Trachiniae*.[63]

Characters of low social status in Greek tragedy, said Maas, do not sing lyrics. In tragedy, in other words, song is a performed marker of high social status. 'Status' hides inexactitude: nearly everyone who sings tragic lyrics is royal. From Aeschylus' Xerxes, Cassandra, Electra and Orestes, through Sophocles' Electra, Heracles, and Antigone, through to Euripides' Phaedra, Helen, Creusa and Ion, it is almost always a marker of royalty inherited by blood. It signifies privilege both by birth status and by emotional role within the play.

A conceptual boundary thus existed between tragic roles which could involve singing and those which could accommodate anapaests but not lyrics. An informative passage is the exchange between the choros and Rhesus' charioteer in the *Rhesus*. After Rhesus' murder, the charioteer arrives to announce it, himself badly wounded, and performs a passionate exchange (728–53). Yet as charioteer and underling, he is given anapaests for the purpose where a high-status character who had been injured and bereaved would typically have been given lyrics.[64]

---

[63] 'Personen niederen Standes (ausgenommen den Phryger in Orestes) erhalten keine Singverse, wohl aber Anapäste, wie die Amme in Hippolytos, oder Hexameter, wie der Alte in den Trachinierinnen.' Maas (1929) paragraph 76, p. 20. Maas's principle was much more recently brought to the notice of a wide English-speaking audience by Lloyd-Jones' translation of this book as Maas (1962) 53–4.

[64] An undated tragic performance attested by a papyrus with musical annotation shows that in later antiquity a character whose status as underling is confirmed by their use of the vocative *despoti* could certainly sing an emotional speech to their mistress: see

Actor's song in tragedy

Lyric metres are a marker of birth status: slaves in Greek tragedy can sing – indeed they sing often – provided that they were freeborn. One of the pervasive vaguenesses about slaves in tragedy is implicit in Maas's formulation: he would undoubtedly say that slaves cannot sing. It is true that slaves by birth (with one possible major exception, the Phrygian eunuch in Euripides' *Orestes*) do not get given lyrics. It would astonish us all if a tragedy were to turn up in which even an important servant like Cilissa in *Choephoroe*, the Corinthian shepherd in *OT*, or the *paidagōgos* in *Ion* sang lyrics, let alone an insignificant attendant.[65] But in the frequent tragic situation where the once free have been enslaved (for example, Hecuba and Andromache in both *Hecuba* and *Troades*, Hypsipyle), their aristocratic birth ensures that they retain the 'privilege' of lyric self-expression in their life of servitude. Indeed, Hypsipyle explicitly contrasts the menial song she sings to the baby Opheltes with the songs she once sang as mistress of her house on Lemnos.[66] Thus the conventions surrounding tragic song only respect what Aristotle's *Politics* Book I would define as 'natural' class boundaries imposed at birth.

In Aristophanes' *Frogs* Euripides' Muse is summoned onto the stage (1305–7). Dionysos regards her as a person of whom it would never be said that she used to *lesbiazein* (1308). This might mean that she was not like the great lyric poets who hailed from Lesbos (Arion, Terpander, Alcaeus, Sappho), or it might be a comment on her sexual behaviour.[67] It is not clear whether she is represented as an ugly old woman, a scruffy young one, or as a vulgar prostitute, but 'we can be sure ... that she is neither dignified nor attractive'.[68] Her (current) social status is not high, which makes this personification of Euripidean lyric consonant with *Frogs*' portrayal of Euripides as a poet of unheroic individuals (959), colloquial speech (978–9), and 'democratized' tragedy in which women and slaves speak as much as 'the master of the house' (949–52).[69]

The Muse apparently dances to accompany Aeschylus' performance of his spoof of Euripidean lyrics. The first passage seems to parody

---

Eitrem, Amundsen, and Winnington-Ingram (1955) 10. But the low-status singer, interestingly, is still using anapaests.
[65] A lonely exception is Østerud (1970) who seems unaware of Maas's hypothesis, and perversely argues that these lyric iambics are more suited to the character of the nurse in *Hippolytus* than to Phaedra.
[66] Fr. 1 ii 9–16, in Cockle (1987) 59. On Hypsipyle's song for Opheltes see also Wœrn (1960) 6–7, who regards it as a song to *entertain* children rather than a lullaby.
[67] Dover (1968a) 351–2.
[68] Dover (1968a) 351.
[69] On which see Hall (1997).

Euripides' choral style (1309–24), but from 1331 onwards Aeschylus sings in the manner he explicitly ascribes to Euripides' monodies (*ton tōn monōidiōn diexelthein tropon*, 1330). Dover says that this female persona is, like the unpersonable Muse, 'of low social status':[70] his evidence is that she sings of going to the market to sell flax (1350–1). Yet she is certainly no household slave: she has her own attendants (*amphipoloi*), whom she instructs to light her lamps and fetch her water (1338). This parody of a Euripidean singing character has unheroic, domestic concerns and may have to work herself. But there is no evidence that she contravenes Maas's principle. Like Euripides' Electra in *Electra*,[71] Hypsipyle,[72] and Ion,[73] she may have fallen on hard times and is singing while she works, but there is no evidence that she is 'of low social status' by birth.

So the free/unfree class boundary is upheld even in Aristophanes' parody of solo actors' singing in Euripides' controversial 'democratized' tragedy. Thus one of the ways in which a tragedian evoked the social universe instantiated in his plays was by implementing a taboo on slaves by birth breaking into lyric metres. This tragic phenomenon was presumably not a reflection of the realities of Athenian life. There is no reason to suppose that lyric music was not sung in classical Athens as often by slaves as by the free; in *Clouds* the sophist-educated Pheidippides refuses to sing at a symposium on the ground that he is no woman grinding grain (1358), and there is evidence that other intellectuals would have agreed with him (see Σ *Clouds* 1358, Plato *Prt.*, 347c–e, Plut. *Alc.* 2.6). In elitist quarters singing was sometimes seen as a banausic activity unfit for the *eleutheros*. Aristotle, at any rate, argued that the Spartans had got it right (*Politics* 8. 1339a41–b10): they acquire good taste by listening to others. Free men, rather than learning to perform themselves, might instead enjoy the fruits of another's study. Here Aristotle raises the example of the poets' portrayal of Zeus:

The poets do not depict Zeus as playing and singing in person. In fact we regard professional performers as belonging to the lower classes, though a man

---

[70] Dover (1968a) 358. On the Muse of Euripides see further Hall (forthcoming).

[71] The audience will already have this iconoclastic play in mind, since Aeschylus has quoted it in the foregoing parody of Euripidean choral lyric (Eur. *El.* 435–7 = *Frogs* 1317–18).

[72] The Muse of Euripides is given potsherds to play (*ostrakois*, 1305), almost certainly in direct parody of the castanets or rattle (*krotala*) Hypsipyle had played to the baby Opheltes as she sang to him in Euripides' *Hypsipyle* fr. 1 ii 9 (see note 66, above). See also the quotation of *Hypsipyle* (fr. 752 N²) at *Frogs* 1211–13. Since *Hypsipyle* was performed between 412 and 407 (a scholion to *Frogs* 53 says it was performed with *Phoenissae* and *Antiope*), it would have been relatively fresh in the mind of any regular theatre-goer at Athens in 405 BCE.

[73] See above, note 27.

Actor's song in tragedy

may play and sing for his own amusement or at a party when he has had a good deal to drink.

Even pre-tragic poets do not portray many immortals as singing (with the important exceptions of Apollo and the Muses), which in itself may illuminate the dearth of lyric singing by divinities in tragedy before the *Rhesus*. In the *Homeric Hymn to Apollo* (189–206) the Muses sing, several female and youthful divinities dance, Apollo plays the *kithara*, while Zeus and Leto *watch*, perhaps because they are older and more dignified.

Yet other sources confirm that citizen men were expected to sing in the context of the symposium. The repertoire of well-known songs for performance after the paean and libations included the compositions of the great lyric poets, extracts from tragedy, and lyrics from comedy. Although lengthy virtuoso performances may have been restricted to guests with musical skills above the average, every participant was probably expected to perform a stanza as he held the myrtle branch.[74] In Theophrastus' *Characters* a sign of the surly (*authadēs*) man is that he 'always refuses to sing, perform a speech, or dance' at symposia (15.10).[75] It is in a travesty of a sympotic context that Polyphemus drunkenly sings solo in Euripides' satyric *Cyclops* (503–10). But Polyphemus is hardly a cultured individual, and the text of the *Characters* elsewhere indicates that singing was not something a refined man would indulge in at whim: type of song, context, and *dignity* were critical.

It was one thing to sing an elegant skolion to fellow symposiasts. It was quite another to memorize the songs associated with lower-class entertainments such as conjurors' shows (*thaumata*). These were favoured by children, and featured females playing the *aulos* and dancing (Xen. *Symp.* 2.1). In the *Characters* the man who does his learning too late, the *opsimathēs*, attends these shows repeatedly in order to learn the songs off by heart (*ta aismata ekmanthanein*, 27.7). Perhaps, as Ussher suggests, the songs were like those composed by the 'poets of shameful songs' with whom Philip of Macedon surrounded himself, and to which he was said to be addicted.[76] Singing in an inappropriate public context is criticized in the Theophrastan definition of the *agroikos*, the 'boor', a term which elsewhere is found in tandem with terminology

---

[74] Pellizer (1990) 179; Parker (1997) 3–4;
[75] Ar. *Clouds* 1355–8, 1364–72, *Wasps* 1222 with scholion *ad loc.*, Xen. *Symp.* 7.1, where Socrates leads the singing. According to Cicero, Themistocles' refusal to play the lyre at feasts earned him the reputation of being *indoctior* (*Tusc. Disp.* 1.2.4). See Ussher (1960) 133.
[76] Ussher (1960) 230. On the performances called *thaumata*: Isocr. *Antidosis* 213.

defining the *aneleutheros*:[77] the boorish man is liable 'to sing (*aisai*) at the baths' (*Char.* 4.14).[78]

IV

For the parody of Euripidean monody in *Frogs* the singing persona whose identity Aeschylus assumes is a woman. In Aeschylus female singers (Hypermestra[?], Antigone and Ismene, Cassandra, Electra, Io) outnumber male (Xerxes, Orestes). Singing in Euripides seems to be a female (and barbarian) prerogative: with a few exceptions (notably Theseus in *Hippolytus*, see below), lyric utterance is particularly associated with women (Phaedra, Electra, Hecuba, Andromache, Cassandra, Polyxena, Evadne, Helen, Andromeda, Hypsipyle, Creusa, Jocasta, Antigone, Agave, Iphigeneia in both her plays). Singing males include the barbarians Polymestor and the eunuch in *Orestes*, the children of the heroines of *Alcestis* and *Andromache*, the youths Hippolytus and Ion, and the aged Peleus in *Andromache* and Oedipus in *Phoenissae*.[79] It is a distinctive and remarkable feature of Sophoclean heroic protagonists that they sing lyrics when in physical pain or extreme emotional turmoil, apparently regardless of gender. Ajax sings a great lament, which Sophocles ironically prefaces with the information that this hero regarded high-pitched lamentation as 'unmanly' (317–20). Heracles sings in *Trachiniae*, and so do Antigone, Creon, Electra, Philoctetes, and Oedipus (see Calame, this volume), although the brevity of Oedipus' lyric musical utterances in *OC* has been attributed to his identity as an old man, who could not be expected 'at the very close of his life to sing with the necessary vigour'.[80] But Aeschylean and Euripidean singers are generally the 'others' of the free Greek man in his prime.[81]

---

[77] In Aristophanes fr. 706 the man who is both *agroikos* and *aneleutheros* cannot speak in a dignified way in public.

[78] This view to be found articulated elsewhere: Artemidorus asserts that it is not a good thing to sing at the baths (1.76), and the barbarous Triballians are said to behave in an ill-bred way in the baths (*Etymology* s.v. *Triballoi*). See also Seneca *Ep.* 56.2 (... *et illum cui vox sua in balneo placet*), Petronius *Sat.* 73, Ussher (1960) 61–2.

[79] Oiax probably sang a lament for his brother in Euripides *Palamedes*: see fr. 588 N² and Webster (1970) 162.

[80] Owen (1936) 152: Owen's article disscusses Sophoclean actors' songs in detail. Neither actor's song nor its socio-political dimensions receives much attention in Scott (1984) and (1996).

[81] Barner (1971) 314 agrees that Aeschylean and Euripidean singers sing for similar reasons and are similar theatrical types. The main difference is, of course, that Aeschylean singers all sing during exchanges with the choros. But it is just possible that the paradosis may give us a distorted view of Aeschylean song: according to Philostratus' *Life of Apollonius of Tyana* 6.11.219c, one of Aeschylus' improvements to tragedy was that he 'invented dialogues for the actors, discarding the long monodies' (*to tōn monōidiōn mēkos*).

Actor's song in tragedy 113

A tendency to gender song as feminine is apparent in ancient (and more modern) thought,[82] from the symbolism embodied in the Muses, to Aristides Quintilianus' schematization, which he attributes to 'the ancients', whereby melody is the female partner in bringing music to life and rhythm is the male partner (1.19).[83] If the Hibeh Papyrus' fragmentary treatise on musical modes is a contemporary's response to Damon, then the masculinity specifically of tragic actors and their singing had been impugned by the early fourth century: it is denied that the enharmonic mode can bestow bravery on tragic actors, for they are not 'a manly lot'.[84]

Ritual, especially ritual lament, is important here. A few tragic songs delivered by actors are work songs (Ion) or perverted wedding songs (Cassandra in *Troades*, Evadne in *Supplices*). But the ancients seem to have believed that most tragic songs were fundamentally threnodic.[85] The ritual lament which informs so many tragic songs had traditionally been a female obligation.[86] But the Platonic Socrates' gendered objection to tragic performance in Book 10 of the *Republic* is significant here. He argues that tragedy encourages types of behaviour and emotional expression which are inappropriate in a man and only befit a woman; it is particularly reprehensible and 'feminine' to luxuriate in watching distressed heroes delivering long speeches or 'singing and beating themselves' (*aidontas te kai koptomenous*, 10.605c10–e2). Plato is presumably thinking of tragic lamentation – the combination of song and gesture denoted by the noun *kommos*. The passage is suggestive because singing (*aidein*) has entered the vocabulary referring to tragic behaviour inappropriate in men; this will resurface, as we have seen, in Aristotle's distinction between Odysseus and Melanippe in the *Poetics*.

Famous performances of tragedy in later antiquity usually involve female singing roles. The actor who terrified the barbarians in Spain was performing a song of the Euripidean Andromeda.[87] At the beginning of the Christian era the Argive actor Leontos performed Euripides'

---

[82] Segal (1994) 17–34.
[83] Winnington-Ingram (1963). *Tines de tōn palaiōn ton men rhuthmon arren apekaloun, to de melos thēlu* etc. The theory is dependent on the Aristotelian view of mammalian reproduction: 'feminine' melody is formless, lifeless and inactive material which needs to be shaped and put in order by the active 'masculine' principle of rhythm, thus producing music.
[84] Grenfell and Hunt (1906), pt. 1 no. 13, pp. 45–58, col. ii. For a more contemporary English translation see Anderson (1966) 147–9.
[85] So a scholion on Eur. *Andr.* 103 ('A monody is the song of a character doing a *thrēnos*'), and the *Suda*'s gloss of *monōidein* as *to thrēnein*: 'for all the songs from the stage in tragedy are properly *thrēnoi*'.
[86] See especially Foley (1993) 101–43.
[87] See note 38, above.

Hypsipyle in front of King Juba II of Mauretania (Athen. *Deipn.* 8.343e–f).[88] Leontos' performance was so poor that Juba composed an epigram to reprove him, criticizing the actor's *voice*: Leontos had been eating too many artichokes.[89] Juba says that his own vocal gifts had been ruined by over-eating, but that Bacchus used to love his voice (*gērun*), a term which, along with the cognate verb *gēruō*, is often found in contexts to do with expert *singing*. To have the voice of Orpheus is to have a *gērus* (Eur. *Alc.* 969); in Pindar *gēruein* is regularly the term used of the performance of lyric poetry; the middle form *gēruesthai* often means, absolutely, 'to sing'.[90] It was Leontos' failure in the role of Hypsipyle which provoked this epigram on the inter-relationship of voice and diet, so outstanding vocal form was thought to be required for the role of Hypsipyle. The papyri confirm that her role was a heavily musical one similar to that of Euripides' *Helen*, and certainly an inspiration behind Aristophanes' parody of Euripidean actors' lyrics in *Frogs*.[91]

Another example is provided by Plutarch's report of the death of Crassus (*Vit. Crass.* 33.2–4). The head of the slaughtered Roman general was brought into the presence of the Parthian king Orodes on an occasion when a tragic actor (*tragōidiōn hupokritēs*), Jason of Tralles, performed 'the part of Euripides' *Bacchae* which is about Agave' (*aiden Euripidou ta peri tēn Agauēn*). Jason handed his 'Pentheus' costume to one of the choros, and seized Crassus' head. Assuming the role of the frenzied Agave, and using Crassus' head as 'a grisly prop',[92] he sang the words from her lyrical interchange with the choros, 'We bear from the mountain a newly cut tendril to the palace, a blessed spoil from the hunt' (*Bacch.* 1169–71). This delighted everyone. But when the dialogue was sung where the choros asks, 'Who killed him?', and Agave responds, 'mine was this privilege' (1179), the actual murderer sprang up and grabbed Crassus' head, feeling that these words were more appropriate for him to utter than for Jason. The distinctive sung exchange of *Bacchae*, where Agave's sung utterance over Pentheus' head represents Bacchic *mania*, was thus a party-piece in antiquity.[93]

Or take Euripides' *Electra*. Plutarch records that after the battle of

---

[88] See Cockle (1987) 41.
[89] For other ancient sources on the effect of certain dietary items on the voice see Flashar (1967) 546.
[90] *Hymn. Hom. Merc.* 426 and *Theocr.* 1.136 (of birdsong), Pind. *Isthm.* 1.34, Eur. *Hipp.* 213 (of Phaedra, who is delivering lyric anapaests in contrast with her nurse's recitative anapaests), Aesch. *Suppl.* 460.
[91] See above, notes 66, 72.
[92] Braund (1993) 468–9.
[93] On the variety of dramatic entertainments offered at dinner parties, especially in the Roman imperial era, see Jones (1991) 185–97.

Aegospotami, at which Athens lost the Peloponnesian war in 404 BCE, the Theban Erianthus proposed to raze Athens to the ground and sell the Athenians into slavery. But the city was saved by one Phocion at a banquet where Lysander and the other allied generals were assembled: he performed the *parodos* (*tēn parodon*) of Euripides' *Electra*, which begins with the female choros' address to the distressed princess: 'O Electra, daughter of Agamemnon, I have come to your rustic court...' (167–8). This song is shared with a soloist: Electra responds to the choros in this first strophe, lamenting her shabbiness and her absence from Hera's festivals (175–89). Phocion is thus supposed by Plutarch to have performed Electra's sung lament.[94] The evocation of Electra's pitiable plight affected the generals; they connected it with the parlous state in which Athens found herself, and decided against destroying the city (Plut. *Vit. Lys.* 15.2–3). Plutarch therefore remembers a female tragic role which we know was distinguished by its pathetic singing. Perhaps the same applied to the actor Polus' celebrated rendition of Sophocles' *Electra* (another role characterized by extensive song), in which he 'method acted' by utilizing his 'real living grief (*luctu*) and lamentations (*lamentis*)', as he handled the urn containing the ashes of his own dead son (Aulus Gellius 6.4).

Electra has a singing role in all four plays involving her by all three tragic poets. This raises the possibility that certain mythical characters were more likely than others to be made to sing by the tragedians. Clytemnestra, unlike Electra, never seems to sing lyrics, although Aeschylus in *Agamemnon* gives to her (as to Athena in *Eumenides*) anapaestic lines in an exchange with the choros.[95] Parker has remarked that Clytemnestra here subverts expectation precisely by failing to use even lyric anapaests: 'in this aberrant specimen of the genre the dead man's wife, instead of joining in the lament, uses recitative anapaests'.[96] Perhaps anapaests could be recited in a grand and declamatory manner more suitable than lyric song for indomitable masculinized females.[97]

---

[94] Diodorus (16.92) reports that a tragic actor famous for the power of his voice (*megalophōnia*) sang at another important symposium with military overtones, held by Philip of Macedon the night before his assassination. Neoptolemus (on whom see also the references in Stephanis (1988) no. 1797, 321–2), was ordered to choose a piece pertinent to the King's planned expedition against Persia. Unfortunately it is not clear whether his song was originally designed to be delivered by a male or female character, nor, indeed, whether it was from a monody or a choral lyric (*TrGF* vol. II, no. 127). See Pat Easterling's discussion in the present volume.
[95] On which see Peretti (1939) 181.
[96] Parker (1997) 57.
[97] This notion is certainly latent in Pintacuda's discussions of both Clytemnestra and Medea (1978: 114, 171–3).

It is striking that tragedy's other 'manly' female, Euripides' Medea, is likewise given anapaests but never lyric song:[98] the wife-dominated Jason, on the other hand, is likely to have performed a monody in an anonymous tragic *Medea* (tr. fr. adesp. 6 N²). Clytemnestra does not even sing lyrics in Euripides' *IA*, where as a morally unimpeachable grief-stricken mother, listening to her daughter's heart-rending monody, she had certainly found a suitable occasion (Clytemnestra's introductory anapaests: 1276–8. Iphigeneia's anapaests and monody: 1279–1310).

Were Hecuba and Andromache famous as singing characters? Certainly their roles in *Trojan Women* were renowned for their emotive potential. In his *Life of Pelopidas* (29.4–6) Plutarch describes the legendary cruelty of Alexander of Pherae, the fourth-century tyrant who killed his own uncle; he used to bury enemies alive, or encase them in the hides of wild animals and set his hunting dogs on them. But at a production of *Trojan Women* he was forced to leave rather than let the people see him weep 'at the sorrows of Hecuba and Andromache'. He subsequently sent a message to 'the actor' (*tragōidon*) to say that his departure was no reflection on the actor's performance (*agōnizesthai*). These two female characters, of course, are both singing roles in *Trojan Women* and in other tragedies, perhaps an inheritance from their performance of dirges for Hector in the twenty-fourth book of the *Iliad*.

Certain female characters seem almost pre-programmed to sing (Electra, Hecuba, Iphigeneia, Cassandra). With others there is no consistency, and the choice of speech or song may partly depend on the extent of the 'interiorization' of a woman's character in an individual play, for monodists, especially in Euripides, tend to be deeply self-absorbed and self-referential.[99] Helen, who also performs a lament in *Iliad* 24, stands out in Euripides' *Trojan Women* as the only woman in Troy who does *not* sing: Hecuba, Cassandra, and Andromache are lyric roles, but this cynical rhetorician of a Helen is confined to the iambic trimeter. What a difference, therefore, in the play of but a few years later, Euripides' *Helen*, where the heroine can hardly be stopped from lyric expression, at least in the first third of the drama (164–78, 191–210, 229–52, 348–85).

If the performance of dirges impugned a man's masculinity, the question arises of the extent to which tragic heroes with laments are

---

[98] What Euripides might have done is shown by the song Ennius seems to have given Medea at some point during the crisis over the death of the children (fr. 282 in Vahlen (1903) 70).
[99] See Damen (1990) 134–5.

Actor's song in tragedy 117

effectively 'effeminized'. There can be little doubt that this applies to Xerxes. He may even sing in a high pitch, like the Phrygian eunuch in *Orestes*, whose 'chariot melody' (1384) was in the high-pitched Phrygian mode: the same actor who played the eunuch almost certainly took the part of Electra, who was also required to sing in a high-pitched voice (Dion. Hal. *Comp.* 11).[100] The pseudo-Aristotelian *Problem* 11.62 asks, 'Why do children, women and eunuchs and old men speak in a shrill voice (*phthengontai oxu*)?' The dirge in *Persians* may even programmatically announce both the high pitch of melody to which it is sung (it is 'Mariandynian', 937), and the type of instrument (a Mariandynian *aulos*, traditionally of high pitch) used to accompany it.[101] The actor singing Xerxes will thus be performatively confirming the earlier implications that he is effeminate, including the statement of the messenger that he was given to wail (*kōkuein*) in a shrill manner designated by the term *oxu* – that is, lamenting in a high-pitched voice appropriate to a woman.[102]

Barbarian males are often given song (see below), but in extant tragedy and in the fragments (e.g. of *Erechtheus*) adult Athenian men, with the exceptions of Theseus in *Hippolytus*, and Sophocles' Salaminian Ajax, do not sing lyrics. Was it felt appropriate that the mythical ancestors of the hosts at the City Dionysia should maintain the appearance of dignity by sticking to the iambic trimeter? In *Hippolytus* however, Theseus delivers some lyric lines after the discovery of Phaedra's death (between 817–51). But he might actually be the exception who proves the rule, because the pattern of his delivery is two lyric lines alternating repeatedly with two iambic trimeters. The lyrics never become continuous, but are restrained by the repeated insertion of iambic (and thus probably spoken) lines.[103] This metrical pattern is frequently found in epirrhematic scenes, where choral song alternates with actor's spoken trimeters or *vice versa*. It is also common in female – male 'duets', where women have lyrics while their performance partners mostly have iambic trimeters. Examples are the recognition scenes in *IT*, *Helen* and in Sophocles' *Electra*, where Electra sings, Orestes speaks, and she fails to persuade him to join her (except for a lone bacchiac at 1280) in the feminine emotional self-expression of which

---

[100] See the references in note 25, above. The Phrygian in *Orestes* was certainly regarded as a eunuch in later antiquity: see Terentianus Maurus, *de Metris* (2nd century CE), 1960–2.
[101] See the scholion on *Pers.* 917 and Comotti (1989) 33.
[102] See Hall (1996a) 143.
[103] Schadewaldt (1926) 147–51, has some sensitive comments on the unusual metrical structure of Theseus' monody.

her lyrics are the vehicle.[104] In Euripides' Theseus a similar struggle between lyric and iambic, between song and speech, is located within one individual.

V

There are only three possible exceptions to Maas's principle. They are the Phrygian eunuch in Euripides' *Orestes*, the Egyptian herald in Aeschylus' *Suppliants*, and the nurse in Sophocles' *Trachiniae*. To argue backwards, Deianeira's nurse almost certainly does not sing: the slightest of emendations restores her to spoken iambic trimeters.[105]

But there is little doubt that the Egyptian herald sings. The Danaids have been terrified by the sight of their cousins rowing into shore. Between 825 and 871 there is a long lyric sequence. Internal evidence proves that the Danaids cannot sing several of the groups of lines (836–42, 847–53, 859–65). They are having an interchange with an opponent who threatens them with extreme violence, including decapitation. Critics have long been tempted to invent a choros of Egyptians here, in order to remove the alleged problem of a low-status singing character.[106] Yet immediately afterwards, an aggressive herald sent by the sons of Aegyptus speaks in iambic trimeters to both the choros of Danaids and to Pelasgus, and many scholars now infer that the Danaids' singing adversary is the solo herald.[107]

Perhaps Henderson was correct to argue that the status of heralds had always been ambivalent: neither servants nor equals of kings.[108] But it may be more important that the singer is a barbarian. His lyrics represent anger and uncontrolled physicality. His lyrics are neither work song, wedding song nor lament: he sings because he is violent and because he is not Greek. He is in a tradition of singing stage *barbaros* going back at least to Aeschylus' Xerxes,[109] and forward to Euripides' Phrygian eunuch, and the barbarian characters given *oratio*

---

[104] Willink (1989) 46–7 makes some perceptive remarks on these 'recognition' duets. On singing in Sophocles' *Electra* see Webster (1970) 173–4.
[105] See L. D. J. Henderson (1976) 19–24; Easterling (1982) 183.
[106] E.g. Maas (1929). The singing herald is replaced with a choros by Johansen and Whittle (1980), a decision they try to justify in vol. III, 171–4.
[107] E.g. Popp (1971) 242; Taplin (1977) 217 is rightly dismissive of the subsidiary choros theory.
[108] Henderson (1976).
[109] And almost certainly beyond Aeschylus to Phrynichus. Nothing is known of the cast of Phrynichus' *Sack of Miletus*, but the eunuch who spoke the iambic prologue of his *Phoenissae* (fr. 8) may have sung later, and the play must have included members of the Persian royal family.

recta within Timotheus' flamboyant Salamis aria, his *Persians*.[110] It may also be significant that the same actor who played Danaus must have performed the herald's role; the playwrights may have exploited the distinctive timbre of a particular actor's voice in establishing links between the characters he took in a play. Pavloskis has suggested that in *Supplices* the duplication suggested the foreign character of both Danaus and the herald, in contrast with the Greek Pelasgus.[111]

Yet it is debatable how far the herald's language characterized him as a *barbaros*: some have thought that the actual noises are supposed to replicate barbarian speech, or a barbarian accent on Greek speech similar to the caricatured Scythian pronunciation used by the archer in Aristophanes' *Thesmophoriazusae*.[112] It is more likely that an exotic type of utterance was implied symbolically by certain features, including the recurrent word-doubling (836, 838, 839, 842, 860, 861, 863 – also a feature of the *exodos* of *Persae*), the syntactical strangeness of the verbless sentence of 838–42, and the exoticism of *barin* and *ichar*.[113]

The Phrygian slave in Euripides' *Orestes*, whatever he owes to the 'New Music' of Timotheus, helps to protect this Aeschylean exception to the exclusion of low-status singers, since he, likewise, is an overwrought male barbarian. Non-Greekness seems to prompt an Athenian tragedian to think in terms of song; it may be significant that Greeks thought that in barbarian tyrannies there was no secure distinction between slave and free.

Polymestor may offer a closer parallel to the Egyptian herald and to the Phrygian than has been appreciated. He is a ruler of sorts and as such might be expected to sing a 'blind' scene, but even his status as king is ambivalent: he is a barbarous Thracian horseman (710), who lives in the mountains without a polis, and who has no claim to aristocratic birth. He is only once called 'king', and then it is by Agamemnon in a fit of cynical flattery (856). He is, however, called 'barbarian' and 'you there', and no fewer than nine times he is just 'the Thracian', which subliminally associates him with one of the commonest slave ethnic names in Athens.[114] As a violent barbarian male,[115] whose ethnicity is compounded by physical agony, the poet's decision to make him sing becomes almost over-determined. Collard's account of Polymestor's

---

[110] See Hall (1995a) 60–70.
[111] Pavloskis (1977–8) 116. For arguments along similar lines see also Damen (1989).
[112] Garvie (1969) 56–7. On the Scythian archer's voice, see Hall (1989a).
[113] Johansen and Whittle (1980) vol. III, 174.
[114] Hall (1989) 109–110
[115] I cannot imagine why the only moderately recent substantial study of monody in tragedy classifies Polymestor as a Greek (Barner (1971) 262–3).

monody is one of the more perceptive descriptions in existence of a tragic song, and one of the few discussions of monody in the English language:[116] 'His crippling physical pain is conveyed by theatrical entry on all fours ... and a changed mask now all bloody ... Irregular shrieks of agony and despair; cries of hate; broken, illogically ordered thought, mostly phrased as imploring questions; staccato delivery (the monody has no connective particles between clauses whatsoever).'[117] The exaggerated extent of the asyndeton is unimaginable in spoken iambic trimeters, and is reminiscent of Aristotle's objection to lack of connection in the speech of the orator, a reprehensible habit he says they borrow from actors (*Rhet.* 3.1413b).

VI

One of the most significant issues ever raised by Vernant was the need to examine the processes whereby Athenian tragedy *transformed* reality while assimilating it into its own medium – what cultural materialists would call the processes of artistic 'mediation': 'No reference to other domains of social life ... can be pertinent unless we can also show how tragedy assimilates into its own perspective the elements it borrows, thereby quite transmuting them.'[118] It is important to be aware of the particular codes conditioning such processes of transformation, and then to ask what those codes reveal about the society operating them.

Work of this kind has been done on the *content* of the tragedies: we now understand better how light is cast on issues of concern to the democratic city-state by being refracted through the prism of the heroic mythical past. But I hope this paper has shown that insufficient attention has been paid to the relationship of tragedy's aural *form* – its actors' musical and metrical performance codes – to the society which produced it.

Even from this cursory look at some actor's songs some interesting results have emerged. Song versus speech was both an emotionally and an ideologically laden distinction. Singing in the fifth-century theatre seems to be a human, rather than divine, form of self-expression. Solo song is affected by social status, for it distinguishes rulers from 'ordi-

---

[116] An important exception is Collard's review of the bibliography on monody and analysis of Evadne's song in his edition of *Euripides' Supplices* (Collard, 1975) ii, 358–62. There are also some excellent points made in Barlow's accounts of the imagery in Euripidean monody (Barlow (1986) 43–60), and of its diction and style (Barlow 1986a) 10–22. Parker (1997), 514–18, offers an admirably succinct review of the metrical features of Euripidean monody.
[117] Collard (1991) 187.
[118] In Vernant and Vidal-Naquet (1988) 31.

Actor's song in tragedy 121

nary people', and individuals born into slavery from those enslaved by misfortune. Solo song is also implicated in tragic distinctions determined by gender: Plato's Socrates had much more to complain about in Sophocles (where male protagonists regularly *aidein* and *koptesthai*) than in Euripides, where they do not. Song could imply barbarian ethnicity. Besides Sophocles' Ajax, Athenian men tend not to sing, except in the case of Theseus' half-hearted lament in *Hippolytus*. Certain characters (especially virgins like Electra) seem almost preprogrammed to sing in tragedy, while others (especially the 'manly' matrons Clytemnestra and Medea) do not. Female tragic roles with important sung elements seem to have been particularly popular choices as star turns in later antiquity.

Tragic song and metre, therefore, are not to be separated from the sociology of tragedy, and what is relevant to the sociology of tragedy is relevant to the sociology of the polis. Acknowledging the ideological implications of mode of delivery and metrical form suggests further questions, not least relating to Athenian imperialism. Attic tragedy is a remarkably inclusive genre, with a sponge-like ability to absorb other genres inherited from other parts of the Greek-speaking world. This feature must have ideological implications for a city-state setting itself up in the sixth century as the cultural centre of the Greek-speaking world, and in the fifth as the leading imperial power. A way of looking at tragedy could be to see it as not only aesthetically 'panhellenizing', but effectively as imperialism expressed on the level of form.

Athens had no distinctive poetic genre of its own, despite the Peisistratean attempts to hegemonize Homeric epic. The Dorians had choral lyric and anapaestic marching songs, the eastern Aegean had monody, the Ionians had iambos: in tragedy the Athenians invented an inclusive new genre which assimilated them all. Many of the types of delivery of both speech and song associated with other Greek-speaking communities, and to be heard all over Hellas, now came to be appropriated and heard in composite performances in the theatre of Dionysus at Athens. It may even be that tragedians could pay far more explicit compliments to other (friendly) communities by their inclusion of certain genres of song than we are remotely aware.[119] Thus when

---

[119] Long ago Denys Page argued that genre, form and ideology were inseparable. According to his view of Euripides' *Andromache*, choice of metrical form and sung performance were inextricably bound up with Athenian politics and its imperial programme. He argues that *Andromache* was first produced at Argos at a time when Athens was seeking to secure Argive support against Sparta. The grounds are that (i) there was a tradition of 'Doric threnodic elegy' at Argos, of which the Argive poet Sakadas was the chief representative poet; that (ii) the play was not produced at

Aeschylus chose to effeminize the great King of Persia through *kommos* and to prevent him from using the 'rational' discourse of iambic speech, the decision may have been literally 'consonant' with the same fifth-century imperial Athenian version of the world which in tragedy produced metrical and musical panhellenism performed on the level of genre. As Diomedes the grammarian said, there is much to be learnt by singing lyrics as we read them, even though we do not know the tragedian's original tune.[120]

Athens (so a scholion on line 445); and that therefore (iii) the elegies sung by Andromache strongly suggest an Argive first production, and constitute a sung compliment, by inclusion of a genre unusual in tragedy, to the Argive poetic tradition: Page (1936) 223–8.

[120] Several people provided invaluable help when I delivered this paper both in 1990 and 1996. Important references are owed to Helene Foley, Simon Goldhill, Peter Wilson, and Oliver Taplin. I would like in particular to thank Pat Easterling for her perceptive criticisms and abundance of references, especially those in note 38.

Part II

The drama of performance

5 Performative aspects of the choral voice in Greek tragedy: civic identity in performance

Claude Calame

'The separation of roles between actors and spectators, the establishment of a mythical storyline, the choice of a specific place of meeting, these are the features that little by little changed a ritual into an institutionalized theatrical event. From that point on the public came to watch and to be moved "at a distance" by means of a myth familiar to it and of actors who, in their masks, represent it.' This ambiguous statement concludes the reference to ancient Greece in an article which a semiotician of the theatre devotes to the ritual origins of dramatic representation in his recent *Dictionary of the Theatre*.[1] In the context of this being a concluding statement we can take for granted that the final 'it' refers back to the myth that the actors are thought to represent. Nevertheless, the scholar aware of the position from which the actors speak in a classical Greek tragedy, thought of as performance, would prefer to read here a reference back to the public. Is it not the public that the actor in Athenian tragedy, and more particularly the choros, represents under his mask?

1. Performative aspects of the choral voice in tragedy

'The choros is, in a word, the idealized spectator.' That was the conclusion August W. Schlegel famously drew from his examination of the role assumed by the members of the choros in Greek tragedy.[2] This

---

[1] Pavis (1987) 338–40 (an article entitled 'Théâtre et rituel'). This paper is based on my synthetic essay 'Fonctions énonciatives et performatives du choeur tragique: le *je/nous* choral aux Grandes Dionysies' which I worked up for the sixth 'Coralie' meeting under the title *Choreia* which was organized by the Department of Classics at Harvard University in May 1996. A part of it was delivered as the G. F. Else Lecture at the University of Michigan, Ann Arbor, in March 1998.

[2] Schlegel (1846) 76–7. The definition of the tragic choros proposed by Schlegel is discussed in particular by Kranz (1933) 219–25, and again by Hose (1990) 1.32–7; see also Hall, this volume (esp. n. 1). When they write 'le choeur, être collectif et anonyme, dont le rôle consiste à exprimer ... les sentiments des spectateurs qui composent la communauté civique', Vernant and Vidal Naquet (1972) 14 are giving a new shape to the same idea.

125

summary claim is often quoted, but it needs to be nuanced. On the one hand, in Schlegel's view the choros in its role as idealized spectator communicated the passions aroused by the drama while at the same time reducing their impact. On the other, the members of the choros must be thought of as standing for the whole of humanity. In this role it would represent not so much the public as the poet and his thought. The choros, as mouthpiece both of the ideal spectator and of the writer of tragedy, essentially represents, in the final instance, 'the common spirit of the nation, and so the universal human sympathy'.

Who then is it that in the last analysis speaks the tragic choral texts when they are enacted? Who then is it that sings through the voice of the members of the choros? What sort of a person speaks with what sort of authority in the words of the choros? There have been lengthy treatments of this question, but it is one that must be faced by any discussion of the role of the tragic spectacle in a culture which seems to achieve its political and democratic aims in and through performance.

But what does performance mean, unless that every means of achieving the end of communication involves action in which the body is engaged as well as the mind? In a 'song culture' (and Greek, and more particularly Athenian, culture was a song culture), this very broad idea of performance, as it is defined in the introduction to this volume, applies in particular to the musical re-enactments with singing and dancing that make up tragic drama; and the notion of performance is even more relevant for the choral parts of tragedy in which the voice evokes the authority of the group and the rhythm of the dancing has to involve its body.[3] In this paper which takes up the question of the effect of choral action on the civic community gathered in the theatre and on their shared values and their social and institutional practices, I will concentrate on the linguistic side of performance, on the 'performative' aspect of the language in the strict sense defined by Emile Benveniste. I will therefore consider a statement to be performative if it 'denotes the act performed from the fact that Ego pronounces a phrase containing the corresponding verb in the first person of the present tense'.[4] Expressed in simpler terms, a performative utterance corresponds to a

---

[3] In relation to ideas of authority and mimesis, understood as 'dramatic re-enactment', Gregory Nagy has recently developed the idea of performance in order to explain the basis of different forms of Greek poetry: see Nagy (1996) 1–38. For the idea of 'embodying discourses' see Goldhill and von Reden (this volume).

[4] This is the definition given by Benveniste (1963) 3–12, reprinted in (1966) 267–76. Benveniste takes up and renders more precise the idea developed by Austin (1975) 4–7, 67–71, for whom in a 'performative sentence' or 'performative utterance', 'the issuing of the utterance is the performing of an action'. For the broad definition of performance see Goldhill above, p. 1.

speech act: as they pronounce such utterances speakers accomplish an action which is entirely a matter of language, they invest all their authority in that act of speaking. From the linguistic point of view performative utterances are marked by the use of the first person (often defined by reference to someone who is the second person), by use of the present tense or of the modal tenses of wishing and ordering, by use of the deictic 'here', and above all by use of verbs explicitly referring to the word spoken: I order, I swear, I call upon, I pray, I sing.

These general reflections must be made more precise in two respects: in relation to the idea of the spectator and to the complex nature of the choral voice in tragedy.

First, contemporary theorists who concern themselves with texts and textuality have taken up the notion of the 'idealized spectator' ('idealisierter Zuschauer') and reformulated it as the 'model reader' or, transposing that concept to the theatre, as the 'ideal or virtual spectator'.[5] In this use, the ideal reader or spectator is a purely textual figure constructed by a series of discursive strategies. These same strategies relate this fictive figure to the real public, the actual empirical spectator. By these linguistic means, which create a relationship between the internal face of discourse (the uttered enunciation) and its external face (the empirical communication), the spectator is brought, at every new performance of the text, to perceive and understand it in relation to the community of belief to which he or she belongs. The figure of the ideal reader or spectator has in this way been added to the scheme of communication as Roman Jakobson, in particular, conceived it. This virtual figure is then placed in front of the ideal author, similarly a purely textual figure.[6] In the particular case of Athenian drama as performance, to insert the ideal spectator into the traditional scheme of communication and to try to give him a precise position will prove to involve a serious misunderstanding. In diagram 1, however, we offer an attempt to do it, as a theoretical possibility.

Second, in an earlier study of the relations between melic choral songs and Athenian choral odes, I have tried to define the nature of the voice of female choruses in some tragedies with reference to and by

---

[5] The idea of the 'Lettore Modello' has been elaborated particularly by Eco (1979) 50–66 and (1992) 67–88. For the way in which Aristotle, despite his claim at *Poetics* 1450b 15–16, makes the spectator of classical tragedy a mere reader, see Hall (1996).

[6] Jakobson (1963) 87–99 (originally (1961)). As applied to language Jakobson's scheme of communication has undergone substantial reformulation; see especially Grize (1990) 27–32. I borrow here the scheme which Adam (1991) 26–8 has elaborated by introducing the figures of 'virtual author' and 'ideal reader' and I have inserted into it the distinction between utterance and uttered enunciation which I explain in Calame (1995) 3–26.

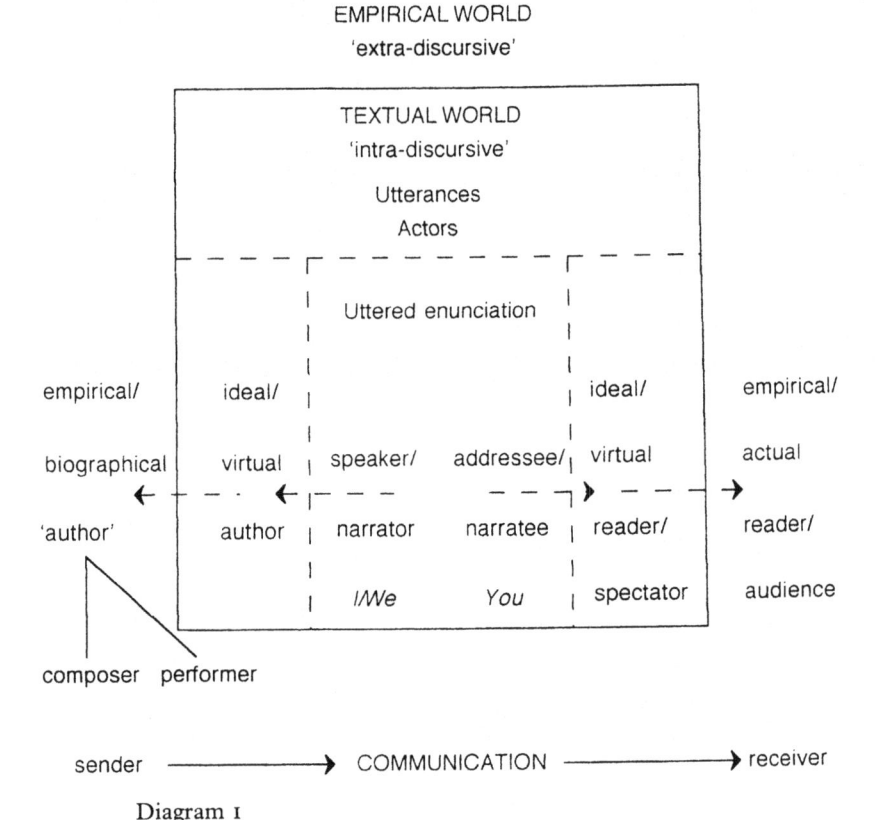

```
                    EMPIRICAL WORLD
                     'extra-discursive'
    ┌─────────────────────────────────────────────┐
    │              TEXTUAL WORLD                  │
    │              'intra-discursive'             │
    │                 Utterances                  │
    │                  Actors                     │
    │     ┌ ─ ─ ─ ─ ─ ─ ─ ─ ─ ─ ─ ─ ┐            │
    │     │    Uttered enunciation   │            │
    │     │                          │            │
empirical/│ ideal/ │               │ ideal/    │  empirical/
    │     │        │               │           │
biographical│virtual│ speaker/ addressee/│virtual│ actual
    ←─────│───←────│── ── ──   ── ── ──│──→────│──→
'author'  │ author │ narrator  narratee│ reader/│  reader/
    │     │        │                   │        │
    │     │        │  I/We      You    │spectator│  audience
    │     └────────┴───────────────────┴────────┘
    └─────────────────────────────────────────────┘
        ╲
composer  performer

sender  ─────────→  COMMUNICATION  ─────────→  receiver
Diagram 1
```

contrast with earlier practice of choral and ritual poetry.[7] Given the collective character of the voice of the chorus members, who usually sing in unison, distinguishing the features that determine the vocal nature of the choros must end up being artificial. Nevertheless it is possible to make out three complementary dimensions of the choral voices of tragedy in performance.

• A ritual dimension which makes the choros members interact (συναγωνίζεσθαι is Aristotle's expression in *Poetics*) with the dramatic action and with the actors who perform the action on stage. This

---

[7] Calame (1994/5). I give there a full bibliography of earlier studies of the problem discussed here of defining the voice of the tragic choros. I merely give here the references to Aristotle's famous discussion of the role of the choros and of *katharsis*: *Poetics* 1456a 25–7, 1449b 24–8.

interactive dimension often takes the form of cult songs which allow the members of the choros, by means of the ritual, to act on the attitude of the actors in the face of events. In this way the group of members of the choros can have a certain practical influence on the development of the dramatic action.
• A 'hermeneutic' dimension, in as far as the words of the choros often involve narrative and description. The *choreutai* give information about what has gone before the action that the spectators have seen, or about the spatial setting in which the action takes place; in their gnomic remarks they also comment on the action that occurs.
• An 'affective' dimension which allows the members of the choros to express (usually intense) emotions provoked by the action occurring on stage. The passions which the public must experience, according to Aristotle's statement, seem to be delegated to the choros. This process of delegation may explain the mysterious phenomenon of *katharsis* in which the strong emotions of pity and fear provoked by tragedy seem to be purified in their very expression.

The emotional aspect of the voice of the community in the choros members returns us to the spectators: by way of the dramatic performance the reactions of the ideal spectator, inscribed in the text with reference to a fictional action, would induce similar reactions in the actual public which has come together in the theatre to honour Dionysos Eleuthereus. By analogy, it might be suggested that in the hermeneutic dimension the choral voice corresponds to that of the ideal author and returns itself to the real author, to the biographical author: he is the omniscient narrator who knows the ins and outs of the action he manipulates. This is made even more probable by the author not appearing on the stage in classical tragedy but in some way delegating his authority to the real (but masked) performers, that is the actors and choros members. Furthermore there is little doubt that, in its ritual action, the choros is also made part of the plot of the drama played under male and female tragic masks; the group therefore acts like one of its protagonists. The choros is no longer ideal spectator, nor virtual author, but actor. In fact, in the dramatized text, in the text in performance, the ideal or virtual figures, who, in epic poetry for instance, would belong to the uttered enunciation and be then just textual figures, are made 'real' in the stage *mimēsis*; the narrative and fictional action with the protagonists who react in the utterance itself is made 'real' in the same mimetic way. As a result of this *mimēsis*, the ritual which the members of the choros accomplish in the *orchēstra* as they enact the performative aspect of their voice, reacts to the dramatized fictional narrative and is therefore also a fictional action.

II. Choral reference and choral authority in tragedy

In the course of a still more recent debate the question of the role and the authority of the words of the choros in the performance of tragedy has also been examined on the level of utterance. John Gould hypothesized that 'the choros brings to the fictional world of tragedy an alternative experience to that of the hero, and one that is of its essence both "collective" and "other"'; and in response Simon Goldhill said more specifically that 'the collective voice [of the choros] has a particular role to play in the *agōn* of attitudes that makes up tragedy. The choros requires the audience to engage in a constant renegotiation of where the authoritative voice lies.'[8] So what is the authority of the choral voice, that voice which in the majority of the tragedies of Sophokles and Euripides known to us is assumed by a group of young girls or women by means of the distance which wearing a mask produces? In those textual games played by word and action on gender and on the mask, in the many dimensions in which its voice plays a part, does the figure of the tragic choros coincide principally with the ideal spectator or with the actual spectator, with the virtual author or, as performer, with the real author, or just with the figure of a (masked) actor engaged in a dramatic plot?

In a study of choral performance centred on the performative aspect of the choral voice, it is essential to recall once more that choral odes in tragedy take up not only the rhythmic, dialectal and lexical forms of archaic choral melic poetry, but also its ritual forms. In as far as archaic and classical melic poetry is ritual and cultic speech, the choral odes of tragedy can also be considered as cultic speech acts. In terms of language, the inheritance of the performative dimension of melic poetry is revealed by the features we have mentioned: use of present and modal tenses (optative, imperative and above all 'future'), spatial indications of the *here* (and *now*) through deictics such as ὅδε, and above all the alternate forms of *I/we* and *you* (sing.)/*you* (pl.) applied to verbs expressing the act of utterance, the act of the ritual song. Engaged in these ritual speech acts, the members of the choros of melic poetry, like those of tragedy, are led to describe their own vocal action, along with its musical and choreographical aspects. This type of description has made Albert Henrichs characterize the choral activity of tragic choruses by the happy term 'self-referentiality'.[9] It is still appropriate to

---

[8] Gould (1996) 219; Goldhill (1996) 255.
[9] Henrichs (1994/5). Henrichs enlarges his enquiry to melic poetry in Henrichs (1996), and goes into more detail in Henrichs (1996a). The performative force of self-referential futures in Greek poetry has been most recently stressed by Faraone (1995).

nuance this self-referential procedure with the help of the distinctions that have just been introduced.

In relation to language use, the process of reference involves both intra-discursive and extra-discursive reference. By the numerous ways in which their odes make self-reference, the members of the choros of an Athenian tragedy are able to point both to the textual and 'ideal' figures inscribed in their words (and engaged in the intra-discursive and textual world) and to biographical and 'real' people taking part in the tragic performance in the here and now of the cult rendered to Dionysos (and engaged in the external and extra-discursive world). Given the melic ancestry of the choral forms of tragedy, it is important not to forget that in melic choral poetry the biographical person of the author or composer (Alkman, Pindar, Bacchylides) is distinct from the actual group of performers, often female, who sing and dance the song in the circumstances of a defined ritual. The melic poet was not limited to composing the song for the choral group, he was also employed to instruct the group in the song, assuming the function of *(choro)didaskalos*. During the execution of the choral work it was the *chorēgos*, the choros-leader, who was responsible for seeing that that instruction was carried out. In tragedy this role of leader of the choros was taken on by a *koruphaios* whose voice, despite modern distinctions, could often not be distinguished from that of the members of the choros.[10]

In these circumstances, the ritual and performative dimension of the performance of a tragic choros is not purely a matter of the role that the group of choros members play as actors involved in a dramatized plot. For it is also a matter of the choros being the virtual author and, in as far as the choros members are the actual performers of the text, the biographical author, along with the audience which in the end, by way of numerous intermediaries, he addresses. If the identity of the person who takes on the *I/we* forms, and thus the position of the discursive authority, is far from certain in melic choral poetry, the configuration of the authority of the choral 'subject' in tragedy is even more difficult to get a grip on.[11]

All this notwithstanding, it is with the complex process of 'authorial'

---

[10] The role of the leader or of the *chorēgos* in relaying the authoritative voice of the poet has been detailed by Nagy (1990) 360–81, who takes up and bases himself upon the thesis developed in Calame (1977) 92–143, 386–411 (= (1997) 43–73, 221–43). The complicated relations between choros and *koruphaios* are the subject of some sensible remarks by Kaimio (1970) 31–5.

[11] For the contradictory answers given to the question of the person taking on the *I/we* in lyric it will be enough to look at the different studies collected in Slings (1990) together with the complementary remarks of Gentili (1990).

and performative *mimēsis* that I will try to do battle here. I base my argument on an analysis of two tragedies which I have chosen because their choral group represents figures very different from the 'ideal spectator' and from the Athenian civic community that the choros has been thought to stand for. In Sophokles' *Oedipus the King* the choros is a group of old men in a Thebes which in tragedy represents a sort of 'anti-city' in opposition to Athens. In Euripides' *Hippolytos* the choros is a group of women in the 'mini-Athens' of the little city of Troizen.[12]

III. The choros of *Oedipus the King* and the performative question: 'myth and ritual'

Taking advantage of recent illuminating studies, I begin with the interventions of the choros and its leader in Sophokles' *Oedipus the King*. As it enters the *orchēstra*, the choros of old men of Thebes addresses a prayer to Zeus. This is an indirect prayer, in the Pindaric manner, since its addressee is the word (ἀδυεπὲς φάτι 151) of the king of the gods; and at the end of the first strophe of the *parodos*, in ring position, the voice of Zeus is relayed by that of Apollo (ἄμβροτε φάμα 157) who has himself been invoked in the middle of the strophe as god of Delos and as the god Paian. The performative dimension of the beginning of this choral ode comes out as much in the double address, in the vocative, to the divine word, which frames the strophe, as in the demand that it become real in favour of the 'I' (εἰπέ μοι 157) or in the ritual cry direct to the attention of the god Paian of Delos (ἰήιε Δάλιε Παιάν 154).[13]

The ritual character of the performance represented by this first choral intervention is underlined by the fact that the voice of the choros takes up immediately from the prayers of the priest of Zeus which punctuate the prologue. Most of the priest's part in the exchanges with Oedipus can be described as ritual acts: '*we* are sitting at your altars' (15–16) with a 'we' that includes 'I', the priest, and '*these* (οἵδε) chosen young men' (18–19) that the public has before its eyes and who accompany the Theban dignitary. An analogous formula is repeated in the middle of an address to Oedipus that takes the form of a prayer to the god (31–2); Oedipus addresses his reply to this prayer to the whole

---

[12] The functions of Thebes as the space of 'the other' in Athenian tragedy has been studied by Zeitlin (1990). On Troizen as a 'remote Athens' in tragedy see Vidal-Naquet (1992). The specificity of female choral voices is illustrated by Easterling (1988). See also Taplin, this volume.

[13] The innumerable parallels to the ritual refrain which punctuates the different types of paian are given by Käppel (1992) 65–70 (see also 31–42).

body of young men, treated like a choral group (ὦ παῖδες οἰκτροί 58–9, compare 78–9); finally, in a last performative formulation (ὦ παῖδες, ἱστώμεσθα 147–50) the priest and the young men stand up again and express the wish that by means of the oracle he has given Apollo may become, like Oedipus in the first prayer (51), the saviour of the town. The last reference to the plague which afflicts the city polluted by the murder of Laios serves in a way to introduce the choral ode which immediately follows this mention of the god who purifies and heals.

After its initial address to the oracular voice of Zeus and then to that of Apollo, the choral ode of the *parodos* develops along the traditional lines of a prayer. In its poetic expression the singing of the prayer takes on the tripartite structure of what has been known since antiquity as a 'cletic hymn': a direct appeal to three divinities, Athena who is carefully designated by her relationship with Zeus who dominates this whole choral ode, Artemis who sits in the agora, and naturally the archer Apollo; reference is then made to past interventions by these deities to avert misfortune from the city and they are finally asked to intervene in the same way on this occasion (ἔλθετε καὶ νῦν 158–67).[14] We are therefore dealing with a cultic prayer, with all the linguistic and structural marks of the act of verbal ritual that go to make it up. This cultic prayer relates to the dramatic action, if it is true that the address to Pheme simply takes up the mention of Kreon's consultation of Apollo's prophets at Delphi (85 and 95–7), and if it is also true that Athena was effectively honoured at Thebes as protector of the Seven Gates giving access to the city and that Athena was worshipped as Eukleia. But this prayer could also be understood in an Athenian context, outside the action of the drama: Delian Apollo, apparently unknown at Thebes, refers us to the Delian League sanctuary, and Athena, daughter of Zeus and tutelary deity of Athens, reigns over the first two thirds of this choral prayer, invoked at its beginning (πρῶτά σε 159) and at its end (187–8) to do good to a polis which is never clearly identified.[15] The real audience could then feel even more concerned as

---

[14] The structure of the cletic hymn (*invocatio, epica laus, preces*) and its relation to the structure of prayers has been the subject of many studies; see in particular Des Places (1959), Bremer (1981). For a good demonstration of the way in which Zeus assures his domination in the choral odes of *Oedipus the King* see Segal (1995a) 185–98.

[15] It is because she protected the gates of the city that the Theban cult of Athena Onka has been related to the appeal to Athena by the choros, but it has to be admitted that it is hard to identify the two temples of Athena to which the priest of Zeus makes allusion at the beginning of his intervention (20–1). See Schachter (1981) 130–2, and the complementary remarks of Zeitlin (1993) 160–1, on the role of Athena in *Antigone*. As for Artemis, the identification with the Theban Artemis Eukleia (Paus. 9.17.2) is far from certain; see Schachter (1981) 104 and Bollack (1990) II. 98–100.

it is certainly culturally sensitive to the power of oracles and of cultic speech.

However, in the final strophe and antistrophe of the *parodos*, which is still dominated by the authority of Zeus, it is Dionysos and not Athena who appears in the invocation of three protecting deities, and this leads us back to Thebes and to the site of the dramatic action. The act which invokes Dionysos presents him as the eponymous god of this land (τᾶσδε γᾶς, 210). Oedipus makes no mistake when he immediately takes up the choros's prayers (αἰτεῖς, 216, using the second person singular) to address a solemn appeal to all the citizens of Kadmos' city. Oedipus' words combine the performative engagement of the first person singular with orders given to the Kadmeans addressed in the second person plural (ὑμῖν προφωνῶ, 223, ὑμᾶς 256, ὑμῖν 273). The *koruphaios* then hastens to insert himself into this address (276): the boundaries between the community of Theban citizens, the choral group of old men of the city, and the *koruphaios* who leads their ritual song are decidedly fluid. That the civic community is included by the terms of the utterance in the group of members of the choros is rendered still more probable because their choral ode does not simply display the specific features of a paian, and not just those of a prayer, but echoes the paian sung by the wives and mothers of the Theban victims of the plague that has struck the city.[16]

Stasimon after stasimon, the choral interventions by the old men of Thebes are almost obsessively dominated not only by the weight of Zeus' power, but above all by the echoes of the prophetic voice from Delphi. The *koruphaios* shares this obsession when, in accordance with his role in presenting actors whose mask does not allow their identification, he introduces Tiresias to the stage: inspired by the divinity the seer is the only man who can grasp the truth (297-9); the *koruphaios* even compares him to Apollo himself (284-6).[17] But at the end of his intervention (461-2) Tiresias, faced by a doubtful Oedipus, even goes so far as to suspect his own divinatory art of lying.

The members of the choros immediately take up Tiresias' provocative expression of doubt, and make the order of Apollo's oracle announced by Kreon at the beginning of the play the theme of the first stasimon (463-7). Announced by Oedipus himself (86), invoked by the choros in the introduction to the *parodos* (158), the word from Parnassos im-

---

[16] The relation between the parodos and a paian has been stressed particularly by Rutherford (1994/5).

[17] On the role of oracles and oracular voices in *Oedipus the King* see generally Segal (1981) 236-41 and Pucci (1992) 16-30. On the role of Tiresias in relation to knowledge based on sight, see the references which I give in Calame (1996b).

placably pursues any who try to escape (473–6). But faced with the intelligence of Zeus and of his son Apollo, the members of the choros in their turn also doubt the words spoken by the wise seer, treat them as merely reproaches (μεμφομένων, 505–6) dependent upon the relative wisdom of men rather than a 'right word' (ὀρθὸν ἔπος, 505) displaying itself by proofs. Reducing the truth of the word of the seer inspired by the divinity to the relativity of its human dimension involves the choros in questioning its own human word. By refusing to attack the reputation which Oedipus has established, the members of the choros are left able to define their performative voice only in a negative way: 'I do not know what to say' (ὅ τι λέξω δ' ἀπορῶ, 486). Overcome by trouble and doubt, the ritual speech act represented by the song of a choros that Creon will assimilate to the community of citizens (513) seems without effect. From now on the choros and its leader can only express allegiance to Oedipus and a refusal to accuse him (660–3, 689–91, 834–5).[18]

So it is that during the second stasimon the choros comes to ask the question that is fundamental to its self-referential and performative voice: 'why should I dance?' (τί δεῖ με χορεύειν; 896). It is not just the choral voice, but the very activity of the choros as ritual actor that is dramatically questioned here. This shocking phrase, placed in the mouth of one whose function is precisely to sing and dance in a choros, has stimulated many commentaries. It has been noted that this question by the members of the choros about the legitimacy of their own performance originates in the doubts expressed by Jocasta in the previous scene with regard to the truth of the prophecies (see especially 720–5 and 857–8). Those doubts provoke the choros in the first part of its ode to affirm once more the legal order which Zeus, elevated to sole god, guarantees (871, 880, 881). The performative voice of the choros serves the god while at the same time it does not cease to fight, for the good of the city, against the *hubris* of the tyrant. The two performative verbs which establish this contract of reciprocity (αἰτοῦμαι, οὐ λέξω, 880–1) stand in opposition to the questioning of choral activity; an end to choral activity is envisaged only if impiety triumphs and justice is scorned.[19]

---

[18] Note that if Creon addresses the choros when they finish singing as citizens (513), at the end of his speech he hails (σοῦ, 522) the *koruphaios* alone, who then takes on the ignorance which the choros has professed (οὐκ οἶδα, 530). But subsequently, in a speech which is generally attributed to the choros because of its melic form, the speaker uses the *I* form (691–2), although in a final speech, which because of its iambic form is supposed to belong to the *koruphaios*, it is the *we* form that is used!

[19] On this famous passage see Burton (1980) 160–9, Segal (1981) 25–6 and Henrichs (1994/5) 65–73. The controversial question of the relation of this stasimon to the action has recently been treated by Sidwell (1992).

The development of the second antistrophe of this choral song confirms that the vocal acts of the choros correspond to an action undertaken in the context of cult rendered to gods. Here it is a case of cultic honours for Apollo at Delphi or in his Phocian sanctuary at Abai or for Zeus at Olympia. In this way the spatial perspective of the choros is no longer Theban or Athenian but acquires a panhellenic dimension. This enlarged spatial point of view means that the choral voice is placed between the enunciative authority of the actor taking part in a fictional drama, and the social position of the actual public. But the end of the choral ode brings us to Thebes: to cast doubt upon the oracles given to Laios is to contest both Zeus' power and the honours due to Apollo. The threat of stopping dancing at a choros is simply a response to the failing of the divine (ἔρρει δὲ τὰ θεῖα, 910). It has a direct impact upon the course of the dramatic action, since Jocasta has scarcely heard this choral song before she speaks out (ἱκέτις ἀφῖγμαι, 920) in prayer to Apollo, asking him, on behalf of the community (ἡμῖν, 921), for deliverance. She has no more doubts about the power of the god, even if she carries on speaking ironically about the oracles of the gods (μαντεύματα, 945–7, 952–3).

It is hardly a surprising thing to claim, that the choros sees its songs and dances, in a self-referential way, as cultic acts. It is sufficient to recall that in classical Greece choral activity was one of the four fundamental elements that made up every festival for a divinity.[20] As Henrichs, whose analysis I repeat here, has well demonstrated, the interpreters of the second stasimon of *Oedipus the King* have long been divided between those who think that it is only within their role in a drama that choros members can question their choral activity, and those who unmask the same choros members to identify them as Athenian citizens refusing to serve in a choral group from this point on. However the performative role of the self-referential voice of the masked choros members allows affirmation that 'as a performer of ritual dance, the choros exists simultaneously inside the dramatic realm of the play and outside of it in the political and cultic realm of the here and now'.[21] Seen against the dramatic action unfolding in Thebes in response to Jocasta's doubt, the choros's confidence raises questions for the spectators who are themselves worshipping the god of tragic music. The choral voice of the group of actors engaged in the (intra-discursive) fic-

---

[20] See Calame (1992).
[21] For the contrasting positions see Bain (1975) and Stinton (1990) 253 n. 45 (maintaining that the reference is internal) against Dodds (1996) (who maintains that it is external). Henrichs (1994/5) 65–71 gives an exhaustive discussion of the problem. Note also Bollack (1990) III. 581–4, and Hölscher's important contribution (1975).

Performative aspects of the choral voice

tion played out between the stage and the *orchēstra* invites the (extra-discursive) spectators to take on the position of the *I/we* of the choros, which corresponds to the performative dimension of the mimetic actor. The Dionysiac context clearly lends itself to this sort of interrogation which by means of cultic acts involves the relations of the actors as well as the spectators with the gods.

The way the fictional action of the drama slips into the extra-discursive situation is particularly clear in the changing verbal register of the second strophe and antistrophe of this same second stasimon. Because of the invocation to Zeus to divert the threat weighing down the oracles given by Apollo, which closes the stasimon, echoing the evocation of 'father Olympos' (867), the deictics (ἐν τοῖσδε, τοιαίδε (πράξεις) and τάδε, 892, 895, 900) seem to relate the impious practices to which they refer to the practices which the spectators have before their eyes. But by employing generalizing forms (τις, τίς ἀνήρ and πᾶσι βροτοῖς, 882, 892, 901) the denunciation by the choros takes on a gnomic function, and its general validity is underlined by its referring outside the text, as I have mentioned, to the panhellenic sanctuaries of Delphi and Olympia. By this slippage the performative voice of the choros takes on a double reference, while also acquiring a kind of hermeneutic dimension. Such a repeated use of the deictic *hode* can refer both within and outside the discourse.[22] The effect of having the issue of trust raised by fictional circumstances which, through the use of deictics, are given a general force and made to apply outside the text, is to make the ideal spectator give voice to the performative utterances of the choros – a virtual spectator with whom the real spectators can identify. As for the author's role, in principle attached to the hermeneutic voice of the choros, it is appropriate to defer discussion of that for a while.

It has often been noted that the third choral ode in *Oedipus the King* contrasts with and is complementary to the second stasimon. It is complementary in as far as the same mountain themes are taken up again, but it contrasts in as far as, like Oedipus after his exchange with Jocasta and the messenger from Corinth, the choros would be making a grave mistake about the true identity of the king of Thebes. Although sensible, the self-referential identification of the choros with the figure of the prophet would place the members of the choros in a position which contradicts their previous attribution of true knowledge to the gods

---

[22] On an analogous play between the situation constructed in the text and the actual situation of communication in the *Works and Days* see the suggestions and references in Pucci (1996) and Calame (1996b). The frequent movement from the local to the universal in classical tragedy is discussed by Segal (1995b).

alone. The heavy tragic irony of Oedipus' reassuring words would be developed in the song of a choros which, mistaken in its faith in Oedipus, would substitute a flight to an idyllic countryside, which will prove fatal, for its ignorance of the real fate of the hero.[23]

In fact by invoking not Olympos but Kithairon the choros once more places itself in the perspective of the fictional action. It takes on their performative voice to promise the Theban mountain a choral hymn. Kithairon is presented as the father, nurse and mother of Oedipus at the same time. Described in a series of future forms as a choral dance taken on by the speaker (χορεύεσθαι πρὸς ἡμῶν, 1094), the ode addressed to Kithairon is set at the full moon of the next day. By this delay, ironically or not, the choros displays a remarkable lucidity since they anticipate the desire which Oedipus expresses after his identity has been revealed and he has blinded himself: to leave the town of his ancestors and live on the Kithairon that is 'my Kithairon, the mountain that my mother and father, alive, designated as my tomb' (1452-3). From this point on, by their clairvoyance, the future odes of the choros cannot fail to please Phoibos, who is invoked by the ritual cry introducing the paean (1096). Taking up the mountain associations suggested by the invocation of Kithairon, the choral evocation of the putative parents of Oedipus associates Pan, Loxias, Hermes, even Dionysos himself with the Nymphs who frolic in the mountain valleys (1098-109). The third stasimon, with its central invocation of Apollo, brings Oedipus, who has just declared himself 'child of fortune' (1080), the response of a perceptive prophet: after the destructive revelation of his identity under Apollo's seal of knowledge, Oedipus will neither be able nor wish to be anything other than the son of Kithairon.[24] It should not be forgotten that this short third stasimon comes at the point of transition to the reversal that the information given by the old slave of Laios will provoke. In their hymn to Kithairon the *choreutai* draw us by means of their cultic speech act into the domain complementary to rite, the domain of myth. A myth which, for all that it is itself a fiction centred in this case on a space exterior but related to the plot of the drama, is quickly shown to be cruelly effective.

From the point of view adopted here the fourth stasimon calls for two comments. Sung at the very moment when Oedipus becomes

---

[23] See Sansone (1975) of the supposed tragic irony of this stasimon, along with commentaries by Bollack (1990) III. 698-723, Henrichs (1994/5) 71-3, and Segal (1995a) 190-4. Pucci (1992) 128-32, on the other hand, insists that the choros recognizes the semi-divine origin of Oedipus.
[24] The problem of Oedipus' identity is taken up by Pucci (1992) 78-89. See also Ahl (1991a) 145-52.

aware of his real identity and consequently of his double crime, this ode is essentially carried by the hermeneutic function of the choral voice. On the one side the double interjection that frames it, addressed at the beginning to the generations of men and at the end to the son of Laios (1186, 1216) only serves to underline in a performative way the validity for all mortals of Oedipus' destiny, made into an *exemplum* (παράδειγμα, 1193). By moving from *you* (pl.) refering to mortals (ὑμᾶς, 1187) to *you* (sing.) of the 'unhappy Oedipus' the choros stress the performative dimension of their negative judgement (οὐδὲν μακαρίζω, 1195) and also of their groanings (ὀδύρομαι, 1218). The reference within the discourse to the fate of the man whom the *choreutai* call 'my king' (1201-2) is thus included in the reference outside the discourse to the brusque reversal of fortune which threatens all men. Among mortals susceptible to experience the *metabolē* from happiness to unhappiness which Aristotle defines as proper to the good tragic plot, citing precisely the example of Oedipus, there are also the spectators newly constituted as an ideal audience which refers back also to the actual public.[25] Such is the double reference of the pronoun *you* (ὑμᾶς) in the address at the opening of the choral ode. On the other hand, at the end of its last ode the choros shows that it follows the movement of this abrupt reversal of fortune as it anticipates, by the expression which it uses to designate its own unhappiness, Oedipus' self-blinding (1219-21). In this context we find the invocation of Zeus alone, the god who rules over men's destiny. In the face of Zeus even the person who has been able to outsmart the prophetic voice of the sphinx must bend (1196-201).[26]

But the role of the choros does not finish with the fourth stasimon. The messenger who announces Jocasta's suicide makes his address precisely to the whole choros. When he asks that all should listen and hear (ἀκούσεσθε, εἰσόψεσθε, using second person plural and future, 1224), all 'the honoured of this earth' (1223) reply (cf. the form ᾔδειμεν in 1232), rather than the *koruphaios* alone. Similarly at the beginning of the second *kommos* it is the choros which sings in anapaests in reaction to the spectacle of Oedipus blinded (ὦ δεινὸν ἰδεῖν πάθος, 1297).[27] And

[25] Aristotle *Poetics* 1431a 13-15, 1453a 7-22. On Aristotle's idea of tragic reversal see Dupont-Roc and Lallot (1980) 215-16, 238-49.
[26] Segal (1995a) 194-6 cogently demonstrated that in relation to 'time which sees all' (1213) the appeal to Zeus in this stasimon embodies all that the choros has previously been able to affirm about his power in the face of the instability of the human condition. On the relation between the user of 'I' in this stasimon and the voice of the author see Kaimio (1970) 95-6.
[27] For metrical analysis of this complicated lyric exchange see the commentaries of Dawe (1982) 229, 255, and Bollack (1990) 1.327-8.

when Oedipus in turn employs a lyric rhythm marked by dochmiacs to speak of his pain, he first addresses himself to the *koruphaios*, using the singular (ἰώ φίλος, followed by a series of forms in the second person singular, 1321–6), and then to all the choros members, using the plural (φίλοι, 1339, 1341; ἀπάγετε, 1340, 1341). Beyond the focalization of Oedipus' remarks on a tragic blinding which is the consequence of the paradoxes of his vision, the *koruphaios* insists on the auditory and visual aspect of the drama which unfolds in his hearing and before his eyes (1312 echoing 1224 and 1297): he treats the horrible sight as belonging both to him and to all men (ἐγώ, ἀνθρώποις, 1297–8). This is another reference to an ideal spectator, but one in the position of *I/we* not that of *you* (sing.)/ *you* (pl.), as a strict application of the scheme of communication would lead one to expect.

Finally, after the spectacle of the terrifying reversal of fortune experienced by Oedipus has been narrated by the messenger to the choros and accepted by the choros and the *koruphaios* face to face with the tragic hero, he is, at the end of the tragedy, presented by the choros to the people of Thebes (1254–30). Although some have cast serious doubt on the authenticity of these concluding verses, they place Oedipus' fate within the Delphic maxim on the changeability of human fortune.[28] Such a placing already determined the movement of the first famous strophe of the fourth stasimon in which Oedipus' lot became paradigmatic of the illusory character of the *eudaimonia* experienced by mortals (1186–95). After invoking first the unhappy hero and then Zeus himself, the members of the choros addressed their Delphic commentary to 'generations of mortals' while here, at the end of the play, they address it to the 'people of Thebes'. The words of the choros construct the figure of the ideal spectator through the community in which the dramatic fiction is placed, and the real spectators of the tragedy perhaps become that ideal spectator. But from the point of view of utterance, the figure of the virtual spectator oscillates between the position of *I/we*, in which it is identified with that of the choros, and that of *you* (sing.) / *you* (pl.). In this enlargement of the recipients of its speeches outside the discourse, the choral *I/we* has the opportunity to include the ideal author, the omniscient narrator, in the speaking position. The performative and the hermeneutic voice of the choros are here combined.

---

[28] The authenticity of these final lines of the play is discussed by Dawe (1982) 247, and Bollack (1990) IV.1038–54. For the exceptional change from singular to plural in Oedipus' address to the choros/*koruphaios* after verse 1321 see Kaimio (1970) 227–8, who also discusses the final verses at 171–2.

IV. The female choral odes of the *Hippolytos*: the power of the gods

From Aristotle on it has been said that in Euripides the choros was losing the central role which it plays in Sophokles' tragedies.[29] The tendency attributed to Euripides of making choral interventions simple musical interludes is certainly not to be found in the *Hippolytos*, a play in which not only do the gods and their power play a major role in the plot, but where the members of the choros also intervene at all the crucial moments.

The choros of the *Hippolytos* are young women of good family from Troizen, the little city in which the action takes place. Phaedra calls the 'noble girls of Troizen' (710) in a speech which moves into the singular (ὑμεῖς, 710; ἔλεξας or ἐλέξατε, 715; σύ, 724; ὄμνυμι, in the choros's response, 713); this shifting shows the way the *koruphaios* can speak for the whole choros.[30] However, in the fourth and last stasimon (1267–81), at the moment when Theseus declares, using a performative verb (ἐλέγξω, 1267), that he will give a surprise to his son, whose abrupt change of fortune and imminent death he interprets as just punishment from the divinity (δαιμόνων συμφοραῖς, 1267; terms taken out of the mouth of the *koruphaios*, 1255–6), these wives of citizens address Aphrodite in a brief song. This ode is made up of a single strophe sung and danced in a dochmiac rhythm indicative of strong emotions. The prevailing view has been that this is a hymn to Aphrodite and Eros. In fact this choral ode gives only the first part of a hymn or prayer, the *invocatio*.[31] By this means, the ode gives a definition of the ways in which the goddess of amorous desire intervenes, while at the same time describing the field of her application: undivided sovereignty, thanks to Eros' bewitchment of maddened hearts, over animals, over men and over the gods, at sea as well as on land. The two second-person verbs which frame this ode (σύ ... ἄγεις, 1271–2; κρατύνεις, 1281) have an attributive force which, without question, transforms the performative force of this hymn into a commentary on the dramatic action. In fact, scarcely has the hermeneutic voice of the choros completed the ode than Artemis appears to explain the meaning of the action and

---

[29] See Hose (1990), and the Aristotelian reflections cited in n. 7 opposing Euripides to Sophokles over the συναγωνίζεσθαι of the choros.
[30] For the alternation of singular and plural in an actor's address to the *koruphaios* see Kaimio (1970) 207–8, as well as, on this particular passage, Barrett (1964) 294.
[31] For this stasimon as a hymn see Barrett (1964) 391–3, who also gives a metrical analysis of it. For the structure of the hymn and its relationship to prayer see the references in n. 14.

remove from her servant all moral blame: like Phaedra, Hippolytos is a victim of the will of Kypris. This name, which has sealed the choral ode at both ends in a ring structure (1269, 1281), continues to punctuate Artemis' long intervention (1304, 1327, 1400, 1417). When the choros announces the arrival of Hippolytos in agony on the stage, in an anapaestic rhythm which will run through the hero's words, they show that they understand Phaedra's death, as well as Hippolytos', to be a product of the gods (1346), just as Theseus in what will be his last speech, recognizes the harmful power of the goddess Kypris (1461).[32]

However, this hermeneutic voice, which mixes with the performative voice of the choros to relate the unfolding of the action to the divinities who drive it, can be seen from the very beginning of the play. Indeed it can be seen immediately in the preliminary words of the complementary choros of Hippolytos' followers. These young men enter the stage in a sort of first parados, led by the young hero himself. Through his performative words that engage his followers in singing for Artemis (ἕπεσθε ἀείδοντες, 58) in collective honours (μελόμεσθα, 60), Hippolytos presents himself as the *koruphaios* or *chorēgos* of the group of which he is the head; taking on the identificatory role that usually belongs to the *koruphaios*, Aphrodite sees in this choral group 'the *kōmos* which honours the goddess Artemis with his songs (ὕμνοισιν, 54–6)'. The use of this Pindaric term to designate the choros reminds us that this first song of glorification addressed to Artemis balances the last stasimon addressed to Kypris. A chiasmic structural opposition places this ode after Aphrodite's prologue, while the last choral ode comes immediately before the long explanation given by Artemis at the end of the play.[33]

This opening choral ode, which glorifies Artemis, the daughter of Leto and Zeus, the most beautiful of young girls, is not in every respect a hymn. Although it asks the goddess to 'rejoice' (χαῖρέ μοι, 64, 70), it is but the introduction to the ritual offering presented in performative manner by Hippolytos himself in the following verses (σοὶ τόνδε... στέφανον... φέρω, 73–4). This ode and these cultic actions in honour of Artemis are put in direct contrast with the speech of the old slave

---

[32] Hose (1990) II.128–30 emphasizes the function of this stasimon in relation to the power of Aphrodite. The role plaid by Aphrodite in *Hippolytos* is analysed by Zeitlin (1985); see also Blomquist (1982).

[33] In his commentary Barrett (1964) 167–9 gives several examples of tragedies with secondary choruses, and also stresses that Hippolytos plays the role of leader of the choros formed by his *prospoloi*. Ancient and modern scholars have been uncertain as to the exact composition of this choros: see Diggle (1984) 209 (apparatus to line 61). For the sense and usage of *kōmos* in Pindar see especially Burnett (1989).

(ὡς πρέπει δούλοις, 115) who points to the presence of Kypris and the need that she be recognized (101) before giving her remark a performative turn. In marked opposition to the *neoi* (114) and strong contrast to Hippolytos, who has just personally sent Kypris away (Κύπριν ... ἐγὼ χαίρειν λέγω, 113, with a probable play on the word χαίρειν), the servant adopts the collective *we* form and the performative future in addressing Queen Kypris and her statue in a brief ritual salute (ἡμεῖς δὲ ... προσευξόμεσθα ... δέσποινα Κύπρι, 114–17). After the prologue in which she has herself expressed her anger with Hippolytos and his scorn for her, Aphrodite is continuously present on the stage and in the action, thanks to the ritual words of the choros which, on the other hand, also summons the presence of Artemis.

From this standpoint, the *parodos* itself presents some hesitations (121–75). As if concerned to increase the dramatic tension which drives the plot, the young women of Troizen in this song merely summon Phaedra, whom they treat as a young girl (ὦ κούρα, 141), directly. Asking questions about the malady which consumes the dying queen, they evoke divine powers: Pan, Hekate, the Korybantes, Diktynna – all powers capable of possessing people (ἔνθεος, 141) and making them beside themselves.[34] In using a hermeneutic voice which employs the past interrogative, the *choreutai* avoid any mention of Aphrodite. When they evoke more human causes to explain the trouble gnawing at Phaedra's heart, it is appeal to Artemis that they advise, not to Kypris. The failure of the interpretation given here by the choros is certainly a matter of dramatic tension.

The uncertainty continues in its dialogue with the nurse in which the choros/*koruphaios* presents itself as a collective individual (ὁρῶμεν, 268; ἡμῖν, 269; βουλοίμεθ᾽ ἄν, 270); the nurse replies in similar terms (γυναῖκας, 301). But as soon as Phaedra has revealed her love for Hippolytos the veil over the origin of her malady is lifted: it is Kypris. The nurse first recognizes it when she attributes to the goddess of love a more than divine power (359–61; see also 443–5 which anticipates what the choros will sing in the last stasimon); then it is the turn of the *koruphaios* to realize that what was confused (ἄσημος, 371; cf. 269) is no longer, and that for Phaedra *tuchē* and the will of Kypris are the same thing; finally, in her long speech, Phaedra has not the least hesitation in attributing her own madness to Kypris (397–402), whom she finally invokes in her sovereign power. Indeed, in the dialogue in iambic

---

[34] The relationships between the various divine powers evoked by the choros and the natural world and possession are detailed by Barrett (1964) 189–90. The relations of Hippolytos and Phaedra with the external world are studied by Segal (1965).

trimeters, the nurse as well as Phaedra addresses the *koruphaios* explicitly as the collectivity of women of Troizen (354, 373); and, as for the *chorēgos*, she addresses one of the *choreutai* (ἄιες ὤ, 362), no doubt in a generic manner, in a strophe in dochmiacs, before turning to Phaedra to recognize that the heroine is the victim of a fate wished on her by Aphrodite.[35] The frequency of this kind of address and question from one member of the choros to another in Euripides' tragedies shows that, even if these verses were sung by the *chorēgos* alone, her 'I' (ἔγωγε, 364) refers to the collectivity of the choral group of women of Troizen, in the number of whom Phaedra will end up counting herself (419)!

To recognize the absolute power of a deity is also to invoke it, to call for its presence in a ritual manner. So the *first stasimon* (525-62) responds to the last appeal for help that the nurse addresses to Kypris, before Phaedra herself reports the catastrophe which has struck her (522-3, 565). The first stasimon is an ode which takes the form of a hymn to Eros, evoking the tragic fate known in tradition from Iole and Semele, and asking for protection from the destructive powers of Aphrodite.[36] By pronouncing these performative words in the form of a wish for a favour to themselves (μή μοι ... φανείης, 528), the members of the choros will not prevent the tragic death of Phaedra; just before her suicide the heroine attributes to Kypris the death which the goddess has wanted and announced from the beginning (47-50).

This suicide is described immediately, as soon as it has occurred, at the end of the ode of distress and complaint that forms the *second stasimon* (732-75). The women of Troizen too set the desire for death that seizes Phaedra in relations to the impious love that the goddess Aphrodite has inspired (764-5). At the end of this ode, in a new dialogue with themselves, the members of the choros pose the tragic question *par excellence* (about their own performance!): 'what are we to do?' (τί δρῶμεν; 782, alternating with the first person singular in 788).[37]

The reply given to the fundamental question of the tragic hero, when

---

[35] The form of this choral intervention, in lyric response with Phaedra who in her turn complains of her lot and wonders which divinity to turn to (668-79), is discussed by Barrett (1964) 224-6, who attributes it to the *koruphaios*, as Kaimio (1970) 140 also hesitatingly proposes with many examples of consultations within a choros.

[36] For a brief commentary on the dramatic function of this choral ode and for thorough bibliographical references see Calame (1996d) 13-16, 167-8. See also Hose (1990) II.156-9, and Cerbo (1993).

[37] The division and attribution of replies in this exchange in iambic trimeters which follows the second stasimon are far from certain: see Barrett (1964) 311-13. Kaimio (1970) 110-11 gives other examples of passages where replies were spoken by different choros members.

posed by the members of the choros, can only be choral; a short song of lament over Phaedra's lot (811–16), an expression of intense fear as they glimpse the further trouble which is to come with the curse uttered by Theseus against his son (φρίσσω, 855, cf. 881), and above all a song full of pathos addressed to the power of the gods. This short ode announces the *third stasimon* (1102–50). There has been a long controversy about its beginning because the double evocation of the troubles which the gods visit upon men is taken on in its first part by a male speaker (κεύθων, 1105; λεύσσων, 1106), and in its second development by feminine forms (μοι εὐξαμένα, 1111; μεταβαλλομένα, 1117).

Even if ancient commentators attribute the whole ode to the main choros formed by the women of Troizen, the most elegant solution is to divide the first and second pairs of strophe and antistrophe between the masculine choros of followers of Hippolytos and the female choros of women of Troizen. To those who point out the frequent use in Greek of masculine participles by female speakers, I would note that the division is too systematic to be random. To the commentator who shows that in all other cases known to us where the secondary choros alternates with the principal choros the ode of the first is explicitly announced, I respond that here the introduction is made by Hippolytos when, in the immediately preceding verses, he addresses his companions, asks them to follow him (προείπαθ' ἡμᾶς καὶ προπέμψατε, 1099), and shows what sort of people they are – young men of the same age (νέοι ... ὁμήλικες, 1098); they therefore have the choral status which the women of Troizen seem to recognize in them when they evoke their intervention at the moment of Phaedra's suicide (πρόσπολοι νεανίαι, 784). As for the γάρ (1120) which appears hardly, as taken strictly it should, to indicate a causal relationship between the second and the first strophe, the best explanation would seem to be that the hope disappointed by the sight (λεύσσων or λεύσσω according to the manuscripts, 1121) is just a particular case of the sight (λεύσσω, 1107) of the chance of human destiny.[38] It is worth adding that the second

---

[38] The problem did not escape the scholiast (on 1102: II.117 Schwartz) who refers the use of masculine forms to the voice of the poet! Cf. also Poll. 4.111. Kühner and Gerth (1989) 83–4 give examples of the use of masculine forms in a generalizing way to designate women, and in tragedy of participial forms in the masculine as attributes of women speaking of themselves in the first person plural; verses 1103–10 (pronounced by the choros in the singular and not by the 'Chorführerin') would thus constitute an exception. The objections to dividing the stasimon between two choruses, which I have tried to deal with briefly here, are gone into in detail and with full references by Barrett (1964) 365–9, to which add Hose (1990) II.16, and Sommerstein (1988) 23–41. For the emotive aspect of the voice of the choros in these verses, in reaction to events of the drama, see Kaimio (1970) 68–9.

strophe, whose speaker is masculine, insists on the masculine qualities of Hippolytos as hunter, while the second antistrophe, which can be attributed to the women of Troizen, introduces us to the feminine world of poetry inspired by the Muse and of the young girls competing to be the young wife of the hero.

With the evocation of the misfortune which, with the lot of her son, strikes also Hippolytos' mother, and with the critical question posed at last to the protectors of the conjugal pair, the Charites, who drive the hero from his dwelling, the feminine perspective finally pervades the epode of this third stasimon (1142–50). That perspective takes a performative turn in the address to the Graces which is certainly that of the married women who make up the choros of Troizenian friends of Phaedra; this in contrast to the unmarried young companions and followers of Hippolytos. However that may be, dividing the lines of the third stasimon between male and female choruses according to the criterion of the gendering of their perspective has an enormous advantage: in an ode which is above all a gnomic commentary on the fragility of human happiness in the face of the all-powerful gods, it reserves the performative interventions to the choros of women – the expression of a wish that the prayer to *moira* be answered (1111–13) and the final appeal to the Charites who are partly bound up with Aphrodite, particularly in marriage (1148–50).[39]

Kypris dominates the action of *Hippolytos*, as she herself declares when she presents herself in the first lines of the prologue, saying that she reigns over mortals and over heaven (1–2). The recognition of the power of Aphrodite is made complete in the *fourth stasimon* (1267–81). As has been seen, without constituting a prayer, it uses the form of a hymn to define the field and manner of action of the goddess. Only young wives can fully experience the power of a divinity that intervenes with most force at the moment of consummation of marriage. Undoubtedly the geographical position of the members of the choros on 'this extremity (τόδ' ἔσχατον, 373, cf. 1159) of the land of Pelops' that is Troizen, contributes to the easy demonstration of the destructive consequences for animals, humans and gods of this discretionary divine power. But it will be left to Theseus, the founding king of Athens, both to bring the action back to the land of the city of the

---

[39] On the relations of the Charites with Aphrodite see, for example, *Kypr.* frr. 4 and 5 Bernabé, with the references which I have given in Calame (1996d) 45–6, 180–3. Several readers of this stasimon have wrongly imagined that the epode was sung by a group of unmarried girls, cf. Barrett (1964) 375–6. On the hermeneutic function of this ode as a whole see Hose (1990) II.159–62.

spectators and, in a final address to Kypris, to denounce the evils she has brought about (1459–61).[40]

Once it has struck the one who tried to ignore it, the pain is shared by all citizens. Tears flow in torrents. The grief is even deeper, indeed, when the narrative concerns the hero (1462–6). Whether or not the anapaests which the choros deliver to conclude the play are genuine, they only generalize the lesson that has been formulated in the third stasimon by directing the grief provoked by the action that has just been seen upon the community of citizens.[41] Is this to say that by way of these verses, in this passage from fictional dramatic action to a general situation with extra-discursive significance, the choros of the *Hippolytos* becomes an ideal spectator with links to the real spectator? This is a complex question. Whether it turns itself into a giver of lessons or whether it simply appears as a warner of the implacable power of a divinity, the choros could also be the spokesman for the virtual author bearing some relation to the biographical author, whose choice of a choros of women does not fit with the accusation of misogyny made against him since antiquity ...[42] What is more, the performative and ritual dimension of the voice of a choros aware of the effects of the power of the gods on the hazards of human life and its changes in fortune adds to its hermeneutic aspect. Performative and ritual, the choral voice in a way gets bound up with the prematrimonial ritual foreseen by Artemis after Hippolytos' heroic death. The institution and the performance of this rite by mature girls is a way of honouring Hippolytos in compensation for the evils he has suffered (1423–30). As they consecrate their hair to Hippolytos at the moment of marriage the girls of Troizen are called upon to keep his memory by laments; but these threnodies evoke the odes of the *choreutai* themselves.[43] With

---

[40] Although its formulation is contested, 1459 can refer only to Athens: cf. Barrett (1964) 416–17, and on the problem posed by the mention of Athens in the third stasimon (1123) Barrett (1964) 373–4, and Diggle (1984) 256 and 271. Segal (1988) 110–35 discusses the way in which the last scene of the tragedy transforms private affliction into public spectacle.

[41] Barrett (1964) 417–18 discusses the authenticity of the final anapaests. The general problem posed by the extra-discursive reference and the authenticity issue of the final lines of classical tragedies is well raised by Roberts (1987). The relations between the world of the play and the world of the theatre in *Hippolytos* has been studied by Easterling (1991).

[42] On this see particularly March (1990). On the way the audience can perceive the moral value of the action played on the stage, see Sourvinou-Inwood (1997) 175–84.

[43] Taking up the reflections of Pucci (1977) on the rhetorical resolution of the violence at the end of *Hippolytos* and of Foley (1985) 30–56 on the saving effects of ritual in Euripidean tragedy, Goff (1990) 105–29 has shown how the prematrimonial rite instituted

Hippolytos, the young man who acts like a young girl, the ritual aimed at the young women of Troizen sanctions the move into the matrimonial state which the hero refused. With Phaedra, the ritual odes of the adult women of Troizen establish the power of Aphrodite within the very institution of marriage. This curious coincidence, by aetiological play, between ritual heroization of the protagonist of the play and the ritual significance of the odes of the choros can bring us to some provisional conclusions.

v. **The choral odes of tragedy as civic performances**

One more moment from *Hippolytos* will help to draw this paper to a conclusion. From the point of view of the significance of the words of the choros, and despite the uncertainty in establishing the precise text in the two key passages, it is surprising to have the choros and then Theseus himself connect the young hero victim of Aphrodite with the territory of Athens (1121-5, 1459-60); Phaedra had insisted on the fact that the tragic action was happening on the liminal Peloponnesian territory of Troizen.[44] The solution to this apparent contradiction can be found in the messenger speech. The messenger suggests that Hippolytos' suffering will affect Theseus, whom he addresses, and also the citizens who live in the marginal territory of Troizen and those who reside in the city of Athens (1157-9). In saying this, the messenger not only establishes the relationship henceforward expected between the two cities, but, because the citizens of Athens correspond with the real audience of the play, he makes a reference to Athens which can be equally understood as extra-discursive. This double reference becomes broader still when, in their last ode, the choros says that the mourning provoked by the tragedy is that 'of all the citizens' (1462). Directed here to the public, this complex referential process recalls that which marks the spatial position of the forms *I* and *we* in Pindar, divided between the city of the poet and the city in which the choral celebration of the addressee of the ode takes place.

Similarly, the *you* (sing.) / *you* (pl.) that the *I/we* of the choros/ *koruphaios* addresses in the tragedies chosen here corresponds to a multiple position. It is occupied by the protagonists in the action, for whom the choros often reserves a hermeneutic voice of doubled emotion, by the gods evoked, usually ritually, by a voice that is naturally

to honour the memory of the hero took the place of the ritual of tragic representation for the benefit of the public and so of the civic community.

[44] On the difficulties of establishing the text of these passages see Barrett (1964) and Diggle (1984) *ad locc.* (see note 40).

performative, and by men in general – but never, directly, the spectators. Spectators are called in only in a mediated way by some general summonses to citizens or mortals to see or feel as the choros does; they appear only as ideal spectators or auditors inscribed in the virtual addressee for whom Oedipus, like Hippolytos a fictional figure, is offered as a *paradeigma*.

But the discretion in direct communication the choros demonstrates in no way prevents the real spectator from acting and reacting effectively in the here and now of the dramatic representation. That representation is itself the *mousikos agōn* of a long festival made up of different cult honours given to Dionysos by the city. Consequently, apart from a few generally indirect addresses, the actual spectator, because of his situation in the theatre in relationship to members of the choros, seems above all invited to assume the position of the choral *I/we*; that position is the position of a performer who is engaged in *mimēsis* and therefore 'virtual'. This process of identification, in which the public is called to address itself to the actors or to the gods with the thoughts and feelings of the choros, is rendered the more probable by the fact that the spectators in classical Athens had themselves received a musical education based essentially on choral activity. By way of the *I/we* of the choral speaker in tragedy, the spectators who take part in a festivity in honour of Dionysos in the theatre in some way delegate part of their choral competence and authority to the choros which is at the heart of the dramatic representation.[45] By means of the performative dimension of the choral odes, and in combination with their emotive component, the public is undoubtedly invited to *sunagōnizesthai* with the dramatic action presented to it. Although on the level of utterance the real public is absent from the *you* (sing.) / *you* (pl.) position (addressee/listener), it places itself in the position of the *I/we* of the choros (speaker/ narrator).

The effect of the performative side of the choral voice is to confer a reality upon the dramatic fiction. As performances with a cultic aspect, the odes of the choros of tragedy place the *muthos* acted in the theatre of Dionysos into the field of ritual with all its pragmatic function and social and ethical significance.[46] In these conditions, the *I/we* of the choral performance of tragedy, with its ritual and collective components, is

---

[45] Without bringing any new perspective on the question of musical and choral education, Lonsdale (1993) 44–75 offers a longer treatment of this question, but one which fails to mention the still fundamental work of Marrou (1964) 69–81. Note also Bacon (1994/5).

[46] On the logic which links 'myth' and 'ritual' to produce social effects see my suggestions in Calame (1996c) 162–77. For tragedy and its critical mediation between myth and ritual see for example Goldhill (1986) 265–86.

even more suitable for welcoming into the text the extra-discursive reality of the civic community assembled in the theatre-sanctuary to give cultic worship to Dionysos. It is in this sense of delegating ritual competence and partially identifying the spectator with the action taking place on the stage, through the medium of the play of masked drama, that the numerous overlaps, by this time of a rather refined kind, between the cult acts in tragedy and tragedy as cult act are to be understood.[47]

But does the choral *I/we* of tragedy, particularly when it is borne by a hermeneutic voice which describes and comments on the stage action, revealing aspects that cannot be seen, not refer back above all to the ideal author, the omniscient narrator? And beyond this discursive figure, does this *I/we* of the choros not hide the real author whose name can no longer appear in the dramatic text in the form of the *sphragis* familiar in archaic poetry? In relation to the famous verses of Aristophanes on the essentially educative function granted to contemporary tragedy, several pieces of evidence attribute to the earlier tragic poets, such as Phrynichos or Aeschylus, the function later taken on by the citizen *khorodidaskalos*.[48] The realization of the tragic performance seems therefore to be centred on the preparation of the choros formed from young citizens. From contemporary texts onwards, this preparation is referred to as *didaskein*, that is as teaching.[49] If the real author does address the public, he does it, as Herodotos says of Phrynichos, through the *poiein*, the poetic creation, and the *didaskein*, the training of the choros. But there is a certain incoherence in declaring that in consequence the poet and his public are both, through the figures of virtual author and virtual spectator, in a position to become the *I/we* of the choros. The traditional scheme of communication, as reformulated at the beginning of this paper, puts these two figures in opposition; but

---

[47] From Burkert (1966) to Seaford (1994) 368–405 many studies have examined the relationship between the rituals played out in tragedy and cult. See the review of Easterling (1988a).

[48] See notably Aristophanes *Frogs* 1009–39 and 1500–3, with the references given by Dover (1993) 15–16. Tragic poets as dancers: Plutarch *Quaestiones Convivales* 732f (= Phryn. 3 T 13 Snell), and Athenaios 1, 21af (= Aeschylus T 103 Radt) with Aristophanes fr. 696 Kassel-Austin, where Aeschylus says of himself that he has created the choreographic moves for his tragic choruses. Other testimonies pointing in the same direction in Pickard-Cambridge (1968) 90–1, 291, 303–4.

[49] Hdt. 6.21.2 (= Phrynichos 3 T 2 Snell), Aristophanes *Frogs* 1026 (= Aeschylus T 120, 1026 Radt (about the *Persai*)), Plato *Protagoras* 327d, etc. The word διδάσκειν is employed in the same sense in the *Didaskaliai*! See Herington (1985) 24–5, 87–8, 183–4. With regard to the tragic choros, Winkler (1990b) has even hypothesized that the choral roles in classical tragedy were taken on by a group of ephebes. The role of the choros in poetic διδάσκειν has recently been redefined by Nagy (1996) 39–58.

in the utterance of the choral texts of tragedy they seem, on the contrary, to get superimposed. On the other hand, it should be added that the choros cannot be entirely identified either with the ideal author or with the virtual and then real audience. Quite often the *choreutai* prove to know less about the action played out than the spectators, not to mention the omniscient narrator, would know. This is most probably a matter of dramatic tension and mimesis to behold through the play.[50]

It is important to remind oneself here that, in melic choral poetry, the position of the speaker/narrator is as often taken on by the group of *choreutai* who are in fact performing the poem as by its 'author'. This draws attention to the fact that in choral poems of the archaic and classical period the figure of the ideal author is mirrored on the extra-discursive level in a biographical author and an actual performer. This real 'author' has for the choros the same function of master of music that he has in tragedy – his authority is choral and didactic. Thus the *I/we* of choral odes in classical drama, in its appeals to the protagonists of the action, to the gods, or to men of whom the spectators make themselves part, carries and assumes, in the performance of the ode here and now, both the voice of the real audience (with its ritual role), and that of the biographical poet (with his educative function). In melic poetry, the use of the language of community allows, for example, a female choral group to express itself in a song composed by a male poet; it explains how, notwithstanding differences of social status and of gender, the public can take on the words of the choros, not only as the 'you' but above all as 'I'.

The particular features of choral performance, both melic and tragic, make it necessary to abandon the scheme of communication offered earlier and substitute that shown in diagram 2.

The construction in the text of a virtual spectator, who blends into the figure of the ideal author by way of the virtual performer, facilitates the actual public coming to occupy the position of the choral speaker. In particular the polymorphism of the collective choral voice serves to explain how the choros and the audience can react in the face of protagonists who occupy a different space and time, and engage in heroic action, as do those of dramatized fictitious legends. The interventions of the tragic *choreutai* engage in a real polyphony, in the Bakhtinian meaning of the word. Masked productions and, more generally, the context of the cult in honour of Dionysos, have the effect of referring back to the public as spectator, as 'you', the drama in which it is invited

---

[50] For the concept of *mimēsis* conceived as 'imitating in the sense of a process, an activity', see Else (1986) 104.

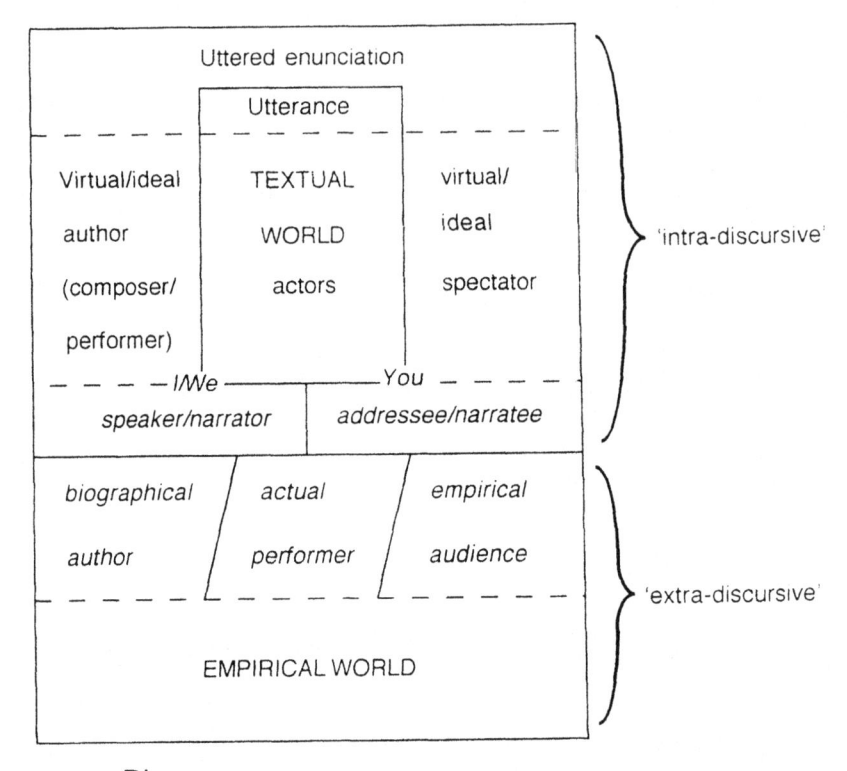

```
┌─────────────────────────────────────────┐  ⎫
│         Uttered enunciation             │  ⎪
│      ┌──────────────────┐               │  ⎪
│      │    Utterance     │               │  ⎪
│──────┼──────────────────┼───────────    │  ⎪
│ Virtual/ideal │ TEXTUAL │  virtual/     │  ⎪
│               │         │               │  ⎬ 'intra-discursive'
│ author        │  WORLD  │  ideal        │  ⎪
│               │         │               │  ⎪
│ (composer/    │  actors │  spectator    │  ⎪
│               │         │               │  ⎪
│ performer)    │         │               │  ⎪
│ ─ ─ ─ ─ ─I/We─┴─────You─┴─ ─ ─ ─ ─      │  ⎭
│   speaker/narrator   addressee/narratee │
│                                         │  ⎫
│ biographical │ actual   │ empirical     │  ⎪
│              │          │               │  ⎪
│ author       │ performer│ audience      │  ⎬ 'extra-discursive'
│─ ─ ─ ─ ─ ─ ─ ┴─ ─ ─ ─ ─ ┴ ─ ─ ─ ─ ─ ─   │  ⎪
│                                         │  ⎪
│          EMPIRICAL WORLD                │  ⎭
└─────────────────────────────────────────┘
```

Diagram 2

to take part as choral actor, as 'we', notwithstanding distinctions of social status and gender.

From the emotional point of view, this procedure of reflexive distancing of proximity, thanks to the cult rendered to Dionysos, is able to account for the phenomenon of *katharsis*, which has been so much discussed: the emotions ritually expressed by the choros have an essential part in this. They could be 'purified' by the fact that they are in some way delegated from the audience and assumed by the masked *choreutai*. The affective collaboration which is required of the public in its participation in the action through the intermediary of the choros, leads to the abandonment of the idea of 'communication' and the substitution of the larger notion of 'intersubjectivity' recently proposed to define the relationship of choros and actors in *Hippolytos* itself. 'Interaction' would be here the key concept.[51]

---

[51] Cf. Zeitlin (1985) 235–6 and 250 n. 65. The concept is extended to 'the sacred space of the Athenian State Theater' by Nagy (1994/5).

If, with Charles Segal, one sees the choral odes of tragedy as representing hypotheses which clarify the sense of the dramatic action, one must add that these hypotheses, borne by the hermeneutic voice of the choral group, generally correspond to ritual speech acts.[52] With its double value, taken up from the *I/we* of melic poetry and reinforced by the occasional division between *koruphaios* and choral group, the position of the speaker of choral odes in tragedy lends itself to being occupied either by the author as the master of song or by the spectators performing their cult act in the theatre of Dionysos. Both are summoned to take part in the collective masked mimetic voice of the *I/we* of the choros to give the 'mythic' action played out on the stage a ritual and performative interpretation, a participant interpretation with a real social effect. Thanks to the performative voice of the choros as virtual performer, thanks to this performative dimension which lines up the hermeneutic and the affective dimensions of the tragic choral songs, the actual audience is called on not to adopt the position simply of ideal listener, as the classic scheme of communication would lead one to expect, but to be active at the side of the virtual author. By the device of the ritual choral performance and of the virtual positions that it constructs, the tragic poet, in conformity with the position assumed by Aeschylus, Sophokles and Euripides at Athens, is indeed the educator of the Athenian civic community, itself 'in performance'.

Translated by Robin Osborne

---

[52] Segal (1995a) 196-8. Note in this connection the carefully nuanced remarks of Kranz (1933) 220-3, who concludes 'So [the choros] is very far from being another "Character".' See also Kaimio (1970) 92-103, who develops Kranz's hypothesis that the voice of the poet is particularly clear in the final strophe of stasima, in judgements formulated in the first person singular.

6 Actors and voices: reading between the lines in Aeschines and Demosthenes [1]

Pat Easterling

Καὶ νὴ τοὺς θεοὺς τοὺς Ὀλυμπίους, ὧν ἐγὼ πυνθάνομαι Δημοσθένην λέξειν, ἐφ' ὧι νυνὶ μέλλω λέγειν ἄξιον καὶ μάλιστ' ἀγανάκτειν. ἀφομοιοῖ γάρ μου τὴν φύσιν ταῖς Σειρῆσιν. καὶ γὰρ ὑπ' ἐκείνων οὐ κηλεῖσθαί φησι τοὺς ἀκροωμένους ἀλλ' ἀπόλλυσθαι, διόπερ οὐδ' εὐδοκιμεῖν τὴν τῶν Σειρήνων μουσικήν. καὶ δὴ καὶ τὴν ἐμπειρίαν καὶ τὴν φύσιν μου γεγενῆσθαι ἐπὶ βλάβηι τῶν ἀκουόντων. Aeschines 3.228

Now I most emphatically declare that there is not a single item among the claims which I gather Demosthenes intends to make which annoys me more than this. He draws a comparison between my character and that of the Sirens, who brought destruction, he says, [not enchantment] to their hearers, which is the reason for the discredit which attaches to the music of the Sirens. In the same way, according to him, my oratorical flow acted to the detriment of my audience. Trans. Saunders (1975)

There is no trace of this comparison in the published version of Demosthenes' response to Aeschines in the dispute over the crown (18); for whatever reason Demosthenes decided not to use it – or maybe it was Aeschines' invention in the first place.[2] For my purposes ownership is not the most important point: either way, the music of the Sirens is a memorable image for the voice of the actor/orator, and its associations – glamour, power, danger – are relevant to the two related questions that I attempt to deal with in this paper, namely what is the logic of Demosthenes' critique of Aeschines *qua* performer, and how far can this be related to contemporary perceptions of actors in public life.

There are two relevant sets of speeches: Demosthenes 19 and Aeschines 2, which deal with the second Athenian delegation to Philip (346; the case was heard in 343), and Aeschines 3 and Demosthenes

---

[1] Several other contributions to the Colloquium have helped me re-model this paper for publication, especially those by Andrew Ford and Jon Hesk. Simon Goldhill's unpublished discussion of 'the contest of voice' in Aeschines and Demosthenes has been particularly relevant to my topic and I am glad to have access to it.
I am grateful, too, to the anonymous readers for some points of detail.

[2] Cf. 19.196–8 and Aeschines 2.153–7 (below, pp. 162–3 for a comparable (though more elaborate) mis-match. In general see Wankel (1976) 51 with n. 123.

18, *On the crown*, delivered in 330. In the case on the embassy, Demosthenes was prosecutor and Aeschines was acquitted by a very narrow margin, having also been successful the previous year in his prosecution of Demosthenes' associate Timarchus; although the later dispute was formally a case made by Aeschines against Ctesiphon for proposing the award of a crown to Demosthenes, and Demosthenes was speaking in defence of Ctesiphon, no one was in any doubt that this was a trial of strength between the two rivals.[3] This time Aeschines lost, and after his defeat he left Athens for good. In neither case should we expect the choice of detail, however irrelevant it may seem, to be in any way casual or trivial: everything suggests that it should be taken as part of a calculated and artful design, and the way the speakers represent each other's performance must have implications for the way they want their own to be perceived.

The express purpose of Demosthenes' attack on Aeschines in both speeches is to show that while presenting himself as an Athenian patriot he has betrayed the city by taking bribes from Philip, a pattern of behaviour which Demosthenes traces back to the time of the delegation in 346. His startlingly abusive account of Aeschines' life story in 18 is directed towards a single main goal, the demonstration of Aeschines' venality: if his upbringing and all his early experience can be shown to have prepared him to be a paid subordinate, a *misthōtos*, then he is no fit person to be a leading politician, since he could be corrupted by Philip, even when the safety of Athens itself was at issue.[4] So there is a clear rhetorical point in suggesting that Aeschines has had a series of demeaning jobs as his only training in statesmanship: assistant in the schoolroom where his father worked,[5] attendant at the low-grade orgiastic ceremonies presided over by his mother,[6] clerk to minor magistrates,[7] member of an undistinguished acting troupe that toured the deme festivals.[8] Of course Demosthenes finds plenty of ways of making

---

[3] As Aeschines points our (3.56), the court was packed: 'I give you your answer, Demosthenes, before the members of the jury, before other Athenian citizens in the circle of the court, and before other Greeks, who are making a point of listening to this case – I observe that their numbers are not small, in fact greater than anyone can remember in a public case...' Cf. Dyck (1985) 42. On the political context see Cawkwell (1969); Ryder (1975).

[4] Cf.18.131, 262, 284; 19.200, 249 for emphasis on Aeschines as a 'hireling'; Dyck (1985) 45. The whole of 18 257–65, contrasting the two speakers' life-stories, illustrates the strategy well.

[5] 19.249, 281; 18.129, 258.

[6] 19.199, 249; 18.259–60. There may be a glancing reference to mysteries at 18.122 (καὶ βοᾶις ῥητὰ καὶ ἄρρητ' ὀνομάζων).

[7] 19.70, 95, 200, 249, 314; 18.127, 209, 261.

[8] 19.200, 246–50, 255, 337–40; 18.127, 129, 139, 180, 209, 242, 259–65, 267, 313.

these activities sound degrading or ludicrous and uses a rich variety of abusive words to ridicule Aeschines' occupations[9] (*grammatokuphos* 'hunched over your accounts' (18.209), *iambeiophagos* 'devourer of iambic verses' (18.139),[10] *autotragikos pithēkos* 'perfect tragic ape' (18.242); but in both speeches there may be a sub-text, informed by a more complex strategy and conveying a different message.

It is interesting that all but the schoolroom story are linked through the importance attached to Aeschines' voice. When Aeschines helped his mother at her cult gatherings it was he who 'read the books aloud' while she performed the ritual 18.259; cf. 19.199) and prided himself on giving the 'loudest cry ever heard in the rite'.[11] 'I can well believe it', says Demosthenes ironically, 'with a penetrating voice like his, it must have been a super-resonant (*huperlampron*) ritual cry' (18.259-60). And when he was clerk to the Council it was his job to dictate to the herald the form of prayer read at the opening of every Assembly (*exēgeito ton nomon touton toi kēruki* 19.70).[12] Was the possession of a fine voice perhaps an advantage to an official in this capacity?

When it comes to the ridicule of Aeschines as actor, Demosthenes' tactics are particularly elaborate. He has a great deal to say about Aeschines' voice, and this is part of a complex of associations that seems designed to deconstruct any power an actor might have in influencing his audience. The sub-text, of course, is that the voice of a performer (whether actor or orator) is indeed a force to be reckoned with. So there might be an advantage for the opponent in linking it with unglamorous occasions, like small-time cult meetings or what can be represented as minor bureaucratic chores, and in suggesting that in its theatrical instantiation it was grotesquely inappropriate. I am less concerned here with the question of historical fact – did Aeschines or didn't he have an exceptionally memorable voice[13] – than with how the

---

[9] For the comic vocabulary cf. Harding (1994) 215-16.
[10] The reading *iambeiographos* is less likely; see Wankel (1976) *ad loc.*
[11] Cf. Hall (1995) 48.
[12] Harris (1995) 30-1. Cf. the remark about heralds at 19.338.
[13] The whole ancient tradition certainly took this for granted, but the influence of Demosthenes' speeches must have been crucial in shaping the tradition; see Wankel (1976) on 18.129. The best evidence that Demosthenes took seriously the danger of Aeschines' vocal powers as compared with his own is the remarkable passage in 19.216-17, where he warns the jury not to be influenced 'if his voice is fine and loud and mine poor; it's not a competition for speakers or speeches that you have to judge today'. Cf. 19.206-8. The language in 19.337-40, 18.308-9, and 18.313 also seems to have a strong motivating force behind it. It is not irrelevant that Aeschines won the case against Timarchus and was acquitted in the embassy case. See in general Katsouris (1989) 57-60 and 97-109; Hall (1995) 46-9.

Actors and voices

power of a performer's voice might be viewed, and Demosthenes gives a remarkable range of evidence.

19.337–40 is a telling passage: placed crucially near the end of the speech, it draws attention to Aeschines' threatening power as a speaker. In 336 Demosthenes has suggested the sort of challenge that needs to be given to Aeschines, concluding with the idea that he will have only his voice to offer, with no content in his words. But this is not enough: the jury must be warned that they need to resist the appeal of Aeschines' voice. It would be inconsistent of them to take notice of his fine-sounding voice now, when the issues are public affairs of the greatest importance, considering that when he took part in enacting the horrors of Thyestes and the Trojan war, they hissed him off the stage and very nearly stoned him, with the result that he gave up the theatre job altogether. There may be some equivocation here: Demosthenes may be talking about one or two entire productions that failed to please their audiences, rather than about Aeschines' performance in particular, and the whole account is quite vague.[14] At any rate, although it might hardly seem important to make so much of the speaking powers of an allegedly failed minor actor, Demosthenes finds it necessary to

[14] At 19.337 ὅτε μὲν τὰ Θυέστου καὶ τῶν ἐπὶ Τροίαι κάκ' ἠγωνίζετο can be read either more generally, with κακά as the subject, as 'when the horrors ... were performed' or, with Aeschines as subject, 'when he was performing the horrors ...' *Was* Aeschines a failure as an actor? The question is as hard to answer with conviction as the question about his voice (n. 13 above). The main point of the remarks about Aeschines as tritagonist is that he was a subordinate, hired for pay (which was no doubt the way many actors started their professional careers). On the whole question of the terminology see Pickard-Cambridge (1988) 132–5 and Wankel (1976) on 18.129. The reference in 19.247 to Theodorus and Aristodemus as putting on *Antigone* has often been taken (wrongly) to imply that these famous performers were in the same troupe instead of each leading their own. It is much more likely that they each had the play in their repertoire (the Greek text certainly suggests this: Ἀντιγόνην δὲ Σοφοκλέους πολλάκις μὲν Θεόδωρος, πολλάκις δ' Ἀριστόδημος ὑποκέκριται) and that Aeschines acted for both; to be chosen, even as third actor, for the troupe of either might indeed have been to his credit as a performer. (On the political connections of these two actors see below.) The main point in the context here is Aeschines' subordinate role and then his moral degeneracy: he had the opportunity to learn sound principles form Creon's speech in Sophocles, but he evidently didn't learn them, to judge by the way he treated Timarchus. In 19 it is only in 337–40 that there is any claim that Aeschines was unpopular, but it may have been the shows rather than his acting in particular that failed. The more explicit claim about the disastrous performances of the 'Groaners' in 18.262 is also quite vague about Aeschines, and again the emphasis is on the degrading nature of his formative experiences. We know that he gave up acting, but as Harris points out (1995, 31) he married money, and this (combined with his political ambitions?) may have been the reason why he left the profession. For an attempt to challenge the ancient evidence on Aeschines as an actor see Dorjahn (1929–30), and on Demosthenes' general willingness to make untrue allegations (e.g.) Cawkwell (1969).

make the case again, twice: first by drawing a distinction between heralds, who need good voices, and ambassadors, who don't, and then, most remarkably, by advising his audience to 'shut out' Aeschines' voice and listen to it with hostility. This is how he rounds off his case: 'Most human powers may be thought to stand for themselves, but that of speech is broken (*diakoptetai*) by an audience which stands against it. Such must be the hearing you give a man like this, wicked, corrupt and false in every word' (340). This is strong language, and the placing of this passage in the speech as a whole suggests that the opponent's voice is to be seen as something special.

It now becomes easier to see the logic of earlier references: the passing remark in 200 that Aeschines had had a paid job as a tritagonist in someone else's acting troupe, and the more elaborate one in 246–50, the famous reference to Aeschines playing Creon when he worked as a subordinate to well-known lead actors like Neoptolemus and Aristodemus. In 255 the disparaging comments on Aeschines' voice production (*phōnaskia*) and histrionic reciting of Solon in his speech against Timarchus are not strictly about his acting but contribute to the cumulative effect: in all these contexts the voice is to be associated not with glamour and power but with artifice or with the mere 'tradesman' skills of a herald or a hired third actor.[15]

The same strategy is used in 18 (258–64), where in his account of Aeschines' demeaning jobs, culminating in his career as an actor, Demosthenes implies that all that Aeschines with his fine voice was fit for was to hire himself to an inferior troupe nicknamed the 'Groaners' (*barustonoi*)[16] led by two otherwise unknown actors, who made a poor living (at the deme festivals, presumably) and were badly treated by hostile audiences (as in 19, this is all pretty vague, but it is given specificity by being associated with particular individuals, and there are a couple of references to parts played by Aeschines – Cresphontes, Creon, Oenomaus,[17] 18.180 and 242 – which are probably there for the same purpose).

In this speech, just as in 19, reference to Aeschines' voice is made at a climactic moment in the peroration (306–8). Demosthenes contrasts

---

[15] For demeaning sexual associations with the organ of speech cf. Aeschines' allegations about Demosthenes (n. 30 below).

[16] 'Roarers' (Pickard-Cambridge); 'Ranters' (Saunders); 'Growlers' (Harris). Pickard-Cambridge (1988) 169 cites a long list given by Pollux (4.114) of terms for bad actors, almost all relating to their voices. There are on independent records about the two actors with whom Aeschines allegedly played, Simycas (if that is the correct form) and Socrates.

[17] There must have been something notorious about this show; cf. the story attributed to Demochares that Aeschines had a fall when taking the part of Oenomaus.

his own public-spiritedness with Aeschines' recent lack of involvement in politics, a withdrawal punctuated by sudden (but carefully stage-managed) speeches in the Assembly, which may be striking but do no good to anybody: 'At this point his silence breaks into a sudden cyclone of speech, and with voice-training in top form (*pephōnaskēkōs*) and gathering together words and phrases he lets out a loud stream of them without stopping for breath ...'(308). 'Without stopping for breath' (*apneustei*) draws further attention to the technical skill of one trained in elocution; the idea is continued in the references to training in 309 (*meletē* and *epimeleia*). If this kind of thing came from a 'just soul', says Demosthenes, it would do some good, but there is no sign of good actions in Aeschines' case: the only context in which he has distinguished himself is in harming the Athenians, which is precisely when 'your vocal brilliance and your memory stand out, and you become the best of actors, a true tragic Theocrines' (313).[18] The superlatives *lamprophōnotatos, mnēmonikōtatos, aristos* mark a resounding climax, which brings together the ideas of the loud and brilliant voice, the elaborate training (since memory was as important for the speaker as voice-production) and the dubious stage career. The expressive idea of the 'just soul' must gain some of its resonance from a rather Gorgianic play on the contrast between 'soul' or 'heart' (*psuchē*) and 'voice' (*phōnē*) which is made twice (287 and 291, prepared for already in 280–1) in an impassioned passage a few paragraphs earlier. Here, in a comparison between himself and Aeschines, Demosthenes has pointed out that he, and not Aeschines for all his brilliance, was chosen to speak the funeral oration over the war dead after Chaeronea: what was wanted was a speaker who would feel and express the 'true grief of the *psuchē*' and not give a 'vocal pretence of lamentation' (287); Aeschines in fact went even further in demonstrating his failure to feel anything in his *psuchē*: 'raising his voice in an elaborate and cheerful display of elocution' (*eparas tēn phōnēn kai gegēthōs kai larungizōn*).[19]

The image of the actor and his voice thus has enormous rhetorical potential: it can be made to suggest all that is most suspect about the orator (naturally the speaker's opponent, not the speaker) and *his* voice, and this may be one reason why so much use is made by Demosthenes of the imagery and language of theatre in both speeches, in addition to what he says directly about Aeschines' career as an actor. The job of an actor is to learn to play any part, however shameless, with brazen

---

[18] Trans. Saunders (1975). See *Or.*58 in the Demosthenic corpus for Theocrines, who must have been well known as a sycophant.
[19] See Wankel (1976) *ad loc.* for the meaning of *larungizein*, which seems to suggest an artificial style of delivery.

confidence,[20] so someone trained to use his voice in that way will be particularly dangerous: at 19.199, after telling the shocking story of Aeschines' drunken violence at a party where a female captive from Olynthus was allegedly whipped for refusing to sing, he goes on 'yet he will dare to look you in the eye and utter an account of his life in his splendid voice – it makes me choke'.[21]

This idea of playing fictive roles can be given different nuances: with the emphasis on artifice, for example, – all training and show and no content, as in what Demosthenes has to say about voice-production,[22] – or on deception, on fraudulent misleading of audiences, as at 19.120, when he suggests that Aeschines takes on court cases as readily as if they were plays, without needing witnesses,[23] or in the passages in 18 (287, 291) where 'voice' and 'soul' are set in contrast, or in the passage on the Sirens in Aeschines (quoted above). There is also the contrast between fantasy and reality, as in the climactic remarks about the brilliant distinction of Aeschines as performer – in speaking against the interests of the Athenians (18.313).[24] All of these nuances have their usefulness for the orator attempting to undermine his opponent as a speaker.

But there were good things about having a great voice. A performer, whether actor or orator, with an outstanding, professionally trained voice could give intense pleasure to large audiences in open-air theatres and places of assembly, and in choosing to belittle Aeschines' powers (or to construct an argument against him in which the voice, rightly or wrongly, became a critical factor) Demosthenes had a delicate path to tread. He might want to show that there was nothing appealing or glamorous about Aeschines' connections with the theatre and that on

---

[20] But lead actors might opt to play a grandly shameless figure like Clytemnestra rather than a mean villain like Menelaus; see Pavloskis (1977) and Damen (1989) for factors that may have influenced the assignment of parts between the three speaking actors.

[21] Cf.19.206–9, where shamelessness and Aeschines' loud voice are linked; at 19.126 Aeschines' action in going off on the delegation to Philip is put down to corrupt motives: his powers as a speaker are linked with his claim to be a patriotic statesman and found wanting ('our clever schemer with the wonderful voice', trans. Saunders).

[22] 19.255, 336; 18.280, 308–9. As Wankel (1976) points out on 18.280, references to *phōnaskia* can also suggest lack of experience: the speaker is still practising to be an effective orator. On voice-training for actors see Aristotle *Probl.* 11.22; Pickard-Cambridge (1988) 167–71.

[23] Cf.19.216–17: Philip is the *chorēgos*, and his witnesses will perform as he directs; 19.314: Aeschines' new life-style and costume as one of 'Philip's close friends'; cf. Wilson (1996) 321. The tragic tag in *muri' ergastai kaka* (repeated at 337) no doubt recalls Aeschines the tragic actor and adds to the impression of falsity conveyed here; 18.15: Aeschines acts a part; 18.284: Aeschines pretends to have been a friend, rather than a hired agent, of Philip's.

[24] Cf.19.337, quoted above.

Actors and voices 161

the contrary because (in his case) they were socially demeaning they were evidence of his poor qualification for statesmanship, but at the same time he needed to avoid giving the impression that theatre as such was a bad thing or that the profession of an actor was inherently suspect. He also had to allow for the fact that in practice some star actors did have influence in the wider world, beyond that of audiences in Attic theatres.[25] The charisma of the famous and therefore rich and influential performer was something to be appropriated by the speaker rather than simply denied, particularly in a culture in which audiences were used to allowing overlap in functions between actors and orators, and in which lavish quotation from the poets was something to be admired in a court case.[26]

There are other performers besides the 'Groaners' mentioned in the speeches, and it is interesting that what is said about them suggests no belittling – on either Demosthenes' or Aeschines' part – of actors *qua* actors. Taking part in a poor production may have been a thing to earn ridicule, but actors and acting are certainly not denigrated, nor is their social standing called into question (just as participating in mystery cults is fine if you are an initiate and not an attendant).

The case of the actors Aristodemus and Neoptolemus is particularly interesting, since these were people Demosthenes had every reason to want to criticize. There is no doubt that he thought that they had misled the Athenians with encouraging accounts of Philip's eagerness to be friends with them, and he refers to this several times in 19 (12, 18, 94, 315). But he seems to have no way of using their professional activities against them, beyond saying at 94 that Aristodemus and Ctesiphon (not an actor) 'took the leading role' (*tēn prōten epheron*) in the deception of the Athenians. The implication is that they were extremely successful in giving the Athenians a glowing picture of Philip's friendly attitude. Aeschines, indeed, claims that Demosthenes himself was initially well enough disposed to Aristodemus to propose the award of a crown to him when he reported Philip's desire for peace, and that he took the initiative in getting Aristodemus excused his professional engagements so that he could join the embassy (2.15–19).[27] In his speech *On the peace*, delivered in 346, Demosthenes had been more

---

[25] For the evidence see Pickard-Cambridge (1988), esp. 279–81; Csapo and Slater (1995) 221–74. Aristodemus as member of an embassy is certainly not an isolated case.
[26] See the papers by Ford and Hesk (pp. 201–56); Wilson (1996). For an example of Demosthenes' technique of self-dramatization see Yunis (1996) 268–77 on Demosthenes 18.169–79.
[27] There is probably no reason to doubt Aeschines here since Demosthenes keeps off the subject.

explicit about the activity of Neoptolemus. The strongest point to emerge there is Neoptolemus' persuasiveness with the Athenian public. Demosthenes claims that those to blame for taking too much notice of him were the Athenians themselves: 'If you had been watching tragic actors at the Dionysia and the debate had not been about safety and matters of public interest you would not have listened with so much favour to him and so much hostility to me' (5.7). (Later events proved Demosthenes right about Neoptolemus' true agenda: he sold his property at Athens and went to live in Macedonia.)[28]

Aeschines' reply to Demosthenes' *On the embassy* includes a number of references to actors (though not to his own acting career), which confirm the impression that they might be public personages with real political influence or connections with the great, though Aeschines' strategy is to mock Demosthenes by demonstrating that he too was under the spell of Aristodemus. (As well as the account in 15–18, mentioned above, there is a nice touch at 51, when he recalls Demosthenes remarking that Philip was no better looking than Aristodemus.) One passage in particular seems designed to imply that Aeschines as a speaker is to be compared with a performer at the top of his profession, the admired comic actor Satyrus. At 156 he purports to quote what Demosthenes said about him and Satyrus; it is worth putting Aeschines' account side by side with the relevant passage in Demosthenes 19 (where the words – unsurprisingly – don't appear), to see what could be made out of a story about a famous actor. Demosthenes (of course) uses it to draw a contrast unfavourable to Aeschines:

After Philip's capture of Olynthus, when he was celebrating the games at Mount Olympus [Dion], he collected all the artists he could to attend the ceremony and the general gathering, gave them a dinner and crowned those who had won prizes. He asked our friend, Satyrus the comic actor, why he was the only one not to put down any public request. Did he feel any want of public spirit in Philip himself? Had he detected any personal ill-feeling? Satyrus' reply, it is said, was that he didn't happen to want anything the others asked for, and what he would like to put down was the easiest thing in the world for Philip to do to please him, but he was afraid he might not be granted it. Philip told him to say what it was, and with a certain youthful extravagance declared he wouldn't refuse him anything. [Satyrus asked for the ransom of the daughters of a friend of his, Apollophanes of Pydna.] 'Now', he went on, 'since the capture of Olynthus they have been prisoners, and are in your hands, and of an age to be married. The request that I make to you is to hand them over to me ... I shall get nothing out of it. I shall give them each a dowry and find them husbands, and not allow them to meet a fate which is beneath myself or their

---

[28] More on Neoptolemus in Stephanis (1988) s.v.; Easterling (1997) 218–22.

Actors and voices 163

father.' At this the guests at the party gave a loud shout of applause, which shamed Philip into agreeing, although this Apollophanes had been one of the killers of Philip's brother, Alexander.

Let us draw a comparison between this party of Satyrus's and the party enjoyed by Aeschines in Macedonia ... (19.192–6, trans. Saunders (1975))

Then follows his account of the outrageous behaviour of Aeschines and his friends in trying to force a well brought up Olynthian woman to sing for them (above, p. 160). When Aeschines tells the story (2.153–7) he does so in order to recall how the jury had been so disgusted by Demosthenes' false allegations that they made him stop half-way through, but he is also interested in putting words into Demosthenes' mouth:

But do you remember [Aeschines says to the jury] that unspeakable verbal trickery which Demosthenes offers to the young and is now using against me, how he mourned and wept for Greece, and sang the praises of the comic actor Satyrus for asking Philip, at a party, for some friends of his whom he found in captivity digging Philip's vineyard in chains; and then after the preamble he went on at the top of his harsh, unpleasant voice to the effect that it was appalling that the actor of parts like Carion and Xanthias should show such breeding and nobility, while I who represented the greatest of all cities and preached sermons to thousands in Arcadia could not control my violence, got drunk and quarrelsome when Xenodocus, one of Philip's friends, gave us a party ... (2.156–7, trans. Saunders (1975))

The reference to 'thousands in Arcadia' in Aeschines' audience, juxtaposed with the disparaging remarks about *Demosthenes*' voice, looks like a neat way of deconstructing his opponent's mockery of his powers as a performer, without making any reference to it in detail, and at the same time appropriating all the good associations of the successful Satyrus. In neither of his speeches against Demosthenes does Aeschines in fact make direct mention of his own voice (though the reference to the 'music of the Sirens' in 3.228 is probably another indirect and teasing allusion). Silence may imply that he regards his voice as an asset that needs no defence: its value will be demonstrated in the delivery itself. As with his counter-criticisms of Demosthenes as a performer, the implicit message is that performance matters and that Aeschines has the upper hand in this department.[29] The overall impression is certainly that actors are to be reckoned with, and Aeschines makes interestingly different use from Demosthenes of the contrast between play-acting and the real world.

At 2.34–5 Aeschines describes the conduct of the first embassy:

[29] Cf. Hesk in this volume. (pp. 206–7, 210–11, 224–5).

when it was Demosthenes' turn to speak before Philip (and expectations had been created of a great speech) he suddenly became tongue-tied (Aeschines uses the theatrical term *ekpiptei* 'dried'), and Philip encouraged him to go on when he recognized what the trouble was: he mustn't think, as if he were in the theatre, that he'd experienced a catastrophe, but he must calmly and systematically recover the thread and say what he had intended. But once Demosthenes had got upset and lost his place in his script he wasn't able to recover himself, and when he tried to speak again the same thing happened to him. 'When there was complete silence the herald told us to withdraw.' (A properly trained speaker, with well-practised powers of memory, ought not to have needed a script ...) Again, at 111–12 Aeschines describes Demosthenes' second speech before Philip, a ludicrously embarrassing display of flattery, which caused his fellow-ambassadors to hide their faces and provoked exceptional merriment in the audience. Demosthenes' own 'harsh and disagreeable, (*anosion* 'unholy') voice (2.157) was too high-pitched (if that is the meaning of 3.209–10); he was also too inclined to 'act out' his meaning on the platform (3.167). Then there is the claim, following on from the 'Sirens' passage, that all there is to Demosthenes is his tongue: take that away, and he'll be no more use than an instrument without anyone to play it (3.229).[30] These teasing details may be hints that when it comes to images of failed actors Demosthenes fills the bill better than Aeschines.

For anyone interested in Greek performance culture the fourth century is particularly important as the period when two decisive developments took place. The growth in interest in Attic theatre and its practitioners, well-documented for Sicily and South Italy, was given a very strong impetus by the Macedonian kings from Archelaus onwards, and the most telling theatrical event recorded in the generation after the Peloponnesian War was the introduction in 386 of revived old plays at the City Dionysia. This must presuppose a growing demand for re-performance, based no doubt on practice at some of the deme festivals and on developments outside Attica, and it seems clear, too, that particular leading actors were developing their own repertoire. As soon as it becomes normal for actors to move around the Greek-speaking world, making contracts with different festival organizers or patrons on their own account, there is no limit to the different contexts in which drama might be performed. A touring actor and his troupe might enter

---

[30] This passage should perhaps be compared with Aeschines 2.23 and 88, where in a not too veiled way he accuses Demosthenes of practising fellatio, and each time draws attention to where his *voice* is projected from.

Actors and voices 165

a competition with old or new full-length plays, or the actor might put on a solo performance (e.g. of favourite arias) in a public context such as a theatre, or for private after-dinner entertainment, and there must have been plenty of possible variations on such arrangements, as when visiting actors used the backing of local musicians and choruses. When the occasions for dramatic performance become as flexible and varied as this, the way is open for actors to use the networks of patronage, and to adopt some of the patterns of organization and life-style, already well established for musicians, athletes, rhapsodes and others, and it is interesting to see actors developing institutional links with these other types of performers when the guilds of *Technitai* get established.[31]

The texts of Demosthenes and Aeschines reflect, however obliquely and distortingly, a world in which top actors are potentially players on an international stage in the 'real world' of inter-city relations, and in which the very existence of the travelling media star affects the way sophisticated societies define their cultural values.[32] But weren't actors merely the latest recruits in a tradition of travelling virtuosi that stretched back well into the archaic period? Was there anything to differentiate them from other performers? Two things may have made them stand out: the obvious fact that the actor's skills and training were very like those of the public speaker (and both were concerned with the slippery art of using words to persuade large audiences, relying on their vocal powers to give them special charisma and influence[33]); and the fact that the imaginary world projected by drama had the power to shape the public's feelings and experience more comprehensively than those media in which the role of the performer was relatively more stable. There is also a broader consideration, the power of the words themselves: as the most memorably phrased ideas of the most popular plays became part of the educational heritage, along with the poetry of Homer and Hesiod and the sayings of the early 'masters of truth', the

---

[31] Evidence and discussion in Csapo and Slater (1995) esp. ch. IV, Easterling (1997), Ghiron-Bistagne (1976), Green (1994), le Guen (1995), Pickard-Cambridge (1988), Stephanis (1988), Taplin (1993), Trendall (1991), Wilson (1996).

[32] The political implications of performance, too, must have been greatly complicated when texts originally designed to be played to democratic audiences at Athens were received elsewhere by audiences with quite different traditions.

[33] See especially Hall (1995); also the Introduction to this volume, and the papers by Ford and Hesk. On actors' voices see Pickard-Cambridge (1988) 167–71 and the famous passage in Aristotle's *Rhetoric* (1403b) on the importance of the use of the voice and its qualities of volume, harmony and rhythm: the performers who pay attention to these 'nearly always win the prizes in dramatic contests, and just as nowadays the actors have greater influence than the poets so it happens in political contests, owing to the debased nature of our forms of government' [i.e. that speakers' voices had a disproportionate influence in law-courts and assemblies].

actor's utterance could claim significance and authority.[34] Theatrical performance mattered, both at home and abroad, and it is no accident that the Greek language itself became permeated with the imagery of the theatre.

[34] See Wilson (1996), esp. 315.

7 Aristophanes: the performance of utopia in the *Ecclesiazousae*

Froma I. Zeitlin

1. Performance

Given the theme of this volume, 'performance culture and Athenian democracy', which focuses on what might be called the 'theatricalization' of civic experience in a wide variety of institutional contexts and discursive practices, then Aristophanes' *Ecclesiazousae* might serve as an exemplary proof text to substantiate these claims.[1] Old Comedy is perhaps the single art form most identified with the democratic city of the fifth century. As a species of public performance, wholly rooted in its contemporary political and social milieu, the genre claims an impudent freedom to represent virtually every aspect and space of civic life – law-court, Assembly, marketplace, theatre, temple, gymnasium, symposium. The plays also often take us behind the scenes, as it were, to give us a glimpse of the degree to which these spaces and those who act within them are in fact themselves actors, primed to play their roles in a stratified society of competitive public display, including their performance in the comic theatre itself. In its zeal to expose the pretensions and impostures of its elite citizen body (as well as to express the forbidden yearnings and ambivalent fantasies of the common people), Old Comedy, as is commonly observed, also delights in a self-conscious awareness of its own theatricality and exploits the implications of self-representation in wicked parodies of dramatic and other conventions.

The opening of the *Ecclesiazousae* conducts this comic operation in a paradigmatic way on two fronts at the same time. The costuming, rehearsal, and role playing of women, who are donning male dress in order to infiltrate the all-male Assembly, confront the issue of performance in the public arena in the first instance and, in the second, the issue of gender difference in a city with a highly codified division

---

[1] This essay is a much expanded version of a previous communication, entitled 'Utopia and Myth in Aristophanes' *Ecclesiazousae*,' presented at the Quebec meeting of the Fédération Internationale des Etudes Classiques (FIEC) in 1993.

between the sexes. By means of the women's masquerade, the play makes clear that 'the workings of the theatre are directly linked to the workings of government'.[2] To carry off their disguise, the women need to look like men, dress and comport themselves like men; they also need to speak like them, rehearsing their lines, shaping their idiom and rhetoric to a masculine norm. This scene demonstrates, as elsewhere in Aristophanes, an awareness of the difference in speech patterns between men and women in both style and substance, but the very idea of a rehearsal itself suggests that any and all appearances in the Assembly – as in other public venues – could be considered a species of performance. Thus, Old Comedy and the *Ecclesiazousae* in particular puts on a fine show of the terms in which this book's project is conceived: *schēma* (figure), *epideixis* (display), *agōn* (contest) – and *theōria* (viewing).[3]

Comedy generally works both sides of the street in a series of mirroring and ironic reflections. If the rehearsal scene pokes fun at women pretending to be orators, their version of public speaking also parodies the real thing, revealing 'expert orators' careful preparations and transparent attempts to appear spontaneous', including the 'topos of inexperience at public address' (110–23, 150–3).[4] Even Praxagora's harangue before the Assembly, criticizing the current state of political affairs, makes use of a number of well-known rhetorical themes,[5] whose purely conventional nature is brought to the fore, when incongruously uttered by female voices. The mimetic exercise, however, has larger implications than a comic display of women performing as men with satirical gestures to both sides, since its stated aim, in penetrating the masculine space of the Assembly, normally closed to women, is to reverse the gender roles once and for all in the conduct of political affairs. Hence cross-dressing itself is the fundamental point of entry into the conduct and outcome of the plot and consequently deserves to take centre stage in our enquiry.

But first, let us note that there is no critical consensus as to the significance of this masquerade. Taaffe, at one pole, relies on Judith Butler's arguments about the performativity of gender when she asks whether the notion of women dressed as men implies that 'the tradi-

---

[2] Taaffe (1993) 103.
[3] See the discussion of these terms in the introduction to this volume.
[4] Ober and Strauss (1990) 264.
[5] Ober and Strauss (1990) 264–5. The rhetorical topoi they mention are: (a) I have an equal share in this country, just as each of you does; (b) the polis is being ruined because of people's willingness to follow evil leaders; (c) you citizens mistrust those who truly love you, but trust those who care nothing for you; (d) you care too little for state, too much for private affairs, and (e) you change public policy too often. See also the analysis in Rothwell (1990) 82–92.

Performance of utopia in the *Ecclesiazousae* 169

tional division of authority, based on sexual difference, no longer functions normally'. 'Does the play', she continues, 'therefore show an evanescent illusion of gender that exists in the rapidly changing Athens' of this period in the early fourth century? Even more, she would go so far as to claim that the scene is meant to demonstrate that 'gender definitions and representations can be constructed and taken apart easily'.[6] In this reading, masculinity and femininity are claimed to be unstable categories, liable to permutations and reversals through a series of consciously adopted gestures, costumes, and actions. *Schēma* makes the man!

At another pole, given the transparency of the disguise and the women's bumbling efforts in rehearsal, it could be argued with Saïd 'that costume never modifies anything but appearance and has no power to transform character' in any way. 'Even if they are dressed as men', it is claimed, 'women are incapable of expressing themselves in a manly way and never stop talking like women', even though, under Praxagora's tutelage, it is acknowledged that 'they do overcome these errors and play their role in a convincing way in the Assembly of which they have only heard tell'.[7] From this perspective, the performance would consist precisely in demonstrating the impossibility of escaping a gendered identity that both defines and is defined by any effort at its evasion either in costume or speech.

In a different vein, which qualifies both of these contrasting views, others have wondered whether the women's success in the Assembly is in fact more 'natural' than might be assumed. After all, Praxagora's skill as an orator in miming political speech is occasioned by the fact that seductive rhetoric itself is understood in a way as already feminized through the cosmetic enhancement of speech that gives it a deceptive allure.[8] When, for example, the women ask 'how will a female-minded association of women address the people'? Praxagora can reply: 'Quite well... For they say that the youths who are buggered the most are the most skilful speakers' (110–14)[9]. That is, 'even among the orators, the most "womanly" are also the best speakers', which implies that 'real women should be better still'.[10] In any case, Agyrrhios, a prominent politician, is said to have had to borrow a beard from one Pronomos, because formerly he was a *gunē* (woman, 102–3). Applied to a pederastic partner, the pejorative label, *gunē*, might seem to imply a direct equivalence between the *erōmenos* and a woman,

---

[6] Taaffe (1993) 103.   [7] Saïd (1979) 35, and more generally, see Saïd (1987).
[8] Rothwell (1990) 77–101.   [9] Textual citations are from the edition of Ussher (1973).
[10] Ussher (1973) 90.

reinforced by the fact that the women preparing for the Assembly rightly consider beards an indispensable part of their masculine attire. At the same time, when the other women ask Praxagora how it is that she speaks with such skill, how it is she is so *sophē* (clever) and *deinē* (eloquent), she puts forth the claim that she learned her rhetoric by listening to the orators when she was quartered temporarily with her husband on the Pnyx (241-6).[11] Who then is the model for whom in the arena of rhetoric and public speaking? Women for men, or men for women?

There is a partial validity to each of these readings, depending on which aspect of cross-dressing or role reversal is chosen for emphasis. In the first place, a transvestite disguise on the comic stage must be evident to the spectators or the transgressive point of the humour is lost,[12] but in this case it also must succeed with its internal audience or the plot would founder before it begins. Moreover, since the aim of the women's intrigue in the first place is to vote themselves as rulers of the state because of the qualities of leadership they claim as specifically feminine (the basis of Praxagora's speech in the Assembly), their disguise is only a temporary expedient, meant to be discarded as soon as they triumphantly return home. Even so, they can never quite look like 'real' men. Despite the fact that they had tried to emulate the masculine ideal by standing in the sun as much as possible beforehand and ceasing to depilate their body hair (as standards of feminine beauty required), the men at the Assembly remarked on their pale-faced appearance, but took them to be shoemakers, who, like other artisans spent their time indoors (385). Between the two poles of strict gender definition there are obviously recognizable gradations, which for men, especially, extend to the categories of artisans and more particularly, to effeminates, a favourite butt of Aristophanic satire.

At the same time, the very premise of a plot that stages women, who take over public leadership from men, already suggests not just the failure of masculine policies, but of manliness itself,[13] an inference that can be performed on the comic stage when male characters in turn are

---

[11] They were refugees, probably during the reign of the Thirty, but the reference is not entirely clear.

[12] Gruber (1986) 27, and see, more generally, Garber (1992): these concerns have been central also to the performance artists discussed in this volume's introduction.

[13] See, for example, Zeitlin (1985), now (1995), 366, in connection with the *Frogs*. 'Aristophanes, not untypically, assumes that when things go badly for men and masculine interests, the cause lies in a decay of moral and aesthetic values, from which he slides easily into hints of effeminacy and all that that charge implies.'

compelled to don female attire.[14] The logic of cross-dressing therefore works in two opposite but complementary ways – to empower the women and to subject the men to public embarrassment. To make the point clear, the *Ecclesiazousae* overloads this message: first, since the women have stolen their husbands' clothing for their own disguise, the men have nothing to wear but the feminine garments their wives have left behind, and second, is the scatological nature of the succeeding scene that prompts the men's urgent need to come outside in the first place. Loss of virility and hyperfemininity go hand in hand, instantiated not just in the exchange of costumes, but in the relative ease with which women, true to their reputation for clever plotting, dupe the men and prove them gullible fools. I will return to these points.

Whether the play is taken, for example, as a satire of current political practices and philosophical principles, or a disconcerting symptom of waning morale in the public city of men, or just a carnivalesque divertissement of topsy-turvydom, or finally, a mixture of all three,[15] it should be emphasized, however, that once the rule of women is put into operation and the plot acts out its social consequences for male and female alike, the outcome shows that gender boundaries are accordingly *both* breached *and* reinforced – providing we recall that Aristophanic comedy, like all Athenian theatre, is performed by male actors for a male audience, whether women were present in the theatre or not.

My aim in this essay, therefore, is not to focus on the more obvious (if contested) aspects of performance in the play, as discussed above, but rather what we might learn about its ideological patterns from the

---

[14] In the *Lysistrata*, where women take over the Acropolis in response to men's mismanagement of public affairs in the conduct of the war, the women briefly provide the magistrate with feminine props to seal their verbal victory over him (550–5). The *Thesmophoriazousae*, an extended exercise in males dressed as women, has Euripides rather than politics *per se* as its target. On this play, see Zeitlin (1981) now in (1995).

[15] The range of critical evaluation of this play (and its 'message') is still more extensive, with many gradations of opinion in between, including other suggestions such as a satire of contemporary theories of utopia (often with reference to Plato's *Republic*, composed twenty years later, although this suggestion is now largely discredited). Needless to say, Aristophanes' own views are a continuing topic of debate for those who insist on this line of questioning, as is the state of the genre of Old Comedy at this late date. See the convenient summaries of Rothwell (1990) 1–25, especially 7–10, and David (1984) 1–2. More recently, see Ober and Strauss (1990), who point to the recent institution of a series of legal reforms and a renewed emphasis on 'regaining a sense of a socio-political consensus (*homonoia*) among citizenry polarized along class lines by the bloody reign of the Thirty. For fuller development see, Ober (1998).

conduct of the plot itself. I would like to shift attention to the performative nature of utopia itself as an imagined world of 'what if' and its coincidence in the theatre with a 'play world', which constructs a comic version of another totalizing social reality for Athens in the real space and time of the theatrical performance. While the *Birds* situates its state-building fantasy elsewhere in an imaginary avian realm in the heavens, the *Ecclesiazousae* has come down to earth. Even more, it takes place in Athens itself before an Athenian audience to propose a radical new style of government through the women's plan to put themselves in charge and legislate the abolition of both private property and the institution of marriage. The play therefore directly represents to the citizen audience an image of its collective self on stage, but from a reversed point of view, by which the concerns of contemporary life are filtered through the antics of a comic plot that translates its make-believe into the immediacy of the theatre and gives life and form to abstract ideas and conceptual frames of action. Praxagora, with the connivance of her author, would have us believe in the novelty of her invention. But it is a distinctive feature of the genre of Old Comedy that an outrageous innovation in the present also looks to the past, to the mythico-ritual basis of civic existence. There is just such a myth, I will argue, which is screened behind the fiction of the play, one with profound implications in the ideology of the city and its imagined prehistory. The tacit presence of this myth not only brings the contradictions of the plot and its vexed issues into sharper focus but also underwrites the entire scenario. Indeed, its import goes beyond the comic stage to join up with two momentous civic artefacts, whose influence in shaping the cultural attitudes of the period can hardly be overstated: the tragic theatre in Aeschylus' *Oresteia*, and the sculptures on the Parthenon, whose general iconographical programme, I will suggest, directly pertains to the gynaecocratic situation of the *Ecclesiazousae* and the terms of its enactment. My question, in short, is 'what is being performed in and by the *Ecclesiazousae*'?

II. Paradoxes of the plot

In the many and varied interpretative approaches to the *Ecclesiazousae*, one consistently shared observation has been to note the paradox of the scheme that the women put into action once they have gained power. This paradox is twofold: it revolves around the oppositions of conservatism versus innovation on the one hand and individual self-interest versus public spirit and concern for the community, on the other. Praxagora, the instigator of the women's revolution, argues that it is women who are the bedrock of tradition and continuity in the city. By contrast with their male counterparts who, in their zeal for novelty are at the mercy of every foolish scheme that comes along, women can assure the salvation of the city, precisely because they are 'truly conventional natural-born conservatives'.[16]

Our *tropoi* are better, Praxagora claims in her first exhortation to the women, because we do things according to the *archaios nomos*, by time honoured custom, just as we have always done. We dye wool in hot water, sit down while we cook, carry burdens on our heads, just as we always have. Women celebrate the Thesmophoria, their special festival, just as before, and likewise bake flatcakes, annoy their husbands, enjoy their lovers inside the house, buy little extras from the market on the side, retain their fondness for unmixed wine, and finally, delight in getting laid, just as before (214-28). In this self-characterization that mixes the homely details of household tasks with the perennial clichés about the foibles of the female sex in the comic theatre, Praxagora can point to other, more solid, virtues that equip women to rule: maternal concern for their soldier sons, skill in raising money for city management, and as arch-deceivers themselves, not being susceptible to others' political deceptions. Above all, the women can promise a life of happiness and prosperity for all citizens, a goal which the state has failed to achieve.

The bill passes not only because the disguised women, who have crowded out many of their menfolk, gain a majority of the votes; but, in keeping with current political policy, its appeal also lies in the fact that this is the single remaining scheme the city has *not* tried before. In other words, handing over the city to the community of women in the name of civic stability is yet another novelty in a long list of desperate attempts to save the polis in its time of need. Just how novel it is will be revealed in Praxagora's plan of such clever invention (*sophou tinos exeurēmatos*, 577) that it may have been the stuff of dreams, but it has never been *enacted* or decreed before in public, either in the political arena or in the theatre (578-80). Political policy and comic ingenuity converge. The audience of citizens in both instances require their poets and politicians to come up with some new-fangled idea each time to pique their interest and keep their attention.

This clever woman does not disappoint expectations. Her radical scheme of civic reform institutes community of property in order to ensure equal benefits for all and goes so far as to include community of sex as well. In the name of the *oikos*, the conservator of archaic values,

---

[16] The phrase is Parker's (1967), 21, introducing lines 221-8.

the line between *polis* and *oikos* disappears to make the city a single unified household (*mia oikēsis*, 674). In the name of radical democracy, egalitarian ideals are pushed to their furthest degree to create a harmonious commonwealth, where all will share in satisfying their material needs: plenty of clothing, shelter, food, drink, and sex (ἀλλ' ἕνα ποιῶ κοινὸν πᾶσιν βίοτον, καὶ τοῦτον ὅμοιον, 594). Political, economic, and social life will undergo drastic change: no lawsuits, no courts, no venal informers; no line between rich and poor, but also an end to the institutions of marriage and patrilineal kinship in the polis.

This happy scheme then is meant to eliminate private interests in favour of public sharing. In effect, the new law aims to create an economy of satiety and a peaceful existence, with plenty of libidinal opportunity for all under the hegemony of a benevolent feminine nurturance. In the second part of the play, the requirement to turn in one's household utensils into the common store meets with some resistance in the figure of a sceptic, who tries and fails to dissuade his neighbour from obeying the law, hoping nevertheless to cadge a free dinner for himself along with the law-abiding citizens (729–875). But, as the comedy approaches its conclusion, the new regime seems to falter more seriously in the two scenes that stage a rivalry between older women for the sexual favours of a young man. The first is between an old woman and the young man's sweetheart (877–1048), the second between the young man and a pair of ugly hags who, each vying for his attention, nearly tear him apart (1049–111). To guarantee equality, this time between old and young, Praxagora had earlier decreed that the old folks will have first priority in access to sex before the young and beautiful may couple with their own kind (611–33).

But by putting this principle into practice on stage for the benefit of old women and not old men (as is more usual in comedy), various problems immediately arise. We seem, as many have claimed, to have returned precisely to the very social ills the gynaecocratic plan had intended to eliminate from the city when men were in charge. The women's vaunted solidarity has broken down. In the Assembly, the disguised Praxagora had claimed that unlike men, women can keep secrets; they need no contracts or witnesses to their transactions, since they freely borrow and repay among themselves (441–54). Now it looks as though women are all too ready to invoke the tyranny of legal sanctions – and why? For sex, of course. Libidinal desire takes precedence over the peaceable sharing that made a female community into a model for the state.

Yet, how are we to read this outcome? Is their usurpation of male power and privilege responsible for the turnabout in their behaviour, so that women are now mimicking their men folk in the very kinds of self-interested competition they had formerly decried? Hierarchical political position, in other words, is the essential factor that dictates the role to be played. Or conversely, does the *agōn*, which pits one woman against another in the pursuit of gratification – whether old against young in a conflict between generations or one between the two competing hags – only confirm men's suspicion that the imperatives of female sexuality would lead to just such contests, were it not kept under control by the normative rules of society? Once again, the matter is undecidable. Comedy generally insists on this view of women's sexual nature even as it also consistently expects its male politicians to abuse their powers over the citizens. What counts is the play's version of democratic politics. In the wake of the new policy which enforces community of property as well as granting free feeding and free sex, the plot seems here to have reached a low point of degradation, one that in the name of a hyper-egalitarianism proves to yield only chaos and violence, not the salvation, the *sotēria*, the city has been seeking.

A double paradox then. The first between the old and the new, tradition and innovation, an appeal to stability to effect revolution; the second in the short-lived ideal of communal values that gives way to a single-minded pursuit of private interests, on both sides, whose effects, most would say, are not fully mitigated by the servant girl's closing invitation to the joyous civic banquet which rounds out the play. At the very least, despite the observance of formal comic conventions in the structure of the plot, the ambiguities at the end suggest that 'the play offers no answer as to whether the new regime was a success or a failure'.[17]

For some critics, these apparent contradictions are in keeping, if in somewhat extreme form, with comedy's well-known licence for dramatic inconsistency in the name of farcical play and laughter-producing nonsense. When not dismissed as an escapist farce simply played for laughs, however, the play is sometimes taken as a sign, even as a proof, of the failing powers of the comic poet in this late stage of his career. Aristophanes is deemed 'aging or overtired', or 'elderly and peevish', described as the 'broken man who could sink to the tired dirtiness of the *Ecclesiazousae*'.[18] Perhaps, as one ingenious critic surmises, Aristophanes may even have suffered a stroke.[19]

---

[17] Ober and Strauss (1990) 269.
[18] Respectively, Murray (1933) 181 and 198; MacDowell (1995) 308; Taylor (1926) 210.
[19] Dover (1972) 195 n. 7. Lest these simplistic judgements be ascribed to outworn critical standards, a recent voice goes even further to complain that there is no intrinsic connection between 'the two themes of women at the Assembly and the communistic

For others intent on taking the play as an accurate barometer to gauge the climate of its times, the emphasis falls on the supposed idea of a demoralized Athens after its defeat in the Peloponnesian war, some thirteen years before. Even if the historical facts suggest a better state of affairs, the city in the play is shown as foundering in a morass of social and economic ills, engendered from within. Its citizens are all selfish egotists, goaded by poverty or, more generally, deaf to appeals to civic virtue and the rule of law.[20] Above all, the lunatic illogic of the play is taken as both a satire on and a symptom of the lamentable disarray in public policies – unreliable and foolish lawmakers, an unending string of half-baked ideas taken up and discarded in rapid succession, whether in public policy or in philosophical utopian speculations of the intellectual elite. In this topsy-turvy world of comic role reversals, fantasy not only provides a welcome respite from everyday woes; it is the fantasy itself that mirrors the condition of the very society it aims to amuse. Reality overtakes representation; comic conventions and topical reference merge to reflect the decline both of the community and of the genre. Whereas utopian schemes of a free and just society and dreams of a Golden Age of abundance and satisfaction of material needs constitute the very backbone of the plots of Old Comedy – a fact that accounts for its happy merger of festive celebration and political satire – the *Ecclesiazousae* is judged by many as the final *reductio ad absurdum* of the entire comic pattern.

Above all, it is contended, the critical distance between an imagined elsewhere and the actual space of the city of Athens is erased. This conjunction does not bring the longed-for rejuvenation of the body politic in the exercise of a creative if anomic energy. It does not unblock a stalled economy, both material and social, in the exuberant and liberating schemes of the comic hero. Rather, as Auger observes, it does away with the 'symbolic system of the city which is founded on codified exchanges', whether in the marketplace, at the altars (no gods are ever mentioned), in the exchange of women, or in politics. Marriage is abolished, and implicitly, sacrifice too, along with agriculture,

---

organization of property and sex'. He thinks it 'an obvious hypothesis that Aristophanes originally planned a play about women attending the Assemble, but after writing 557 lines, found that he had exhausted the subject; he therefore thought up a second subject, communism, in order to complete a comedy of normal length, but did not bother to alter anything in first half of play to prepare the way for the second half'. This was a fault, he continues, 'but it is a fault that is not likely to have troubled the audience much, since both subjects in themselves are entertaining'. MacDowell (1995) 320.

[20] On egotism, see Rothwell (1990) and Saïd (1979), and the introduction to this volume, p. 9.

which is to be conducted by slaves.[21] The line between public and private is erased, as is the analogical exchange between household and state.[22] All differentiation disappears into the collective, all symbolic meanings are 'beaten back into the materiality of consumable goods',[23] exemplified in the scene where kitchen utensils are personified and lined up to parody the solemn procession (*pompē*) of Athenian participants in the Panathenaiac festival (730–45).[24] Finally, in this most obscene of Aristophanes' extant work, the desublimated body reigns supreme, subject to a vertiginous mix of oral, genital, and anal fantasies, evoked in various combinations.[25]

The *Ecclesiazousae* is the third and last play in Aristophanes' surviving comic repertory that resorts to the theme of women in charge, and, as though in ascending or descending order (depending on how one reads the impact of women's claims to power in the city), this is the one that goes to the furthest extreme. It raises the matter of cross-dressing to new levels of self-conscious theatrical play, complicates the social definitions of masculine and feminine identity, and, above all, it takes the unusual step of leaving the women in power to enforce their utopian scheme, which by dissolving the institution of marriage and of the individual *oikos* itself, ensures the permanence of their rule in the new social order.

The comic exuberance of role reversal normally resides in its temporary duration – a source of revitalizing energy that closes on a reconciliation between male and female elements, and more importantly, a return to the accepted norms in the restoration of masculine dominance. In both the *Lysistrata* and the *Thesmophoriazousae*, women may challenge their male counterparts and compel them to come to terms with feminine demands. But the final scenes are transactions between

---

[21] Auger (1979) 90.
[22] Saïd (1979) 47. She further points out that letters of the alphabet, symbolically used in the jury system to assign the place of tribunal and the rank of the judges, have become just what they mean, each letter of the alphabet now standing literally for the initial of the dining hall where the meal is to be served (e.g., B = Stoa Basileia).
[23] Auger (1979) 90–5. See also Carrière (1979), Saïd (1979), and Saxenhouse (1992).
[24] See Ussher (1973) 178.
[25] Ober and Strauss (1990) and Ober (1998) give the most positive (and most ungendered) reading of the play, suggesting that its topic theme is 'egalitarianism and its limits', a matter high on the public agenda in the early years of the fourth century (how to 'use political equality to mediate social inequalities both legally and on the ideological plane'), and the poet's aim is to confront the citizen spectators with contradictions in their political system and its ideological goals. But it hardly disturbs the more general pessimistic assessment of the message(s) of the *Ecclesiazousae* to conclude that 'the fact that the play does not end in utter disaster might ... be taken as a guarded vote of confidence in an egalitarian socio-political order', Ober and Strauss (1990) 266–7.

men – whether between the men of Athens and Sparta in the *Lysistrata*, or in the second case, Euripides' collusion with his kinsman to engineer the latter's escape from the Scythian policeman. Earlier in the *Thesmophoriazousae*, the kinsman had been surrounded by women, who having penetrated his disguise, threaten him bodily harm. But the official representative of masculine law and order takes over, albeit in the effeminate figure of Cleisthenes, who both aids in detecting the kinsman's transgressive costume and sends for that same policeman to guard the prisoner until the magistrate's arrival. By contrast, under the dispensation of the new law, the captivity of the young man in the *Ecclesiazousae* at the hands of the old hags is a sign of an enthralment to women, which, despite his protests, he cannot subvert or avoid, now or in the future.

Finally, all three comedies emphasize the theme of *sōteria* (salvation). The *Lysistrata* and the *Ecclesiazousae* concoct their schemes in order to save the city, in the first instance, from the ruinous effects of war, and in the second, from the ruinous effects of greed and poverty. The *Thesmophoriazousae* modulates the theme to confront Euripides and his kinsman with the need to re-enact the poet's well-known *sōteria* plots in the interests of the two men's own salvation. The young man in the *Ecclesiazousae* requires the same, and, in fact, as he is dragged off by the two hags, he calls directly on Zeus *sōtēr* for rescue, but to no avail, although the aim of the women's plan, as Praxagora had argued in the first place, was to bring salvation to the ailing city. The point is made explicit. The young man's piteous cry, 'o poor unlucky, thrice unlucky, me,' *o dusdaimōn, trikskakodaimōn* (1098) is matched in reverse by the serving girl's apostrophe to the *makarios dēmos*, blessed citizenry, the *eudaimōn gē*, the lucky land (1112–14), whom she has just invited to the joyous feast. The price men must pay for happy feeding, it seems, must be paid in advance by unhappy sex, and if men are to enjoy a maternal bounty of inexhaustible nurture in filling their bellies, the women may, in a final reversal of roles, exact (or extort) sexual enjoyment from them as their reward.

This spectre of sexual coercion is precisely what Praxagora's husband, Blepyros, had initially feared when confronted by his neighbour Chremes with the news that the *Ecclesia* had voted to hand over the city's governance to the women (465–70). Performance of another sort is very much on his mind. But Praxagora subsequently relieved his anxieties, reassuring him that, as an older and uglier man, he will benefit from the new laws and have first rights to enjoy the favours of young women (611–29). Blepyros may go off with the dancing girls at the end to enjoy the festivities, following the lead of the servant girl.[26] In so doing, the play may gesture briefly to the typical comic pattern of rejuvenated masculine strength that symbolizes renewed fertility in the city and a new vigour invested in the body politic, which elsewhere in comedy is often, in fact, enacted in the form of a marriage. But the reversal of this pattern in the figures of an old woman and a non-compliant young consort seems to tilt in the opposite direction to signify sterility, and according to the unhappy young man, it even portends death.[27]

Why then does Aristophanes promise sex to older men but actually stage the reverse? What logic links the theme of gynaecocracy to the two paradoxes I have outlined – the apparent discrepancy between conservatism and innovation, on the one hand, and on the other, the reversal of communal ideals of civic harmony into yet another and more graphic instance of self-interested greed, one which now escalates into a physical violence that replaces the desired image of civic wholeness with the contrary model of a Dionysiac *sparagmos*? My response is to suggest that certain long-lived cultural scenarios may be lurking behind the social engineering of utopian schemes that finds its fullest and for some, its most self-defeating, exemplar in the spectacle (and spectre) of an Athens and its male citizen body given over to women's rule. I therefore propose that we listen for responsive chords whose echoes we might hear in the comic conventions of mythic plots and philosophical utopian schemes, as these are performed in the theatrical milieu. Even closer to home, behind the seeming inventive resources of free comic play, we may well detect resonances of the stories that Athens tells about itself, about its own traditions and its city's foundation. In short, within the *Ecclesiazousae*'s glittering comic manipulation of the performances of Athenian citizenry, there is a further, older story, as I hope to demonstrate, that the play inevitably also enacts. It is this level of performance with which the remainder of this chapter will be concerned.

[26] It is assumed, but not certain, that Blepyros is the celebrant in question.
[27] See, for example, Saïd (1979) 60, Auger (1979) 94, and Carrière (1979) 106. On rejuvenative motifs in Old Comedy, see Cornford (1914) 90–3, and more recently, on the correlation of old age and time past in myth and utopia, see Carrière (1979) 90–2. Some assess the ending more positively as an outburst of a wild comic energy: Konstan and Dillon (1981) 382, and cf. Sommerstein (1984) 320, and Henderson (1987) 119–20, and (1996) 150. Bowie (1993) sensibly suggests that 'one should probably not choose either pole here', but all his arguments about the licence granted to old women in Greek culture cannot, in my opinion, overcome the savagery of the invective and the negative associations of their sexuality.

III. Utopia and myth

By taking this approach to the *Ecclesiazousae*, my emphasis lies on the conception and construction of a plot that acts out the terms and consequences of gynaecocratic rule. Given a play whose premise is to erase the lines of difference in the city, I prefer to maintain the lines of difference between the imaginary and the real in assessing what motives might lie behind the play, succumbing neither to a wholly 'sociological illusion' nor to one that is simply 'textual', as Vidal-Naquet has memorably put it.[28] Neither a literal rendition of reality nor a purely metaphorical signifier, the figure of 'woman' acting in the theatre must be considered in the light of the more ambiguous and ambivalent negotiations between past and present, convention and originality, theme and variation, on which the genre of Old Comedy depends.

The mediating force between the imaginary and the real is precisely the double-sided interplay between myth and utopia, between a return to the past and a projection of defined social rules for the future that meet in the prospect of a magical renewal of a decadent society and its liberation from an unhappy and chaotic present in the proposition and fulfilment of some great comic idea. That past, as we have come to understand it, is typically represented as the pre-Olympian age, or the age of Kronos, the time before Zeus came to power.[29] Its characteristics are articulated in archaic poetry, in Homer and especially in Hesiod, in the myth of the Five Ages, the contrasting visions of the just and unjust city, and the account of Prometheus and Pandora.[30] These same themes and patterns are reflected also in aspects of certain festivals (including the Kronia in Athens) which at certain times of the year celebrate the carnivalesque reversal of roles – of gender, social class, and status – in forms of controlled anarchy, not unlike the *Ecclesiazousae* itself in many of its details.[31] This age of Kronos is two sided. It participates in a cultural schema of human development that leads from savagery to civilization, from the raw to the cooked, from anarchy to the establishment of social rules. But the price to be paid for these benefits is a surrender of a primitive, natural state of origins, of freedom, spontaneity, abundance, peace, and justice in favour of a regime of libidinal constraints, social hierarchies, unequal divisions, and those inescapable necessities of toil, pain, old age – and above all, of mor-

---

[28] Vidal-Naquet (1979) 5–6. See also Loraux (1991) 19.
[29] See especially, Carrière (1979) 85–118.
[30] See especially, Auger (1979) 72–8.
[31] One these rituals of reversal, see the full discussion of Versnel (1994) 115–35, with copious bibliography.

tality.[32] Utopia, the brilliant concoction of a counter-reality, shares in the same aspirations and the same ambivalences that attend the age of Kronos. In their search to reinstitute or, better, to reinvent a juster society, as filtered through contemporary democratic ideals, utopian schemes that answer to the concerns of contemporary politics harness the archaic powers of myth to a purposeful design.[33] The *Birds*, that other full-blown utopian fantasy, directly engages with this pattern, since the new regime depends on displacing the gods in favour of the birds, who, it is argued, preceded the Olympian deities now in power. There are echoes of the Gigantomachy throughout and Prometheus appears on stage at the end. In this relapse to an earlier theogonic state, the comic hero, Pisthetairos, even ends up by installing himself as the new universal *tyrannos* over Zeus. In short, if I may use psychoanalytic terms, Old Comedy places the 'id' of unrepressed desire, characteristic of the age of Kronos, over the 'superego' of Olympian realities in the present day, and mixes a nostalgic desire for innocent origins with a self-centred will to mastery.[34] In its imposition of new laws as a condition for procuring that new society, comic utopias may therefore tend, as Jean-Claude Carrière has put it, to produce a disturbing best of worlds or even a dangerous *dystopia* that ends not in progress but in regress, or at least, in an ironic ambivalence about the limitless extent of human desires.[35] These concepts deserve fuller elaboration. But in the limited space at my disposal, I want to pursue a particular version of a story that belongs to this age of Kronos, one that is directly situated in the local traditions of Attica and which I hope may cast instructive light on the utopian project of the *Ecclesiazousae* and the logic of its paradoxical comic performance.

IV. The age of Kekrops

In this myth, we are in the age of Kekrops, the first king of Athens. He is of autochthonous origins, a hybrid figure, part human, part serpent, who played a key role in establishing the basic institutions of the Athenian way of life that marked the passage from nature to culture, from savagery to civilization. In keeping perhaps with that hybrid form,

---

[32] On Kronos, see especially, Vidal-Naquet (1986) 363–4 and further, Versnel (1994) 90–9, 106–14, with exhaustive discussion and bibliography.
[33] On utopia, Golden Age, and the myth of Kronos in comedy, see especially the excellent analysis of Carrière (1979) 85–118, and see too Auger (1979).
[34] On nostalgia for origins and the will to mastery, see the provocative remarks of Konstan (1990) in his subtle analysis of utopian ideas in the *Birds*.
[35] Carrière (1979) 101.

Kekrops seems to represent both sides of the divide. He consolidates or commemorates the earlier age by instituting rituals that honoured the old gods who came before Zeus. Specifically, he erects the first altar to Kronos and Ops (Rhea) and founds the festival of the Kronia, whose defining feature was precisely the temporary reversal of roles: masters and slaves, men and women. At the same time, during his reign, Kekrops transforms the social organization of the people whom he has organized into a settled community, 'inventing many laws for humans' as the scholiast to Aristophanes' *Ploutos* 773, specifies. The particular story I have in mind is set in the frame of a transition to the Olympian order. Its source is of late provenance, Augustine in the *City of God* (18.9), quoting Varro, but its typology is familiar in mythic accounts of the archaic and classical period and the assumptions that govern it can only refer to the workings of a democratic city.[36]

The ostensible motive for the myth is the naming of the city which stems from the dispute between Athena and Poseidon for control of Athens. Two portents announce their rivalry: a mysterious olive tree that suddenly appears on the Acropolis and a source of gushing water. Kekrops sent to the Delphic oracle to find out what this meant and what was to be done. Apollo replied that the olive signified Athena and the spring Poseidon, and that it was up to the citizens to decide from which of the two gods (whose symbols these were) the city should take its name. Kekrops then called together the citizens of both sexes – for at that time it was the custom that women too should have a part in public deliberations. The men voted for Poseidon and the women for Athena, and because the women outnumbered the men by exactly one, Athena won the victory. The women, it seems, did not. Quite the contrary. In response to Poseidon's wrath (he flooded the land), Kekrops decreed that 'the women must lose the vote, no child shall take the mother's name, and they themselves cannot be called Athenian women, *Athenaiai*'. The same scholiast to the *Ploutos* who had claimed that Kekrops 'brought the Athenians out of a state of wildness (*agriotēs*)

---

[36] The citation is from Varro's *de gente populi Romani* (fr. 7, H. Peter (1837–1914), *Historicorum Romanorum Reliquiae*, vol. II, 13). Pembroke (1967) 27, remarks on assessing the provenance of Varro's tale: 'What is certain is that variations and combinations of these stories were circulating over a period of centuries. It makes no difference whether the process was predominantly oral, or literary, and no reason why the story in Varro, or an earlier version of it, should not be taken as model rather than the copy.' In any case, as Castriota (1992) 148, argues, there may be a reference to this version in in Xen. *Mem* 3.5.9–10, where the adjudication (*krisis*) of the dispute involves *hoi peri Kekropa*. Attributed to Socrates, the remark may well indicate the story was known in the fifth century. See further below on the sculptures of the west pediment of the Parthenon and Castriota's more general argument.

Performance of utopia in the *Ecclesiazousae* 183

into tameness (*hēmerotēs*)', specifies that this autochthonous king was the inventor of marriage: 'Some say he found men and women having intercourse quite casually, so that no son could tell who was his father, no father who was his son. Kekrops accordingly drew up the law making them cohabit openly and in pairs. He also discovered the two natures of the father and the mother'. Or, as another source puts it, 'Kekrops legislated that women, who before mated like beasts (*thēria*), be given in marriage to one man'.[37]

This story is an exemplary version of the 'invention of patriarchy' which both taught men their role in sexual reproduction and established the rules of patrilineal kinship in a system of monogamous marriage that brought women under the sexual control of their mates and sons under the jurisdiction of their fathers.[38] The striking significance of this myth, we should note, lies in the correlation of all the terms – in the political, social, and religious spheres. To vote in the political process is equivalent to or matched by claims to the rights over progeny, and in this primitive city which has not yet established the rules of the sexual division of labour or the distinction between public and private domains, between *oikos* and polis or even between mortal women and goddesses, women exercise more power than men. The women's numerical majority of a single extra vote is not only a face-saving device to account for the embarrassing anomaly of a goddess' victory in what will later become a city of men. It also assumes a sufficient difference between the sexes and their respective interests to promote an unquestioning loyalty to one's own kind. But 'more' is also 'stronger', and in this tale of ostensible parity between the sexes in their mutual rights to vote, there is more than a hint of gynaecocracy, or more accurately, matriarchy, recalling a time when women were in charge, indulged in sexual freedom to mate as they pleased, and by a mother's prerogative gave their names to the children they bore. Instituting the *oikos*, hitherto unknown, will put her and keep her in her place, and to make certain of her subordinate status, she can no longer be called an *Athenaia* in gendered symmetry with an *Athenaios*, a change that both reinforces her exclusion from the political sphere of action and obviates any semantic confusion with the tutelary goddess or the official name of the city.

---

[37] John of Antioch in *FHG* IV, p. 547, F 13.5. Other sources, in addition to the scholion on *Ploutos* 773, include Klearchos of Soloi [pupil of Aristotle] quoted by Athenaeus, 13.555d (= *FHG* II, p. 319, F 49); Justin 2.6; Charax of Pergamum (*FGrH* 103 F 38); Nonnus, *Dionysiaca* 41.383. Also schol. *Il* 18.483. For discussion, see Pembroke (1967) 26–7, 29–32, Vidal-Naquet (1986) 216–17, and Tyrrell (1984) 28–31.
[38] See, especially, Pembroke (1967) 26–7, and Tyrrell (1984) 28–30.

The relevance of this story to the plot and the title of the *Ecclesiazousae* should be obvious.[39] The women go to the Assembly. This is the first essential step. They vote themselves into power – unanimity of opinion is a given – and their plan, as it turns out, entails consequences that are perfectly consistent with the conditions of the first stage in the reign of Kekrops: dismantle the individual *oikos*, and with it, the rights of private property along with the institution of monogamous marriage. With the dissolution of matrimony comes sexual freedom and its inevitable outcome – no man will be able to recognize his own children and no children their father. Blepyros immediately voices this anxiety about the new arrangements that dispense with an already threatened paternal authority: 'If indeed, everyone in the younger generation will consider all older men to be their fathers', he says, 'then sons will take this as a licence to beat up any old man, since they already do this to their own fathers' (638–9).[40] Finally, in addition to the abrogation of patrilineal kinship is the spectre of incest that arises from the decree that gives priority in sex to the older generation, provoking the young girl's exclamation: 'If you put this law into effect, you'll fill the land with Oedipuses' (1038–42). In short, the women's decree will produce fatherless offspring, encourage sexual promiscuity, and lead to the mixing of generations, but it is also coupled with the promise of abundance, prosperity, and freedom from toil that identify the conditions of the primitive community and the age of Kronos.

This gynaecocratic scheme gives an especially elegant demonstration of the dialectical relationship between myth and utopia, the archaic and the revolutionary, the primitive and the decadent. The basis of the women's decision to seek power in the city, let us recall, rests on the archaic traditions they claim to represent, the old ways they maintain until now, and their initial maternal concerns. We might be returned to Hesiod's depiction of the Silver Age, where men never grew up and stayed beside their mothers for a hundred years. But those feminine values (and the women's expertise in management) derive from their status in the *oikos*, itself the sign of reliable conservatism in the present time of the politically impotent city. What is coded as myth and a primordial state of affairs is represented in the plot as an insurrection

---

[39] Rothwell (1990) 9 n. 43, seems to be the only critic to suggest, even if just in passing, that the age of Kekrops might be a possible source for the plot of the *Ecclesiazousae*.

[40] This anxiety about sons beating their fathers shows another, more threatening aspect of the age of Kronos (who himself had violently replaced his own father), one that is a common preoccupation of Aristophanic comedy, as in the *Clouds* or the *Wasps*, where the scales are always weighted in favour of the triumph of the older generation (of men), especially in libidinal renewal.

against male authority and an outlandish situation of role reversal to overturn an existing order. In fact, much of the humorous irony as well as the anxiety in the play relies on the mirror effect of reversals, when egalitarian principles prove to be just what they mean and old women demand the same privileges that had been promised to men. This neat turnabout in the distribution of sexual favours is not one, of course, that Blepyros, intent on securing his own benefits with a younger and prettier girl in the new dispensation, had ever seriously contemplated.[41] The old women, accused of being on the threshold of death, represent the old in its most threatening form, and in the confrontation between the old and the young, the question of the 'new versus the old' recurs now in embodied form, where the women revert to 'type' by disclosing a voracity of appetite that social constraints had previously kept under control. It is precisely the framing of utopia as a scheme that engages the simultaneously innovative *and* regressive rule of women which accounts, I suggest, for the problems critics have faced in evaluating the structure of the play. And it is precisely the unstated ambivalence about the mixture of masculine desire and anxiety that dictates the mostly negative responses of modern day critics, who displace that ambivalence from the substance – what is really at stake – (the *acting out* of female libido) to critique of the form (the patterns of *action* in the comic genre).[42]

In the mythic perspective, men have not yet acquired the social markers of paternity and property that define their masculine identity. They have not yet learned Aristotle's precept as enunciated in the *Politics* that men are by nature more fit to command than women (*Pol.* 1.12.1, 1259b 1–2), nor that the relationship of male to female is by nature superior, one governing and the other governed (*Pol.* 1.5.7, 1254a 13–14). From the point of view of present time, however, gynaecocracy, as earlier observed, marks the logical result in a city where the men are no longer fully men. The initial ploy of cross-dressing when women steal their husbands' clothes and don false beards, and the men in turn have no other choice than to put on their wives' saffron dresses and Persian slippers already attests to this state of the affairs, and the play on several occasions scornfully makes an

---

[41] The new rules for sex, proposed by Praxagora, are set on equal terms, but the emphasis here (611–30) and later at Praxagora's triumphal exit centres on pleasures for men (689–709). By contrast, the official decree read out by the hag specifies only women's rights (1015–20). The ground has clearly shifted.

[42] The issue at stake is not the gender of the individual critic, but the degree to which critics interiorize (or 'naturalize') the very cultural assumptions they are aiming to explicate.

explicit point of men's effeminacy. The spectators confront neither heroic nor civic values; there is no gesture to the manly arts of war or agriculture. They are shown no other life for men except one that shuttles between the house and the Assembly, where the credulous citizens prove as flighty and unstable as women are supposed to be, unable to penetrate the disguise of these pale-faced interlopers and all too ready to vote the women into power. No wonder the city needs its real women when there are no men worthy of the name and when the leading politician, we may recall, is himself accused of having borrowed a beard because he once was a woman. This is an extreme example of the general rule as expressed in the *Lysistrata*, where the women claim they have heard the men themselves going about the streets saying publicly 'there is no man in this town' (524). This prior effeminization, this condition of being less than a man, is an essential prerequisite for any scenario, tragic or comic, where women gain the upper hand. For when in defiance of social norms women take charge, the logic of gender opposition goes into effect and decrees that men must have already descended from superior to inferior status, their masculine deficits having already been defined by the exhibition of feminine strength (how otherwise could women enforce their will?).

In the comic idiom, the power game is played above all on the field of sex. All three plays featuring 'women on top' link female assertions of power to the cultural construction of women's libidinal desires and use that sexuality as the underlying source of comic ambivalence which drives the plot. The *Lysistrata* stages a sex strike precisely in order to bring husbands back to the marital bed; the women of the *Thesmophoriazousae* resent Euripides' disclosure of their sexual secrets on the tragic stage, because it prompts men in the audience to suspect their own wives and hence, among other restrictions, to inhibit their amorous affairs. The *Ecclesiazousae* opens with Praxagora's soliloquy on the lamp, the 'light of the indoors', which illuminates all the hidden recesses of women's domain, whether for sex in the boudoir, pilferage of household stores, or genital depilation (1–16). As this most openly obscene of all Aristophanes' plays proceeds, the true import of gynaecocracy is revealed in the apparently seamless connection established between political and sexual enfranchisement. This association implies that women, once given the freedom of political speech, will also exercise a sexual freedom that can outstrip and finally deflate phallic power once and for all. That same lamp, which knows how to keep women's secrets indoors, is brought outside to be used as a beacon signal, summoning the women to a predawn rendezvous to put their plan for infiltrating the Assembly into effect.[43] The double threat of women in charge culminates in the need to pack all these anxieties in the staging of the worst possible scenario of the female grotesque body – ugly hags, Empousas, smeared with white lead, looking like monkeys, creatures who have come up from the dead, and worse, demonic figures, who pounce on their unwilling victim (e.g., 904, 935, 1056, 1071–2). The hapless fellow himself expects to die and prays for an even worse fate to finish off his pursuer:

> If I die, as is probable, sailing here with these two whores,
> bury me at the very mouth of the harbour, and this one here, from
> the top of her body, pouring tar into her, still alive, and then
> pouring molten lead in a circle around her ankles, put her on top
> as the representative (*prophasis*) of a *lēkythos*.
>
> (1105–11)

This hyperbolic comic turn caps the grotesque scene of the tug of war on stage with a series of obscene references that equate the act of sex with death and liken the old woman, her face painted with white cosmetics, to a funereal lekythos that, fastened to its base like a statue, is to be placed upside down as a monument over his grave.[44] The coupling of sexuality and anti-fertility in the coupling of an old woman and a young man in metaphors that exploit the cultural associations between marriage and death would seem to indicate that comic rejuvenation has not taken place, for either sex, despite the slapstick virtues of the scene, which would play so well in the comic theatre. The new situation of women in charge was designed to reverse the city's fortunes, both moral and economic, and to fulfil a promise of abundance and plenitude for all. But it only seems to intensify the theme of the city's blocked reproductive powers, embodied earlier in the male figure of Blepyros, who, when compelled to appear in women's dress, when he emerges from the house, prays to Eileithyia, the midwife goddess, to relieve his constipation – and let him give birth to a turd.[45]

Praxagora's later excuse to her husband for her absence was a claim

---

[43] The reference to the lamp as a beacon, as Bowie (1993) 255, observes, may appropriately recall Clytemnestra's connections to such fire signals at the opening of Aeschylus' *Agamemnon*. On the *Oresteia* and the *Ecclesiazousae*, see further below.

[44] Earlier, in the scene between the first hag and the young man, he had pretended that her lover would be jealous if he gave her a kiss, a lover he describes as a 'painter who decorates *lēkythoi* for the dead' (996). Slater (1989) suggests that these references to cosmetics and white ground *lēkythoi* also apply to the painting of theatre masks.

[45] On this extended scene (311–72) and other excremental references (e.g., 78, 433, 464, 595, 640, 870–1, 1059–62), see Bowie (1993) 258, who justifiably suggests that these are signs of disorder and infertility in the male world.

to have been attending a pregnant friend who was just giving birth to a male child (549). This, of course, is not true in this case, but Praxagora's alibi points to the one usual source of political empowerment for women in the polis as mothers of citizen sons. This is one of the arguments, in fact, which the disguised Praxagora makes to the Assembly for giving political rule to women, since mothers, not fathers, are the ones who are most concerned with preserving the lives of their soldier boys (233–5), and who better than a mother, she says, to assure the provision of food (233–5)?[46] Whether giving, saving, or sustaining life, maternal concerns legitimate women's hegemony in the household and the assurance of prosperity in the new political regime, founded, as Taillardat puts it, on a 'politics of the belly'.[47] But when, on the analogy of motherhood, women's selfless concern for the welfare of the state turns into self-interested concern for sex, the psychological anxiety that arises in the situation stems from the threatened transgression of the tabooed line between maternity and sexuality. The young girl – who has a self-interested claim on the young man herself – expresses this panic in terms unequivocal enough to drive off the first hag:

> He isn't old enough to sleep with you;
> You'll be his mother rather than his wife.
> If you establish this to be the law (*nomos*),
> You'll fill the country up with Oedipuses.
>
> (1039–42)

Most critics simply assume that the pairing of an old woman and a young man is contrary to 'nature' and that these scenes illustrate a *reductio ad absurdum* of an egalitarian scheme that would use *nomos* to legislate *physis*.[48] But while we hear a great deal in the play about laws and decrees (*nomoi* and *psēphismata*), we should beware of assuming some idea of immutable 'nature' as its counterpart, especially in a society where by convention men tended to marry wives far younger than themselves and the bloom of youth was hyperidealized in and of

---

[46] On the respect for mothers in comedy, see Lévy (1976) 108, Henderson (1987) 111, and Loraux (1993) 228. Auger (1979) also notes the significance of maternity in the *Ecclesiazousae*, but interprets it pejoratively as a reduction of women's functions. The analyses of both Auger (1979) and Saïd (1979), which appear in the same volume and overlap in some important details, are among the best treatments of the *Ecclesiazousae*. Nevertheless, they seem to replicate the ideological attitudes of Athenian men, judging women somehow as an inevitable source of degradation and failure.

[47] Taillardat (1965) 395–8, and Saïd (1979) 43–5, 49–50.

[48] On conflicts in comedy between 'nature' and law, see, Carrière (1979) 90–3, and Saïd (1979) 58–60.

itself. At any rate, it is worth noting that the word, *physis*, or its equivalent, is never even mentioned in the play. This is not to overlook the fact that lewd old women (and not men) are often subjected to scurrilous abuse in comedy,[49] nor that the public legislation of private instincts is also not at stake. But the issue is far more one of social propriety, which dictates, as the saying goes: 'A woman who leaves the house should be at a stage of life when those who meet her ask not whose wife but whose mother she is' (Hypereides *apud* Stob. 74.33). Hence, it is more the promiscuous mixing of categories, old and young, parents and children, along with the confusion in public and private domains, that testifies to the anarchic aspects of the age of Kronos (and Kekrops). Embodied in the figure of a sexualized crone, these overtake and undermine the blissful utopian dream of a unified primitive community, fostered by fantasies of a benevolent maternal imago.[50]

If the play then ends in the triumph of a gynaecocratic rule, it also bears the stamp that marks this and many other 'myths of matriarchy' of this kind with the ideological overload that relates how in the past women once ruled. Such myths are normally found in 'societies where there also exist a set of cultural rules and procedures for determining sexual dimorphism in social and cultural tasks'. Women once had power, so the story goes, but they abused it through 'trickery and unbridled sexuality', thus fostering 'chaos and misrule'. The men, therefore, rebelled. They assumed control and took steps to institutionalize the subordination of women. The point of the myth is not the recording of some historical or prehistorical state of affairs, as Bachofen would have liked (and instantiated with this play, among others), but rather the demonstration that women are not fit to rule, only to be ruled.[51] This myth is 'not a memory of history, but a social charter', which 'may be part of social history in providing justification for a present and perhaps permanent reality by giving an invented "historical" explanation of how this reality was created'.[52]

The scenario enacted in the time of Kekrops, involving a radical reform of social and political arrangements, and its reverse, as performed

---

[49] See Oeri (1948) 7–12, Taillardat (1965) 49–50, and Henderson (1987). Carson (1990) 144–8, has excellent remarks on the Greek belief that 'a woman' s life has no prime, but rather a season of unripe virginity followed by a season of overripe maturity, with the single occasion of defloration as the dividing line'.
[50] On the significance of incest, although framed somewhat differently, see Saxonhouse (1992) 14.
[51] Bamberger (1974) 276, 280.
[52] Bamberger (1974) 267.

in Aristophanes' *Ecclesiazousae*, when women venture out of their homes to take over the rule in the city, only confirms the same pattern of women's 'misrule' and on the same grounds. In addition to lusty desire, women are tricky. They dress as men and lay their plots, claiming as a virtue that they cannot be deceived in office because they are such arch-deceivers themselves (236–8). Some critics have posited some greater role for women in post-war Athens,[53] or a greater psychological interest in their portrayal.[54] It may even be argued that by their initial cross-dressing, women have somehow turned into men. If they *look* like men to take over the Assembly, they must also eventually *act* like men when they take over the state.[55] But if topical concerns, both with new forms of legislation and the renewal of civic harmony, lend a timely atmosphere to the play, there is no doubting, I think, that the construction of the plot obeys the rules of an already prescribed scenario. These hyperfeminine women portrayed in the comic theatre are only reverting to the predictable terms enshrined in the cultural imaginary, in which women, indeed, are perceived as being too close to nature, to the imperious demands of the belly, whether for food or for sex. In turning from maternal nurturing to sexual predation, or rather in combining the two, they are only doing what they would always do, it seems, if given half a chance. Hence Kekrops invented marriage. For all the on-stage cross-dressing and gender games, what the performance of the *Ecclesiazousae* finally enacts is also the oldest message of all about gender propriety.

v. The *Oresteia*

This pattern of a 'myth of matriarchy' may sound familiar to some ears. I confess I used it once before in general terms in a piece I wrote a long time ago on the *Oresteia*, with the aim of demonstrating how closely the conduct of the trilogy followed this basic outline. I later realized, however, that the same myth of Kekrops might also be operating behind the scenes, as it were, to situate the ending of Aeschylus' trilogy in a more local frame of reference, one that would align it directly with the

---

[53] Lévy (1976) 111. Some argue for a higher proportion of mature women in the population, owing to the high casualty rates of Athenian men in the naval campaigns of 410–404. See Strauss (1986) 70–86, 82 n. 3, and Taaffe (1993) 131. The comedies of 'women on top' begin in 411 with the *Lysistrata*, however, and continue well down into the fourth century.

[54] Tschiedel (1984) 47, ascribes this interest to the influence of Euripides on Aristophanes.

[55] Tschiedel (1984) 39.

city of Athens, its patron goddess, and hence reinforce the ideological validity of the decisive part taken by Athena's city in the resolution of Argive Orestes' case.[56] The status of Athena herself is at issue here. For however Athens may glory in Athena's prestige, a certain paradox resides in the fact that this city of patrilineal kinship is named for and belongs to a female divinity, and more than one mythic tradition attempts to account for this disturbing anomaly.[57] Aristophanes puts it neatly with a comic twist in the *Birds*: 'How could a city be well ordered where a god is born a woman, wears complete armour, and Cleisthenes has a spindle?' (829–31). Although the *Eumenides* shows an Athena firmly ensconced in power, the crisis in the city which claims her attention replays several significant elements in the myth of Kekrops – including conflict between different deities and opposition between male and female interests on both human and divine levels. The similarity of pattern to the terms of this myth, if I am correct in my surmise, would lend powerful support to what we have assumed to be Aeschylus' 'inventive' solutions regarding Athena's successful mediation between Apollo and the Erinyes.

Bachofen himself invoked the myth of Kekrops in support of his theory of matriarchy as indeed he did for the *Eumenides*, but he only juxtaposed the two on the basis of 'mother right' without noting the more extensive resemblances between them.[58] The myth of Kekrops and the *Oresteia*, let us recall, both relate how women by exercising power, lost it, along with their superior position in the household and their self-assertion in sexual affairs. In this reading of the *Oresteia*, Clytemnestra's bid for political power would be the correlative of the 'right to vote', since, in the first play, the choros honours her authority (*kratos*) as regent in her husband's absence (*Ag.* 258–60), and in the second, Orestes, after killing his mother and Aegisthus, proclaims his victory over the twin 'tyrants' (*Choe.* 973). The 'domestication' of the Erinyes in Athenian cult, however, functions to reduce their juridical power over men's affairs, and they are defeated, of course, in their defence of a mother's rights. Apollo's telling argument, echoed by Athena, that the father is the only true begetter and the mother merely a receptacle-nurse is but a more extreme version of the Kekropian law, which decreed that henceforth children will be known only by the name of their fathers.

Both the myth of Kekrops and the *Eumenides* share the setting of a

[56] What follows is a slightly expanded version of what I added to the original essay (1978) when revising it for publication in Zeitlin (1995) 115–18.
[57] Loraux (1981) 60–1, and see too (1981a) 119–52.
[58] Bachofen (1867 [1954]) 158.

juridical dispute between competing male and female claims and both share the logic that insists on the intrinsic links between political and domestic hegemony. Both are also clear in identifying the basic source of women's power as maternal dominance. Hence the solution that emerges is to attenuate (or deny) that power, while at the same time reserving honour for a virginal goddess (Athena). She is finally the key figure in both contests, whether in the role of adjudicated (myth of Kekrops) or in that of adjudicator (*Eumenides*).

In Aeschylus, the jury that is to decide the case of Orestes is made up of Athenian citizens, who, as in the quarrel between Athena and Poseidon, are summoned to arbitrate a dispute between opposing divinities (Apollo and the Erinyes). But, as in the earlier story, there is a risk that the matter might not reach a definitive outcome, as indeed would have been the case in the Athens of Kekrops, had there not been an extra vote on one side to tip the balance in favour of Athena. Our play anticipates the dilemma of such a judicial impasse, even though it is no longer a literal matter of female enfranchisement. The *Eumenides* establishes in advance a means of resolving a tied vote and, in the face of its actuality, promptly puts it into operation. Athena, we note, is the one who takes the lead on both accounts and for her own interests. Whether we understand the text to mean that she will cast a vote, if the other votes are equal, or that she will declare a tied vote to be an acquittal, it is she who sets the rules and she who exercises her judgement in favour of Orestes, when the situation arises, claiming as her justification that 'but for marriage [i.e. for myself], I am always for the male with all my heart, and strongly on my father's side' (*Eum.* 737–8).[59]

From the juridical perspective, the provision for breaking a tied vote might seem a necessary precaution to ensure the proper functioning of a jury in a law-court. But viewed through the lens of the myth of Kekrops, both the provision itself and Athena's reasons for putting it into practice take on a different cast. Underlying the explanation for Athena's victory over Poseidon is the assumption that males and females pursue their own quite separate interests, each group bound to maintain solidarity by siding automatically with their own kind.[60] It

---

[59] The status of Athena's vote is a source of continuing debate, along with the question about the number of jurors. For recent discussion of both sides of this debate, see Sommerstein (1989) 221–2, and Seaford (1995) 209–12. Whatever solution is adopted (and I lean to the idea that the jurors' votes were equal), it does not affect my argument, since the parallels between the two stories are not exact. My point is simply that the emphasis on setting the rules in case of a tied vote denotes, and perhaps hints at, the same preoccupation we find in the earlier myth.

[60] E.g., Aesch. *Suppl.*, 640–5; Ar. *Thesm.*, 520–6; Eur. *Hel.*, 329.

is only on this basis, in fact, that the myth of Kekrops can resolve the paradox of how a female divinity came to hold power in a city of men. But in the *Oresteia*, it seems, Athena returns the favour. She repudiates any allegiance to a feminine cause (since she has no mother) and explicitly declares her partisanship of men and masculine institutions. Whereas the goddess had initially profited from the women's loyalty to gain possession of the city, she now both upholds (and extends) the law of Kekrops that had decreed the primacy of the paternal bond and the significance of marriage, and she uses her tie-breaking power to acquit Orestes and thereby side with the male. Athena thus ratifies again, as it were, the reorganization of the city's structure that followed in the wake of her original victory for control over Athens, a victory that put an end to women's significance in procreation and politics and brought that particular version of a myth of matriarchy to an end.

Augustine's reaction (*City of God* 18.9) to the justice of this ultimate outcome is illuminating – and also tantalizing:

And when Athens was struck by the conquered male, it was compelled to avenge the victory of the victorious female, being more in awe of the waters of Neptune [Poseidon] than of the weapons of Minerva [Athena]. Nor did she defend the women who had voted for her; when they lost the right of suffrage for the future, and their sons were cut off from their mothers' names, she might at least have seen to it that they had the privilege of being called Athenians and of bearing the name of the goddess, since they had given her the victory over the male god by their votes. What comments, and how lengthy, might be offered on this subject, if only my discourse were not hurrying on to other themes! [61]

Aeschylus' version of the same dilemma as the myth of Kekrops is framed for different ends (the foundation of the law-court and the cult of the Eumenides). At the same time, because it recalls (and partially reverses) the terms of this earlier myth of origins, the *Eumenides* gains additional authority by placing a distinctive Athenian stamp on the strategy of myth-making that appealed for its prestige to more general cosmogonic and theogonic contests between Olympian and pre-Olympian (or chthonic) forces. If the outcome of the *Oresteia* also judges and justifies Athena, as I suggested in the conclusion to that earlier essay, it also, we might add, justifies the male citizens' endorsement of her hegemony over their affairs from the time of Kekrops up to the present day.

If my argument is correct that both the *Ecclesiazousae* and the *Oresteia* share a common mythic pattern in their enactment of competition

---

[61] Tr. Sanford and Green (1965).

between male and female in the public domain, the two, as representatives of dramatic genres, also share the idea of re-enacting that competition in a staged version of the city's two major arenas for performance before an audience of its citizens: the Assembly, in the first instance, and the law-court, in the second. Both arenas are indeed the loci where the rules of democratic procedure are put into practice and where the rhetorical *agōnes* of debate and competing discourses have more than a little in common with the conventions and experience of the theatre itself. Assembly, law-court, and theatre are all sites of visual display. In turning now to architectural sculpture, which, unlike theatre, of course, occupies a permanent place in the spectator culture of fifth-century Athens, the issue of performance takes a different turn. But the visual arts too may at a certain level be subsumed into an expanded definition that takes account of the narrative propensities of Greek art for telling a story, whether in painted pictures or in architectural sculpture (pediments, metopes, friezes), or, more precisely, in framing a significant moment and thereby capturing the essence of that story in a single scene, replete with a cast of characters, whose identities are meant to be recognized by distinctive attributes or props. At the same time, given the static nature of any visual artefact, it could also be said that monumental art itself provides a setting, a permanent stage against which the drama of everyday life or the ceremoniousness of public ritual are played out. The Parthenon can be viewed as just such a setting, a particularly egregious example of the city's representation of itself and its sustaining myths in visual form.

VI. *The Parthenon*

The *Oresteia* and the *Ecclesiazousae* are separated by sixty-five years. The first – the tragedy – is most often taken to express the state of visionary optimism following the victory over the Persians to laud the triumph of civilization and the institution of the law-court. The second, by contrast, – the comedy – supposedly follows a momentous defeat to civic morale, not entirely overcome by the economic improvement of more recent years and the restoration of democracy after the Rule of the Thirty. The outcome of one is not matched by the outcome of the other, and in the *Ecclesiazousae* the gods are nowhere to be found. There is a suspicious resemblance, however, between the Erinyes in the *Eumenides* and what they would do to their male victim (Orestes) and the series of hags we have met at the end of the *Ecclesiazousae*, one of whom finally triumphantly drags the fellow off stage.

This comparison could and should be developed further.[62] But I would like to turn now to an important monument in the city, whose time of construction and completion spans the interval between the tragic and comic works. The monument in question is the Parthenon, and the aspect which concerns us is the west pediment, which depicted the contest between Athena and Poseidon. Badly damaged in the explosion of 1687, we are aided in restoration by a pre-existing drawing. There is no archaeological consensus as to the identification of all the figures on the pediment, except for Poseidon, Athena, and Kekrops in the centre, nor can we be certain of the exact version of the myth that was used.[63] But I am intrigued by a recent hypothesis put forth by David Castriota. He notes the unusual predominance of female figures on the pediment, arguing that seven or possibly eight of the adult figures are female. By contrast, it is likely that only three or at most, four other figures could have been mature male citizens. If the figures in the corners represented rivers or springs, the outside parameters would still consist of a ratio of six women to two or three males. Furthermore, Castriota notes, these females are accompanied by children, thus emphasizing the women's significance as mothers. What might be the reason for this arrangement, he asks, unless it were 'a means of stressing the women's majority support for Athena, as well as suggesting one of the punishments they incurred to placate Poseidon – the loss of matrilineal succession?' With this reading, Castriota sees a further link between the west pediment and the metopes on the same side, which depict the Amazonomachy. Hence, as he concludes, the two themes represent variants of potential threats to male hegemony, one from outside (Amazons) and one from within (Athenian mothers).[64] Since the east pediment depicted the birth of Athena from Zeus's head, we are back on familiar territory with regard to the history of the city and its insistence on establishing male priority in reproduction and in assuring paternal lineage.

---

[62] The entrance of Penia (Poverty) in Aristophanes' very last play, *Ploutos*, is explicit on the analogy between ugly old women and Erinyes, an image borrowed from the tragic stage. Not knowing her identity, one of the male interlocutors exclaims: 'She is probably an Erinys from tragedy, she has both a mad and tragic look' (ἴσως Ἐρινύς ἐστιν ἐκ τραγωιδίας; βλέπει γέ τοι μανικόν τι καὶ τραγωιδικόν, 423–4).

[63] The judges of the dispute vary in other sources: The twelve Olympian gods (Apoll. *Bibl.* 3.14.1; cf. Ovid *Met.* 6. 70–82), Zeus alone (Hyginus *Fab*, 169), or Kekrops as single arbiter or witness (Xen. *Mem.* 3.5.10; Callimachus fr. 194. 66–8). See also Parker (1987) 198–200.

[64] Castriota (1992) 145–51, with extensive bibliography on the identification of the figures and the myth represented on the pediment.

Our earliest extant written source for Kekrops' role in cultural foundations turns up first only in the fourth century, at the hands of those Attidographers, who were intent on constructing a systematic account of the early history of Athens and its social and political institutions. Hence the similarities in pattern I have noted between the *Oresteia* and the *Ecclesiazousae* with regard to the circumstances of a common myth could be explained as constructed after the fact, owing to the deductions of later historians in making a coherent narrative from hints in already extant texts. But, if Castriota's theory is correct about the iconography on the west pediment, then this version of the women's role in Athena's victory over Poseidon in the age of Kekrops would already be attested by the middle of the fifth century. In fact, it must be earlier still, or else how would the tableau be legible to an Athenian gazing at the Parthenon, the crowning monument of his city?

VII. *What does an Athenian (man) want?*

The *Ecclesiazousae* showcases performance at different levels – the performance of gender, the performance of politics, the performance of utopian schemes. It displays and plays with Athenian role-modelling with immense comic verve. It makes a joke of civic (and sexual) performance. But throughout this essay I have emphasized also the teleological and normative aspects of a mythic scenario, seen also in the cultural productions of tragedy and iconography, which endeavours to create and sustain the solid ideological basis of Athenian masculinity. The force of this mythic scenario draws all these cultural productions into its orbit with a depressing regularity. This scenario allows women to take charge in response to (or rebellion against) transgressions of the social order, which in the first instance are always initiated by men, but then stages a sequence of events that suggest the cure may be worse than the ailment. The ending either demonstrates the need to displace feminine power in favour of a male-centred city, as in the *Oresteia*, or as in the *Ecclesiazousae* (the major focus of this essay), there is just enough uncertainty about the results of the women's legislation to compromise, if not undermine, the entire idea.

A significant residue remains in the reading of Aristophanic comic theatre, one that is located, not so much in the product, but in the process itself of playing. In other words, the performance itself in its duration and not just in its predictable conclusion. That residue invariably gives rise to an interpretative conundrum where it remains difficult to assess the quality of the *spoudaiogelaion*, the serious in the midst of laughter. It is still more difficult to gauge the effects of a double-edged satire that holds up a mirror to all parties concerned, a mirror, whose optic includes both reflections and projections – of ambivalent desires and fears – and all at the same time. Simon Goldhill has written cogently of these issues in his recognition of the polyphonic resonances of comedy, particularly those that represent an inverted and parodistic world.[65] As a result, the pleasure and playfulness of the comic performance is in a constant and unresolvable tension with the normative projection that grounds the play's mythic enactment. In its staging for the city, it is this tension which the *Ecclesiazousae* performs – and it is in responding to this tension that the spectators perform their role(s) as a diversified audience of citizens. Here, finally, is how the *Ecclesiazousae* is a proof text of the 'theatricalization' of civic experience.[66]

[65] Goldhill (1991) 167–222.
[66] My heartfelt gratitude to Simon Goldhill for performing his usual roles as exemplary critic and creative editor.

Part III

Rhetoric and performance

8 The rhetoric of anti-rhetoric in Athenian oratory[1]

Jon Hesk

'This morning, I listened to some of the comments that the Labour party was spinning in the media. I understand that it is in the nature of politics to oppose. By opposition, one questions, and by questioning one elicits for the common good knowledge that can make policies work better. To mislead the country and paint a picture that is not true is not to oppose but to spin yarns. Spinning yarns is not the traditional role of the Opposition. To spin yarns in the media is to mislead the public and the business community. Yarn spinning wrecks confidence in the country; it makes the country look inadequate and international investors become suspicious. To spin yarns is not clever. It is too self-interested and too self-serving. When the election comes, the electorate will not be fooled.'[2]

'Before the hon. Member for Cunninghame, North (Mr. Wilson) leaves with his electronic device, could you confirm, Madam Speaker, that there is a ban, enforced by yourself, on electronic devices? When an hon. Gentleman has a message from Mr. Mandelson on his electronic device, which he reads at the Dispatch Box, I suspect that that is a new departure for the House.'[3]

The Labour party under Tony Blair is the party of 'soundbites' and 'spin doctors'. The Conservative party under John Major was revealed to be the party of 'sleaze'. Or at least, these are the images of political deceit, trickery and corruption which emerged and informed the arguments and analyses of politicians and journalists in the last two years of Major's government. Recent workers in political science have shown how different countries and different political climates defy any attempt to write a monolithic account of how and why political skulduggery occurs, increases or becomes an 'issue'.[4] But individuals or institutions

---

[1] I am grateful to Simon Goldhill and Malcolm Schofield for reading and helpfully commenting on drafts of this essay. I would also like to thank all the participants in the colloquium on which this volume is based.
[2] Nirj Deva (Conservative MP for Brentford and Isleworth) quoted in *Hansard*, 26 November 1996.
[3] Ian Bruce (Conservative MP for South Dorset) quoted in *Hansard*, 11 March 1997.
[4] See the following collections of essays: Ridley and Doig (1995); della Porta and Mény (1997); Levi and Nelken (1996); Ridley and Thompson (1997). For important observations on 'bribery' in Athenian politics and its representation in the orators, see Harvey (1985).

201

which take up stances *against* corruption (or, more rarely, are happy to admit to *being* corrupt) are often doing so for strategic reasons of self-legitimation and self-promotion in a variety of competitive environments.[5] In this sense, the exposure and pursuit of scandals is crucially implicated in processes of political *performance*. Today's political scientists soberly reflect that corruption and deceit can no longer be regarded as tools exclusive to totalitarian regimes, 'developing' democracies or a few rotten apples in the 'developed' democratic barrel. They could also add that 'show trials' can take place in 'developed' democracies too.[6]

But if political scientists have started to examine actual instances of democratic 'sleaze' and (to a much lesser extent) the 'discourse' of corruption, they are not doing the same for 'spin'. To be sure, we have had countless books and television programmes which document how 'spin' works and what a 'spin doctor' does.[7] But these accounts are *part* of a phenomenon or 'discourse' which requires explanation. Why is 'spin' now a key topos in the rhetoric of politicians or the assessments of the Fourth Estate? There have always been press officers and political statements designed for mass communication in the media. So why have 'spin' and 'soundbite-politics' suddenly become objects of scrutiny and vexed argument? And what does it mean for modern democratic culture that it has apparently become so concerned with its own processes of performance and communication?

I do not intend to answer these questions about modern democracy seriously. But I have raised them in order to provide a clarifying frame for the real concerns of this essay.[8] I want to argue that the democratic

---

[5] See Levi and Nelken (1996) 2.
[6] The strategic and theatrical quality of recent anti-corruption campaigns was most recently and blatantly demonstrated in Britain when Labour and the Liberal Democrats encouraged the television journalist Martin Bell to stand as an independent 'anti-sleaze' candidate against the Tory MP for Tatton, Neil Hamilton. Hamilton was under investigation for having taken bribes. Bell held a press conference on Tatton Common but as the cameras and reporters arrived, he was confronted by Hamilton and his wife. A surreal argument between the two candidates was performed in the midst of a scuffling *corona* of Media personnel. The television image was of two men and a woman duelling in an empty field for the benefit of attending journalists. Thanks to Dr Neil Reynolds for reminding me of this piece of theatre. As I write, it is becoming clear that Labour was covering up its own difficulties with 'sleaze' and as the party of government is now staging 'clean-up' operations.
[7] The BBC screened a *Panorama* documentary on (predominantly Labour) techniques of 'spin' on the eve of the 1996 Labour Conference. Earlier in the same year, Channel 4 screened an American documentary about Democratic and Republican techniques. For an insider's account of Westminster 'spin' and 'soundbite' techniques and Media collusion with them, see Jones (1995). For a fictional account of spin in action by a political commentator see Anonymous (1996).
[8] The particular examples of 'sleaze' and 'spin' rhetoric will no doubt soon fade from the memory, but newly topical examples will readily come to readers' minds.

oratory of classical Athens is crucially concerned with its own modes and techniques of performance. Athens certainly was a 'performance culture' but what I am calling democratic oratory's 'rhetoric of anti-rhetoric' can show us that Athens' elite and demos see their performance culture as having a particular quality which raises particular problems and opportunities. The 'rhetoric of anti-rhetoric' is meta-discursive and self-conscious. And the meta-discursive strategies which I will discuss lend support to the notion of Athens' democratic 'performance culture' as a 'self-reflective critical discursive system' which Goldhill outlines in the introduction to this volume.[9] The orators deploy reflections on rhetorical performance which, when we listen to them, help us to understand what was seen to be at stake in the legal and political contests which constituted Athenian democracy. Indeed, these anti-rhetorical reflections help to explain why the Athenian democracy preserved itself for so long. Here, I will be indebted to the excellent work of Josiah Ober, but I hope to raise some further issues which he does not address.[10]

Before I turn to the Athenian texts, I need to make some more remarks about 'spin' in contemporary British politics because they clarify my argument. The second of my opening quotations refers to an incident which occured in the House of Commons during the weeks running up to the 1997 General Election. The Labour MP Brian Wilson was caught receiving information on an electronic pager. This information was then deployed by him to make an allegation of 'sleaze' in the form of a 'point of order'. Ian Bruce made out that Wilson was receiving messages from Peter Mandelson – Labour's most powerful and ruthless 'spin doctor'.[11] Another Tory MP accused Wilson of receiving electronic messages from Labour's 'Dirty Tricks Department' and demanded to know on whose behalf Wilson was 'merely the messenger boy'.[12]

It is clear that the notion of 'spin' provided the Tory party with a useful network of images with which to undermine the Labour party's developing self-representation as a modernized party. My first quotation is just one example of the way in which the Consevative party and its supporting agencies sought to counteract Labour's 'anti-sleaze' strategy by representing Labour as an organization which had embraced

---

[9] See Goldhill 'Introduction', p. 10.
[10] See Ober (1989), (1994).
[11] Mandelson became 'Minister without Portfolio' in the Labour administration. Journalists were then worried that his lack of 'Portfolio' made him unaccountable to Parliament. *Private Eye* magazine nicknamed him 'The Spinning Minister'.
[12] Nicholas Winterton (Conservative MP for Macclesfield) quoted in *Hansard*, 11 March 1997.

the modern environment of technology and high-speed media communications in order to manipulate it with lies and hollow rhetoric. The trivial spats over the use of mobile phones and pagers were a brief side-show. But these exchanges were reported in the news media and, taken with the first quotation, they demonstrate a number of important points.

Firstly, to identify and attack 'spin' is not simply another way of accusing an opponent of lying or using fancy rhetoric. It is a rhetorical and strategic response which provides a negative 'gloss' on Labour's attempt to represent itself as 'New Labour'; a born-again centrist party of the nineties. It attempts to redescribe Labour as 'new' only in so far that it will utilize modern technology and the rhetorical armatures of corporate public relations and the advertising industry. 'Spin' gets its currency as a term of abuse precisely because 'new' techniques and technologies are seen as aids to the Labour party's public performance. And here 'performance' must mean two things. There are the 'first order' performances; Commons speeches, television interviews and battle-bus tours. But the *technai* of 'spin' are also seen more generally as the manipulative and disingenuous means by which Labour enhances its 'second order' performance in polls and public opinion. Thus 'anti-spin' rhetoric is reliant on a perceived presence of new *technai* and their effect on modes and standards of political performance. Even the apparently unimportant exchange about electronic pagers constitutes an element in a significant set of attacks, debates and counter-strategies about performance. And this discursive focus on performance translates into an argument about how democratic politics should be conducted and who is fit to serve in its offices.

Crucially, the 'anti-spin' rhetoric glosses this use of modern modes of communication and performance as politically bankrupt. The use of 'spin' means a party that will do and say anything to get into power. It means a party that will lie and smear its way towards the short-term goal of victory rather than argue on the basis of the long-term goals of national interest and collective prosperity. As Nirj Derva puts it, to 'spin' is to opt out of doing 'democracy' fairly, properly and traditionally.

In addition to this, accusations of 'spin' are similar to allegations of 'sleaze' in that they raise concerns about accountability and deception. 'Spin' often seems to make the elected representative the 'mere messenger boy' of unelected men who control strategy and policy decisions from the wings of the political theatre. And as in the first quotation, 'spin' can itself be 'spun' in order to connote the artful dissemination of untruths and evasions of the truth.

Indeed, Nirj Derva's gloss on 'spin' as 'the spinning of yarns' illustrates a further point I will be making in connection with Athenian oratory. The gloss may not seem very clever or original. And if one has the patience to trawl through *Hansard*, one finds that attacks on Labour 'spin' are predominantly a Tory topos. An association between 'spin' and outright deception is also a recurring theme. And yet, Derva's pun is unique. His particular *way* of identifying 'spin' and glossing it as lies is an original intervention. We may still wish to describe this as a topos but it is not *formulaic*. We might rather describe Derva's attack as unique but not idiosyncratic. I will argue that it is crucial to understand that Athenian democratic culture's topoi of 'anti-rhetoric' are often similarly to be characterized as *both* commonplaces at one level *and* as creative, unique strategies at another. At other times, speeches deploy completely unique strategies to 'unmask' an opponent's tricks. And it is the requirements and dynamics of a *performed* contest between individual elite actors in a democratic setting which motivate this interplay between topology and originality.

Finally, while this concern to gloss an opponent's political performances as amounting to a new and dangerous mode of deceptive communication is undoubtedly a *strategic* gloss (a 'spin' on 'spin') it is not to be viewed as the invention of a few party strategists at Tory Headquarters. 'Spin' has developed meanings and currency in British political exchange because our Media have identified its operations and introduced them to us. The notion of political 'spin' was named and identified by journalists in the United States long before we had heard of the term here. But at the same time as Blair was described as subjecting his party to 'Clintonization', so the British Media focused on Labour's new penchant for something called 'spin'.[13] Contrived political manipulation of the Media has been happening in Britain for decades. But it is important to realize that the public representation of 'spin' as something 'new' goes hand in hand with a perception that Labour have harnessed performative techniques which are in some sense 'alien' to British political discourse. Despite the presence of American products and culture in all aspects of British life, and despite 'the special relationship' between the two countries, Britain's political

---

[13] Although Labour are now in power, the identification between technology, spin and 'New Labour' persists. Labour's Deputy Prime Minister John Prescott is generally regarded as closer to 'Old' Labour's ideology. Lobby journalists report his antipathy to Mandelson's power and tactics. In August 1997, Prescott appeared to express that antipathy publicly and one television reporter summed up the situation in these terms: 'All the pagers, lap-top computers and the like are clearly powerless when faced with the "Prescott Factor".'

206   Jon Hesk

and Media elite continue to identify certain modes of behaviour as 'American' and then exploit deep-seated British fears or prejudices concerning 'Americanization'.

Athenian democracy bore little resemblance to modern Western democracies and I will not rehearse all the differences between them here.[14] Suffice it to say that I will make no attempt to equate British democracy with the very different conditions at Athens. But it is striking and potentially helpful to note that the extant Athenian legal orations exhibit self-reflexive concerns which have similarities with the topoi concerning 'spin' which I have been discussing.

The idea of an opponent dangerously and deceptively harnessing a *technē* of speech and performance is explicitly raised by Aeschines in his speech *On the Embassy* – a speech which, like the oration of Demosthenes to which it responds, is replete with meta-discursive strategies concerning rhetoric and deception:

> You hear the witnesses under oath and their testimony. But these unholy arts of speech (*tas d' anosious tautas tōn logōn technas*), which this man offers to teach our youth and has now employed against me ... (Aeschines 2.56)

Demosthenes teaches *technai* of speech to Athens' youth and Aeschines goes so far as to represent this technology as 'unholy'. Here he perhaps invokes the same sense of religious transgression as that conveyed by the pre-procedural curse against deceit of the demos which was proclaimed before meetings of the *boulē* and *ecclēsia*.[15] Aeschines goes on to mimic one of Demosthenes' attacks on him, referring to his shrill

---

[14] For good accounts of the differences and similarities between Athenian and modern Western democracy see Finley (1973); Ober (1989) 3–10; Farrar (1992); Cartledge (1993) 175f.; Roberts (1994), 47f. See also the essays collected in Ober and Hedrick (1996). On questions of 'participation', see Osborne (1985); Carter (1986); Sinclair (1988).

[15] For the strong evidence that the curse forbad deceit of the demos, see Andocides 1.31; Aeschines 1.23; Demosthenes 19.70–1, 20.107, 23.97; Dinarchus 1.47–8, 2.16; Lycurgus 1.31; Aristophanes *Thesmophoriazusae* 295–372. For a reconstruction of the curse see Rhodes (1972), pp. 36–7. There was also a law against 'deception of the people' (ἀπατὴ τοῦ δήμου). This is associated with 'preliminary charges' (*probolai*) against sycophancy and treason. See Aristotle *Constitution of Athens* 43.5, with Christ (1992). For ideologically and symbolically charged citations of the law see Demosthenes 20.100 and 135. See also Demosthenes 49.67, where the law is cited to reinforce a view of an opponent's deceptions as religiously transgressive. Herodotus 6.132–5 relates that the general Miltiades was prosecuted 'because of deception of the people' (τῆς Ἀθηναίων ἀπατῆς εἵνεκεν) some time after the battle of Marathon. Whilst disagreeing over the procedure used, commentators assume that this refers to a specific charge of 'deception of the people'; Harrison (1971) 54; Hansen (1975) 69; Macdowell (1978) 179; Rhodes (1979) 105. For our only certain use of the law see Xenophon *Hellenica* 1.7.35 (invoked against those who had called for the execution of six generals after Arginousae).

The rhetoric of anti-rhetoric in oratory   207

and unholy voice (157). So often it is Aeschines' career as an actor and his trained voice which Demosthenes attempts to disparage.[16] But here, Aeschines attempts to trope Demosthenes' deceptive *technai* of rhetoric as akin to a mimetic theatrical performance and he implicitly connects these *technai* with the paideutic practice of sophistry and the industry of logography.

This kind of 'self-reflexivity' where the orator foregrounds his opponent as a technologist of performance has a *strategic* and *antagonistic* quality.[17] As Ober and others have noted, the forensic orators frequently represent themselves as innocent of various procedures associated with rhetorical training and preparation.[18] Often this self-representation will correlate with an attack on the speaker's opponent on the grounds that he, by contrast, is heavily implicated in rhetorical procedures. Ober rightly stresses that such claims to innocence or ignorance of rhetorical preparation describe a 'dramatic fiction'. No speech in our extant corpus could possibly be described as the spontaneous creation of a semi-educated man who was 'unfamiliar with public speaking'. Although he does not characterize them as 'meta-discursive' or 'self-reflexive', Ober views extant oratory's strategies concerning speaking ability and rhetorical training as germane to the continued existence of the democracy. Alongside other topoi (for example, those concerned with wealth), these strategies show that 'the members of the educated elite participated in a drama in which they were required to play the roles of

---

[16] See Easterling in this volume for discussion, references and bibliography. The denigration of an opponent as a theatrical performer falls in line with Aristotle's displeasure at having to admit *hupokrisis* ('delivery') as an important element of rhetoric. See Aristotle *Rhetoric* 1403b35–1404a13. See also 1403b20–35 where he states that *hupokrisis* is a matter of how the voice should be used in expressing emotion. He then points out that those who use vocal techniques properly nearly always carry off prizes in dramatic contests and as in his own time actors have greater influence on stage than poets, so it is with political contests (*politikous agōnas*), owing to the corruption/moral bankruptcy of forms of government (*dia tēn mochthērian politeiōn*).

[17] There has been a (sometimes justified) recent tendency to attack critical works which concentrate on texts' apparent elements of 'self-reflexivity' or 'meta-discursive' aspects as ahistorical or banal. See Seaford (1994a) who in the context of criticism on tragedy expresses 'the vain hope that self-reflexivity is an idea whose time is up'. My analysis in this essay should go some way towards demonstrating that this hope is misguided when 'meta-discursive' elements in prose and poetic texts are approached with certain questions and contexts in mind.

[18] See Demosthenes 27.2–3, where a young Demosthenes asks for a fair hearing having proclaimed his own youth and inexperience and the cleverness, ability and preparedness (*paraskeuē*) of his opponents. Other examples of this combination of topoi ('plea for a hearing' and 'I am unskilled') in extant speeches; Antiphon 3.2. b2, c3; Andocides 4.7; Lysias 19.2; Isocrates 8.5; Demosthenes 18.6–7, 37.5, 38.2, 57.1. For further examples of these two topoi and the 'my opponent is a skilled speaker' topos see Ober (1989) 170–7. See also Dover (1974) 25–8; Ostwald (1986) 256–7.

208   *Jon Hesk*

common men and to voice their solidarity with egalitarian ideals'.[19] This drama policed the political ambitions of the elite. At the same time as the Athenians gained the benefit of having educated men serve in advisory roles of the state, they kept these advisors on a tight leash and restrained the tendency of the educated elite to evolve into a ruling oligarchy.

In the law-court, the speaker attacks his opponent as a deceptive sophist, a 'clever speaker', a logographer (or reliant on one), a magician with words and so on. And in Ober's terms, the 'logical corollary' of this is the self-representational claim to be 'inexperienced' in speaking.[20] In order to keep the disingenuous and strategic quality of these self-representations or invectives firmly in mind, I want to designate them with the phrase 'the rhetoric of anti-rhetoric'.[21] At the same time, my loose analogy with modern 'anti-spin' rhetoric only goes so far. My first three sections deal with the orators' attacks on opponents as 'types' of rhetorical technician – sophist, logographer and so on. But the last two sections address oratory's focus on 'rhetoric' in a much broader sense of the word. My fourth section will show how a speaker can expose the deceptive 'rhetoric' of a citizen's presentation of self in everyday life.[22] My fifth and final section returns to the sense of 'rhetoric' as a dangerous *technē* in Athens' law-courts. But here the orator's 'anti-rhetoric' will be seen to expose, not the opponent's conformity to a deceptive 'type', but rather his deceptive manipulation of common strategies of argument.

1. Speech-writing and 'cleverness'

In his speech *Against Meidias*, Demosthenes anticipates the charge that he has written and practised his oration.[23] He argues that it would be

---

[19] Ober (1989) 190–1. See also 153–4, where Ober argues that regular mass participation in the Athenian dramatic festivals educated the citizenry in the process of colluding in these 'dramatic fictions'. See also Ford in this volume for an account of the orators' performances of Homeric and dramatic poetry as strategic engagements with mass and elite conceptions of poetic performance and education.

[20] Ibid. p. 174.

[21] I have borrowed this phrase from Valesio (1980) who uses it to describe a persistent trope in renaissance tracts and Shakespearean speeches.

[22] Here I have deliberately purloined the title to Goffman (1969). For Goffman's reading of self-presentation in modern western society as a 'theatrical' and 'performative' process and its relevance to Athens, see the introduction of Goldhill in this volume, pp. 13–14.

[23] There is some doubt as to whether this speech was ever actually delivered. For the evidence and the arguments see MacDowell (1990) 23–8; Wilson (1991) 187. See also Ober (1994).

foolish of him not to prepare himself and adds that it is effectively Meidias who has written the speech for him through his crimes.[24] A rhetorical treatise attributable to Anaximenes of Lampsacus indicates that it was a common tactic to deride speakers for writing their oration and for intensive training or preparation.[25] However, Anaximenes does recommend a suitable reply to such derision: 'We must come to close quarters about suggestions of that sort, in a tone of irony, and about writing the speech say that the law does not forbid one to speak a written speech oneself any more than it forbids one's adversary to speak an unwritten speech.'[26] As to the charge of having learnt and practised a speech, Anaximenes recommends the following:

If they say that we study and practise speaking, we shall admit the charge and say: 'We who study speaking are not litigious (*philodikoi*), whereas you who do not know how to make a speech are proved to be making a malicious prosecution (*sukophantōn*) against us now and have done so before.' So we make it appear to the advantage of citizens if he too learnt to be a *rhētōr* as he would not be such a wicked blackmailer (*sukophantēn*) if he did.[27]

---

[24] Demosthenes 21.191–2: 'Perhaps too he will say something of this sort; that my present speech is all carefully thought out and prepared. I admit, Athenians that I have thought it out and I should not dream of denying it; yes, and I have spent all possible care on it (*memeletēkenai*). I would be a wretched creature if all my wrongs, past and present, left me careless of what I was going to say to you about them. Yet the real composer of my speech is Meidias. The man who has furnished the facts with which the speeches deal ought in strict justice to bear that responsibility, and not the man who has devoted thought and care to lay an honest case before you today.' Although Demosthenes is happy to use it of himself here, the verb μελετάω and its cognates, meaning 'to practise oratory', is elsewhere used in a derogatory sense to characterize opponents as manipulative and skilled speakers. See the attack on Aeschines' oratorical *meletē* at Demosthenes 18.308 and 19.255.

[25] Anaximenes *Ars Rhet.* 36.37 (p. 88, 3–5) in the text of Fuhrmann (1966): ἐὰν δὲ διαβάλλωσιν ἡμᾶς, ὡς γεγραμμένους λόγους λέγομεν ἢ λέγειν μελετῶμεν ... 'If they try to slander us by saying that we read out written speeches or practise them beforehand ...' On the disputed dating and authorship of what is more commonly known as the *Rhetorica ad Alexandrum*, see Kennedy (1963) 114–24. Kennedy follows the majority view that the treatise was written in the late fourth century.

[26] Anaximenes *Ars Rhetorica* 36.37 (p. 88, 5–10): χρὴ πρὸς τὰ τοιαῦτα ὁμόσε βαδίζοντας εἰρωνεύεσθαι καὶ περὶ μὲν τῆς γραφῆς λέγειν, μὴ κωλύειν τὸν νόμον ἢ αὐτὸν γεγραμμένα λέγειν ἢ ἐκεῖνον ἄγραφα· τὸν γὰρ νόμον οὐκ ἐᾶν τοιαῦτα πράττειν, λέγειν δὲ ὅπως ἄν τις βούληται συγχωρεῖν. The sophist Alcidamas implies that speeches were learnt by heart when written out and not read from a text held in the hand during proceedings. See Alcid. 15.11, 18, 21, 34, in the text of Radermacher (1951). For the possibility of a logographer advising on delivery as well as, or instead of actually writing the speech, see Dover (1968) 151. See also Lavency (1964).

[27] Anaximenes *Ars Rhetorica* 36.39–40 (p. 88, 14–20): ἂν δὲ φάσκωσιν ἡμᾶς λέγειν μανθάνειν καὶ μελετᾶν, ὁμολογήσαντες ἐροῦμεν· ἡμεῖς μὲν οἱ μανθάνοντες, ὡς φής, οὐ φιλοδικοί ἐσμεν, σὺ δὲ ὁ λέγειν μὴ ἐπιστάμενος καὶ πρότερον ἑάλως συκοφαντῶν· ὥστε λυσιτελὲς φανεῖται τοῖς πολίταις κἀκεῖνον μανθάνειν ῥητορεύειν· οὐ γὰρ ⟨ἂν⟩ οὕτω πονηρὸν οὐδὲ συκοφάντην αὐτὸν εἶναι.

Interestingly, Anaximenes claims that even a charge of teaching others how to plead or of composing their dicanic speeches can be deflected by replying that everyone, as far as he can, helps his friends with instruction and advice.[28]

This last piece of advice is not taken up in any of our extant public speeches. Nobody admits to having written speeches for others or having taught them. Nor does anyone ever admit to buying a written speech. But there are occasions when orators openly or tacitly admit their opponents' abusive labels of 'cleverness at speaking' (*deinotēs legein*) or 'being a *rhētōr*'. In these instances (some well documented by Ober) the speaker draws a contrast between a rhetorical activism which is deceitful and harmful to the polis and the honest, beneficial activism which (of course) he has always adhered to.[29] In his speech *On the Crown*, Demosthenes admits to Aeschines' charge of *deinotēs*, but rejects his other charges of deception (*apatē*), sophistry and wizardry (*goēteia*) as applicable to Aeschines rather than himself (18.276). He goes on to make it clear that unlike Aeschines, he always uses his skill in the public domain and for the good of the demos (277–84). In his speech *Against Ctesiphon*, Aeschines tacitly admits that he is an able speaker by nature (*phusis*) when he 'anticipates' Demosthenes' claim that his *phusis* is like that of the Sirens whose charming voices bring destruction (3.228–9).[30] Aeschines deflects this picture by arguing that, while strictly unfounded, such an accusation would be understandable coming from an inarticulate general (*stratēgos*) who was jealous of his ability. But, he continues, it is intolerable to hear this attack from a man who 'is made up of words' (*ex onomatōn sunkeimenos*) and who would be as useless as a reed-less *aulos* if you took out his tongue.[31]

---

[28] Ibid. 36.42 (p. 89, 4–8).
[29] Ober (1989) 187–91.
[30] On the significance of the Sirens comparison see Easterling in this volume. Although Demosthenes' extant speech (18) in reply frequently accuses Aeschines of being a clever and deceptive speaker, he never likens him to the Sirens. Adams (1919) 487 suggests that Demosthenes omitted his comparison when he revised his speech for publication. See also Dover (1968) 178. The difficulty (I would say impossibility) of determining the relationship between published speeches and their performed 'originals' has generated much discussion; see Kennedy (1963) 206; Adams (1912); Dover (1968); Usher (1976); Hansen (1984); Harris (1995) 10–15. Ober (1989), 49 suggests that orators and logographers would not revise speeches substantially for fear of being mocked by opponents or losing clients.
[31] Aeschines 3.229: 'But if the charge really had to be made, it was not for Demosthenes to make it, but for some general who, although he had rendered distinguished services to the state, was not gifted with the power of speech, and for that reason was envious of the natural endowments of his opponents in court, because he knew that he had not the ability to describe one of all the things he had accomplished, but saw in his accuser a man able to set forth to the hearers in all detail how he had himself administered things which had not been done by him at all. But when a man who is

This is just one example of Demosthenes' and Aeschines' constant tussle over the training, quality and effects of their voices and I will have cause to return to their focus on vocal performance below.

Cleverness and ability in speech and preparation: these are notions which the speaker *can* admit as applying to himself. Demosthenes admits to having written out his speech for *himself* but no extant oration follows Anaximenes' recommendation that a speaker should admit to having trained others or to having written their speeches.[32] And on the evidence we have, it seems that admissions of preparation and rhetorical skill are confined to high-profile *rhētores* such as Demosthenes or Aeschines, spoken *in propria persona*. Legal speeches written for clients do not seem to contain such admissions, despite (or perhaps because of) Anaximenes' recommendations. In the case of well-known career politicians, their standing was perhaps so high and the 'fiction' of their inexperience so obviously fragile, that the demos gave them the licence to attempt the reassurance that their transparent involvement with the *technai* of speech was all in a just cause.

II. Sophistry and witchcraft

Alongside the accusation of writing for others, there was another charge levelled at any elite speaker, whatever the extent of his involvement in political and legal discourse, which could not be admitted, even implicitly. This was the accusation of being a sophist, with all its apparent connotations of cunning and deceit. It seems that whoever you were, this label could not be admitted or given a positive colouring. Like the accusation of sycophancy and writing for others, a charge of sophistry had to be denied, ignored, or denied and turned back on the opponent who tried to pin it on you.[33] Aeschines and Demosthenes

---

made up of words, and those words are bitter and useless – when such a man takes refuge in "simplicity" and the "facts", who could have patience with him? If you treat him as you might an *aulos*, and take out his tongue, you have nothing left!' On this and similar passages concerned with voice and gesture I have learnt from Goldhill (Unpublished).

[32] It seems likely that Anaximenes' recommendation that these particular charges be admitted is polemical. Scholars have generally viewed the *Ars Rhetorica* as a 'sophistic' text. See Kennedy (1963) 115f. Whilst I would argue that anyone teaching rhetoric or writing speeches for others could be labelled 'a sophist' (hence Isocrates' and Aristotle's anxieties to attack and distance themselves from sophistry), Anaximenes is attempting to find and promote a topos which admits and neutralizes accusations of sophistry and logography. For him, such practices should not be taboo. This would explain why he promotes this topos when (as we will see below), unlike admissions to preparation and writing one's own speech, admissions to sophistry and writing for others are not found in extant oratory.

[33] See Aeschines 1.125, 175, 3.16 and 202: Demosthenes 18.276, 19.246–8 and 250. For a variation on 'he's a sophist' see Lysias fragment 1.5 in the text of Thalheim (1901)

constantly accuse each other of being sophists in the five speeches relating to the trial of Timarchos, the embassy to Philip and the crowning of Demosthenes.

They also abuse each other, in the context of alleged rhetorical ability or sophistry, with names denoting witchcraft and magic.[34] Demosthenes is described as a *goēs* ('wizard') several times by Aeschines. The term implies trickery and delusion of an audience through magic arts but, as Burkert and Bowie have emphasized, it is also associated with un-Athenian identity and behaviour.[35] It is thus a perfect term of abuse to connote sophistry since many notable 'sophists' were foreigners. The public texts of Athens can be seen to be identifying a technique of performance as 'deceptive communication' and classifying it as alien to normative Athenian identity.

Just as the Spartans are castigated for their dishonesty and deceptive speech in late fifth-century Athenian drama and historiography, so the oratory of the fourth century tropes 'sophistic' technique in public trials and debates as the infiltration of 'un-Athenian' activity.[36] But if this aspect to the representation of 'sophistry' reminds us of the Tory exploitation of the American associations of 'spin', there is also a peculiarly ancient Greek resonance to this connection between rhetoric and witchcraft. Dinarchus, Aeschines and Demosthenes all utilize a cultural analogy between the deceits of sophistry or rhetoric and the spell-binding effects of magic which we see theorized in the writings of Gorgias, Plato and Isocrates.[37] Again these terms (*goēs* and *baskanos*)

---

with the translation and discussion of Millett (1991) 1–3. An alleged ex-pupil of Socrates is accused of systematically cheating a range of creditors. The speaker glosses this behaviour as 'the life of the sophist'.

[34] Demosthenes is described as a *goēs* at Aeschines 2.124, 153, 3.137 (in conjunction with *magos*) and 207. *Goēs*, *pharmakeus* and *sophistēs* are used of Eros at Plato *Symp.* 203d. Demosthenes prefers a different word for a magician against Aeschines – *baskanos*; see 18.132 and adjectivally at 119, 139, 242, 317. See also 21.209, 25.80, 83. No other orator uses it. Whereas *goēs* seems to be a general term connoting trickery and working magic, *baskanos* more specifically connotes malevolence. It is derived from the verb βασκαίνω which can mean 'to bewitch' or 'give the evil eye'. As at Demosthenes 18. 242, Aristophanes uses *baskanos* in relation to sycophancy and slander; see Aristophanes *Knights* 105, *Wealth* 571. It would seem that Demosthenes attempts to trump Aeschines' deployment of *goēs*, by using an analogous, but more specifically loaded term. At Demosthenes 18.257–9 Aeschines is mocked for reading texts during his mother's shady nocturnal rituals, and it is implied that his howling voice was trained in this context. Perhaps *baskanos* is meant to evoke this past.

[35] Burkert (1962) 55; Bowie (1993) 114–15.

[36] I discuss the Athenian construction of Spartan 'dishonesty' in Hesk (1997) 13–50.

[37] See Dinarchus 1.66, 92 where, again, Demosthenes is the *goēs*. On the link made between magic and rhetoric in Gorgias, Plato and Isocrates see de Romilly (1975). For the specific links made by Plato between *apatē*, sophistry, rhetoric and *goēteia* see Burkert (1962) 50–1.

are non-negotiable; neither Aeschines nor Demosthenes can admit to being 'wizards' of speech.

Where the label 'sophist' crops up as a term of abuse throughout extant oratory, Aeschines and Demosthenes often offer extended vignettes of the other's sophistry. Demosthenes tells his jury that Aeschines never acted in a play from which he quoted in a previous legal clash. He 'hunts up' quotations thereby demonstrating that *he* is the sophist and the last person who should accuse others of sophistry (19.246–50). Demosthenes is responding to Aeschines' speech *Against Timarchus*, in which he is compared to the 'sophist' Socrates. In that speech, Aeschines reminds the jury that they put the sophist Socrates to death for being the teacher of the oligarch Critias (1.173). If Socrates was executed for teaching Critias, the jury should not sanction Demosthenes' advocacy: for this is a man who takes vengeance on *idiōtai* ('private citizens') and *dēmotikoi* ('friends of the people') for their *isēgoria* ('freedom of speech').[38] Aeschines then draws a vivid picture of Demosthenes the sophist, a man who uses his law-court performances as object-lessons in deceptive rhetoric for his young students. He imagines Demosthenes boasting about his successful displays of deception to his pupils and urges the jury to keep strict control of him, as if he were a racehorse.[39] Ober analyses this passage well, highlighting the way in which Aeschines warns the jury that sophistry is a threat to the democratic ideal of *isēgoria*.[40] It should also be emphasized that Aeschines represents a vote for Demosthenes as a vote for his intention to transform the people's court into his private school for rhetorical deception.

These vignettes derive their force from an interplay between commonplace and creative strategy. Both Demosthenes and Aeschines

---

[38] Aeschines 1.173: 'Did you put to death Socrates the sophist, fellow citizens, because he was shown to have been the teacher of Critias, one of the Thirty who put down the democracy, and after that, shall Demosthenes succeed in snatching companions of his won out of your hands, who takes such vengeance on private citizens and friends of the people for their freedom of speech?'

[39] Ibid. 175–6: 'So I do beg you by all means not to furnish this sophist with laughter and patronage at your expense. Imagine that you see him when he gets home from the courtroom, putting on airs in his lectures to his young men, and telling how successfully he stole the case away from the jury: "I carried the jurors off bodily from the charges brought against Timarchus, and set them on the accuser, and Philip, and the Phocians, and I suspended such terrors before the eyes of the hearers that the defendant began to be the accuser, and the accuser to be on trial; and the jurors forgot what they were to judge and what they were not to judge, to that they listened." But it is your business to take your stand against this sort of thing, and following close on every step, to let him at no point turn aside nor persist in irrelevant talk; on the contrary, act as you do in a horse race, make him keep to the track – of the matter at issue.'

[40] Ober (1989) 172.

mobilize the 'he's a sophist' topos but they often extend and 'particularize' the commonplace. This creative 'spin' on an opponent's techniques of 'spin' serves a double purpose. It distinguishes its author's performance. The jury has heard all these anti-rhetorical topoi before but *this* speaker is doing something different. He knows the 'script' but he departs from it and develops it. At the same time, the departure from the 'script' serves to make the speaker's attack more authoritative. The opponent is a sophist, but a creative vignette of his activities appears to raise the attack above the level of conventional name-calling. Aeschines wants to convince the jury that he is not just tapping into a set of commonly-held prejudices which have worked well in the past. He makes his accusation sound 'truthful' by describing what *this particular sophist* does at the demos' expense.

While we have examples of anti-rhetorical charges being admitted and given a positive colouring, the charge of being a sophist was *non-negotiable*. It seems that the charge of being a logographer, in the sense of writing for others, was similarly impossible to admit. Thucydides represents Cleon criticizing his audience for listening to *ecclēsia* speeches as if they were spectators of sophistic displays rather than deciding on national and international policy.[41] And Aristophanes certainly portrays sophistic teaching and logography as a threat (albeit laughable) to honest and just legal and political transaction.[42] We can see that the cultural image of the sophist connoted the display of, and instruction in self-serving deception at the same time as 'sophistry' became identifiable as a new technology and a distinctive form of education.[43]

Whilst Ober does observe that an orator can admit to *deinotēs* or being a *rhētōr* and write those roles positively, he does not mark a difference between terms connoting rhetorical deceit which can be neutralized and those which cannot. The distinction is not important for Ober because he is primarily concerned to demonstrate that the subgroup of the citizen elite who are perceived to be *rhētores* have a licence to admit and defend their own eloquence and experience at the same time as they are attacked for it. He does not ask himself why an orator can admit to being *deinos legein* but not to being a *sophistēs*. I now turn to that question.

[41] Thucydides 3.38.7.
[42] For the most pertinent references and sensible discussion, see Murphy (1938) 71–8. A mass of bibliography could be given. See Dover (1968a) xxviii–xxvii, (1972) 109ff.; Cartledge (1990a) 35–8; O'Regan (1992); Bowie (1993) 112–24; MacDowell (1995) 125ff.
[43] On the history of the word *sophistēs* and its increasingly pejorative connotations in the classical period, see Guthrie (1971) 24–37.

III. Performing 'democratically'

We saw that Demosthenes had no trouble in redefining his *deinotēs* positively and democratically. And Aeschines was able to turn the charge that he had the *phusis* of a Siren into a modest admission that his eloquence was indeed a matter of *phusis* – a positive *phusis* with all its implications of an ability which has not been acquired artfully or artificially. Other speakers who go to court can be subject to the full range of meta-discursive abuses, but unlike *rhētores* they have to maintain the 'inexperience' topos at all times. However the *rhētōr* can and must deny that he writes speeches for others, teaches and uses the *technai* of rhetoric as a sophist, or transforms the courtroom or *ecclēsia* into a sophistic laboratory of deception. The *rhētōr* is allowed to be more 'rhetorical' than anyone else but he is constantly subject to the suspicion that his 'rhetoric' exceeded the limits imposed by *isēgoria*. One of Ober's fundamental questions is why, given the obvious dangers and deceptions which rhetorical expertise brought to the democracy, *rhētores* were allowed to operate at all. The answer is not simply (as Ober formulates it) that egalitarian suspicion of rhetoric's deceptive potential kept a useful elite's deployment of rhetoric in check. Rather, the inadmissibility of being a peddler or a recipient of logography and sophistry reveal and reinforce the limits of democratic rhetorical licence.

The terms *sophistēs* and *logographos* are not abusive, inadmissible terms just because they describe elitist occupations. In their strategies of suspicion and denigration the orators represent sophistry and logography as practices which valorize the end of winning an argument over and above the means and motives through which that end is achieved. Aeschines even represents 'Demosthenes the sophist' as using the legal process as a forum for the didactic display of his powers of deception. In the speech *Against Lacritus*, Demosthenes' client similarly accuses his opponent of being a 'perfidious sophist' (*ponēros sophistēs*) who considers himself a great deceiver of juries and takes money for teaching others to do the same (35.40–3).[44]

When we set these attacks on sophistry against the orators' definitions of what makes a good upstanding *rhētōr*, it becomes clear that sophistry and logography are demonized because they are perceived as lacking an ideological priority of commitment to the demos. In the speech *Against Ctesiphon*, Aeschines warns his jury that they will be deceived by Demosthenes if they focus on the pleasing sound of his speech rather than the obvious defects of his *phusis* and the real 'truth'

---

[44] On this see Ober (1989) 170–1.

(*alētheia*) (3.168). Aeschines goes on to outline some predictable qualities for the *dēmotikos rhētōr*; he must be freeborn, he must have an ancestrally inherited love of democracy, he should be 'moderate' (*metrios*) and 'self-controlled' (*sōphrōn*), have 'manly courage' (*andreia*) and never desert the demos (169–70). He should also be of good judgement (*eugnōmōn*) and an able speaker (*dunatos eipein*). For his *dianoia* should prefer what is best and both the *paideia* of the *rhētōr* and the *paideia* in *logoi* should persuade his listeners. But, Aeschines continues, if the *dēmotikos rhētōr* cannot have both, *eugnōmosunē* should always be preferred to *logos* (170). This check-list of attributes is of course introduced in order to demonstrate that Demosthenes does not match up to any of them; amongst other failings Aeschines contrasts his initial status as a trierarch with his eventual emergence as a logographer, and a corrupt one at that. Furthermore, Demosthenes may be *deinos legein* and produce *kaloi logoi* but his life is *kakos* and his deeds are *phaula* (174–5).

Sophistry and logography produce a speaker whose valorization of winning a case or an argument by all means (especially deceptive ones) makes him antithetical to the democratic ideal of the speaker whose speaking ability is subordinate to his political *eugnōmosunē*. This speaker is allowed to deploy a *paideia* in rhetoric to articulate his good advice, but if a speaker moonlights as a paid teacher or consultant himself, then it is assumed that any apparent *eugnōmosunē* is simply a dishonest rhetorical effect of his priority to display the invincibility of his *deinotēs* and successful deployment of *apatē* through the arts of rhetoric. To be sure, Aeschines' invocation of Socrates indicates that the sophist and his deceits can be associated with 'oligarchic tendencies'. But oratory's consistent demonization of the logographer and the sophist constitute an ideological isolation of practices which are deemed to privilege self-serving rhetorical deceit of juries and assemblies over and above any other concern. Rhetoric must only be harnessed in the service of articulating wisdom, good judgement and genuine democratic commitment. One is reminded of Derva's distinction between proper 'opposition' for the 'common good' and mere 'yarn-spinning'.

The ideological terrain mapped out by these anti-rhetorical topoi and the areas of negotiation and inadmissibility which that terrain reveals, can help us to assess the force and contextual significance of Plato and Aristotle's discussions of rhetoric. It is clear, although too infrequently observed, that many of Plato's grounds for condemning contemporary rhetorical theory and practice develop meta-discursive reflections on political and legal discourse which had already been articulated in Thucydidean speeches and Aristophanic comedy.[45] Plato's characterization of contemporary rhetoric as a form of deceptive flattery analogous to cookery and cosmetics is a theoretical development of late fifth-century democratic culture's own anti-rhetorical critiques and self-authorizations.[46] But where Plato attempts to carve out a 'true' or 'philosophical' *technē* of rhetoric in the *Phaedrus*, or where (as his detractors gleefully point out) he appropriates the seductive operations of *peithō* for the maintenance of law and social order in his ideal polis, he effectively proposes the same subordination of rhetoric to the articulation and achievement of 'the good' which is implied by the orators' definitions of acceptable *deinotēs* and the good *rhētōr*.[47] This is not to say that the orators share the same definition of wisdom, or the same political ideals or goals as Plato. Nor can we argue that Plato's complex arguments against contemporary rhetoric and in favour of a 'philosophical' rhetoric are doing the same 'work' as the meta-discourse of the orators. But the notion that rhetoric's deceptive and destabilizing potential can only be contained if it is kept subordinate to knowledge, wisdom and a constitutional status quo is a notion which is shared between the strategies of *rhētores* and Plato's philosophy. Plato wishes to expose contemporary rhetoric and sophistry as false discourses of knowledge and subordinate the art of persuasion to dialectical wisdom and self-knowledge.

The orators authorize their commitment to democracy by legitimating a notion of rhetoric which is subordinate to, and in the service of, good judgement and advice. For both the orators and Plato, sophistry presents as a discourse which has no prior commitment to 'truth' or agreed moral and political ends: it is only concerned with achieving victory for an individual in any debate and demonstrating that it can do

---

[45] Yunis (1996) provides a refreshing, if limited, account of the ways in which Plato takes up the images of the flattering, deceptive demagogue and the fickle, easily led demos which are projected by Aristophanes and Thucydides.

[46] See Plato *Gorgias* 463a–c, 464c–d, 481d, 521a. For the comic image of the demos as misled by the flattering deceits of demagogues see Aristophanes *Knights* 763–1110, 1340–4. See Aristophanes *Acharnians* 370–8 and 634–5 where we have the ironic, 'didactic' image of the demos as prone to the deceptive demagogic flattery and the dubious self-representation of the comic playwright as the man who exposes such flattery for what it is. See also Thucydides 2.65.8–10, where Pericles is praised for not resorting to flattering rhetoric and his successors are condemned for it. For the special contribution of Thucydides and Aristophanes to Athenian democracy's problematic confrontation with the powers and perils of rhetorical deception see Hesk (1997), 222–34.

[47] See Plato *Phaedrus* 259e1–261a5. On the *Phaedrus*' complex subordination of rhetoric to philosophy and ethical goals, see Ferrari (1987), especially 39–45 and 204–32; Murray (1988); Halliwell (1994); Yunis (1996) 172–210. On the role of rhetoric in the *Laws* and *Republic*, see Popper (1966) 138–46 and 270–2, Vickers (1988) 143f.; Yunis (1996) 211–36.

so. Where the orator represents himself as having a prior knowledge and political commitment which shapes and delimits his use of rhetoric, Plato represents all orators as lacking in 'true' knowledge or as practitioners of sophistry. But both Plato and the individual orator mobilize their model of good subordinated rhetoric and contrast it with the false, falsifying and insubordinate rhetoric of everybody else.

The orators' demonization of sophistry and their self-representation as harnessing *deinotēs* and speaking ability for good political and moral ends also finds its analogue in Aristotle's attempt to carve out a theory of legitimate civic rhetoric. Aristotle argues that what distinguishes the sophist from (his vision of) the rhetorician is not a 'difference in faculty (*dunamis*) but in moral purpose (*prohairēsis*)'.[48] For Aristotle the faculty of public speaking only becomes sophistry when its intentions and effects are deemed to be politically and morally undesirable.[49]

My qualification to Ober's characterization of anti-rhetorical topoi demonstrates that Athenian democracy's legal discourse does not straightforwardly associate *technai* and powers of rhetoric with *apatē*. Rather, the two related practices of logography and 'sophistry' are singled out as deceptive practices because they are seen to represent the prioritizing of personal victory over and above commitment to the values and integrity of the demos and a concomitant disregard for legitimate methods of persuasion. The Athenians both utilized rhetorical skill and fostered continuing articulations of its powers to deceive, bewitch and stupefy. According to Ober, they reaped rhetoric's benefits and kept its threat to their constitutional system in check. I would add that this was not simply a process of articulating what Ober calls 'ambivalence and balance'.[50] There is no ambivalence surrounding the orators' representations of sophistry and logography. Rather, the elite orator develops and responds to an ideological demand that rhetorical skill be subordinated to a regime of political and moral 'truth'. The sophist and the logographer are imagined and invoked as inadmissible actors because they stand for rhetorical practice unchecked by long-term commitment to this regime.

IV. Dishonest deportment

Ober focuses on Attic oratory as evidence for answering questions about how Athens maintained and reproduced its democracy and the apparent sovereignty of mass over elite. But there is another perspec-

---

[48] Aristotle *Rhetoric* 1355b18-21 in the text of Kassel (1971). Garver (1994) 206-31 unpacks this distinction with reference to Aristotle's ethical philosophy.
[49] See Garver (1994) 208.
[50] Ober (1989) 187.

The rhetoric of anti-rhetoric in oratory 219

tive on Athenian oratory which is stressed by those critics who seek to use these speeches as 'evidence' for the 'sociology' or 'discursive practices' of Attic society.[51] If we are to give a full account of Athenian culture's confrontation with the possibility of deception – what Detienne calls the 'ambiguity of speech' – we need to address political and legal discourse's involvement in the negotiation of disputes between individuals.[52] High-profile politicians and lower-profile litigants participated in 'democratic discourse' but at the same time they were using the law-courts and the *ecclēsia* to fight each other for status and recognition in the wider community. Of course, in many private cases it is clear that large sums of money were at stake. But wealthy individuals also used the courts to seek redress and renewed gains in an elite contest of manhood and honour.[53] Here, the citizen performs in court in order to enhance or rehabilitate his general 'performance' in the eyes of the city.

It is from this perspective that we must view some highly individual strategies and counter-strategies through which speakers expose an enormous variety of lies and tricks on the part of their opponent. These strategies cannot be described as topoi, and I suspect that their force derived from their relative novelty and singularity; their particularity served to highlight and isolate the singular (often exceptional) 'dishonesty' of the individuals against whom they were directed. They all invoke cultural norms and accepted paradigms of behaviour but, unlike the anti-rhetorical arguments I have just discussed, they are not even recognizable as commonplaces. While these strategies focus on the dishonesty of the opponent, and they are certainly 'meta-discursive', they cannot all be described as 'anti-rhetorical' strategies in the narrow sense which I have been using. In the remainder of this essay, I will discuss two examples of this broader 'rhetoric of anti-rhetoric'.

---

[51] Here I am thinking particularly of the following studies: Dover (1974), (1978); Nouhaud (1982); Humphreys (1985); Foucault (1987); Halperin (1989); Millett (1991); Cartledge (1990); Osborne (1985a), (1990); Winkler (1990a); Todd (1990), (1993); Cohen (1991), (1995); Hunter (1994); Hall (1995); Wilson (1997).

[52] Detienne (1967) 51–80.

[53] Recent studies have highlighted the use of the law-courts as a forum for feuding and competition over public status and reputation. Out extant Athenian forensic speeches participate in, or else draw on the language and protocols of, what has been termed a 'zero-sum' game. In accordance with this model of social rivalry, the male citizen elite (and mainly the inner wealth-elite of the liturgical class) extend their rivalries and squabbles as high-profile citizens to the public stage of the law-courts. This extension occurs, as Cohen (1995) 141 puts it, in order to 'avenge dishonour or outmanoeuvre an enemy'. See Winkler (1990a) 178ff.; Cohen (1991) 171–202, (1995) 63–70. See Aristotle *Rhetoric* 1382b where Aristotle articulates a zero-sum principle of social competition in his treatment of fear. See also the sophistic extract *Anonymus Iamblichi* DK 89 17–20, where it is stated that nobody likes to give honour to someone else because they think that they are themselves being deprived of something.

My first example of a non-standard, meta-discursive strategy comes from the Demosthenic speech *Against Stephanus I*. This strategy does not interrogate the opponent's honesty with respect to his involvement in *technai* of public speaking. This time it is the nascent formation of 'physiognomic' enquiry (the ancient 'meta-discourse' of performance *par excellence*) at Athens during the late fifth and fourth centuries which provides an important frame for thinking about the strategy's force and the social behavioural assumptions which give it a foundation.[54] Whether directly informed by the theory and practice of this new 'science' or simply an inevitable product of Athens' 'surveillance culture', the peroration of the Demosthenic *Against Aristogeiton I* makes it clear that legal oratory could make good use of physiognomic assumptions:

One more thing I have to say before I sit down. You will soon be leaving this court-house, and you will be watched by the bystanders, both aliens and citizens; they will scan each one as he appears, and detect by their looks (*phusiognōmonēsousi*) those who have voted for acquittal. What will you have to say for yourselves, Athenians, if you emerge after betraying the laws? With what expressions and with what looks will you return their gaze? (Demosthenes 25.98).[55]

This passage is an outrageous spin on the topos of reminding a jury that their decision will be judged by bystanders or the rest of the demos.[56] This speaker actually warns the jury that when they leave the

---

[54] Winkler (1990a) 199–200, defines the ancient 'science' of physiognomics as 'the informal practice of reading people's "natures" by the observation of their physical characteristics and style'. On the problems of defining certain ancient practices as 'scientific' see Lloyd (1970) 125ff. This kind of practice, and the assumptions on which it rests, can be traced back to Homer *Iliad* 13.275–87. Evans (1969) lists passages informed by physiognomic assumptions in Homer, and other archaic poets.

Most surviving physiognomic texts date to the second century CE and after (Förster (1893), Gleason (1995), Barton (1994) 95–131). However, two pseudo-Aristotelian treatises on human physiognomy date to the fourth century BCE. See Lloyd (1983) 18–26; Armstrong (1958) 52f. Galen *Anim. mor. corp. temp.* 7 claims that Hippocrates invented physiognomics, and the Hippocratic corpus certainly contain physiognomic material: see Hippocrates *Epidemics* 2.5.1, 16, 23, 2.6.1. Porphyry *Life of Pythagoras* 13 claims that Pythagoras used physiognomic analysis. Cicero *On Fate* 5.10 and *Tusculan Disputations* 4.37 relate a story of Zopyrus' physiognomic diagnosis of Socrates as stupid and fond of women. Diogenes Laertius 6.16 (= Caizzi fr. 1), lists a *Peri tōn sophistōn phusiognōmonikos* as a work by Antisthenes.

[55] This speech may not be by Demosthenes. Kennedy (1963) 207–8 and Ober (1989) 358 regard it as genuine.

[56] Surprisingly, this passage is not mentioned by Winkler (1990a) or Gleason (1990), (1995). Nor is the passage discussed by Cohen (1991) or (1995) which both cite other parts of the speech extensively. Hunter (1994) 232, note 41 does cite the passage in her list of references to the perceived importance of bystanders in democracy as witnesses to events which have a bearing on trials and as viewers of the courtroom conduct of litigants and juries. Dinarchus 1.30, 66 and 2.19 remind the jury of the judgemental surveillance of bystanders. See also Bers (1985) 8 on the *thorubos* of bystanders at trials.

The rhetoric of anti-rhetoric in oratory 221

court, onlookers will even be able to distinguish which of them has voted for an acquittal through physiognomic scrutiny. He even attempts to make them self-conscious about what facial expression those who vote for Aristogeiton will adopt when confronted with this scrutiny. Physiognomy was clearly a strategic resource for the fourth-century litigant.[57]

It is with this resource in mind that I turn to the speech *Against Stephanus I* (Demosthenes 45). This oration was delivered by Apollodorus in an indictment against a witness in a previous trial.[58] Stephanus is alleged to have given false testimony on behalf of his friend Phormio who had been involved in a previous legal battle with Apollodorus. At one point in the speech, Apollodorus accuses Stephanus of greed, money-seeking flattery, covetousness and insolence (65–7). He then makes the following observations concerning Stephanus' behaviour in everyday public life:

Neither should the appearances which this man fashions as he walks with a sullen face along the walls be properly considered as signs of self-control, but rather as signs of misanthropy. In my opinion, a man whom no misfortune has befallen, and who is in no lack of the necessaries of life, but who nonetheless habitually maintains this demeanour, has reviewed the matter and reached the conclusion in his own mind, that to those who walk in a simple and natural way and wear a cheerful countenance, men draw near unhesitatingly with requests and proposals, whereas they shrink from drawing near in the first place to affected and sullen characters. This demeanour (*schēma*), then, is nothing but a cover for his real character, and he shows therein the wildness and bitterness of his disposition. (68–9)[59]

Apollodorus believes that the demeanour (*schēma*) of his opponent in public life is relevant to the case in question. As Goldhill discusses in

---

[57] See Barton (1994) 99 on the relationship between physiognomics and rhetoric at Rome: '... the basic elements of the system were morally persuasive. The methods of physiognomics reveal themselves as developments of traditional τόποι of praise and blame which worked to persuade the audience to identify with the speaker against the categorised Other.'

[58] This speech is generally held to be the work of Demosthenes and written for delivery by Apollodorus. See Trevett (1992) 50–76. There seems to be a difficulty in giving this speech to Demosthenes when other 'Apollodoran' speeches in the Demosthenic corpus have been ascribed to a previously unknown orator; namely Apollodorus himself. Why did Apollodorus write the other speeches and not this one?

[59] Οὐ τοίνυν οὐδ' ἃ πέπλασται καὶ βαδίζει παρὰ τοὺς τοίχους οὗτος ἐσκυθρωπακώς, σωφροσύνης ἄν τις ἡγήσαιτ' εἰκότως εἶναι σημεῖα, ἀλλὰ μισανθρωπίας. ἐγὼ γάρ, ὅστις αὐτῷ μηδενὸς συμβεβηκότος δεινοῦ, μηδὲ τῶν ἀναγκαίων σπανίζων, ἐν ταύτῃ τῇ σχέσει διάγει τὸν βίον, τοῦτον ἡγοῦμαι συνεωρακέναι καὶ λελογίσθαι παρ' αὑτῷ, ὅτι τοῖς μὲν ἁπλῶς, ὡς πεφύκασι, βαδίζουσι καὶ φαιδροῖς, καὶ προσέλθοι τις ἂν καὶ δεηθείη καὶ ἐπαγγείλειεν οὐδὲν ὀκνῶν, τοῖς δὲ πεπλασμένοις καὶ σκυθρωποῖς ὀκνήσειεν τις ἂν προσελθεῖν πρῶτον. οὐδὲν οὖν ἀλλ' ἢ πρόβλημα τοῦ τρόπου τὸ σχῆμα τοῦτ' ἔστι, καὶ τὸ τῆς διανοίας ἄγριον καὶ πικρὸν ἐνταῦθα δηλοῖ.

the introduction to this volume, the term *schēma* is a fundamental expression in Athens' agonistic culture of performance and surveillance – not least because it develops technical senses which connote the learning and composition of 'postures' and 'figures'.[60] Apollodorus makes it clear from the outset that he believes Stephanus' appearance to be manufactured or affected. Stephanus is described as walking by the city walls with a sullen facial expression (ἐσκυθρωπακώς) and he fashions appearances (*ha peplastai*). Apollodorus assumes (perhaps deliberately and falsely) that this spectacle is familiar to the audience. The ascription of the adjectives σκυθρός, σκυθρωπός or the verb σκυθρωπάζω to a subject or subject-group seems to connote a range of emotions manifested in a frowning facial expression; solemnity, sadness, sullenness and anger.[61] It is hard to determine exactly what sort of expression Apollodorus is seeking to convey with 'ἐσκυθρωπακώς'. However, it is clear that Stephanus is represented as having some kind of fixed countenance of gravity. Apollodorus thinks that the audience would be likely to interpret this expression and other unspecified airs and graces as 'signs of self-control' (*sēmeia sōphrosunēs*). Stephanus gives off the appearance of being self-controlled, moderate and modest; his body-language is easily correlated with a moral and political disposition which was greatly valorized by Athenian culture.[62]

According to Apollodorus, everybody is likely to infer from a person's facial and bodily signs to an internal character or disposition. Of course, this is a rhetorical move on Apollodorus' part and can give us only partial insight into the extent to which Athenians deployed a 'folk' physiognomics as an embedded social practice. Nevertheless, there is a case to be made for Apollodorus raising the issue precisely *because* he knows that he must deal with a general perception of Stephanus' appearance as connotative of an upright moral character. Stephanus does not look or behave like a cheat and, for his prosecutor, there is a lot riding on these conclusions – conclusions surely derived from the collective practice of a social semiotics of the body. There can be no certainty of the extent to which Athens was truly a 'face-to-face' society where everyone in the jury had heard about Stephanus or had seen him going about his daily business.[63] But Apollodorus' staged scrutiny of

---

[60] See Goldhill Introduction, p. 4–5.
[61] Cf. Eur. *Hipp.* 1152 (sadness or solemnity); Ar. *Lys.* 7 (anger or sulleness); Aeschin 2.36 (anger or sourness), 3.20 (solemnity); Pl. *Symp.* 206d5 (discontented frowning).
[62] On *Sōphrosunē*, see North (1966), especially 85–149.
[63] Cf. Ober (1989) 148–51 on rumour as a democratic and acceptable form of proof in the orators and their use of the 'you all know' topos. On the question of whether the notion of Athens as a 'face-to-face' society was reality or ideality see Finley (1973) 17–

The rhetoric of anti-rhetoric in oratory 223

Stephanus' facial expressions and demeanour evokes the notion of a 'surveillance culture' (whether it be a rhetorical myth or an oppressive social reality) which Winkler, Cohen and Hunter all detect as crucial to Athenian legal discourse.[64]

Having set up Stephanus as a man who looks upright, Apollodorus offers his audience a different interpretation of his opponent's physical appearance. Stephanus has suffered no personal misfortune and is not lacking in life's necessities. This biography somehow debars Stephanus from the honest deployment of the physical signs of *sōphrosunē*. Apollodorus explains that those who walk simply and *naturally* and maintain a cheerful or bright expression are often approached by others with requests and proposals However, people will not approach those who appear affected or sullen/solemn. Apollodorus infers that Stephanus has represented himself in this way so that he can deter any demands from other citizens. And he will go on to claim that Stephanus has never performed a single act of private or civic generosity in his life (69–70). The demeanour commonly associated with *sōphrosunē* is nothing more than a cover (*problēma*) for a very different internal disposition; in reality it confirms Stephanus' 'misanthropic' temper (*misanthrōpias*) and the 'wildness and bitterness of his disposition' (*to tēs dianoias agrion kai pikron*). Apollodorus' argument here dovetails uncannily with a section of the Aristotelian *Physiognomics* which explores the drawbacks of an 'expression method' of physiognomic interpretation; this is a method which the author distinguishes from an equally flawed 'zoological' approach.[65] The Aristotelian soberly points out that two men with radically different dispositions (*dianoiai*) can exhibit the same facial expression; there is often nothing to tell the difference between the expression of a courageous man and that of an impudent

---

18, (1983) 28–9 (reality); Osborne (1985) 64–5 and Ober (1989) 31–3 (ideality). Recent work on the unlikeliness of a real face-to-face society at the level of polis structures would suggest that gossip and rumour about a litigant might not always filter from deme communities to the mixed-deme audiences of the assembly and law-court juries. For the impact of Athenian law enacting a shift from face-to-face relations in villages to the polis where such relations no longer existed in reality see Humphreys (1985) 350f. The possibility that, at the level of social reality, there could rarely have been anything like an absolutely 'common report' concerning all but the most prominent political individuals seems to follow from the following observation of Ober (1989) 32: 'When a rich Athenian entered the people's court as a litigant, he could not count on having a single fellow demesman on the jury, and the rest of the jurors were likely to be strangers.'

[64] See Winkler (1990a) on elite 'surveillance culture'. On neighbourhood gossip, rumour and surveillance, see Cohen (1991) 49–55, 64–9, 90–5. On gossip and rumour as a means of social control in Athens, see Hunter (1994) 96–119.

[65] See Armstrong (1958) 53–5.

one. Similarly, a man of generally gloomy disposition can have a good day and therefore look cheerful.[66]

Apollodorus destroys any unequivocal link between a specific set of physical signs and the character-type which they are commonly held to signify. But he does not disrupt the workings of the assumptions which ground physiognomic interpretation. Apollodorus is very careful to provide a plausible causal account of how the signs of *sōphrosunē* could also connote a completely different (in this case, totally antithetical) moral disposition. Stephanus is not simply held to have hidden his misanthropy and malignity behind a mask of moderation and modesty. Rather, the commonly recognized signs of *sōphrosunē* are given a functional role in the practice of misanthropy. To appear unapproachable is to *be* unapproachable; to want to be unapproachable without mitigating personal circumstances is to be misanthropic and rude. Hence the signs of unapproachability, which happen to be the same as those of *sōphrosunē*, are often proof that a man does not wish to take part in the 'give-and-take' of everyday public life. The misanthrope can perpetuate his disposition by warding off demands from others with his sullen looks. At the same time he can hide that disposition because its physical manifestation usually signifies a positive character-type. In short, Apollodorus exposes Stephanus' public self-representation as a clever but disingenuous theatrical performance.

Athenian oratory does not abound with physiognomic-style assumptions and interpretations.[67] But we have seen that, within their specific battles, Demosthenes and Aeschines are fond of diagnosing an inner disposition, *phusis* or *ēthos* from the quality and strength of each other's public-speaking voice.[68] They also mock, mimic and analyse each other's physical gestures within the performative context of the law-court. They even mock and imitate (through words and gestures) each other's strategies of (verbal and gestural) mockery and imitation.[69] Often the opponent's quality of voice or use of mimicry and gesture is represented as leading an audience away from the truth or the real

---

[66] Aristotle *Physiognomics* 3 in the text of Förster (1893).
[67] However, Evans (1969) is too pessimistic in claiming that Attic oratory is virtually silent in relation to physiognomic assumptions or strategies.
[68] See Aeschines 2.34–5, 3.228–9; Demosthenes 18.308–10, 19.336. For Demosthenes' stress on Aeschines' voice being that of an actor, see Easterling in this volume.
[69] See Demosthenes 18.232–3. Goldhill (Unpublished) sums it up: 'As he accuses Aeschines of using *schēmata*, he shows – imitates – the *schēmata*: unless the deictics have no force. This is an imitative performance of *schēmata* which accuses its opponent of an imitative performance of *schēmata*. Performance is itself the means and matter of debate.' See also Aeschines 2.156–8. For more on Demosthenes and Aeschines' focus on performance see Ford and Easterling in this volume.

issues at hand. As Easterling discusses in this volume, Demosthenes makes particular play of Aeschines' career as an actor.[70] Demosthenes also claims that Aeschines' voice and articulation signify dishonesty and hidden criminality (19.207–10).

There are one or two occasions where the litigant has to deny the negative character-trait which is implied by the way he walks and talks about town. A plaintiff in a Demosthenic speech has to explain that his habit of 'fast walking and loud talking' is not, as his opponents claim, a sign of bad character but an unavoidable natural trait, and he appeals to his general reputation for support (37.52, 55–6). And at the same time as Apollodorus exposes the fraudulence of Stephanus' outward appearance in the manner I have just discussed, he later asks the jury to excuse his own 'fast walking and loud talking' as an unfortunate affliction of *phusis*. (45.77). He may partly have embarked on his extraordinarily detailed 'physiognomic' exposure of Stephanus' deliberately misleading appearance in order to distract the jury from his own 'physiognomic reputation'.[71]

In his analysis of Stephanus' everyday *schēmata* before the trial and outside the confines of the law-court, Apollodorus does not simply give his opponent a permanent disposition of mean misanthropy. He also represents Stephanus as habitually dishonest and duplicitous in his relationship with other citizens. This was obviously a good argument to deploy against a man accused of having given false testimony. An implied probability argument and an implied argument from character are rolled into one. The argument has no near parallel in extant oratory. And yet, at the same time as it is highly unusual, it is very 'typical' in terms of its appeal to ideologically and morally charged notions of *sōphrosunē*, wildness (*agriotēs*) and reciprocity.[72] It is also a classic (and classically manipulative) example of the interrelationship between a culture of surveillance and the strategic articulation of physiognomic assumptions. Finally, and most importantly for my purposes, the passage demonstrates how a speaker can confront and represent the problem of the citizen who lies to the *dēmos* with a meta-discursive strategy that is strikingly unusual, thereby creating the impression that the strategy is not a strategy at all. Apollodorus creates the impression that the conventional topoi of anti-rhetoric are both inadequate as

---

[70] See again Demosthenes 18.232–3. See also 19.120 and 337–8 with Easterling in this volume. Aeschines 2.156–8 tropes Demosthenes' shrill voice and mimicry as tools of slander.
[71] 'Physiognomic reputation' is also at work at Demosthenes 54. 32ff. and Lysias 16.18f.
[72] See North (1966) on *sōphrosunē*; Cartledge (1993) 50–5 on savagery and 'wildness'; von Reden (1995) on reciprocity.

descriptions of Stephanus and unnecessary as typical strategies of invective. With Stephanus, we have a man who lives and breathes dishonesty in order to remain true to his socially unacceptable self. He is able to *be* misanthropic by hoodwinking everyone into assuming that he is *sophrōn*. There is, Apollodorus implies, no need for the name-calling ('sycophant', 'sophist' and so on) which juries hear every day, and such name-calling would fail to capture the extraordinary truth of Stephanus' life of deception. Apollodorus' physiognomics of deceit attempts to authorize its truth-status by virtue of its distinctive distance from the standard topoi of invective used against 'dishonest' opponents.

v. The lying topos

Apollodorus conjures up an image of his opponent's dishonesty by focusing on his (strategic) performances in Athens' thoroughfares and meeting places. This is not an attack on Stephanus' use of rhetorical *technai* in the limited domain of the law-court and as such it is a marked departure from the anti-rhetorical topoi which I have already discussed. But there are occasions where a speaker actually distances himself from the deceptive connotations of rhetorical *technē* by foregrounding his opponent's use of commonplaces and by 'unmasking' the lies which such topoi conceal. There are several examples of this anti-rhetorical strategy in extant oratory but I only have space to discuss one in detail.[73] They all deal with different topoi and they all serve to undermine an opponent by representing an argument he has used (or will use) as a mere commonplace which has *become* a commonplace precisely because it has proved itself an effective means of disguising guilt. If topoi were the means by which mass and elite colluded in dramatic fictions, the orators occasionally argue that topoi constitute the fiction of an opponent's innocence. This is a form of self-conscious 'anti-rhetoric' which commentators have overlooked, and I will offer one illustration of its force from Demosthenes' speech *Against Boeotus II*.

The 'as you all know' topos is a particularly frequent commonplace which is introduced through a recurring set of phrases.[74] The topos is used to represent a piece of information about an individual as truthful

[73] Other examples: Antiphon 5.4–5 (on the 'plea for a hearing' topos) with Usher and Edwards (1985) 70; Demosthenes 21.136–7 (on the 'have you ever seen me doing this' *topos*) and 141–2 (on the 'inexperience' topos).

[74] See Ober (1989) 147–9 for discussion and examples. The most interesting creative expansion of the 'as you all know' topos has to be Aeschines 1.127–30. For this appeal to *Pheme* see the discussion of Ford in this volume.

by common report or rumour.⁷⁵ It is also used to introduce exemplifying lines of poetry, legal statutes or historical events.⁷⁶ In the *Rhetoric*, Aristotle claims that speech-writers use this *topos* to drum up assent from everyone, including those who do not really know the information being expressed as common knowledge, because the latter would be too ashamed to reveal their ignorance.⁷⁷ The topos' function and effectiveness has also been associated with 'the fiction that the entire polis was the sort of face-to-face community that in reality existed only at the level of the demes' and the fact that *phēmē* (rumour) was regarded as expressive of a highly democratic and egalitarian mode of proof.⁷⁸ But in their analysis of the topos as a recurrent fictionalizing and authorizing strategy, critics have failed to remark on an occasion when the topos' fictionalizing function is interrogated within practical Athenian rhetorical discourse itself.⁷⁹ In the second speech *Against Boeotus*, Demosthenes' client Mantitheus issues this warning concerning the rhetorical tactics of his opponent:

> And he is such a criminal that, if he has no witnesses to prove a fact, he will say that it is well known to you, men of the jury. This is something which is done by all those who do not have a clean argument. If he should try any such device (*technazēi*), do not tolerate it; expose him. What anyone of you does not know, let him assume that his neighbour does not know it either. Let him demand that Boeotus prove clearly whatever statements he may make, and not run away from the truth by declaring that you know things about which he will have no just argument to advance; since I, for my part, men of the jury, although you all know the way in which my father was compelled to adopt these men, am nonetheless suing them at law, and have brought forward witnesses responsible for their testimony. (Demosthenes 40.53–4)

Mantitheus anticipates Boeotus' possible use of the 'as you all know' topos and represents it as something crafted (*technazēi*) by all those who have nothing to say that is fair or sound. The topos is viewed in terms of a contrivance deployed by a non-specific mass of speakers who use it as a veil for 'reality'. The speaker explicitly connects his opponent with 'the many' who use the topos and describes his opponent's

---

⁷⁵ See above, notes 63 and 64.
⁷⁶ On the orators' use of 'as you all know' for history see Pearson (1941); Perlman (1961); Nouhaud (1982). On orators using the topos to introduce citations and references to drama and poetry, see North (1952); Perlman (1964); Ober and Strauss (1990) 250–5.
⁷⁷ Aristotle *Rhetoric* 1408a32–6. Ober (1989)149 connects this interpretation of the *topos*' manipulation of the masses with Hyperides 4.22 where the orator claims that even children know which of Athens' *rhētores* had taken bribes.
⁷⁸ Ober (1989) 150–1. On the question of whether the notion of Athens as a 'face-to-face' society was reality or ideality see above, note 63.
⁷⁹ See, however, Dorjahn (1935) 291 who gives a passing reference to my passage as evidence that the 'as you all know' topos was 'finally turned into an abuse'.

228   *Jon Hesk*

likely deployment of it as a method of 'running away from the truth' (*apodidraskein tēn alētheian*). Mantitheus associates the topos with the failure to provide supporting witnesses. As with Demosthenes' depiction of Aeschines' histrionic rhetoric an opponent's rhetoric is marked as deceptive through its representation as a substitution for the provision of testimony.[80] In this instance, however, a specific strategy is being dismantled.

Furthermore, Mantitheus does not simply gloss the 'as you all know' *topos* as a cover for the presentation of unsubstantiated lies as common facts; he offers a methodology to the audience for interpreting the legitimacy of any occurrence of information represented as common knowledge. He asks each jury-member to consider whether Boeotus' 'commonly knowns' are known to him personally. If they are not, the juror is to assume that his ignorance is not private to himself but shared by the rest of the jury and therefore deduce that the 'as you all know' *topos* has been used to present a fiction or an unsubstantiated claim in terms of a common rumour which is actually non-existent. In asking the jurors to infer from their own ignorance that of their fellow judges, the speaker attempts to demolish any possibility that an individual will not be party to a body of communally held knowledge. He therefore takes advantage of a democratic notion that common report is necessarily defined as knowledge held by *all* individuals in the polis without any exception. This passage could be read as a deliberate playing off between a social reality on the one hand and an ideality on the other. If it was actually possible, at polis level, for a citizen not to be party to a particular item of *phēmē*, then Mantitheus destroys that possibility by introducing the ideal conception of *phēmē* as something which has to be known by absolutely everyone for it to count as forensically and civically legitimate; 'real' *phēmē* as opposed to Boeotus' plans for a topologically contrived *phēmē*.[81]

Mantitheus' meta-discursive interrogation of the 'as you all know' *topos* can be compared instructively with Andocides' summing up of a defensive account of his part (or lack of it) in the profanation of the Mysteries in 415 BCE. In his speech *On The Mysteries*, which was delivered in 399, Andocides rounds off his long narrative of events that occurred some sixteen years previously with this request: 'Gentlemen, recollect as to the truth of my words and those of you who know must

[80] See Demosthenes 19.120 where he suggests that Aeschines' rhetorical and theatrical skill can render the need for witnesses redundant and, by implication can be effective in masking the fact that he has no witnesses.
[81] See above n. 63 on the likelihood that not everybody was party to a particular item of *phēmē*.

teach the rest who do not' (Andocides 1.69). In this instance the speaker is unafraid to admit that not everyone will know his story of events that occurred some years before. He actually instructs those jurors who know and remember to inform those who do not. He still adheres to the spirit of the 'as you all know' topos, because he constructs an image of a group of cognoscenti, implying that there are younger jurors who would not have been old enough in 415 to know details of the events in question. But he is careful to take the diverse competence of his audience into account and as such, provides an example of the way in which orators did not always simply repeat topoi or feel a necessity to play along with the 'dramatic fictions' which they both reflected and reproduced. Often it was advantageous for speakers to stage an exposure of such fictions (to show *how* an opponent was using established rhetorical elements to deceive) as part of their *own* self-representing strategy.

Conclusions

As spaces for the contest and performance of *logoi*, Athens' law-courts provoke strategic constructions of, confrontations with and 'solutions' to, the 'ambiguity of speech'. Fragment 226 of the orator Hyperides articulates this 'ambiguity' and the anxiety it generates: 'There is no stamp of men's intention on their face' (*charaktēr oudeis epestin epi tou prosōpou tēs dianoias tois anthrōpois*). With its stress on the absence of an external marking (*charaktēr*) for determining inner disposition, this dislocated phrase reads like a gnomic warning from the *Theognidea* and even more like the many reflections on the impossibility of detecting lies and 'true' character from words and external appearances which we find in Euripidean tragedy.[82] In yet another swipe at Aeschines, Demosthenes characterizes deceit as peculiarly threatening for Athenian democracy because of its dependence on the performance of *logoi*:

'A man can do you no greater injustice than tell lies. For in a political system based on speeches, how can it be safely administered if the speeches are not true?' (Demosthenes 19.184)[83]

The need for the democratic speaker to disambiguate speech, to stamp himself as honest and his opponent as a liar, gives rise to a proliferation

---

[82] See Theognis 119–28; Euripides *Electra* 367f., *Hippolytus* 927f. At Euripides *Medea* 515–19 the heroine asks Zeus why he has not offered a clear *charaktēr* on the human body which would be a mark of counterfeit virtue.

[83] οὐδὲν γὰρ ἔσθ' ὅ τι μεῖζον ἂν ὑμᾶς ἀδικήσειέ τις, ἢ ψευδῆ λέγων. οἷς γάρ ἐστ' ἐν λόγοις ἡ πολιτεία, πῶς, ἂν οὗτοι μὴ ἀληθεῖς ὦσιν, ἀσφαλῶς ἐστι πολιτεύεσθαι;

of meta-discursive strategies which invoke the manifold possibilities and techniques of deception. Some of these strategies are frequent and standardized enough to be called topoi. Others are commonplaces with unique and creative descriptions coming out of them. Others still are highly original for the extant corpus. It may be no accident that the exceptional strategies which I have described are deployed against citizens whom we could not class as *rhētores*. Stephanus and Boeotus are not recognizable or plausible as 'professional' technicians of deceit and it is therefore important that their dishonesty be constituted by distinctive strategies rather than conformity to 'types' of deceptive performer.

The agonistic nature of democratic public discourse generated its own 'theory' of (mis)representation and performance. The orators assess the recently formed *technai* of rhetorical pedagogy and consultancy in political theoretical terms and find them to be inappropriate to 'democratic' performance. They warn of speech's 'ambiguity' and at the same time offer (albeit self-interested) reflections on the ways in which deceptive communication (whether verbal or physical) should be detected, policed and classified. Fifth-century dramatists and historians highlighted the dangers and opportunities which rhetorical performance and 'the ambiguity of speech' presented.[84] Thucydides' Mytilinean Debate, Aristophanes' *Knights* and the *Acharnians* even invite an audience to view anti-rhetorical arguments as potentially deceptive strategies in themselves.[85] In the fourth century, the orators seem to sustain and develop this atmosphere of suspicion amongst their audience. Undoubtedly they did so to compete, curry favour and fulfil democracy's ideological requirements. But in doing so they also kept the demos aware of the ways in which dissembling and manipulative performances throughout the various spaces of the city could rob them of their apparent sovereignty. In this sense, 'the rhetoric of anti-rhetoric' was more than a *strategic* meta-discourse. It was a meta-discourse which heightened mass vigilance and suspicion over the very individuals who used it as rhetorical strategy. When British Conservatives accuse Labour of 'spin', they are in a glass house throwing stones. But instead of falsely blaming America for inventing 'spin', British citizens should perhaps thank American journalists for first identifying its performances and subjecting them to surveillance.

---

[84] Most recently, Halliwell (1997) stresses that Tragedy engages with rhetoric's powers and perils, rather than simply harnessing its new formulae and strategies as creative resources.

[85] See Hesk (1997) 221–34.

9 Reading Homer from the rostrum: poems and laws in Aeschines' *Against Timarchus*

Andrew Ford

In a few surviving orations from fourth-century Athens, speakers quote Homer and other poetry *in extenso* and comment at length on the verse. Such passages are a valuable reminder that Athenian literary culture was sustained not only by many public performances at state-sponsored festivals, but also by a series of more or less informal re-performances of poetry by citizens among each other. The present paper considers such presentations of poetry in legal contexts for what they say about the uses of literary culture in the democratic city. It aims to show that displaying poetic sophistication to an audience constituted as an arm of the Athenian state was a complex affair. For if we have inherited from the Greeks the idea that a knowledge of ancient traditions, and especially of old poems like Homer's, helps to fashion good citizens, we have inherited certain problems with it as well. It is far from clear what benefits an acquaintance with ancient verse actually confers, and it may be thought difficult to reconcile the pursuit of literary culture, requiring as it does leisure and often the means for formal education, with the egalitarian aspects of democratic theory. My particular focus will be Aeschines' *Against Timarchus*, for it is one of those orations that offers a flurry of poetic quotations and also exhibits a certain tension in the presentation of elite literary culture to a mass audience.[1] It is furthermore a speech very much concerned with rhetorical performance,[2] both its own and that of its target. It is in such publicly engaged, high-stakes works – rather than in the hostility to poetry by withdrawn elites like Plato or in the abstract and universalizing formalism of well-travelled metics like Aristotle – that we may examine why sophistication in poetry was valued and how it was accommodated to democratic ideology.

My argument proceeds in three stages. I shall first (in Part 1) nuance the much-quoted ancient claims for Homer's centrality in Athenian

[1] Remarked and discussed by Ober (1989) 177–81. Cf. Ober and Strauss (1989) esp. 250–5.
[2] On the 'meta-discourse' of Athenian oratory, see Hesk, this volume.

culture by drawing attention to their social implications and considering the realities they covered over. This will make clear that beneath the consensus of Homer as the common *paideia* of the Greeks was a constant competition over how to interpret the poems, one that played out differently among different social groups. I will then turn (in Part II) to the practices of rhetoricians and orators in regard to poetry. Here I shall argue that the way certain sophisticated Greeks interpreted Homer was very closely allied to the way a skilled orator like Aeschines interpreted the laws of Solon: in both cases one had to do with arguing for a particular 'reading' of a text that was often old and not perfectly clear in its implications. This will suggest that at least one benefit of acquiring literary expertise was that it made a speaker more agile in persuading others how to 'read' certain texts. Finally (Part III), I shall illustrate this hypothesis by comparing the strategies by which Aeschines used Homer and other canonical poets to represent himself and his opponent to an audience of Athenian judges.

I. Reading Homer in the democratic city

The incorporation of Homer into democratic education and culture may seem at first glance perfectly intelligible and indeed inevitable, given his ancient authority in history, science, and morals. Public performances of Homeric poetry had been a part of Athenian civic life at least since the Peisistratids, and the democracy retained epic recitations at festivals such as the Panatheneia and Brauronia. So identified had Homer become with democratic festivals that by the fourth century it was common to forget the role of the Peisistratids in all this (not forgotten by [Plato] *Hipp.* 228b) and to ascribe these institutions to the work of 'our fathers' or 'forebears' (Lycurg. *In Leocr.* 102, Isoc. *Paneg.* 4.159) or even Solon (Dieuch. *FGrH* 485 F 6). Festival performance, along with informal presentations by travelling rhapsodes, must have made Homer familiar to a large number of citizens in this spectacle-loving society. Comedy's travesty of epic indirectly attests to its centrality, and Homer's presence behind so many tragic texts justifies the verdict that there was 'a large degree of continuity throughout the fifth and fourth century in the important place of music, dancing, poetry, and in particular Homer in early education'; in principle, Homer's importance was based on 'a notion of poetry not as esoteric art or mere entertainment, but as a medium for important, general and true utterance to the city'.[3]

---

[3] Goldhill (1986) 140, 141. His ch. 6 traces Homer's omnipresence in Athenian culture of this time. Cf. Todd (1990) 164.

So much seems to be proclaimed by 'Aeschylus' in *Frogs* (1054 f.): 'what a schoolteacher [*didaskalos*] does for children, poets do for them when they grow up'. Yet not every member of Aristophanes' audience had had the benefit of a *didaskalos*, Athenian education notoriously depending on individual means and initiative. Hence, the notion of poetry as a common possession and of Homer as the universal educator may be less an accurate description of social reality than the sort of thing a democratic audience expected to hear. (Contrast, e.g., Heraclitus' esotericism or the in-group elitism of Theognis [681] and Pindar [*Ol.* 2.83-92]). It was therefore prudent for Athenian teachers to say that they made their students memorize 'the works of good poets' because they contained 'many admonitions, admiring descriptions and encomia of good men, with the result that the child may desire to emulate their deeds' (*Prt.* 325e f.).

The absence of public education is but one indication that alongside the ideology of Homer as everyman's poet was an inevitable stratification in the knowledge of epic. Simply by virtue of its notional omnipresence, epic could serve not only as a medium of cultural exchange but also as an arena for winning social distinction by amassing 'cultural capital'.[4] The young men who were 'crammed' (διακορεῖς, *Laws* 810e 10) with poetry at school were likely to find it at least as useful in 'dinner party and banquet society' as in the agora.[5] When Nicias told his son Niceratus that he had to learn the *Iliad* and *Odyssey* by heart to become a 'good man' (*anēr agathos*, Xen. *Symp.* 3.5-6), a charitable bystander would no doubt assume this was because of the valuable civic lessons therein. But Nicias appears to have insisted on the *whole* poems, something requiring a good deal of leisure, means, and access to texts; whatever moral lessons Niceratus may have imbibed, the social distinction conferred by a polished and extensive familiarity with the common classic would not have hurt his chances of being taken for a worthy man. It was perhaps possible for the unschooled (and largely illiterate)[6] to gather a fair knowledge of Homer from rhapsodes at festivals (though Isocrates snobbishly estimates that less than half the audience cared to stay awake on such occasions: *Paneg.* 12.263). There were also frequent displays in the agora (Xen. *Symp.* 3.6). Like teachers, rhapsodes had every reason to act as 'praisers' of Homer, advertising

---

[4] Superbly discussed by Guillory (1993). How systems of education can perpetuate inequality is valuably explored in many works of Bourdieu, esp. (1984); cf. Goldhill (1991) 169 on education in late fifth-century Athens as 'a source of conflict rather than social stability'.

[5] Connor (1971) 29; cf. 163-8 on culture and education among the 'new politicians'. For a valuable reading of the Douris cup on these lines, see Lissarrague (1987) 130, 132.

[6] The low estimates in Harris (1989) remain the fullest discussion.

how the poet had educated Greece and was worth studying for the conduct of human life (*Resp.* 606e; for 'praisers of Homer', cf. *Ion*, 536d, 541e, 542b, *Prot.* 309a–b, *Laws* 810e–811a, Xen. *Mem.* 1.3.3). But in the circles where Niceratus met and dined with Socrates, Antisthenes, and Euthydemus (a collector of Homeric texts), it was fashionable to say that rhapsodes were the most stupid of men because they did not know the deeper meanings of Homer such as could be learned (at a fee) from Stesimbrotus of Thasos and the like.[7] If literary refinement could express social position, we need not be surprised at an anecdote (Plut. *Alcib.* 7) ascribing such passionate devotion to Homer on the part of Alcibiades that he thrashed one schoolmaster who did not own a copy of Homer and would praise another extravagantly if he were able to edit him. Homer's greatness is reaffirmed at the same time as Alcibiades asserts his right to judge schoolteachers.

A sophisticated familiarity with notionally common literary culture was useful for communicating and competing within elite groups at private occasions such as symposia; but it had a further use if it were displayed to the public, either by way of advertising a teacher's rare insights or as an indication of the style of life that went on in certain houses. Public displays of such 'higher' forms of literary culture provoked both popular resentment and elite contempt.[8] Still, a wide range of the Athenian population must have become to some degree familiar with sophisticated ways of reading: the *Frogs* amply shows that at least the most striking ideas of literary savants flowed out from the houses of the wealthy and intellectually ambitious, from the gymnasia and the schools, and percolated down to the agora where Socrates found no shortage of people willing to debate what a given poem meant (Pl. *Apol.* 22a–c).

These details I add to our picture of Homer in the democratic city do nothing to diminish the more general truth that the 'system of representations by which the city lived extracted from the Homeric epic examples that still had real meaning ... and made Athenian history a repetitive gesture in which the battles of the present copied those of the past and foreshadowed those to come'.[9] They do, however, make us realize that if Homer was common coin in the democratic exchange of

---

[7] Xen. *Symp.* 3.6; *Mem* 4.2.10, on which see Richardson (1975) 74. Further on the use of Homer as a badge of culture in Ford (1997).
[8] Resentment: [Xen.] *Ath. Pol.* 1.13. Contempt: Isocrates on the 'vulgar sophists' who rehearse the same stale trivialities about Homer and Hesiod 'all over the place' (*Panath.* 12.18–19); Plato's ironic praise of 'modern' education which publicly expounds the hidden truths of poetry (the example is *Il.* 16.201) to cobblers and the like (*Theaet.* 180d).
[9] Loraux (1986) 145.

ideas, each transaction was also a social exchange of status and ideology. Homer was pervasive in Athens in the sense that many different levels of Homer-expertise were on offer, and competitions in interpreting his texts engaged the citizens at least as much as widespread proclamations of his greatness. Indeed, one of the major tasks of the quintessentially Athenian art forms – tragedy, comedy, and the funeral oration – was to rewrite for the city heroic traditions that were hardly imbued with democratic values or institutions.[10]

When we turn to the study of rhetoric, however, it is a little more difficult to understand why, as it appears, Homer and other poets continued to be studied. I wonder whether Cleon, for example, would agree that 'the most important part of a man's education is to be an acute [*deinos*] critic of what the poets have said, to understand and distinguish what is well said from what is ill, and to justify oneself on this matter when challenged' (Pl. *Prt* 339a). After all, in practical terms Homer was arguably the *least* useful text for a clear-eyed student bent on eminence in the city (*Prt.* 318e).[11] His archaic and polyglot diction did little to prepare an orator to face an audience keen to leap on solecisms, barbarisms, and mispronunciations.[12] His stories had very little to do with the great democratic and religious myths, to say nothing of those staples of democratic oratory, Marathon and Salamis.

Nevertheless, Aristotle recommends that orators cite the poets as authoritative and well-known witnesses (*Rhet.* 1375b28ff.), and it seems a fair supposition that the plethora of poetic exempla in his *Rhetoric* (far outnumbering his citations of orators)[13] was not uncharacteristic of how the art was presented to students. One might suppose that orators would need to know the poet who served as a common point of reference, yet it is unclear that the advice to cite poets was actually much put into practice. The fine survey of S. Perlman has shown that quotations of poetry are relatively infrequent in our surviving oratorical texts, mostly concentrated in four speeches.[14] This scarcity may be explained in various ways,[15] but it is still worth asking how

---

[10] Goldhill (1986) 143ff., (1991) esp. 167–76; Loraux (1986) 145ff.; Wilson (1996).
[11] Cf. Gomperz (1912) 127.
[12] Hence we may understand why, as North and Perlman show, the most often cited poetry after Homer comes from the plain, Attic, and gnomic *rhēseis* of Euripides (the ποιητῇ ῥηματίων δικανικῶν, Ar. *Peace* 534).
[13] North (1952) 6–7, 22.
[14] Perlman (1964) esp. 162: Aeschines I (*Timarchus*), which provoked a reply in Demosthenes 19 (*Embassy*).; also Dem. 18 (*On the Crown*) esp. 315, 322, and Lycurgus *Against Leocrates*. See now the fine study by Wilson (1996).
[15] The relative scarcity of poetic quotation would seem to pose a challenge to those who assume that quoting Homer was like quoting the Bible, a sure-fire way to gain audience support (e.g. Dorjahn (1972)). Perlman's explanation for the rarity (1964) 161 is a

familiarity with the poets was translated into effective rhetorical practice. If the impact of the sophists may be described as a 'revolutionary influence on the control, formation and dissemination of knowledge', and as offering 'new and different techniques for approaching the procedures of democratic authority',[16] we might try to specify how their teaching of Homer effected these ends. Helen North has admirably documented the importance attributed to studying poetry in rhetorical education, but admits too that 'It is often difficult to discover precisely what relation existed between the studies of poetry which formed so prominent a part of the Sophists' curriculum and their rhetorical instruction'.[17]

I wish to suggest that the continued study of Homer had a real practical importance for the would-be democratic orator in that it developed two useful skills. The first was that the very antiquity and obscurity of the poems taught certain Athenians how to read closely and interpret difficult texts, and that this skill could usefully be transferred to the decipherment of old laws and the exposition of recent ones. Secondly, the general irrelevance or distance of the Homeric world from Athens sharpened the skill in re-using traditions to speak to present social and political arrangements. To see this it is first necessary to consider by way of two examples what actually might go on when Athenians interpreted Homer.

The most basic skill required to read or recite Homer is understanding the *glossai*, the embedded traditional language made obscure by time, sometimes to the poet or performer himself. This oldest strand in Homeric expertise had by the end of the fifth century moved from being the rhapsodes' special lore to become the tedious staple of Athenian boys' education.[18] But the simplicity and antiquity of glossing should not let us take it for granted. For glossing is of

---

combination of a 'deep-rooted antagonism toward experts' with the development of an independent oratorical-prosaic style. North (1952) 24 says that poetry was most useful in epideictic oratory, and that forensic (i.e. the bulk of our evidence) and deliberative speakers were inhibited from quoting by convention and conservative prejudice. Yet in the face of such antagonism and prejudice, why take the poets as models to begin with, and why continue to pay lip-service to their value through the fourth century? My own explanation would take off from anecdotes such as the one North herself cites ([Plut.] *Lives of Orators* 845c), in which Demosthenes rose up at an Olympic festival and silenced orators praising Macedon by quoting ancient poems on the glory of Thebes and Olynthus. I suggest that poetic quotation was most impressive when it seemed to be the 'spontaneous' impulse of a well-bred and educated citizen; hence it was more common in oral than written eloquence.

[16] Goldhill (1986) 226, 227; on their techniques see now O'Sullivan (1992) ch. 3.
[17] North (1952) 2.
[18] Pfeiffer (1968) 12, 41.

course translation from the archaic into the contemporary, so that Homer always required *interpretation* and not just memorization or recitation to become part of the citizens' cultural equipment. A brief look at Plato's Callicles shows how quickly glossing certain terms could become ideological in the democratic city. Callicles derides the 'philosophical' man because he 'shuns the city centre and its agora, where "men become distinguished", as the poet says' (*Gorg.* 485d: φεύγοντι τὰ μέσα τῆς πόλεως καὶ τὰς ἀγοράς, ἐν αἷς ἔφη ὁ ποιητὴς τοὺς ἄνδρας ἀριπρεπεῖς γίγνεσθαι). As the underlined phrases show, Callicles defends the active political life by glossing the words of Phoenix describing Achilles as a lad 'still unacquainted with war *and the agorai, where men become distinguished*': οὐδ' ἀγορέων, ἵνα τ' ἄνδρες ἀριπρεπέες τελέθουσι, (*Il.* 9.441). Part of Callicles' glossing is for clarity, and no doubt also to display his easy familiarity with Homeric idiom: Homer's ἵνα, 'in which place', becomes the prosaic ἐν αἷς; ἀριπρεπέες is given its Attic form and ἄνδρες is given an article; the archaic/poetic τελέθουσι becomes γίγνεσθαι. But quite significantly Homer's ἀγοραί, 'assembly place(s)', is kept[19] and cunningly glossed with τὰ μέσα τῆς πόλεως to exploit its fifth-century connotation of 'marketplace' where ideas, knowledge, and power were exchanged. If the poet of men 'good with the spear and in council' valued the agora as one arena for winning distinction, Callicles is only too happy to read this as a commendation of demagogic politicians who bravely descend to the market places of ideas to win eminence. His modern and unsettling (cf. 500c) ambitions gain thereby the sanction of tradition and the veneer of heroism.[20]

Another example of disingenuous glossing shows how flexible it could be in ideological battles. Xenophon (*Mem.* 1.2.58–9) records two quite opposite political interpretations being read into the same Iliadic passage. In an anti-Socratic pamphlet, Polycrates[21] had accused Socrates of hating the democracy, and illustrated this by saying the philosopher 'often' cited verses from *Iliad* 2 in which Odysseus restrains the kings and subdues the troops. At issue particularly was the contrast between Odysseus' mild rebuke to the nobles (*Il.* 2.188–91)

---

[19] As Callicles is glossing, there might be something to be said for τῆς ἀγορᾶς, which would be a further clarification of the epic use of the plural for a single assembly.

[20] What is original with Callicles is his choice of proof text, not the misreading he gives it: Unjust Logos in *Clouds* 1055–7 makes the same slippery point: 'I don't condemn spending time in the agora, for Homer made Nestor an *agorētēn*, as he did all the *sophoi*'. See further Dover (1968a) on *Clouds* 991.

[21] Xenophon's antagonist is almost certainly Polycrates in his *Accusation of Socrates*; cf. Schol. Aristeides III.480.29ff. Dindorf.

and his harsh reproach to the common soldier (198–202).[22] The latter lines run:

ὃν δ' αὖ δήμου τ' ἄνδρα ἴδοι βοόωντά τ' ἐφεύροι,	198
τὸν σκήπτρῳ ἐλάσασκεν ὁμοκλήσασκέ τε μύθῳ·	
δαιμόνι', ἀτρέμας ἧσο, καὶ ἄλλων μῦθον ἄκουε,	
οἳ σέο φέρτεροί εἰσι· σὺ δ' ἀπτόλεμος καὶ ἄναλκις,	201
οὔτε ποτ' ἐν πολέμῳ ἐναρίθμιος οὔτ' ἐνὶ βουλῇ.	202

And whenever he came upon one of the common men making a din	198
he curbed him with his sceptre and addressed a speech to him: 'Sir! Take your seat quietly and listen to the commands of others who are your superiors; but you are useless in attack and defence,	201
and never of any account either in war or in council.'	202

From Xenophon (1.2.58), who quotes the passages in question, we gather that Polycrates had Socrates 'interpret the lines as if The Poet sanctioned beating common people and the poor': ταῦτα δὴ αὐτὸν ἐξηγεῖσθαι, ὡς ὁ ποιητὴς ἐπαινοίη παίεσθαι τοὺς δημότας καὶ πένητας. Glossing Homer's δήμου ἄνδρα (v. 198) with τοὺς δημότας καὶ πένητας makes Socrates vividly anti-democratic and elitist; rendering τὸν σκήπτρῳ ἐλάσασκεν with παίεσθαι removes any possibility of construing Odysseus' action as something less that *hubris* against a citizen. Woe to anyone who commended such texts to the youth of Athens.[23]

Xenophon denied that Socrates could have offered any such interpretation, since he was poor himself; and he counters with a reading of the passage by a 'democratic and people-loving' Socrates (δημοτικὸς καὶ φιλάνθρωπος, *Mem.* 1.2.60). This Socrates paraphrased the lines quite differently: 'it is necessary to prevent by any means' (πάντα τρόπον κωλύεσθαι, that is, even hitting/ushering with the sceptre) those who are 'useless in word or deed, and can offer no support to the army or the city or the people when need arises' (τοὺς μήτε λόγῳ μήτ' ἔργῳ ὠφελίμους ὄντας μήτε στρατεύματι μήτε πόλει μήτε αὐτ' τ' δήμῳ, εἴ τι δέοι, βοηθεῖν ἱκανούς). Here Xenophon is glossing, in reverse order, the final clauses in Odysseus' speech (*Il.* 2.201–2). Homer's war/council dichotomy (οὔτε ἐν πολέμῳ | οὔτ' ἐνὶ βουλῇ, v. 202) becomes the contemporary and readily intelligible 'word/deed' opposition (μήτε λόγῳ

---

[22] Xenophon's quotation omits 192–7 (irrelevant plot summary) and significantly cuts off just before the very anti-democratic 'not all of us Achaeans here are kings, many-kingship is a bad thing' (2.203ff.).

[23] Polycrates had branded Socrates with being the teacher of Alcibiades: Isoc. *Busiris* 5f. Aeschines also presented Socrates as a threat to the democracy for teaching Critias (1.173).

μήτ' ἔργῳ). Xenophon then combines this dichotomy with the preceding antithesis in 2.201 (ἀπτόλεμος καὶ ἄναλκις, 'useless in attack and defence') into a tricolon crescendo that shifts from Homer's martial world to democratic Athens: μήτε στρατεύματι μήτε πόλει μήτε αὐτ' τ' δήμῳ (?!). (I can only assume that the last clause is extrapolated from Homer's βουλῇ in v. 202.) There is also a subtle moderation of Odysseus' charge that the common soldier is *never* of any account (οὔτε ποτ', 2.202) into εἴ τι δέοι, which implies that the worthless man will let the city down in a crisis.

Having democratized Odysseus' harshness by converting its object from the (inherently, naturally) worthless to the politically 'useless',[24] Xenophon's Socrates adds that the useless must be restrained no matter what their station: 'even if they should be very rich' (that is the βασιλῆα καὶ ἔξοχον ἄνδρα at 2.188 are sat down too) or 'arrogant'. If 'arrogant' (θρασεῖς) be a gloss alluding to Thersites (who enters the *Iliad* immediately after Odysseus' speech: 2.211ff.), Socrates declares himself opposed equally to elite and demagogic interference in the Assembly. All in all, this teacher of the young shows himself in favour of an orderly but still democratic Assembly; there is nothing in this to corrupt the children of an Athens where Assemblies were policed by Scythian archers in the fifth century and by marshals (*proedroi*) in the fourth.

These passages show both the complexities involved in glossing Homeric poetry and the possibilities it offered ingenious interpreters to bend it to their purposes. Hence, as we credit ancient proclamations of Homer's great authority for the democratic city, we must recognize that those who made a special study of Homer were likely to be more resourceful and persuasive in putting these notionally common texts to work for themselves.

My next step is to argue that, whatever the reasons given for studying old poetry past primary schooling, the reading skills that some Athenians sharpened in rhetorical studies and practised among their peers could have given them a practical advantage in litigation. That archaic laws could at times need real linguistic decipherment is clear from Lysias 10.16 ff. in which the speaker goes through a series of archaic 'Solonian' laws and has to gloss a number of their terms with synonyms from the contemporary legal lexicon. This is a rather isolated example,[25] but the obscurity and complexity of such codes as the Solonian

---

[24] Xenophon's μήτε ... ὠφελίμους is the antithesis of those values signified by the democratic sense of χρηστός, on which see Ober (1989) 13.

[25] But cf. Ar. *Clouds* 1185 ff. where Pheidippides hopes to cancel a debt by appealing to 'old Solon, that friend of the common man' and what he meant by the old expression *henē kai nea* (first used by Solon according to D.L. 1.57).

law of inheritance were notorious, and even led some political theorists to conclude that Solon had been deliberately 'unclear and complicated' in order to make the people ultimately powerful as judges, while others held that the acknowledged obscurity was simply the result of the difficulty of framing general laws.[26] A link between literary and legal glossing is suggested in the famous testimonium to the rote learning of Homeric *glossai* at school (Ari. *Dait.* Fr. 233 KA). Ehrenberg valuably observed that what goes on in this passage is that the modern young man may be bored with Homer but is very excited at picking up arcane legal terminology such as *iduous* and *opuein* – both of which one may note were to be found in the Solonian laws on inheritance.[27]

Even when the laws at issue were not ancient, one might hazard that a trained manipulator of texts would be more adept at extracting from the archives laws that were relevant to his case or that could be made relevant on a certain interpretation. Now this might be thought to be a trivial or even non-existent advantage, for there was nothing to prevent any citizen from seeking out a legal text for himself, just has he was free to hunt up access to Homer;[28] Harris has observed that repeated service on juries could create a pool of quite experienced judges.[29] But most Athenian jurors gained their experience of the laws in the context of some speaker interpreting it for them. There was no neutral approach to the laws and no interpretation without partisan colouration (just as there was no access to the Homeric poems 'in themselves' without ideological framing).[30] Hence I propose that the literary education of orators helped them take an important role in educating assemblies and courts about the law. To illustrate how this worked I

---

[26] E.g. *Ath. Pol.* 9.2 (Solon 'neither *haplōs* nor *saphōs*'), on which see Ruschenbusch (1957), Rhodes (1981) ad loc., Osborne (1985a) 40–44, Lewis (1993), Harris (1994) 138. Aeschines adverts to this issue to help him interpret a 'law' at 1.24, but most relevant for our purposes is the deployment of the idea in Lycurgus *Against Leocrates* 102–3: 'I would like to commend Homer to you as a witness. For so worthy a poet was he in your fathers' estimation that they instituted a law to the effect that, out of all the poets, his poems alone should be performed at each Greater Panatheneia. They thereby demonstrated to the Greeks how they valued the noblest deeds, and this was fitting. For the laws, on account of their brevity cannot teach but only prescribe what should be done; whereas poets who imitate the actual lives of men, picking out the noblest of their deeds, persuade men by the full demonstration that accompanies their account.'

[27] Ehrenberg (1962) 289.

[28] For a recent account of access to laws by litigants and jurors, see Boeghold (1996) esp. 205–6 and Lane Fox (1994) 140–1 on West (1989). On 'experts in Athenian law', Todd (1996).

[29] Harris (1994).

[30] Further in Hedrick (1994).

will turn to Aeschines and consider how he interprets laws in *Against Timarchus*. It is not always easy to separate law from interpretation in this text, especially because the oration is often our sole or principal source for the legal matters it discusses. But a look at how Aeschines organizes his exposition and at a few clear instances of his glossing laws will suggest that the skills of this schoolmaster's son were not forgotten when he came to 'teach', as he puts it (1.196), the law to a democratic jury.

II. Glossing the law in *Against Timarchus*

When Aeschines found himself indicted by political opponents around 346 BCE, he discovered the means for counter-attack in a provision of Athenian law that debarred any citizen who had prostituted himself from participating in public life in a number of ways, including addressing the people's Assembly. It happened that Timarchus, who was prosecuting Aeschines, had lived a notoriously profligate life and had been active in civic politics; he thus seemed vulnerable to being formally denounced before the Assembly as a prostitute who had violated these provisions and then tried in court.[31] Aeschines' *Against Timarchus* represents his successful prosecution:[32] despite the assistance of Demosthenes, Timarchus became subject to arrest and severe punishment should he pursue his suit or be politically active in any way.[33]

From a strictly legal point of view, it is true that 'Aeschines rested his case against Timarchus squarely on the law which punished male prostitutes who addressed the Assembly or served as magistrates'.[34] Certainly, Aeschines began the speech by having this law read out to the court (1.2–3) and he returns to it often.[35] But something else is also going on in *Timarchus*, for the actual discussion of this law (1.28–32) seems buried in a much wider survey of (not always directly relevant) laws in 1.6–36. Moreover, even this conscientious legal discussion occupies less than a sixth of the entire speech. This makes sense since

---

[31] On the law and proceedure, see Harrison (1968–71) 2.171, 204–5, Hansen (1987) 117, Rhodes (1972) 2.5, Dover (1978) 20–9, Halperin (1990) 94–5.

[32] I read *In Tim.* suspecting that published orations had a loose relationship to what was actually said in court. However, the 'genre' of the political oration/tract clearly aims at recreating a plausible oral performance.

[33] On the legal outcome: Bonner (1993) 81ff., Harrison (1968–71) 2.205 with 229–31, Hansen (1976) 66–7; cf. Dem. 19.200, 257.

[34] Harris (1994) 133.

[35] E.g. 1.28–30, 40, 73, 81, 186, 195.

prostitution was not illegal *per se* in Athens, and Athenian attitudes towards activity we call homosexual were, to say the least, complex.[36] It is hardly surprising that Aeschines was not content with saying that, on account of what Timarchus may once have done behind this or that closed door, the hitherto active and well-known figure (as is clear from the invidious survey of his political career: 1.106-15) should be banished from public life. My discussion of *Timarchus* will set Aeschines' treatment of the law in the context of this more elaborate assault. In this section I will be concerned with how the orator constructs from a variety of legal texts an allegedly Solonian ideal of the worthy citizen and orator which goes beyond any single legal issue to condemn the entire life and character of his opponent.

That Aeschines will require a certain amount of creative reading or application of old texts to the present case is indicated by the way he introduces Solon, Draco and the other ancient law-givers as 'prescient' (ὅσην πρόνοιαν περὶ σωφροσύνης ἐποιήσατο ὁ Σόλων ...) in their concern to inculcate 'virtue'[37] through their laws (1.6-7). To attribute prescience to Solon is to suggest that the explicit word of the law fits Timarchus with uncanny exactness so that no interpretative adjustment is needed. This proves not to be so. Aeschines not only will strongly gloss the laws he cites, but he will also marshal them into a structured drama of his own making, suggesting that Solon composed his code by proceeding systematically through the stages of a citizen's life from cradle to coming of age. This organized presentation, he assures us, is only for the sake of clarity (1.8) and in any case follows the *explicit* language of the law (διαρρήδην, 1.7, a word that often recurs in the following chapters).[38] On closer examination, however, it will appear that we are being given an artificial synthesis of laws and interpretations designed to add up to an ideal ('Solonian') prescription of the citizen's proper education and conduct through life. It hardly needs to be added that Timarchus will fall short of these standards in every respect, or that his prosecutor's persona will gradually blend into that of revered moral preceptor.

Aeschines' artful structuring comes into play immediately as he

---

[36] On *Tim.* and Athenian sexual attitudes: Dover (1978) 19ff., Halperin (1990) 88-112, Winkler (1990) 45-70, Cohen (1991) 171-202, with the discussion of Wallace (1994) 145, 151-2.
[37] *Sōphrosunē* is surely the keynote of the speech, occurring some 28 times in various forms. I often signal its variable nuances (Dover [1974] 119-23) with 'virtue', which is appropriately vague, high-minded, and suggestive of conservative sexual habits.
[38] Aeschines is cited from the edition of Martin and de Budé (1927). The new Teubner edition by Dilts reached me too late for study, though I have accepted 'Timarchus' in the dative at 1.18.

Reading Homer from the rostrum

assembles the first set of laws, those concerning children. These are divided into two parts: first, those having to do with early upbringing, and then laws protecting children from sexual aggression. A fair amount of interpretation seems required to claim that the first group of these laws (in 1.9–12) was aimed at an 'education in virtue', setting out the requisite activities and nurture for a free child (περὶ τῆς σωφροσύνης τῶν παίδων ... ἃ χρὴ τὸν παῖδα τὸν ἐλεύθερον ἐπιτηδεύειν, καὶ ὡς δεῖ αὐτὸν τραφῆναι). Whatever actual laws the clerk read out in 1.12 we cannot now recover,[39] but from Aeschines' description of the legislation as 'publicly inscribed [ἀναγράψαντες] and handed over to the people for safekeeping', we can assume that they were to be found in the state archives and perhaps on public stelae too. The provisions (1.9–11) are a mixed bag ranging from rules for the operation of schools[40] to the minimum age for *chorēgoi*,[41] but all fit his construct since they have to do with occasions in which boys are away from their fathers and in the presence of other boys and men. Still, Timarchus' upbringing is not legally at issue, however sordid it may have been. This set of laws, however, does allow Aeschines to extract by way of interpretation what 'the law-giver' thought was the right way to raise a citizen.[42] For example, he infers from 'explicit' regulations on the hours schools may be open and what adults may be present that Solon was wary of pedagogues: ὅμως ἀπιστῶν φαίνεται, καὶ διαρρήδην ἀποδείκνυσι (1.9). It is also his own generalization when he sums up the series of regulations as reflecting the law-giver's belief (ὁ νομοθέτης ἡγήσατο) that the useful citizen is produced by a 'fine upbringing' (καλῶς τραφέντα 1.11). All this, of course, will make a stark contrast with Timarchus' extraordinary early life. At the same time, Aeschines himself becomes the mouthpiece of tradition, prescribing the proper education for Athenian citizens at a time of curricular debate and uncertainty.[43]

Having finished with upbringing, Aeschines turns in 13–18 to three laws that might cover sexual and criminal offences against children, none of which are exactly pertinent to the main charge. The first (1.13)

---

[39] Like the other laws in this text, the version at 1.12 is an editorial fabrication: Drerup (1898) 297, 314.

[40] The school regulations seem authentic, though they should not be over-interpreted: Pélékidis (1962) 31–2, Schmitter (1972) 111.

[41] The rule for *chorēgoi* seems a fourth-century innovation, see Rhodes (1993) 625–6 on *Ath. Pol.* 56.3.

[42] On the motives, methods and necessity of inferring absent law-givers' intentions, see Hansen (1990), Thomas (1994) esp. 123–4, (1995).

[43] As can be seen from the debates joined in Aristotle *Politics* 7–8, and numerous passages in Plato, Isocrates, Alcidamas, etc.

explicitly (διαρρήδην γοῦν λέγει ὁ νόμος) prescribes death for the father or guardian who sells the sexual services of a boy. Another (1.14) imposes 'the gravest penalties' on anyone who panders a free-born boy or woman.[44] Finally, he manages to bring in the law against *hubris* as 'summing up all such laws'. While *hubris* often had a sexual side,[45] Aeschines needs to gloss the law to make it relevant here: its 'explicit' (ἐν ᾧ διαρρήδην γέγραπται) punishments for *hubris* against child, woman, and man must 'presumably' include hiring out such persons for sex (ὑβρίζει δὲ δή που ὁ μισθούμενος, 1.15). Aeschines then has the text read out (1.16) to draw a further inference from its surprising provision – 'something a hearer may well wonder at' – of protection for slaves. Although the clause is quite irrelevant here, it allows him another inference: the law-giver made *hubris* against slaves actionable not for their sake, but because 'he wished to accustom Athenians to steer as far as possible away from the crime against free persons' (1.17).[46] From this *a fortiori* argument follows another quite relevant one: the law-giver 'believed' that the man who committed *hubris* against anyone at all was unfit to be a citizen.

Dover suggests that the strategy behind this legal mish-mash was to throw sand in the jurors' eyes and intimate that Timarchus merits 'the gravest penalties' in the present case, suggesting capital punishment.[47] Dover's analysis is acute as usual, though disenfranchisement (*atimia*) was all Aeschines needed for his purposes, and all he got. At least an additional benefit of his strategy is that he has made Solonian law associate the integrity of the citizen's body with the health of the body politic.[48] There is no chance that Timarchus' behaviour is a personal style; his life is such as the law-giver foresaw, despised, and tried to legislate against. With this in place, Aeschines can turn to his second class, laws governing young men, and come at last to the law visiting *atimia* on prostitutes who would speak to the Assembly (1.19–21). In listing the disabilities imposed by this law (1.19), he interlards selective quotation with a series of prejudicial inferences that make the law-giver

---

[44] On the laws in 1.13 and 1.14, see Dover (1978) 27–9.
[45] Cohen (1987) 5–8, (1991) 176–80, Fisher (1992) 109ff.
[46] On Aeschines' use of the *hubris* law, see Dover (1978) 34–9. Demosthenes also infers an *a fortiori* argument from the law as he quotes it (21.45ff.): if *hubris* against a slave is punishable, insulting a *chorēgos* must be a far greater crime; cf. Murray (1990) 145, Wilson (1991), Fisher (1992) 58ff. On extracting the original *hubris* law from the orators' exegeseis, I am persuaded by Harris's scepticism in *CP* 87 (1992) 77–8 rather than MacDowell's optimism (1990) 263ff.
[47] Dover (1978) 27–8 on 1.72 conflicting with 1.14.
[48] Cf. Halperin (1990) 94–5, 102–5, Winkler (1990) 56–61.

utterly hostile to the defence.[49] With a remark that Timarchus has dared to violate these 'established, fine and virtuous' laws, he reiterates once more his tripartite scheme (1.22), and moves on to the final stage, laws concerning 'the rest of the Athenians'.

For the analytical reader, Aeschines' 'three ages of man' pretence will collapse immediately, since he begins this final section with a set of miscellaneous practices and laws for running Assemblies. The audience, however, is being swept up into a dramatic fiction in which Solon (who, as 'everybody knows', wrote a poem on the ages of man) made up all these laws in sequence: '*first*' (1.7) he regulated early upbringing; then youth, but 'not yet speaking to the boy himself' (1.18); once they become citizens, Solon addresses the young men themselves through the laws (1.18–19); finally, 'once he had finished with these laws, he examined how best to conduct Assemblies' (1.22).[50] By subtly imposing this drama on his series of laws, Aeschines depicts the last laws on rhetors and Assemblies as Solon's ultimate provisions for the city's good.

Aeschines develops his theme for this last section by zeroing in on the beginning of a certain law (1.22): 'How does the law-giver begin' his culminating legislation, he asks, and answers: νόμοι ... περὶ εὐκοσμίας. The specific provisions that immediately follow (1.23) include such things as the preliminary cathartic rites of the Assembly, the order in which heralds and ambassadors are received,[51] and how speakers are to be recognized in the Assembly. These provisions, mostly well attested, are as creditably authentic as they are legally irrelevant. But one of them gave Aeschines a word he wanted to pounce on. In the fourth, fifth, or even sixth century, any of these procedural rules could perfectly well have been inscribed under the heading *eukosmia* in its old sense of 'good order, good management'. Aeschines, however, wants to take περὶ εὐκοσμίας as 'decent' or 'decorous' behaviour, and so glosses the phrase by saying the law-giver 'first took up the matter of virtuous conduct': ἀπὸ σωφροσύνης πρῶτον ἤρξατο (1.22). Aeschines will seize on this sense of *eukosmia* to collect a series of provisions

---

[49] See Dover's analysis (1978) 24–5. Dem. (22 *Androtion* 30–2) deduced Solon's purpose in this law as having been not to chastise prostitution but to preserve the democracy from falling into the hands of a cabal of reckless and lewd men.

[50] The transition from description to narrative fiction had already begun with a piece of speculative aetiology at 1.13: 'the ancients were provoked to making these laws [covering sexual crimes] when unbecoming acts actually occurred' (sc. despite the excellent provisions for primary education just enumerated).

[51] Cf. *Ath. Pol.* 43.1, 26–7.

(some very recent) which suggest that the orator is bound to a special code by which to conduct his life, his body and his attitudes. By this final group of laws he will remove Timarchus' offensive past acts utterly from the realm of *ta idia* and associate them with his public decorum, suggesting that both are a threat to the 'orderly' conduct of democracy. The word *kosmos* will be exploited to link incorrect posture and attitude to incorrect democratic government.[52]

In another oration, *Against Ctesiphon*, Aeschines complained at length about the present 'indecent behaviour of rhetors' (τῶν ῥητόρων ἀκοσμία), and held that they violated Solonian laws on the subject (οὓς ἐνομοθέτησεν ὁ Σόλων περὶ τῆς τῶν ῥητόρων εὐκοσμίας, 3.2–4). Some commentators are willing to credit this,[53] but a close look at what is actual quotation and what is interpretation in *Timarchus* suggests that the 'law on rhetorical comportment' is another Aeschinean construct, analogous to the 'Solonian' law περὶ τῆς εὐκοσμίας τῶν παίδων (1.8) cobbled together from miscellaneous regulations for schools, gymnasia, and the like. The 'law on rhetorical decorum' in 1.22–36 seems to have been constructed out of three blocks of law: certain procedures for running an Assembly, the law on testing the qualifications (*dokimasia*) of public speakers under which the present case is being prosecuted, and a recent one involving the *proedroi*.

One of the key props for this synthesis is the herald's traditional proclamation opening an Assembly, with a qualifier added: 'who *above the age of fifty* wishes to address the Assembly?' (1.23). The inclusion of an age-clause is a peculiar, but apparently authentic detail.[54] Aeschines deduces from it that the law-giver wished to teach the young to respect their elders and to encourage older men to share their wisdom even if they are less assertive than they once were (1.24).[55] Moreover, the fact that this clause had apparently fallen into disuse or neglect gives

---

[52] Hence at 1.192 convicting Timarchus will be the 'foundation of *eukosmia* in the city'. Cf. *Prot.* 325d where parents are said to send their children to school more to learn *eukosmia* than letters or *kithara*-playing.

[53] I agree with Ober *CP* (1989) 325 n. 7 that Hansen (1987) 71–2 over-reconstructs this law. Cf. Drerup (1898) 307–8.

[54] It was perhaps moribund at the time: cf. *Ctes.* 4: σεσίγηται μὲν τὸ κάλλιστον καὶ σωφρονέστατον κήρυγμα τῶν ἐν τῇ πόλει· 'τίς ἀγορεύειν βούλεται τῶν ὑπὲρ πεντήκοντα ἔτη γεγονότων;' I think we must accept the expanded version as based on the actual practice of at least some period within memory; it would seem harder to palm off on an audience a doctored proclamation (being brief, easily memorized, and publicly performed at some regular interval) than a law. The evidence outside Aeschines is very slim; discussion in Griffith (1966) 119–20, Lane Fox (1994) 147–9, and historical reconstruction in Hansen (1987) 171 n. 581.

[55] The ideas, though not the ages, can be reconciled with Solon's 'ages of man' poem (27.7–8, 13–16 West).

Aeschines the opportunity to enter on the theme of the decline from the good old days of noble oratory.[56]

Lamenting the decadence of oratorical style was already conventional in the fourth century. In Aeschines the story is told with Timarchus in the role played elsewhere, as in Thucydides, by Cleon.[57] Aeschines ventures that Timarchus' manners on the *bēma* – speaking agitatedly, with an arm outside the cloak – would have been accounted arrogant (θρασύ) in the days of Solon and Pericles (1.25). As evidence, Aeschines misreads the body language of a statue in Salamis where Solon stands with his hand in his cloak, 'showing in what fashion he addressed the demos of Athens' (1.25).[58] By contrast, in a recent performance Timarchus had actually cast off his cloak and leapt around naked like a pancratist, disgusting 'the right minded at least' with 'his foul and shamefully abused body' (1.26). The function of this 'law' on rhetorical deportment is already becoming clear: a moribund custom enshrined in a traditional formula can lead to the suggestion that Timarchus' adventurous style (after all, not everyone in the audience is said to have been disgusted) is something politically harmful and virtually criminal.

The second component of Solon's laws for rhetors, the '*dokimasia* of rhetors',[59] is the key legal text, and it is introduced by Aeschines with another suggestion of Solonian prescience: the law-giver is said to have framed the provision with exhibitions like that of Timarchus in mind (ἃ συνιδὼν ὁ νομοθέτης διαρρήδην ἀπέδειξεν οὓς χρὴ δημηγορεῖν καὶ οὓς

---

[56] It seems to me arguable that Aeschines' paraphrase of 'Solon's Laws on the good comportment of rhetors' in *Ctes.* 2 is nothing more than an expansive inference from the heralds' 'fifty-year' proclamation (the essentials of which I underline): ἐξῆν πρῶτον μὲν τ' πρεσβυτάτῳ τῶν πολιτῶν. ὥσπερ οἱ νόμοι προστάττουσι, σωφρόνως ἐπὶ τὸ βῆμα παρελθόντι ἄνευ θορύβου καὶ ταραχῆς ἐξ ἐμπειρίας τὰ βέλτιστα τῇ πόλει συμβουλεύειν, δεύτερον δ' ἤδη καὶ τῶν ἄλλων πολιτῶν τὸν βουλόμενον καθ' ἡλικίαν χωρὶς καὶ ἐν μέρει περὶ ἑκάστου γνώμην ἀποφαίνεσθαι. This last phrase would in addition be a gloss (cf. Arist. *Rh.* 1394a 21) on the herald's ἀγορεύειν.

[57] Cf. *Ath. Pol.* 28.3 where Cleon's screaming, spewing abuse, and binding this cloak up short is the fall away from earlier orators who had spoken decently (ἐν κόσμῳ). See Rhodes (1993) 352–4 and Connor (1971) 132–4.

[58] Aeschines 'misreads' because (1) the statue may very well have been of Solon rhapsodizing to save Salamis, cf. Solon 1 West and Schol. Aesch. ad loc. (20.62 Dilts); (2) As Demosthenes 19.251 objected, the statue in any case was no more than 50 years old. Demosthenes also mocks Aeschines' preoccupation with posture at 19.255, and it is fascinating to compare a fourth-century sculpture of Aeschines showing him as earnest advisor to the state – with his arm conspicuously folded in his cloak – with the statue of Sophocles commissioned by Lycurgus. See Zanker (1996) 42–50 and compare Goldhill's discussion of *schēma* in the introduction.

[59] As it is called from Aeschin. 1.186, our principal source. I find myself much in agreement with the analysis by Lane Fox (1994) 149ff.

οὐ δεῖ λέγειν ἐν τῷ δήμῳ, 1.27). Aeschines' interpretation of its 'explicit' provisions begins negatively: from the fact that the law had no requirements of wealth he infers that its 'explicit' instructions were aimed at general decorum, against those living 'disgracefully' (*aiskhrōs*, 1.28). This summary gloss[60] puts under a useful description the specific misdeeds enumerated in 1.28–32: impiety to parents, avoiding military service, and debauching or prostituting oneself. While it would be enough if Timarchus could be shown to have committed any single one of these acts, it is important to Aeschines to infer from these specifics a general condemnation of his opponent's way of life.

The third and final piece of the laws on rhetors is admittedly a recent one, but that is because Timarchus' recent 'charming gymnastic exhibition' as an orator (1.33) led 'you' to add to the old laws the institution of special seating for marshals (*proedroi*) to ensure order at the Assembly (1.34). Bringing in this law, elsewhere described as aimed at the 'indecent' behaviour of rhetors (τῆς δὲ τῶν ῥητόρων ἀκοσμίας, *Ctes.* 4), raised the same anxieties about how far to control public address that the Xenophontean Socrates was made to discuss. It had a further advantage in that Timarchus appears to have failed in an attempt to overturn it not long before Aeschines' speech.[61] With this conclusion to his treatment of the laws, Aeschines calls for the clerk to read out what he reiterates are laws for the proper deportment of speakers (τοὺς νόμους τοὺς περὶ τῆς εὐκοσμίας κειμένους τῶν ῥητόρων, 1.34).

Although uncertainty remains as to how far these syntheses of laws, regulations, and procedural rules are Aeschines' pure invention, we have seen enough clear examples of his interpretative glosses on words and phrases to say that his use of the city's texts called on many of the same skills that literary minded Athenians were exercising in reading Homer. It thus seems plausible that when rhetors studied the old poets they were not only pursuing an activity that was useful for entering into common culture and justifiable as moral improvement, but were also developing important skills for the law-courts. I do not wish, however, to reduce the rhetoricians' study of Homer to this single pragmatic function, for I consider it at least equally important that the public discussion of poetry could display the background, tastes and character of the speaker. The exegesis of poetry and law were so close in method because both activities involved constructing out of a mass of tradi-

---

[60] The phrase has been taken as a cover-all term for other provisions not enumerated in 1.28–32. (As Aeschines is our principal source, we cannot be sure this is an exhaustive list.) On the dubious information at Din. 1 *Dem.* 71, cf. Griffith (1966) 136 n. 54, Harrison (1968–71) 2.204–5 and MacDowell (1990) 511.

[61] Cf. Demosthenes 25.90 and Hansen (1983) 30–2, (1987) 37–9.

tional texts an authoritative ethos for both the speaker and the tradition, whether the latter was personified as the Poet or the Law-giver. Indeed, the second half of *Timarchus* shows how close using legal texts to project an interpretation of shared standards was to using poetic texts to project a certain ethos to the city. In my final section I turn to Aeschines' quotations of Homer, Hesiod, and other poetry to show that the way one presents poetry is also a part of *eukosmia*.[62]

III. Teaching poetry and teaching law

In his peroration (1.196) and in his prologue (1.8), Aeschines sums up his task in *Timarchus* as 'teaching the laws' and examining the life of Timarchus. Yet I have noted that the laws occupy only 1–36, and the examination of Timarchus' character is finished about half-way through at 1.116. The burden of the rest of the speech is, as Aeschines says (1.117), refutation of anticipated counter arguments and 'an exhortation of the citizens to a life of noble virtue' (παράκλησις τῶν πολιτῶν πρὸς ἀρετήν). It is for this moral exhortation that Aeschines clearly wishes his speech to be remembered: two years later he summed up *Timarchus* as that 'exhortation I delivered, a call to virtue always to be remembered' (τὴν τῆς σωφροσύνης παράκλησιν ... ἀειμνήστως παρακέκληκα, 2 *Embassy* 180f.).[63] The epithet 'always to be remembered' invokes poetic traditions of immortalization, and quite appropriately: the latter part of *Timarchus* presents itself as a parainetic address in prose. Aeschines borrows from the poetic tradition of parainesis its hectoring persona, its task of moral precepting, and the words of many of its poets. In the second half of *Timarchus*, as was usual in early oratory, poetic forms are being taken over into a newly matured medium; there is particular interest, however, in Aeschines' self-consciousness about how poems are to be used and interpreted.

Aeschines begins quoting the poets as witnesses, as Aristotle advises. They are brought in just where he most needs witnesses, when he anticipates the (quite legitimate) charge that he has no hard evidence for Timarchus' deeds apart from vulgar rumours (1.125).[64] His response (1.127–30) is that truth often underlies rumours, and for this reason Rumour is taken for a god both in the city's altar and among the poets. The altar to Rumour is a clear enough *tekmērion*; to prove poetic admiration for rumour Aeschines begins badly by claiming that Homer

---

[62] On the rhetor's performance as part of persuasion, see Hall (1995).
[63] Cf. Harris (1995) 102–3.
[64] Gossip and rumour are indispensable to Aeschines' case: Hunter (1994) 104–6.

'often' says 'rumour went among the camp' for an event which actually comes to pass in the *Iliad*. The expression φήμη δ' εἰς στρατὸν ἦλθε is nowhere in our texts, but Aeschines may be glossing Homeric phrases in which the archaic *ossa* ('voice, speech') has the sense of rumour.[65] Aeschines is on firmer ground quoting a trimeter from Euripides (865 Nauck) and Hesiod's *Works and Days* 763-4, where he is at pains to point out that Hesiod 'says quite explicitly that *Pheme* is a god, for those who care to listen to him' (Ἡσίοδος καὶ διαρρήδην θεὸν αὐτὴν ἀποδείκνυσι, πάνυ σαφῶς φράζων τοῖς βουλομένοις συνιέναι, 1.129). With that final phrase invoking democratic 'everyman',[66] Aeschines throws open the franchise on poetic interpretation and encourages the audience's aspirations to poetic taste without making his case one only the elite could champion.[67] He also affirms Hesiod's authority quite cunningly: 'you will find that these verses are commended by people who live decorously, since everyone with a desire for public esteem knows that reputation comes from what is said about one': τούτων τῶν ποιημάτων τοὺς μὲν εὐσχημόνως βεβιωκότας εὑρήσετε ἐπαινέτας ὄντας· πάντες γὰρ οἱ δημοσίᾳ φιλότιμοι παρὰ τῆς ἀγαθῆς φήμης ἡγοῦνται τὴν δόξαν κομιεῖσθαι (1.129). Despite the fact that living εὐσχημόνως meant reclining elegantly at supper for some people (cf. Ar. *Wasps* 1210), for Aeschines living democratic life 'becomingly' was simply a matter of being respectful of public opinion (*doxa*).[68] Do this and you implicitly belong to the company of those who esteem estimable poets; one need not be a symposiast or littérateur to be a good citizen.

This instance also shows that quoting poetry at the *bēma* could be hazardous, for Demosthenes later turned the tables and argued that Hesiod's lines applied better to Aeschines.[69] The real pitfall in quoting poetry, however, was to be thought elitist.[70] In *Timarchus* Aeschines

[65] As '*ossa*, Zeus' messenger' at *Il.* 2.93-4. Closest to Aeschines' expression is *Od.* 24.413: ὄσσα δ' ἄρ' ἄγγελος ὦκα κατὰ πτόλιν οἴχετο πάντῃ. The word *phēmē* is not in our *Iliad*.
[66] Cf. Lyc. *Leocr.* 108, after quoting Tyrtaeus: καλά γ', ὦ ἄνδρες, καὶ χρήσιμα τοῖς βουλομένοις προσέχειν.
[67] Although many, Isocrates tells us, found the didactic poets tiresome, all were willing to pay lip-service to their value: *To Nic.* 2.42-3. *Works and Days* 763 is also quoted by Aristotle at *Eth. Nic.* 7.13 1153b27 as expressing popular belief.
[68] Ehrenberg (1962) 302 describes *doxa* as a more acceptable democratic alternative to high-flown *kleos*, which is used especially in tragedy and mockingly for sophists.
[69] Demosthenes turned Aeschines' quotation of Hesiod against him at 19.243ff., and Aeschines countered at 2.144ff. where he went on to quote *Works and Days* 240ff. on the whole polis suffering from the actions of a single wicked man; this quotation he further expanded on in 3.134-6 because be found it fitted Demosthenes 'like an oracle'.
[70] Ober (1989) 171ff., Ober and Strauss (1989) 251-2, Wilson (1996) 311-13.

tries to fend off this charge by finding the snobbish poetry expert enlisted on the other side.

In what proved to be an ineffective tactic, Timarchus had called as a character witness a certain unnamed General of evidently refined manners and education. This allowed Aeschines, somewhat disingenuously, to stigmatize him as an effete 'product of wrestling schools' (1.132). Where there are wrestling schools there is socializing among the leisured and often music,[71] and this General presumed to counter Aeschines' stern impersonation of Solon and Hesiod with a lecture on the subtle ideas of love between men that are to be found in the songs and poems most cherished by Athenians. We can gather (1.132-3) that he began with the story of how the bond between Harmodius and Aristogeiton made the democracy possible; he went on to Homer, and maintained that the exemplary friendship between Achilles and Patroclus had its roots in passion (*erōs*); this was topped off with an 'encomium' to beauty, a hackneyed theme in Aeschines' view, and one calling for 'virtue' to do well. The point of the elegant presentation, Aeschines says, was to show these simple-minded people how paradoxical (ἄτοπον, 134) it would be for them to punish Timarchus when they had the values they had.

After his impressive opening, the General went on to accuse Aeschines of hypocrisy: he brought up certain erotic scandals from his past and capped it all by performing (ἐπιδείξεσθαι) some amatory poems Aeschines had composed (1.135). Aeschines does not deny that he wrote the poems in question, from which we may gather that they were, as is to be expected of the genre, suggestive but not obviously coarse.[72] What he objects to is the distorting interpretation the General puts upon them: τὰ δὲ ἐξαρνοῦμαι μὴ τοῦτον ἔχειν τὸν τρόπον ὃν οὗτοι διαφθείροντες παρέξονται, 1.136). Instead of replying with his own *explication de texte* (his poems, after all, were private: ἐρωτικὰ εἴς τινας ποιήματα, 1.135), Aeschines sets out a series of nice definitions that distinguish the homoerotic feelings of 'fine, virtuous, fellow-loving, and right-thinking men' from what can be expected of the 'licentious, hubristic, and boorish [ἀπαιδεύτου]' sort (1.137). I regret that Aeschines foregoes this chance to skirmish over glossing erotic verselets, but a substantial lesson in public literary criticism is provided in his subsequent correction of the General on what values the heroic texts really teach.

Aeschines insists he is drawn into talking about Homer only because

---

[71] Cf. Dover (1978) 41, citing Ar. *Frogs* 729.
[72] On the likely character of Aeschines' erotic verse, see Dover (1978) 57ff.

the General had insultingly suggested that the jury is completely uncultured (ὡς τῶν μὲν δικαστῶν ἀνηκόων παιδείας ὄντων, 1.141); but 'we have picked up a thing or two' (καὶ ἡμεῖς τι ἤδη ἠκούσαμεν καὶ ἐμάθομεν). Having identified himself with the common man, he is now free to take on the tones of schoolmaster to the republic: 'consider, men of Athens, how great a distinction those universally admired poets draw between the virtuous lovers of virtuous men and those who are uncontrolled and hubristic' (1.141-2). He then makes two points about Achilles and Patroclus: first, he allows that Homer intended us to take them for lovers, but notes, as the General perhaps had not, that he never uses the word *erōs* (1.142-4); in addition, their love can be shown to have been of that ideal kind described in 1.137-8, for what they most valued was their comradeship (1.147). On this reading, Homer was offering a paradigm for noble homoerotic attachment as Aeschines has just defined it (1.146).

Most of this is proved neatly enough from the text: quotations read out by the clerk (as laws were read out) demonstrate Achilles' loyal determination to avenge his comrade even at the cost of death (*Il.* 18.333-5), and the hero's courage is shown by the fact that Thetis had made him aware of this price (18.95-9);[73] the shade of Patroclus rehearses the longed-for times they spent alone, and wishes to be buried beside him (23.77ff.).[74] It all seems at the level of *grammatistai*, though pederasty was not perhaps a theme officially treated at school. But the most striking part of Aeschines' exegesis is his complex and subtle proof that the two were lovers: this, he says, the poet only intimated, concealing the name for their love but expecting the cultured among the audience to 'get' it : τὸν μὲν ἔρωτα καὶ τὴν ἐπωνυμίαν αὐτῶν τῆς φιλίας ἀποκρύπτεται, ἡγούμενος τὰς τῆς εὐνοίας ὑπερβολὰς καταφανεῖς εἶναι τοῖς πεπαιδευμένοις τῶν ἀκροατῶν (1.142).

Noticing, correctly, that Homer is never explicit about *erōs* in this connection in itself requires some expertise (a knowledge of the *whole Iliad*, like that of Niceratus); but far more subtle is the way Aeschines divines proof that Homer made Achilles Patroclus' lover. The proof text is rather unpromising: Achilles' lament that his promise to bring Patroclus back home to his father will now go unfulfilled (*Il.* 18.324-9). Aeschines quotes this text himself (as always, with a disarming που when he himself quotes) and paraphrases it, claiming that it makes it

---

[73] Van der Valk (1964) 328-9 suggests that Aeschines ending of 18.99, ὅ μοι πολὺ φίλτατος ἔσκεν, is a deliberate variant for ὁ μὲν μάλα τηλόθι πάτρης. Still, Aeschines' point is that Homer is never explicit about these things.

[74] For variations from our Homer text, see Leaf (1900-02) ad loc.

obvious that Achilles took charge of Patroclus through love: 'for he had promised that, if Menoetius should *entrust* his son to accompany Achilles to Troy, he would *return* the boy to Opus; from this it is obvious that it was on account of love [*erōs*] that he took the boy under his charge' (ἐπαγγείλασθαι γὰρ εἰς Ὀποῦντα σῶν ἀπάξειν, εἰ συμπέμψειεν αὐτὸν εἰς τὴν Τροίαν καὶ παρακατατιθεῖτο αὐτῷ. ᾧ καταφανής ἐστιν, ὡς δι' ἔρωτα τὴν ἐπιμέλειαν αὐτοῦ παρέλαβεν, 1.143). As Dover remarks,[75] this is a far from obvious inference. But a closer look at the *Iliad* shows that Aeschines relies on a gloss: in his paraphrase he plays on a word from 18.327: 'he said he would *return* the son to Opus crowned with glory' (φῆν δέ οἱ εἰς Ὀπόεντα περικλυτὸν υἱὸν ἀπάξειν). In Homer, the verb means simply 'to bring back home' (LSJ s.v. II); but by Aeschines' time it also had the sense 'return a deposit' (LSJ s.v. III). This commercial sense is activated when Aeschines adds to his paraphrase the unwarranted παρακατατιθεῖτο for Menoetius' 'entrusting' his son to Achilles. This verb was the technical term for laying down a deposit (LSJ s.v. παρακατατίθημι), and, combined with ἀπάξειν, it makes the missing links in the Homer passage: Achilles' language reveals that he contracted to 'undertake the supervision'[76] of Menoetius' son; it was not the base 'purchase' of sex Aeschines has just condemned (1.137), but the ideal love in which a generous soul takes charge of one not yet of age (ἀκύρου, 1.138). Their *philia* was not that of equals (far less, as some maintained, one in which Achilles was the subordinate), but of guardian to guarded. Of course, no sane father would contract with another man to supervise his son unless it were a noble contract, and so this *erōs* must have been of the noble sort that Aeschines practises and Homer, subtly, commends.

The rhetorical effects of Aeschines' Homeric exegesis are complex: it begins as a democratic riposte to a patronizing littérateur, but proffers an accomplished and esoteric reading of its own. Aeschines is motivating the audience to accept his reading by equating being a sound citizen with being among those 'in the know' about poetry. In fact, the bait Aeschines offers the jury is quite tempting, for in a broad sense what he does in this passage is to convert the courtroom into a literary salon. He takes up and explicates many of the same texts that were deployed and debated at aristocratic symposia to show the participants' wit and learning, especially on erotic topics.

Plato's *Symposium* is an obvious case in point, where the company

---

[75] Dover (1978) 53.
[76] With Aeschines' δι' ἔρωτα τὴν ἐπιμέλειαν παρέλαβεν, cf. the office ἡ τῶν ἐφήβων ἐπιμέλεια attested at Din. 3.15.

amuses itself by ringing variations on a theme as hackneyed as the General's: encomia to love. Indeed, the first speech by Phaedrus uses one of the same proof texts as Aeschines (*Il.* 18.96ff.) to demonstrate Achilles' manly devotion to Patroclus (179e).[77] For these hyper-sophisticated gentlemen, the sport is decking out the old theme by weaving together exempla from poets and philosophers that are either unexpected or given a recherché meaning. Phaedrus sets the Achilles paradigm off against the love stories of Alcestis and Orpheus, nicely distinguishing between the quality of the attachment and the rewards from the gods in each case: Alcestis' man-like courage[78] was rewarded by her coming back from the dead (bypassing Euripides' version in which Heracles has to fight for her);[79] Orpheus, by contrast, died at the hands of women because he was a little too effeminate (179d; rather a precious explanation compared to, e.g., Aesch. *Bassarai*). Juxtaposed with these is an uncanonical account of Achilles as rewarded for his love by transportation to the isles of the blest (in Pindar, *Ol.* 2.78ff., but not in Homer). Phaedrus goes on to show his Homeric expertise by taking up what was evidently a hot topic: who was who's lover in the *Iliad*. His view is that Aeschylus 'talked nonsense' in making Achilles the lover of Patroclus.[80] If Aeschines could adduce a subtle proof for the Aeschylean view, Phaedrus is equally adept at reading the great text in the opposite sense: he notes that Homer says Achilles was 'the fairest' of the heroes,[81] and that Homer says he was younger than Patroclus (*Il.* 11.786ff.). Unlike earnest Aeschines, Phaedrus' point is to paint Achilles as the model *eromenos*, but both performers exhibit their qualities in the way they cite poetry.

In this light it becomes clear that Aeschines and the General are not so much appealing to a universal familiarity with Homer as exhibiting to the audience their sophisticated familiarity with the text. Each may be said to be capping the other's reading in sympotic fashion. The same may be said of their discussion of Harmodius and Aristogeiton, which was not only a standard legend for democratic orators[82] but a drinking song with a potent history of interpretations. Perhaps originating in aristocratic dining circles of post-Cleisthenic Athens, the scholion was by the later fifth century a piece of popular verse that

[77] Evidently a well-thumbed passage: in *Apology* 28c Plato has Socrates adduce Achilles' preceding words to his mother on the worthlessness of a life without honour (*Il.* 18.70ff.).
[78] Cf. A. M. Dale, *Alcestis* xi.
[79] Cf. the moral Lycurgus draws from Euripides's *Praxithea* (*In Leocr.* 101).
[80] Aesch. *Myrmidons* Fr. 288f.
[81] *Il.* 2.673-4 would be most suited (cf. *kallistos*), but cf. the many expressions of Ajax' being second only to Achilles in *demas* and *erga* (*Il.* 17.279-80, *Od.* 24.17-18 etc.).
[82] Cf. Arist. *Rh.* 2.24 1401b10ff.

could be broadcast from the comic stage to many who would never attend a proper symposium. But its meaning was never stable, and it continued to offer scope for sympotic play as well as a target for historical revisionism.[83] Aristophanes seems to have toyed with its democratic use by pairing it with the aristocratic *Admetou melos*,[84] and Plato's after-dinner performer Pausanias ingeniously drew out its sociopolitical import as showing that *paiderasteia* is the practice of freedom-loving peoples (*Symp.* 182c). Still, it was a game to be played carefully in public: Hyperides (*Phil.* 3) attests to a law forbidding anyone to speak ill of the pair or to 'sing disparagingly' about them. Aeschines is playing a safely democratic version of this game when he calls them 'benefactors of the city' and insists that they were educated by a 'lawful and virtuous love, whatever name one cares to put on it' (ὁ σώφρων καὶ ἔννομος, εἴτε ἔρωτα εἴτε ὄντινα τρόπον χρὴ προσειπεῖν, τοιούτους ἐπαίδευσεν).

The second half of *Timarchus*, then, uses cleverness about poetry in several ways. It first of all adds the sanction of Homer and the poets to the construction of sexuality Aeschines wishes to advance. At the same time, its subtlety offers those who think of themselves as right-minded to think of themselves as sophisticated too, for the right-minded views are there in Homer if one is willing to look at him in the right way. Finally, it attempts to make this blend of good manners and right reading characteristic of the speaker himself. He is not a snob like the General, but knows what everyone knows about Homer – that his poems are good and worth imitating. If it takes a certain subtlety to see this, it is not so much that Homer is subtle as he is discreet: he does not toss around the word love, nor do his characters. So too the good critic is not so much subtle as discreet: like Homer, Aeschines is discreet about sex; in his version of 'virtuous love' the lover puts off 'talk of love' until the boy is of an age to respond appropriately (1.140).[85] Refinement is shown in the way one reads a poem, courts a boy, or speaks in court.[86] All these qualities might be comprehended under the 'Solonian' term *eukosmia*, the proper, decorous and right bearing of body, mind, and polity.[87]

---

[83] E.g. Thucydides 1.20, on which see Ober (1994a) 105.
[84] So Reitzenstein (1893) 26 n. 1, cited on Ar. *Pelargoi* 444 KA.
[85] So far is Aeschines from Timarchus' immodesty that it makes him blush to discuss Timarchus even in the most euphemistic terms, 1.53 f.
[86] See Easterling, this volume, on the significance of even the physical voice in gauging a performer's worth.
[87] Cf. the reproach at 1.169 of Demosthenes' *akosmia* in slanderously misrepresenting Alexander's performance at a symposium to the *Boule*. In 1.189 the *akosmia* of Timarchus' way of life (*tropos*) reveals the *hexis* of a soul that despises the great laws and virtue.

The final piece of poetry Aeschines discusses lets the audience in on the point that glossing is not only a game but a matter of giving life and force to abstract or fictional texts. Insisting on the relative unimportance of proof in cases of this kind, he quotes from Euripides' *Phoenix* (812 Nauck) on the necessity of judging men by their associates. It is a germane enough text in any case, but he gives an extra twist to its first line, 'Many times ere now have I been chosen to be a judge of speeches' (ἤδη δὲ πολλῶν ᾑρέθην λόγων κριτής). 'These words are spoken by a man who has been the judge of many cases [*pragmata*], just as you jurors now are' (1.153). No theatre-going citizen could have failed to notice that these words, spoken by a heroic character in a heroic age, needed a little translation to apply to them in a democratic court.[88] Here Aeschines wants them to notice that they are translating, since their task will be to apply old and miscellaneous statutes to the forceful suppression of one of themselves. The judgement they are called to deliver on Timarchus is interpretative and aesthetic as much as legal; it is a matter of 'reading', a sense of style: their verdict will show not only that they make good laws but that they know 'how to distinguish what is fair from what is foul' (κρίνειν τὰ καλὰ καὶ τὰ μὴ καλὰ δύνασθε, 1.118). For Aeschines, the ability to distinguish between τὰ καλὰ καὶ τὰ μή is not a matter of elite aesthetics, but basic civic knowledge embodied in the laws and acquired when citizens are-enrolled in their demes (1.18).[89] But this democratically shared ability to judge is not unlike what the sophists had long ago promised to teach about poetry: συνιέναι ἅ τε ὀρθῶς πεποίηται καὶ ἃ μή, καὶ ἐπίστασθαι διελεῖν τε καὶ ἐρωτώμενον λόγον δοῦναι (Pl. *Prot* 339a). Such were the powers of glossing poetry to the people.[90]

---

[88] On the passage, see Bers (1994) 191. Demosthenes also critiques this quotation in learned fashion (19.245) on which see Wilson (1996) 315.

[89] Cf. the peroration to Aeschines' most crucial public address (3.260): ὦ γῆ καὶ ἥλιε καὶ ἀρετὴ καὶ σύνεσις καὶ παιδεῖα, ᾗ διαγιγνώσκομεν τὰ καλὰ καὶ τὰ αἰσχρά, with Dem.'s riposte 18.127–8.

[90] I thank Simon Goldhill and Robin Osborne for organizing the conference on performance where my ideas were much refined in stimulating company. Josh Ober greatly improved an early draft of this paper which arose from the happy experience of our teaching a seminar on the theory and practice of Athenian oratory. Finally, Edward M. Harris' acute and sceptical critique of part of my text was as gracious as it was helpful since he will not agree with many of my conclusions; thanks too to his student, James Mulkin, who is preparing a commentary on *Timarchus* and helped me correct and clarify several points.

10 Plato and the performance of dialogue

Sitta von Reden and Simon Goldhill

Socrates tells the story of Leontius while explicating the tripartite system of the soul in Book IV of the *Republic*. One day, Leontius, son of Aglaion, was coming up from the Peiraeus, when he saw some corpses, and the public executioner standing near by. He felt a strong desire to look at them, but at the same time felt disgust and turned away. For a while he struggled and kept his hands over his eyes, but eventually was overcome by his desire to watch; he opened his eyes, ran up to the corpses and said, 'there you are, you devils, satisfy yourselves with that lovely spectacle' (*tou kalou theamatos*, *Resp.* 439e). In the *Republic* this memorable anecdote is introduced to demonstrate the conflict between parts of the soul and to identify a third part which controlled desire but which seemed to be something different from reason: a feeling, like shame or disgust, that was based on the knowledge of what was right and acceptable.[1] This is called here *to thumoeides* (441a); yet as the discussion of the *Republic* proceeds it is described more precisely as a force which strives for power (*kratein*), victory (*nikan*) and good repute (*eudokimein*), or *to philotimon* or *philonikon*: 'that which loves honour or victory' (581ab). It corresponds to the second – warrior – class in the ideal city who excel in courage (*andreia*) and an unfailing sense of what is right and lawful (*nomimon*).[2] Intriguingly, a textually corrupt comic fragment may fleetingly suggest that Leontius had entered public awareness in connection with a perverse attraction to pale, thin bodies 'like corpses'.[3] His desire (*epithumia*) to feast his eyes may not just be a morbid curiosity but also perceived as a more specifically erotic compulsion.

---
[1] Annas (1981) 125 f.; Irwin (1997) 131–2.
[2] 429c–430c (cf. 580d). These 'lovers of honour' take over in the second constitution which is one removed from the best and called timocracy. Its rulers are described also as lovers of gymnasia and hunting (549c).
[3] Schol. Arist. Av. 1406 (Theopompus Comicus, Kassel–Austin fr. 25; cf. Kock vol. I, fr. 24 both with discussion of its connection with *Resp.* 439e). The name 'Leontius' is a probable emendation for the unmetrical 'Leontinus'. The sense of the fragment is difficult: 'with a good complexion and beautiful, like a corpse' seems to link the thin, pale poet Leotrophides and, possibly, the interests of Leontius. But it is hard to be more than extremely tentative here.

The connections between control and what is right, the eyes and desire, provide the central matrix to a story Plato has Socrates tell about himself, a story which deploys the same vocabulary of 'honour' and 'control'. In the *Charmides*, when encountering Charmides for the first time, Socrates says that the boy after sitting down between Critias and himself (155d):

> gave me such a look with his eyes as passes description, and was just about to ask his question, and when all the people in the palaestra surged round about us in a circle, then, my friend, I saw inside his cloak and caught fire, and I was no longer within myself but thought Cydias was the wisest in love-matters – who in speaking of a beautiful boy recommends someone to 'beware of coming as a fawn before a lion and being seized as his portion of flesh'; for I too felt I had been caught by such a beast.

Like Leontius, Socrates feels a marked discrepancy between his desire to watch and another feeling that persuades him not to submit to the desires of his gaze. The feeling of inappropriateness that makes Leontius turn away from the dead bodies despite his (sexual) attraction to them is in Socrates' story pictured as a fawn in danger of being devoured by a wild beast; and just as Leontius' eyes are excoriated as the *kakodaimones*, 'the devils', which overcome his own sense of shame, Socrates feels he has been seized (*healōkenai*) by a violent power. Yet in contrast to the story of Leontius, which is told to clarify a psychological topography, Socrates' first-person story complicates any simple divisions. It is no accident that the first encounter with Charmides takes place in front of Critias and an audience of bystanders in the gym (155d). On the one hand, the silent audience of men and boys stands for what might be regarded as the ordinary frame of reference for that part of the self that 'loves honour and victory'. In their eyes, Socrates would assert his masculinity and his very status as a male citizen by winning over the boy. On the other hand, Critias, who would become famous as the violent and hated head of the Thirty tyrants, is a very different viewer. By the time of the writing of the dialogue, although not its setting, he was a person who had most unequivocally broken the frame of social control, and his regime could stand as an icon for what happened when *philotimia* turns into *hubris*, when ambition becomes transgression. What happens to him when watching Socrates courting the boy, but refraining from the usual further sexual advances, and – just – 'doing philosophy'? What should a tyrant learn about the treatment of boys from this scene?[4]

Socrates, however, with all the self-consciousness of a first-person

---

[4] On tyrants and their paradigamtic violent treatment of boys, see Aristotle *Politics* esp. 1314b.

narrator, finds that the sight of Charmides makes him 'not within himself'; and the figure who most often rejects the moral guidance of poets (in his apologetic search for who is really 'the most *sophos*' in the city), now thinks Cydias the poet is precisely 'the most *sophos*' when it comes to erotic matters. Socrates for all that he does not simply enact the part of erotic pursuer within the public gaze, conforms to the (sympotic) image of the lover taking advice and solace from the performance of poetry – with all the ironies that creates for the philosopher Socrates. Socrates in short plays a double role both in front of the bystanders who see him aflame and barely holding back, and in front of the readers/listeners of the dialogue who are made the witnesses of the terms of his inner struggle.

What is the function of a scene which so boldly parades its own theatricality? On the one hand, since Socrates was put to death explicitly for 'corrupting youth' (as well as introducing new gods), and, implicitly, it may be assumed, in part at least for his connections with the tyrants led by Critias, this scene of philosophical self-control must be read as a function of Plato's apologetics for his master, a rhetoric designed to exculpate Socrates by his performance of *sophrosunē* before the very figures he is said to have corrupted. Critias cannot learn the lesson he is being offered. As the discussion of the dialogue will later revolve around the definition of *sophrosunē* and knowledge, so the performance of *sophrosunē* by the first-person narrator becomes part of the knowingness of the dialogue's didactic thrust. How (not) to be ... On the other hand, the scenario, replete with images and vocabulary of watching, seems to problematize the meaning of self-control within the matrix of a performance culture. It draws attention to, without fully exploring, the powerful and dangerous reciprocity between audience and performance, the different exchanges that take place between them, and the role which that reciprocity plays in the formation and public display of the self.

More precisely, it raises the question of what *to thumoeides* (*to philotimon/to philonikon*) might be, whose judgement it follows and what role the eyes play in the political and personal process of forming the soul. Charmides gives Socrates his 'look that surpasses description' at the moment he wishes to learn the cure for his headaches (155b). He deliberately uses his eyes to seduce Socrates to impart his knowledge. (And so Socrates notes Charmides' every blush, giggle, and argumentative gesture.[5]) The bystanders laughably rush to crowd in on Socrates' conversation with the beauty (155b) and watch in their eagerness to learn and to control the exchange. Indeed, Critias re-enters the

[5] E.g. 156a4; 158c5; 159b1; 160e1; 162b11; 162d1.

conversation precisely because he 'competitively pursues honour before Charmides and the other bystanders' (ἀγωνιῶν καὶ φιλοτίμως πρός τε τὸν Χαρμίδην καὶ πρὸς τοὺς παρόντας ἔχων 162b-c), and also, significantly for the future tyrant, because he cannot control this urge any longer (μόγις δ' ἑαυτὸν ἐν τῷ πρόσθεν κατέχων τότε οὐχ οἷός τε ἐγένετο ... ὁ δ' οὐκ ἠνέσχετο). Both *agōniōn*, which implies anxiety as well as competitiveness, and *philotimōs*, mark the agonistic search for status as the aim of dialogue's performance. Tellingly, both for the representation of Critias and for the discourse of performance, the future tyrant's dissatisfaction with his ward's answers is described here by Socrates as μοι ἔδοξεν ὀργισθῆναι αὐτῷ ὥσπερ ποιητὴς ὑποκριτῇ κακῶς διατιθέντι τὰ ἑαυτοῦ ποιήματα, 'he seemed to me to be angry with him just as a poet is with an actor who muffs his compositions'. Critias is not a teacher like Socrates (with his model of midwifery), but wants his pupils to rehearse a taught lesson, like an actor with a playwright's lines: the performance of Socratic dialogue is thus – this is the reader's challenge – to be distinguished from that paradigm of performance, the scripted drama. Similarly, when the previously confident Critias is drawn to share Socrates' *aporia* – which 'spreads like a yawn between spectators' (169c4-5) – 'because of his customary feelings for his good repute (*eudokimōn*), he was ashamed before the bystanders' and 'tried to cover his loss of control with an obscure mumble' (169c): ἅτε οὖν εὐδοκιμῶν ἑκάστοτε, ᾐσχύνετο τοὺς παρόντας ... ἔλεγέν τε οὐδὲν σαφές, ἐπικαλύπτων τὴν ἀπορίαν. The audience's observation, coupled with the pursuit of reputation before such observation, leads to the collapse of man-to-man straight talk.

Conversely, Socrates agrees to pretend privileged medical knowledge in order to catch sight of Charmides' body. (The first-person narration is again important for the self-conscious marking of positionality and the gaps between words and desire in the exchange of dialogue, as Socrates 'plays doctor'.) His deception allows him to present himself as being caught by desire, but also as being controlled by another force. Commentators often read Charmides' headache as a metaphor for his craving for knowledge; but what is lost from the erotics of exchange if it is read solely and simply as a philosophical metaphor? The seductive play between Socrates and the youth does not merely allude to the problematical relationship between philosophy and desire, knowledge and beauty, learning and watching, but in the performance of social exchange that is involved in philosophy as process, it allows the dangers of desire to resound in the playfulness of its language even as it traces the attempt to maintain a philosophical control. In a similar way, after the drama of Charmides' entrance into the gym (surrounded by lovers, and to the confusion and amazement of the watchers[6]), Socrates uses markedly erotic language for his interest in the boy's soul: Critias has commented that however beautiful Charmides' face is, if he took his clothes off, he would seem faceless, so fantastic is his body. Socrates immediately asks if his soul matches his form, and when he hears that the boy is indeed noble, comments 'Why haven't we taken the clothes off (*apodunai*) that part of him, then, and gazed (*theāsthai*) at it, before his form (*eidos*)?' (154e). The soul is to be stripped naked and stared at. Metaphor and innuendo allow desire to be heard in language, even as the argument leads towards the discussion (and display) of self-control.

Both the story of Leontius and the opening scene of the *Charmides* suggest that Plato took a more complex approach to the politics of watching than appears from his sometimes unequivocal criticism of the theatre-culture of Athens. In the *Laws* he opposes *aristocratia* to '*theatrocratia*'. Music, he argues there, has deteriorated since the pleasure of the audience had become the criterion of quality. The lawlessness (*paranomia*) of music first instilled boldness into the audience, leading it to think itself capable of passing judgement without knowing the difference between good and bad (701a). Then, the licence in *mousikē* carried over to freedom in politics where the conceit of the wisdom of everybody in everything made the populace so fearless as no longer to listen to the opinion of the better (701b). The notion of *theatrocratia* thus on the one hand related democracy to what it was, that is, the rule of the people, but on the other it represented the demos as above all a mass – and mere – *audience* of theatrical displays. Theatre is the sign and catalyst of the dangers of democratic collectivity. The reference to the theatre not only undermines the sincerity of political performance, but also renders politics a performance that is written not by independent playwrights but by the judging audience.

The watching and judging mass audience is represented as the heart of democracy also in the *Republic*. Here audience rule is introduced in order to caricature democratic education purported to be taking place in the public fora of democracy.[7] The permanent active involvement of a large part of the citizen body in the decision making processes, and the absence of a state-run system of formal education, endowed the public fora with an educational function that was not just ideological.[8]

---

[6] *Ekplexis* and *thauma* are the standard terms for the psychological effect of seeing beauty on a viewer.
[7] Cf. *Ap.* 25b, and below.
[8] Ober (1989), 156–91; cf. Thuc. 2.41.2; Aeschin. 3.246.

Yet Plato strategically (mis)represents that link, first, by presenting the watching audience as the self-proclaimed teachers of the performing individuals, a sarcastic inversion of the normative model, and, secondly, by rendering the public gaze not as a means of political control but as an example of the power of uncontrolled desire (492b–c):

> When the multitude, sitting together at the assemblies or in the law-courts or in theatres and camps, or any other public gathering, with a great uproar censure some of the things that are said or done and praise others, both in an excessive way, by shouting and clapping – and wherever they are, the rocks and the region send back an echo, doubling the volume of the praise and the censure... What sort of private education will hold out against this – who will not be overwhelmed and swept away, carried by the current of such praise and censure wherever it may lead?

The passage falls into sharper relief against the background of a discussion in the *Lysis* where the educational and erotic effects of praise are briefly analysed. Here, Hippothales, the older lover of young Lysis, is reproached by Socrates for praising his beloved with an *encomium*. For by creating in the beloved a feeling of high-mindedness which he had not yet displayed, praise extinguishes the boy's tractability and thus his interest in the lover/teacher (*Lys.* 206a). Moreover, in a brilliant sophistic inversion, Socrates even claims that praise of a beloved is really only praise of the praiser (205e): the more a beloved is praised the more glory (*kosmos*) will redound on the successful lover; and the unsuccessful lover will seem to have lost all the more. Hence all praise 'tends (*teinein*) to the praiser'. Neither praiser nor praised thus truly comprehends the unsatisfactory economics of praise.[9] Praise in the public sphere, too, increased the ignorance of the people praised. In the *Menexenus* the *epitaphios logos* is criticized for puffing up the audience thinking themselves to be better than they were.[10] But in the *Republic* Plato fully inverts the dynamics of censure and praise by rendering the audience the encomiasts and 'teacher' of the individual on stage. Just as Hippothales corrupts his lover by his excessive praise, and is unaware of what he does, the democratic audience corrupt their *rhētores* by their applause and hisses. Plato ironizes the democratic pretensions to public teaching by intimating an analogy between the sexual desires of the lover – teacher and the desires of the mass audience as teachers. The audience, driven by its desire for spectacle, aims to control the performance it is watching so as to heighten its pleasure, and to control

---

[9] The fullest discussion of the dynamics of erotic praise remains the *Phaedrus*, on which see the exemplary analysis of Ferrari (1986).

[10] See esp. *Menex.* 235a–c; cf. Loraux (1986) 315; Nightingale (1995) 107.

the emotions of the individuals it praises. Against the background of the perceived sexual reciprocities and symbolic asymmetries involved in traditional one-to-one teaching in gymnasium and palaestra, the democratic model of education in the public fora corrupts the hierarchy between teacher and pupil by relinquishing the moulding of minds to the gaze of a sexually uncontrolled mass.

Yet despite the attacks on the theatricality of democracy and the concomitant problematizing of the erotic exchanges of the gym and symposium, Plato did not abandon the cultural paradigm of watching as a form of understanding, nor indeed of desire as a motivational force for teaching as well as learning. As Nussbaum has argued in some detail, throughout the Platonic corpus the beautiful as the incarnation of goodness is not made accessible to the reasoned part of the soul alone. While in the *Republic*, the Platonic Socrates urges that true knowledge can only be acquired by dialectical argument, the *Phaedrus* and the *Symposium* give more room to desire as an energy that makes the soul receptive to the vision of truth.[11] The encounter of the souls with the truth, moreover, is represented as an overwhelming sight. Plato conveys these spectacles within the imagery of myth,[12] even – paradigmatically – via seductive mythic imagery aimed against the seductive status of images.[13] In the myth of Er the soul when approaching the judges in the sky is told 'to listen and to watch everything in the place' (ἀκούειν τε καὶ θεᾶσθαι πάντα τὰ ἐν τῷ τόπῳ, 614d). In the episodes that follow the vocabulary of watching strongly emphasizes their relation to performances in the theatre (*theas* 615a; *etheasmetha* 615d; *theamatōn* 615d; *tēn thean* 619e). In the *Phaedrus*, too, a myth is told in which the souls travel to the sky where they become witnesses of blissful spectacles (*makariai theai*, 247a). They take their stands at the outer rim of heaven and, while carried around by its revolution, behold (*theōrousi*, 247c) the spectacles outside.

It is thus not just a superficial analogy when in the *Republic* the philosopher is described as a *philotheamōn* ('a lover of sights') but one to be contrasted with the *philotheamones* ('lovers of sights'), theatre-goers who satisfy their desire for watching colours, shapes and beautiful sounds, but whose minds are incapable of seeing beauty itself (475e).

---

[11] Nussbaum (1982) 100ff.; cf. *Phdr.* 251a–f.
[12] On myth as the readers'/listeners' spectacle, as well as on the following, see Mattéi (1986) 77–8.
[13] The Image of the Cave in the *Republic* is especially important here. Its alluring and elusive doubleness – its challenge to the seductions of the perceptual world via a seductive image – both aims to imbricate the reader into its (mythic) conceptual apparatus, and yet challenges the reader to go beyond the temporary attractions of that apparatus. The philosopher's vision is both the promise and the limit of the scene.

The difference is broadly characterized. There are, on the one hand, people whose desire and sense of beauty lead them to philosophy, and whose reason and spirit are capable of controlling the base sorts of desire. These would watch in silence the performances of virtue and, in the continuous process of forming their souls, increase their sense of shame and decency (cf. *Laws* 816de). There are, on the other hand, the mass of people who are incapable of discrimination and of controlling their base desire for sexual satisfaction and visual entertainment. As theatrical and other performances were controlled in democracies by the judgement of mass audiences, they had a detrimental effect both on the quality of the performances themselves and on their audiences. Plato constructs a strict reciprocity between the nature of the performance and that of the audience, whether in the theatres of theatocracies or the theatres of truth.

There is, then, a broad frame for the question of the role of performance in philosophical dialogue and the role of watching in the process of creating a philosophical self. Now, it has often been noted that Plato's evaluation of *mimēsis* is shifting and full of unresolved tensions: on the one hand, he acknowledges the positive effects of watching (theatrical) performances of virtue on the soul, but on the other he regards them as false and deceptive replications of true virtue and therefore detrimental to the mind; the shift between Book III of the *Republic* where non-frivolous mimetic arts are accepted in the ideal city, and Book X where it seems all poetry is banned, remains difficult.[14] The philosopher faced a double problem both within the culture of his contemporary society and within the performative tradition of wisdom represented by the figure of the sage.[15] On the one hand the human was the only being in which virtue or goodness could made itself visible to the eye, but on the other hand there was *a priori* no way of controlling the gap between the human as a true image of virtue and his/her capacity of enacting it playfully or falsely (or ironically). In a way, Plato's struggle over performance resumed, at the level of the body, the much debated problem of the relation between truth, lies and representation.

There is a considerable literature on the conflict between philosophical dialogue and the performative arts expressed in, and represented by, Platonic dialogue. Also the dramatic settings have come into

---

[14] *Resp.* 393cd, 395c, 396cd vs. 595ab, 597eff.; see Murray (1996) 3ff., for discussion and a useful selection of the voluminous further literature, to which can be added Janaway (1995) and from a different perspective Prendergast (1986).

[15] Martin (1993) 124.

Plato and the performance of dialogue 265

focus as part of the philosophical content of any particular dialogue.[16] This paper, however, takes a different perspective in that it aims first to investigate more broadly how Plato positioned himself in and against a political culture in which power and authority were determined by competitive performances in the public space, and second to discuss how performance of dialogue and philosophy come into conflict in and around the erotic. It has been argued persuasively that the philosophers of fourth-century Athens acted outside and in opposition to the space where communication, politics and education took place in democratic Athens.[17] It is striking thus that many of Plato's dialogues are set in places beyond and outside the public fora of politics: private houses, places outside the city walls, semi-private niches in gymnasia and palaestra. The public spaces of politics and the battlefield are limned as absent presences to define the space of philosophy. Only the *Apology* sets Socrates fully in a democratic institutional space – the law-court – and tellingly the *Apology* shows the limits and (im)possibilities of a philosopher acting in an arena in which communication is controlled by a democratic audience. At the same time, the use of standard political terms such as 'advising' (*sumbouleuō*), or 'busying oneself in affairs' (*polupragmonō*) to describe Socrates' discourse outside the deliberative fora indicates Plato's intention to assign political value to the discourse that is in a conventional sense private and nonpolitical.[18] Given the profoundly political nature and representation of philosophical dialogue it is unlikely that Plato easily dispensed with performance as a way of authorizing his own discourse.

The contrast between the private or semi-private settings of the dialogues on the one hand, and Socrates' intimate engagement with the public, political (discursive) space on the other, constitutes the dialogues as a form of *performance in exile*. What is more, much as the aporetic dialogues defer any conclusiveness through the slippery promise of further discussion in another place, another time, so too the dialogues' careful framing devices and establishment of different internal audiences promote in the reader an awareness of a performance *on the self* – as the reader becomes a judging, participating spectator of his own performance also. The dialogues thus not only introduce and redefine spectatorship in (and through) philosophical discourse, but as a series contain a metadialogue about watching,

---

[16] We have learnt in particular from Ferrari (1987); Nightingale (1995); Halperin (1992).
[17] Carter (1986) on the *apragmones* in general; on the philosopher Steiner (1995), Too (1995), Nightingale (1995).
[18] See e.g. Yunis (1996), especially 154. This is not to imply that Plato saw a way forward in real politics or aimed to educate a new generation of Athenian politicians.

listening and reading, which does not offer conclusions but encourages the audience to look at themselves for an answer. As Ferrari has put it, the multiple representation and re-representation of voices force the reader into a dialogue with the dialogues and makes him realize his own role as 'interpretive performer'.[19]

In what follows, we shall look at the politics of performance in two further Platonic dialogues, the *Laches* and the *Lysis*, and, by way of contrast, a long speech of Isocrates, the *Panathenaicus*. Like the *Charmides*, the *Laches* and the *Lysis* are both conventionally dated to the early period of aporetic dialogues. Each takes place in a highly charged, semi-private, but intensely political space, the *Lysis* in the gymnasium, the *Laches* in or around the palaestra. Each depicts and discusses a developed sense of how to perform within the exchanges that make up society. And in each case, the reciprocity of seeing and being seen as well as the representation and transformation of selves within the gaze of others are woven into the dialogue as spectacle. The *Laches* is a useful starting point as it seems to be especially concerned with the politics of spectacle and the construction of a citizen ideal (and is consequently most often accused of a lack of philosophical weight or detail). We shall see, however, that the *Laches* is exemplary in its use of dialogue to represent and explore the formation of a politicized group of men: it uses the dynamics of a group interaction to analyse the recognition of a man and his manliness within a group, and to promote a new idea of citizen activity. In contrast with this Platonic image of men's talk, Isocrates' *Panathenaicus* depicts a rhetoric teacher at work with his *équipe* of students. Through its representation of interactive dissent, of committed interpretation, and its strongly normative account of Athenian and Spartan political systems, Isocrates' text projects a model of civic identity and the performance of political argument that contrasts sharply and tellingly with Plato's oblique and shift relationship to the political centre of the polis. Finally, the *Lysis*, which further explores the dynamics of erotic exchange we have seen in the *Charmides*, uncovers how an eroticism runs through the verbal exchanges of the males in the gymnasium, an eroticism which threatens to undermine philosophical claims of dialogic control and progress. Together, then, these texts not only represent fascinating and different accounts of the performance of verbal exchange within the democratic polis – the city of words – but also do so in a way which raise important questions for the political and philosophical positioning of Plato in his use of dialogue.

[19] Ferrari (1987) 211.

II

The focal question of the *Laches* is *andreia*, 'masculine courage', and whether it can be acquired by exercises in hoplite fighting. This question is posed explicitly within the context of the education of children, and the transmission of values between the generations. Lysimachus, son of Aristeides, and Melesias, son of Thucydides, have taken their sons to watch an expert in the display of heavy-armour fighting (*machomenos en hoplois*) performing in front of a large crowd (179d–180a; cf 183c). Aristeides and Thucydides are famous political figures of the generation of Pericles: Lysimachus and Melesias regret that they have not lived up to their celebrated fathers. They have also taken Nicias and Laches, the two most prominent generals of Athens after Pericles, in order to be their advisers of how best to instill *andreia* into their sons. The dialogue is thus immediately positioned in the highest echelons of Athenian society and against the background of *philotimia* which runs also through the *Charmides*. The dialogue begins with the very word *tetheasthe* – 'you have just watched'[20] – and it should be noted that *andreia*, in contrast to its usual English translation 'courage', encapsulates and genders the very essence of what is implied in the notion of performance culture.[21] *Andreia* indicates manly excellence, and its association with courage in battle says less about any specialized usage of the term than about the fact that the battlefield was the site where Greek manhood was traditionally formulated.[22] In the battlefield a Greek soldier asserted conspicuously and competitively his place in the collective, and it was the collective which, in turn, bestowed honour (*timē*) and glory (*kleos*) on its most courageous citizens.[23] It is not surprising therefore that Lysimachus worries most of all that, if their sons do not receive proper instruction in *andreia*, they will remain as *aklees* as their fathers (179d). It is the admiration of the citizen body which Lysimachus is seeking for his son and which defines *andreia* for him. Significantly, Lysimachus' initial concern about asking advice

---

[20] See Burnyeat (1997) on the importance of first words; see also the accumulation of *etheasasthe*, *theasasthai*, *thean*, *suntheatas* in 179e, and the continuous occurrence of the vocabulary of seeing and watching within the dialogue.

[21] Stokes (1986), with reference to Méron (1979), emphasizes the importance of the difference between *andreia* and 'courage', but uses this observation mainly in order to establish that the openness of the term allowed Socrates to create confusion about its precise meaning in his interlocutors; see esp. 36–7 and 44–8.

[22] Stokes (1986) 44–8, gives a lexical overview of the meaning of *andreia* and contrasts the term with *tolma* and *thrasys* referring later in the dialogue more narrowly to 'bravery' or 'daring'.

[23] Dover (1974) 161–7; Goldhill (1986) 145.

from the generals is phrased as a recognition that (178a5) 'some people mock (*katagelōsi*) such requests and do not say what they think'. The collective dismissal of laughter (as with the mocking of Hippothales in love in the *Charmides*, and as will be seen in a more developed form in the *Lysis* also) provides the background to the question of how to obtain the collective approval of fame. And the hope of 'straight talk' – ever an ideologically charged value in democratic Athens – establishes a normative social context for Socrates' irony.

Hoplite warfare gradually changed its political symbolism in fifth-century Athens as maritime warfare and the advantages of peltast fighting increased the political importance of the *thetes*. But it remained the hoplite who embodied most unequivocally the values of *andreia* as well as citizen male status.[24] It was also the hoplite who represented the class to which Plato addressed his dialogues and with which Socrates identified himself in the dialogues, although many of the young nobles in Socrates' company will have been *hippeis* by birth. Equipping oneself at one's own expense for the battlefield and seeking private education for one's sons outside the public fora of Athens were very much two sides of the same coin.

Lysimachus, Melesias, Nicias and Laches have come to watch a performance of hoplite exercise in the city. By the end of the fourth century both military training and the theatrical display of hoplite military manoeuvres in gymnasium and theatre were central parts of a publicly financed *ephēbeia*. In the much discussed chapter 42.2 of the *Ath.Pol.* it is said that the people elected two athletic trainers and instructors to teach the ephebes to fight in heavy arms (*hoplomachein*) in the gymnasium.[25] In the second year, an assembly was held in the theatre and the ephebes gave a display of their hoplite drills. At the end of the ceremony they received a shield and a spear from the state, while at the end of the two years they were received into full citizen status. It has proved immensely controversial to stretch back the evidence of the *Ath.Pol.* to the earlier classical or even archaic period. Allusions to an ephebic oath in fifth-century texts render it likely that there was some equivalent of the Lycurgan ephebate earlier in the classical period, but there is no conclusive evidence about its precise nature.[26] Given Xenophon's reference to exclusively private military training in Athens (Xen. *Mem.* 3.12.5) and the existence of an ephebic oath in the fifth century, it is reasonable to suppose that the *ephēbeia* in the first half of

---

[24] See the classic statement by Vidal-Naquet (1986).
[25] Winkler (1990b) 25–35 for discussion and lengthy bibliography of the debate.
[26] Loraux (1986), Siewert (1977), Winkler (1990b), esp. 30; cf. Aesch. *Pers.* 956–62; Soph. *Ant.* 663–71; Thuc. 1.144.4; Ar. *Arch.* 995–99; *Peace* 596–8.

the fourth century was a practice – and probably therefore an ambition and sign of distinction – of the sons of those who could afford it.[27]

The theatrical enactment of hoplite warfare by young men in either theatre or gymnasium, moreover, is attested for fifth-century Athens in vase-painting and later literary sources,[28] though again the evidence is fraught with uncertainty. Athenaeus, when discussing the origins of war-dances does not relate a single one to Athens (Athen. 14. 629a–631e). But Plato in the *Laws* mentions dances in hoplite armour (*enhoplia paignia*) not only for Crete and Sparta, but also for Athens (*Leg*.796b). Winkler has argued that the choros of tragic performances consisted of young men in military training, and Borthwick suggests that Attic ephebes performed pyrrhic dances at the Panathenaia.[29] If this was indeed the case, theatrical displays of hoplite warfare enacted by young ephebes regularly brought on stage the difference and tensions between age-classes as well as between social and economic unequals in a democratic society.

Nicias in the *Laches* itself suggests that *en hoplois machesthai* was a useful exercise for a young man if he wanted to excel in real warfare. For it would help him the moment the ranks broke up and a man had to prove himself in face-to-face combat. It would also make him ambitious (*philotimos*) to aspire to the higher accomplishment of becoming manager of the troops and general (182ab). Far from being part of general military training, *en hoplois machesthai* is to be regarded as a way of distinguishing oneself in a competitive democratic society.

Laches, however, for his part distinguishes between such performances and 'the real thing' of battle, pointing out that neither has he seen any such performance artist behaving heroically on the battlefield, nor has he heard of such performers daring to show their arts in Sparta, the epitome and pinnacle of hoplite culture. What's more, he recalls how Stesilaus, the performer whose display (*epideiknumenon*) they have been watching, despite his own self publicity (183d1), gave a 'real show' (*alēthōs epideiknumenon*) against his will in battle. For he was equipped with a remarkable weapon (a cross between a spear and a scythe) which in the course of fighting from a trireme became entangled in the rigging of a passing freight vessel, and was left dangling by the warrior to the laughter and applause (*gelōs kai krotos*) first of those on the freight ship and then even of his comrades in the trireme. A coward, concludes the general (184b–c), who has done his exercises

---

[27] Winkler (1990b) 29; Pritchett (1974) 208–13.
[28] *P Oxy*. 2738; Dion. Hal. 7.72.7; Borthwick (1970), Pritchett (1974), Winkler (1990b) 55–6.
[29] Winkler (1990b); Borthwick (1970) 318.

famously will become all the more conspicuous (*epiphanesteros*) for what he truly is; but the brave man must do something exceptional indeed to avoid the jealousy aroused by the pretension to such skills in exercises. Only a prodigious act of heroism will prevent such a man becoming a laughing stock (*katagelastos*), if he is known for his skill in exercises. Between *philotimos* and *katagelastos*, loving honour and becoming a laughing stock, hoplomachic exercise thus becomes in all senses a contest of *andreia*, the performance of masculine excellence.

Much more than simply 'courage' and 'education' is thus at stake in the *Laches*. The opening scene raises the question of how to gain recognition as a man and how to assert one's social position in the theatre of a competitive society. Lysimachus and his companion do not represent ordinary Athenians but want their sons to be looked at and up to. Does exercising (for) a civic role (e.g. hoplomachy) teach how to become a citizen worthy to be looked at? And if not, in what ways does this qualify the status of such citizens? As the two generals, Laches and Nicias, argue about the merits of hoplomachic exercises, what is at stake are the very paradigms of social performance.

Although they have defined themselves within the patterns of a performance culture, Lysimachus and Melesias do not believe that the collective was capable of instilling into their sons that excellence for which it praised itself. They condemn their fathers for not having looked after their education despite their own distinction (179d), and they feel ashamed that now, in turn, their private dining company (179b) failed to be a school for their sons as they had no *erga* to tell about.[30] In their despair they have called upon Nicias and Laches to join them in watching the show of hoplomachy, and to discuss their problems with them. There is a marked emphasis on the communality of their endeavour (***sunparalabein***, ***suntheatas***, ***sumboulous***, *koinōnous*, 179e), and formal agreement of the two generals is necessary to have them enter the *koinōnia* (180ab). When Laches suggests co-opting Socrates, it takes again some formal introduction to bring the community about. Socrates' pre-existing social ties with Lysimachus are emphasized (180e), his pedagogical competence is asserted (180c), and his valour as a soldier, which Laches had been able to watch (*etheasamēn*) in the battle of Delium, is praised by so competent a judge as the general himself (181b). The care of this social manoeuvring to create a

---

[30] In criticizing the democratic educational practice Lysimachus and Socrates are quite on the same trajectory; cf. *Prt.* 319e, *Grg.* 503bc; 515cff.; *Menex.* 93aff., *Alc.* 1 118c. where Socrates expresses similar criticism about leading Athenian politicians. Stokes (1986) 113, also notices that in the last resort Socrates and Lysimachus have more in common than the 'best' philosopher and the best generals; for which, see below.

Plato and the performance of dialogue 271

group is clearly part of Plato's apologetics. Socrates is to be seen not merely as the educator of Critias but also as the consultant of the great generals of the past, lauded for his bravery as a soldier ('a real man') and chosen as an adviser for the educator of the young. Socrates indeed is said (181a) to have 'kept up his father's status as the best of men' (ὀρθοῖς τὸν πατέρα, ἄριστον ἄνδρα ὄντα), precisely the failed hope of the fathers who summon him; and to have won 'fine praise' (ἔπαινος καλός), the aim of these parents for their children. As the performance of *philia* (181c) is paraded, so too the status of Socrates is glorified.

The formation of the small, carefully selected *koinōnia/sunousia* (cf. 196b, 201c) stands in conscious opposition to the arbitrary crowd of citizens in which education was supposed to be taking place in the city of Athens.[31] Laches says explicitly that there is no need to decorate (*kosmein*) oneself with empty speeches in such a gathering (*sunousia*): in the intimate group of friends, one could speak honestly and frankly and did not have to worry about the appearance of difficulty as one would in the law-court (196b). In the mouth of Euripides' Hippolytus such comments about the small group and its different requirements of linguistic performance are a marker of a privileged self-positioning, a worrying proclamation of elite separation from the mass.[32] Here too the claim has a rhetorical effect, since it is used by Laches to criticize Nicias' apparent unwillingness to recognize his own *aporia* (the parallel with Critias in the *Charmides* is patent), an unwillingness γενναίως ὁμολογεῖν ὅτι οὐδὲν λέγει, 'nobly/honestly to agree he has no argument'. 'Straight talk between gentlemen' is an ideological protocol of the self-recognition and policing of the elite group.

---

[31] *Sunousiai*, like *sussitiai*, were semi-formal and socially competitive groups in which favours and obligations were exchanged. The various social, religious and economic functions, as well as the intense emotional involvement, that were implied in joining such a group can be inferred from a little speech preserved in the corpus of speeches of Lysias. The speaker seems to have formally joined a group of friends (8.6) for *suneinai kai dialegesthai* 'company and coversation' (5) who apparently had also been together on a mission to Eleusis (5), cooperated in some credit operation (10), and expected legal aid of each other (18). The friendship had turned sour and the highly emotional speech reveals the rationale on which such associations were predicated: equal education, equal wealth, equal reputation and an equal number of friends (7); see also Sayre (1995) 157ff. On the political implications of *sunousiai* for Socrates, and on the social background, see Robb (1993). In associating *sunousiai exclusively* with traditional, oral, intergenerational education between families – as against the the professional aociations formed by sophists (including, in the eyes of the public, Socrates; see also Isocrates, discussed below) – Robb underestimates how *sunousia* could be a contested concept which Socrates is keen to appropriate for his own purposes.

[32] Eur. *Hipp.* 986–9, on which see e.g. Goff (1990) 42–3; Lloyd (1992) 47–9; Goldhill (1986) 233–4.

Socrates, in his failed attempt to defend himself and his practices before a mass democratic court, also contrasts the *sunousiai* between himself and his pupils with the assemblies of 'all Athenians' who pretended to be the teachers of the young (*Ap.* 25c) – which adds a certain bite to Laches' contrast between their *sunousia* and the law-court.[33] In the *Laches*, however, the emphasis on the *koinōnia* of the participants has a further double function, beyond the very performance of its construction as a significant social setting for the discussion of manhood and distinction. On the one hand, it establishes a hierarchy of the participants, which, as Laches asserts, renders any posturing – social performing – unnecessary. There is both a hierarchy of age-groups and of military achievement: the two sons are *meirakia*, adolescents shortly before their ephebic training; their parents are old men beyond military age, while Nicias, Laches and Socrates (the youngest of the three, 181d) are of full citizen age. Lysimachus and Melesias, moreover, confess to have achieved nothing, the two sons may do so potentially, while Laches and Nicias are *stratēgoi* of highest rank. Socrates' military achievement, introduced in the form of praise by one of these generals, neatly matches his status of being part of, but youngest within, the age group of privileged speakers. Together with the bonds of friendship and kinship tying the group together, this creates a speech situation in which the hierarchy between the participants seems non-negotiable. On the other hand, the apparent hierarchy provides only the backdrop for Socrates' ascent towards the most authoritative position in the dialogue. The apologetics consist not only in Socrates' participation in this group but in his intellectual dominance of it.

Let us return, however, to the beginning to look in more detail at the construction of this *sunousia*. Lysimachus observes that not with everybody could they discuss as important an issue as the education of their sons. For some people would simply laugh at them (*katagelōsi*), and when asked for advice (*sumbouleusētai*) would not say what they thought (οὐκ ἂν εἴποιεν ἃ νοοῦσιν), but guessing what the other wished to hear, would speak against their own opinion. To Nicias and Laches, by contrast, he felt he could talk freely (*parrhēsiazeusētai*), and not only had they the necessary discernment but would also on their part speak frankly their own opinion (178b). *Parrhēsia*, 'free speech', so often a political watchword of democracy over and against tyranny, here becomes a term defining the elite group over and against the institutions for the exchange of words in the democratic *polis*. Lysimachus

---

[33] Cf. *Tht.* 150d; and *Plt.* 257a–258a where the most elaborate description of the mutual ties of the participants is given.

establishes three conditions necessary for getting proper advice: (a) that between the partners discussing there is freedom and a common understanding of the problem, rather than the one laughing at the other; (b) that the person advising has enough *gnōmē* for giving advice; and (c) that he says what he thought rather than aiming to please the person asking. These conditions, especially since they are put into the language of political rhetoric (*parrhēsia, sumboulē, gnōmē*, etc.), appeal to the model of good Athenian deliberation as it was exemplified by the Thucydidean Pericles.[34] But they also echo Plato's requirements for philosophical discourse. Throughout his work he insists that the philosopher has to have knowledge before putting knowledge into words, that those who aimed their speeches at their audience, rather than at the truth, were sophists not philosophers, and that the philosopher is laughed at by ordinary people who do not have the same level of understanding.[35] Lysimachus without quite such theoretical grounding has found it quite enough to turn to the two most distinguished citizens/generals for proper advice. Yet although his conditions are expressed in a non-philosophical perspective they are sufficient to set a frame within which Nicias and Laches fail and Socrates succeeds (or at least does not fail).

At first Socrates politely steps back from the privileged position of speaking first: since he is the youngest and least experienced it is only correct to have Nicias and Laches take the lead (181d); if he had anything to add he might try to explain it (*didaskein*) later and to persuade (*peithein*) them to take his view. Socrates hides himself in the language of a good citizen, but at the same time indicates that political instruction is for him not advising equals (*sumbouleuein*) but teaching (*didaskein*). For the time being, however, the two generals have the prerogative of giving their speeches first and, after the brief *agōn* described above, Lysimachus turns to Socrates. By asking him to act as the arbitrator, as it were, in their council (καὶ γὰρ ὥσπερ τοῦ διακρινοῦντος δοκεῖ μοι δεῖν ἡμῖν ἡ βουλή), he explicitly shifts the discussion to the public space of deliberative rhetoric. Since the two generals have

---

[34] Yunis (1996) 136ff. and *passim*, has suggested that some of Plato's attack on rhetoric makes sense as a response to Thucydides. If one accepts an early date of the *Laches* and the appearance of the *Histories* in the 390s, the *Laches* could be included in such a case.

[35] As Nightingale (1995) 178-80 shows, laughter is for Plato an image of distorted exchange between people talking at different levels of comprehension. Thus in the *Republic* the philosopher returning to those imprisoned in the cave would produce laughter (516e-517a); and in the *Theaetetus* Socrates observes that those who had occupied themselves with philosophy would appear to be ridiculous speakers when they went into the law-courts (172c; cf. 174a-175b); cf. Mader (1977) 31-3; more generally Halliwell (1991), and for the later tradition Goldhill (1995) 14-20.

argued opposite positions on the benefits of hoplomachy, he wishes to hear with whom Socrates will cast his vote (ποτέρῳ τοῖν ἀνδροῖν σύμψηφος εἶ 184d). Socrates now hits back: 'would he really decide the matter on what the majority said?', he asks, aiming at the very heart of democratic decision making. He turns away from Lysimachus (184e) to establish a new role for himself and a new communicative space, first, by redefining the parameters of the discussion (are we talking about hoplomachy or about something more general? 185bc) and secondly by changing the form of the debate from *agōn* to dialogue.[36] Not only does the change of form make the comparison with law-court or council impossible but the transposition of the problem renders it painfully obvious that Lysimachus had just been playing *bouleutērion* in such important a question as the education of his son (185a). And, as if in tacit confirmation of this dramatic shift, Nicias and Laches comply with the new conditions: Nicias, by saying that it is not others but oneself whom one is asked to judge when talking with Socrates (187e–188a); and Laches by despising all *logoi* that are not in harmony with the *erga* of the speaker (188de) as well as by conceding that from a teacher it was in truth virtue (*aretē*) that one had to expect rather than age (*hēlikia*) or public reputation (*doxa*, 189b). Democratic advising has turned into hierarchical teaching, and judgement by an audience into self-judgement. A process of agonistic speech-making with its possibilities of display, victory and *philotimia*, has become a dialogue which will end not merely in *aporia* about the definition of *andreia*, but also in the promise of necessary further education 'tomorrow' (*aurion* 201c bis), as the scene of judgement turns into deferral for further reflection (and thus a challenge to the audience of the dialogue as much as to the audience in the dialogue).

The dialogue thus restarts with the conventional hierarchies under erasure. Laches and Nicias willingly submit to Socrates' elenchus which in a short while reveals that the generals fail on the very account on which they had been chosen as advisers and speakers. Confronted with the first aporia, Laches realizes that he is incapable of saying what he thinks (ἃ νοῶ μὴ οἷός τ' εἰμὶ εἰπεῖν, 194b; cf. above 178c) and that there is no harmony between his *erga* and his *logoi* (193e cf. above 188d). In the following exchange, which begins emphatically with the question of whether Nicias might be able to say something or whether he says

---

[36] We are not convinced by Rutherford (1995) 84, who sees here only an expression of Plato's dislike of set speeches where the listener has no real chance to stop the speaker and ask questions.

things only for the sake of an argument (λόγου ταῦτα ἕνεκα λέγει, 196c), Laches fiercely attacks his rival so as to make him fail as badly as he himself. So it is not even Socrates but his fellow general who blames Nicias for 'embellishing himself with words' (197c), 'dodging his way and hiding his own perplexity as if they were in a law-court' (196b), and pretending to be wise but simply babbling nonsense (195a). And indeed, Nicias cannot say what *andreia* is any more than Laches (199e). Little wonder that the two generals fall out with each other, so that Laches finds nothing but laughter (*katagelan*, 200b; cf. above 178a) directed both at Nicias and at Damon whose clever phrases the general had just been plagiarizing. Nicias sticks a little more to his semi-philosophical tack by observing that Laches was incapable of 'looking at himself, but only at others' (οὐδὲν πρὸς αὐτὸν βλέπειν ἀλλὰ πρὸς τοὺς ἄλλους, 200b; cf. 197c) – a 'typical human deficiency'.[37] The implicit irony of the remark, given Laches' infallible eye for true and false *andreia* in hoplite warfare,[38] is a lure for further reflection for an attentive audience.

Finally, however, unlike the breakdown represented in some later dialogues, *koinōnia* is easily re-established with the agreement that all need Socrates as a teacher, and with the agreement to organize such teaching, not caring even if it prompts laughter from others to see old men going back to education (201a–b). The (imagined) laughter of spectators thus ends up by confirming that this *sunousia* stands out against the collective of the city and its misunderstandings. As the dialogue began with a worry about being laughed at for seeking advice, so it ends with a willing acceptance that laughter may indeed dog their pursuit of understanding, but this will be a sign of the group's transcendence of the judgement of the many (καὶ ἡμεῖς οὖν ἐάσαντες χαίρειν εἴ τίς τι ἐρεῖ, κοινῇ ἡμῶν αὐτῶν καὶ τῶν μειρακίων ἐπιμελείαν ποιησώμεθα, 'And so we shouldn't give a damn if anyone says anything, but arrange the tuition of ourselves and the young men in common'). The frame of judgement has shifted.

The opposition between *logoi* and *erga*, 'words/arguments' and 'deeds/reality', has often been noted by comentators as a thematic concern of this dialogue, which further connects its debates to a paraded public political issue (and may even be seen as a response to

---

[37] As Stokes observes, although Nicias can flash with some philosophical phrases, his inability to learn is as great as Laches' (Stokes (1986) 112).
[38] See above 181a (*etheasamēn* Socrates at Delium); 183d (*etheasamēn* the *hoplomachomenos*, in his fight against the trading vessel).

e.g. the Thucydidean highlighting of such terminology[39]). Indeed, the frequent recurrence of key notions of political rhetoric, such as *sumbouleuein*, *parrhēsia*, *gnōnai* etc., broadens the dialogue's involvement with political discourse. This leads in two particularly important directions. First, Lysimachus' attempt to identify the private debate between Socrates and the generals with a discussion in the *boulē* not only allows Socrates to reject the comparison in favour of his idea of dialogue, but also establishes the discussion as a political display that rivals other political displays of the work. The two old men come to watch the *machomenos en hoplōi* and after engaging in a number of other displays, and discussions of displays, arrive at the conclusion that Socrates has given the best one. There is a politicized turn here against the institutions of the polis in which the figuring of Socrates plays a key role.

Second, commentators have also repeatedly noted that there is little of 'philosophical substance' in the short exchange, and that Socrates leaves the conversation at the intellectual level of his interlocutors. The *aporia* is certainly swiftly recognized and the need of further discussion acknowledged. In part, this stems from the representation of Socrates as a 'good citizen/soldier' in the opening section of the dialogue, and from Socrates' questions which follow immediately from what his interlocutors have said or from popular reasoning – as Socrates plays his role. Plato has scripted a very particular type of performance for the young Socrates amid his elders and betters. The gap between *logoi* and *erga* grounds such role playing, as it grounds Socratic irony, even when it is directed towards the comprehension of the performance of the adult male in the polis.

Stokes gives the meaning of the *Laches* an incisive turn when he draws attention to the fact that at the end of the dialogue Socrates encourages his audience to look for a man less ignorant than they themselves, rather than for *andreia*, let alone *aretē* (200e). This search was the one that Socrates prosecuted throughout his life and which Plato has him portray in the *Apology*.[40] From the beginning, the *Laches* dramatizes the search for a man, that is, the kind of person who not only the boys but also their fathers had better become, and who might be their best teacher. For the two old citizens, such a man was *andreios*, courageous, but also more generally, outstanding in the eyes of the

---

[39] Some commentators note the presence of the theme, but do not relate it to Thucydides; cf. Stokes (1986); O'Brien (1963). Yunis (1996) 136ff., persuasively argues that Thucydides provides 'one part of the complex background' to the *Gorgias* and the *Menexenus*, but does not discuss the *Laches*.

[40] Stokes (1986) 112; cf. *Ap.* 21b–23b.

collective. This is why watching displays of *andreia* in the public space and engaging in the test of these displays is of such importance to them. Yet in the course of the dialogue the test of displays of *andreia* or virtue more generally takes a different direction. Via a series of conventional possibilities of identifying the *anēr* in the first part (the *hoplomachomenos*, the figures of Nicias, and of Laches as distinguished generals, of Socrates as hoplite) the dialogue constitutes a new search which not only redefines the man searched for but also the way he might be recognized. The dialogue does not call into question the gaze as a way of perceiving virtue embodied, for all that the collective and its representatives are seen as an inadequate frame of evaluation. But it urges the audience to look at the effects on themselves in order to identify the nature of a performance. Socrates is not a wise man, but by his performance and his demonstration of his own and others' lack of wisdom, he makes the audience realize their own lack of wisdom and their need to search for a different teacher: to reconstruct themselves. In the absence of a wise man this must do. At least, until tomorrow. It is, we might say, a different kind of audience control, which neither follows the model of the sage nor the model of democratic mass instruction. The *Laches* in its brief scope seeks to establish through its dialogue a new ideal of performance for the citizen.

III

The politics of Plato's dialogic technique are highlighted by contrast with a quite remarkable passage of Isocrates, which gives a different sense of how performance, politics and the cultural strategies of verbal exchange may be discussed. This is Isocrates's great speech the *Panathenaicus*, begun in 342 BCE when the author was ninety-three, it is claimed.[41] The speech begins as a eulogy of Athens, the city of the writer, which is conjoined with an attack on Sparta. The praise and the attack are both conducted in terms of political policy, constitution and national character. After some 199 chapters of this, the writer turns suddenly and quite remarkably to the moment of writing itself (200): 'I had just written what you have just read', he writes, 'and was revising it with three or four young men who customarily spend time with me. As we went through it, it seemed good to us and lacking just its conclusion, when it occurred to me to call one of my former students who had lived under an oligarchy, so he could point out any mistakes I had

---

[41] *Panath.* 17; 268–70. For an astute account of the discourse of autobiography in Isocrates, see Too (1995).

made.' Although poets sometimes represent the moment of creation or inspiration, it is extremely odd indeed for a political pamphlet, especially after two hundred chapters of argument *in persona*, to turn to represent its own composition in this way. We are invited into the teacher's study with his pupils around him. The student is duly called and, the teacher reports, praises the speech lavishly (201), but, when pushed, attempts to argue that the representation of Sparta is ridiculously biased (202): for 'Spartans had discovered the best way of life, and lived by it *and* displayed it to mankind.' Isocrates again reflects on the moment of composition and the effect of his pupil's comment (203): 'This brief and brusque assertion was the reason why I did not conclude my speech where I had intended. I thought it would be shameful and terrible for me if when present (*paron*) I should overlook one of my pupils using poor arguments.' The orator's response to the audience's criticism is to turn immediately to counter-attack and the author promptly launches into a violent tirade (204–15) against his pupil (which the pupil accepts with good grace and tact, as fictional pupils do). Indeed, the pupil confesses that he had spoken only in praise of Spartan athletic practices and was motivated by his own perplexity (*aporia*) because he could not simply praise his master as he was accustomed to do – a comment which, the teacher notes (218), 'concealed the extreme harshness of his previous remarks with culture and sense, and defended his other points with more control than his previous outspokenness (*parrhēsiasamenon*)'. *Parrhēsia*, lauded in Plato's *sunousia* of the *Laches*, has become here a pupil's lack of educated dissimulation before his authoritative teacher (and the writer), as the need for extreme care in rhetorical self-positioning is emphasized as a criterion for effective participation in social discourse.

It may look at first sight as if the figure of the pupil has been introduced merely to dramatize in a striking way a possible objection to the previous argument and to crush it. Dramatizing the 'you may object', or the 'someone might say' strategy typical of forensic oratory.[42] But there is much more. For Isocrates goes on to point out that he has an even more crushing attack to make on Spartan training practices, an attack he then demonstrates at length (218–29). This reduces 'the widely experienced and highly trained student' (219) to silence and departure – which in turn prompts a further extraordinary anatomy of the audience response from the writer (219–20): 'The young men present did not have the same judgement on the scene as I. They

---

[42] For an argument on how Isocrates' writing here may relate to the conventions of oratory, see Gray (1994), whose discussion of this speech is the fullest currently available.

Plato and the performance of dialogue 279

praised me for speaking more vigorously than they had expected, and for competing (*agōnizesthai*) nobly. They also despised him. Their judgement, however, was faulty and they were wrong on both of us.' The orator rejects his rhetorical success as an audience's misreading. (Reading the audience, part of an orator's skill according to the handbooks, is raised to a highly developed demonstration of mastery here.[43]) His reason is that on the one hand the young man had in fact gone away wiser about not merely the Spartans' nature but also himself ('he had experienced the message of the inscription at Delphi to "know yourself"'[44]); whereas he himself had spoken effectively but without the wisdom of his years and all too like a rash youth. Indeed, after dictating the speech to an amanuensis, and re-reading it more calmly after three or four days, not only is he distressed about what he said immoderately about the Spartans, but also confesses that (232) 'I had spoken with contempt and extreme bitterness and altogether without understanding.' The crushing retort to the pupil – with what rhetorical manoeuvring or disingenuousness? – is partially withdrawn because of its extreme tone. Although tempted to rub it out or burn it, out of pity for his old age and the work he had put in, he decides to invite his pupils to hear the whole speech with its new ending, doubts and all, and to judge whether it should be destroyed or circulated. At first, perhaps unsurprisingly, it simply receives the praise and applause 'such as successful epideictic displays win', τετυχηκὼς ὦνπερ οἱ κατορθοῦντες ἐν ταῖς ἐπιδείξεσιν (233).

In the following audience discussion, however, the same pro-Spartan pupil nervously opens a further debate, and offers a long speech (235–63) in which he too regrets his former reaction, and offers a lengthy counter-reading of the speech, which claims that his *own* first reading had been wrong. The voice of the audience gets to perform a critique, a reading, both of a previous reaction and of the master's further and previous performance. (The *Panathenaicus* gives the lie to two assumptions underlying much performance criticism: that an audience has one direct, immediate response to e.g. a play; and that this response should be privileged.) Although at first sight, Isocrates was attacking Sparta, he claims, in fact on closer reading it was clear that Isocrates was also praising Sparta for precisely that which Spartans themselves were proud of. We wish to focus not on the substance or the politesse of the

---

[43] See e.g. Aristotle *Rh.* 1.2.3–6 for the statement of principle, and for a sparky discussion of this issue with regard to the *Panathenaicus*, Gray (1994).

[44] The closeness to the Platonic is (as often in Isocrates) marked in the shared turn to the Delphic maxim as a teaching principle, especially in contexts of the pain of learning.

pupil's re-reading,[45] but first on a passage where he justifies and comments on his strategy of re-reading. We will need to quote at length (244-7):

> It was, then, with such an intention (*dianoia*) that you composed the overall strategy of your speech. If I thought you would no longer engage in what has been said and leave this speech without critical revision (*anepitimēton*), I would not undertake to speak further. But as things are, I do not think you will be concerned that I have not declared on the matter I was summoned here to offer advice (*sumboulos*). For when you called us together, you did not seem to me to be serious about it. Rather, you had chosen to compose a speech unlike others. To those who read lazily (*tois rhathumōs anagignōskousin*), it would seem simple and easy to comprehend (*katamathein*). To those who go through it with care trying to see what others have missed, it would clearly be hard to comprehend (*duskatamathēton*), and full of much history and philosophy, and of all sorts of complexity (*poikilia*) and fiction (*pseudologia*), not the fiction which, with evil, usually harms fellow citizens, but that which, with education and culture (*paideia*), benefits and pleasures the listeners.

The pro-Spartan, since he has, he believes, determined Isocrates' intention via the structure of the speech, first proposes that Isocrates' writing demands a double level of reading. On the one hand, there are lazy political readers who will think the speech simple and easy to follow, *haploun ... kai rhadion katamathein*. On the other, there are those who will see its artifice as a philosophical and intellectual stance: it will be difficult and hard to understand, *khalepon kai duskatamathein*. The reason for this is that the speech is full of deceptive intricacy, *poikilia*, and false speaking – *pseudologia* – not the false speaking that harms one's fellow citizens (*tous sumpoliteuomenous*), but one which with proper education or culture – *meta paid[e]ias* – can both benefit and pleasure them *ophelein kai terpnein*. Isocrates' speech can perform both sides of what after Thucydides is so often seen as a mutually exclusive polarity of aims in writing prose.[46] Isocrates can be both pleasurable and instructive. The complexities of the place of deception – the recognition of deception – within the democratic ideology of open governance are laid bare by this version of Plato's 'noble lie'.[47] If the community values straight talk, man to man, what place for the

---

[45] See Tigerstedt (1965) 179ff. with further references to earlier debates on the senility of Isocrates for daring such a structure for a speech. More careful is Gray (1994) who is attacking in particular Kennedy (1989) and Eden (1987).
[46] This clearly picks up the opening two chapters of the speech which opposes the pleasures of myth to the work of advice. For a useful collection of passages on the opposition of 'pleasure' and 'benefit' in history writing especially, see Hunter (1983) 48–9.
[47] See Hesk in this volume.

recognition of the need for indirection and manipulation in language – for both speaker and audience? Isocrates' performance as an orator produces different kinds of performance from his listeners or readers. Indeed, the pupil continues by marking the paradox that by his very exposition of the strategy of the speech he may be accused of lessening its effect, because the more patent and intelligible it becomes the less its honour among those who study hard to appreciate its true meaning (247):

> You will say that I have not let things stand in the manner you designed them. Rather, I have not perceived that by explaining the power of what was said and expounding your intention (*dianoia*), as I make the speech more clear and more intelligible, I make it less distinguished. For by producing understanding in those who don't know, I make the speech empty and deprived of the honour which would come to it from those who labour at it and take pains for themselves.

Despite this suggested justification of esoteric or elite understanding (which could well be seen as a critique of Plato's didactic strategies), he goes on to conclude that there is a political reason (or analogy) for not composing according to such hidden and restrictive methods, as the pupil and reader proceeds to question the strategies of performance of the master and orator (248):

> When your city deliberates about matters of the greatest importance, there are times when those who seem to be wisest miss what is required, and times when some chance person from those who are thought trivial and despised comes up with a solution and seems to say what is best. So it would not be surprising if something similar is happening in the present circumstances. You think you will get the greatest reputation (*eudokimein*), if you conceal for the longest time the purpose with which you worked out your speech; I think, however, that you will do best if you can reveal the intention (*dianoia*) of your speech as soon as possible to everyone, especially the Spartans . . .

Because of the way in which democracy's process of judgement often involves errors and misunderstandings, Isocrates should cut out the artifice and explain as clearly as possible the concept – *dianoia* – the *Grundgedanke* – according to which the speech was composed. His hope of 'good reputation' (*eudokimein*) in the public arena will be best achieved by following the principles of democratic openness in deliberation. Thus, the fictional character asks the author to dispense with the veils of fiction. To come clean. To tell it how it is.

Now, orators traditionally invent opponents' words, often imagining responses to a speech, but here we have a fully dramatized version of an exchange, in which a fictional character discusses the strategies of fiction adopted by the author and encourages – but worries about – a practice of 'non-lazy' reading, and recognizes 'simplicity' and 'singleness' as a lure for those without knowledge, but concludes, none the less, that in democracy, it is better to be direct about policy.[48] Yet look at the response, as once again Isocrates dramatizes an audience's engagement with a speech and his masterful comprehension of the scene (264–5):

> When he had spoken and asked those present (*tous parontas*) to declare their opinion on the question about which they had been summoned, they did not merely applaud as they usually did for a speech which pleased them, but shouted out that he had spoken remarkably, and thronged around him and praised him, envied him, congratulated him, and had nothing to add or take away from what he had said. They agreed with him and advised me to do what he had urged. Nor did I stand by in silence, but I praised his nature and training. As for the rest, I uttered not a word about what he had said, neither how his interpretations (*huponoiai*) had hit upon my intention (*dianoia*), nor how he had missed, but I let him stay with the position he had formed for himself.

First, all the other pupils tumultuously acclaim the pupil's version of the master's discourse, and the master himself praises his nature and training – *phusis* and *epimeleia*.[49] He will not be a mere bystander to the throng of the spectators as they demonstrate the pupil's achievement of public recognition (*eudokimein*) in the praise and congratulations of the collective. The group dynamics are emphasized here in this *sunousia* of the orator. But the master then distances himself from the collective praise: 'But beyond that I uttered not a word about the sentiments he had expressed, neither how his interpretative reading (*huponoia*) had hit upon my concept (*dianoia*), nor how it had missed it; but I allowed him to stay with the position he had formed for himself.' Asked as a matter of policy for a clear expression of his concept, the author dramatizes the appeal ... and his own studied and continued ambivalence towards such a claim.[50] The oration self-reflexively and self-consciously *performs*, as it discusses, the ambivalence of reading practice in the space constructed by the politics of openness promoted by democracy, on the one hand, and the rhetorical and philosophical recognition of the deceptiveness of logos, on the other. The movement

---

[48] The unparalleled complexity and length of this dramatic writing make it hard to agree with Gray (1994) that it rehearses simply the conventional rhetorical strategy of establishing a negative position for contrast and warning.
[49] *Epimeleia* was the term also for the training that the participants of the *Laches* sought (201b5).
[50] This ambivalence makes it hard to see the scene either as 'a complete palinode' (Tigerstedt (1965) 196) or as simply 'an affirmation' that the pro-Spartan has just missed the point, as Gray (1994) argues.

Plato and the performance of dialogue 283

towards *dianoia*, the meaning, the concept, the intention, of a speech, is framed by the pedagogic exchange (as Yun Lee Too has shown[51]), but also by what could be called a politics of reading practice. As Athens and Sparta are compared and contrasted, the speech dramatizes the possibilities of different political reactions to its own rhetoric, and in strikingly self-reflexive manner, sets in motion not merely counter-readings within the text but also an explicit discussion of the strategies of representation themselves. We are shown the community at work over *logoi*. Reading as a politically led and politically framed activity. And at the crucial moment, the ironic master withdraws from an authorizing gesture – and thus turns back on the reader the task of using his or her interpretive skill, *huponoia*, to determine the sense of the speech. Or rather invites the reader to engage in the community of readers reading – the *agōn* of meaning – under his tutelage and indirect direction.

Thus, finally, in the last paragraphs of the work, rather than rehearse once more the political arguments he has made about Sparta and Athens, Isocrates turns to a final methodological homiletic, and enjoins his readers first 'not to trust their own opinions, nor to think true the judgements of lazy readers', and second 'not hastily to make public what they do not know about, but to wait till they can agree with those who have much experience of public performance (*tōn epideiknumenōn*)'. The dramatization of criticism in the *sunousia* of Isocrates has become the injunction to avoid simple judgements and readings, and to see how mastery of public performance is hard won through the process of criticism within the teacher's circle.

The contrast between Plato and Isocrates is, we suggest, instructive. Both offer a first-person narration that dramatizes the *sunousia* of men at work over the scene of language within a didactic context. Both texts are apologetic and competitive, Isocrates more explicitly so. Both narrators ironize their position as teachers and authorities with considerable self-consciousness and self-reflexiveness, though the mask of Socrates for Plato adds a further level to the drama of representation. Both offer performative texts about performance. Both explore in part at least the nature of *epideixis* in the polis and its connections with reputation (*eudokimein*), the pursuit of status (*philotimia*), and the constructions of different audiences and the interplays between audiences and performance. Yet Isocrates seems to stand in a quite different relation to the institutions and languages of the *polis*. His account of the glories of Athens over and against Sparta (so unlike Plato's

[51] Too (1995), though she surprisingly does not discuss this passage.

mocking funeral oration in the *Menexenus*), his acceptance and training of the public orators of the Assembly and law-court, his desire to hold his place and authority within the rhetorical institutions of the city, in short, his 'civic identity',[52] betoken a sense of *koinōnia* and *sunousia* that strikingly emphasizes the oblique and difficult relations between Platonic dialogue and the *polis*. Isocrates and Plato show different possibilities for an engagement with the culture of performance through dialogue.

IV

Our final text travels again to the gym, indeed to a newly built wrestling school near the spring of Panops, where Socrates is invited in to where a group of young males are exercising in words and with their bodies, and where *eros* is much in the air. Plato's *Lysis* is an aporetic dialogue, where what *philia* is – 'friendship' is the usual if wholly insufficient translation for a term which implies at least the mutual and reciprocal obligation of social and familial bonds and duties – is not successfully defined but where the journeying towards the failed definition is instructive. It is not by chance that this pursuit of *philia* takes place in the erotically charged environment of a group of young men, who are engaged in a complex round of physical activity – training the body and the self, as Foucault would put it[53] – nor is it by chance that it is led by Socrates, the famously ugly lover of Beauty itself. The aporia of the dialogue will be, as Socrates puts it in the final paragraph of the work, that 'we think we are friends of one another – and I count myself in your group – but we can't yet find out what a friend is' (223b). There is, in short, a certain tension between what the dialogue represents – the performance of 'being *philos*' or 'becoming a *philos*' – and its question about the definition of a *philos* – a tension absolutely integral to the text. We want to emphasize this from the start, because the standard philosophical discussions of this dialogue fail to mention, let alone account for the framing of this work, its sense of men engaged in the business of *philia* as they talk about *philia*.[54] We want to explore the significance to the dialogue of its sense of performance, and for this purpose we have chosen to emphasize one paradigmatic passage which to our knowledge has not been adequately commented on. If the performance of dialogue in the *Laches* aims to redraw the map of civic

---

[52] A term borrowed from Too (1995).   [53] Foucault (1987); (1988).
[54] See e.g. Bolotin (1979).

performance, the *Lysis* shows how the performance of dialogue can question philosophic procedure itself.

Hippothales, who has invited Socrates into the gym, is in love with Lysis. Socrates asks him how he talks to his object of desire, and he hears how Hippothales has written poems in praise of his loved one, and his loved one's talents, and his father, and his family. 'Ridiculous fellow, you are, Hippothales', comments Socrates, 'why do you compose and sing an encomium for yourself, before you've won?' 'I'm not writing or singing for myself', retorts the hurt lover. 'You are', continues Socrates, 'the songs certainly all refer to you. For if you win the love of a boy like that, your words and songs and what's really your victorious encomium will be your own glorious adornment. If he flees you, the greater the good you will seem to be deprived of, and the more ridiculed you'll be.' And he gradually draws out the danger of puffing up the pride of a potential lover with such praises. We have already discussed this passage in terms of the dynamics between praiser and praised as a paradigm of the difficulties of the relationship between performance and audience, and we have already noted how the fear or accusation of being *katagelastos*, 'a laughing stock', signals the dynamics of status in the public sphere: it is a term that is repeated at key points throughout this dialogue. Hippothales is crushed by the argument that praise of a boy redounds on the praiser; and asks Socrates how he should speak properly to a beloved, and Socrates replies tellingly (206c3–6): 'It isn't easy to say. But if you want to bring him into a conversation perhaps I could show – *epideixai* – how you ought to converse with him instead of all the stuff they say you talk and sing.' The conversation to come is to be a demonstration, an *epideixis*, of how to talk to someone you want to make your boyfriend. We – Hippothales and us – like so many later comic figures, are to watch a teacher of desire's tricks winning over a loved one . . .

There follows some neat manoeuvring to get Lysis and a boy of the same age, Menexenus, to sit with Socrates. First, we are treated to a description of the gym, with the boys dicing, some of them in the courtyard, some by the changing rooms. And typically, as we have seen, Socrates sees a group of observing bystanders too (206e8–9): τούτους δὲ περιέστασαν ἄλλοι θεωροῦντες, 'and others stood around them, watching (*theōrountes*)'. Lysis is picked out because of his looks (*opsis*), and when Socrates and his pals sit opposite in a quiet spot to begin a discussion, Lysis himself keeps turning around and glancing in their direction (θάμα ἐπεσκοπεῖτο ἡμᾶς), showing that he wants to come up and join them (although he is too shy). It is only when Menexenus sees (*eiden*) them and comes up, and Lysis sees (*idōn*) him, that the boys join the Socratic circle. Others come over too to stand and watch (*ephistamenous*) – and thus form a new group of observing bystanders – and when Hippothales sees (*heora*) them, he uses them as a cover so that Lysis won't see (*katopsesthai*) him. Thus, Socrates 'stares at' (*apoblepsas*) Menexenus, and begins... There is an elaborate game here of placement and glances, articulating the social politesse of looks and group formation in the charged, erotic, competitive atmosphere of the gym.

Menexenus, however, is quickly called off by his personal trainer, and it is Lysis who takes up the exchange, and is put through the elenchus by Socrates, to prove with nice sophistic flair that even – especially – his parents aren't his *philoi*. This exchange, based as it is on the principle that the reason for friendship is usefulness, has been the focus of some philosophical analysis,[55] but its conclusion, like its opening, is usually and regrettably ignored (210e1–211a5):

I listened to him and stared (*apeblepsa*) towards Hippothales, and I nearly made a mistake. For it occurred to me to say, '*That's* how you talk to a boyfriend – humbling and diminishing him, not like you, puffing him up and pampering him.' I saw (*katidōn*) he had been thrown into a state of competitive angst (*agōniōnta*) and confusion (*tethorubēmenon*) by what had been said, and I remembered that he did not want Lysis to notice him as a bystander (*parestōs*). So I caught myself and restrained my speech.

This clearly picks up the aim of the promised *epideixis* of erotic display, and thus significantly frames the first discussion of Lysis. Hippothales has been secretly listening in on this lesson of how to win over a boy – his boy – and Socrates thinks to bring him in to rub home the message, but catches himself in time to preserve the fragile triangle of love talk and overhearing. Socrates seems to let us into his process of thought in the elenchus as it is performed, shares with the reader the privileged access of the first person narration, as the lover is not merely given a lesson in how to win over a boy, but also is reduced to painful struggle and confusion in his voyeuristic exclusion. Like Critias listening to the elenchus of Charmides, Hippothales is reduced to a state of anxious competitive confusion. Watching Socratic performance is disturbing, as Socrates here ironically notes.

Meanwhile, Menexenus returns, and sits down next to Lysis from where he'd got up (211a1–5): 'So Lysis, really sexily and in a friendly way, concealed from Menexenus, quietly said to me "Socrates, do the

---

[55] See e.g. Price (1989) 1–14 (with bibliography).

argument you did to me on Menexenus, too".' The beautiful boy speaks secretly to Socrates, and most importantly, speaks *mala paidikos*, 'quite like a boyfriend', 'sexily',[56] and *philikos*, 'like a friend'. Socrates' dialectic has clearly had its desired and announced effect on the boy. The elaborate dance of who sits where, who stands, who is looking at whom, who is listening to whom, culminates in a little drama of secret words between teacher and young beauty, words which in asking Socrates to continue the exchange of argument with Menexenus, also performs in its tone at least – *mala paidikos kai philikos* – a come-on to the older man. Indeed, the two are interrupted shortly and sharply by Ctesippus who comes up and asks (211c10–12) what they are doing in secret conclave and 'could we all share the conversation?'

The aim of the discussion of *philia*, then, is to show to a concealed lover how to win over a boy by humbling him, and the watching lover observes with pain and confusion as the boy responds precisely *paidikos* and *philikos* to such treatment. The erotics of argument are clearly marked here. The argument is not just about 'friendship', as contemporary philosophers would have it, but is performing 'friendship'. It is demonstrating, more precisely, how Socrates is, as he says later, 'absolutely sexual about the obtaining of friends', πρὸς δὲ τὴν τῶν φίλων κτῆσιν πάνυ ἐρωτικῶς [ἔχω] – phraseology that ironically twists the emotive language of relationships to an almost paradoxical degree (as the translation of *erōtikos* by 'sexual' rather than the more discrete 'passionate' is meant to indicate). The scene, which so carefully represents the bodily movements and reactions of the participants, making groups, making connections, sitting, standing, watching, watching who is watching, overhearing in agony, is designed to showcase Socrates' words *doing something* to the boy, having an effect. So, after Socrates does his argument on Menexenus and reduces Menexenus also to aporia, Lysis interrupts with an answer to a question, and (213d3–5) 'blushed as soon as he had said it', comments Socrates, 'for it struck me that the words had escaped him unintentionally, because he was concentrating so much on our talk – as he clearly had been all the time he was listening'; and in response to Socrates' conclusion that the genuine and not the pretended lover should be favoured, 'Lysis and Menexenus gave a faint nod of assent, but Hippothales turned all sorts of colours out of pleasure' (222b1–2). Throughout the dialogue there

---

[56] Although *paidika* is a normal term for the junior partner (object of desire) in male–male erotic liaisons, some translations offer 'boyishly' here for *paidikos*, which misses the point of the coquettishness.

is a constant recognition of and concentration on not just the microsociology of the group in the gym but especially the bodily reactions – the somatics – of the performance of argument, blushing, secret whispers, laughing, watching, being watched, watching oneself being watched. Body Talk. The philosophers of the gym are very much Of The Body. It's quite a performance.

What we wish to stress is that the descriptions of the performance of the dialogue as it proceeds are not a background to the philosophical discussion, not local colour nor supportive material. Rather, the philosophical discussion is explicitly labelled as an epideictic example of how to perform the role of lover for the audience's instruction. Thus, when the conclusion of the dialogue is reached, the aporia needs careful articulation. (222b2–7):

> We broke up our company (*sunousia*), and as they departed, I said, 'Now, Lysis and Menexenus, we have become laughing stocks (*katagelastoi*), you, and I, an old man. For these people [the bystanders, *hoi periestōtes*] will go away and say that we think we are *philoi* of one another – for I do place myself in your group – but we can't yet find out what a friend is.'

On the one hand, with some irony, Socrates remarks the group dynamics: the *periestōtes*, the bystanders, split away; the *sunousia*, the company, is broken up.[57] The discussants have become, however, a group of *philoi*, and the bystanders, the wider group, will – according to Socrates' self-mockery – call them a 'laughing stock', that key sign of the group's disapprobation. The very conjunction of the 'old man' and the youths becomes part of this ironic distance from the expectations of the easy transmission of wisdom in a public forum (not to mention any suggestion of erotic disapprobation of such a grouping). On the other hand, the disjunction between the failed work of definition and the successful personal interactions raises a sharp question for the boundaries of philosophical reading. The arguments about *philia* cannot be properly understood apart from the demonstrations of *philia* at work. The exemplary performance in the gym shows the inadequacy of philosophical argument to account for such performance. Philosophy, like dicing, exercising and gossiping, is here part of the scene of social exchange, and, like other aspects of social exchange in the *polis*, it finds *eros* a specifically difficult and dangerous topic to bring into its ambit. It is, in short, the tension between social performance and philosophical performance that signifies here, and to repress either aspect distorts Plato's writing.

---

[57] The same phrase *dialuein sunousian* is also used at the end of the *Laches* (201c1–2).

V

Plato's critique of theatre and rhetoric as dangerous institutions in the democratic city of words has been much discussed in recent years. What we have tried to show in this chapter is how the performance of dialogue itself can become a theme and a problem in Plato's writing in a way that has wide political and intellectual implications. By his dramatization of the scene of exchange, his construction of particular group dynamics, his articulation of the tensions between argument and performance, the involvement of the self and the bystanders at the scene of performance, Plato marks a specific and complex site for the politics of his writing in and against the institutions and languages of democracy. In recent years, several scholars have tried to use a notion of dialogue, informed by the Bakhtinian project, to suggest that Plato may not be as simply anti-democratic and authoritarian as many post-Popperian critics would have it. Dialogue as a (politicized) challenge to authority, univocality, and control. Plato's writing, however, is constantly and profoundly informed by his deeply ambivalent engagement with the politics and philosophy of performance, and the way in which Plato's dialogic technique engages with the discourse of power needs careful historical and cultural analysis. It is a contribution to that dialogue which this chapter has attempted to offer.[58]

[58] We had great pleasure in writing together. Thanks for sharing in our dialogue to John Henderson (who first pointed SDG towards the *Lysis* many years ago), Thomas Johansen, Malcolm Schofield and Chris Rowe.

Part IV

Ritual and state: visuality and the performance of citizenship

11 Processional performance and the democratic polis

Athena Kavoulaki

In recent years the notion of 'performance' has become particularly popular as a category and general approach. Although the main impulse (especially in relation to the study of cultures) has been given by cultural anthropology,[1] related trends have developed almost concurrently in a number of fields as a result of a general dissatisfaction with traditional structural analysis and of a desire to recapture a 'living quality', the social dimension of cultural phenomena through an emphasis on the conditions under which these phenomena are meaningful.[2]

Occasion, audience, context, effect, as well as the role of the performer, are focal points in performance analysis, which purports to describe the social pattern, rather than the essence or nature of human activity.

A major advantage of the current surge of interest in performance is the attention it gives to areas which have been overlooked by conventional approaches. In relation to ancient Greek culture, manifestation rituals such as processions are a characteristic example: despite their ubiquity in the ancient world, a ubiquity well attested in the surviving remnants, processions have been relatively neglected as an object of study, figuring mainly in antiquarian works of the beginning of the century.[3] The invitation, however, to contribute an article on processions to a book on performance in classical Athens can be taken as indicative of an orientation towards 'occasions in which a culture or society reflects upon and defines itself, dramatizes collective myths and history, presents itself with alternatives, and eventually changes in some ways while remaining the same in others'.[4]

In the case of processions, however, the performance perspective

---

[1] Singer (1959) coined the term 'cultural performance' and gave the main impulse. For other later major contributions see Turner (1974) and (1982); Schechner (1988).
[2] Generally on performance theory in anthropology and related disciplines see Ortner (1984) 143-5, Bell (1992) 37-46, Carlson (1996) 13-75.
[3] E.g. Leacock (1900), Pfuhl (1900), Eitrem (1920) 56-108.
[4] MacAloon (1984) 1 with slight alterations.

needs to be applied not 'from outside', as a methodological model which considers the pragmatics of social phenomena, but from 'inside', as part of the definition, experience and function of the ritual in ancient Greek culture. More particularly, processional ritual shares with theatrical performances – performances *par excellence* – an explicitly declared emphasis on viewing: processions as well as theatre (θέατρον) (along with a number of other occasions) are 'viewing occasions', 'spectacles', θεωρίαι, θέαι.[5]

This use of cognate terms marks the central role of the viewer in both theatre and processions and confirms modern theories which perceive audience as a constitutive factor of performance. Acknowledging the presence, taking responsibility in front of an audience, implies a degree of consciousness in performance which works from both sides: of performers as well as spectators.[6] It is this heightened consciousness in acting and in discerning the acting which has been suggested as a fundamental universal element of performance.[7] Apart from the social and psychological factor, there is also the physical dimension: performance is physically inscribed, it becomes a mode of the body. If Barba is right, the foundation of performance in pre-expressive, physiological stimuli and responses is also a universal mode.[8] As regards processional performance in ancient Greek culture, the evidence suggests that it was based indeed on differentiated movement, on a distinct mode of movement which separated it from other performances (and actions) and which – due to its specificity – could be recognized and even deployed as a deception device.[9] To move in procession means, thus, to perform, that is to differentiate behaviour in front of the eyes of a beholder, be that the self, an invisible supernatural entity, or a human collectivity.

The last major parameter for the definition of performance is a connection to a special context, a 'frame' which in a way 'sets' performance 'apart' from other everyday activities.[10] In the case of ancient Greek processions, the frame was provided by the special occasion (involving time and place) on which a procession took place, such as the festivals of gods and heroes, weddings and funerals, victory

---

[5] See (e.g.) Ar. *Wasps* 1005, Xen. *Hier.* 1.12, Theophr. *Char.* 5.7, Xen. *Eph.* 1.2.2.
[6] Cf. Carlson (1996) 15, 38–42.
[7] See Blau (1993) 250f.
[8] See Barba (1991).
[9] Polyain. 5.5. νόμῳ πομπῆς βαδίζοντες.
[10] The concept of frame is due to Goffman (1975); the importance of context has been stressed by folklorists, anthropologists and sociologists alike; see (e.g.) Burke (1957), Singer (1959), Bateson (1972) and Bauman (1986).

celebrations, receptions and farewell ceremonies. Central to the programme of all these events was a perambulatory activity which could take several different names (πομπή, πρόσοδος, ἀγωγή, εἰσαγωγή, ἐκφορά, ἔκδοσις) and which involved a collectivity of people, distinctively dressed and carrying symbols and ritual objects, moving along a defined route for reasons of performing a significant act or of accomplishing a significant change at the end of the journey.[11] The use of objects, symbols or costumes has an 'alerting' quality which implies the attraction of spectators and the interchange between performers and spectators. The interaction could be accomplished all along the way or especially at the specific locations at which the procession could stop usually for the performance of music, singing and dance in connection with other ritual acts such as sacrifice.[12] Both the visual impression of colourful objects and choreographic movement, as well as the acoustic impression of instrumental and often vocal music show that processional performance was an elaborate event with symbolic and highly aesthetic qualities.

The multiplicity of functions and effects that a procession could have, is a first indication of the complex ways in which performance could work in ancient Greek culture. To make things even more complicated, processional performance was in constant and concurrent interaction with other kinds of performances and especially theatrical performances, with which it had obvious affinities: at its most basic the theatrical performance consisted of an array of people (*choros*) moving along the *parodos* (cf. the term *prosodos*), reaching a *stasis* (station) to perform a ritual singing and dancing (*stasimon*) in honour of a god, and finally exiting (*exodos*).[13] This basic structure, which parallels the structure of processional ritual, as well as the pragmatic situation of an audience attending suggest a close connection between theatre and processions. In cultures where theatre remains unknown, it is the processional performance which provides the pre-theatrical or pre-dramatic material.[14] In the Greek world the poetic *logos* or rather *dia*-

---

[11] I shall not dwell on the details of composition, arrangement, route etc. of ancient processions; for a good exposition see Bömer (1952). My aim here is to bring to the fore socio-religious and socio-political aspects of processions which have not been highlighted so far and which stand in relation to a wider context.

[12] See (e.g.) the famous procession of the Molpoi (Sokolowski (1955) 50, *SIG*³ 57) which included many stations (*staseis*) which Gödecken (1986) attempts to retrace; also the procession to Eleusis: sacrifices along the way *IG* II² 1078, Plut. *Alk.* 34.4.

[13] The chorus as the nucleus of the theatrical performance: cf. the organization of the classical festival in terms of chorus (the poet ᾔτει χορόν, the archon ἐδίδου χορόν; see Pickard-Cambridge (1988) 84).

[14] See Kakouri (1974); for the prehistory of the Greek theatre which shows the importance of processions see Stoessl (1987); cf. also Herington (1985).

logos 'grafted' the processional structure and led to the development of the theatrical form.[15] Athens, both typical and atypical, was the *first* polis which established theatrical *agōnes* as well as the *best* polis in ἄγειν μυστήρια καὶ πομπάς (conducting mysteries and processions, Plut. *Lyk.* 30). Athens' distinction in advancing performances in a climate of developing democracy merits an attempt at a closer study which will be pursued below, after a brief discussion of the recurrence of processions in the various cultures and political systems.

The general picture and some theoretical conclusions

Processions are neither culturally nor politically specific. They turn up in cultures all over the world and in all historical periods and regimes.[16] The earliest extant religious texts attest to the performance of magnificent processions in the ancient civilizations of Assyria and Babylonia, where no sharp distinction between sacred and profane obtained, and gods and kings had a share in all major ceremonies.[17] Similar was the situation in Egypt,[18] to which Herodotos (2.58) ascribes priority in the performance of the ritual in relation to Greece. According to Herodotos, Greece started practising processions νεωστί (lately). Despite the historian's assurances, and although the process of acculturation is hard to discern, there is no doubt about the antiquity of the custom in the Greek world: in Minoan – Mycenean iconography processions are extensively portrayed and Linear B tablets provide related linguistic evidence.[19] From the archaic times onwards the sources are plentiful and the development of the ritual can be traced throughout antiquity.

---

[15] As it relates to the origins of tragedy, contemporary scholars agree that the singing of the τραγῳδοί must have been associated with the *processional* arrival at the locus where the ritual singing would take place: cf. Burkert (1966); Seaford (1994) 238–51; Sourvinou-Inwood (1994); similarly for comedy: cf. Adrados (1975) (the *kōmos*, placed at the centre of his reconstruction, is in effect connected with perambulatory activity); Ghiron-Bistagne (1976) 207–98 also on an original *kōmos*. West's hypothetical suggestion (1990) 21 points to the power of processions to gather the community. Well-documented comparative material from other cultures shows the foundation of theatre in processional performances and in their fertilization with narration and mimetic action; the Islamic theatre developed among the Shia Muslim communities is probably the best example: see Chelkowski (1985).

[16] They have been even conjectured for Paleolithic times: Schechner (1988) 159–60. Cf. Burkert (1985) 52 for Neolithic evidence relating to phallic processions.

[17] See Pongrantz-Leisten (1994) (especially the introduction for the general picture).

[18] See Stadelmann (1982).

[19] Minoan–Mycenean iconography: see Marinatos (1986) 25–7, 32–5 and Marinatos (1993) 31–6 and 51–75. For the ancient Greek view on the origin of *pompai* from Crete: see Didymos Chalk. *apud* Lact. *Inst.* 1 22. 19. Linguistic evidence: *θρονοελκτήρια in Pylos (PY Fr 1222), θεοφόρια in Knossos (KN Ga 1058).

Further onwards in time, in the processional rituals of Byzantium and Western Europe – whether it is Renaissance Venice or Victorian England for example – a sense of continuing tradition may be intriguingly felt, a tradition which nourishes perhaps even modern manifestations of religion and politics.[20] On the other hand, resistance to established modes of power can also take the form of processional activity, as the numerous radical demonstrations suggest. Finally, evidence from completely different strands of tradition, from Muslim communities in the desert or from native communities in Sri Lanka for instance,[21] further confirms the ubiquity of processional performance and its power in the articulation of socio-political and religious life.

The need to perform processions is inseparably linked to the spatial co-ordinate of life. Space is a major parameter in the experience of the world, and the definition of a group, smaller or larger, is to a large extent dependent on the space at its disposal which enables its very existence. The procession demarcates space and symbolically appropriates it.[22] The group builds a relation to spatial environment and organizes space, but at the same time it organizes itself through the arrangement of the procession: in the space which is available to the community human relations are formed and power associations are manipulated and negotiated.[23] The procession can play, thus, an instrumental role in shaping the forces of social interaction, but the potential processional configurations and corresponding formations of relations are perhaps countless. The dynamics of human relations created in and through the procession can vary in accordance with a number of interrelated factors: the participants of the procession and their social roles and identities, the route chosen for the procession with its toponyms (place names), the order and composition of the procession and the participants' relative positions in it, the symbols or other narrative apparatuses used, its (possible) commemorative aspect, and finally its pragmatic dimension, that is the mode of interaction with onlookers.

The geographical and historical expansion of the ritual suggests that it does not have an intrinsic political character (monarchical, oligarchic, democratic or other). Power relations articulate and are articu-

---

[20] To offer a specimen only of related bibliography, I refer to Janin (1966), Muir (1981), Marin (1987), Gehring (1979).
[21] See Bechoffer (1988). Cf. Geertz (1981) (Indonesia).
[22] Cf. a late fourth-century decree from Kolophon (text and comments in Robert (1969)) in which territorial sovereignty is combined with an act of thanksgiving to the gods expressed in πρόσοδον καὶ θυσίαν.
[23] Cf. Connor's (1987) 47–9 hypothesis in relation to Solon's reforms.

lated by processions.[24] Processions mediate in their formation. The ritual, in other words, does not support or confirm an order of things but this order is shaped through and by ritual action.[25] It is from this point of view that processions are important in democratic Athens – not as an intrinsic democratic phenomenon, but as a field of political fermentation and an arena of contestable interests which may lead to new developments.

Processions and democratic politics in classical Athens

At the end of his study on Athenian processions Pfuhl concludes that Athenian processions differ from those of the rest of the Greek world.[26] The restricted comparative material, that Pfuhl provides,[27] cannot convince, and an overview of non-Attic material (such as Nilsson's work of 1906) proves that there is much correspondence and analogy in the rituals of the Greek poleis. As Parker has shown in relation to Spartan religion,[28] the ethos may change from place to place but the basic forms and structures of ritual remain the same. This is certainly true of processional ritual which occupied a prominent place in the festival calendar and life of all Greek poleis and which has indeed been suggested to have played an instrumental role in the formation of the Greek polis in general. According to de Polignac's model[29] the performance of public processions from the centre to the periphery (an extra-urban sanctuary) unified the social space and encouraged the integration of the social body which periodically reaffirmed its control over the territory. Although Athens originally seemed to be an exception to de Polignac's model due to the centripetal Panathenaic procession, recent studies have brought to the fore the history and significance of other centrifugal Athenian processions (like the Oschophoria and Skira processions, and most importantly the Eleusinian Mysteries) and have shown their crucial role in the shaping of Attic territory.[30] In Athens as in the other ancient cities, processions underlined the

---

[24] Concerning the relation of ritual and power: the one-way manipulation model has long been shed; scholars now talk about 'communication in two directions' (Connor (1987) 41), 'poetics of power' (Geertz (1981) 123), 'play of forms' or 'redemptive hegemony' (Bell (1992) 82, 84).
[25] For ritual as a shaping force see practice theory in general, and for a good exponent Bell (1992); my treatment of ritual owes much to her analysis.
[26] See Pfuhl (1900) 111.
[27] See Pfuhl (1900) 108–10.
[28] See Parker (1989).
[29] See de Polignac (1995).
[30] See Osborne (1994); Sourvinou-Inwood (1997a).

unity between the various points of the territory, radiating in multiple directions.

Pfuhl, however, (who explicitly connects Athenian processions with Athenian artistic innovation)[31] may have had a point which seems to find some support from the sources: Athenian processions *were* distinguished – not for their nature, however, but for their excellence: they were κάλλισται (most beautiful), πολυτελέσταται (most extravagant), σεμνόταται (most stately), ἱερώταται (most holy) (Ar. *Clouds* 307, [Pl.] *Alk.* 148e, [Xen.] *Ath.* 3.2, Plut. *Lyk.* 30). In general, the form and elements of a procession are the outcome of a double process: on the one hand, a procession is the product of a diachronic development which can be traced back to history, that is to the debts of tradition, to possible processes of cross-cultural fertilization and to other factors such as environmental conditions; on the other hand, there are the effects of synchronic preferences, events and current historical developments which give the ritual its final shape. The memorable Athenian processions were, in this latter sense, a product of Athenian democracy, and this fact recommends some reflection upon the relation that may have or could have existed between processional performances and the general socio-political atmosphere.

The Panathenaic festival has been characterized as a 'major political' celebration.[32] Such a characterization introduces modern distinctions, different from ancient perceptions, but still it is indicative of the significance of the feast for the Athenian polis, a feast which celebrates not only the patron deity of the city but also the very existence of the city in its present (fifth-century) form, that is the *synoikismos* (union into one city-state) of the Attic land. Within the context of the festival the procession was a focal point: its importance and popularity, obvious in the number of extant relevant sources, make it a good reference case,[33] although it must be noted that it shared many common features with processions in other πάνδημοι ἑορταί (public festivals), such as τὰ ἐν ἄστει Διονύσια (City Dionysia).

The Panathenaia, penteteric or annual, is a feast for the city and by the city. The procession is organized by state officials, by the *hieropoioi* or later by the *athlothetai*.[34] The space traced by the procession is the central axis of the polis, unifying in one movement the commercial,

---

[31] Pfuhl (190) 111.
[32] Cf. Bömer (1952) 1894: 'man darf die Panathenaia als die grosse politische ... Pompe bezeichnen'.
[33] For a historical reconstruction of the procession and the whole festival see Pfuhl (1900) 3–33, Deubner (1932) 22–35, Parke (1977) 33–50; for a recent comprehensive exposition see Neils (1992).
[34] See Sokolowski (1969) 33; *Const. Ath.* 54.6ff., 60.1.

political, historic and religious centre of the community: starting from the Dipylon Gate – a transitional point between the *asty* and the wider periphery – the procession crosses the Kerameikos, the commercial district (the most distinguished burial site outside the wall), moves across the multifunctional (commercial, cultural, political, religious[35]) centre of the agora, and along the Panathenaic way it reaches the Akropolis, the religious heart of the polis. Various locations are incorporated into the route which is not simply linear and unidirectional. We hear explicitly of the Eleusinion on the way to the Akropolis and of the Hermai in the Agora where dances take place;[36] the chain of interrelations between spatial foci is, thus, increased. The demarcation of public space is one aspect of the choice of the route. The other aspect is the success in stirring up the community which gathers in the agora at the centre of the city. The procession is, thus, a call to the community as a whole and stands in relation with the living and the natural environment.

At the same time, the body which forms the procession is no other than the civic body, the civic community. All ages and all sexes are represented in the procession, from the young *kanēphoroi* (basket-bearers) to the old *thallophoroi* (shoot-bearers). Most importantly, the whole population is represented, metics and citizens alike, and probably even slaves, who may have not participated in the procession, but who were probably there as *theatai* (spectators) in the agora.[37] Participation was also organized on an egalitarian basis: the *pompeis* (participants in the procession) were arranged in groups according to deme.[38] Even if the whole population did not process to the Akropolis, the majority attended the feast, by watching, dancing, and most importantly eating, consuming the large amounts of meat sacrificed in honour of the goddess and distributed to the people. This all-inclusive character is combined with an emphasis on beauty: the procession had to be ἀξιοθέατος (worth seeing, Xen. *Hipparch.* 3.1.2); the *kanēphoroi* – who could be numerous – were elaborately dressed, the *pompeia* (processional apparatus) were choice items, often of precious materials, and the participating old men were selected among the most

---

[35] Implying Olympian and chthonic and including the sphere of the dead.
[36] Route: Thuc. 6.56ff., Dem. 34.39, Paus. 1.2.14 et al.; archaeological evidence has confirmed the literary sources. Locations along the route and events: Xen. *Hipparch.* 3.2, Philostr. *VS* 2.1.5, Schol. Ar. *Knights* 566, Paus. 1.29.1; cf. Himer. 3.12.
[37] Metics in Athenian public *pompai*: Ael. *Var. Hist.* 6.1; Poll. 3.55, Harp. s.v. σκιαδηφόροι, σκαφηφόροι and μετοίκιον, Phot. s.v. σκάφας, σκαφηφορεῖν and ὑδριαφόροι, Hsch. s.v. σκαφηφόροι. Slaves: according to Bekker *Anec. Gr.* 1.242 they took part in the Panathenaia carrying an oak tree branch through the agora.
[38] At least in Sokolowski (1969) 33 B. (Cf. the arrangement of the public *ekphora* according to tribe: Thuc. 2.34).

handsome.[39] The long row of cavalry men and young hoplites increased the magnificence of the spectacle and intertwined beauty with power, while the musicians increased the overall aesthetic value of the procession with their melodies.[40]

This emphatic splendour in the manifestation of the whole social body (characteristic mainly of the Panathenaia but also of other major Athenian processions) may not relate simply to aesthetic preferences; an association with popular self-assertiveness emanating from the experience of the relatively young democracy may also carry some truth. If it is so, this association exists at counterpoint with the principle of hierarchy, which permeates the ordering of people, and with living aristocratic ideals: the *kanēphoroi* are daughters of noble Athenians and precede the daughters of metics who follow as *skiadēphoroi* (parasol-bearers) or *diphrophoroi* (stool-bearers);[41] the state officials precede in prominent positions and have a special share in the sacrificial animals (distinct from the majority),[42] and the priestess of Athena, receiving the procession on the Akropolis, comes from the *genos* of the Eteoboutadai. At the same time, the power of the public body, emphasized by the presence of troops among the participants, interacts with the power of the Athenian *archē* (hegemony, empire) manifested in the procession through the participation of embassies from the colonies and (from at least 425/4 BCE) the allies.[43] The interplay created is strong,[44] but still it is placed in a context with an all-inclusive dimension which moderates the structures of dominance. The *archē* is manifested and celebrated but the creators of the *archē*, the Athenian people, demesmen and metics, are also celebrated. Contrast Twain's concluding thoughts on the parade for Queen Victoria's Jubilee: 'the capitalist, the manufacturer, the merchant, and the workingmen' were not represented in the vast parade which 'suggested the material glories of the reign finely and

---

[39] Plural number of *kanēphoroi*: Sokolowski (1969) 33 B.15; Stratokles' decree in the *Life of Ten Orators* 852; dress: Roccos (1995). *Pompeia*: Thuc. 2.13.4, Andok. 4.13.4, Dem. 22.78, Paus. 1.29.16, Plut. *Alk.* 13, Philoch. ap. Harp. s.v. *Thallophoroi*: Ar. *Wasps* 540 with schol., Ar. *Ekkl.* 728ff., Xen. *Symp.* 4.17, Hsch. and Phot. s.v.
[40] Military bodies: Thuc. 6.56ff., Dem. 4.26 and 21.171ff., Xen. *Hipparch.* 3.2–5 and *Hipp.* 11.1–12. Musicians, mainly kitharists: Poll. 8. 113; cf. Haldane (1966) 99–101; Nordquist (1992) 144–54.
[41] See Ar. *Ekkl.* 728ff., *Birds* 1550ff., Ael. *Var. Hist.* 6.1.
[42] Mentioned in Sokolowski (1969) 33.
[43] Schol. Ar. *Clouds* 386, *IG* I^3 71; in *IG* I^3 14 cow and armour, the same in *IG* I^3 46.
[44] Osborne (1994a) has argued for an interplay between 'democracy and imperialism' in the sculptural programme of the Parthenon and especially in the relation of the Parthenon Frieze to its wider context; he takes the procession of the frieze to be that of the Panathenaia. More recently, with evidence from the iconography of processions, Neils (1996) has also supported the connection of the Parthenon frieze with the Panathenaic procession.

adequately. The *absence* [emphasis mine] of the chief creators of them was perhaps not a serious disadvantage.'[45]

At the Panathenaia the polis celebrates itself ἐν πομπεῖ, not in the form of a parade. There is much difference. As Lacey (*apud* Dunlop (1932) 21) has put it: 'a perambulation alone is not a procession: a procession means going somewhere to do something'. A parade implies demonstration for review or inspection.[46] A collectivity is arranged to file past spectators with the single purpose of being seen and inspected. At the end of the journey the parade reaches a point of dissolution at which the members disperse and disappear. The parade marches in order to impose, to make an impression – whatever that may be. The Red Square parades during the anniversary celebration of the October Revolution, or – to some extent – even the parade of the war orphans through the *orchēstra* in classical Athens (Isokr. *Peace* 82, Aischin. *In Ktes.* 154) are distinct from a *pompē*.

A procession like the Panathenaic one does indeed make an impression and attracts attention, but its main purpose is to form a relationship with the divine, an attempt which culminates at the end of the journey, the point at which a significant act – usually a sacrifice – is accomplished. The procession is an invitation for the attention of the superhuman,[47] and as such it admits an aspect of incompleteness in human society which first draws together, and then turns towards the divine for a meeting and a relationship[48] which is perceived to empower the society. By presenting itself, the marching community becomes a gift (δῶρον [Pl.] *Alk.* ii 148e) in which the god / hero rejoices (ἀγάλλεται Ar. *Peace* 399), or an ἀνάθημα (dedication), such as the *pompē* and sacrifice that the Orneatai dedicated to Delphi (Paus. 10.18.5).[49] The community ἀνάκειται τῷ θεῷ (is dedicated, offered to the god) because the whole community asks for the deity's reciprocal protection: πέμπηται ἡ πομπὴ παρεσκευασμένη ὡς ἄριστα τῇ Ἀθηνᾷ καθ' ἕκαστον τὸν ἐνιαυτὸν ὑπὲρ τοῦ δήμου τῶν Ἀθηναίων ('so that every year the procession is led arranged in the best way in honour of Athena for the sake of the Athenian people', Sokolowski (1969) 33 B. 3–5).

---

[45] *Apud* Merritt (1984) 182.
[46] Cf. Marin (1987) 222–4.
[47] Divine or heroic in ancient Greek culture. But I shall normally use 'divine' (or 'divinity' or 'deity') to imply both aspects in order to avoid repeating the disjunction 'divine/heroic'.
[48] Cf. the concrete vision of this meeting in Pind. *Nem.* 7.44–7 ἐχρῆν δέ τιν' ... ἡροΐαις δὲ πομπαῖς θεμισκόπον οἰκεῖν ἐόντα πολυθύτοις.
[49] For the votive character of many of the processional representations on vases, and in sculpture, see Lehnstaedt (1970) 137ff. who also discusses the 'Weihecharakter der *Pompe*'.

The procession, however, remains always an attempt. The community, hierarchically arranged, approaches the divinity but divine reciprocity cannot be guaranteed. Hekabe in the *Iliad* (6.286–311) led the Trojan women in supplication to Athena, but Pallas Athene denied their supplication (ἀνένευε Παλλὰς Ἀθήνη). As a result the community perished, Hekabe and the royal family included. This is a different equality achieved through the procession, an equality in impotence before omnipotence, a democracy in which the power of the demos lies in the potential of the communal movement to gain favour for all.

At the same time, the procession is itself a manifestation of divine authority. Divine power is inscribed upon the community, as the various symbols carried along suggest. While moving, the community is already under the influence of the deity. Unlike the parade, the procession does not only seek to impose but is already imposed, does not only lead but is also led – a *pompē*, both actively and passively charged.

The procession, thus, establishes a reciprocal or double relation of call and response. The procession is articulated as a response *to* the authority of the divine but it articulates at the same time a call *for* the response of the divine. The directions of this double movement may receive different emphasis according to the occasion. Cases of *eisagōgē* (introduction) emphasize the presence or rather entry and action of the divinity which calls for the reaction of the community.[50] Sacrificial processions emphasize the approach and call of the community. But both sides are there in any case and support the formation of a relationship, whenever an opportunity is given either on the occasion of major public festivals or on a number of other occasions which might not have attracted more than the minimum group of religious officials but which were still necessary for the preservation of reciprocity.[51] In other cases, the processional performance and the relation aimed at could serve the interests of sub-groups within the city. Extant votive offerings, for example, depict families hierarchically presented in front of the divinity,[52] a response to and an invitation for a relationship with the deity. Set against this background of less conspicuous and less wide-ranging processional performances, the public festival emerges as a synthesis of all these different interests and attempts, a natural culmination of common experiences and needs, and not simply as an isolated sensational performance.

[50] See (e.g.) the introduction of Asklepios in 420/19 BCE: *IG* II² 4960; and the *eisagōgē* of Dionysos from Eleutherai: Paus. 1.38.8; Schol. Ar. *Ach*. 243 (cf. the annual celebration of the εἰσαγωγὴ ἀπὸ τῆς ἐσχάρας: Pickard-Cambridge (1988) 60).
[51] Cf. Jameson's paper in this volume.
[52] See Van Straten (1992) 274–81, (1995) 60–1 and *passim*.

To unite all interests, to encompass all is itself a success of the 'dialogue' articulated through and by the procession, a 'dialogue' which operates on two levels, human and divine. If the success of the operation on the divine level cannot be taken for granted, neither can it be taken on the human level. Individual interests can press with counteraction. The unidirectional movement and purpose of the procession enhances solidarity but cannot create it without a basis of common benefit.[53] As with divine reciprocity, so with human interaction the processional performance is an open procedure; it cannot secure an integrative result.

The establishment of fifth-century democracy is itself marked by one failure and one success in the 'dialogue' or reciprocity attempted by processional performance conducted in the heart of the city. In late sixth century at the Great Panathenaia of 514 BCE the tyrant Hipparchos was executed by the so-called *tyrannoktonoi* (tyrant-slayers); the murder was carried out while Hippias (who was the original target) διεκόσμει ὡς ἕκαστα ἐχρῆν τῆς πομπῆς προϊέναι ('arranged the order in which the several parts of the procession should move forward', Thuc. 6.56ff.; cf. Hdt. 5.56). Whatever the reasons for the murder, obviously there was no basis for unity. The schism broke out at the moment when an attempt at oneness took place. It was some time after this schism that social reform was introduced. In contrast to the *tyrannoktonia*, at the end of the fifth century reparations for the disruption of democracy by the Thirty were conducted through processional ritual (Xen. *Hell.* 2.4.39–40, Lys. 13.80–1).[54] The exiled democrats after their victory at Peiraieus are able to enter the *asty* again. Unity has not yet been achieved but after the defeat of the Thirty the climate is good for an attempt at reintegration. They decide to enter in procession which – like the Panathenaic procession – reaches the Akropolis and offers sacrifice to Athena. After the *charisteria* to the goddess, the democrats call an *ekklēsia* where the power of *logos* completes the attempt. Democracy is re-instituted and normality is reintroduced after a period of *anomia* and *asebeia* (lawlessness and impiety).

In the last example the combination of procession and speech in one sequence makes more explicit the 'discourse' conditions[55] that

---

[53] Cf. Bell (1992) 221f.
[54] On this episode cf. also Strauss (1985) 69–72.
[55] 'Discourse' conditions and not simply discourse: I would like to dissociate myself from models which see ritual as a kind of language only and imply a dichotomy between thought and action. Practice theory has castigated this dichotomy and talks about the creation of a 'ritual environment' and a 'ritual body' through the repetition of ritual (Ortner (1984) 144–66, Bell (1992) 98–114).

processional performance helps establish. With the entry of the democrats a new interactive process started which eventually led to transformation and re-stabilization. Interaction implies call and response, action and re-action; both sides are equally important in the process.[56] But for the new interactive process *to start*, it is essential that the possibility of entering and setting up a performance is open. During the Thirty no entry of new forces was allowed, in an effort to control environment and discourse; in a similar manner, the tyrants (especially Hippias), exercising their power to arrange and control the people, met with counter action which led to the possibility of introduction of new measures. The possibility of entering and performing means the possibility of *new* conditions of contact (especially when the body entering is a foreign collective body), which *may* lead to some change. Creating the opportunity to receive and the potential to gather and attend new performances implies (and presupposes) an openness that only a broad socio-political perspective can establish and endure. In Athens the gradual development of such conditions of openness enabled the establishment of an institution[57] – the dramatic festivals – which at regular periods permitted a collectivity to enter a public space processionally and to set up a public performance and dialogue with the community. This newly emerged possibility is probably what most closely relates processional performance with Athenian democracy, and what brings in the third parameter of the relation, the theatrical performance.

With the establishment and development of the new institution, processional performances are ultimately built into a new, more complicated performative context. They continue to address the community, but at the same time they enter a new type of interaction with the standard processional practice of public life. In the new theatrical context the performers do not come from outside but from within the community. They perform, however, having first departed from their ordinary identity: the ritually disguised performers hint at the community (or part of it) being already in the process of trans- (or trance) formation, incarnating others and the Other, hiding themselves under masks which – resembling the dead – rise up to educate the living with experience from a world beyond.

To attempt to establish new conditions and interrelations through

---

[56] I shall explore the importance of reaction in my discussion of Ar. *Birds* below.
[57] It is important to stress that Athens was the first to *establish* dramatic performances. There are traces of early dramatic performances in other parts of the Greek world (see Stoessl (1987) 58–115), but only Athens institutionalized theatre at that time.

ritual (and particularly processional) performance is of significance: processional performance is not simply communication; rather it is something more or other than communication:[58] it involves and targets a new or renewed body, movement, way of life and rhythm of life; the ritual procession affects body and environment, it addresses all senses, it activates both cerebral hemispheres; through traditional movements, symbols and songs, it stirs up memories, shapes and figures of the past living into the present, an evocation of presence and absence at the same time.

Processions in Athenian drama[59]

To perform processions in the theatre is both close to and far from observing the ritual in a non-theatrical context. Familiar schemes and patterns operate, and general structuring principles govern the theatrical enactment, but the theatrical examples are often variations of, accretions to or contrasts to the general pattern; the familiar model forms the background against which the theatrical cases operate. More importantly, the relations shaped through and by the ritual are extraordinary: they involve direct contacts between divinities, humans and heroes of a past era and create power adjustments of a different order. For this reason direct analogies or parallels with processions outside drama could lead to simplifications or even misjudgements concerning the interpretation of the plays and especially their relation to political power outside. Even in such a well-known case as the end of Aischylos' *Eumenides* the generally accepted connection of the enacted ritual with one particular historical festival, namely the Panathenaia, is on the one hand restricted to a few features only,[60] and on the other risks obscuring some important facts about the dramatic situation.

In the third play of the Aischylean trilogy the main issue is not simply the acquittal of Orestes but the dynamics of superhuman power: divine action and its conflicting results for human life encapsulated in

---

[58] Practice theory has found the notion of communication problematic (Bourdieu (1977) 106, 120, 156; cf. Rappaport (1979) 202–4) and stresses that ritual is something other than linguistic communication.

[59] Many aspects pertaining to this issue, as well as points made above, are discussed in much greater detail in my forthcoming book based on my doctoral dissertation which had the title ΠΟΜΠΑΙ: *Processions in Athenian Tragedy*.

[60] The analogy has been overstressed since Headlam's (1906) interpretation of the φοινικόβαπτα ἐσθήματα as characteristic of the metics in the Panathenaic ceremony. But the role of the metics and the colour of their chitons is attested generally ἐν ταῖς πομπαῖς, and not only in the Panathenaic one (e.g. Poll. 3.55, Harp. s.v. σκαφηφόροι, Suda s.v. ἀσκοφορεῖν).

Orestes' deliverance and the ensuing danger for Athens. With the arrangement of the procession (1003ff.)[61] a re-ordering of powers has been completed and a balance of divine powers has been achieved and can be made manifest.[62] It is this balance which may arouse expectations of positive consequences for the human community. Framed by both celestial and chthonic powers, the procession provides some assurance for the protection of the human community. In this context the role of Athena and Athens proves to be crucial not only for the ordering of human relations but also for the reconstitution of cosmic powers. It is this *cosmic* balance which guarantees and indirectly confirms the salvation of both Orestes and Athens.

In the new order Olympians retain the primary role, represented by Athena who leads (1003, 1022). The Erinyes, associated throughout the trilogy with death and blood, receive their place in the procession as 'metics' (1011), honoured but in a way also subordinated, or at least dependent. Athena herself, however, sees the need to contain the power of the Erinyes and makes them part of the body of society (embracing gods, men and nature) as represented emblematically in the procession. The Erinyes and generally the power associated with death prove to be necessary for the stability of society, and their proper acknowledgement in a wider hierarchical order renders benefits. In the procession this order receives its first material formation and opens up the possibility of positive reciprocity.

The hierarchical order in this procession has hardly anything to do with the hierarchical order of a historical panathenaic procession. In the historical case hierarchies are arranged according to a temporary dominant scheme of social human powers. In the theatrical world the procession articulates a model of power relations among cosmic powers diachronically influencing human communities. The balance created has a much wider potential range and consequence than any immediate historical schema. A topical relevance, however, is also incorporated in the theatrical spectacle which gives the Erinyes the position of metics and includes the Areopagites as the human escort to the Erinyes (1010–11). The characterization of the Erinyes as 'metics'

---

[61] For the problems relating to the composition of the procession see Sommerstein (1989) *ad* 1021–47. A detailed reconstruction is not necessary for my argument here; suffice to say that Athena must be at the head and the Erinyes at the back of the procession according to Athena's instructions in the play.

[62] Earlier in the play a sharp and unbridgeable distinction was drawn between chthonic and Olympian divinities: on this issue cf. Sidwell (1996) 48–9. Lebeck (1971) 142 observes that the prologue, referring to the harmonious union between old gods and new, prefigures the play's resolution.

(1011) and the Areopagites as ἀστῶν τὰ βέλτατα (the best of the citizens, 487), may encourage an interrelation between cosmic (poetic) hierarchies and social (historical) hierarchies. More important than the term 'metics', however, – which is metaphorical and is in some instances replaced by terms meaning residents or citizens (ξυνοικήτωρ 833, ξυνοικίαν 916, γαμόρῳ 890) – seems to be the inclusion of the human representatives in the wider cosmic schema of the procession. Both as dikasts and as representatives of the whole Athenian people (λεώς 638, 681), the inclusion of the Areopagites[63] brings the social dimension into the spectacle but does not wholly impose it. It mainly supports the creation of an interplay between historicity and transcendence which gives the scene its power and effect, both synchronic and diachronic. But it is an interplay (let it be stressed), and its significance as such should not be lost in favour of a panathenaic or any other narrow, regional connection.

Cases such as this scene provide an insight into the complicated texture of ancient drama which is neither a reproduction of the scenario of a standard myth nor a reflection of reality. Through an activation of traditional ritual patterns of the past, ancient theatre articulates visions, dreams or even experiences of the present, which cannot be otherwise articulated, and opens up visionary possibilities for the future. The ἀστικὸς λεώς (people of the city, 997) in its totality (cf. 1025ff.), in the play and outside, now and then, can move to prosperity under the guidance of the divine *pompos* (escort) and in the middle of a balancing cosmic structure. The ritual draws this potential benefit for all, which comes from a collective *syntaxis* with the divine but which still requires and remains a collective appeal: εὐφαμεῖτε πανδαμεί ('auspicious words, all you people', 1038).[64] If something receives some affirmation in the play it is this relation with the divine order, and the potential of rituals to shape it, even though not to guarantee it.

Obviously, even such a 'clear' or 'easy' case as the *Eumenides* resists attempts at drawing simple connection lines. More importantly, it does not support a simple viewing of an affirmative or subversive relation to an external reality. The polarity 'affirmation – subversion' itself fails to

---

[63] The procession includes Athena's *prospoloi* too (1024); but I emphasize the Areopagites because they are repeatedly called λεώς, Ἀττικὸς λεώς, πολισσοῦχοι etc. (see 638, 681, 1010); the context makes it explicit that the *dikastai* are described. For the arguments against a crowd of extras besides the Jurors see Taplin (1977) 394 and 412.

[64] Cf. also the wish for *euphrosyne* which aims at the prevalence of the positive side, a result achieved mutually: εὔφρονας εὔφρονες (992), ὑπ' εὔφρονι πομπᾷ (1034), ἵλαοι καὶ εὐθύφρονες (1040). Moreover, while the Erinyes sing blessings, Athena replies with warnings (921ff.).

Processional performance and the polis 309

do justice to the tragic perspective.[65] Instead of giving 'yes' or 'no' answers, ancient theatre (and especially its ritual structures) seems to delineate more the 'how';[66] and this is ultimately what performance is about: not static appearance, but active procedure, operation – procession or progression in time and space if you like. The workings or operations of ritual in the theatre, however, are rather unpredictable: they can surprise with the variety of directions that they can take, even if these directions follow well-trodden patterns. Euripides' *Bakchai* will serve as an example.

It has often been remarked that the main action in the *Bakchai* follows the festival pattern, that is *pompē, thysia, agōn*.[67] The processional structure, however, is not only introduced at a climactic point in the play (965ff.), but it forms its very beginning: a group of religious worshippers led by the god himself enter the city in order to introduce the rites of the god (55–167). Their *parodos* is a processional *eisodos* (entry) and a processional performance which seeks to interact with the community: τίς ὁδῷ, τίς ὁδῷ; τίς/ μελάθροις; ('who is in the road? who in the road? who in the palace?', 68f.).[68] With their dances and songs through the city the choros announces and manifests the rites and calls the community to respond. The arrival of the choros and their guide signals the entry or the intervention of a new force into Thebes; the rest of the play will explore the effect, worked through performance, that this force can cause.

At first instance, the coming of the group and their leader seems to have no strong impact. There is no collective response to their call, an indication of the unusual situation at Thebes. It provokes, however, the reaction and resistance of the king (233ff.). Pentheus' reaction both

---

[65] The social functions of the performative process in general are much debated not only among classicists but much more among anthropologists and sociologists. The answers given tend to move along the lines of the polarity mentioned. Anthropologists usually see performance as reinforcing the cultural givens in traditional societies; see e.g. Turner (1982) 20–60. Classicists often debate the democratic or aristocratic ideals of the theatre (see below p. 313 and n. 83). Goldhill (1990) has argued for ambiguity and a de-stabilizing force in tragedy. The on-going debate suggests that monolithic answers cannot apply. Recently Easterling (1997) 28 has judiciously urged that we should 'accept that right from the start the plays will have been open to very diverse political readings'; see generally there her treatment of the interplay between the heroic ambience and fifth century socio-political issues in tragedy.

[66] The shift from the 'what' to the 'how', from the 'essence' of a culture to its praxis is one aspect of the great popularity of the performance perspective in many cultural fields; see Carlson (1996) 191–7. Cf. George (1989) for an approach to similar attitudes from a post-modern perspective.

[67] See (e.g.) Foley (1985) 205–18 referring to earlier bibliography.

[68] Cf. Dodds (1960) *ad loc.*; cf. also Seaford (1996) 37–9 (the ritual background of processional movements in historical festivals).

differentiates from and represents the community. Even if Thebes has been struck by Dionysos' influence, at the beginning of the play the community as a whole has not recognized the god, the king resists, no conditions of positive reciprocity exist.[69] The group of foreign women and the stranger arrive in order to revert the situation – through ritual performance, direct contact and exchange. Even if resisting at first, Pentheus is gradually drawn into an agreement with the stranger, which at the crucial point leads to the formation of a *pompē* (912–76, cf. 1046f.). With the *pompē* the *peripeteia* is under way. In the procession the balance of power changes; the god is the *pompos* (965, 1047), the leader and dominant figure to whom Pentheus has surrendered both identity (by putting on the maenad's dress, 915) and power to control movement and route. Obviously, power relations have changed but Pentheus has played a role in that with his willingness to be led by the stranger. It is a degree of *complicity* on his part that made this change possible.

The god receives the position of the *pompos*, the position that divine supremacy justifies and that is traditionally ascribed to divinities: not only as recipients but also as leaders of human communities like Athena in the *Eumenides* (1022) or Apollo in the hymn (*h. Ap.* 514–16 ἦρχε δ' ἄρα σφιν ἄναξ Διὸς υἱὸς Ἀπόλλων ... οἱ δὲ ῥήσσοντες ἕποντο, 'and the lord Apollo, son of Zeus, showed them the way ... and they followed'). The beneficial leading role of the divinity, however, presupposes honorific acknowledgement and a relation of positive reciprocity. In the *Eumenides* the Erinyes participate in the procession only after such a common basis has been established. Pentheus, on the contrary, enters on false premises. Isolated from the community and looking for his own satisfaction, Pentheus enters a relationship which fails to serve either a personal or a communal interest. If Pentheus seems to be tyrannical, it is also because he fails to build a relationship with Dionysos in the interest of his people.[70]

Or so it is from one side. Because by participating in the *pompē* of the god, Pentheus is consecrated to the god,[71] becomes a follower and victim of the god,[72] participant in the god's *theōria* (cf. 1047).[73]

---

[69] There are indications that the male community of Thebes gradually changes (196, 441–51, 721, 770) and Pentheus becomes almost isolated in his rejection.

[70] Cf. Seaford (1996) 47f.

[71] Already expressed at the preparations for the *pompē*: σοὶ γὰρ ἀνακείμεσθα 934 with Dodds (1960) and Seaford (1996) *ad loc.* Cf. Eur. *Herakl.* 601: the *parthenos* moves to sacrifice and Iolaos admits that her body κατῆρκται.

[72] For Pentheus' death perceived, from different angles, as a sacrificial killing see for instance Dodds (1960) xxvii–viii, Seidensticker (1979) Burkert (1983) 176–8, Seaford (1996) 39–44 and *passim*.

[73] Participant in the viewing of the god (924), in the *theōria* procession and in the *theōria* (viewing, spectacle) on Mt Kithairon (1047). On the term *theōria* and its ancient (relating to *theos*) and modern (relating to *thea*) etymology see Boesch (1908) 1f.

Processional performance and the polis

Through Pentheus the power of the god can be viewed and experienced. It is Pentheus' reaction and final submission, his participation in the *theōria*, which mediates in the collective re-orientation of Thebes towards Dionysos (at the great cost of the royal family who originally failed – with their resistance – to mediate in the relation of the polis with the divine).

The fact that the *pompē* is a *theōria* is important.[74] *Theōriai* were regularly organized, especially on the occasion of major panhellenic festivals, such as the Delia.[75] Representative groups *(theōroi* or *theōriai)*[76] from the various poleis would be officially sent to the celebrating centre in order to participate in the festivities; as a typical act of homage, they would arrive in procession and offer solemn sacrifice.[77] More widely, they would participate in all activities and events which would honour and 'commemorate' the god (μνησάμενοι *h. Ap.* 150). The term and practice of *theōria* aligns most closely the aspect of viewing with participation: watching the *heortē*, seeing what was taking place, meant actually participating in the *heortē*. In the Homeric hymn to Apollo the epitome of the festival is given in a picture which insists on the aspect of viewing: the god participates as a pleased spectator[78] and the human participants strive to delight him with their spectacle (ἐπιτέρπεαι, τέρπουσι *h. Ap.* 146, 150).[79] To a human spectator, the human celebrants would also seem to participate in divine nature in this panegyric context: φαίη κ' ἀθανάτους καὶ ἀγήρως ἔμμεναι αἰεὶ / ὅς τότ' ἐπαντιάσει' ὅτ' Ἰάονες ἀθρόοι εἶεν ('whoever comes upon the Ionians, when they are gathered, might think they were forever immortal and ageless', *h. Ap.* 152–3). The conditions which allow such a positive rapprochement of the human and the divine sphere are based on mutual benefit and pleasure;[80] the *theōria* of the festival means participation in joy, in sharing in enjoyment along with the god (*h. Ap.* 146–73). In the *Bakchai*, the *theōria* procession also leads to a 'festival', to the viewing of

---

[74] On *theōria* generally see Ziehen (1934). Seaford (1996) on 1047 has to accept that for the classical period the term *theōria* is associated with processions and that the *theōria* of mystic viewing is known only from late texts.

[75] On *theōria* processions see Nilsson (1951) 167f.

[76] On the meaning of the word *theōros* in ancient Greek see Boesch 1908, 5f.; he concludes that the word has two principal associations: (a) with viewing, (b) with religious office.

[77] For an example see the information on the Delia in Thuc. 3.104. A vivid picture of the arrival of a Delian *theōria*: Plut. *Nik.* 3.5–6 τήν τε πομπήν τῷ θεῷ καὶ τὸν χορὸν ἄγων (sc. Nikias) κεκοσμημένον πολυτελῶς καὶ ᾄδοντα διὰ τῆς γεφύρας ἀπεβίβαζε.

[78] The god may also participate as *synchoreutes* in the midst of the human community, according to Plato *Laws* 654a, 665a.

[79] Cf. Lonsdale (1993) 51–72.

[80] Cf. for a different festival occasion Pindar fr. 94b. 3–4 ἥκει γὰρ ὁ Λοξίας πρόφρων ἀθανάταν χάριν Θήβαις ἐπιμείξων.

and participation in conditions manifesting and celebrating divine (and particularly Dionysiac) power. Already by donning the maenad's dress and joining the *pompē*, Pentheus starts having visions of Dionysos' 'other' nature (920–2). But for the formation of the *pompē* (and the participation in the *theōria*) no basis of positive reciprocity would have existed, so it led to an experience not of the beneficial but of the tremendous, negative power of the divine.

The procedure which allows this experience is 'viewing', *theōria*, implying and incorporating all the possible vantage points: viewing the worshippers from the point of view of the divinity, viewing the divinity among the worshippers, viewing the worshipping community as divine or 'other' and recognizing the power of the divine. Whichever the perspective (and there may be many more), each has its own value, and it is this evaluation of viewing which makes the action – the performance – of the performers (divine or human agents or other) also valuable. The multiplicity of viewing points should check any attempts to give an easy assessment of Dionysiac activity in the play. If the rites on Mt Kithairon reveal the wildness of the god, there are also the rites of the choros, the foreign women who arrived at Thebes in order to introduce the god's worship. Throughout the play the choros continue their performance, establishing in the midst of Thebes a distinct mode of Dionysiac performance which may not be part of the *theōria* on Mt Kithairon (though intertwined with it in 977–1023), but which is part of the *theōria* in the theatre. The choros' singing and dancing brings forth complementary sides and aspects of the god and stands in interaction with other events in the play,[81] complicating the *theōria* of the audience. Moreover, while the choros observing the rites of the god remain intact, the royal family and the world of Thebes are heavily tormented under the influence of the god.

How would the interaction of all these sides be seen and appreciated, and what possible connections with the world of the audience could be made? Recently, the destruction of the royal family and the establishment of public rites has been seen as a procedure instrumental for the generation of the polis and for the operation of the democratic polis in particular;[82] in other words, the subversion in the play could function as an affirmation of the collective values of the polis community. This may well be so. But the complicated interaction of performances in the play may leave or create some room for further qualifications. How

---

[81] Cf. Seaford (1996) 28–30.
[82] See Seaford (1994) and Seaford (1996) 44–52, with support from Aristotle' remark *Pol.* 1319b25.

would the role of and cost for the royal family be evaluated in this procedure for example?[83] Instead of seeking single answers or even instead of insisting upon such questions, it may be worth concentrating on the power of the play to illuminate the way in which a given situation may be formed, transformed or reformed through the same performative means which strategically applied, or interpreted, can lead to varied, and always fluid, results.

To illustrate this composite potential of ritual performance and to end with a comic note, I shall give a brief example from comedy.

Aristophanes' *Birds* closes with a great ceremony celebrating the return of Peisetairos[84] from Olympos. After the end of the 'Gigantomachy'[85] which he successfully conducted against the gods, he confirms his power by taking the symbols of Zeus' power and by receiving Zeus' (fictitious) daughter Basileia as wife; victorious and proud for having taken the heir to Zeus' throne in marriage – a marriage which legitimates control over the heritage – he returns and enters *Nephelokokkygia* in a glorious wedding procession, ultimately effecting and displaying the beginning of his sovereignty. Before he comes in, a *kēryx* announces and describes his coming (οἷος οὔτε παμφαὴς/ ἀστὴρ ἰδεῖν ἔλαμψεν... 'no all-shining star has ever gleamed in such a way', 1709–17) and asks the Birds' community to receive him (δέχεσθε 1708). He comes in and the Birds give him not simply a hero's but a god's welcome. Literally: as Kleinknecht argued long ago, this is the first detailed literary example of an *apotheosis*[86] which is a phenomenon associated mostly with the Hellenistic and Roman times. According to Kleinknecht's linguistic analysis the scene abounds in cultic and hymnetic linguistic formulae which actually recur in the extant descriptions of the apotheosis of Hellenistic and Roman rulers. As Kleinknecht has noticed, however, the formulae used are not novel inventions of Hellenistic and later times which Aristophanes here, as if in a visionary way, anticipates; they are well-known traditional patterns, established and used in the context of divine and heroic cult of the archaic and classical times, and especially characteristic of divine epiphanies. They are transposed here – for the first time according to

---

[83] For an evaluation of the role of noble families in tragedy in relation to the persistence of aristocratic ideals see Griffith (1995).

[84] The *paradosis* is almost unanimous on the form *Peisthetairos*; *Peisetairos* is an emendation (and for the reasons see Dunbar (1995) 128f.). I use it only because it has become standard in English bibliography but I feel sympathy with Kakrides' scepticism (Kakrides (1987) on 644).

[85] On the mythical patterns behind the *Birds* see Hofmann (1976) 79–90; Bowie (1993) 152–66; for a concise exposition Dunbar (1995) 7–9.

[86] Kleinknecht (1937) 297.

the extant sources – to a different context in which a human, and not a heroic or divine figure, is honoured. The kinaesthetic dimension, which has not been explored by the German scholar but is crucial for the effect of both the ritual and the scene, reveals another side: Peisetairos' entry is modelled upon and develops traditional patterns of processional movements – employed in victorious and wedding contexts but also substantially connected with the divine and heroic world – which have been here reworked and recombined to enable the reception of a human with superhuman honours – the standard processional pattern of entries of rulers, kings and emperors of later times.

The procession performed is both victorious and bridal. This pairing is usual, and a good parallel example is the Hesiodic fragment 211M–W relating Peleus' return to Phthia with the spoils from the sack of Iolkos and with a wife. The wedding processions, as well as the victory celebrations, were occasions on which – contrary to sacrificial examples – the distinction of an individual (or a couple) was brought forward.[87] The exaggerated μακαρισμοί (blessings) attested in the Hesiod fragment mentioned above, or the likening of Hektor and Andromache to gods during their wedding procession (ἴκελοι θεοῖς Sapph. 44.23L–P, cf. Sapph. 111L–P) suggest a similar atmosphere. In this case, however, the tendencies of the ritual are taken to an extreme (a comic extreme) in which metaphors and similarities are presented as identities. In the enacted *hymenaios*, for example, the mythological paradigm prevails at the expense of other traditional features, e.g. the praise to the bride. This emphasis can hardly fail to suggest an association between Zeus' and Hera's *hieros gamos* and the new divine couple.[88] In this context the bridegroom is presented as if in the place of a god. His promotion becomes the focus of the scene and the song. Prominent wedding symbols, such as torches, are completely played down, while his symbols of triumph, that is the thunderbolt, the thunder and the lightning, receive particular attention (1744–52). The extended praise to these attributes and to Peisetairos' power is also contrasted to the very brief acclamation to the bride (just line 1724), although she normally has a large (perhaps the larger) share of praise.[89] It is apparent that in the enacted wedding it is not the couple (as it should be), but the human partner, Peisetairos, who becomes exceedingly elevated, in an effort to subject the marital to the triumphant side of the ritual.

---

[87] But always in the context of a wider cosmic hierarchy; for the wedding see Oakley and Sinos (1993) 28–30 and *passim* (also figs. 64, 65); for the victory celebration see below.
[88] Cf. also Hofmann (1976) 152–3.
[89] See Sappho frgs. 105, 107, 108, 114, 116 and 117L–P; Theokr. 18; Cat. 61 and 62.

Like the wedding ritual, victory celebrations of archaic and classical times were also centred around a processional movement in which the distinguished person held a prominent position.[90] Songs and acclamations created a jubilant atmosphere, and the τήνελλα καλλίνικε (*tēnella*, the noble victor) refrain would bring forward the mythological prototype of victors, the hero Herakles.[91] An association between Peisetairos and Herakles, who received apotheosis after death for his help in the Gigantomachy and his life of *ponos* (toil), has indeed been detected in the pattern of the *Birds*. Yet, unlike Herakles, who while in life referred his victories to Zeus and the other gods[92] and who was received in Olympos only after death, and unlike ordinary human victory celebrations which were also placed within the context of a divine or heroic act of worship (an *anathēsis*, or a sacrifice),[93] Peisetairos celebrates his triumph without any reverence to the gods but rather replacing the gods. Having won not an *agōn* with human rivals but a true *theomachia*, he ends up in a ceremony in which all songs, ritual symbols, and smells are returned to Peisetairos and to his newly-acquired attributes. His entry is announced with a formula typical of divine epiphanies (1708): δέχεσθε τὸν τύραννον ὀλβίοις δόμοις ('welcome the king to the blessed palace').[94] The traditional response is approval; and he secures it. So he enters as a victorious super-god in a *hieros gamos* which promotes his distinction and which commences his era – a true triumph! All, of course, happen in the context of a utopia in which the triumphant hero is an old and ugly bird-man, the receiving community are birds and the sovereign city is a 'Cloud-cuckoo-land' suspended in the air between heaven and earth. The ridicule and implausibility of the context justify the comedy of the epiphanic triumph, but it is the *way* in which this triumph is achieved that interests us here.

---

[90] For artistic representations see Webster (1972) 152–7, Valavanis (1991).
[91] The honorific *prosphonesis* of Herakles in Archil. fr. 324W; its use in Olympia: e.g. Pind. *Ol.* 9.1–4; cf. Buhmann (1972) 53–6.
[92] See Pind. *Ol.* 10.35–39; Pind. fr. 140a; Soph. *Trach.* 237–8, 754.
[93] E.g. Pind. *Ol.* 9.112, *Nem.* 5.53 and Schol. ad loc.; cf. Blech (1982), 114; Kall. fr. 384.35–9; Ath. 8.610a; cf. Pickard-Cambridge (1962) 37–8. Νίκη or νῖκαι leading animals to sacrifice: see *LIMC* s.v. *Nikē* nos. 340–3.
[94] Cf. the cry δέχεσθε τὰν θεόν which accompanies the appearance of the statue of the divinity in Kallimachos *Hymn* 5. 137–8. Cf. also Sophokles' cultic epithet Dexion for having accepted Asklepios (*TrGF* 4. T 69). In cases of epiphanies the subject of δέχεσθε is the human community. But in the double process of call and response shaped by the procession (see above, p. 303) the address can be reversed: from the community to the deity/ hero. As such the δέξαι motif is a well-known hymnal convention which is recurrent in Pindaric poetry, especially (but not only) when the god (sanctuary or altar) is the destination of the *kōmos*: see Heath (1988) 190. Cf. also δέχνυσο θυηπολίην in Heliod. 3.2.3; for the antiquity of the tradition see also Wilamowitz (1932) 2.354.

The triumph ascribed to Peisetairos is owed not only to his action but also to the receiving community's re-action, their willingness to confer honour upon him. The positive reaction of the choros is prominently reflected in the bridal song which includes a repeated emphasis on the benefits for the new polis and the race (γένος) of the bird (1725–8). The potential effects that a marriage could have on the community seem to have been an issue taken seriously under consideration, and the occasion on which the community could express its view was the wedding procession. The whole point in the presentation of this procession is to provoke and hence to display the affirmative communal reaction which is a measure of the honour of the new 'ruler' and a proof of the comic hero's triumph.

The community's reaction is the ultimate target of the processional ritual and a major purpose for its performance not only in this scene but also on all relevant occasions in ordinary (non-theatrical) life. In cases of divine *eisagōgai* or epiphanies, as in those of weddings and victories, a new agent is to be introduced into the community; the introduction of a new power or a new affiliation may be taken as a threat to established relations and balance of power. The introduction is thus attempted in a processional mode so that, on the one hand, the transition is facilitated, and, on the other, the invitation to the community and the interaction may win the community's reception and not rejection.[95] The community's reaction is both constitutive and indicative of the power and position of the new agent in the new community. The conditions for Peisetairos' entry are prepared, thus, in such a way that a positive contact is achieved and a glorious welcome is organized.

The collective response which Peisetairos receives is not the product of an instant moment, but the outcome of a long procedure. Already at the beginning of the play Peisetairos has used the power of speech to persuade (εἰ πίθοισθέ μοι 'if you would trust me', 163; 465ff.) the Birds to accept him and to secure his position and role among them mainly by promising the increase of their power. At the end of the play, when the unexpected (and utopic) has been achieved, the Birds attribute their power to the seemingly all-powerful. And although just before the *exodos* the Birds, more in their identity as *choreutai*, reassure the audience that in Attica ἡ γλῶττα χωρὶς τέμνεται ('the tongue is always cut away', 1705), in *Nephelokokkygia* Peisetairos – having first won over the Birds with rhetoric and having been publicly proclaimed *tyrannos* –

---

[95] Otherwise the community may suffer from reciprocal violence: see e.g. the case of the victor Oibotas of Dyme: Paus. 6.3.8; 7.17.6–7; the aition for the *phallephoria*: Schol. Ar. *Ach.* 243.

Processional performance and the polis 317

enters with the most wholehearted approval of the Birds! Does not his success deserve a good feasting, having flown away (ἀνεπτόμεσθα 35) from trials (40–2) and from borrowers (115–16),⁹⁶ acquired wings (655, 801–5), thrown away Athens' profit-makers and parasites (903–1057, 1337–469) and even (almost)⁹⁷ overthrown Zeus? The play ends with an all-inclusive *panegyris* after the utopian success of the old man who resists, overthrows and affirms all negative tendencies inherent in contemporary Athenian society and whose action – to reverse established privileges and hierarchies and to acquire power – both nourishes and problematizes dreams and aspirations of his (and others') age.

Social phenomena have roots which turn both backwards and forwards. Past debts are easier to discern, although in this case they are skilfully interwoven in the multiple interplay of motifs in the concluding scene. Apart from general echoes of *tyrannis* (1708),⁹⁸ the specific mode of Peisetairos' entry involves a political parody which gives the scene a distinct tone: a 'play' of evocations of Peisistratos' second coming to Athens, known mainly through Herodotos 1.60.⁹⁹ As in Peisistratos' case, Peisetairos returns escorted by a daughter of Zeus in a way of divine epiphany; Peisistratos' entry was a trick (μηχάνημα) and Peisetairos' success was based largely on his trickery and mainly on his trick to found a birds' city.¹⁰⁰ For his return Peisistratos seems to have used Herakles as a model,¹⁰¹ and Herakles – as mentioned above – is also behind Peisetairos' victorious distinction. More importantly, in order to be received Peisistratos used a cultic formula closely parallel to that in the *Birds*: ὦ Ἀθηναῖοι, δέκεσθε ἀγαθῶι νόωι Πεισίστρατον, τὸν αὐτὴ ἡ Ἀθηναίη τιμήσασα ἀνθρώπων μάλιστα κατάγει ἐς τὴν ἑωυτῆς ἀκρόπολιν ('Athenians, give a hearty welcome to Peisistratos, whom Athena herself has honoured beyond all men and brings back to her own citadel').¹⁰² The 'trick' was εὐηθέστατον (Hdt. 1.60), but it suc-

---

⁹⁶ This aspect is usually overlooked by commentators.
⁹⁷ Behind the comic reversal, Zeus' power is discernible in the scene: see Kakrides (1987) on 1757 and Dunbar (1995) 13f., and on 1755 and 1764.
⁹⁸ Sommerstein (1987) 3 and on 1708 probably goes too far; he overlooks the point of comic caricature and the element of trickery combined with naturalness characterizing the comic hero.
⁹⁹ On the association of the two incidents cf. also Bowie (1993) 165.
¹⁰⁰ But not only on that: the synergy of 'insiders' (see Prometheus) proved also instrumental.
¹⁰¹ As Boardman (1975) has argued. Herakles a model for tyrants: Isokr. *Philipp.* 109–10.
¹⁰² Cf. also the context of the address (Hdt. 1.61): ἤλαυνον ἐς τὸ ἄστυ, προδρόμους κήρυκας προπέμψαντες, οἳ τὰ ἐντεταλμένα ἠγόρευον ἀπικόμενοι ἐς τὸ ἄστυ, λέγοντες τοιάδε... οἱ μὲν δὴ ταῦτα διαφοιτῶντες ἔλεγον, αὐτίκα δὲ ἔς τε τοὺς δήμους φάτις ἀπίκετο ὡς Ἀθηναίη Πεισίστρατον κατάγει, καὶ ⟨οἱ⟩ ἐν τῶι ἄστεϊ πειθόμενοι τὴν γυναῖκα εἶναι αὐτὴν τὴν θεὸν προσεύχοντό τε τὴν ἄνθρωπον καὶ ἐδέκοντο Πεισίστρατον.

ceeded. In the play Peisetairos' plan prevails and the community glorifies; but they are birds, ὄρνιθες, and ὄρνιο still stands in modern Greek for 'stupid'.[103]

More intriguing perhaps than traces of past history are associations with present and future developments. The attribution of cult to historical figures is not unprecedented. Important individuals received heroic honours after death in some cases, and a prominent example is the cult of the Sicilian tyrants.[104] Another, perhaps less well-known, example is Hagnon, honoured in life as oikist in Amphipolis; but Hagnon was displaced by Brasidas after the latter's victory: the community received Brasidas with honours as if he were an athlete; later they heroized him (Thuc. 4.121; 5.11). However, the more radical change came in the fourth century. It was around fifteen years after the *Birds* when Lysander was made – according to the tradition – the first human to receive divine honours.[105] And in 307, after years of democratic institutions, Athens would welcome Demetrios Poliorketes in a way similar to Peisetairos' reception.[106] There is no doubt that for such developments to occur the basis of common interests, necessary for the unfolding of interaction rituals, had changed. No matter how we evaluate such developments, regressive or progressive (necessary, anyway, in the given historical conditions), it is important to see that they were articulated through methods of interaction which in different conditions and by different agents could lead to different results.

How, then, would the concluding ritual performance be evaluated in the context of the play's composite structure allowing ample interplay and a mixture of even contradictory elements[107] and in the context of past and future historical circumstances? If the enacted ritual performance has the potential to parody the past, satirize the present and intimate the future, while at the same time – in the context of a utopia – it can create an engaging celebration of life *as it is*, with all its sides and contingencies, good and bad, both disillusioning and rejoicing, does not this potential deserve close attention, perhaps more than any

---

[103] Having said that (which is the one side of the coin), I do agree with Connor's (1987) analysis of Herodotos' passage which shows *how* such a response is achieved.
[104] See Malkin (1987) ch. 6 generally and Malkin (1987) 238–40 on the Sicilian tyrants, 230–2 on the case of Hagnon mentioned just below.
[105] See Plut. *Lys.* 18; Bommelaer (1981).
[106] See Ath. 6.61–3 referring to earlier sources (mainly Douris). On ruler-cult see Habicht (1970).
[107] A clear example is Peisetairos' hate of *polypragmosyne* in Athens and provocation of *polypragmosyne* among the Birds (cf. also 471). For another example see n. 97 above. On 'inconsistencies' and 'undetermined points' in the play see, for example, Dunbar (1995) 10–14. It is this 'looseness' (or, from a different angle, cleverness and realism) which prevents any easy assessment of characters and action in the *Birds*.

monolithic questions of the affirmative or subversive effect of the ritual? Ritual action is based upon traditional schemata which are familiar and for this reason able to create a sense of bonding and of shared cultural identity, but which may leave much room for a multiplicity of effects due to their generic nature.[108] Ancient theatre builds upon these ritual schemata, and it is interesting to follow their traces and try to see how the interaction between ritual practice and theatrical adaptation can help understanding the workings of culture.

Some conclusions

The performance of ritual both inside and outside theatre seems to suggest that it would not lead to a static, non-changeable result. Ritual performance can provide the means to effect transformation but never total transformation. Under given circumstances a performative attempt can take a specific direction, but the possibilities are numerous and are to a large extent dependent upon situational factors.

In the case of processional ritual a collective *anathēsis* (offering) in the face of and in an approach to divine power seems to enhance communal ideals and to promote a vision of unity. In an oxymoronic way, collective powerlessness before divine power can serve the empowerment of the community as a whole. In ancient Athens such unificatory movements interacted with democratic objectives, as long as the community referred to a transcendent sphere which claimed τιμή (honour) but allowed much room for the operation of inclusiveness, interchange and multiformity involving both order and disorder. Different situations, however, and shifting interests could reshape the balance of power and lead to re-articulations of social groupings. If visions of unity may seem to emanate even from differing processional schemata in traditional societies, this may be so because – as Herbert Blau notes[109] – absolute unity is non-existent, and for this reason sacred ritual tends to evoke it. Indeed, under certain circumstances processional performances themselves may function as major challenges for the explosion of dissidence.

Whether for unity or disunion, in ancient Greek society the way to affect minor or major alterations passes through the channel of performance which involves a ritualized body (the biological centre of all operations, material or mental) structuring, and being restructured

---

[108] Taviani (1991) 266f. has used the Rorschach test in order to show 'the personal and unforeseen meanings' that may emerge from the viewing of spatial rhythms, colours and symmetry.
[109] See Blau (1993) 262.

by, a ritualized environment. In the complicated network of cultural performances the importance of *processional* performance needs to be stressed, not least for its potential to illuminate the nature of performance. As other kinds of performances, processions constitute a bodily-centred dynamic force with the potential to affect the environment, shape relations and power associations and attempt changes by way of interaction.

If in traditional societies performance, implying physical interaction and direct contact, proved crucial for social formation and transformation, in the modern world of long distances and global effects, technologically assisted audio-visual media seem to have acquired a role in similar processes. A thoughtful comparison of operations and effects may yield interesting results. A first approach seems to suggests that, since traditional performances could both uphold, subvert and modify communal or democratic ideals, the prospects for the operation of audio-visual media remain open. Then as well as now, it must be remembered, change comes (also) from within.

12 The spectacular and the obscure in Athenian religion

Michael H. Jameson

Ritual is by its very nature performative.[1] For the ancient Greeks, animal sacrifice (*thusia*), a combination of words and acts, was the central and essential ritual, and it is on sacrifice that this essay will focus. Other clearly performative actions such as procession and dance may be viewed as elaborations of aspects of *thusia*. Indeed, the word can be applied to whole festivals. There are other rites referred to as *orgia* (secret or mystic), for which animal sacrifice need not be directly relevant, or in which it is performed in an abnormal fashion or even excluded; these, in effect, play against the expectations of normal sacrifice. Athletic and musical or poetic competitions do not stand as independent ritual acts but always have a cultic, and thus ultimately a sacrificial, context.[2]

The public and demonstrative character of pagan religious practice has made it difficult for the interpreters of classical Greece to come to terms with its religion. Post-reformation European culture had little sympathy for this aspect of religion as opposed to the personal and inner-directed. For long it was common to speak of the religion of the polis as essentially civic or political (which, though tautological, it surely was) rather than properly religious. Exceptions were allowed for mysteries and certain supposedly older civic cults. So it has been said of the rites associated with the old temple of Athena on the Akropolis of Athens in contrast to those tied to the glittering Parthenon, seen as a symbol of Athenian imperialism, that 'It is clear from the participants in these two sacrifices that if either of them had any religious meaning, it was the modest one in the "Old Temple" of Athena.'[3]

---

[1] Cf. Rappaport (1979) 175–6.
[2] On the distinction between ritual and drama, see Rappaport (1979) 177.
[3] C. J. Herington (1955) 32, following Mommsen (1898) 119, and Deubner (1932) 27. Simon (1983) 61 continues in the same vein in finding less 'religious meaning' in the sacrifices performed on the Great Altar on the Akropolis and thought to be associated with the Parthenon, but only Herington raises doubts about the religious meaning of all the Panathenaic rites.

In the past few decades openness to studies of pre-modern, non-western societies has encouraged both tolerance and appreciation of this alien kind of religion. Festivals, sacrifices and other public ceremonies have come to be seen as reflecting, expressing, even creating the society's conception of itself and its place in the cosmos. Here, it is said, we come closest to apprehending the nature of Greek culture as a whole. 'Polis religion' **is** Greek religion.[4] Such a view fits well with the rewarding attention currently being paid to the performative aspects of Greek culture and which is responsible for the genesis of the present volume. The gains this approach has offered to our understanding are beyond doubt but it may be that by concentrating on the public and the spectacular, the aspects of performance to which most of our information leads us, we risk over-simplifying and thus overlooking other important and complementary dimensions.

Let us begin with a brief review of the evidence for sacrifice as performance. The main elements in all normal sacrifice, public and private, were: (1) the procession (*pompē*) accompanying the sacrificial animals to the altar in a sacred area; (2) the sacrifice proper, which includes prayers, the ritual gestures of pouring libations, offering grains or cakes, slaughter of the animals, burning of certain parts on the altar fire and taking of omens, and eating of roasted innards (*splanchna*) by those who have participated in this stage; (3) the division of the rest of the meat with, in public sacrifices, parts or shares reserved as honours to religious and civic functionaries, followed by consumption of the meat by the participants or their passing the meat on to others. Although modern accounts of classical sacrifice have put great emphasis on the communal meal following upon sacrifice, it is clear from the various options available for most sacrifices that in the classical period, at least, the meal was no longer, if it had been earlier, an essential feature of the ritual process.[5]

The entire procedure of sacrifice was highly visual and dramatic, probably much more so than we can appreciate from verbal descrip-

---

[4] See especially Sourvinou-Inwood (1988), (1990). For a particular festival, the Great Dionysia at Athens, interpreted as a theatre for the interplay of social norm and transgression, see Goldhill (1990).
[5] Robin Osborne points out that the prominent role of women in this public activity also distinguishes it from the ordinary; cf. Osborne (1993a). Reconstructions and intepretations of Greek sacrifice are legion. A few references: Hubert and Mauss (1964, Engl. transl.; first published in French in 1899) drew on Vedic practice; Burkert (1983) 3–7, briefly, before elaborating an ambitious theory; the essentials in Parker (1996a) and Jameson (1988); Detienne and Vernant (1989), various essays; Peirce (1993) and Van Straten (1995), both treating particularly of representations in art.

tions and artistic representations, the latter mostly in the small frame of Attic vases. Actually seeing ritual was a prime component in participation. Normal experience is made clear by the citation of Athenian laws that ban a woman caught in adultery from attending rites at which even foreign and slave women (and *a fortiori* virtuous Athenian women) are permitted to be spectators and supplicants.[6] Hubert and Mauss's idea that in normal sacrifice the procession and the actions leading up to the actual slaughter constitute a process of sacralization, bringing something from the profane world and making it over to the world of the gods, is useful for understanding many of the elements involved. Everything – the victim itself (hung with fillets and sometimes with horns gilded), the sacrificers crowned and costumed, and the sacred place where the killing and burning occur – is marked out from the ordinary, conceptually and visibly. The sacrificers demonstrate the transaction to the gods and to the community at large, and the whole process is a representation to themselves of their appropriately doing honour to the gods.

Performance usually implies an audience and it is the relationship between performer and spectators and listeners that is the subject of most of the studies in this volume. But we should note that there are types of sacrifice such as those used in rites of purification or for the obtaining of favourable signs (καλλιερεῖν), in which the victim is not a source of meat for consumption and the performance requires witnesses (*martyres*) rather than an audience (*theatai*). It is important that they are known to have been done rather than that a community participate in them. This is an aspect that we will want to pursue further but for the present let us continue our consideration of the normal and the most common ritual by far.[7]

For a small community, or for a group of modest size within a large community, a high degree of participation could be expected in the second stage of sacrifice, at the sanctuary itself. The Attic organization of the Mesogeioi announced honours to its officials and benefactors at its annual festival of Herakles, once at least explicitly 'before the sacrifice' (*IG* II² 1244, 3–5), an indication that this was when most of the members might be expected to be gathered together. This was an im-

---

[6] [Dem.] 59.85 θεασομένην καὶ ἱκετεύουσαν εἰσιέναι (cf. Aeschin. 1.183). I take 'supplicate' here to refer to the individual's address to the deity through prayer or offering. The alleged illegal and impious officiant in this case, Neaira's daughter Phano, should have 'refrained from these rites ... from seeing (ὁρᾶν) and sacrificing (θύειν) and performing any of the customary ancestral actions on behalf of the city'.
[7] On rites sometimes termed *sphagia*, see Burkert (1989) 59–60, Jameson (1988), (1991).

portant venue for rewarding *philotimia* ('pursuit of public repute') and *eusebeia* ('piety'). The relevant community congratulates and defines itself.

How the meat of sacrificial animals was distributed, that is, who was entitled to what, was important socially because it recognized membership in a defined community (not necessarily identical with the political community) and status and privilege within it. Awards of choice cooked parts are described in Homer (e.g., *Od.* 14.437). Parts or shares, or multiple shares, more often of uncooked meat, are prescribed for functionaries and honorands in classical and Hellenistic inscriptions.[8] But assignment of meat, cooked or raw, was not crucial for the ritual nor conspicuous as performance to more than a small circle, which is not to deny the importance of knowledge of the fact within the community.

Homer's description of the Pylians on the beach feasting after sacrifice to Poseidon (*Od.* 3.4–9) reveals a community, in this case male and 'political', which has moved directly from sacrifice to cooking and feasting, the whole operation being to some degree a spectacle and a performance. (4500 men in nine *hedrai* feasting on the beach is so heroic in scale that it is hard to guess what prosaic reality may have been like.) Aside from the few honours awarded, the feast was 'equal' (e.g., *Il.* 1.468) and hierarchy was obliterated. But even in Homer meat could be removed to be consumed later elsewhere. So Achilles in his tent has meat ready to eat and to offer to his guests (*Il.* 9.205–21).

As the character of Greek communities changed, becoming larger, more diverse and more complex and as political roles became more narrowly defined, the constituent elements of the community required roles in cult. By the classical period, in democratic Athens and the culturally more or less egalitarian cities of the relatively developed parts of the Greek world, those aspects of sacrifice that could engage the widest range of the community had been expanded and made more prominent. This can be seen primarily in the first stage, the procession, and at the beginning of the third when meat was distributed from numerous animals to the community as a whole.

The obviously spectacular character of the procession in democratic societies needs little elaboration here.[9] The Parthenon frieze shows its triumphant invasion of temple sculpture. The great city *pompē* incorporated within it various elements of the society, female as well as male, metic as well as citizen, and assumed the participation of an

---

[8] Cf. Puttkammer (1912); J.-L. Durand in Detienne and Vernant (1989) 104–5.
[9] See Graf (1996) and Kavoulaki in this volume.

extraordinary number of spectators.[10] The Panathenaic route is not what one might expect for a procession moving from the grove of the hero Hekademos (the Academy) to the Akropolis. It ignores the old agora and the older civic buildings east and north of the Akropolis and enters the city from the northwest via the Kerameikos district at which point most of the participants assembled.[11] The Peisistratids in the sixth century may have deliberately routed it through the still largely empty (classical) agora where there was ample space for assembling and viewing. Numerous post-holes of various date are found along the Panathenaic Way in the agora, some of which may have been for bleachers or shelters for spectators.[12]

A couple of details are worth noting. As in the modern military and para-military parade, identification of the individual participating units was important. We suppose that the Athenian demesmen marched together or with their respective tribes, just as it was through their deme membership that they received their shares of meat (*IG* II² 334, 25–7). A Hellenistic inscription from Ilion requires that the tribesmen escort their tribe's cow for Athena and wether (male sheep) for Zeus Polieus and carry their cakes (*pemmata*). The name of each tribe is to be written on its cow.[13] A second point is the development of a class of ritual equipment which, whatever its original or notional function in ritual performed at the sanctuary, came to be thought of as primarily conspicuous wealth to be displayed in the procession, the *pompē*, and so was referred to as *pompeia* (e.g., Andoc. 4.29). The procession had become an end in itself (cf. Kavoulaki *supra*, pp. 293–320).

The central actions of the second stage probably had changed little: prayers, ritual gestures, the actual killing of the animals, the expert cutting up of the carcase, and the observation of signs, all had to be entrusted to reliable specialists. For the last two actions Attic comedy gives the impression that there may have been a growth in the number of specialized *mageiroi*, who handled the meat, and *manteis* who interpeted the signs derived from sacrifice. Sanctuaries, however, were not designed as theatres for the spectacle of sacrifice, though the huge altars of Sicilian tyrants must have functioned as large smoke and smell machines, whose operations were to be seen, sensed and marvelled

---

[10] See especially Maurizio, forthcoming, on the Panathenaic procession.
[11] See, e.g., Robertson (1992) 97–8 and Maps 2 and 3.
[12] Thompson and Wycherley (1972) 126–7; Camp (1986) 45–6, fig. 28.
[13] Presumably in paint, whitewash or charcoal. Sokolowski (1955) 9.20–4, who cites J. Vanseveren's comparison with *Inscriptions de Délos* 1520: in the *pompē* of the Apollonia at Delos an ox is to carry the inscription: 'The corporation of the Beryttian Poseidoniasts on behalf of Marcus Minatius' (*RPh* 62 [1936] 252–4).

at even from afar. Traditional priests remained the key figures, but Athens at least charged civic officials and bodies of ten representing the ten tribes (notably the various *hieropoioi*) with much additional sacrificing and the assisting of priests at more important ceremonies. The fortuitous engagement in any of this could give The Man of Petty Ambition much joy (Theophr. *Char.* 21.11). The core of sacrifice remained a spectacle, but one limited in the degree to which it could be expanded.

Communal sacrifice in the classical period put much store on distribution of meat after the sacrifice. The reactionary Isocrates (7.29) can complain that the democracy adds festivals solely for the free meat. The very fact of distribution of shares or parts of meat raw points to alternatives to a common meal taking place on the spot immediately after the sacrifice. Dining arrangements were made only for representative sacred and civic officials, and probably not always even for them. It seems likely that in the archaic polis temples with interior hearths or separate buildings in sanctuaries served as dining rooms.[14] In later centuries, a communal meal, al fresco or in the group's building, remained practical and at times desirable for smaller communities of sacrificers.[15] For large groups, a polis as a whole or one of its major divisions such as the Athenian tribe (*phulē*), it was not.[16] Participation *en masse* meant families and individuals bringing their own sacrificial animals or other food, as at the Diasia for Zeus Meilichios[17] and as did women at the Thesmophoria.[18] But an important consequence of public distributions of meat was that it enabled the majority to dine privately, 'aristocratically', in their own homes, often enough in *andrōnes*, the specialized dining rooms which prove to be surprisingly common in the classical private house.[19] Dining in small groups, whether by public officials or private persons, evolved its own rites of prayer, libation and food offerings, followed by the distinct ritual patterns of the symposium.

Parallel to the dining together of mortals was that of the gods. A

---

[14] On buildings for dining, see Goldstein (1978), Bergquist (1990). On public dining, see Bruit Zaidman (1995) briefly, Schmitt Pantel (1992) fully. And various papers in Murray (1990), Slater (1991).

[15] Cf. Ferguson (1944) on the *orgeones*.

[16] The generous public meals offered by Hellenistic benefactors are another matter, and interestingly the bulk of the meat on these occasions may not have not come from sacrificed animals; cf. the inscription of the Athenian Iobacchoi of the second century AD where contractors supply pork for the meals while no sacrifices are listed, *IG* II² 1368, Sokolowski (1969) 51, *SIG*³ 1109.

[17] Jameson (1965) 159–66.

[18] Parker (1987) 145.

[19] Cf. Jameson (1990) 188–91.

portant venue for rewarding *philotimia* ('pursuit of public repute') and *eusebeia* ('piety'). The relevant community congratulates and defines itself.

How the meat of sacrificial animals was distributed, that is, who was entitled to what, was important socially because it recognized membership in a defined community (not necessarily identical with the political community) and status and privilege within it. Awards of choice cooked parts are described in Homer (e.g., *Od.* 14.437). Parts or shares, or multiple shares, more often of uncooked meat, are prescribed for functionaries and honorands in classical and Hellenistic inscriptions.[8] But assignment of meat, cooked or raw, was not crucial for the ritual nor conspicuous as performance to more than a small circle, which is not to deny the importance of knowledge of the fact within the community.

Homer's description of the Pylians on the beach feasting after sacrifice to Poseidon (*Od.* 3.4–9) reveals a community, in this case male and 'political', which has moved directly from sacrifice to cooking and feasting, the whole operation being to some degree a spectacle and a performance. (4500 men in nine *hedrai* feasting on the beach is so heroic in scale that it is hard to guess what prosaic reality may have been like.) Aside from the few honours awarded, the feast was 'equal' (e.g., *Il.* 1.468) and hierarchy was obliterated. But even in Homer meat could be removed to be consumed later elsewhere. So Achilles in his tent has meat ready to eat and to offer to his guests (*Il.* 9.205–21).

As the character of Greek communities changed, becoming larger, more diverse and more complex and as political roles became more narrowly defined, the constituent elements of the community required roles in cult. By the classical period, in democratic Athens and the culturally more or less egalitarian cities of the relatively developed parts of the Greek world, those aspects of sacrifice that could engage the widest range of the community had been expanded and made more prominent. This can be seen primarily in the first stage, the procession, and at the beginning of the third when meat was distributed from numerous animals to the community as a whole.

The obviously spectacular character of the procession in democratic societies needs little elaboration here.[9] The Parthenon frieze shows its triumphant invasion of temple sculpture. The great city *pompē* incorporated within it various elements of the society, female as well as male, metic as well as citizen, and assumed the participation of an

---

[8] Cf. Puttkammer (1912); J.-L. Durand in Detienne and Vernant (1989) 104–5.
[9] See Graf (1996) and Kavoulaki in this volume.

tions and artistic representations, the latter mostly in the small frame of Attic vases. Actually seeing ritual was a prime component in participation. Normal experience is made clear by the citation of Athenian laws that ban a woman caught in adultery from attending rites at which even foreign and slave women (and *a fortiori* virtuous Athenian women) are permitted to be spectators and supplicants.[6] Hubert and Mauss's idea that in normal sacrifice the procession and the actions leading up to the actual slaughter constitute a process of sacralization, bringing something from the profane world and making it over to the world of the gods, is useful for understanding many of the elements involved. Everything – the victim itself (hung with fillets and sometimes with horns gilded), the sacrificers crowned and costumed, and the sacred place where the killing and burning occur – is marked out from the ordinary, conceptually and visibly. The sacrificers demonstrate the transaction to the gods and to the community at large, and the whole process is a representation to themselves of their appropriately doing honour to the gods.

Performance usually implies an audience and it is the relationship between performer and spectators and listeners that is the subject of most of the studies in this volume. But we should note that there are types of sacrifice such as those used in rites of purification or for the obtaining of favourable signs (καλλιερεῖν), in which the victim is not a source of meat for consumption and the performance requires witnesses (*martyres*) rather than an audience (*theatai*). It is important that they are known to have been done rather than that a community participate in them. This is an aspect that we will want to pursue further but for the present let us continue our consideration of the normal and the most common ritual by far.[7]

For a small community, or for a group of modest size within a large community, a high degree of participation could be expected in the second stage of sacrifice, at the sanctuary itself. The Attic organization of the Mesogeioi announced honours to its officials and benefactors at its annual festival of Herakles, once at least explicitly 'before the sacrifice' (*IG* II² 1244, 3–5), an indication that this was when most of the members might be expected to be gathered together. This was an im-

---

[6] [Dem.] 59.85 θεασομένην καὶ ἱκετεύουσαν εἰσιέναι (cf. Aeschin. 1.183). I take 'supplicate' here to refer to the individual's address to the deity through prayer or offering. The alleged illegal and impious officiant in this case, Neaira's daughter Phano, should have 'refrained from these rites ... from seeing (ὁρᾶν) and sacrificing (θύειν) and performing any of the customary ancestral actions on behalf of the city'.

[7] On rites sometimes termed *sphagia*, see Burkert (1989) 59–60, Jameson (1988), (1991).

potent metaphor was *theoxenia*, literally 'hosting the gods', and other language associated with a widespread ritual corresponding to the Roman *lectisternium*.[20] A couch or couches were spread and a table with food set alongside; the setting might be the god's shrine, by the god's image, or images might be fetched for the purpose. It could take place after a sacrifice or, at its simplest, require only the placing of some foodstuffs on a table without couch, image or sacrifice. In most cases mortals did not feast close by or in association with the gods. It is more than a coincidence that this ritual is seen to be common, whatever its origins and earlier history, at a time when dining in small groups was becoming a widespread social, and to some degree, ritual practice in the Greek cities. In most cases, spectacle was not part of the procedure, although at Magnesia on the Maiandros in the Hellenistic period we hear of the images of the Twelve Gods being carried in procession and set up in a structure erected for their entertainment.[21] The procedure might lend itself to spectacle but for the most part it was enough that it was known to have been carried out. We hear of priests being complimented for their preparation of tables, a sight to be seen and admired in a closed space by only a few people at a time.

Against the centrifugal tendency to dine away from the sanctuary stands a requirement found in a number of cult inscriptions that the meat be consumed on the spot. This is indicated most commonly by the phrases οὐ φορά, οὐκ ἀποφορά – 'no carrying away', or δαινύσθων αὐτοῦ – 'let them dine right there'.[22] But while this is the most frequent comment on the disposition of the meat, it is very rare when compared to the usual silence on the subject, with the implication that shares of sacrificial meat could be disposed of as one wished. Meat could be consumed by a group elsewhere than its sanctuary, by the household at home, given to friends or relations or sold to butcher shops.[23] In the great majority of sacrifices, how the meat was disposed of was, in terms of ritual, a matter of indifference. However, the occasional requirement of feasting on the spot points to a desire to continue the group's presence in the sanctuary, that is to prolong and complete the drama of delivering a gift to the gods and then feasting gratefully on the gods' bounty. Against the normal dispersing of the sacrificers, there was a

[20] Cf. most recently Jameson (1994).
[21] *SIG*³ 589, Sokolowski (1959) 32.41–5.
[22] For the last, *SIG*³ 1024, Sokolowski (1969) 96, 26. Generally, see Goldstein (1978) 51–4; Scullion (1994) 99–112; Jameson (1994) 45. Dow (1965) 208–10 unpersuasively sees purely secular considerations at work, to prevent cult personnel from being favoured.
[23] Cf. Rosivach (1994), concerned primarily with the acquisition of animals.

sense that in certain cases it should not happen. It is not clear why the requirement was applied to some sacrifices and not others, and to judge from the insertion of the requirement at a number of points in the sacrificial calendar of the Athenian deme of Erchia after the whole text had been cut, the advisability of its application was debatable.[24]

If the 'no carrying away' provision draws attention to attempts to maintain or prolong a performative if not spectacular aspect of sacrifice, we should now consider information that points in a different direction. This will require attention to detailed sacrificial prescriptions. In two Attic sacrificial calendars of the fifth century we find the terse declaration that the meat from certain victims sacrificed by the organization is to be sold. The first calendar, very fragmentary, is that of the deme of Skambonidai in the city and dates from c. 460 BCE.[25] While there are several references to public distribution of meat (including meat from the Dipolieia and the Panathenaia festivals), there are also two references to selling the meat raw (ἀποδόσθαι ὠμά), first a full-grown sheep sacrificed at the Synoikia festival on the Akropolis (C 16–19) and then a ram or lamb at the otherwise unknown festival Epize[phyra] in the Pythion, presumably for Apollo (C 19–22). In both cases a single victim is sacrificed, which would not provide enough meat to satisfy the many demesmen living nearby, to the north of the Akropolis. It seems that rather than struggle with the question of who was to receive what little there was, the deme decided to sell the meat as soon as the ritual had been completed.[26]

The same intention is expressed in different language in another calendar, attributed to the deme of Thorikos in south Attica.[27] Though

[24] Daux (1963); SEG 21. 541; Sokolowski (1969) 18. Bruit Zaidman (1995) 202, speaking of those specially delegated in the archaic city, writes 'Sacrificial meat eaten in the sanctuary, far from being sacred, is in a sense desacralized by the division made between human and divine portions. The human portion of the beast, though, when consumed by representative humans with other food in the sanctuary, has a ritual value and special function.' Our sources do not tell us what that value and function were.

[25] IG I³ 244, Sokolowski (1969) 10.

[26] The Synoikia in ancient and modern scholarship are explained by the *synoikismos* of Attica by Theseus. If we take the latter to be ahistorical, Noel Robertson's connection of the name with *oikoi*, 'lodges', of phratries (1992), especially 32–43, is attractive. He can point to the biennial sacrifice during this festival to Zeus Phratrios and Athena Phratria in the city's revised calendar, Sokolowski (1962) 10, C 31–58. But the deme's sacrifice on the Akropolis remains unexplained.

[27] It is preserved on an inscription now at the Getty Museum in Malibu. Known earlier from imperfect copies it was first published from autopsy by Georges Daux (1983) and (1984), SEG 33. 147. It is certainly from south Attica and I will refer to it as from Thorikos though the attribution to that deme is not beyond question. I hope to publish a revised text shortly. For discussion of the contents, see especially Whitehead (1986) 194–9, Parker (1987).

published as from the fourth century BCE, probably because of the use of the Ionic alphabet, it has been recognized as dating from around the first phase of the Peloponnesian War.[28] The word πρατός, 'to be sold', occurs six times, applied to sacrificial animals (lines 9, 11–12, 23, 26, 35, and Right Side, Addendum 1, line 3).[29]

This calendar is not otherwise interested in what happens to the sacrificial animals once they have been offered to the gods; no priestly perquisites are mentioned, though we should not suppose for that reason that they were not taken. In only one other instance is the fate of the meat mentioned. A piglet is to be burnt whole (ὁλόκαυτος), probably for Zeus Polieus in connection with a 'Before Ploughing Ceremony' (Prerosia) at a place called Automenai(15).[30] That is also the only time the source of the animal is specified. It must be bought as the great majority of sacrificial animals here and elsewhere surely were. Specifying that this should be done would seem, like the specification of holocaust, to have a ritual rather than a practical motivation – the victim, a purificatory offering, is to come from beyond the circle of worshippers.

In the six sacrifices from which the meat is to be sold, there is no obvious ritual reason for avoiding consumption either in the sanctuary or at home. One sheep was sacrificed to Zeus Meilichios at the Diasia festival (34–5), probably not locally but at the god's shrine at Agrai on

---

[28] D. M. Lewis ZPE 60 (1985) 108, n. 3 (cf. IG I³ 256 bis, p. 958) proposed a date of 440–430 BCE.

[29] This last reading has not been reported previously. The text prepared by Dunst (1977) before the stone became available for autopsy restored π[ρατόν at the end of line 27, following the word Πυανοψίοις, a well-known festival of Apollo. This was accepted by Labarbe (1977) 59, 61, and, with a query by Parker (1987) 144. Daux had confirmed the *pi* on the stone but restored the incomplete Π[οσειδῶ, there being no room for *ni*, and none appearing, on the right side. It is now clear that Ἀπόλ]λωνι and a full-grown victim for the Pyanopsia can be read on the left side in Addendum 1. I am inclined to think that only Neanias is sacrificed to on the 16th of the month, perhaps in connection with the Apatouria, and that Πυανοψίοις is followed not by the requirement that the flesh be sold but by a word relevant to that festival, i.e., π[ύανα, the distinctive mixture of boiled seeds that characterized the festival, Deubner (1932): 198–201. The entry for the country Dionysia in Posideion (31) is even more laconic: Διονύσια and no more. At some point it was felt that the chief god of the festival must be named and his sacrifice specified, and this led to Addendum 1 on the left side. Even if π[ύανα is not right, I would hesitate to restore π[ρατόν since it would be the only instance here of one victim's flesh being sold while that of one or more others was kept; see the discussion below.

This use of πρατός of sacrificial animals is unique, aside from a rather vague reference, 'whenever they (sc. *thusiai*) are not for sale' (ὅκα κα μὴ ὦντι πρατα ...) in a Hellenistic inscription from Thera, IG XII 3, 330, 227; Schwyzer (1923) 227.

[30] A lamb is sacrificed to Zeus at the same place (47–8). That Automenai may be a place name is a possibility mentioned and rejected by Daux (1983) but accepted by Parker (1987) 144, but see now S. Scullion ZPE 121 (1998) 116–19.

the outskirts of the city of Athens, as by the deme of Erchia.[31] If Zeus Meilichios is thought to be chthonic (not in itself a sure guide to consumption), Zeus Kataibates, who comes down in the form of lightning, is not. He receives wethers (castrated adult male sheep) at two different places where lightning has struck (11–12, 25–6). Two more sacrifices from which the meat was to be sold were of ewes for Athena, though the first entry (23) was cancelled at some point by neatly cutting a line through the three words Ἀθηναίαι οἶν πρατόν. The second ewe is in an addendum on the right side of the stele, next to the entries on the main face for the month Hekatombaion; in the addendum there seems to be a reference to the Panathenaia, celebrated at the end of this month, which makes it likely that the offering was to Athena.[32] Finally there is another victim to be sold, a full grown sheep, in a lacunose passage at the very end of Hekatombaion, written in an erasure (9). While it is not impossible that it too was connected with the Panathenaia, in the clearer examples of the meat being sold only a single victim is specified for the festival. The relationship of the main text to the addendum at this point is unclear. It is interesting that two of the six examples in this calendar that included the requirement that the meat be sold may have been subject to debate, with one cancelled and another substituted for a previous entry. We have noted revisions to the 'no carrying away' provision at Erchia. The sacrifice of the Skambonidai on the Akropolis, the sacrifices to Zeus and potentially the other examples from Thorikos have one thing in common, that each ceremony involves only a single god and a single victim. As we have seen, the one apparent exception, the sacrifice to Athena at Thorikos in line 23, coming after sacrifices to three other figures, was cancelled.

The simplest reconstruction we can make of what went on at these sacrifices is that the appropriate priest (accompanied by whatever attendants were customary) went to the sacred place, two of which were probably no more than little enclosures surrounding the spot where a thunderbolt had struck, and two probably in the city of Athens (Zeus Meilichios and, for the Panathenaia, on the city's Akropolis). There he prayed, sacrificed, and then having followed the customary procedure and removed for himself his traditional perquisites, con-

---

[31] *SEG* 21.541, 37–43, Sokolowski (1969) 18.

[32] There is also reference in this entry to a local place name, Μυκηνος (accentuation is uncertain) where later in the calendar, in the month Mounychion, Dionysos receives a tawny or black goat (45–6). It is conceivable if not likely that the ewe for the Panathenaia was also sacrificed there, and not in Athens. I read, without indicating doubtful letters, Μυκηνω[ι] τέ[λεον – – –/– – –]/αν οἶν Παναθ[ηναί]/οις θύεν πρατ[όν.

veyed the remainder to a butcher shop for sale. (Perhaps the *mageiros* accompanied the priest and cut the animal up at the sanctuary.) Parker observed that the Zeus and Athena sacrifices were made at outlying sites in the deme and therefore were 'not suitable occasions for a *hestiasis* [a public feast]'.[33] We should note, furthermore, that the simple alternatives of dividing the meat up on the spot or back at the deme centre were also rejected. While the Diasia for Zeus Meilichios and the Panathenaia in the city were convenient for demesmen living there (fewer, however, before the Peloponnesian War than afterwards), they were a long haul for those still living in south Attica. And yet the Panathenaia was a festival that many from all over Attica attended, though by the later fourth century participation in the annual (as opposed to the quadrennial) festival seems to have needed some boosting.[34] It may be that with solid shares of beef available to any Athenian who made his way to the city on the 29th of Hekatombaion it was not worth the trouble for deme officials to arrange a feast or to share out the meat of their lone ewe.

There were, it seems, situations where the organization making the sacrifice was conscientious about performing the ritual but so few of its members participated that it was more advantageous for the meat to be sold and the proceeds returned to the organization's coffers, no doubt for use for future sacrifices. The opposite to this prescription, the insistence on consumption on the spot, prolongs the existence of a sacrificial community to achieve a particular effect. But neither requirement suggests that communal participation followed by feasting together was the norm. The principal aim of the Thorikos and the other deme calendars was the conscientious performance of a complex schedule of sacrifices. Unfailing attendance at the rites by members of the organization was not expected, and participation and spectacle, while desirable, were not of the first importance. Knowledge that these rites were being performed at the right time, in the right place with the right victims, was. The inscriptions themselves take on the task of declaring and making visible the community's recognition of its obligations.[35] The inscriptions are spectacular, and the large, handsome, *stoichedon* lettering of the fifth century texts, in particular, confirms this function.

Ample support for this perhaps obvious conclusion can be found in

---

[33] Parker (1987) 145.
[34] Cf. *IG* II² 334, Lykurgan measures for enhancement of the annual Panathenaia which included rewarding demes with meat according to the number of members who marched.
[35] Cf. Osborne in this volume.

the frustrating scraps that have survived from the grandest effort of the Athenians to organize and display their ritual obligations, the consolidated calendar of sacrifices prepared around 400 BCE and set up as walls of *stēlai* in the Royal Stoa in the agora.[36] The ancient controversies over the revisions, reflected in Lysias 30, centred on the dropping or reduction of traditional sacrifices and the inclusion of new sacrifices. They provide a valuable glimpse of what must have been an on-going process. It is a fair assumption that the newer sacrifices were ones that had attracted recent interest and might be expected to draw attendance while those that were relegated to infrequent performance in a cycle of years or perhaps eliminated altogether had a smaller, precarious constituency. Inevitably certain festivals associated with particular families would become neglected if the families died out or were reduced in strength. At the same time, openness to new cults and new forms of ritual was more characteristic of Greek paganism, and indeed of most non-literate religions than is usually allowed.[37]

Despite the charges against the draughters, Nikomachos and his associates, what strikes us in examining the fragments of the code is the number of minor and obscure cults that were maintained conscientiously by means of the sacrifice of a single, modest victim. Who would have suspected that a wether was supplied to the pre-Kleisthenic *phulē* of the Gleontes and *trittus* of Leukotainioi to be sacrificed on the day before the main sacrifices of the Synoikia?[38] The approach adopted by the draughters was, it seems, to reorganize the festival calendar and the financial arrangements so as to be able to keep up the widest possible array of sacrifices. A system of cycles was elaborated, so that while some sacrifices were annual, others were performed in alternate years, or every four years (as the Great Panathenaia, like the festival at Olympia, had long been); these cycles are also seen in the fourth-century calendar of the Marathonian Tetrapolis, to which we will return.[39] Another

---

[36] No full edition of the texts exists. One promised by Sterling Dow, who produced several important preliminary studies, never appeared. The largest and most discussed fragment is Sokolowski (1962) 10 (first published by J. Oliver (*Hesperia* 4 [1939] 19–32); cf. also Sokolowski (1969) 17. For the text, interpretation of ritual details and bibliography Hardy Hansen (1990) is the most recent and useful study of the calendar, though the bulk of his work was done in the 1960s. A group of Eleusinian sacrifices is examined in detail by Healey (1990). For discussion of the revision of the laws to which the calendar belongs, see Ostwald (1986) 511–14, Robertson (1990), Rhodes (1991). The accumulated body of laws reviewed at the end of the 5th century were regarded by the Athenians as Solonian but the resulting code reflects aims and practices of c. 400 BCE. For the Solonian calendar, see Parker (1996) 43–55.

[37] Cf. Parker (1996) 214–17; Jameson (1997).

[38] Sokolowski (1962) 10, A 31–43.

[39] IG II² 1358, Sokolowski (1969) 20.

practical feature was the conversion of many, perhaps most, of the the perquisites of priests and other officiants into cash. The parts and shares of the sacrificed animals, the allowances for grain, wine and so on, are all dutifully listed and their equivalence in cash set beside them. No one was to be deprived of his traditional privilege which may have been felt to be part of the proper performance of the rite, but it was to be represented largely by payment in coinage. No doubt this was easier to administer than the assigning of the particular honours. The meat from these numerous minor sacrifices would have been sold and the income returned to the city, but we do not see this happening since the surviving fragments record expenditures, not income.[40]

The impression one gets is that few Athenians other than those charged with their performance (and assured of some form of reward) were likely to participate in a great many of the rites for which the polis had a responsibility. The eyes of the Athenian public were fixed largely on the great festivals of the city such as the Panathenaia in which it participated as marchers in the *pompai*, as recipients of meat from the sacrifices, and as spectators of processions and competitions (*agōnes*). All Athenian families could also claim a place in the rites of civic units (tribes and demes) and in those of older, groups putatively based on kinship, the phratries; many were also tied to *gene* ('clans') and to independent associations of *orgeones* and to *thiasoi*. Women had a role in many polis and local festivals, and the festivals of Demeter and Artemis were predominantly theirs. How much any individual or family participated on any occasion would have varied with their particular circumstances, as too would the degree that any of the performances partook of the public and spectacular, which no doubt would have been enhanced if, for instance, an unusual number of animals became available.

The Athenian, however, was aware of and, indeed, seems to have demanded, the maintenance of a much larger network of ritual performances than any one person could engage in. This is what may be referred to as 'the obscure', those many obligations discharged at the right time and place and by means of the right animals sacrificed in the right ways. Thanks are offered in decree after decree because someone performed their ritual obligations well and according to ancestral practice (καλῶς καὶ κατὰ τὰ πάτρια, e.g. *IG* II² 1247, 6–7). For most people one suspects these rites had little or no correlation with myth and might involve supernatural figures not equated precisely with

---

[40] Contrast *IG* II² 1496, records of the income from the sale of sacrificial skins for a few years in the fourth century.

members of the familiar, limited panhellenic or pan-Attic cast of characters. The goddess Kourotrophos is a good example.[41] The many gods and goddesses, heroes and heroines, of as large and well-populated a land as Attica could only have been apprehended dimly by most people but a sense of their being properly recognized was thought to be essential for the survival of the city. In fact, some must always have been fading away while others were being reinterpreted and newcomers were being established.

Between the great public festival on or below the Akropolis and the small sacrifice in a simple enclosure in a corner of the countryside there was a continuum – the basic ritual acts and personnel differed only in scale, as did participation. Exclusivity of membership and participation served to define the community (and a community might honour an outsider with an invitation). But there were also groups in which membership was defined not only by birth and status but also, or only, by shared knowledge or experience. Most obvious are the mysteries, whether in the charge of the polis or of private groups, such as the *genos* of the Lykomidai, or, as with the Eleusinian Mysteries, a combination of the two.[42] Certain sights seen (especially important for Eleusis) and actions performed distinguished the admitted and the excluded. Here performance was prominent, sometimes spectacular, such as the procession of initiates from Athens to Eleusis, but the central elements were hidden and the very fact of their obscurity defined the participants. This is an example of what has been called 'advertised secrecy'.[43]

At one time such secrecy may have been characteristic of admission to a new status within the society, as in moving from one age group to another by means of rites of passage.[44] In classical Greece, however, it is most characteristic of the status of women defined by their exclusive rites, especially the Thesmophoria and the Munychian and Brauronian

---

[41] Price (1978) 101–32 for the testimonia; intepretation is debatable.

[42] On ancient mysteries in general, see Burkert (1985) 276–304 and (1987). On the personnel of the Eleusinian mysteries, Clinton (1974). On the Lykomidai, Parker (1996) 305.

[43] Levy (1990), especially 335–40. The differences between the use of 'advertised secrecy' in the Nepalese city studied by Levy and in classical Athens are instructive: in Bhaktapur secret knowledge and performance characterized and defined the various groups with their separate and complementary roles in the ritual life of the city. (In Arnhem Land in northern Australia the identity and relationships of neighbouring societies are defined by control of secret ritual knowledge and the degree to which elements are shared, Keen [1994]). While the ritual roles of certain Athenian *genē* are comparable to the groups in Bhaktapur and certain rites were in their charge and hidden from the public, we do not detect claims to secret knowledge except in cults specifically described as mysteries.

[44] So Burkert (1987) on the origin of the mysteries.

rites of Artemis. The Eleusinian Mysteries are distinctive in their abolition of gender distinction in major rites for Demeter and not only in their openness to all Athenians and residents of Attica but, by the fifth century BCE, the active encouragement to participation of all Greek-speakers. It is an interesting paradox that the most fiercely and vociferously protected secrets of Athenian religion were of a cult for which the Athenians proselytized energetically and which was rivalled in this respect only by the competitions of the Panathenaia and the Dionysia. At the same time it was the state cult in which the religious well-being of the individual participant was most clearly a goal. Its complexity mirrors that of contemporary Athens.

Even within recognized public festivals that did not involve the initiation and secret knowledge we associate with mysteries, there were hidden procedures to which ancient sources, learned rather than epigraphic or official, apply the language of mysteries. This is true, for example, of the Plynteria, the spring-cleaning for Athena on the Akropolis, which includes 'the rites not to be spoken of' (τὰ ὄργια ... ἀπόρρητα, Plut. *Alc.* 34.1), and the Arrephoria, involving a night-time descent and return from the Akropolis by two young girls.[45] Thus, in addition to any of the usual public elements such as procession and sacrifice, there were also particular ritual acts performed by selected individuals out of view of the public. The statue, dress and surroundings of Athena had to be prepared for the new year and while this was going on there could be danger to the goddess and the city. The public had to be excluded. Whereas a large pattern of more or less routine rituals did not need spectators, these 'mystic' rites banished spectacle and spectators.

A vigorous religious life for a large polis required everything from public ritual to public mystery, and both performance and the awareness of performance at many levels. Public performance employing spectacle to reach a large community stands at one end of a continuum. Secrecy, the ultimate in obscurity, would seem to be at the opposite extreme but is used primarily to put up a conspicuous screen around a performance and spectacle reserved for a distinct group. The advertising of secrecy is itself a performance. Between the public spectacle and the secret lies the great majority of ritual actions, what we have termed the obscure – more common, diffuse, and varied. In fifth- and fourth-century Athens the observance of a great many, largely obscure rituals produced a crowded calendar of sacred time and a dense map of sacred space.

---

[45] For the sources, Deubner (1932) 9–17.

336 *Michael H. Jameson*

The performance and knowledge of distinct sets of rituals by the constituent social groups within a society or a wider cultural area commonly help to define the groups and to construct the larger community through their complementary roles.[46] This would seem to apply well to the social units that made up the Athenian democracy, the tribes, demes, phratries and *gene*, despite their different origins and functions, the first two essential building blocks of the Kleisthenic structure, the latter two pre-Kleisthenic but of continuing social and religious value to the democracy. Ritual activity was crucial for any Greek social entity. Although we emphasize social and political functions, for its members it might almost be said that the *raison d'être* of the group was the offering of sacrifice to a particular supernatural figure or group of figures.

The ten new tribes of Kleisthenes, whose members came from three groups of demes from different parts of Attica, provided the structure for the army and for the annual Council of 500. Concentrating on honours to their eponymous heroes, they fit the model well enough, though some of the heroes had been the object of cult before the creation of the Kleisthenic tribes named after them.[47] The 139 demes among which all the territory of Attica was divided, were created or recognized by Kleisthenes and served as the source of an Athenian's identity (as the community to which one's paternal ancestor had been attached in 506 BCE).[48] They collected the cults of their local territory while also reaching out to a number of key sites beyond, which points to active communities whose interests were not confined to the territory assigned to the Kleisthenic demes.[49] To a degree we cannot estimate, they were the continuation of traditional, local ritual communities comparable spatially and ritually to the demes; others may have inherited the obligations of regional groupings such as the Marathonian

---

[46] For the student of classical Athens, Levy (1990) is exceptionally valuable, in part because of the size and complexity of the society he examines.

[47] On the tribes and their heroes, see Kron (1976), and on the religious implications of Kleisthenes' reforms in general, Parker (1996) 102–21.

[48] This is not the place to engage in the arguments as to whether the deme was essentially a group of citizens who lived together in 506 BCE or a continuous stretch of Attic land attached to those citizens. For a largely agricultural and pastoral society the distinction may not make much sense.
  On deme cults and their relationship to those of the polis, see Mikalson (1977), Whitehead (1986), Parker (1987), (1996).

[49] The Thorikians went to Poseidon at Sounion (lines 19–20) and probably to Agrai for Zeus Meilichios and perhaps to the Akropolis for the Panathenaia (as discussed above). The Erchians sacrificed to Zeus Epakrios on Mt Hymettos (E 59–64) and went to Agrai (A 37–43) and Athens (A 1–5, B 1–5, G 13–18, D 13–17). Discussion of the location of the Thorikian sacrifices in Whitehead (1986) 196–7.

Tetrapolis, which survived the reforms of Kleisthenes and consisted of four contiguous demes from different tribes. Its continuing validity is shown by the comprehensive sacrificial calendar inscribed in the mid-fourth century BCE.[50] All the surviving deme calendars, however, were the products of basic units of the democracy, set down many years after the creation of the demes themselves. Even the Tetrapolis calendar included the four separate deme calendars in addition to that of the Tetrapolis as a whole.

With the Kleisthenic reorganization in place, the major deme festivals probably served to define the new community (or reaffirm the continuation of a pre-existing community) and to strengthen the identification of the citizens with their demes.[51] Thucydides (2.16) speaks of the Athenians up to the Peloponnesian War living largely in the country (ἐν τοῖς ἀγροῖς, which covers villages as well as dispersed farm houses) and their distress at 'leaving their houses, their sacred places (*hiera*) which had been passed on to them continuously from their ancestors since the time of the ancient organization (of Attica, i.e. before the *synoikismos*), transforming their way of life, each person in effect abandoning his own polis'. The religious life of the extra-urban demes would seem to have corresponded on a small scale to that of the polis.

The consequences of the withdrawals from the countryside during the Peloponnesian War on the settlement patterns of Attica have been much debated.[52] It seems to me inescapable that changes occurred and that the urban centres of Athens and the Piraeus probably grew more populous. It may no longer have been clear that the ancestral demes were the communities in which the Athenians lived their lives and through which they realized their identity as Athenians (though the demes furnished the mechanism of registry). We have seen reason to doubt widespread participation in all but a few major festivals for most deme members.

It is not evident that Kleisthenes or the democratic leaders who came

---

[50] *IG* II² 1358, Sokolowski (1969) 20. Discussion in Whitehead (1986) 190–4. Parker (1996) 331–2. The late Gerald M. Quinn's 1971 unpublished Harvard dissertation is entitled 'The Sacrificial Calendar of the Marathonian Tetrapolis'. An unsolved puzzle is the finding place of the calendar, at Koukounari in the hills west of Marathon and the three other demes. I should record that in 1965 a *stēlē* base was visible at the site of the excavations (Richardson [1895]), which rather argues against the inscription having been brought to Koukounari for a secondary use.

[51] Cf. Parker (1996) 114–15, Osborne (1996) 296–9.

[52] A balanced account in Whitehead (1986) 349–63. Osborne (1985) 16–17 saw the settlement pattern as virtually unchanged throughout the classical period. But the continuing importance of Attic land does not mean it was always exploited and settled in the same way.

after him were concerned with the viability of demes as communities. The ability of the demes to meet their sacrificial obligations was not ensured by any outside authority. Erchia in the fourth century had apparently to adopt a system of five liturgists to pay for its many if small annual sacrifices.[53] The problem is unlikely to have been unique to Erchia. Records of deme activity diminish greatly by the third century BCE and soon disappear. Meanwhile the cults of *genē*, phratries and independent and elective groups such as those of *orgeones* and *thiasoi* continued and seem even to be increasing. With respect to the traditional cults of the Attic countryside it may be suggested that the conception of proper ritual programmes and the measures taken to maintain them at all levels were more significant than the actual participation in the performance. This points to a view of religion which, while still very different from that, say, of the post-reformation western world, is also distinct from what had been traditional in Greece.

Another clue that suggests that the model of the tightly integrated, traditional city discussed above is imperfect for classical Athens is the employment of specialized knowledge and secrecy. Where social units compete and collaborate in the realm of ritual and symbol to constitute the society as a whole, there is likely to be much secret and expert knowledge, either restricted to the group and its specialists or shared selectively with other groups.[54] In Athens, while many rituals were in the charge of the priests of particular *genē*, no doubt jealous of their position and their privileges, and certain performances were hidden from the public, we do not detect claims to superior or secret knowledge, except in those few cults specifically defined as mysteries. The vague if frequent assurance that performance was 'according to ancestral practice' (κατὰ τὰ πάτρια) is as close as we come. The history of the specialized interpreters of ritual known as exegetes is much disputed but what should not be controversial is their very limited role in Athenian religious life.[55] This is consistent with the very restricted part played by Greek priests in general. 'Greek religion might almost be called a religion without priests', as Walter Burkert has said.[56] No one was barred from sacrificing – any Athenian, man or woman depending on the cult – was eligible for the newer democratic priesthoods.[57] Priests were of a particular cult at a particular place, for example, of Apollo Delphinios at the Delphinion in Erchia.[58] What the priest controlled was access to space rather than knowledge, whether his

---

[53] Dow (1965).   [54] Cf. n. 43, *supra*.   [55] Bibliography in Nilsson (1967) 636–7, 864.
[56] Burkert (1985) 95.   [57] Aleshire (1994).
[58] *SEG* 21. 541, A 23–30, Sokolowski (1969) 18.

authority came from hereditary membership in a *genos* or appointment by a public body. The spatial aspect of the large network of 'obscure' ritual the Athenians tried to maintain in the classical period deserves attention.

By the fourth century it is arguable that the Athenian arrangements, the product of continuing political debate, were more 'political' than social, addressing the needs of the Athenian as citizen rather than as a demesman. Political decisions had brought together a great variety of cults in a comprehensive city calendar which, with the city's money, guaranteed that the supernatural interests of the demos were met. If the city calendar was, to state the obvious, in the first instance an organizing of time to serve Athenian religious interests, it was also a partial cultic map of Attica. For the local demes, place may well have been more important than date since the city's calendar necessarily took precedence, while in terms of territory the polis barely intruded into that of the demes (I do not know that any polis cult was celebrated in the territories of Erchia or Thorikos). The local calendars were maps of the deme's cultic obligations conceived of spatially; usually identification of the site was implicit in the identification of the cult and separate specification of place was not needed.

This spatial dimension of the supernatural had a long history and it is interesting that it was still strongly felt at a time when traditional group ties, with their associated cults, were probably weakening. For Greece attention to issues of sacred space in recent years has been directed largely to the dark and disputed origins of the polis.[59] But of course the social and symbolic use of space continued to evolve. The changing character of sacred space in the fully developed, and, in the view of some, declining, polis is largely unexplored territory which we can only point to here. In interpreting classical religious practice and attitudes we need to keep in view the 'modernizing' contemporary forces as well as the integrative traditions of the past.

The demos of the city organized, adapted and preserved the sacred space and time of the city as a whole. Early in the democracy it seems likely that each local demos shouldered the burden of the indispensable but largely invisible performance of ritual over the landscape of Attica. In the last analysis, it was the securing of supernatural favour to the citizen and his family by means of regular observance of many obscure rituals, that was democratic government's major obligation to the people. The observances themselves were, for the most part, ancient. Their arrangement in the classical period was the result of a long pro-

---

[59] Cf. de Polignac (1995), Alcock and Osborne (1994).

cess that kept pace with the changing society. Some citizens active at the level of their demes seem to have taken the lead in preserving regular ritual activity in the parts of Attica to which they were attached. But it may have been as much as Athenian citizens as it was as deme members that they came to see their obligations to the 'gods and heroes who occupy the polis and *khōra* of the Athenians' (Dem. 18.184, cf. Din. 4.64), a view of sacred space that encompassed Attica as a whole as well as their own particular territory.[60]

[60] I was unable to attend the conference in person but I have profited from the comments of Robin Osborne and from discussions with Allaire Brumfield and Robert Levy. [Too late for use in this paper, I became aware of Jan Bremmer, 'Religions secrets and secrecy in classical Greece', in H. G. Kippenberg and G. G. Stroumsa eds. *Secrecy and Concealment* (Leiden, 1995) 71–8.]

13 Inscribing performance

Robin Osborne

'*Inscribed upon the Cross we see in shining letters "God is love"*'*

What exactly *do* we see inscribed upon an Athenian decree? In this paper I look at how what the Athenians recorded on stone related to what they did in the Council and Assembly. I argue that what was inscribed was only a version of the words spoken in the Assembly, and that editing of various kinds occurred before inscription. What is more, what you read in an inscription is by no means a complete description of what went on to occur, for successfully carrying out a decree presupposes numerous actions which the decree itself often fails to order. In trying to account for why decrees operate in this world of their own, which is identical neither to the performance in the Assembly nor to the performance following the Assembly, I consider the relationship between the discursive matter which dominated the Assembly's time, the arguments brought to persuade the people for or against any particular action, and the words finally inscribed, drawing attention to the particular reticence of inscribed formulae. I explore the reasons for this reticence, with particular reference to honorific decrees, and suggest that it betrays both a particular attitude towards the achievement of honours, an attitude influenced by parallels with victories in games, and a particular democratic political position.

We can have some confidence that we know what went on in the Athenian Assembly. Once the sacrifice, curses, and prayers had been carried out, votes were taken on which of the Council's proposals needed further debate and then the debates themselves followed.[1] The

---

* From the hymn 'We sing the praise of Him who died' by Thomas Kelly, published in 1815. Frank Collquhoun (*A Hymn Companion* (London, 1985) 84) describes these lines as 'a strikingly imaginative touch. The Gospels tell us that over the cross was written, "This is Jesus the King of the Jews," the sentence of condemnation. To the eye of faith the inscription reads quite differently. It is transfigured into letters of gold and reads, "God is Love" – the message of salvation.'
[1] On all this see Strauss (1985) 74–5, Hansen (1991) 142.

Council motion was first read out and then, in response for the call for volunteers to speak, citizens got up and tried to persuade the 6000 or so who were assembled that the Council's motion was or was not a good idea or to persuade them that it needed some addition or modification. This procedure may not have remained unchanged over time – Aiskhines claims that older men had been given priority in speaking in past time[2] – but there is no good reason not to believe that the pattern goes back to the 450s at least, which is when we begin to have inscribed decrees preserved in some quantity. But what, out of all this, gets put on stone?

On many occasions Assembly decisions led to nothing on stone at all. Many of the most important Athenian decisions produced no work for stonemasons: most obviously the Athenians never recorded on stone decisions to go to war or decisions to send a fleet, though the expenses arising from such decisions did often get inscribed. We can deduce from what survives, and from comparing that to Athenian decisions known from literary sources, that Athenians were more inclined to record on stone decisions of permanent or on-going importance, but going any further is problematic precisely because only very important decisions not recorded on stone survive in the non-epigraphic record.

In the case of those decisions of the Assembly which do get recorded, it would seem at first sight that what the Athenians recorded on stone was who took the decision (the Council and the People in cases where the procedure described above is carried out without hitch), which magistrates were in control, what the Council proposed, and who it was from the Council who acted as front man for it, along with any amendment which was agreed, and the name of the person who proposed that amendment. The well-preserved decree honouring Oiniades of Palaiskiathos in 408/7 BCE is an excellent example of this.[3] It is easy to imagine that these are the actual words of the *probouleuma*, modified only in accordance with the request made in the amendment, and that that amendment is recorded in the very words of its proposer Antikhares. But is that really what we have got here? and why have the Athenians adopted this form of record?[4]

---

[2] Aiskhines 1.22–3, on which see Lane Fox (1994) 147–8 and Ford p. 246 above.
[3] ML 90/*IG* i³ 110/Fornara 160.
[4] As will become apparent, my concern is with classical Athenian practice. Athenian practice itself changed over time, and practice elsewhere varied considerably. In the Roman period there are decrees which come very much closer to being, if not verbatim records of proceedings at a public meeting, at least very full minutes of the meeting. See Rhodes with Lewis (1997) 561–2 citing e.g. *SEG* 12.226, 24.614, and *IG* xii.9 906.

Other fifth-century decrees show that there is indeed a question here. I want to take three examples and argue in turn (a) that we may see on a stone only a much abbreviated or otherwise edited version of the *probouleuma* that (a member of) the Council proposed to the Assembly; (b) that either a *probouleuma* or an intervention made from the floor of the Assembly might be edited in such a way as to become virtually incoherent; and (c) that the selection of what gets recorded makes it impossible to understand why the Athenians took the decision that they did, and that this effectively depoliticizes Athenian decisions, discouraging their reopening.[5]

(a) I begin with the decree regulating Athenian relations with Phaselis, for which a date shortly before 450 BCE remains orthodox.[6] The decree opens by declaring itself to be the decision of Council and People, and then identifies the magistrates responsible – the *prytaneis* are identified by tribe, the Secretary and President by name. Then we are given a proposer's name. So far, so standard: this is a decree that fits into the middle of the development of prescripts as described by Alan Henry (though we will come to wonder about his motivations for changes): 'Down to the end of the fourth century the development of the prescript proceeded along orderly and logical lines: from the simple statement of legal sanction, through a period when the function of the prescript was simply to record the responsible officials, to a time when the greater publicity given to stones no longer confined to the Acropolis occasioned the refinement of details of date and venue.'[7] But immediately after the prescript we get a publication clause: 'inscribe the decree for the Phaselites'. Can Leon really have begun like that? Could a proposal to agree a judicial treaty with Phaselis really have been presented as a proposal to publish an agreement? Even if it did begin with a publication clause can it really have referred to what was to come merely as 'the decree' rather than 'this decree' or 'the following decree'? – it is 'this decree' that occurs when the publication clause is repeated at the end, where the officer to be responsible (the Secretary of the Council), the material of the inscription (a stone stele) and the source of the money for it (the Phaselites) are all recorded. In the fourth century it appears that the Athenians, on some occasions at least, both recorded the terms of an agreement with another city without any preamble (as Tod 101), and also made a separate record of the As-

---

[5] Some of the material examined here was examined also by Laqueur (1927), who used it to arrive at rather different conclusions involving extensive editing of texts before inscription; his views and their basis are carefully scrutinized by Billigheimer (1938).
[6] ML 31/*IG* i³ 10/Fornara 68.
[7] Henry (1977) 105.

sembly decision to adopt them, detailing some of the circumstances in which they were adopted. So, in the case of the alliance with Khalkis in 377 BCE a record of the alliance follows a proposal by one Pyrrhandros to accept the terms: 'Pyrrhandros proposed: concerning what the Khalkidians say, to bring them to the people at the first Assembly, and to contribute the opinion of the Council that the Council thinks they should accept the alliance from the Khalkidians ...' (Tod 124). What the Phaselis decree would appear to do is in between these two separate forms: it acknowledges the fact that Leon was the one who put forward the proposed agreement, but strips out all preamble other than the injunction to inscribe which serves to explain the presence of the terms on stone.

(b) My second example is one where scholars have indeed much debated the form of the decree: the decree about establishing a priestess of Athene Nike and doing building work in her sanctuary.[8] What survives begins with a mention of the demos and the end of a proposer's name. It proceeds to establish a priesthood of Athene Nike, to put gates/doors on the sanctuary according to the specifications of Kallikrates and a tender in the hands of the *poletai*, to determine the pay and perquisites attached to the priesthood, and to build a shrine to the specifications of Kallikrates and a stone altar. It then records a rider proposed by one Hestiaios establishing a committee of three members of the Council to help Kallikrates draw up the specifications and report to the Council on the tendering process. An excellent example of the way in which the fifth-century Assembly decided particular measures (the building work) and general rules (priestess) indiscriminately, when in the fourth century the latter would be a matter of law, this inscription is remarkable for the 'illogical' order in which the items are presented. Whether, with Meritt, we regard even the first proposal here as a rider, or whether, with Meiggs and Lewis, we think of the first proposal as the substantive measure,[9] the way in which the items tumble over one another is hard to transpose into an Assembly context: did someone really get up and present a proposal in this form? When they and others had spoken in favour of the four or five separate decisions with, presumably, separate arguments but arguments which must surely have grouped matters relating to the priestess and matters relating to the sanctuary, was the proposal then restated still in this order?

(c) My third example, the Methone decree, brings out once more the incoherence which results from the omission of arguments, and it

---

[8] ML 44/*IG* i^{3}35/Fornara 93. On the building work see now Mark (1993).
[9] Meritt *Hesperia* 10 (1941) 307–15, ML pp. 110–11.

Inscribing performance

also brings out the political implications of that omission.[10] In this case the Council do not make a single proposal but ask the Assembly to settle between alternatives – whether to reassess the tribute immediately or whether the Methonaians should pay only the *aparkhē* on their current assessment (lines 5–9, decision in lines 29–32). It is even more pressing in the case of a question like this from the Council that factors relevant to the decision be rehearsed, yet, as indeed is usual in the case of 'open' *probouleumata*, no grounds for discussion are offered, no hint given of what is at issue. Two forms are regularly used in fifth-century inscriptions to indicate purpose or motive: the 'since ...' and the 'in order that' form; but neither is here in evidence.[11] That the Council offered alternatives to the Assembly is, one might think, of less lasting significance than the reasons which caused the Athenians to take the decision they took, but it is the Council's questions alone that make it onto stone. By omitting the arguments the inscribed record obscures the political issues: we are given no hint of what the Council thought might weigh in favour of one or the other option, let alone of any argument used in the Assembly debate. We might reckon that the Council failed to make a recommendation because it was itself split on the question, and hence that this was a particularly live issue, but the deadpan presentation of alternatives in the inscribed record throws a veil over the arguments. Reading the inscribed records can never have been a way of giving oneself a political education.[12]

Epigraphists talk of the development of a 'chancellery style' in Athenian inscriptions from the end of the fifth century. I suspect that the reasons for the use of the phrase 'chancellery' are epigraphic: because it is the inscriptions that the scholars are interested in it is in inscriptional terms that they have sought to account for (ir)regularities. My three examples, however, make at least the beginnings of a case for thinking that what gets inscribed may indeed be 'chancellery', that we cannot assume that there is no gap between the words spoken in the Assembly and the words recorded on the stone. In the light of this we should perhaps reckon the Oiniades decree as an example not of the words of the *probouleuma* 'modified only in accordance with the request

---

[10] ML 65/*IG* i³61/Fornara 128.
[11] For 'Since...' See e.g. ML 58A.3/*IG* i³52/Fornara 119; for 'in order that' see e.g. ML 46.8/ *IG* i³34/Fornara 98.
[12] It is worth noting a comparable gap between what the Athenians will have needed to know to make their decisions and what is said in the case of the record of debates in Thucydides. Although Thucydides, unlike the Methone decree, does record arguments employed, the arguments he records frequently operate at a very general level, even when the Athenians must have been presented with specific information in order to make their practical choices.

made in the amendment' but of the way in which inscriptions do *not* record the words of the *probouleuma*. Although the recording of the rider here allows us to see what is happening, the chancellery change to the body of the decree itself obscures a point of at least some political significance. The gap between what was proposed and argued for in the Assembly and what was recorded on stone is politically important.

The political importance of this gap between what happened in the Assembly and what was recorded is enhanced by the way in which the Athenians themselves treated what was inscribed upon the stone as the 'official text'. Although from the end of the fifth century Athens kept an archive of Assembly decisions, it seems to have been the text on stone which was regarded as the official text. One of the best demonstrations of this is the so-called charter of the Second Athenian Confederacy (Tod 123). Not only does this inscription make provision (lines 31–5) to 'take down' any stele which is unfavourable to the allies,[13] but at lines 12–14 a clause was deliberately erased: here, therefore, we see an inscription on stone being treated as definitive, and that stone being amended, in a way which 'falsifies' it as a historical document, without any measure ordering its amendment being recorded on the stone itself.[14] The Assembly's decision has been translated into a distinct inscribed record which is itself then subject to explicit editing by the Assembly in order to ensure that past decisions which continue to have current force continue to reflect accurately current Athenian political views.

The special status of the text on stone needs to be understood in the light of where inscriptions were put up. The vast majority of Athenian decrees which do not directly relate to a particular location (laws on silver coinage to the mint, grain laws to the agora, and so on) were put on display on the Acropolis. This is a fact which we have come to take for granted, but it is a fact that should cause us some surprise. The Athenian Acropolis can never have been a thoroughfare or a leisure centre. People strolled through the agora and milled about in its stoas, it was a place where people gathered to hear what the Council was up to, as at the beginning of Plato's *Menexenos*, or to gather the latest gossip from the courts. But for most Athenians visits to the Acropolis can only have happened on high days and holidays, and high days and

---

[13] Compare [Aristotle] *Constitution of the Athenians* 35.2 on the Thirty taking down the laws of Ephialtes and Arkhestratos about the Areopagites, and below on the reinscription of decrees knocked down by the Thirty.

[14] Compare, in the fifth century, the erasure of an early preamble and its replacement by a later one when the treaties with Leontinoi and with Rhegion were renewed in 433–2 (ML 63, 64). More generally see Thomas (1992) 86, 122–3, 135 and Rhodes with Lewis (1997) 3 n.4.

Inscribing performance 347

holidays which were Acropolis specific will have occurred even less frequently than meetings of the Assembly on the Pnyx. What is more, the non-Athenians who are the subjects of many of the inscriptions put up on the Acropolis, and for whom the treaties made with and honours given to other non-Athenians might be held have an important exemplary role, will have had fewer occasions still to climb up to the Acropolis, unless simply as sightseers.

The importance of the Acropolis for the display of inscriptions cannot be because it was a convenient central place – not by chance, I suspect, was the Charter of the Second Athenian Confederacy, a document which required frequent working on, put up instead in the agora. The importance of the Acropolis as a place of display must be related to its religious importance. Just as early inscribed laws are all from religious contexts, whether or not their provisions have to do with religion,[15] and just as it seems to be religious visibility, rather than magisterial accountability, which lies behind the inscription of Athenian financial records,[16] so with Athenian decrees, it is arguably for a divine as much as a human public that they are displayed. By inscribing them and erecting the stelai on the Acropolis, political decisions are taken from the sphere of debate, from the political world of the Pnyx and the agora, and replaced set before the eyes of the gods, as records of human achievement inviting protection. If we find the depoliticizing performed by the inscribed record odd, it is perhaps that we underestimate how far the Acropolis is from Athenian politics. Incribing a political decision rendered it, in one very obvious sense, visible. But it may have been done less to ensure visibility than because it was important that it should be part of Michael Jameson's world of the obscure.

If there is a gap between the words of the Assembly and the words inscribed on stone, there is also a gap between the words inscribed on stone and the actions resulting from the Assembly decision. The words recorded in an inscription are clearly not *all* that happens as a result of the decision which they record. Again a trivial feature of the Oiniades honours illustrates this. The inscription records the decision that the secretary of the Council should have the decision to honour Oiniades as *proxenos* and benefactor inscribed on a stone stele and set up on the Acropolis. Since it was indeed so inscribed someone must have paid for it. But the inscription records no decision as to who is to pay. Such an omission is quite frequent in fifth-century decrees; preserved early expense clauses (e.g. *IG* i³ 17.11–12, ML 31.26–7 (restored), 49.18–

---

[15] Thomas (1995/1996); van Effenterre (1994).   [16] Davies (1994).

20, 52.60-1 cf. 45 clause 10, 47.40-1, 87.36, 89.43-4, 94.40) tend to record that it is *not* the Athenians who are paying (but Athenians pay explicitly in e.g. *IG* i³ 7, *IG* i³ 23, *IG* i³ 27), but other decrees record the responsibility of the *poletai* for tendering for the inscription and of the *kōlakretai* for providing the money (e.g. ML 69.25-6, 73.51-2 (rider)). Failure to mention the paying body cannot be explained away on the grounds that the procedure was always the same unless otherwise stated: when Athens honoured Karpathos in the fifth century (*IG* i³ 1454) and decided to inscribe copies of the agreement both on the Acropolis and in Karpathos at the temple of Apollo no provision for who pays was recorded, but the expense of the inscription on Karpathos can hardly have simply gone through routine channels. Even in the fourth century, when there was a fund from which inscription of decrees was paid, decisions about who was to pay were still specifically, but not invariably, recorded.

A particularly fascinating issue concerning a gap between inscribed word and enacted deed concerns the relationship between the inscription already discussed, setting up the priestess of Athene Nike, and the inscription on its reverse (*IG* i³ 36/ML 71/Fornara 139), dated to 424/3 by the name of the secretary. The earlier inscription, as preserved, makes no provision for its own publication or who will pay for it, nor for who will pay the salary assigned to the priestess. In the later inscription it is laid down that it is the *kōlakretai* who are to pay the fifty drachmas to the priestess. The sum was written as a numeral and then that numeral was erased and the sum, together with the following clause specifying who pays this and when, is written in, and is written in Ionic whereas up until the numeral the letters are Attic. Why the change to a different cutter and different orthography after the first had got as far as the fifty dr. sign? What had happened about the pay for the priestess before this second decree was passed? Does the change in cutter mirror a discontinuity in performance, or is it simply a matter of some different cutter, with different views about numerals, taking over where the first had left off? Had the Athenians forgotten to decide first time who was to pay and had the priestess not been paid at all before this second decision had been taken? This latter possibility seems highly unlikely if the earlier inscription dates to the 440s, and even if the earlier inscription were to date to the earlier 420s, as Mattingly has suggested, we might expect some reference to back pay here. If what this later inscription does is simply to change who pays, or when, then it would prove nicely that more had been done than had been laid down in what was inscribed.

We cannot then assume either that what gets onto a stone was for-

Inscribing performance

malized and enunciated in precisely those terms in the Assembly, or that if it was not put on the stone it did not happen.[17] Inscribed decrees operate in a space of their own, which is not identical to any performance in the Assembly or after the Assembly. Negatively, inscriptions fail adequately to record either the words of the Assembly or the actions resulting from them. But these omissions also have positive political implications. In further exploring the way in which inscribed texts perform I want to turn to the question of what decrees say beyond the mere recording of decisions.

Early decrees may record decisions without giving any information about either the circumstances or the reasons for the decision. So the Thespian and Delphian proxeny decrees (*IG* i³ 23, 27) of around 450 BCE give no indication of why the Athenians passed them, and neither of the Athene Nike decrees gives any motive or circumstance for action. Other decrees may give the circumstances but not the reasons: the Praxiergidai decree (*IG* i³ 7) follows a request from the Praxiergidai, and the alliance with the Amphiktyony of *c.* 458 probably announced itself as being 'in accordance with the pronouncement of those from Pylai'. But after around 450 at least some indication of why a measure is being taken seems normal. The people of Sigeion are honoured, perhaps around 450, 'since they are good to the Athenian people' and the writing up of the decree is also explained as being 'in accordance with their own request, in order that it might be written and they might not be wronged not even by a single individual of those on the mainland' (*IG* i³ 17.6–9, 13–15).[18] Most frequently the explanation given for commendation is brief and formulaic – 'because he was a good man and keen to do good to the Athenian people' (*IG* i³

---

[17] On the latter assumption see Rhodes (1993) 2: 'It has long been acknowledged, particularly with reference to decrees honouring individuals, that a text inscribed on stone was not the official text of a decree (which was kept in the archives) [but see below p. 352] but a transcript of it: it seems clear that omission of the δοκιμασία clause from the inscribed text of a decree does not prove that the δοκιμασία was not required at the time of the decree, and more generally we should be very careful in basing arguments on the absence of a standard clause from certain texts.' Compare also Rhodes with Lewis (1997) 3: 'When a state published, or allows an interested individual to publish, a decree, we may assume that the published text is based on (but is not necessarily a complete and *verbatim* copy of) an original text written on papyrus or comparable material'; and *ibid.* 6 'not even an inscribed decree of standard type can be relied on to be absolutely complete: the absence of an item which we might expect to find does not guarantee that the item was absent from the original text in the archives also, or, even if it were absent from the original text also (which we cannot check), that the stage in the procedure to which the expected item would have referred was omitted on the occasion when the decree which lacks the item was enacted'.

[18] Whitehead (1993) 44–7 uses this as a paradigm early honorific inscription in his analysis of the description of virtues in Athenian decrees.

177.4–8). 'In the fourth century as honorary decrees gradually developed a standardized pattern wherein the general reasons for all the honours which were to follow were given in an initial ἐπειδή clause, so too the ἐπαινέσαι provision came to be closely associated with the στεφανῶσαι provision, with which it was frequently combined. In this form there is also usually a summary mention of the honorand's qualities and virtues expressed in a phrase composed of an abstract noun (or nouns) and ἕνεκα.'[19]

The Athenian people can never have honoured an individual or a group without some word being spoken to justify the honour.[20] But it is not only the inscriptions which give no grounds at all for commendation that are problematic: as with U.K. honours lists, the stock phrases of commendation equally invite questions, for to be told that a man has been good to the Athenian people is to invite a request to be told in what the goodness consisted. The extensive descriptions of the virtues of those honoured in which speakers in the Assembly may have indulged have in most honorific inscriptions been reduced to the briefest of acknowledgements of their virtues. Varied services are reduced to uniform terms and only the abstracted goodness of the act, rather than the example of its detail, is, in general, paraded before a wider and deeper public.

This feature of Athenian inscriptions has a political charge. The recording of the Sigeion request that the honours be written up already reveals the value given to publication. The rider to the Oiniades honours, which commend him for being good man, keen to do the city of the Athenians what good he could, and a benefactor of Athenians arriving at Skiathos, shows an interest in the precise terms in which he is described. Such a concern with the exact wording of a description can be paralleled in the slightly earlier honours for the people of Neapolis, where a rider insists that they should not be written up as 'colonists of the Thasians' (ML 89.58–9/*IG* i^3 101). But the rider to the honours for the people of Neapolis is of greater interest still, in as far as it insists on spelling out the services which have earned the honours. Although the initial decree is fragmentary, it is clear that it mentioned the Neapolitans' unwillingness to revolt from Athens, their goodness to Athens and her allies, and their keenness to do good to Athens in word and deed. Axiokhos' rider, although it puts to the Assembly a particular Neapolitan request, adds to their honours only

---

[19] Henry (1983) 7.
[20] Compare Tod 167 with Demosthenes' discussion of the reasons for honouring Leukon at Demosthenes 20.29–40.

an instruction to the Athenian generals to protect Neapolis, but in the process it repeats at far greater length the grounds for praise: 'since they are men good to the army and the city of the Athenians and because they fought against Thasos to help the Athenians besiege it and because they helped in the sea battle and won and have always joined the allies by land and because of the other ways they have benefited the Athenians'. The Neapolitans, to whom the expense of the inscription is charged, are getting their money's worth and the rider is making the decree far more explicitly political than it was in its original formulation.

Other exceptionally full descriptions of the behaviour which led to honours being awarded further display its political importance. When in 407/6 the Athenians, perhaps on the proposal of Alkibiades, decreed honours to Arkhelaos king of Macedon, the description of the services which had merited this ran for some seven lines (now only partially preserved). The honouring of Arkhelaos here is only part of a proposal to get ships built in Macedonia, and it is clear that Athens' military need demands that she do all she can to expedite this. The now incomplete description of the services of Strato, king of Sidon, dating from the 360s, may also have been quite full, but what the inscription itself makes clear is that the statement had been drawn out of the Athenians by ambassadors who had come from Strato. In 327 a similarly full and explicit description of the services rendered to Athens by Mentor of Rhodes was made in the course of inscribing honours for his nephew Memnon, and considerable detail about Memnon's own actions may have been in the part of the inscription now illegible (Tod 199); although the precise political implications of the Athenian act are now not recoverable, it is clear that these honours were, in part at least, a way in which the Athenians marked out their position with regard to Alexander.

The phenomenon of a rider magnifying the description of the honourable behaviour, seen in the case of the Neapolitans, can be paralleled in other cases. The original fifth-century proposal to declare Herakleides of Klazomenai a *proxenos* and benefactor (ML 70) was amended to bestow rights to own land and a house and the same immunity from taxes as was enjoyed by other *proxenoi*; Thoukydides' rider proposing this details the help which Herakleides had given to the Athenian ambassadors to Persia where the main proposal had mentioned standard 'benefaction' and being good to the Athenians. Similarly although little more than Kephalos' rider to the decree for Phanokritos of Parion is preserved, it is clear that, as well as making him a *proxenos*, and not just hailing him as a benefactor, it laid out the reasons for commendation in much greater detail: 'since he announced to the generals that the ships were sailing by, and if the generals had been persuaded the enemy triremes would have been captured' (Tod 116.11–15/*IG* ii² 29). Given that Phanokritos had not actually brought any benefit to the Athenians it was perhaps important, in what may be the only unreal condition in any Attic prose inscription, to emphasize that he would have done but for the generals. And here as in the Neapolitan case laying out the grounds for honours more explicitly brings to the fore the political face of Athenian action.

More is at stake in the writing up of an honorific decree than simply making a record. Honorands often pay for their honours to be inscribed, and to be re-inscribed when the earlier stele has been destroyed. So one of the sons of the Thasian Apemantos pays for the record of the grant of their proxeny to be reinscribed after the original stele had been destroyed under the Thirty (Tod 98/*IG* ii² 6). When re-inscribed it is headed with the five names of the sons, before ever the prescript is recorded. Nor do higher honours trump lower ones, when it comes to having an inscription made. When Herakleides of Klazomenai was given (probably) citizenship in the early 390s the earlier decree was inscribed below the record of the citizenship grant – even though the citizenship grant rendered all the earlier privileges obsolete (ML 70/ *IG* ii² 8 and 65/ Osborne T 27 (Plato *Ion* 541c–d)). Did Herakleides or his sponsors want to ensure that there was a particularly large stele recording the honours to him? Was it more honourable to have repeatedly deserved honour from the Athenians than to have won the honour in one go? Or was a point being made in the internal politics of the years just after 400 BCE by bringing to the fore the Peace of Epilykos?

The most extensive record of honours for a single individual is *IG* ii² 360/*SIG*³ 304. This complicated inscription records two sets of honours for Herakleides of Salamis which between them involve five separate motions to the Assembly. The inscription as we have it opens with a decree of 325/4 proposed by Demosthenes son of Demokles of Lamptrai which makes Herakleides an Athenian *proxenos* and benefactor, gives him rights to own a house and land in Athens, and duties to pay *eisphorai* and serve on campaigns with the Athenians. Not only are the grounds for this laid out in detail – gifts of 3000 medimnoi of grain at 5 dr. a medimnos during a grain shortage and then a gift of 3000 dr. for the purchase of grain – but the honours order not only their own inscription but the inscription of 'the other praises which have been made of him'. There then follow: (2) the inscription of a proposal of Telemakhos son of Theangelos of Akharnai to give him a gold crown and send an ambassador to protest to Dionysios of Herakleia about the taking of Herakleides' sails; (3) a proposal of the same Telemakhos in the Assembly that the Council at its next sitting consider Herakleides; (4) a proposal by Kephisodotos son of Euarkhides of Akharnai in response to this request proposing that Herakleides should be given a 500 dr. gold crown for supplying the people with 3000 medimnoi of grain at 5 dr. a medimnos; and (5) a proposal from Phyleus son of Pausanias of Oinoe that since the Council had been asked to bring a proposal about Herakleides and since he had added to his former benefaction of 3000 medimnoi of grain at 5 dr. a medimnos 3000 dr. for purchasing grain the *proedroi* should put before the Assembly at its next meeting the Council view that he should have a 500 dr. gold crown. The inscription concludes with four crowns, two saying 'The People' and two 'The Council'. Discussion of this decree has tended to focus either on what it tells us about grain crisis in the 320s or on what it does (and does not) reveal about procedure.[21] In terms of my earlier discussion about gaps, it is indeed striking that the definitive Assembly decrees rewrite the *probouleumata* without repeating everything that was in those *probouleumata* – we have to go back to the *probouleumata* to find out how much is to be spent on the crowns. As is common when decrees are combined into a dossier only one full prescript is found and that relates to the final decree (compare ML 65) – only the presence of two crowns saying 'The people' indicates that the earlier decrees were ratified. Particularly curious is the way in which the final decree seems most economically to be considered to depend upon the last motion recorded, the proposal of Phyleus in the Council, yet whereas logically one would expect the *probouleuma* out of which an Assembly motion grows to be recorded, if at all, before the substantive motion to which it has given rise, here it is recorded as if a quite separate matter, at the end of the inscription. *SIG* notes Koehler's remark on the phrase used to refer in the final decree to the earlier motions: 'praise' rather than 'decree': 'The proposer uses "praise", a word of more general significance, because "decrees" or "probouleumata" are both involved without distinction.'[22] But that begs the question of why it is that these *probouleumata* are recorded at all, to which the answer is surely that the advertising of the praise is specifically what the honorand desired, and by tracing the honours through all their stages the two acts for which the honours are given, both of which are mentioned in the decree which orders the others to be published, are celebrated repeatedly.

---

[21] For the former see Garnsey (1988) 154–6, for the latter Rhodes (1972) 66–7, Rhodes with Lewis (1997) 24–5.
[22] 'Voce latius patente ἐπαίνους utitur rogator, quia promiscue ψηφίσματα et προβουλεύματα inciduntur.'

That there was a demand for repeated exposition of honours in order to establish their on-going truth seems further suggested by the way in which the honours for the Samians passed in 405 were not only themselves re-affirmed in 403/2, but Poses, the Samian who seems to have been most behind this, gets himself given 'the book [of the decree]' (Tod 97.21) and a further guarantee that the honours previously voted remained valid.

Even set out at this length, Athenian honours remain laconic and uninformative. Comparison with Hellenistic practice in Athens and in other cities makes this point particularly clearly. Even to cite a small section of the Athenian honours for Phaidros or Kallias of Sphettos or the Olbian honours for Protogenes or the Istrian honours for Agathokles both of late third or early second century BCE makes this point plain.[23] Take just the opening of the honour for Protogenes: 'Resolved by the Council and the People, on the twentieth; the magistrates and the Seven moved: Heroson, father of Protogenes, has performed many great services for the city which involved the expenditure of money and personal exertion, and Protogenes, having taken over his father's goodwill towards the people has throughout his life constantly said and done what was best. First when King Saitaphernes came to Cancytus and asked for the gifts due for his people . . .' That these communities – even third-century Athens – are prepared to spin out the achievements of the wealthy and powerful at such lengths is perhaps a measure of how far they were from the relative egalitarianism of classical Athens.

If inscription, adding riders, and publishing every stage of the proceedings separately were all ways of magnifying the description of honours at Athens, having those honours announced on some public occasion was a further means, enlarging the public addressed beyond that which was politically active. Examination of such proclamation raises a new set of questions about decrees and performance, and moves us from decrees as a record of past performance to decrees as a basis for future performance.

The practice of proclaiming publicly honours that had been given to an individual began in the late fifth century. Announcing the honouring of Thrasyboulos of Kalydon at the Dionysia is one of the distinctly novel, or at least new-fangled, ways in which the murderers of the oligarch Phrynikhos were praised – for those associated with the murder are also among the first recipients of a grant of the right to own land and a house at Athens (ML 85.12–13 (proclamation), 30–2 (right to

---

[23] Phaidros: *IG* ii² 602; Protogenes: *SIG*³ 495, Austin no. 98 (whose translation I cite, with minor changes); Agathokles: Moretti ii. 131, Austin 99.

own land)). Announcing honours became more or less regular for foreign potentates (Evagoras of Salamis (*SEG* 29.86 on), occasionally used for foreigners (particularly if they are given citizenship too) and then later in the fourth century extended to honours for states (*IG* ii² 448 is the earliest) and for citizens (Ktesiphon's honours for Demosthenes first (Aiskhines 3.34) and then *IG* ii² 1629.190-201/Tod 200 for the first epigraphic example).[24] The formula employed for Thrasyboulos of Kalydon is that the announcement should say 'the reason why' (hõv hέv | [εκα]) he was crowned, but four years later when Epikerdes of Cyrene was honoured for giving the city 100 minas the herald was instructed to make an additional proclamation that Epikerdes had given the city 100 minas to help save it and that that was why he was crowned for his manly goodness and goodwill to the Athenians (*IG* i³ 125.23-9). Specifying such a text for the herald never catches on, however, and fourth-century proclamations seem to be limited to mentioning the fact of crowning or alluding to the virtues which have deserved the reward in the usual abstract terms already well established as the inscribed norm.

Proclamation would seem, therefore, to come to stand in a particular relationship to the events in the Assembly which lead up to it. Whereas the Assembly hears both a proposal and arguments for that proposal, what gets proclaimed, like what gets inscribed, is, after the early case of Epikerdes, not a summary of the arguments, but a very brief and formal statement reporting the fact of the crown or the honour.[25] Being honoured by the Assembly becomes just like winning an athletic event: just as victors were 'reported', so too honorands were reported, and on the very same occasions when victors were reported – at competitive festivals. A Panathenaic amphora (BM B144) shows a victor in a horse race being announced, and Pindar makes it clear that victors at the Pythian games were formally announced by a herald (*Pythian* 1.30-3). The similarity between honorands and victors comes out most strongly from the honours given to Spartokos, Pairisades and Apollonios, the sons of Leukon, in 346 BCE. The Athenians decided to have these Bosporan rulers honoured with a gold crown at every Great Panathenaia. The *athlothetai* were charged with the making of the crowns and with announcing that Spartokos and Pairisades the sons of Leukon were crowned for their excellence and goodwill towards the Athenian people, but also with having the crowns inscribed when they were

---

[24] For all this see Henry (1983) 28–33. *IG* ii² 555 exceptionally arranges that Asklepiades of Byzantion be proclaimed in Byzantion.
[25] Whatever one thinks about the decree itself (see Plato *Phaidros* 258a) the proclamation is not a source of glory for the proposer.

dedicated to Athene Polias with the words 'Spartokos and Pairisades sons of Leukon dedicated these to Athena having been crowned by the People' (Tod 167.24–39/*IG* ii^2 212). Victors at the panhellenic festivals could supplement their crown and the announcement of their victory by erecting a statue or having a victory ode composed for them. For those honoured by a city with a crown, the erection of an inscription served as both victor's dedication and victory ode.

This parallelism between victors and honorands may help us to see why the formulae of praise are generally so reticent and go into so little detail about the services for which the reward is given. To be honoured is to have won a competition in virtue and the honour is the prize for a victory. Just as the details of an athletic victory – by how far or how long a time interval someone won a running or chariot race or how long a boxing match lasted – are irrelevant once the victory itself has been achieved, so the details of behaviour which led to honour being given become irrelevant. We see this further reflected in the *philotimia* formula: men are praised not because their giving corn will encourage others to give corn, but because their display of *philotimia*, and the opportunity which it gives for the city to show that it rewards *philotimia*, will lead others to display *philotimia*.[26]

Taking this attitude to public behaviour which is worth honouring is not politically neutral: rather it is politically neutralizing. The circumstances regarded as worthy of honour may themselves be subject to a variety of views, and repeatedly to return to them may encourage debate over whether they really did deserve honour. From time to time, as with the Thirty demolishing the stele honouring those Thasian democrats, even an honour will itself remain controversial. This is still more true, of course, of inscriptions which record dishonour or an agreement imposed by force, as with the agreement which Athens imposed upon Ioulis which the rebels threw down – an agreement which seems also to have recorded the names of transgressors (Tod 142). But in case of honour or dishonour, hiding the circumstances which led to the honour at least reduces the possibility of the issue remaining a live one. It is as if the criteria for public honours are as straightforward and preordained as those for victory in a foot-race.

The de-politicizing of honours may help to explain how it was that Leptines' law, which restricted the scope of honours by ruling out grants of immunity from taxation, could get passed. The idea of, effectively, making grants of *enktesis* and citizenship the only honours which offered on-going material rewards, and hence of making it impossible

[26] Whitehead (1983); see also Henry (1996).

Inscribing performance 357

to give on-going material rewards to citizens, was no doubt one that could be made to appeal both to the poor, since it was a way of preserving public revenues, and to the rich, since it would keep up the pool of those liable to perform liturgies and pay *eisphora* and so reduce the frequency with which others were called upon to use their financial resources to the city's benefit. But the self-interested appeal of this marginal financial attraction would seem hardly sufficient to pursuade any body of people who saw in the passing of honours a major political tool which required a full range of possible variants if it was to deliver its full potential. To an Assembly used to regarding being honoured as like achieving a victory, however, such subtleties might well be invisible. The depoliticizing effect of the way honours were recorded and declared had itself political consequences.

Examination of a rather different inscription, and the way in which it too sets up a future performance which is depoliticized, suggests that the Athenians were perhaps masters of the art of keeping political debate to the Council and Assembly and of reducing the chances that matters might remain public issues. SIG^3 204/IG ii^2 204 records Athenian decisions in 352/1 BCE about the Sacred Orgas that lay on the Athenian border with Megara. The beginning of the decree is lost and our text starts with the setting up of a committee to adjudicate about the boundary of the Orgas. It goes on to assign responsibility for looking after the Sacred Orgas and other Athenian [?sanctuaries] to the Areopagos, the General over the countryside, the *peripolarkhs*, the *demarkhs*, and the Council of 500. It then orders the secretary of the Council to take two identical pieces of tin and write on one of them that it is better and more good to build on one specified bit of the Sacred Orgas and on the other that it is better to leave that bit of Orgas untouched. The *Epistates* of the *proedroi* is then to take these piece of tin, wind wool round them, and deposit them into a bronze hydria. The Treasurer of the Goddess is then to provide one gold and one silver hydria and the *Epistates* is to take one of the pieces of tin from the bronze hydria and put it into the silver hydria and take the other and put it into the gold hydria. Then the *Epistates* of the *Prytaneis* is to seal the two hydriai and any Athenian who wants to can counter-seal them. The Treasurers are then to take the hydriai to the Akropolis. Three men are to be chosen, two from all Athenians and one from the Council to go to Delphi and ask whether the Athenians should act in accordance with what is said in the gold hydria or in accordance with what is said in the silver hydria. When this committee returns the hydriai are to be fetched and the relevant piece of tin to be recovered and read out. The rest of the inscription deals with its inscription, the selection and payment of the committees it has caused to be formed, and the provision of *horoi* for the Orgas. This inscription was effectively exploited by Fontenrose to show something of the attitude towards and expectations of the Delphic oracle. There were perhaps particular reasons for Athens adopting so indirect a means of consulting the oracle at this date, but the inscription is a fine example of the way in which the oracle can be made to decide matters without involving it politically in the major decision. It is similarly a fine example of the way in which the Athenians devised procedures whose elaborateness made visible, through the unnecessarily complicated ritual that it ordained, the impossibility of partiality.[27] This visible impartiality ensured that a matter which they felt they could not decide immediately did not run on as a political issue. Having decided not themselves to decide, they devised a means of reaching a decision in future which did not involve, though it could not of course entirely preclude, raking over the religious and foreign policy issues again. And they did so by pre-inscribing the decision, so that once the oracle had chosen its hydria the decision was already inscribed.

What is inscribed on decrees is not a straightforward record of words spoken in the decreeing body, nor is it a complete script for consequent future action. Much of the language of decrees and of the editing practice may have developed simply through the private initiatives of successive secretaries and might be held to represent a sensible compromise between exhaustive minutes and those that are so laconic as to be quite uninformative. But the practice that evolves is not without its political implications and consequences. Just as Thomas Kelly saw something inscribed upon the cross which was not literally there inscribed, so we should see a particular democratic approach to political decision-making inscribed in Athenian public decrees. Rather than recording a performance or scripting a performance, the publicly displayed texts of Athenian decrees are an independent inscribed performance.[28]

---

[27] Comparison with the elaboration of the system finally evolved for allotting jurors to courts is instructive here: see [Aristotle] *Constitution of the Athenians* 63–5 and Rhodes (1981) 704–5 and 711.

[28] I have been greatly helped by the generous comments and criticisms of Simon Hornblower, Michael Jameson, Robert Parker and Peter Rhodes on earlier drafts of this piece.

14 Publicity and performance: *kalos* inscriptions in Attic vase-painting

François Lissarrague

The practice of inscribing acclamations which publicly celebrate the beauty of a particular individual is known from various literary allusions and a good number of epigraphic examples. Aristophanes twice parodies the habit: he has the Scythian king Sitalkes, in his love for the Athenian people, write up '*Athenaioi kaloi*' on walls; and Philokleon, who is mad keen on the courts, writes '*kēmos kalos*' on a door.[1] In both these cases a public space, a wall or a door, proclaims the writer's passion by describing the loved object with the word '*kalos*'. It is similarly the word '*kalos*' that is always used in the various Hellenistic epigrams which refer to the practice, mentioning names inscribed on pillars, walls or trees.[2]

A late anecdote told by Clement of Alexandria claims that 'Pheidias the Athenian wrote on the finger of the statue of Zeus at Olympia "Pantarkes *kalos*".' Clement adds, in polemical outrage, 'for him it was not Zeus that was beautiful, but his boyfriend (*erōmenos*)'.[3] Although late and suspect, this story, with its conjunction of divine image and reference to a loved one, reveals an interesting bond between two forms of aesthetic pleasure, between human beauty and divine beauty.

Epigraphists are familiar with a number of real examples of these amorous graffiti, although these are often hard to date. They have been found at Athens, both on the Acropolis and on the Stoa Poikile, and at Nemea, in the tunnel leading to the stadium.[4] On Thera there are a number of inscriptions on the rocks above the gymnasium which vary the formula; some are explicitly erotic, while others use *agathos* (most frequently) and *aristos* but only once *kalos*.[5]

---

[1] Aristophanes *Akharnians* 142–3; *Wasps* 97–9.
[2] *Greek Anthology* xii.129, 130.
[3] Clement *Protreptikos* iv.53.4; cf. Overbeck (1868)134 no. 740.
[4] Athenian Acropolis: *IG* i² 1403; cf. *AM* 67 (1942) pl.9.i: the restoration proposed by Oikonomides (1984) seems difficult to accept. On Tyrrhenians in Greece see Gras (1985) 583–700. For Stoa Poikile see Shear (1984) 14–15. For Nemea see Miller (1979) 74, 100–1.
[5] *IG* xii.3 536–49; 536–9 use οἴφειν (Doric for ὀχεύειν); 542 has ἐρᾶται; 540, and 544–6 use ἄριστος; 540 and 547 use ἀγαθός; and 549 uses καλός.

On Thasos acclamations using *kalos* and *khaire* are known from the base of the Doric portico of an unidentified building at Aliki at the south of the island.[6] But the most remarkable collection is that discovered by Yvon Garlan in Kalami bay, also on the south coast of the island. Some sixty inscriptions of the same type are dotted around on a rocky slope just above the water, close below a watchtower. They repeat the names of fourteen young men, varying the adjectives with which they describe them. *Kalos* is most frequent, but other terms used are 'golden', 'not just a pretty face', shapely', 'beautiful face', 'sweet', 'fond of the revel', 'well proportioned', 'charming', 'witty', and 'silver'.[7]

As Garlan and Masson observe in publishing these inscriptions, the terms used apply principally to the bodily beauty, particularly facial beauty (*euprosōpos, kalliprosōpos*), to the youth (*eukharis*) and good proportions (*euskhēmōn, eurythmos*) or to the glamour (*khrusos, arguros*) of the individuals saluted. Other terms, and this is important for our argument, refer to sociability: *philokōmos* (one who likes the *komos*) and *asteos* (urbane). Rarer here, and at the intersection of the two groups, combining physical and social qualities, the term *asteoprosōpos* reveals the background against which the inscriptions are to be understood: it is not a matter of sexual desire pure and simple, but an appreciation of beauty which has a social and ethical side to it.

These epigraphic examples raise at least two issues about the structure of these acclamations as utterances. In most cases the inscriptions proclaim an individual's beauty, but the speaker or writer only very rarely names himself. On a sherd from Mytilene the inscription puts the spoken into writing by announcing: 'Phaestos is *kalos*, so says the writer.'[8] Similarly, on one of the Nemea graffiti, the inscription 'Akrotatos *kalos*' has been finished by another hand with 'of the writer', implying an unnamed writer about whose nature it is hard to be precise.[9] In both these cases the writer, even if explicitly present, remains anonymous. There are, however, a small number of sherds on which the speaker names himself, and in these cases the verb *dokei* is used to introduce him.[10] In any case in the vast majority of these inscriptions it

---

[6] Servais (1980) 46–9.
[7] Garlan and Masson (1982). The Greek terms are: χρυσός, ἀστεοπρόσωπος, εὐσχήμων, καλλιπρόσωπος, ἡδύς, φιλόκωμος, εὔρυθμος, εὔχαρις, ἀστέος, ἀργυροῦς.
[8] *IG* xii.2 268: Φάεστας καλός· ὡς φασί ὁ γράψα⟨ι⟩ς.
[9] This correction seems in fact to reduce the force of the acclamation, whatever sense one gives to it. See the summary of interpretations in *SEG* 32 (1982) 366.
[10] So Agora P.5160 (*ARV* 1561/1): Ἀλκαῖος καλὸς τō[ι] δοκεῖ Μελιτι. Agora P30076/ *Hesperia Supp.* 25 no. 148: Σικελε καλὲ τōι δοκεῖ τōι μοιχοῖ in this case the end of the phrase, τōι μοιχοῖ, has been added by a second hand, undermining the compliment.

Publicity and performance

is the name of the person acclaimed that is important, not the identity of the speaker. When someone writes in a public space what they are doing is leading readers to take up for themselves the words inscribed and to repeat, as they read, that someone is *kalos*.[11] It is not the identification of the speaking subject that is important, therefore, but the object that is acclaimed and ensuring the multiplication of this acclamation. We should add that in archaic culture praise and blame go together. A number of graffiti are undermined by additions made by a second hand which reduce their impact. Others refer themselves directly to derision and play on insult and obscenity. One of the earliest examples, datable to the third quarter of the seventh century, is on a skyphos found in the sanctuary of Zeus on Mount Hymettos. On this one reads, among other things, *P[hil]aides katapugon*. As the editor remarks, 'obscenity is no proof of advanced literacy'.[12] Praise and blame go together in inscriptions.

The second issue is the place where the inscriptions are to be found. The surface inscribed is always a clearly visible one, a door, wall, pillar, or tree, as epigrams show, placed in an open area, a public space, a fort, a gymnasium, a temple or sanctuary – places which ephebes and their admirers pass through. The sight of the body at the age at which it is agreeable (for which see Theognis 1335) is an essential aesthetic and erotic experience in Greek culture, and inscriptions prolong its effect by making the individual perception by a particular older male lover into common knowledge.

On the basis of this rapid survey of 'real' inscriptions and of the practice underlying them, we can pass on to inscriptions painted on pots. Numerous acclamations of beauty are found on Attic pottery. The phenomenon is almost exclusively Athenian and the resultant Athenocentrism must be excused. There is nothing similar on Corinthian, Laconian or East Greek pottery even though painted inscriptions appear on all three. In Athenian pottery the acclamatory inscriptions are integrated into the representation and interact with it to a greater or lesser extent. Vase inscriptions do not stop with reproducing the context to which they refer; painters re-elaborate the mechanism of

---

On the force of τōι see *REG Bull.* (1994) 278. There are a small number of painted insciptions which use the verb *dokei*: see Munich 2447 (*ABV* 425); Louvre F38 (*ABV* 174); London B507 (*ABL* 426.9) ὁ μῦς καλός δοκεῖ; Agora P1386 (*ABV* 351) Εὐμάρες καλός Χ[αρίαι δο]κεῖ; Boston 98.922 (*ABL* 117.2): ho παῖς καλός ἐμοὶ δοκεῖ; London E718 (*ARV* 306): ἀφροδίσια καλὲ τος δοκεῖ Εὐχίροι; Berlin 2316 (*ARV* 1559.1): (a) Αἰσιμίδες καλός (b) δοκεῖ κουννόντι.

[11] On this manipulation of the reader by the inscription see Svenbro (1993).

[12] Langdon (1976) no. 36, p. 47. On the use of '*katapugon*' see Milne and von Bothmer (1953).

acclamation to enhance their own system of representation. On Thera, on Thasos, at Nemea or at Athens, the inscription in public space addresses, from a fixed point, the passer-by to whom it transmits its admiring message. On pottery the inscription circulates with the pot which carries it and the image into which it has been inserted. This produces various discrepancies in the resulting structure of utterance, and these must now be discussed. (Since I concentrate here on a small number of characteristic examples, I must therefore note that generalization is difficult and that observations cannot be systematized since painters display enormous originality in the ways in which they use writing, and their manner of writing becomes part of their overall pictorial style.)

Many different types of inscription are to be found on Athenian vases. There are signatures of painters and potters, captions and names identifying figures represented, words written close to faces, and, finally, acclamations. All these types of inscription are found in the field of the image, with positions and directions which themselves carry significance visually, independently of their linguistic content: words are an image.[13]

Acclamations are not among the earliest inscriptions on pottery. Signatures, dedications, personal names and names of objects are met first. The François vase with its 130 inscriptions is a remarkable example of the practice of writing on pots, and not a single *kalos* is to be found there.[14] The earliest painted acclamations appear in the middle of the sixth century in the workshop of Exekias, a painter who is among those most attentive to the use of writing on images.[15] From this date on, acclamations addressed to young men get more numerous, reaching a peak in archaic red-figure. The latest such inscription is found on a cup attributed to the Codros Painter, of around 420.[16] The inscriptions have all been collected by Beazley to give a long catalogue of young Athenians considered beautiful: there are 91 different names on 141 black-figure pots and 208 different names on 851 red-figure pots.[17] Roughly a thousand vases are therefore at issue, not a negligible number although only a small proportion of the total Attic production.

---

[13] See Lissarrague (1985), (1992) and Hurwit (1990).
[14] Wachter (1991).
[15] Rebillard (1991).
[16] London E 94 (*ARV* 1270.22). A later inscription 'Ganymedes *kalos*' on a pot by the Meidias Painter (*ARV* 1313.11) is considered 'not a real kalos-inscription' by Beazley.
[17] I derive these figures from *ABV* 664–78; *ARV* 1559–616; *Paralipomena* 317–18 and 505–8, and *Beazley Addenda* 2 391–9. I omit the much less numerous women's names (15 on 22 black-figure pots, 20 on 26 red-figure pots). See also the estimates of Klein (1898) 1–31.

Publicity and performance 363

Acclamations on vases produce a sort of playful dialogue between the pot itself and its user. As in the case of graffiti, the speaker is almost never named;[18] the reader, the person using the vase, repeats the acclamation as he reads it. This is not unique to *kalos* acclamations, but occurs in other formulae in which the spectator or user of the pot is verbally implicated. The most common other inscription of this type, found particularly on Little Master Cups, is *'chaire kai piei eu'*, an invitation to drink which is independent of the picture.[19]

Sometimes there are inscriptions which mix together various modes of address. So, on a cup in the Louvre we have *epiluko[s egraph]sen kalos* and on a cup in Palermo *Kha[khrul]ion kalos* in just the place where one would expect rather, after the name of the potter Khakhrylion, the verb *epoiesen*. Another cup, in St Petersburg, carries the inscription *pine k⟨a⟩i cha⟨i⟩re lukis kalos*, putting together two types of acclamation usually kept apart.[20]

There is also a little series notable from the stand-point of utterance. This is of vases which have the simple verb *prosagoreuō*, I address. The word is isolated, with neither subject nor object expressed. All that is uttered is the verbal action, and that verbal action is attributed as much to the pot as to the image. This formula had only a brief popularity: there are nineteen occurrences on drinking cups and alabastra, most of which are attributed by Beazley to the group of Paidikos' alabastra, or connected with the manner of the Euergides Painter.[21] Most of the scenes show athletes or komasts or relate to the symposium. So, on a cup in the Louvre (Fig. 6) two young men advance and sing; they are surrounded by the inscription *prosagoreuō* but that inscription does not come out of the mouth of the singer and cannot be interpreted as his word; rather it indicates utterance, a word put into the image as coming from the vase and addressing the reader – drinker.[22]

Acclamations consisting of a name plus 'kalos' need to be put into

---

[18] δοκεῖ does occur on some vases: see above n. 10.
[19] '*Chaire* is one of the commonest words on vases' (Beazley (1929) 364). This invitation is also found on a mosaic in a dining room at Monte Iato in Sicily: *Antike Kunst* 29 (1986) 72 fig. 3.
[20] Louvre G10 (*ARV 83.3*); Palermo V 655 (*ARV* 113.3); St Petersburg 210, B1412 (*ABV* 669). See Lissarrague (1990) 62–5, fig. 47F.
[21] *ARV* 103–4.
[22] Louvre G82 (*ARV* 98.18 (manner of the Euergides Painter) and 103.6). In his commentary on this cup de Witte (1857) 118–19 and pl. 37 treats the inscription as equivalent to ὁ παῖς καλός. On the function of words as part of pictures see Lissarrague (1990) 123–9. Dover (1978) 118 considers the inscription *prosagoreuō* on a cup in Brussels (R260 (*ARV* 103.4)) to be pronounced by the young man who is masturbating (in front of a krater, not in front of a herm), but the position of the inscription makes this reading impossible.

Fig. 6

this larger context of utterances. If they are compared to graffiti known from epigraphy, two important differences are revealed. There is practically no painted inscription, as far as I know, that is derisory or insulting – all belong to the field of praise.[23] The existence of condemnatory graffiti and ostraka shows that they belong to a more formal and institutional genre. But above all there are quite a number of vase inscriptions that proclaim the beauty of a young man, of a *pais*, but do

---

[23] See Klein (1898) 4, 169 and fig. 46 for a cup formerly in the van Branthegem collection which bears the inscriptions 'kakos'. Comparison of kalos names and ostraka was suggested by Klein (1898) 3 and by Immerwahr (1990) 59–65. See Slater (unpublished). I am grateful to Niall Slater for showing me the manuscript of his article, in which he reaches conclusions similar to my own.

not give the young man's name. Formulae of the type *ho pais kalos* are much more numerous than those which do name the boy in question. Beazley does not list these because they have no prosopographic or chronological significance, but they are very frequent. Although it is impossible to give a total number, an order of magnitude can be suggested on the basis of a sample. When Lucien Bonaparte published his *Museum étrusque* in 1829, in which he made an inventory of all the vases found at Vulci, he reproduced all the inscriptions found on the vases in facsimile. 70 of the 194 inscriptions are kalos inscriptions, and of these only four include a proper name, suggesting around 5 per cent of kalos names among the acclamatory inscriptions. This very approximate calculation needs to be checked against other samples, but it shows clearly that painters wrote *ho pais kalos* much more frequently than they named specific individuals.[24] This is an important point, since it draws attention to a peculiarity of vases: not a single graffito read *ho pais kalos*, that formula is found only on painted pottery. This peculiarity implies a specific usage, not to be found in gymnasia or garrisons, which has been developed in a context where vases were used and circulated and in particular in the context of the symposium.

The question of who is to be regarded as uttering the specific acclamation has often been discussed in relation to painted kalos names. Some have supposed that the frequency of such and such a name on the works of a particular painter indicates a relationship between the painter and the young man in question. Others have thought that the names reflect specific orders. Neither of these explanations is in fact required by the evidence: the same name is found repeated in the work of several painters, and the dispersal of vases counts against the idea of specific orders. Some occasional examples involving the names of artisans working in the Kerameikos[25] are to be seen as exceptions which prove the general rule that the *kaloi* are prominent and fashionable young men who were known by everyone in Athens. It is a matter of advertisement and of shared knowledge. This interpretation is confirmed by the multiplication of the generic formulae of the *ho pais kalos* type. These do not proclaim a personal relationship between painter

---

[24] In the latest London fascicle of CVA (CVA British Museum 9, 1993) Dyfri Williams publishes 59 late archaic cups, of which 9 have a kalos name and 11 have *ho pais kalos*. But several of these cups are fragmentary, and the formula *ho pais kalos* is often repeated several times on a single vase. Counting inscriptions and counting vases is not the same thing.

[25] Thus Louvre F38 (*ABV* 174) includes two inscriptions: *Timagoras epoiesen* and *Andokides kalos dokei Timagorai* and the psykter attributed to Smikros (J. Paul Getty Museum 82 AE. 53, Frel 1983) has an inscription *Euphronios Leagros kalos*. On this question, see now R. Neer, 'Pampoikilos', PhD dissertation, Berkeley, 1998.

Fig. 7

and particular young man or between the man ordering the pot and the young man named, they acclaim beauty in its most celebrated form. By writing *ho pais kalos* the painter increases the field of possibilities offered by this type of proclamation: on the one hand it is left to the user, if he so wishes, to trouble to specify in his own name the proposition that is inscribed; on the other, the figure of the *pais*, because it is indeterminate, can be referred either to what is perceived in the exterior world, in the entourage of the drinker, or in the world of the image and applied to the painted figures. On a cup attributed to the Euergides painter (Fig. 7) a beautiful young man can be seen, wearing a garland, holding a flower in each hand, and surrounded by an inscription which forms a halo and reads, starting from the feet, *ho pais kalos nai*.[26] This phrase could apply to the image or could equally well be addressed to any young man present at the symposium. The regular way

---

[26] New York 09.221.47 (*ARV* 91. 52). The outside shows athletes.

Publicity and performance

in which the letters are disposed around the young man confers on them an ornamental role equivalent to that of the flowers that he holds, and it increases, at the verbal level, the beauty of the image that it exploits.

Because the formula *ho pais kalos* applies to two different fields of reference, it can serve as the interface between the real world and the world represented; it reinforces the links between the two fields, the real and the representation, through the reading that the user performs. There is no contradiction between the generic and the specific uses, they complement one another, and both types are often found together on the same vase.[27] On a pair of jugs (*olpai*) both representing athletes, one reads *Melieus kalos* on one and *chaire pai su kalos nai* on the other, and Beazley correctly observes that 'the artist has not only his athlete in mind: the little cupbearer who will be using this jug will spell out the big clear words and take them as meant for him'.[28]

The same effect is achieved with inscriptions of the type *kalos ei*. These are less common, but are found, for instance, in the work of the Kleophrades Painter, who never uses a specific kalos name.[29] On a hydria in the British Museum attributed to him women are shown washing around a louterion.[30] In the background are the words *kalos ei* in the masculine: it is the spectator rather than the spectacle that is addressed here. On an amphora by the same painter (Fig. 8) on which a rhapsode is shown standing on a dais and singing *hode pot' en tyrinthi*, *kalos ei* is to be read inscribed on the *bēma*.[31] This formula is remarkable here since it can equally well be applied to the singer or taken as addressed to the spectator.

There is more to this case, and we must pause to consider further this inscription, which is not placed by chance. Because it is displayed in large letters on the base this inscription is easier to perceive than inscriptions that are painted in added purple on black glaze; its position makes it look like a real inscription, engraved on the stone, as much as an inscription painted on the surface of the vase. The place of the words in the images is often determined by the desire to achieve such an effect. The painter writes on some object or other whose surface lends itself to easy legibility – on a wineskin, a shield, sometimes even on a vase, thus reproducing recessively the effect of the inscription

---

[27] E.g. London E 46 (*ARV* 315.1, *CVA* BM 9, no. 2).
[28] Beazley (1928) 12 with reference to two *olpai* attributed to the Goluchow Painter (*ARV* 10.1 and 10.2).
[29] Compare Immerwahr (1990) 82.
[30] London E 201 (*ARV* 189.77). Compare a krater once in Naples in the Hamilton collection (*ARV* 500.21) showing the same subject in which the inscription *kalos ei* is found on the bowl of the louterion. On this motif see Durand and Lissarrague (1980).
[31] London E 270 (*ARV* 183.15).

368   *François Lissarrague*

Fig. 8

Publicity and performance 369

on the supporting vase.³² Similarly inscriptions are found on architectural members – on a base, a stele, a boundary stone, a column, a herm, and each of these inscriptions can be taken as belonging to the piece of building that carries it as much as to the vase on which it figures.³³

The medallion of a cup attributed to the Antiphon Painter goes even further in the same direction (Fig. 9).³⁴ Here an athlete is shown pouring oil into his hand. Behind him, on a boundary stone on which he has left his clothes, is written *ho pais naichi kalos* in three lines which are very regularly spaced, and on his thigh, in very small letters, is inscribed *Laches kalos*. Beazley notes that this latter inscription is 'as if he were a statue', and this does indeed correspond to the custom of inscribing the name of the dedicant or of the dead person on the thighs of kouroi.³⁵ Here, however, we have an acclamation, and there is no such inscription in this place on any real kouros. By writing on the athlete's thigh, the painter has in a way made him into a statue, he has made him a living statue, an object of the gaze on two levels, as a representation of an athlete and as a representation of a sculpture representing a victorious athlete. The visual pleasure which this image produces can be compared with a reflection made at the beginning of Plato's *Charmides*: when the beautiful Charmides visits Socrates and his friends they admire his beauty: 'Everyone gazed upon him as upon a statue (*agalma*)'. Socrates cries out 'What a beautiful face he has', and another adds 'Ah, but if he were willing to strip naked, you would not notice his face, his beauty is so complete' (*Charmides* 154c,d). The athlete's body is an aesthetic object *par excellence*, and the acclamation written by the painter on the athlete's thigh associates two levels of experience for the drinker – the beauty of the gymnast and the celebrated figure of Laches. The verbal game which Plato employs at the opening of the dialogue is anticipated by the acclamatory inscriptions

[32] Compare Paris Louvre G 130 (*ARV* 120.1) where in the field of the medallion is written *Euryptolemos kalos*, and on every cup that the drinker holds is written *kalos*. On a fragment of a krater in Copenhagen (inv. 13 365, *ARV* 185. 32, Lissarague (1990) fig. 49) there is a cup with *chaire* written upon it. See also Berlin inv. 31 131 (*ARV* 176.2, Lissarague (1990) fig. 42) where *Kallias ka[los]* is written on a skyphos.
[33] For a base see London E 298 (*ARV* 1581.20); for boundary stones see Moret (1979) 6 n. 13 and Immerwahr (1990) 99–101; for a column see Basle Antikenmuseum (*Para* 436; *Beazley Addenda* 310); for a herm see Boston 68.163 (*Para* 402–3 and 506.17bis).
[34] Berlin F 2314 (with a fragment in Rome, Villa Giulia) (*ARV* 336.14). Beazley (1933) 34 no. 19 notes that 'The cup is pared round and restored... The head is still missing'. My drawing makes use of a photograph which includes the restoration; unfortunately I have not seen this fragment.
[35] See Richter (1970).

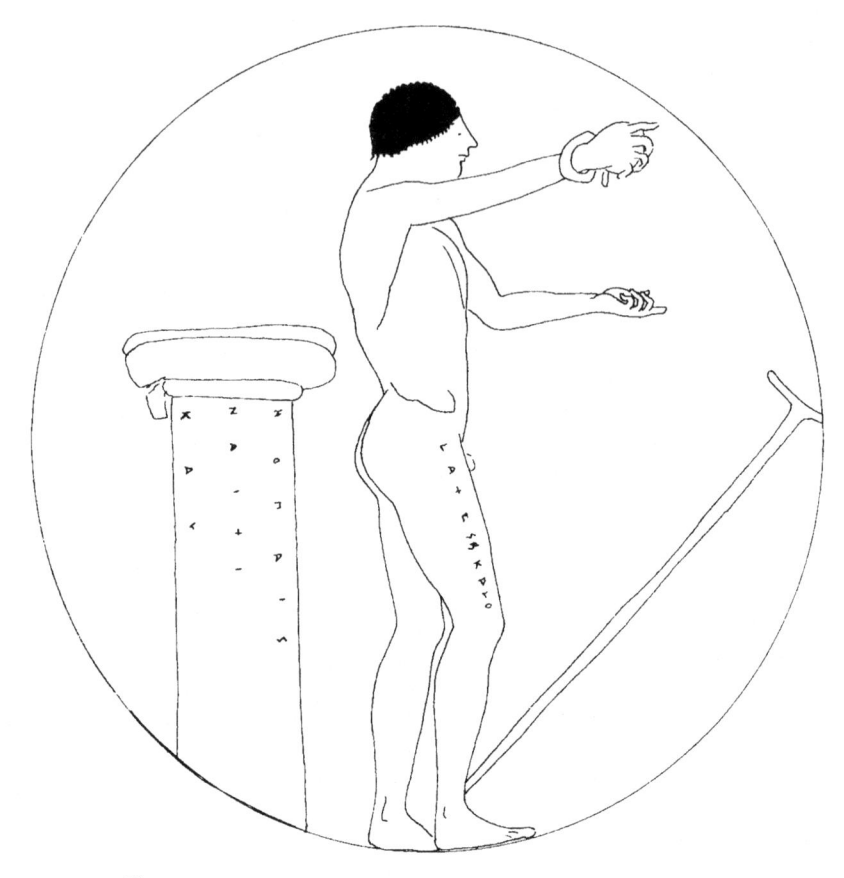

Fig. 9

on late archaic vases. Painters throw in names or generic formulae which drinkers take up in their turn at the symposium, repeating and echoing the admiring words.

The play of the inscriptions and of their interaction with the image creates a public space in which the beauty of young men is spoken of. Those who are admired are sometimes named precisely and the names of certain aristocrats in archaic Athens are found among them; but most often the *pais kalos* is anonymous, enlarging the circle which is thus designated; what began as a purely aristocratic practice is extended and swelled by the multiplication of generic inscriptions which take a particular sense only in the performance, at the symposium when the drinker/reader utters the acclamation, brings it into play, and gives it a

Publicity and performance

Fig. 10

pointed and precise sense.[36] On a drinking vessel the image makes present the beauty of the figures that charm the drinker's heart. Inscriptions of the *kalos* type, mixed in with the image, add a complementary aesthetic level and form an additional ornament in the representation. The inscription on its own comes to function as a figure and an ornament, particularly in the case of Little Master Cups.[37]

[36] The same phenomenon of moving from the generic to the specific can be seen in the inscriptions which appear on the funerary plaques in the work of the Sappho painter: there 'mother', 'father', 'brother' etc. can be read, but the person who uses the pot is well aware of the precise identity of the person commemorated. See Louvre MNB 901 (*ABL* 229.58).
[37] Beazley (1932).

Fig. 11

I end here with a vase that is completely exceptional from this point of view but that in its peculiarities seems to me to confirm this analysis. An oinochoe in Munich (Fig. 10) has decoration only on the shoulder.[38] A white-ground band breaks away from the black glaze of the handle. Fourteen palmettes are painted there in a regular alternation, and between the palmettes a line of writing winds and worms its way, climbing and descending as if to form a plait within the decoration. There is no human figure in this frieze which, uniquely, is made simply of letters and ornaments. The inscription begins from the silhouette of a bird, which seems to launch into flight the following winged words: '*kalos nikola dorotheoskalos kamoidokeinai chateros paiskalos memnon kamoi kalos philos*' which are to be understood as a dialogue: 'καλὸς Νικόλα. Δορόθεος καλός· κἀμοὶ δοκεῖ, ναι. χἄτερος παῖς καλὸς, Μέμνον. κἀμοὶ καλὸς φίλος'. The circle of drinkers and guests makes itself heard here: once more this admiring rumour gets around without revealing the identity of the speaker. That it is marked out as an utterance in the first person does not imply that the words are those of a particular speaker. The opinion, the reputation, gets itself heard, the knowledge is shared which turns Nicolas, Dorotheos and Memnon into celebrities.

---

[38] Munich 2447 (*ARV* 425), related to class of London B632. See Kurtz (1975) pl.57.1, pp. 93–5.

On this oinochoe the graphic disposition of the writing gives it a pictorial value whose equivalent is found in the image on the shoulder of a lekythos showing a figure of Eros flying and holding the palmettes which decorate the vase (Fig. 11).[39] Having Eros fly and having the guests converse are two complementary ways of expressing erotic desire. Painters used image and writing together to give perfume vases and symposium ware graphic trimmings which echo the aesthetic pleasure produced by the young men at the symposium or in the wrestling grounds.

This creation of aesthetic value that can be observed in Athenian imagery at the end of the archaic period is strongly reinforced by the use of generic inscriptions of the *ho pais kalos* type: by freeing themselves from particular names, names which are often aristocratic, the painters allow the spectators to give the generic inscriptions whatever specific sense suits them, and to put the inscriptions to work as they please in a particular situation. Such a practice is not very far from what is involved in the game of *kottabos* in which the vase becomes part of a game in which amorous desire is expressed.

Translated by Robin Osborne

---

[39] Berlin F 2252 (*ARV* 263.54, Syriskos Painter).

Works cited

Abbate, C. (1991) *Unsung Voices: Opera and Musical Narrative in the Nineteenth Century.* Princeton.
Adam, J.-M. (1991) *Langue et littérature. Analyses pragmatiques et textuelles.* Paris.
Adams, C. D. (1912) 'Are the Political "Speeches" of Demosthenes to be Regarded as Political Pamphlets?', *TAPA* 43: 5-22.
Adams, C. D. (1919) *The Speeches of Aeschines,* Cambridge, Mass. and London.
Adkins, A. (1960) *Merit and Responsibility.* Oxford.
Adrados, F. R. (1975) *Festivals, Comedy and Tragedy.* Leiden.
Ahl, F. (1991) 'Pindar and the Sphinx: Celtic Polyphony and Greek Music', in Wallace and MacLachlan (1991) 131-50.
Ahl, F. (1991a) *Sophocles' Oedipus: Evidence and Self-Conviction.* Ithaca and London.
Alcock, S. and Osborne, R., eds. (1994) *Placing the Gods. Sanctuaries and Sacred Space in Ancient Greece.* Oxford.
Aleshire, S. (1994) 'The Demos and the Priests: the Selection of Sacred Officials at Athens from Cleisthenes to Augustus', in Osborne and Hornblower (1994) 325-37.
Anderson, W. D. (1966) *Ethos and Education in Greek Music.* Cambridge, Mass.
Anderson, W. D. (1994) *Music and Musicians in Ancient Greece.* Ithaca and London.
Annas, J. (1981) *An Introduction to Plato's* Republic. Oxford.
Anonymous (1996) *Primary Colours: a Novel of Politics.* London.
Arias, P. E. (1940) *Mirone.* Florence.
Arieti, J. A. (1991) *Interpreting Plato: the Dialogues as Drama.* Maryland.
Armstrong, A. MacC. (1958) 'The Methods of the Greek Physiognomists', *Greece and Rome* 5: 52-6.
Auberson, P. and Schefold, K. (1972) *Führer durch Eretria.* Bern.
Auger, D. (1979) 'Le théâtre d'Aristophane: Le mythe, l'utopie et les femmes', in *Aristophane et les femmes.* Les Cahiers de Fontenay 17: 71-97.
Austin, J. (1962) *How to Do Things with Words.* Oxford.
Austin, J. L. (1975) *How to do things with words.* 2nd edn. Cambridge, Mass.
Bachelard, G. (1964) *The Poetics of Space.* Boston.
Bachofen, J. J. (1867 [1954]) *Myth Religion, and Mother Right. Selected Writings of J. J. Bachofen,* tr. R. Manheim. Princeton.
Bacon, H. H. (1994/5) 'The Chorus in Greek Life and Drama', *Arion* 3.1: 6-24.

Bain, D. M. (1975) 'Audience Address in Greek Tragedy', *Classical Quarterly* 69: 13-25.
Bakhtin, M. (1968) *Rabelais and his World*. Cambridge, Mass.
Bakhtin, M. (1981) *The Dialogic Imagination*, ed. M. Holquist. Austin.
Bal, M. (1996) *Double Exposures: the Subject of Cultural Analysis*. London and New York.
Bamberger, Joan (1974) 'The Myth of Matriarchy', in *Women, Culture, and Society*, eds. M. Z. Rosaldo and L. Lamphere, 263-80. Stanford.
Barba, E. (1991) 'Introduction', in Barba and Savarese (1991).
Barba, E. and Savarese, N., eds. (1991) *A Dictionary of Theatre Anthropology: the Secret Art of the Performer*, tr. R. Fowler. London and New York.
Barker, A. (1984) *Greek Musical Writings: I The Musician and his Art*. Cambridge.
Barlow, S. (1986) *The Imagery of Euripides* 2nd edn. Bristol.
Barlow, S. (1986a) 'The language of Euripides' monodies', in Betts, Hooker and Green (1986-8) vol. I: 10-22.
Barner, W. (1971) 'Die Monodie', in Jens (1971) 277-320.
Baron, D. (1986) *Grammar and Gender*. New Haven and London.
Barrett, W. S. (1964) *Euripides: Hippolytos* (Oxford).
Barthes, R. (1977) *Image, Music, Text*, tr. S. Heath. New York.
Barton, T. (1994) *Power and Knowledge: Astrology, Physiognomics and Medicine Under The Roman Empire*. Ann Arbor.
Bartsch, S. (1989) *Decoding the Ancient Novel: the Reader and the Role of Description in Heliodorus and Achilles Tatius*. Princeton.
Bateson, G. (1972) *Steps to an Ecology of Mind*. San Francisco.
Battcock, G. and Nickas, R., eds. (1984) *The Art of Performance*. Toronto.
Bauman, R. (1986) *Story, Peformance, and Event: Contextual Studies in Oral Narrative*. Cambridge and New York.
Baurain, Cl., Bonnet, C. and Krings, V., eds. (1991) *Phoinikeia Grammata*. Liège/Namur.
Beazley, J. D. (1928) *Greek Vases in Poland*. Oxford.
Beazley, J. D. (1929) 'Some Inscriptions on vases – II', *American Journal of Archaeology* 33: 361-7.
Beazley, J. D. (1932) 'Little-master cups', *JHS* 52: 167-204.
Beazley, J. D. (1933) *Campana Fragments in Florence*. Oxford.
Beazley, J. D. (1955) 'Hydria-Fragments in Corinth', *Hesperia* 24: 305-19.
Bechoffer, W. (1988) 'Processions and Urban Form in a Sri Lankan Village', *Traditional Dwellings and Settlements Review* 1(1): 39-48.
Bélis, A. (1986) 'La Phorbéia', *Bulletin de Correspondance Hellénique* 110: 205-18.
Bell, C. (1992) *Ritual Theory, Ritual Practice*. Oxford.
Benveniste, E. (1963) 'La philosophie analytiane et le langage', *Et. philos* 1 (1963) 3-12 reprinted in E. Benveniste, *Problèmes de la linguistique générale*. Paris. 267-76.
Béquignon, Y. (1937) *La Valleé du Spercheios*. Paris.
Bergquist, B. (1990) 'Sympotic space: a functional aspect of Greek dining-rooms', in Murray (1990) 37-65.
Bernardini, P. A. (1979) 'La dike nella lira e la dike dell'atleta', *Quaderni Urbinati di Cultura Classica* 2: 79-85.

Bernheimer, C. (1989) *Figures of Ill Repute: Representing Prostitution in Nineteenth-Century France*. New York.
Berry, P. (1989) *Of Chastity and Power: Elizabethan Literature and the Unmarried Queen*. London.
Bers, V. (1985) 'Dikastic *Thorubos*', in Cartledge and Harvey eds. (1985) 1–15.
Bers, V. (1994) 'Tragedy and Rhetoric', in Worthington (1994).
Betts, J., Hooker J. and Green J. R., eds. (1986–8) *Studies in honour of T. B. L. Webster*. Bristol: I 1986; II 1988.
Billigheimer, A. (1938) 'Amendments in Athenian Decrees', *American Journal of Archaeology* 42: 456–85.
Blaise, F., Judet de la Combe, P. and Rousseau Ph., eds. (1996) *Le métier du mythe. Lectures d'Hésiode*. Lille.
Blass, F. (1865) *Die Griechische Beredsamkeit*. Berlin.
Blau, H. (1990) 'Universals of performance; or amortizing play', in Schechner and Appel (1990).
Blau, H. (1993) 'Universals of Performance; or Amortizing Play', in Schechner (1993) 250–72.
Blech, M. (1982) *Studien zum Kranz bei den Griechen*. Religionsgeschichte Versuche und Vorarbeiten Berlin.
Blomquist, J. (1982) 'Human and Divine Action in Euripides' *Hippolytus*', *Hermes* 110: 398–414.
Blundell, M. W. (1989) *Helping Friends and Harming Enemies: a Study in Sophocles and Greek Ethics*. Cambridge.
Boardman, J. (1956) 'Some Attic Fragments: Pot, Plaque and Dithyramb', *JHS* 76: 18–25.
Boardman, J. (1975) 'Herakles, Peisistratos and Eleusis', *JHS* 95: 1–12.
Boegehold, A. (1996) 'Resistance to Change in the Law at Athens', in Ober and Hedrick (1996).
Boegehold, A. (1997) 'Group and Single Competitions at the Panathenaia', 95–105 in Neils (1997).
Boegehold, A. and Scafuro A., eds. (1994) *Athenian Identity and Civic Ideology*. Baltimore and London.
Boesch, P. (1908) ΘΕΩΡΟΣ: *Untersuchung zur Epangelie Griechischer Feste*. Berlin.
Bollack, J. (1990) *L'Oedipe roi de Sophocle. Le texte et ses interprétations*. 4 volumes. Lille.
Bolotin, D. (1979) *Plato's Dialogue on Friendship: an Interpretation of the* Lysis, *with a new translation*. Ithaca, N.Y.
Bömer, F. (1952) 'Pompa', *RE* 21.2: 1878–947.
Bommelaer, J.-F. (1981) *Lysandre de Sparte: histoire et traditions*. Bibliothèque des écoles françaises d' Athènes et de Rome; fasc. 240. Paris and Athens.
Bond, G. (1981) *Euripides: Heracles*. Oxford.
Bonner, R. J. (1933) *Aspects of Athenian Democracy*. Berkeley.
Bonzon, S. (1990) 'Sur la "mise en récit" du dialogue chez Platon', in Bonzon et al. (1990).
Bonzon, S. et al., eds. (1990) *La Narration. Quand le récit devient communication. Lieux Théologiques* 12: 205–16.

Borthwick, E. K. (1970) 'P. Oxy. 2738: Athens and the Pyrrhic dance', *Hermes* 98: 318-31.
Bosworth, A. B. (1980) *Commentary on Arrian's History of Alexander* Vol. 1. Oxford.
Bourdieu, P. (1977) *Outline of a Theory of Practice*. tr. R. Nice. Cambridge.
Bourdieu, P. (1984) *Distinction: A Social Critique of the Judgment of Taste*, tr. R. Nice. Cambridge, Mass.
Bowie, A. M. (1993) *Aristophanes: Myth, Ritual and Comedy*. Cambridge.
Bowie, E. (1986) 'Early Greek Elegy, Symposium, and Public Festival', *JHS* 106: 13-35.
Bradeen, D. (1969) 'The Athenian casualty lists', *Classical Quarterly* 19: 145-59.
Braund, D. (1993) 'Dionysiac tragedy in Plutarch, *Crassus*', *CQ* 43: 468-74.
Bremer, J. M. (1981) 'Greek Hymns', in Versnel (1981) 193-215.
Bremmer, J. ed. (1987) *Interpretations of Greek Mythology*. London.
Bremmer, J. (1991) 'Walking, standing and sitting in ancient Greek culture', in Bremmer and Roodenburg (1991).
Bremmer, J. and Roodenburg, H., eds. (1991) *A Cultural History of Gender*. Cambridge.
Brennan, T. and Jay, M., eds. (1996) *Vision in Context*. New York and London.
Brijder, H., Drukker, A. and Neeft C., eds. (1986) *Enthousiasmos: essays on Greek and Related Pottery presented to J. M. Hemelrijk*. Amsterdam.
Bristol, M. (1989) *Carnival and Theatre*. London.
Brock, R. (1990) 'Plato and Comedy', in Craik (1990).
Browning, R. (1963) 'A Byzantine treatise on tragedy', in *Geras: Studies Presented to George Thomson on the Occasion of his 60th Birthday* eds. L. Varcl and R. F. Willetts: 67-81. Prague.
Bruit Zaidman, L. (1995) 'Ritual eating in archaic Greece. Parasites and paredroi', in *Food in Antiquity* eds. J. Wilkins, D. Harvey and M. Dobson: 196-203. Exeter.
Bruit Zaidman, L. and Schmitt Pantel, P. (1992) *Religion in the Ancient Greek City*, tr. P. Cartledge. Cambridge.
Buhmann, H. (1972) *Der Sieg in Olympia und in den anderen panhellenischen Spielen*. Munich.
Burian, P. ed. (1985) *Directions in Euripidean Criticism*. Durham N.C.
Burke, K. (1957) *The Philosophy of Literary Form*. New York.
Burkert, W. (1962) 'Γόης: zum griechischen "Schamanismus"' *RhM* 105: 36-55.
Burkert, W. (1966) 'Greek Tragedy and Sacrificial Ritual', *GRBS*: 87-121.
Burkert, W. (1983) *Homo Necans: The Anthropology of Ancient Greek Sacrificial Ritual and Myth*, tr. P. Bing. Berkeley.
Burkert, W. (1985) *Greek Religion: Archaic and Classical*, tr. John Raffan. Oxford.
Burnett, A. P. (1989) 'Performing Pindar's Odes', *CP* 84: 283-94.
Burns, E. (1972) *Theatricality*. London and New York.
Burnyeat, M. (1997) 'First Words: a valedictory lecture', *PCPS* 43: 1-20.
Burton, R. W. B. (1980) *The Chorus in Sophocles' Tragedies*. Oxford.
Butler, J. (1990) *Gender Trouble: Feminism and the Subversion of Identity*. New York and London.

Butler, J. (1993) *Bodies That Matter*. New York and London.
Butler, J. (1997) *Excitable Speech: A Politics of the Performative*. New York and London.
Buzard, J. (1993) *The Beaten Track: European Tourism, Literature, and the Ways to 'Culture' 1800-1910*. Oxford.
Cairns, D. (1993) *Aidōs: The Psychology and Ethics of Honour and Shame in Ancient Greek Literature*. Oxford.
Caizzi, F. D. ed. (1966) *Antisthenis Fragmenta*. Milan.
Calame, C. (1977) *Les choeurs de jeunes filles en Grèce archaïque I. Morphologie, fonction religieuse et sociale*. Rome. See also Calame (1997).
Calame, C. (1992) 'La festa', in Vegetti (1992) 29–54.
Calame, C. (1994/5) 'From Choral Poetry to Tragic Stasimon: the Enactment of Woman's Song', *Arion* III. 3 1994/5: 136–54.
Calame, C. (1995) *The Craft of Poetic Speech in Ancient Greece*. Ithaca.
Calame, C. (1996a) 'Vision, Blindness and Mask: the Radicalization of the Emotions in Sophocles' *Oedipus Rex*', in Silk (1996) 17–37.
Calame, C (1996b) 'Le proème des *Travaux* d'Hésiode, prélude à une poésie d'action', in Blaise (1996) 169–89.
Calame, C. (1996c) *Thésée ou l'imaginaire athénien. Légende et culte en Grèce antique*, 2nd edn. Lausanne.
Calame, C. (1996d) *L'Eros dans la Grèce antique*. Paris.
Calame, C. (1997) *Choruses of Young Women in Ancient Greece. Their Morphology, Religious Role, and Social Functions*, 2nd edn. Lanham and London.
Camp, J. M. (1986) *The Athenian Agora. Excavations in the Heart of Classical Athens*. London.
Campbell, D. A. (1993) *Greek Lyric V: The New School of Poetry and Anonymous Songs and Hymns*. Cambridge, Mass. and London.
Campbell, M. (1988) *The Witness and the Other World: Exotic European Travel Writing 400-1600*. Ithaca and London.
Carey, C. (1994) 'Rhetorical Means of Persuasion', in Worthington (1994) 26–45.
Carey, C. and Reid, R. A. (1985) *Demosthenes: Selected Private Speeches*. Cambridge.
Carlson, M. (1996) *Performance: A Critical Introduction*. London and New York.
Carpenter T. H. and Faraone C. A., eds. (1993) *Masks of Dionysus*. Ithaca and London.
Carrière, J. (1979) *Le Carnaval et la Politique*. Paris.
Carson, A. (1990) 'Putting her in her place: Woman, Dirt, and Desire', in Halperin, Winkler, and Zeitlin (1990) 135–69.
Carter, L. B. (1986) *The Quiet Athenian*. Oxford.
Cartledge, P. A. (1985) 'The Greek religious festivals', in Easterling and Muir (1995).
Cartledge, P. A. (1990) 'Fowl Play: a Curious Lawsuit in Classical Athens', in Cartledge, Millett and Todd (1990) 41–62.
Cartledge, P. A. (1990a) *Aristophanes and his Theatre of the Absurd*. Bristol.
Cartledge, P. A. (1993) *The Greeks: a Portrait of Self and Others*. Oxford.
Cartledge, P. A. and Harvey, F. D., eds. (1985) *CRUX: Essays in Greek History Presented to G. E. M. de Ste. Croix on his 75th Birthday*. London.

Cartledge, P. A., Millett, P. and Todd, S., eds. (1990) *Nomos: Essays in Athenian Law, Politics and Society*. Cambridge.
Case, S-E. (1990) 'Introduction', in Case ed. (1990).
Case, S-E. ed. (1990) *Performing Feminisms: Feminist Critical Theory and Theatre*. Baltimore.
Castle, T. (1986) *Masquerade and Civilization: the Carnivalesque in eighteenth-century Culture and Fiction*. Stanford.
Castriota, D. (1992) *Myth, Ethos and Actuality: Official Art in Fifth-Century B.C. Athens*. Madison.
Cawkwell, G. L. (1969) 'The Crowning of Demosthenes', *Classical Quarterly* 19: 163–80.
Cerbo, E. (1993) 'Gli inni ad Eros in tragedia: struttura e funzione', in Pretagostini (1993) 645–56.
Chelkowski, P. (1985) 'Shia Muslim Processional Performances', *The Drama Review* 29 (3): 18–30.
Christ, M. (1992) 'Ostracism, Sycophancy and Deception of the Demos: [Arist.] *Ath. Pol.* 43.5', *Classical Quarterly* 42: 336–46.
Christ, W. (1875) 'Die Parakataloge im griechischen und römischen Drama', *Abhandlungen der philosophisch-philologischen Classe der königlichen bayerischen Akademie der Wissenschaften* 13.3: 153–222.
Christo and Jean-Claude (1996) *Wrapped Reichstag: Berlin 1971–95*. Cologne.
Clairmont, C. (1983) *Patrios Nomos: Public Burial in Athens during the fifth and fourth centuries B.C.* London.
Clark, T. (1984) *The Painting of Modern Life*. Princeton.
Clay, J. S. (1992) 'Pindar's Twelfth Pythian: Reed and Bronze', *AJP* 113: 519–25.
Clément, C. (1988) *Opera: or the Undoing of Women*, tr. B. Wing. Minneapolis.
Clifford, J. (1986) 'Introduction: partial truths', in Clifford and Marcus (1986).
Clifford, J. and Marcus, G., eds. (1986) *Writing Culture: the Poetics and Politics of Ethnography*. Berkeley.
Clinton, K. (1974) *The Sacred Officials of the Eleusinian Mysteries*. Philadelphia.
Cockle, W. E. H., ed. (1987) *Euripides, Hypsipyle. Text and Annotation based on a Re-Examination of the Papyri*. Rome.
Cohen, D. (1987) 'Law, Society and Homosexuality in Classical Athens', *Past and Present* 117: 1–21.
Cohen, D. (1991) *Law, Sexuality and Society: the Enforcement of Morals in Classical Athens*. Cambridge.
Cohen, D. (1995) *Law, Violence and Community in Classical Athens*. Cambridge.
Cohen, M. and Prendergast, C., eds. (1995) *Spectacles of Realism: Gender, Body, Genre*. Minneapolis.
Cole, P. and Morgan, J., eds. (1975) *Syntax and Semantics 3: Speech Acts*. New York.
Cole, S. G. (1993) 'Procession and celebration at the Dionysia', in Scodel (1993).
Cole, T. (1988) *Epiploke: Rhythmical Continuity and Poetic Structure in Greek Lyric*. Cambridge, Mass. and London.
Collard, C. (1975) *Euripides' Supplices*. Groningen.

Collard, C. (1991) *Euripides' Hecuba*. Warminster.
Collard, C., Cropp, M. and Lee, K. (1995) *Euripides: Selected Fragmentary Plays I*. Warminster.
Comotti, G. (1980) 'Atene e gli auloì in un ditirambo di Teleste (fr. 805 P.)' *Quaderni Urbinati di Cultura Classica* 15: 57–71.
Comotti, G. (1989) *Music in Greek and Roman Culture* (English translation of original 1979 Italian edition). Baltimore and London.
Connelly, J. (1996) 'Parthenon and *Parthenoi*: a mythological interpretation of the Parthenon frieze', *American Journal of Archaeology* 100: 53–80.
Connor, W. R. (1971) *The New Politicians of Fifth-Century Athens*. Princeton.
Connor, W. R. (1987) 'Tribes, Festivals and Processions: Civic Ceremonial and Political Manipulation in Archaic Greece', *JHS* 107: 40–50.
Connor, W. R. (1989) 'Early Greek land warfare: a symbolic expression', *Past and Present* 119: 3–18.
Cooke, L. and Wollen, P. (1995) *Visual Display: Culture Beyond Appearance*. Seattle.
Copjec, J. (1994) *Read My Desire: Lacan against the Historicists*. Cambridge, Mass.
Corbin, A. (1990) *Women for Hire: Prostitution and Sexuality in France after 1850*, tr. A. Sheridan. Cambridge, Mass.
Cornford, F. (1914) *The Origins of Attic Comedy*. Cambridge.
Coulson, W., Palagia, O., Shear, T., Shapiro, H. and Frost, F., eds. (1994) *The Archaeology of Athens under the Democracy*. Oxford.
Coventry, L. (1990) 'The Role of the Interlocutor in Plato's Dialogues', in Pelling (1990).
Craik, E. M. ed. (1990) *Owls to Athens. Essays Presented to Kenneth Dover*. Oxford
Crary, J. (1990) *Techniques of the Observer: on Vision and Modernity in the Nineteenth Century*. Cambridge, Mass.
Crary, J. (1994) 'Unbinding vision', *October* 68: 21–44.
Cropp, M. (1995) *Erechtheus*, in Collard, Cropp and Lee (1995) 148–94.
Crowther, N. B. (1985) 'Male "Beauty" Contests in Greece: the Euandria and Euexia', *AC* 54: 285–91.
Crowther, N. B. (1991) 'Euexia, Eutaxia, Philopoina: Three Contests of the Greek Gymnasium', *ZPE* 85: 301–4.
Csapo, E. and Slater, W. J. (1995) *The Context of Ancient Drama*. Ann Arbor.
Daltrop, G. (1980) *Il Gruppo Mironiano di Atena e Marsia nei Musei Vaticani*. Vatican.
Daltrop, G. and Bol, P. C. (1983) *Athena des Myron*. Frankfurt.
Damen, M. (1989) 'Actor and Character in Greek tragedy', *Theatre Journal* 41: 316–40.
Damen, M. (1990) 'Electra's monody and the role of the choros in Euripides' *Orestes* 960–1012', *TAPA* 120: 133–45.
Daraki, M. (1985) *Dionysus*. Paris.
Daux, G. (1963) 'La grande démarchie: un nouveau calendrier sacrificiel d'Attique', *BCH* 87: 603–34.
Daux, G. (1983) 'Le calendrier de Thorikos', *AC* 52: 150–74.
Daux, G. (1984) 'Sacrifices à Thorikos', *Bulletin of the J. Paul Getty Museum* 12: 145–52.

David, E. (1984) *Aristophanes and Athenian Society of the Early Fourth Century B.C.* Leiden.
Davidoff, L. (1983) 'Class and gender in Victorian Britain', in Newton, Ryan, and Walkowitz (1983).
Davies, J. K. (1978) *Democracy and Classical Greece*. Hassocks.
Davies, J. K. (1994) 'Accounts and accountability in Classical Athens', in Osborne and Hornblower (1994) 201–12.
Davis, N. (1987) *Society and Culture in Early Modern France*. Cambridge.
Dawe, R. D. (1982) *Sophocles: Oedipus Rex*. Cambridge.
de Bolla, P. (1989) *The Discourse of the Sublime: History, Aesthetics and the Subject*. Oxford.
de Bolla, P. (1995) 'The Visibility of Visuality: Vauxhall Gardens and the Siting of the Viewer', in Melville and Readings (1995).
de Bolla, P. (1996) 'The Visibility of Visuality', in Brennan and Jay (1996).
de Bolla, P. (forthcoming) *18th Century Gardens*.
de Jong, I. and Sullivan, J., eds. (1994) *Modern Critical Theory and Classical Literature*. Leiden.
de Polignac, F. (1995) *Cults, Territory, and the Origins of the Greek City-State*, tr. J. Lloyd. Chicago and London.
de Romilly, J. (1975) *Magic and Rhetoric in Ancient Greece*. Cambridge, Mass. and London.
de Romilly, J. (1980) 'Réflexions sur le courage chez Thucydide et chez Platon', *REG* 93: 307–23.
de Witte, J. (1857) *Elite des Monument Céramographiques*, vol. II. Paris.
Debord, G. (1967) *La Société du spectacle*. Paris. [Retranslated by D. Nicholson-Smith, New York, (1994).]
Décharme, P. (1893) *Euripides et l'esprit de son théâtre*. Paris.
Degrassi, N. (1967) 'Meisterwerke frühitaliotischer Vasenmalerei aus einem Grabe in Polcoro-Herakleia', in Neutsch (1967) 193–231.
della Porta, D. and Mény, Y., eds. (1997) *Corruption and Democracy in Europe*. London.
Demargne, P. (1984) 'Athena', *LIMC* II.
Derrida, J. (1988) *Limited Inc.*, ed. G. Graff. Evanston.
Des Places, E. (1959) 'La prière cultuelle dans la Grèce ancienne', *Revue des Sciences Religieuses* 1: 343–59.
Desclos, M. L. (1992) 'La fonctions des prologues dans les dialogues de Platon', *Recherches sur la philosophie et le langage* 14: 15–29.
Detienne, M. (1967) *Les maîtres de vérité dans la Grèce archaïque*. Paris.
Detienne, M. (1989 [1986]) *Dionysos at Large*, tr. A. Goldhammer. Cambridge, Mass. and London.
Detienne, M. and Vernant, J.-P. (1989) *The Cuisine of Sacrifice among the Greeks*. Chicago.
Detienne, M., ed. (1988) *Les Savoires de l'Ecriture en Grèce ancienne*. Paris
Deubner, L. (1932) *Attische Feste*. Berlin.
Dhoulgeri-Indzessilogou, A. (1994) 'Οι νεότερες αρχαιολογικές έρευνες στην περιοχή των αρχαίων Φερών', in Midrhahi-Kapon, R. (1994) 71–92.
Diamond, E. (1996) 'Introduction', to Diamond (1996).
Diamond, E., ed. (1996a) *Performance and Cultural Politics*. London and New York.

Dieterle, R. (1966) 'Platon, Laches und Charmides. Untersuchungen zur elenktischen Struktur der platonischen Frohhdialoge'. Phil. Dissertation, Freiburg.
Diggle, J. (1974) 'On the Heracles and Ion of Euripides', *PCPS* 20: 3-36.
Diggle, J. (1984) *Euripides: Fabulae* 1. Oxford.
Dihle, A. (1981) *Der Prolog der 'Bacchen' und die antike Überlieferungsphase des Euripides-Textes*. Heidelberg.
Dindorf, L. ed. (1880-1) *Historici Graeci Minores*. Leipzig.
Doane, M. (1987) *The Desire to Desire: The Woman's Film of the 1940s*. Bloomington.
Dodds, E. R. (1960) *Euripides: Bacchae*. 2nd edn. Oxford.
Dodds, E. R. (1966) 'On Misunderstanding the *Oedipus Rex*', *Greece and Rome* 13: 37-49, reprinted in Dodds (1973) 64-77.
Dodds, E. R. (1973) *The Ancient Concept of Progress and Other Essays on Greek Literature and Belief*. Oxford.
Dolan, J. (1987) 'The Dynamics of Desire: Sexuality and Gender in Pornography and Performance', *Theatre Journal* 39: 156-74.
Dolan, J. (1993) 'Geographies of learning: Theatre studies, Performance and "the Performative"', *Theatre Journal* 45: 417-41.
Dorjahn, A. P. (1927) 'Poetry in Athenian courts', *CP* 32: 85-93.
Dorjahn, A. P. (1929-30) 'Some Remarks on Aeschines' Career as an Actor', *Classical Journal* 25: 223-9.
Dorjahn, A. P. (1935) 'Anticipation of Arguments in Athenian Courts', *TAPA* 66: 274-95.
Dougherty, C. and Kurke, L., eds. (1993) *Cultural Poetics in Archaic Greece*. Cambridge.
Douglas, M. (1966) *Purity and Danger*. London.
Dover, K. J. (1968) *Lysias and the Corpus Lysiacum*. Berkeley.
Dover, K. J. (1968a) *Aristophanes' Clouds*. Oxford.
Dover, K. J. (1972) *Aristophanic Comedy*. Oxford.
Dover, K. J. (1974) *Greek Popular Morality in the Time of Plato and Aristotle*. Oxford.
Dover, K. J. (1978) *Greek Homosexuality*. London.
Dover, K. J. (1993) *Aristophanes. Frogs*. Oxford.
Dow, S. (1965) 'The Greater Demarkhia of Erchia', *BCH* 89: 180-213.
Drerup, E. (1898) *Ueber die bei den Attischen Rednern Eingelegten Urkunden*. *Jahrb f. Cl. Phil.*, Supplementband 24.
Dreyfus, H. and Rabinow, P., eds. (1983) *Michel Foucault: Beyond Structuralism and Hermeneutics*. Chicago.
Dunbar, N. (1995) *Aristophanes: Birds*. Oxford.
Dunlop, D. C. (1932) *Processions: A Dissertation together with Practical Suggestions*. London.
Dunn, L. and Jones, N., eds. (1994) *Embodied Voices: Representing Female Vocality in Western Culture*. Cambridge.
Dunst, G. (1977) 'Der Opferkalendar des attischen Demos Thorikos', *ZPE* 25: 243-64.
Dupont-Roc R. and Lallot J. (1980) *Aristote: La Poétique*. Paris.
Durand, J. L. and Lissarrague, F. (1980) 'Un lieu d'image? L'espace du louterion', *Hephaistos* 2: 89-106.

Dyck, A. R. (1985) 'The Function and Persuasive Power of Demosthenes' Portrait of Aeschines in the speech *On the Crown*', *Greece and Rome* 32: 42-8.
Easterling, P. E. (1982) *Sophocles. 'Trachiniae'*. Cambridge.
Easterling, P. E. (1988) 'Women in Tragic Space', *BICS* 34: 15-26.
Easterling, P. E. (1988a) 'Tragedy and Ritual: "Cry 'Woe, Woe' but may the good prevail"', *Mètis* 3: 87-109.
Easterling, P. E. (1991) 'Euripides in the Theatre', *Pallas* 37 (1991) 49-57.
Easterling, P. E. (1994) 'Euripides outside Athens: a Speculative note', *ICS* 19: 73-80.
Easterling, P. E. (1997) 'Constructing the Heroic', in Pelling (1997) 21-37. Oxford.
Easterling, P. E. ed. (1997) *The Cambridge Companion to Greek Tragedy*. Cambridge.
Easterling, P. E. and Muir, J. eds. (1985) *Greek Religion and Society*. Cambridge.
Ebener, D. (1966) *Rhesos. Tragödie eines unbekannten Dichters*. Berlin.
Eco, U. (1979) *Lector in fabula. La cooperazione interpretativa nei testi narrativi*. Milan.
Eco, U. (1992) *Interpretation and Overinterpretation. Umberto Eco with Richard Rorty, Jonathan Culler and Christine Brooke-Rose*. Cambridge.
Eden, K. (1986) *Poetic and Legal Fiction in the Aristotelian Tradition*. Princeton.
Eden, K. (1987) 'Hermeneutics and the Ancient Rhetorical Tradition', *Rhetorica* 5: 59-86.
Eder, W. ed. (1995) *Die Athenische Demokratie im 4. Jahrhundert v. Chr.* Stuttgart.
Ehrenberg, V. (1962) *The People of Aristophanes*. New York.
Eitrem, S. (1920) *Beiträge zur griechischen Religionsgeschichte* 3. Kristiania.
Eitrem, S., Amundsen, L. and Winnington-Ingram R. P., eds., (1955) 'Fragments of unknown Greek Tragic texts with Musical notation (P. Oslo inv. no. 1413)', *SO* 31: 1-87.
Ellis, H. (1929) *Man and Woman*. 2nd edn. Boston.
Else, G. F. (1986) *Plato and Aristotle on Poetry*. Chapel Hill/London.
Elsner, J. (1992) 'Pausanias: a Greek Pilgrim in the Roman World', *Past and Present* 135: 3-29.
Emerson, C. (1997) *The First Hundred Years of Mikhail Bakhtin*. Princeton.
Emlyn-Jones, C. (1996) *Plato: Laches*. Warminster.
Evans, E. C. (1969) *Physiognomics in the Ancient World*. Philadelphia (= *TAPS* 59.5).
Faraone, C. A. (1995) 'The "Performative Future" in Three Hellenistic Incantations and Theocritus' Second Idyll', *CP* 90: 1-15.
Farrar, C. (1992) 'Ancient Greek Political Theory as a Response to Democracy', in J. Dunn ed. *Democracy: the Unfinished Journey, 508 B.C to A.D 1993*. Oxford. 17-46.
Fehling, D. (1968) 'Νυκτὸς παῖδες ἄπαιδες. A. Eum. 1034 und das sogenannte Oxymoron in der Tragödie', *Hermes* 96: 142-55.
Felman, S. (1980) *Le Scandale du corps parlant: Don Juan avec Austin ou La séduction en deux langues*. Paris.
Ferguson, W. S. (1944) 'The Attic orgeones', *HThR* 37: 61-140.

Ferrari, G. R. F. (1987) *Listening to the Cicadas: a Study of Plato's Phaedrus*. Cambridge.
Figueira, T. and Nagy, G., eds. (1985) *Theognis of Megara*. Baltimore and London.
Finley, M. (1973) *Democracy Ancient and Modern*. London.
Finley, M. (1983) *Politics in the Ancient World*. Cambridge.
Fish, S. (1980) 'How to Do Things with Austin and Searle', in *Is There A Text In This Class?* Cambridge, Mass.
Fisher, N. (1992) *Hybris: A Study in the Values of Honour and Shame in Ancient Greece*. Warminster.
Flashar, H. (1967) *Aristoteles Problemata Physica*. Berlin.
Foley, H. P. (1982) 'The Female Intruder Reconsidered: Women in Aristophanes' *Lysistrata* and *Ecclesiazousae*', *CP* 77: 1–21.
Foley, H. P. (1985) *Ritual Irony: Poetry and Sacrifice in Euripides*. Ithaca and London.
Foley, H. P. (1993) 'The Politics of Tragic Lamentation', in Sommerstein, Halliwell, Henderson, and Zimmermann (1993) 101–43.
Fontenrose, J. (1978) *The Delphic Oracle*. Berkeley.
Ford, A. (1997) 'The Inland Ship: Problems in the Performance and Reception of Early Greek Epic', in *Written Voices, Spoken Signs: Tradition, Performance, and the Epic Text*. ed. E. Bakker and A. Kahane. Cambridge, Mass.
Förster, R., ed. (1893) *Scriptores Physiognomici Graeci et Latini*. 2 vols. Leipzig.
Forte, J. (1990) 'Women's performance art: feminism and post-modernism', in Case (1990).
Foucault, M. (1977) *Discipline and Punish*, tr. A. Sheridan. Harmondsworth.
Foucault, M. (1987) *The Use of Pleasure*, vol. II of *The History of Sexuality*, tr. R. Hurley. London.
Foucault, M. (1988) *The Care of the Self*, vol. III of *The History of Sexuality*, tr. R. Hurley. London.
Foxhall, L. and Lewis A. D. E., eds. (1996) *Greek Law in its Political Setting: Justification not Justice*. Oxford.
Fraenkel, E. (1950) *Aeschylus. Agamemnon*. Oxford.
Frel, J. (1983) 'Euphronios and his fellows', in *Ancient Greek Art and Iconography* ed. W.G. Moon. Madison, Wisconsin.
Fried, M. (1980) *Absorption and Theatricality: Painting and Beholder in the Age of Diderot*. Chicago.
Froning, H. (1971) *Dithyrambos und Vasenmalerei*. Würzburg.
Frontisi-Ducroux, F. (1991) *Le dieu-masque: une figure du Dionysos d'Athènes*. Paris and Rome.
Frontisi-Ducroux, F. (1994) 'Athéna et l'Invention de la Flûte', *Musica e Storia* 2: 239–67.
Fuhrmann, M. ed. (1966) *Anaximenis Ars Rhetorica*. Leipzig.
Gabrielsen, V. (1994) *Financing the Athenian Fleet: Public Taxation and Social Relations*. Baltimore and London.
Garber, Marjorie. (1992) *Vested Interests*. New York.
Gardeya, P. (1981) *Das Problem des 'Besten' in Platons Laches*. Würzburg.
Garlan, Y. and Masson, O. (1982) 'Les acclamations pédérastiques de Kalami (Thasos)', *Bulletin de Correspondance Hellénique* 106: 3–22.

Garnsey, P. (1988) *Famine and Food Supply in the Greco-Roman World.* Cambridge.
Garrod, H. W. (1920) 'The Hyporcheme of Pratinas', *Classical Review* 34: 129–36.
Garver, E. (1994) *Aristotle's Rhetoric: an Art of Character.* Chicago.
Garvie, A. (1969) *Aeschylus' Suppliants: Play and Trilogy.* Cambridge.
Gebhard, E. (1973) *The Theater at Isthmia.* Chicago.
Geertz, C. (1981) *Negara: The Theatre State in Nineteenth-century Bali.* Princeton.
Gehring, G. (1979) *American Civic Religion: an Assessment.* Society for the Scientific Study of Religion 3. Storrs, Conn.
Gentili, B. (1979) *Theatrical Performances in the Ancient World.* Amsterdam/Uithoorn.
Gentili, B. (1990) 'Die pragmatischen Aspekte der archaischen griechischen Dichtung', *Antike und Abendland* 36: 1–17.
Gentili, B. and Luisi, F. (1995) 'La Pitica 12 di Pindaro e l'aulo di Mida', *Quaderni Urbinati de Cultura Classica* 49: 7–31.
George, D. (1989) 'On Ambiguity: Towards a Post-Modern Performance Theory', *Theatre Research International* 14: 71–85.
Gevaert, F. A. and Vollgraff, J. C., eds. (1901–3) *Les Problèmes musicaux d'Aristote.* Ghent.
Gevaert, F. A. (1875–81) *Histoire et théorie de la musique dans l'antiquité.* 2 vols. Ghent.
Ghiron-Bistagne, P. (1976) *Recherches sur les acteurs dans la Grèce antique.* Paris.
Gibson, P. and Gibson, R., eds. (1993) *Dirty looks: Women, Pornography, Power.* London.
Gill, C. (1996) *Personality in Greek Epic, Tragedy and Philosophy.* Oxford.
Gill, C. and McCabe, M. M., eds. (1996) *Form and Argument in Late Plato.* Oxford.
Gilula, D. (1996) 'A Singularly Gifted Actor', *Quaderni di Storia* 44: 159–64.
Giuliani, L. (1996) 'Rhesus between Life and Death: on the Relation of Image to Literature in Apulian Vase-Painting', *BICS* 41: 71–86.
Gleason, M. W. (1990) 'The Semiotics of Gender: Physiognomy and Self-Fashioning in the Second Century C.E.', in Halperin, Winkler and Zeitlin (1990) 389–415.
Gleason, M. W. (1995) *Making Men: Sophists and Self-Presentation in Ancient Rome.* Princeton.
Gödecken, K. (1986) 'Beobachtungen und Funde an der Heiligen Strasse zwischen Milet und Didyma, 1984', *ZPE* 66: 217–53.
Goff, B. (1990) *The Noose of Words. Readings of Desire, Violence, and Language in Euripides' Hippolytos.* Cambridge.
Goff, B. ed. (1995) *History, Tragedy, Theory: Dialogues on Athenian Drama.* Austin.
Goffman E. (1969) *The Presentation of Self in Everyday Life.* Harmondsworth.
Goffman, E. (1975) *Frame Analysis: an Essay on the Organization of Experience.* London.
Goldberg, R. (1988) *Performance: Live Art 1909 to the Present.* London.
Goldhill, S. (1986) *Reading Greek Tragedy.* Cambridge.

Goldhill, S. (1990) 'The Great Dionysia and civic ideology', in Winkler and Zeitlin (1990) 97–129.
Goldhill, S. (1991) *The Poet's Voice: Essays on Poetics and Greek Literature.* Cambridge.
Goldhill, S. (1994) 'The failure of exemplarity', in de Jong and Sullivan (1994).
Goldhill, S. (1995) 'Representing democracy: women at the Great Dionysia', in Osborne and Hornblower (1995).
Goldhill, S. (1996) 'Collectivity and Otherness. The Authority of the Tragic Chorus: Response to Gould', in Silk (1996) 244–56.
Goldhill, S. (1996a) *Foucault's Virginity: Ancient Erotic Fiction and the History of Sexuality.* Cambridge.
Goldhill, S. (1997) 'The Audience of Greek Tragedy', in Easterling (1997).
Goldhill, S. (1997a) 'The language of tragedy: rhetoric and communication' in Easterling (1997) 127–50.
Goldhill, S. (Unpublished) 'Reading, Politics and the Body.'
Goldstein, M. S. (1978) 'The Setting of the Ritual Meal in Greek Sanctuaries: 600–300 BCE' Dissertation, University of California, Berkeley.
Gomperz, H. (1912) *Sophistik und Rhetorik.* Leipzig.
Gould, J. (1996) 'Tragedy and Collective Experience', in Silk (1996) 217–43.
Graeser, A. (1975) 'Zur Logik der Argumentationsstruktur in Platon's Dialogen *Laches* und *Charmides.*', *Archiv fhr Geschichte der Philosophie* 57: 172–81.
Graf, F. (1996) 'Pompai in Greece. Some considerations about space and ritual in the Greek polis', in *The Role of Religion in the Early Greek Polis* (Swedish Institute at Athens; ActaAth-80, XIV) ed. R. Hägg. Stockholm.
Gras, M. (1985) *Traffics tyrrhéniens archaïques à Rome.* Rome.
Gray, V. J. (1994) 'Images of Sparta: writer and audience in Isocrates' *Panathenaicus*', in A. Powell and S. Hodkinsion (1994) *The Shadow of Sparta.* London. 223–71.
Green, J. R. (1994) *Theatre in Ancient Greek Society.* London.
Greenblatt, S. (1980) *Renaissance Self-Fashioning: From More to Shakespeare.* Chicago.
Greenblatt, S. (1991) *Marvellous Possessions: The Wonder of the New World.* Oxford.
Greenwood, L. H. G. (1953) *Aspects of Euripidean Tragedy.* Cambridge.
Grenfell, B. P. and Hunt, A. S., eds. (1906) *The Hibeh Papyri.* London.
Grice, P. (1975) 'Logic and conversation', in Cole and Morgan (1975).
Griffith, G. T. (1966) 'Isegoria in the Assembly at Athens', in E. Badian ed. *Ancient Society and Institutions.* Oxford.
Griffith, M. (1995) 'Brilliant Dynasts: Power and Politics in the *Oresteia*', *Classical Antiquity* 14: 62–129.
Griffith, M. and Mastronarde, D., eds. (1990) *Cabinet of the Muses.* Atlanta.
Griswold, C. ed. (1986) *Platonic Writings, Platonic Readings.* London.
Grize, J.-B. (1990) *Logique et Langage.* Paris.
Gruber, W. (1986) *Comic Theatre. Studies in Performance and Audience Response.* Athens and London.
Guillory, J. (1993) *Cultural Capital: The Problem of Literary Canon Formation.* Chicago.

Guthrie, W. K. C. (1971) *A History of Greek Philosophy*, vol. III. Cambridge.
Guthrie, W. K. C. (1975) *A History of Greek Philosophy*, vol. IV. Cambridge.
Gutting, G. ed. (1994) *The Cambridge Companion to Foucault*. Cambridge.
Habicht, C. (1970) *Gottmenschentum und griechische Städte*. Zetemata 14. 2nd edn. Munich.
Haldane, J. (1966) 'Musical Instruments in Greek Worship', *Greece and Rome* 13: 98–107.
Hall, E. (1989) *Inventing the Barbarian: Greek Self-definition through Tragedy*. Oxford.
Hall, E. (1989a) 'The Archer scene in Aristophanes' *Thesmophoriazusae*', *Philologus* 133: 38–54.
Hall, E. (1995) 'Lawcourt Dramas: the Power of Performance in Greek Forensic Oratory', *BICS* 40: 39–58.
Hall, E. (1995a) 'Drowning by nomes: the Greeks, swimming, and Timotheus' *Persians*', in H. A. Kahn ed. (1995) *The Birth of the European Identity* (*Nottingham Classical Literature Studies* vol. II). Nottingham. 44–80.
Hall, E. (1996) 'Is there a polis in Aristotle's *Poetics*?', in Silk (1996) 295–309.
Hall, E. (1996a) *Aeschylus' Persians*. Warminster.
Hall, E. (1997) 'The sociology of Athenian tragedy', in Easterling (1997) 93–126.
Hall, E. (forthcoming) 'Female figures and metapoetry in Old Comedy', in F. D. Harvey ed. *The Rivals of Aristophanes* (forthcoming).
Halleran, M. (1995) *Euripides: Hippolytus*. Warminster.
Halliwell, S. (1984) 'Plato and Aristotle on the Denial of Tragedy', *PCPS* 30: 50–8.
Halliwell, S. (1991) 'Comic Satire and Freedom of Speech in classical Athens', *JHS* 111: 48–70.
Halliwell, S. (1994) 'Philosophy and Rhetoric', in Worthington (1994) 222–43.
Halliwell, S. (1997) 'Between Public and Private: Tragedy and the Athenian Experience of Rhetoric', in Pelling (1997) 121–42.
Halperin, D. (1992) 'Plato and the erotics of narrativity', in *Innovations of Antiquity*, ed. R. Hexter and D. Selden, 95–126. New York and London.
Halperin, D. M. (1989) 'The Democratic Body: Prostitution and Citizenship in Classical Athens', *South Atlantic Quarterly* 88.1: 149–60; revised version in Halperin (1990) 88–112.
Halperin, D. M. (1990) *One Hundred Years of Homosexuality: And Other Essays on Greek Love*. New York.
Halperin, D. M., Winkler, J. J. and Zeitlin F. I., eds. (1990) *Before Sexuality: the Construction of Erotic Experience in the Ancient Greek World*. Princeton.
Handley, E. and Green, J. R. (1995) *Images of the Greek Theatre*. London.
Hansen, H. (1990) *Aspects of the Athenian Law Code of 410/09–400/399 BCE* New York and London.
Hansen, M. H. (1975) *Eisangelia: the Sovereignty of the People's Court in Athens in the Fourth Century BCE and the Impeachment of Generals and Politicians*. Göttingen.
Hansen, M. H. (1976) *Apagoge, Endeixis and Ehpegesis against Kakourgoi, Atimoi and Pheugontes*. Odense University Classical Studies 8.

Hansen, M. H. (1983) *The Athenian Ecclesia: a collection of articles (1976–1983)*. Copenhagen.
Hansen, M. H. (1984) 'Two Notes on Demosthenes' Symbouleutic Speeches', *C&M* 35: 57–70.
Hansen, M. H. (1987) *The Athenian Assembly in the Age of Demosthenes*. Oxford and New York.
Hansen, M. H. (1989) *The Athenian Ecclesia: a collection of articles (1983–1989)*. Copenhagen.
Hansen, M. H. (1990) 'Solonian Democracy in Fourth-century Athens', in W. R. Connor *et al. Aspects of Athenian Democracy*. Copenhagen, 1990, 71–99.
Hansen, M. H. (1991) *The Athenian Democracy in the age of Demosthenes*. Oxford.
Hanson, A. and Armstrong, D. (1986) 'The virgin's voice and neck: Aeschylus, *Agamemnon* 245 and other texts', *BICS* 33: 97–100.
Harder, A. (1985) *Euripides' Kresphontes and Archelaos*, (*Mnemosyne*, Supp. 87). Leiden.
Harding, P. (1994) 'Comedy and rhetoric', in Worthington (1994).
Harris, E. M. (1994) 'Law and Oratory', in Worthington (1994).
Harris, E. M. (1995) *Aeschines and Athenian Politics*. London.
Harris, W. V. (1989) *Ancient Literacy*. Cambridge, Mass.
Harrison, A. R. W. (1968–71) *The Law of Athens*, 2 vols., Oxford.
Harvey, F. D. (1985) '*Dona Ferentes*: some Aspects of Bribery in Greek Politics', in Cartledge and Harvey (1985) 76–117.
Harvey, F. D. (1990) 'The Sykophant and Sykophancy: Vexatious Redefinition', in Cartledge, Millett and Todd (1990) 103–21.
Haslam, M. W. (1972) 'Plato, Sophron, and the Dramatic Dialogue', *BICS* 19: 17–38.
Headlam, W. (1906) 'The Last Scene of the *Eumenides*', *JHS* 26: 268–77.
Healey, R. F. (1990) *Eleusinian Sacrifices in the Athenian Law Code*. New York and London.
Heath, M. (1988) 'Receiving the κῶμος: The Context and Performance of Epinician'. *AJP* 109: 180–95.
Hedreen, G. (1992) *Silens in Attic Black-figure Vase-painting: Myth and Performance*. Michigan.
Hedrick, C. W. (1994) 'Writing, Reading and Democracy', in Osborne and Hornblower (1994).
Helmholtz, H. L. F. (1885) *On the Sensations of Tone as a Physiological Basis for the Theory of Music*. 2nd English edn. London.
Henderson, J. (1987) 'Older Women in Attic Old Comedy', *TAPA* 117: 105–29.
Henderson, J. (1996) *Three Plays by Aristophanes: Staging Women*. London.
Henderson, L. D. J. (1976) 'Sophocles' *Trachiniae* 878–92 and a principle of Paul Maas', *Maia* 28: 19–24.
Henrichs, A. (1978) 'Greek Maenadism from Olympias to Messalina', *HSCP* 82: 121–60.
Henrichs, A. (1984) 'Loss of Self, Suffering, Violence: the Modern View of Dionysus from Nietzsche to Girard', *HSCP* 88: 205–40.

Henrichs, A. (1990) 'Between Country and City: Dionysus in Attica' in Griffith and Mastronarde (1990) 257–77.
Henrichs, A. (1993) 'The Tomb of Aias and the Prospect of Hero Cult in Sophokles', *Classical Antiquity* 12: 165–80.
Henrichs, A. (1994/5) '"Why should I dance?" Choral Self-referentiality in Greek Tragedy', *Arion* 3.1: 56–111.
Henrichs, A. (1996) *'Warum soll ich denn tanzen?' Dionysisches im Chor der griechischen Tragödie*. Stuttgart and Leipzig.
Henrichs, A. (1996a) 'Dancing in Athens, Dancing in Delos: Some Patterns of Choral Projection in Euripides', *Philologus* 140: 48–62.
Henry, A. S. (1977) *The Prescripts of Athenian Decrees*. Leiden.
Henry, A. S. (1983) *Honours and Privileges in Athenian Decrees*. Hildesheim.
Henry, A. S. (1996) 'The Hortatory Intention in Athenian State Decrees', *ZPE* 112: 105–19
Herington, C. J. (1955) *Athena Parthenos and Athena Polias*. Manchester.
Herington, C. J. (1985) *Poetry into Drama: Early Tragedy and the Greek Poetic Tradition*. Berkeley, Los Angeles and London.
Herman, G. (1987) *Ritualised Friendship and the Greek City*. Cambridge.
Herman, G. (1993) 'Tribal and Civic Codes of Behaviour in Lysias 1', *Classical Quarterly* 43: 406–19.
Herman, G. (1994) 'How violent was Athenian society?', in Osborne and Hornblower (1994).
Herman, G. (1996) 'Ancient Athens and the Values of Mediterranean Society', *Mediterranean Historical Review* 11: 5–36.
Hesk, J. (1997) 'Deception, Democracy and Ideology. The rhetoric of Self-Representation in Classical Athens', Ph.D dissertation. Cambridge.
Hesk, J. (forthcoming) *The Rhetoric of Self-Representation: Deception and the Collective in Classical Athenian Culture*. Cambridge.
Hilgard, A. (ed.), (1991) *Scholia in Dionysii Thracis Artem Grammaticum* (= *Grammatici Graeci* Part 1 vol. III) Leipzig.
Hirschkop, K. and Shepherd, D. eds. (1989) *Bakhtin and Cultural Theory*. Manchester.
Hofmann, H. (1976) *Mythos und Komödie: Untersuchungen zu den Vögeln des Aristophanes*. Hildesheim and New York.
Holquist, M. (1990) *Dialogism: Bakhtin and His World*. London.
Hölscher, U. (1975) 'Wie soll ich noch tanzen? Über ein Wort des sophokleischen Chores', in Köhler (1975) 376–93.
Hornblower, S. (1990) 'When was Megalopolis founded?', *ABSA* 85: 71–7.
Hornblower, S. (1991) *A Commentary on Thucydides: books i–iii*. Oxford.
Hose, M. (1990) *Studien zum Chor bei Euripides* vol. I. Stuttgart.
Hoy, D. ed. (1986) *Foucault: a critical Reader*. Oxford.
Hubert, H. and Mauss, M. (1929) 'Essai sur la nature et fonction du sacrifice', in the authors' *Mélanges d'histoire des religions* (2nd edn. Paris): 1–130. (First published in 1899, in Année Sociologique 2: 29–138. English tr. by Halls, W. D. 1964. *Sacrifice: Its Nature and Function*. Chicago).
Huchzermeyer, H. (1931) *Aulos und Kithara in der griechischen Musik bis zum Ausgang der klassischen Zeit*. Emsdetten.

Hughes, A. (1996) 'Comic Stages in Magna Graecia: the Evidence of the Vases', *TRI* 21: 95–107.
Humphreys, S. (1985) 'Social Relations on Stage: Witnesses in Classical Athens', *History & Anthropology* 1: 313–69.
Hunningher, B. (1956) *Acoustics and Acting in the Theatre of Dionysus Eleuthereus = Mededelinger der koninklijke Nederlandse Akademie van Wetenschappen, afd. Letterkunde* 19.9, 303–38. Amsterdam.
Hunt, E. (1982) *Holy Land Pilgrimage in the Later Roman Empire*. Oxford.
Hunt, L. ed. (1993) *The Invention of Pornography*. Cambridge, Mass.
Hunter, I., Saunders, D. and Williamson, D., eds. (1993) *On Pornography: Literature, Sexuality and Obscenity Law*. London.
Hunter, R. L. (1983) *A Study of* Daphnis and Chloe. Cambridge.
Hunter, V. J. (1994) *Policing Athens: Social Control in the Attic Lawsuits, 420–320 BCE* Princeton.
Hurwit, J. (1990) 'The Word in the Image: Orality, Literacy and Early Greek Art', *Word and Image* 6.2: 180–97.
Immerwahr H. (1990) *Attic Script*. Oxford.
Itzin, C. ed. (1990) *Pornography: Women, Violence and Civil Liberties*. Oxford.
Jakobson, R. (1961) 'Linguistics and communication theory', *Structure of Language and its Mathematical Aspects. Proceedings of Symposia in Applied Mathematics* 12: 245–52.
Jakobson, R. (1963) *Essais de Linguistique Générale*. Paris.
Jameson, M. H. (1965) 'Notes on the Sacrificial Calendar from Erchia', *BCH* 89 (1965) 154–72.
Jameson, M. H. (1988) 'Sacrifice and Ritual: Greece', in *Civilization of the Ancient Mediterranean: Greece and Rome* II, ed. M. Grant and R. Kitzinger: 959–79. New York.
Jameson, M. H. (1990) 'Private space in the Greek city', in Murray and Price (1990) 169–93.
Jameson, M. H. (1991) 'Sacrifice before Battle', in *Hoplites. The Classical Greek Battle Experience*, ed. V. Hanson. London.
Jameson, M. H. (1994) 'Theoxenia', in *Ancient Greek Cult Practice from the Epigraphical Evidence* (Swedish Institute at Athens; ActaAth-8o, 13, Stockholm, 1994), ed. R. Hägg: 35–57.
Jameson, M. H. (1997) 'Religion and the Athenian Democracy', in *Democracy 2500? Questions and Challenges* (Archaeological Institute of America, Colloquia and Conference Papers, No. 2), eds. I. Morris and K. Raaflaub: 171–95. Boston.
Janaway, C. (1995) *Images of excellence. Plato's Critique of the Arts*. Oxford.
Janin, R. (1966) 'Les processions religieuses de Byzance', *REB* 24: 68–89.
Janko, R. (1992) *The Iliad: books 13–16*. Cambridge.
Jay, M. (1993) *Downcast Eyes: the Denigration of Vision in Twentieth-century French Thought*, Berkeley.
Jens, W. ed. (1971) *Die Bauformen der griechischen Tragödie*. Munich.
Johansen, H. F., and Whittle. E. W. eds. (1980) *Aeschylus: The Suppliants*. Copenhagen.
Jones, C. P. (1991) 'Dinner Theater', in Slater (1991) 185–97.

Jones, N. (1995) *Soundbites and Spin Doctors. How Politicians Manipulate the Media and Vice Versa*. London.
Kahn, C. H. (1983) 'Drama and Dialectic in Plato's Gorgias'. *OSAPh* 1: 75–121.
Kaimio, M. (1970) *The Chorus of Greek Drama within the Light of the Person and Number Used*. Helsinki.
Kakouri, K. (1974) Προϊστορία τοῦ Θεάτρου: ἀπὸ τὴ σκοπιὰ τῆς Κοινωνικῆς Ἀνθρωπολογίας. Athens.
Kakrides, F. I. (1987) Ἀριστοφάνους: Ὄρνιθες. 2nd edn. Athens-Ioannina.
Käppel, L. (1992) *Paian. Studien zur Geschichte einer Gattung*. Berlin.
Kappeler, S. (1986) *The Pornography of Representation*. Cambridge.
Karp, I. and Lavine, S., eds. (1991) *Exhibiting Cultures: the Poetics and Politics of Museum Display*. Washington and London.
Kasper-Butz, I. (1990) *Die Göttin Athena im klassischen Athen: Athena als Repräsenntantin des demokratischen Staates*. Frankfurt.
Kassel, R. ed. (1971) *Aristotelis Ars Rhetorica*. Berlin.
Katsouris, A. G. (1989) Ρητορική Υπόκριση. Ioannina.
Kavoulaki, A. (1996) 'ΠΟΜΠΑΙ: Processions in Athenian Tragedy', Dissertation Oxford.
Keen, I. (1994) *Knowledge and Secrecy in an aboriginal Religion*. Oxford.
Kennedy, G. (1963) *The Art of Persuasion in Greece*. London.
Kennedy, G. A. (1989) 'Ancient Antecedents of Modern Literary Theory', *AJP* 110: 492–8.
Klein, W. (1898) *Die Griechischen Vasen mit Lieblingsinschriften*. Leipzig.
Kleingünther, A. (1933) Πρῶτος εὑρετής. Philologus Supplement 26,1.
Kleinknecht, H. 1937. 'Zur Parodie des Gottmenschentums bei Aristophanes', *ARW* 34: 294–313.
Köhler, E. ed. (1975) *Sprachen der Lyrik. Festschrift für Hugo Friedrich*. Frankfurt a. M.
Koller, H. (1963) *Musik und Dichtung im alten Griechenland*. Bern and Munich.
Konstan, D. (1997) *Friendship in the Classical World*. Cambridge.
Konstan, D. and Dillon, M. (1981) 'The Ideology of Aristophanes' *Wealth*' *AJP* 102: 371–94.
Kotsidu, H. (1990) *Die musischen Agone der Panathenäen in archaischer Zeit: Eine historisch-archäologische Untersuchung*. Munich.
Kovaks, D. (1994) *Euripidea*. Leiden.
Kranz, W. (1933) *Stasimon. Untersuchungen zu Form und Gehalt der griechischen Tragödie*. Berlin.
Kristeva, J. (1982 [1980]) *Powers of Horror: an Essay on Abjection*, tr. L. Roudiez. Columbia.
Kron, U. (1976) *Die zehn attischen Phylenheroen* (Athenische Mitteilungen, Beiheft 5). Berlin.
Krummen, E. (1993) 'Athens and Attica: *Polis* and Countryside in Greek Tragedy', in Sommerstein, Halliwell, Henderson and Zimmermann (1993) 191–217.
Kuhn, H. (1941–2) 'The True Tragedy: On the Relationship between Greek Tragedy and Plato', *HSCP* 52: 1–40 and *HSCP* 53: 37–88.
Kurtz, D. C. (1975) *Athenian White Lekythoi*. Oxford.

Kyle, D. G. (1992) 'The Panathenaic Games: Sacred and Civic Athletics', in Neils (1992) 77-101.
Labarbe, J. (1977) *Fouilles de Thorikos, I: Les testimonia.* Ghent.
Lane Fox, R. (1994) 'Aeschines and Athenian Democracy', in Osborne and Hornblower (1994) 135-56.
Langdon, M. (1976) *A Sanctuary of Zeus on Mount Hymettos*, Hesperia Supplement 16. (Princeton).
Lanni, A. (1997) 'Spectator Sport or Serious Politics? οἱ περιεστηκότες and the Athenian Lawcourts', *JHS* 117: 183-9.
Laqueur, R. (1927) *Epigraphische Untersuchungen au den griechischen Volksbeschlüssen.* Leipzig.
Larson, J. (1995) *Greek Heroine Cults.* Madison, Wisconsin.
Lasserre, F. (1954) *Plutarque, De la musique: texte, traduction, commentaire.* Lausanne.
Lavency, M. (1964) *Aspects de la logographie judiciaire attique.* Louvain.
Lawrence, A. (1991) *Echo and Narcissus: Women's voices in Classical Hollywood Films.* Berkeley.
le Guen, B. (1995), 'Théâtre et cités a l'époque hellenistique: "Mort de la cité" – "Mort du Théâtre"?', *REG* 108: 59-90.
Leacock, A. G. (1900) 'De rebus ad pompas sacras apud Graecos pertinentibus: Quaestiones Selectae'. *HSCP* 11: 1-45.
Leaf, W. (1900-02) *The Iliad*, edited with English notes and Introduction. 2nd edn, 2 vols. London.
Lebeck, A. (1971) *The* Oresteia*: A Study in Language and Structure.* Washington, D.C. and London.
Leclercq-Neveu, B. (1989) 'Marsyas, le Martyr de l'Aulos', *Mètis* 4: 251-68.
Lefkowitz, M. (1981) *Lives of the Greek Poets.* London.
Lefkowitz, M. and Fant, M. (1992) *Women's Life in Greece and Rome: A Sourcebook in Translation.* 2nd edn. London.
Lehnstaedt, K. (1970) 'Prozessionsdarstellungen auf attischen Vasen'. Dissertation Munich.
Levi, M. and Nelken, D., eds. (1996) *The Corruption of Politics and the Politics of Corruption.* Oxford.
Levine, D. (1985) 'Symposium and the *polis*', in Figueira and Nagy (1985).
Levinson, S. (1983) *Pragmatics.* Cambridge.
Levy, R. I. (1990) *Mesocosm. Hinduism and the Organization of a Traditional Newar City in Nepal.* Berkeley.
Lévy, Edmond. (1976) 'Les Femmes chez Aristophane', *Ktèma* 1: 99-112.
Lewis, D. M. (1993) 'Oligarchic Thinking in the Late Fifth Century', in R. Rosen and J. Farrell eds. *Nomodeiktes: Greek Studies in Honor of Martin Ostwald.* Ann Arbor.
Lewis, S. (1996) *News and Society in the Greek Polis.* London.
Lissarague, F. (1987) *Un flot d'images: une esthétique du banquet grec.* Paris.
Lissarrague, F. (1985) 'Paroles d'images: remarques sur le fonctionnement de l'écriture dans l'imagerie attique', in *Ecritures II* ed. A. M. Christin: 71-93. Paris.
Lissarrague, F. (1990) *The Aesthetics of the Greek Banquet: Images of Wine and Ritual.* tr. A. Szegedy-Maszak. Princeton.

Lissarrague, F. (1990a) 'The Sexual Life of Satyrs', in Halperin, Winkler, and Zeitlin (1990) 53-81.
Lissarrague, F. (1990b) 'Why Satyrs are Good to Represent', in Winkler and Zeitlin (1990) 228-36.
Lissarrague, F. (1992) 'Graphein: écrire et dessiner', in *L'image en jeu*, eds. Ch. Bron and E. Kassapoglou: 189-203. Lausanne.
Lissarrague, F. (1993) 'On the Wildness of Satyrs', in Carpenter and Faraone (1993) 207-20.
Lissarrague, F. and Frontisi-Ducroux, F. (1990) 'From Ambiguity to Ambivalence: A Dionysiac Excursion through the "Anakreontic" Vases', in Halperin, Winkler, and Zeitlin (1990) 211-56.
Lloyd, G. E. R. (1970) *Early Greek Science: Thales to Aristotle*. London.
Lloyd, G. E. R. (1979) *Magic, Reason and Experience: Studies in the Origin and Development of Greek Science*. Cambridge.
Lloyd, G. E. R. (1983) *Science, Folklore and Ideology*. Cambridge.
Lloyd, G. E. R. (1987) *The Revolutions of Wisdom: Studies in the Claims and Practice of Ancient Greek Science*. Berkeley.
Lloyd, M. (1992) *The Agon in Euripides*. Oxford.
Lloyd, M. (1994) *Euripides: Andromache*. Warminster.
Lonis, R. ed. (1992) *L'Etranger dans le monde grec*. Vol. II. Nancy.
Lonsdale, S. 1993. *Dance and Ritual Play in Greek Religion*. Baltimore and London.
Loraux, N. (1981) *L'Invention d'Athènes*. Paris.
Loraux, N. (1981a) *Les enfants d'Athéna. Idées athéniennes sur la citoyenneté et la division des Sexes*. Paris (see also Loraux (1993)).
Loraux, N. (1986) *The Invention of Athens*. Cambridge Mass. (Eng. trans. of Loraux (1981)). 115-39.
Loraux, N. (1990) 'Gloire du Même, prestige de l'Autre', *Le genre humain* 21: 115-39.
Loraux, N. (1991) 'Aristophane et les femmes d'Athènes. Réalité, fiction, théâre. Note preliminaire', *Métis* 6: 119-30.
Loraux, N. (1993) *The Children of Athena*, tr. C. Levine, Princeton.
Loraux, N. (1993a) 'Aristophane, les femmes d'Athènes et le théâtre', in E. Degani ed. *Aristophane. Entretiens sur l'Antiquité Classique*, vol. 38: 203-44. Vandoevres-Geneva.
M.-Klein, B. (1988) 'Die myronische Athena – im Weggehen begriffen?', *Boreas* 11: 43-7.
Maas, M. and Snyder, J. (1989) *Stringed Instruments of Ancient Greece*. New Haven and London.
Maas, P. (1929) *Griechische Metrik*, = A. Gercke and E. Norden eds. *Einleitung in die Altertumswissenschaft*, vol. 1.7. Leipzig and Berlin.
Maas, P. (1962) *Greek Metre*. Oxford.
MacAloon, J. ed. (1984) *Rite, Drama, Festival, Spectacle: Rehearsals toward a Theory of Cultural Performance*. Philadelphia.
MacDonald, B. R. (1982) 'The Import of Attic Pottery to Corinth and the Question of Trade during the Pelonnesian War', *JHS* 102: 113-23.
MacDowell, D. M. (1971) *Aristophanes' Wasps*. Oxford.
MacDowell, D. M. (1978) *Law in Classical Athens*. London.

MacDowell, D. M. (1990) *Demosthenes: Against Meidias*. Oxford.
MacDowell, D. M. (1995) *Aristophanes and Athens: an Introduction to his Plays*. Oxford.
MacKinnon, C. (1987) *Feminism Unmodified*. Cambridge, Mass.
MacKinnon, C. (1993) *Only Words*. Cambridge, Mass.
Macran, H. (1912) *The Harmonics of Aristoxenus*. Oxford.
Mader, M (1977) *Das Problem des Lachens und der Komödie bei Platon*. Stuttgart.
Malkin, I. (1987) *Religion and Colonisation in Ancient Greece*. Studies in Greek and Roman Religion. Leiden.
March, J. (1990) 'Euripides the Misogynist', in Powell (1990) 32–75.
Marin, L. 1987. 'Notes on a Semiotic Approach to *Parade, Cortege*, and *Procession*', in *Time out of Time: Essays on the Festival*, ed. A. Falassi: 220–30. Albuquerque.
Marinatos, N. (1986) *Minoan Sacrificial Ritual: Cult Practice and Symbolism*. Stockholm.
Marinatos, N. (1993) *Minoan Religion*. New York.
Mark, I. S. (1993) *The Sanctuary of Athena Nike in Athens. Architectural Stages and Chronology*. Hesperia Supplement 26. Princeton.
Marrou, H.-I. (1956) *History of Education in Antiquity*. New York.
Marrou, H.-I. (1964) *Histoire de l'éducation dans l'Antiquité I. Le monde grec*. 6th edn. Paris.
Martens, H. H. (1954) *Die Einleitungen der Dialoge Laches und Protagoras*. Kiel.
Martin, R. (1993) 'The Seven Sages as Performers of Wisdom', in Dougherty and Kurke (1993).
Martin, V. and de Budé, D. (1927) *Aeschine. Discours I*. Paris.
Marx, F. (1933) 'Musik aus der griechischen Tragödie', *Rh. M* 82: 230–46.
Masqueray, P. (1895) *Théorie des formes lyriques de la tragédie grecque*. Paris.
Mastronarde, D. (1994) *Euripides: Phoenissae*. Cambridge.
Mattéi, J.-F. (1986) 'The Theatre of Myth in Plato', in Griswold (1986).
Maurizio, L. (forthcoming) 'The Panathenaia: Processing Notions of Athenian Identity', in *Democracy, Empire and the Arts*, ed. K. Rauflaub and D. Boedeker. Cambridge, Mass.
Melville, S. and Readings, W., eds. (1995) *Vision and Textuality*. London.
Méron, E. (1979) *Les idées morales des interlocuteurs de Socrate dans les dialogues platoniciens de jeunesse*. Paris.
Merriam., A. (1964) *The Anthropology of Music*. Northwestern University Press.
Merritt, C. (1984) "The Greatest Spectacle": Processions in the Works of Mark Twain', *American Literary Realism* 17.2: 180–92.
Metzger, H. (1951) *Les représentations dans la céramique attique du IVe siècle*. Paris.
Michaelides, S. (1978) *The Music of Ancient Greece: An Encyclopaedia*. London.
Midhrahi-Kapon, R. ed. (1994) *La Thessalie: Quinze années de recherches archéologiques, 1975–1990*. Athens.
Mikalson, J. (1975) *The Sacred and Civil Calendar of the Athenian Year*. Princeton.
Mikalson, J. (1977) 'Religion in the Attic Demes', *AJP* 98: 424–35.
Miller, M. C. (1997) *Athens and Persia in the Fifth Century BCE. A study in Cultural Receptivity*. Cambridge.

Miller, S. (1991) *Arete: Greek Sports from Ancient Sources.* Berkeley.
Miller, S. G. (1979) 'Excavations at Nemea, 1978', *Hesperia* 48: 71–103.
Millett, P. (1991) *Lending and Borrowing in Ancient Athens.* Cambridge.
Milne M. and von Bothmer D. (1953) 'Katapugon, katapugaina', *Hesperia* 22: 215–24.
Mommsen, A. (1898) *Feste der Stadt Athen in Altertum.* Leipzig.
Monro, D. B. (1894) *The Modes of Ancient Greek Music.* Oxford.
Moravcsik, J., and Temko, P., eds. (1982) *Plato on Beauty, Wisdom and the Arts.* New Jersey.
Moret, J.-M (1979) 'Un ancêtre du phylactère: le pilier inscrit des vases italiotes', *RA* (1979) 3–34, 235–58.
Moretti, J.-Ch. (1991, 1992, 1993) 'L'Architecture des théâtres (1980–1989)', *Topoi* 1(1991), 7–38 (Mainland Greece); 2(1992) 9–32 (Asia Minor); 3(1993) 72–100 (Sicily & S. Italy).
Morrison, J. (1984) 'Hyperesia in Naval Contexts in the Fifth and Fourth Centuries BC', *JHS* 104: 48–59.
Mossé, C. (1995) 'La classe politique à Athènes au IVème siècle', in Eder (1995).
Moutsopoulos, E. (1962) 'Euripide et la philosophie de la musique', *REG* 75: 96–452.
Muir, E. (1981) *Civic Ritual in Renaissance Venice.* Princeton.
Müller, D. (1987) *Topographisches Bildcommentar zu den Historien Herodots: Griechenland.* (Tübingen).
Mulvey, L. (1989) *Visual and Other Pleasures.* London.
Murphy, C. T. (1938) 'Aristophanes and the Art of Rhetoric', *HSCP* 49: 69–114.
Murray, G. (1933) *Aristophanes: A Study.* Oxford.
Murray, J. S. (1988) 'Disputation, Deception and Dialectic: Plato on the True Rhetoric (*Phaedrus* 261–266)', *Philosophy and Rhetoric* 21: 279–89.
Murray, O. and Price, S., eds., (1990) *The Greek City from Homer to Alexander.* Oxford.
Murray, O. ed. (1990) *Sympotica: A Symposium on the Symposium.* Oxford.
Murray, P. (1996) *Plato on Poetry.* Cambridge.
Murray, T. ed. (1997) *Mimesis, Masochism and Mime: The Politics of Theatricality in Contemporary French Thought.* Ann Arbor.
Nagy, B. (1992) 'The Athenian Athlothetai', *GRBS* 19: 307–13.
Nagy, G. (1979) *The Best of the Achaeans.* Baltimore and London.
Nagy, G. (1990) *Pindar's Homer. The Lyric Possession of an Epic Past.* Baltimore and London.
Nagy, G. (1994/5) 'Transformations of Choral Lyric Traditions in the Context of the Athenian State Theater', *Arion* 3.1: 41–55.
Nagy, G. (1996) *Poetry as Performance. Homer and Beyond.* Cambridge.
Nead, L. (1988) *Myths of Sexuality: Representations of Women in Victorian Britain.* Oxford.
Neer, R. (1998) 'Pampoikilos', PhD dissertation, Berkeley.
Neils, J. (1992) 'The Panathenaia: an introduction', in Neils ed. (1992).
Neils, J. (1996) 'Pride, Pomp and Circumstance: the Iconography of Processions' in J. Neils, ed., *Worshipping Athena: Panathenaia and Parthenon.* Madison, Wisconsin. 177–97.

Neils, J. ed. (1992) *Goddess and Polis: the Panathenaic Festival in Ancient Athens.* Princeton.
Neils, J. ed. (1996) *Worshipping Athena: Panathenaia and Parthenon.* Madison, Wisconsin.
Neubecker, A. (1990) 'Altgriechische Musik 1958–1986', *Lustrum* 32: 99–176.
Neutsch, B. ed. (1967) *Herakleiastudien.* MDAI (R) Ergänzungsheft 11. Heidelberg.
Newton, J., Ryan, P. and Walkowitz, J., eds. (1983) *Sex and Class in Women's History.* London.
Nightingale, A. W. (1995) *Genres in Dialogue.* Cambridge.
Nilsson, M. P. (1906) *Griechische Feste von Religiöser Bedeutung: Mit Ausschluss der Attischen.* Leipzig.
Nilsson, M. P. (1951) 'Die Prozessionstypen im griechischen Kult', in *Opuscula selecta ad historiam religionis Graecae*, vol. 1: 166–214. Lund.
Nilsson, M. P. (1957) *Griechische Feste von religiöser Bedeutung mit Ausschluss der Attischen.* Stuttgart.
Nilsson, M. P. (1967) *Geschichte der griechischen Religion. I³. Die Religion Griechenlands bis auf die griechische Weltherrschaft.* Munich.
Nochlin, L. (1989) *The Politics of Vision.* New York.
Nock, A. D. (1944) 'The Cult of Heroes'. *HThR* 37: 141–73.
Nordquist, G. C. (1992) 'Instrumental Music in Representations of Greek Cult', in *The Iconography of Greek Cult in the Archaic and Classical Period: Proceedings of the First International Seminar Ancient Greek Cult (Delphi 16–18 November 1980).* Kernos Supplément 1, ed. R. Hägg: 143–68. Athènes and Lièges.
North, H. (1952) 'The Use of Poetry in the Training of the Ancient Orator', *Traditio* 8: 1–33.
North, H. (1966) *Sophrosyne: Self-Knowledge and Self-Restraint in Greek Literature.* Ithaca.
Nouhaud, M. (1982) *L' utilisation de l' histoire par les orateurs attiques.* Paris.
Nussbaum M. (1982) '"This Story isn't True": Poetry, Goodness and Understanding in Plato's *Phaedrus*', in Moravscik and Temko (1982).
Nussbaum, M. (1986) *The Fragility of Goodness.* Cambridge.
O'Brien, M. J. (1963) 'The Unity of the *Laches*', *JCS* 18: 133–47.
O' Regan, D. (1992) *Rhetoric, Comedy and the Violence of Language in Aristophanes' Clouds.* Oxford.
O'Sullivan, N. (1992) *Alcidamas, Aristophanes and the Beginnings of Greek Stylistic Theory.* Hermes Einzelschriften Heft 60. Stuttgart.
Oakley, J. H. and Sinos, R. (1993) *The Wedding in Ancient Athens.* Wisconsin.
Obbink, D. (1993) 'Dionysus Poured Out: Ancient and Modern Theories of Sacrifice and Cultural Formation', in Carpenter and Faraone (1993) 65–86.
Ober, J. (1989) *Mass and Elite in Democratic Athens: Rhetoric, Ideology and the Power of the People.* Princeton.
Ober, J. (1994) 'Power and Oratory in Democratic Athens: Demosthenes 2, *Against Meidias*', in Worthington (1994) 85–108.
Ober, J. (1994a) 'Civic Ideology and Counterhegemonic Discourse: Thucydides on the Sicilian Debate', in Boegehold and Scafuro (1994).
Ober, J. (1998) *Political Dissent in Democratic Athens: Intellectual Critics of Popular Rule.* Princeton.

Ober, J. and Hedrick, C., eds. (1996) *Dēmokratia. A Conversation on Democracies, Ancient and Modern.* Princeton.
Ober, J. and Strauss, B. (1990) 'Drama, political rhetoric and the discourse of Athenian Democracy', in Winkler and Zeitlin (1990) 237-70.
Oeri, B. (1948) *Der Typ der komischen Alten in der griechischen Komödie.* Basle.
Oikonomides, A. (1984) 'An Etruscan in Fifth-Century Athens', *Ancient World* 10: 127-8.
Ophir, A. (1992) *Plato's Invisible Cities: Discourse and Power in the Republic.* London.
Ortner, S. B. (1984) 'Theory in Anthropology since the Sixties', *Comparative Studies in Society and History* 1: 126-66.
Osborne, M. J. (1981-3) *Naturalization at Athens.* 4 vols in 3. Brussels.
Osborne, R. (1985) *Demos: the Discovery of Classical Attika.* Cambridge.
Osborne, R. (1985a) 'Law in Action in Classical Athens', *JHS* 105: 40-58.
Osborne, R. (1987) 'The Viewing and Obscuring of the Parthenon Frieze', *JHS* 107: 98-105.
Osborne, R. (1990) 'Vexatious Litigation in Classical Athens: Sykophancy and the Sykophant', in Cartledge, Millett and Todd (1990) 83-102.
Osborne, R. (1993) 'Competitive festivals and the polis: a context for dramatic festivals in Athens', in Sommerstein, Halliwell, Henderson, and Zimmermann eds. (1993).
Osborne, R. (1993a) 'Women and Sacrifice in Classical Greece', *Classical Quarterly* 43: 392-405.
Osborne, R. (1994) 'Archaeology, the Salaminioi, and the Politics of Sacred Space in Archaic Attica', in Alcock and Osborne (1994).
Osborne, R. (1994a) 'Democracy and Imperialism in the Panathenaic Procession: The Parthenon Frieze in its Context', in Coulson et al. (1994) 143-50.
Osborne, R. (1996) *Greece in the Making 1200-479 BCE.* London.
Osborne, R. and Hornblower, S., eds. (1994) *Ritual, Finance, Politics. Athenian Democratic Accounts Presented to David Lewis.* Oxford.
Østerud, S. (1970) 'Who sings the Monody 669-79 in Euripides' *Hippolytus*?', *GRBS* 11: 307-20.
Ostwald, M. (1986) *From Popular Sovereignty to the Sovereignty of Law: Law, Society and Politics in Fifth-Century Athens.* Berkeley.
Ousterhout, R. (1990) *The Blessings of Pilgrimage.* Urbana.
Overbeck, J. (1868) *Die antiken Schriftquellen zur Geschichte der bildenden Künste bei den Griechen.* Leipzig.
Owen, A. S. (1936) 'The date of Sophocles' *Electra*', in *Greek Poetry and Life: Essays Presented to Gilbert Murray on his Seventieth Birthday.* Oxford. 145-57.
Page, D. L. (1936) 'The elegiacs in Euripides' *Andromache*', in *Greek Poetry and Life: Essays Presented to Gilbert Murray on his Seventieth Birthday.* Oxford. 206-30.
Palmer, C. (1975) *Miklós Rózsa: A Sketch of his Life and Work.* London and Wiesbaden.
Pantos, P. (1994) 'La Vallée du Spercheios ... aux Epoques Hellénistiques', in Midhrahi and Kapon (1994) 221-8.
Paquette, D. (1984) *L'Instrument de musique dans la céramique de la Grèce antique: études d'Organologie.* Paris.
Parke, H. W. (1977) *Festivals of the Athenians.* London.

Parker, A. and Sedgwick, E., eds. (1995) *Performativity and Performance*. London and New York.
Parker, D. (1967) *Aristophanes, The Congresswomen*, tr. D. Parker. Ann Arbor.
Parker, L. P. E. (1997) *The Songs of Aristophanes*. Oxford.
Parker, R. (1987) 'Myths of Early Athens', in Bremmer (1987) 187–214.
Parker, R. (1987) 'Festivals of the Attic demes', in *Gifts to the Gods* (Boreas, 15) eds. T. Linders, and G. Nordquist: 137–47. Uppsala.
Parker, R. (1989) 'Spartan Religion', in A. Powell, ed. *Classical Sparta*. London. 142–72.
Parker, R. (1996) *Athenian Religion: A History*. Oxford.
Parker, R. (1996a) 'Sacrifice, Greek', in *Oxford Classical Dictionary*. 3rd edn: 1344–5. Oxford.
Patterson, R. (1982) 'The Platonic Art of Comedy and Tragedy', *Philosophy and Literature* 6: 76–93.
Patterson, R. (1985) *Image and Reality in Plato's Metaphysics*. Indianapolis.
Pavis, P. (1987) *Dictionnaire du théâtre* 2nd edn. Paris.
Pavloskis, Z. (1977–8) 'The Voice of the Actor in Greek Tragedy', *Classical World* 71: 113–23.
Pearson, L. (1941) 'Historical Allusions in the Attic Orators', *CPh* 36: 209–29.
Pearson, L. (1962) *Popular Ethics in Ancient Greece*. Stanford.
Pearson, L. (1990) *Aristoxenus. Elementa Rhythmica*. Oxford.
Peirce, S. (1993) 'Death, Revelry, and Thysia', *Classical Antiquity* 12: 219–78.
Pélékidis, C. (1962) *Histoire de l'Ephébie Attique*. Paris.
Pelling, C. B. R. ed. (1990) *Characterization and Individuality in Greek Literature*. Oxford.
Pelling, C. B. R. ed. (1997) *Greek Tragedy and the Historian*. Oxford.
Pellizer, E. (1990) 'Sympotic entertainment', in Murray (1990).
Pembroke, S. (1965) 'The Last of the Matriarchs: A Study in the Inscriptions of Lycia', *Journal of Economic and Social History of the Orient* 8.3: 217–47.
Pembroke, S. (1967) 'Women in Charge. The Functions of Alternatives in Early Greek Tradition and the Ancient Idea of Matriarchy', *Journal of the Warburg and Courtauld Institute* 30: 1–35.
Penley, C. ed. (1988) *Feminism and Film Theory*. New York and London.
Peretti, A. (1939) *Epirrema e tragedia*. Florence.
Perlman, S. (1961) 'The Historical Example, Its Use and Importance as Political Propaganda in the Attic Orators', *SH* 7: 150–66.
Perlman, S. (1964) 'Quotations from Poetry in Attic Orators of the Fourth Century BCE', *AJP* 85: 155–72.
Petrey, S. (1990) *Speech Acts and Literary Theory*. New York and London.
Pfeiffer, R. (1968) *History of Classical Scholarship: From the Beginnings to the End of the Hellenistic Age*. Oxford.
Pfuhl, E. (1900) *De Atheniensium pompis sacris*. Berlin.
Phelan, P. (1993) *Unmarked: the Politics of Performance*. London.
Phelan, P. (1997) *Mourning Sex*. London.
Pickard-Cambridge, A. (1962) *Dithyramb, Tragedy, and Comedy*, 2nd edn, revised by T. B. L. Webster. Oxford.

Pickard-Cambridge, A. (1968) *The Dramatic Festivals of Athens*, 2nd edn. Oxford.
Pickard-Cambridge, A. (1988) *The Dramatic Festivals of Athens*, 2nd edn, revised with supplement and corrections by J. Gould and D. Lewis. Oxford.
Pintacuda, M. (1978) *La Musica nella tragedia Greca*. Maggio.
Poizat, M. (1992) *The Angel's Cry: Beyond the Pleasure Principle in Opera*, tr. A. Denner. Ithaca and London.
Polacco, L. et al. (1981, 1990) *Il teatro greco di Siracusa* (i, Rimini; ii, Padua).
Polignac, de F. (1995) *Cults, Territory and the Origin of the Greek City-State*. Chicago.
Pollitt, J. J. (1974) *The Ancient Greek View of Greek Art*. New Haven.
Pongratz-Leisten, B. (1994) *Ina Sulmi Irub: die kulttopographische und ideologische Programmatik der akitu-Prozession in Babylonien und Assyrien im I. Jahrtausend v. Chr.* Baghdader Forschungen. Mainz.
Popp, H. (1971) 'Die Amoibaion', in Jens (1971) 221–75.
Popper, K. (1966) *The Open Society and its Enemies, vol. 1, The Spell of Plato*, 5th edn. London.
Possetto, P. and Sartoro, G., eds. (1995) *Teatri Greci e Romani*. Rome.
Pötscher, W. (1959) 'Die Funktion der Anapästpartien in der Tragödien des Aischylos', *Eranos* 57: 79–98.
Powell, A. ed. (1990) *Euripides, Women, and Sexuality*. London.
Pratt, M. (1977) *Towards a Speech-Act Theory of Literary Discourse*. Bloomington.
Pratt, M. (1992) *Imperial Eyes: Travel Writing and Transculturation*. London.
Prendergast, C. (1986) *The Order of mimesis*. Cambridge.
Pretagostini, R. ed. (1993) *Tradizione e innovazione nella Cultura greca da Omero all' età ellenistica. Scritti in onore di Brunto Gentili*. Vol. II. Rome.
Price, A. W. (1989) *Love and Friendship in Plato and Aristotle*. Oxford.
Price, T. H. (1978) *Kourotrophos. Cults and Representations of the Greek nursing Deities*. Leiden.
Pritchett, W. K. (1974) *The Greek State at War*. Vol. II. Berkeley.
Pucci, P. (1977) 'Euripides: the Monument and the Sacrifice', *Arethusa* 10: 165–95.
Pucci, P. (1992) *Oedipus and the Fabrication of the Father*. Baltimore and London.
Pucci, P. (1996) 'Auteur et destinataire dans les *Erga* d'Hésiode', in Blaise et al. (1996) 191–210.
Puttkammer, F. (1912) 'Quo mode Graeci victimarum carnes distribuerint.' Dissertation Königsberg.
Radermacher, L. (1951) *Artium Scriptores*. Vienna.
Randall, J. H. (1970) *Plato: Dramatist of the Life of Reason*. New York.
Rappaport, R. A. (1979) *Ecology, Meaning, and Religion*. Richmond, California.
Rau, P. (1967) *Paratragodia: Untersuchung einer komischen Form des Aristophanes Zetemata* 45. Munich.
Raven, D. S. *Greek Metre: an Introduction*. 2nd edn. London.
Rebillard, L. (1991) 'Exékias apprend à écrire', in Baurain et al. (1991) 549–64.
Redfield, J. (1985) 'Herodotus the Tourist', *CP* 80: 97–118.
Reeve, C. D. C. (1989) *Socrates in the Apology*. Indianapolis.

Reinelt, J. and Roach, J., eds. (1992) *Critical Theory and Performance.* Ann Arbor.
Reiner, E. (1983) *Die Rituelle Totenklage bei den Griechen.* Tübingen.
Reitzensten, R. (1893) *Epigramm und Skolion.* Giessen. Reprint, 1970. Hildesheim.
Rhodes, P. J. (1972) *The Athenian Boule* (revised edn 1985). Oxford.
Rhodes, P. J. (1979) 'ΕΙΣΑΓΓΕΛΙΑ in Athens', *JHS* 99: 103–14.
Rhodes, P. J. (1991) 'The Athenian Code of Laws, 410–399 BCE', *JHS* 111: 87–100.
Rhodes, P. J. (1981) *A Commentary on the Aristotelian* Athenaion Politeia (re-issued with addenda 1993). Oxford.
Rhodes, P. J. (1993) 'One treasurer oligarchic, many treasurers democratic?', in *Tria Lustra* eds. H. D. Jocelyn and H. Hurt: 1–3. Liverpool.
Rhodes, P. J. with Lewis, D. M. (1997) *The Decrees of the Greek States.* Oxford.
Rhodes, R. (1995) *Architecture and Meaning on the Athenian Acropolis.* Cambridge.
Richardson, N. J. (1975) 'Homeric Professors in the Age of the Sophists', *PCPS* 21: 65–81.
Richardson, R. B. (1895) 'A Sacrificial Calendar from the Epakria', *AJA* 10: 209–26 (also in *Papers of the American School of Classical Studies at Athens* 6 [1890–97] 374–91).
Richter, G. M. A. (1970) *Kouroi: Ancient Greek Youths.* London.
Richter, L. (1983) 'Die Musik der griechischen Tragödie und ihre Wandlungen unter veränderten historischen Bedingungen,' in *Die griechische Tragödie in ihrer gesellschaftlichen Funktion.* ed. H. Kuch: 115–39. Berlin.
Ridley, F. F. and Doig, A., eds. (1995) *Sleaze: Politicians, Private Interests and Public Reaction.* Oxford.
Ridley, F. F. and Thompson, B., eds. (1997) *Under the Scott-light: British Government Seen Through the Scott Report.* Oxford.
Ritchie, W. (1964) *The Authenticity of the Rhesus of Euripides.* Cambridge.
Robb, K. (1994) *Literacy and Paideia in Ancient Greece.* Oxford.
Robert, L. 1969. *Opera minora selecta: epigraphie et antiquités grecques,* vol. II. Amsterdam.
Roberts, D. H. (1987) 'Parting Words: Final Lines in Sophocles and Euripides', *Classical Quarterly* 81: 51–64.
Roberts, J. T. (1994) *Athens on Trial: the Anti-Democratic Tradition in Western Thought.* Princeton.
Robertson, N. (1990) 'The laws of Athens, 410–399 BCE: The evidence for review and publication', *JHS* 110: 43–75.
Robertson, N. (1992) *Festivals and Legends: The Formation of Greek Cities in the Light of Public Ritual.* (Phoenix, Supplementary Volume 31). Toronto.
Roccos, L. J. (1995) 'The Kanephoros and her Festival Mantle in Greek Art', *American Journal of Archaeology* 99: 641–62.
Roesch, P. (1982) *Etudes Béotiennes.* Paris.
Roesch, P. (1989) 'L'aulos et les aulètes en Béotie', in *Boiotika* ed. H. Beister and J. Buckler: 203–14. Munich.
Romer, F. E. (1983) 'When Is a Bird Not a Bird?', *TAPA* 113: 135–42.

Romm, J. (1992) *The Edges of the Earth in Ancient Thought*. Princeton.
Roos, E. (1951) *Die Tragische Orkhestrik im Zerbild der Altattischen Komödie*. Lund.
Rose, P. (1992) *Sons of the Gods, Children of Earth: Ideology and Literary Form in Ancient Greece*. Ithaca and London.
Rosen, S. (1993) *The Quarrel between Philosophie and Poetry*. New York.
Rosivach, V. (1994) *The System of Public Sacrifice in Fourth-Century Athens* (American Classical Studies, 34). Atlanta.
Rösler, W. (1986) 'Michail Bachtin und die Karnevalekultur in antiken Griechenland', *Quaderni Urbinati di Cultura Classica* 23: 25–44.
Rothwell, K. (1990) *Politics and Persuasion in Aristophanes' Ecclesiazousae*. Leiden.
Rouse, J. (1994) 'Power/Knowledge', in Gutting (1994).
Rowe, C. J. (1996) 'The *Politicus:* Structure and Form', in Gill and McCabe (1996).
Rowe, G. (1966) 'The Portrait of Aeschines in the *Oration on the Crown*', *TAPA* 97: 397–406.
Ruschenbusch, E. (1957) '*Dikastērion pantōn kurion*', *Historia* 6: 257–74.
Russell, D. and Winterbottom, M. (1972) *Ancient Literary Criticism*. Oxford.
Rutherford, I. (1994/5) 'Apollo in Ivy: the Tragic Paean', *Arion* 3.1: 112–35.
Rutherford, R. B. (1995) *The Art of Plato*. London.
Ryder, T. T. B. (1975) 'Introduction', in Saunders (1975).
Ryle, G. (1966) *Plato's Progress*. Cambridge.
Saïd, S. (1979) 'L'Assemblée des Femmes: Les femmes, l'économie et la politique', in *Aristophane et les femmes. Les Cahiers de Fontenay* 17: 33–60.
Saïd, S. (1987) 'Travestis et travestissements dans les comédies d'Aristophane' *Cahiers du groupe interdisciplinaire du théâtre antique* 3: 217–46.
Saïd, S. (1993) 'Tragic Argos', in Sommerstein, Halliwell, Henderson and Zimmermann (1993) 167–89.
Sanford, E. and Green, M. (1965) Translation of Augustine *City of God*. Cambridge, Mass.
Sansone, D. (1975) 'The Third Stasimon of the Oedipus Tyrannos', *CP* 70: 110–17.
Sansone, D. (1988) *Greek Athletics and the Genesis of Sport*. Berkeley.
Saunders, A. N. W. (1975) *Demosthenes and Aeschines* (translations of Demosthenes 18 and 19, Aeschines 2 and 3). Harmondsworth.
Saxonhouse, A. (1992) *Fear of Diversity. The Birth of Political Science in Ancient Greek Thought*. Chicago.
Sayre, K. M. (1995) *Plato's Literary Garden. How to Read Platonic Dialogue*. Notre Dame and London.
Schachter A. (1981) *Cults of Boiotia. 1. Acheloos to Hera. Bulletin of the Institute of Classical Studies* Supplement 38.1. (London).
Schadewaldt, W. (1926) *Monolog und Selbstgesprach: Untersuchungen zur Formgeschichte der griechischen Tragödie*. Berlin.
Schauenberg, K. (1958) 'Marsyas', *RömMitt* 65: 42–66.
Schauenberg, K. (1972) 'Der besorgte Marsyas', *RömMitt* 79: 317–22.
Schechner, R. (1977) *Performance Theory*. London and New York.

Schechner, R. (1988) *Performance Theory*, revised and expanded edition. London and New York.
Schechner, R. (1990) 'Magnitudes of performance', in Schechner and Appel (1990).
Schechner, R. ed. (1993) *The Future of Ritual*. London.
Schechner, R. and Appel, W., eds. (1990) *By Means of Performance*. Cambridge.
Schlegel A. W. (1846) *Sämtliche Werke V. Vorlesungen über dramatische Kunst und Literatur* vol. 1 ed. E. Böcking. Leipzig.
Schlesier, R. (1993) 'Mixtures of Masks: Maenads as Tragic Models', in Carpenter and Faraone (1993) 89–114.
Schlesinger, K. (1939) *The Greek Aulos*. London.
Schlesinger, K. (1959) *The Greek Aulos: A Study of its Mechanism and of its Relation to the Modal System of Ancient Greek Music*. London.
Schmitt Pantel, P. (1992) *La cité au banquet, histoire des repas publics dans les cités grecques* (Collection de l'école française de Rome, 157).
Schmitter, P. (1972) *Die Hellenistische Erziehung im Spiegel der New Komodia und der Fabula Palliata*. Bonn.
Schneider, R. (1996) 'After us the savage goddess: feminist performance art of explicit body staged, uneasily, across modernist dreamscapes', in Diamond (1996).
Schwyzer, E. (1923) *Dialectorum Graecorum exempla epigraphica potiora*. Leipzig.
Scodel, R. ed. (1993) *Theater and Society in the Classical World*. Ann Arbor.
Scott, W. C. (1984) *Musical Design in Aeschylean Theater*. Hanover and London.
Scott, W. C. (1996) *Musical Design in Sophoclean Theater*. Hanover and London.
Scullion, S. (1994) 'Olympian and Chthonian', *Classical Antiquity* 13: 75–119.
Seaford, R. (1977–8) 'The "Hyporchema" of Pratinas', *Maia* 29: 81–94.
Seaford, R. (1988 [1984]) *Euripides: Cyclops*. Oxford.
Seaford, R. (1994) *Reciprocity and Ritual. Homer and Tragedy in the Developing City-State* (Oxford).
Seaford, R. (1994a) Review of Rabinowitz 'Woman as Fetish', *TLS* 4787.
Seaford, R. (1995) 'Historicizing tragic ambivalence', in Goff (1995) 203–21.
Seaford, R. (1996) *Euripides: Bacchae*. Warminster.
Searle, J. (1969) *Speech Acts*. Cambridge.
Searle, J. (1977) 'Reiterating the differences', *Glyph* 1: 198–208.
Searle, J. (1983) 'Review of J. Culler *On Deconstruction*', in *New York Review of Books* Oct. 27th: 74–9.
Segal, C. (1965) 'The Tragedy of *Hippolytos*: the Waters of Ocean and the Untouched Meadow', *HSCP* 70: 117–69.
Segal, C. (1981) *Tragedy and Civilization: an Interpretation of Sophocles*. Cambridge, Mass.
Segal, C. (1988) 'Theatre, Ritual, and Commemoration in Euripides', *Hippolytus*', *Ramus* 17: 52–74, reprinted in Segal (1993) 110–35.
Segal, C. (1993) *Euripides and the Poetics of Sorrow. Art, Gender, and Commemoration in* Alcestis, Hippolytus, *and* Hecuba. Durham N.C.
Segal, C. (1994) 'The gorgon and the nightingale: the voice of female lament and Pindar's twelfth *Pythian Ode*', in Leslie C. Dunn and Nancy A. Jones, *Embodied Voices: Female Vocality in Western Culture*. Cambridge.

Segal, C. (1995) 'Perseus and the Gorgon: Pindar Pythian 12.9-12 Reconsidered' *AJP* 116: 7-17.
Segal, C. (1995a) *Sophocles' Tragic World. Divinity, Nature, Society.* Cambridge, Mass.
Segal, C. (1995b) 'Classics, Ecumenicism, and Greek Tragedy', *TAPA* 125: 1-26.
Seidensticker, B. (1979) 'Sacrificial Ritual in the *Bacchae*', in *Arktouros: Hellenic Studies presented to Bernard M. W. Knox on the occasion of his 65th birthday*, eds. G. Bowersock, W. Burkert, and M. C. J. Putnam: 181-90. Berlin and New York.
Servais, J. (1980) *Aliki*. Vol. 1. Paris.
Shapiro, H. A. (1992) 'Mousikoi Agones: Music and Poetry at the Panathenaia', in Neils (1992) 52-76.
Shear, T. L. (1984) 'The Athenian Agora: Excavations of 1980-1982', *Hesperia* 53: 1-57
Sidwell, K. (1992) 'The Argument of the Second Stasimon of the Oedipus Tyrannus', *JHS* 112: 106-22.
Sidwell, K. (1996) 'Purification and Pollution in Aeschylus' *Eumenides*'. *Classical Quarterly* 46: 44-5.
Siewert, P. (1977) 'The Ephebic Oath in Fifth-century Athens', *JHS* 97: 102-11.
Sifakis, G. (1967) *Studies in the History of Hellenistic Drama*. London.
Silk, M. S. ed. (1996) *Tragedy and the Tragic. Greek Theatre and Beyond*. Oxford.
Silverman, K. (1988) *The Acoustic Mirror: The Female Voice in Psychoanalysis and Film*. Bloomington.
Simon, E. (1983) *Festivals of Attica: an archaeological commentary*. Madison.
Simon, G. (1988) *Le Regard, l'être et l'apparence dans l'optique de l'antiquité*. Paris.
Sinclair, R. K. (1988) *Democracy and Participation in Athens*. Cambridge.
Singer, M. ed. (1959) *Traditional India: Structure and Change*. Philadelphia.
Sinos, R. (1993) 'Divine selection: epiphany and politics in Archaic Greece', in Dougherty and Kurke (1993).
Sivan, H. (1988) 'Holy Land Pilgrimage', *Classical Quarterly* 38: 528-35.
Slater, N. (unpublished) 'The vase as ventriloquist: *Kalos*-inscriptions and the Culture of Fame'.
Slater, N. (1989) 'Lekythoi in Aristophanes', *Ecclesiazousae*, *Lexis* 3: 43-51.
Slater, W. ed. (1991) *Dining in a Classical Context*. Ann Arbor.
Slings, S. R. ed. (1990) *The Poet's I in Archaic Greek Lyric*. Amsterdam.
Snyder, D. (1980) 'Plato's Symposium as Dionysiac Festival', *Quaderni Urbinati de Cultura Classica* 33: 41-56.
Snyder, J. M. (1979) 'Aulos and Kithara on the Greek Stage,' 75-95 in T. Gregory and A. Podlecki eds. *Panathenaia: Studies in Athenian Life and Thought in the Classical Age*. Kansas.
Sokolowski, F. (1955) *Lois sacrées de l'Asie Mineure*. Paris.
Sokolowski, F. (1962) *Lois sacrées des cités grecques. Supplément*. Paris.
Sokolowski, F. (1969) *Lois sacrées des cités grecques*. Paris.
Sommerstein, A. (1984) 'Aristophanes and the Demon Poverty', *CQ* 34: 314-33.

Sommerstein, A. (1987) *Aristophanes: Birds*. Warminster.
Sommerstein, A. (1988) 'Notes on Euripides' *Hippolytos*', *BICS* 35: 23-41.
Sommerstein, A. (1989) *Aeschylus: Eumenides*. Cambridge.
Sommerstein, A. (1994) *Aristophanes Thesmophoriazousai*. Warminster.
Sommerstein, A. (1997) 'The Theatre Audience, the *demos*, and the *Suppliants* of Aeschylus', in Pelling (1997) 63-80.
Sommerstein, A., Halliwell, S., Henderson, J. and Zimmermann, B., eds. (1993) *Tragedy, Comedy and the Polis*. Bari.
Sourvinou-Inwood, C. (1988) 'Further Aspects of Polis Religion', *AnnNap* 10: 259-74.
Sourvinou-Inwood, C. (1990) 'What is polis religion?', in Murray and Price (1990) 295-322.
Sourvinou-Inwood, C. (1994) 'Something to do with Athens: tragedy and ritual', in Osborne and Hornblower (1994) 269-90.
Sourvinou-Inwood, C. (1997) 'Tragedy and Religion: Constructs and Readings', in Pelling (1997) 161-86.
Sourvinou-Inwood, C. (1997a) 'Reconstructing Change: Ideology and Ritual at Eleusis', in *Inventing Ancient Culture: Historicism, Periodization and the Ancient World*, eds. M. Golden and P. Toohey. London and New York.
Sperber, D. and Wilson, D. (1986) *Relevance: Communication and Cognition*. Cambridge.
Sprague, R. K. (1973) *Plato, Laches and Charmides*, trs. with introduction and notes. Indianapolis and New York.
Stadelmann, R. (1982) 'Prozessionen', in *Lexicon der Ägyptologie* 4: 1160-3.
Stallybrass, P. and White, A. (1986) *The Politics and Poetics of Transgression*. London.
Stehle, E. (1997) *Performance and Gender in Ancient Greece*. Princeton.
Steiner, D. T. (1994) *The Tyrant's Writ: Myths and Images of Writing in Ancient Greece*. Princeton.
Steiner, W. (1995) *The Scandal of Pleasure*. Chicago.
Stephanis, I. E. (1988) ΔΙΟΝΥΣΙΑΚΟΙ ΤΕΧΝΙΤΑΙ. ΣΥΜΒΟΛΕΣ ΣΤΗΝ ΠΡΟΣΩ-ΠΟΓΡΑΦΙΑ ΤΟΥ ΘΕΑΤΡΟΥ ΚΑΙ ΤΗΣ ΜΟΥΣΙΚΗΣ ΤΩΝ ΑΡΧΑΙΩΝ ΕΛΛΗΝΩΝ. Herakleio.
Stewart, A. (1990) *Greek Sculpture: an Exploration*. Vol. 1. New Haven and London.
Stinton, T. C. W. (1990) *Collected Papers on Greek Tragedy*. Oxford.
Stoessl, F. (1987) *Die Vorgeschichte des griechischen Theaters*. Darmstadt.
Stokes, M. C. (1986) *Plato's Socratic Conversations. Drama and Dialectic in Three Dialogues*. London.
Strauss, B. (1986) *Athens after the Peloponnesian War. Class, Faction, and Policy, 404-386 BCE*. London.
Strauss, B. S. (1985) 'Ritual, Social Drama and Politics in Classical Athens', *American Journal of Ancient History* 10: 67-83.
Stumpf, H. C. (1896) 'Die pseudo-Aristotelischen Probleme über Musik', *Abhandlungen der königlichen Akademie der Wissenschaften zu Berlin* 1896, no. 3, 1-85.
Sutton, D. (1987) 'The Theatrical Families of Athens', *AJP* 108: 9-26.
Sutton, D. (1989) *Dithyrambographi Graeci*. Munich and Zurich.

Svenbro, J. (1993) *Phrasikleia: an Anthropology of Reading in Ancient Greece.* Ithaca and London.
Taaffe, L. K. (1993) *Aristophanes and Women.* London and New York.
Taillardat, J. (1965) *Les images d'Aristophane: Etudes de langue et de style,* 2nd edn. Paris.
Taplin, O. (1977) *The Stagecraft of Aeschylus: The Dramatic Use of Exits and Entrances in Greek Tragedy.* Oxford.
Taplin, O. (1993) *Comic Angels and Other Approaches to Greek Drama through Vase-painting.* Oxford.
Taplin, O. (1996) 'Comedy and the Tragic', in Silk (1996) 188–202.
Taplin, O. (1998) 'Narrative variation in vase-painting and tragedy: the example of Dirke', *Antike Kunst.*
Taviani, F. (1991) 'Views of the Performer and the Spectator', in Barba and Savarese (1991) 256–67.
Taylor, A. E. (1926) *Plato. The Man and his Work.* London.
Taylor, A. E. (1934) *Philosophical Studies.* London.
Tennenhouse, L. (1986) *Power on Display: The Politics of Shakespeare's Genres.* New York and London.
Thalheim, T. (1901) *Lysiae orationes.* Leipzig.
Thalmann, J.-P. (1980) 'Recherches aux Thermopyles', *Bulletin de Correspondance Hellénique* 104: 757–60.
Thomas, R. (1992) *Literacy and Orality in Ancient Greece.* Cambridge.
Thomas, R. (1994) 'Law and the Lawgiver in Athenian Democracy', in Osborne and Hornblower (1994).
Thomas, R. (1995/1996) 'Written in stone? Liberty, equality, orality and the codification of law', *BICS* 40 (1995), reprinted in Foxhall and Lewis (1996) 9–31.
Thompson, H. A. and R. E. Wycherley (1972) *The Athenian Agora, XIV: The Agora of Athens.* Princeton.
Thür, G. (1995) 'Die athenischen Geschworenengerichte – eine Sackgass?', in Eder (1995).
Tigerstedt, E. N. (1965) *The Legend of Sparta in Classical Antiquity.* Vol. 1. Uppsala.
Todd, S. C. (1990) 'The purpose of evidence in Athenian Courts', in Cartledge, Millett and Todd (1990) 19–39.
Todd, S. C. (1993) *The Shape of Athenian Law.* Oxford.
Todd, S. C. (1996) 'Lysias *Against Nikomakhos*: The Fate of the Expert in Athenian Law', in Foxhall and Lewis (1996).
Todd, S. C. and Millett, P. (1990) 'Law, Society and Athens', in Cartledge, Millett and Todd (1990) 1–18.
Todorov, T. (1984) *Mikhail Bakhtin: The Dialogic Principle,* tr. W. Godzich. Manchester.
Too, Y. L. (1995) *The Rhetoric of Identity in Isocrates: Text, Power, Pedagogy.* Cambridge.
Trendall, A. D. (1967) *The Red-Figured Vases of Lucania, Campania and Sicily.* Oxford.
Trendall, A. D. (1986) 'Two Apulian calyx-kraters with representations of Amphion and Zethos' in Brijder, Drukker and Neeft (1986) 157–66.

Trendall, A. D. (1988) 'Masks on Apulian Red-Figured Vases', in Betts, Hooker and Green (1988) 137–54.
Trendall, A. D. (1991) 'Farce and tragedy in South Italian vase-painting', in *Looking at Greek Vases* eds. T. Rasmussen and N. Spivey: 151–82. Cambridge.
Trevett, J. (1992) *Apollodoros the Son of Pasion*. Oxford.
Tschiedel, Hans J. (1984) 'Aristophanes und Euripides. Zur Herkunft und Absicht der Weiberkomödien', *Gräzer Beitrage* 11: 29–49.
Turner, V. (1967) *The Forest of Symbols*. Ithaca.
Turner, V. (1969) *The Ritual Process*. Chicago.
Turner, V. (1974) *Dramas, Fields and Metaphors*. Ithaca.
Turner, V. (1982) *From Ritual to Theatre*. New York.
Turner, V. (1990) 'Are there universals of performance in myth, ritual, and drama?', in Schechner and Appel (1990).
Tyrrell, W. (1984) *Amazons: A Study in Athenian Mythmaking*. Baltimore.
Uhlig, G. ed. (1983) *Dionysii Thracis Ars Grammatica* (= *Grammatici Graeci* Part 1 vol. 1) Leipzig.
Usher, S. (1965) 'Individual Characterization in Lysias', *Eranos* 63: 99–119.
Usher, S. (1976) 'Lysias and his Clients', *GRBS* 17: 31–40.
Usher, S. and Edwards, M. (1985) *Greek Orators 1: Antiphon and Lysias*. Warminster.
Ussher, R. G. (1960) *The Characters of Theophrastus*. London.
Ussher, R. G. (1973) *Aristophanes: Ecclesiazousae*. Oxford
Vahlen, J. (1903) *Ennianae Poesis Reliquiae*. Leipzig.
Valavanis, P. 1991. 'Τήνελλα Καλλίνικε: Prozessionen von Panathenäensiegern auf der Akropolis', *AA*: 487–98.
Valesio, P. (1980) *Novantiqua: Rhetorics as a Contemporary Theory*. Bloomington.
Van der Valk, M. H. (1964) *Research on the Text and Scholia of the Iliad*. Vol. II. Leiden.
Van Effenterre, H. and van Effenterre, M. (1994) 'Ecrire sur les murs', in *Rechtskodifizierung und soziale Normen im interkulturellen Vergleich*, ed. H.-J. Gehrke. Tübingen.
Van Gennep, A. (1960) *The Rites of Passage*, tr. M. Vizedom and G. Caffee. London.
Van Straten, F. T. (1992) 'Votives and Votaries in Greek Sanctuaries', in *Le Sanctuaire grec*. Entretiens sur l' antiquité classique 37: 247–90.
Van Straten, F. T. (1995) Hiera Kala: *Images of Animal Sacrifice in Archaic and Classical Greece*. Religions in the Graeco-Roman World 127. Leiden, New York, and Cologne.
Vegetti, M. (1988) 'Dans l'ombre de Thoth. Dynamiques de l'écriture chez Platon', in Detienne (1988).
Vegetti, M. (1992) *Introduzione alle culture antiche III. L'esperienza religiosa antica*. Turin.
Vernant, J.-P. (1980) *Myth and Society in Ancient Greece*, trans. J. Lloyd. Brighton.
Vernant, J.-P. (1985) *La mort dans les yeux*. Paris.
Vernant, J.-P. and Vidal-Naquet P. (1972) *Mythe et tragédie en Grèce ancienne*. Paris.

Vernant, J.-P. and Vidal-Naquet, P. (1988) *Myth and Tragedy in Ancient Greece*, tr. Janet Lloyd. New York.
Versnel, H. (1981) *Faith, Hope and Worship. Aspects of Religious Mentality in the Ancient World.* Leiden.
Versnel, H. (1987) 'Greek Myth and Ritual: The Case of Kronos', in Bremmer (1987).
Versnel, H. (1994) *Inconsistencies in Greek and Roman Religion.* Vol. II. Leiden.
Vickers, B. (1988) *In Defence of Rhetoric.* Oxford.
Vidal-Naquet, P. (1979) 'Preface, Aristophane et les femmes', *Les Cahiers de Fontenay* 17: 5–6.
Vidal-Naquet, P. (1984) 'La Société platonicienne des dialogues', in *Aux origines de l'Hellénisme. La cîte et la Grèce. Hommage à H. van Effenterre.* Paris.
Vidal-Naquet, P. (1986) *The Black Hunter: Forms of Thought and Forms of Society in the Greek World.* Princeton.
Vidal-Naquet, P. (1992) 'Note sur la place et le statut des étrangers dans la tragédie grecque', in Lonis (1992) 297–313.
von Möllendorf, P. (1995) *Grundlagen einer Ästhetik der Alten Komödie.* Tübingen.
von Reden, S. (1995) *Exchange in Ancient Greece.* London.
von Reden, S. (1997) 'Money, Law and Exchange: Coinage in the Greek Polis', *JHS* 117: 154–76.
Vos, M. F. (1986) 'Aulodic and Auletic Contests', 122–130 in Brijder, Drukker and Neeft (1986) Amsterdam.
Wachter, R. (1991) 'The Inscriptions on the François Vase', *Museum Helveticum* 48: 86–113.
Walkowitz, J. (1980) *Prostitution and Victorian Society.* Cambridge.
Wallace, R. W. (1994) 'Private Lives and Public Enemies: Freedom of Thought in Classical Athens', in Boegehold and Scafuro (1994).
Wallace, R. W. (1995) 'Speech, Song and Text, Public and Private. Evolutions in Communications Media and Fora in Fourth Century Athens', in Eder (1995) 199–218.
Wallace, R. W. and MacLachlan, B., eds. (1991) *Harmonia Mundi: Musica e Filosofia nell' Antichità. Biblioteca di Quaderni Urbinati di Cultura Classica 5.* Rome.
Wankel, H. (1976) *Demosthenes: Rede für Ktesiphon über dem Kraus.* Heidelberg.
Webster, T. B. L. (1967) *The Tragedies of Euripides.* London.
Webster, T. B. L. (1970) *The Greek Chorus.* London.
Webster, T. B. L. (1972) *Potter and Patron in Classical Athens.* London.
Weis, A. (1992) 'Marsyas', *LIMC* VI.
West, M. L. (1966) *Hesiod. Theogony.* Oxford.
West, M. L. (1987) *Introduction to Greek Metre.* Oxford.
West, M. L. (1987a) *Euripides' Orestes.* Warminster.
West, M. L. (1990) *Studies in Aeschylus.* Beiträge zur Altertumskunde 1. Stuttgart.
West, M. L. (1992) *Ancient Greek Music.* Oxford.
West, M. L. (1992a) 'Analecta Musica', *ZPE* 92: 1–54.
West, W. C. (1989) 'The Public Archives in Fourth-Century Athens', *GRBS* 30: 529–43.

Whitehead, D. (1983) 'Competitive Outlay and Community Profit', *Classica et Medievalia* 34: 55–74.
Whitehead, D. (1986) *The Demes of Attica*. Princeton.
Whitehead, D. (1993) 'Cardinal Virtues. The Language of Public Approbation at Athens', *Classica et Medievalia* 44: 37–75.
Wilamowitz, U. (1932) *Der Glaube der Hellenen*, 2 vols. Berlin.
Wiles, D. (1997) *Tragedy at Athens*. Cambridge.
Wilkins, J. (1993) *Euripides: Heraclidae*. Oxford.
Williams, L. (1993) 'A provoking agent: the pornography and performance art of Annie Sprinkle', in Gibson and Gibson (1993).
Willink, C. (1989) 'The Reunion Duo in Euripides' *Helen*', *CQ* 39: 45–69.
Wilson, P. J. (1991) 'Demosthenes 21 (*Against Meidias*): Democratic Abuse', *PCPS* 37: 164–95.
Wilson, P. J. (1996) 'Tragic Rhetoric: the Use of Tragedy and the Tragic in the Fourth Century', in Silk (1996) 310–31.
Wilson, P. J. (1997) 'Leading the Tragic *Khoros*', in Pelling (1997) 81–108.
Wilson, P. J. (forthcoming) *Choregia*. Cambridge.
Wilson, P. J. and Taplin, O. (1993) 'The "Aetiology" of Tragedy in the Oresteia', *PCPS* 39: 169–180.
Winkler, J. J. (1990) *The Constraints of Desire: the Anthropology of Sex and Gender in Ancient Greece*, New York/London.
Winkler, J. J. (1990a) 'Laying Down the Law: the Oversight of Men's Sexual Behaviour in Classical Athens', in Halperin, Winkler and Zeitlin (1990) 171–209.
Winkler, J. J. (1990b) 'The Ephebes' Song: *Tragōdia* and the *Polis*', in Winkler and Zeitlin (1990) 20–62.
Winnington-Ingram, R. P. (1963) *Aristidis Quintiliani de Musica Libri Tres*. Leipzig.
Wœrn, I. (1960) 'Greek Lullabies', *Eranos* 58: 1–8.
Worthington, I. ed. (1994) *Persuasion: Greek Rhetoric in Action*. London and New York.
Young, J. (1993) *Holocaust Memorials and Meaning*. New Haven.
Yunis, H. (1996) *Taming Democracy: Models of Political Rhetoric in Classical Athens*. Ithaca and London.
Zanker, P. (1996) *The Mask of Socrates: The Image of the Intellectual in Antiquity*, tr. A. Shapiro. Berkeley.
Zarilli, P. (1986) 'Towards a Definition of Performance Studies I and II', *Theatre Journal* 38: 372–6; 493–6.
Zeitlin, F. I. (1978 [1995]) 'The Dynamics of Misogyny: Myth and Mythmaking in the *Oresteia*', *Arethusa* 11: 149–84. (Also in *Women in the Ancient World: The Arethusa Papers*, ed. J. Peradotto and J. P. Sullivan (Albany, N.Y.) 1984).
Zeitlin, F. I. (1981) 'Travesties of Gender and Genre in Aristophanes' *Thesmophoriazousae*', in *Reflections of Women in Antiquity*, ed. Helen Foley, 169–217. [Revised in Zeitlin 1995.]
Zeitlin, F. I. (1985) 'The Power of Aphrodite: Eros and the Boundaries of Self in the *Hippolytus*', in Burian (1985) 52–110 and 198–207, reprinted in Zeitlin (1995) 219–84.

Zeitlin, F. I. (1990) 'Thebes: Theater of Self and Society in Athenian Drama', in Winkler and Zeitlin (1990) 130–67.
Zeitlin, F. I. (1993) 'Staging Dionysus between Thebes and Athens', in Carpenter and Faraone (1993) 147–82.
Zeitlin, F. I. (1995) *Playing the Other: Gender and Society in Classical Greek Literature*. Chicago.
Zeitlin, F. I. (1995a) 'Art, memory, and *kleos* in Euripides', *Iphigeneia In Aulis*', in Goff (1995).
Ziehen, L. (1934) 'Theoria', in *RE* 5.A2: 2228–33.
Zimmermann, B. (1992) *Dithyrambos: Geschichte einer Gattung*. Göttingen.

Index

abuse, 361, 364; in law-courts, 156-60
Academy, 325
acclamations, on vases, 359-73; on buildings and rocks, 359-60
Achilles, 251-4, 324
Acropolis, at Athens, 21, 25, 60-2, 78 n.73, 300, 304, 321, 325, 328, 330-1, 334, 335, 336 n.49, 346-7, 357, 359
actors, status of, 23, 161; manliness of, 113; famous individual, 35; singing by, 26, 27, 102-3; as virtuoso performers, 103-4, 113, 121; separation from spectators, 125; in public life, 154-66, 225
Adonis, 333
adultery, 323
Agathon, 37, 42, 89
age, 246-7, 274, 276, 288, 361
agōn, 2-3, 8, 25, 168
agora, essential feature of city, 34-5; at Athens, 25, 300, 325, 331, 346
Agrai, 329
Agyrrhios, 169
Aigai, 42
Aischines, 8, 22; as actor, 37; attacked by Demosthenes, 210-15, 224, 228-9, 250; on Demosthenes, 86; 154; (1) *Against Timarchus*, 155, 213, 231-2; 240 n.26, 241-56, 342; (2) *False Embassy*, 206-7, 249; (3) *Against Ktesiphon*, 154-5, 163-4, 210, 215-16, 246, 247 n.56, 256 n.89, 355. *See also* Demosthenes
Aischylos, 2, 67, 150; in Sicily 41; on *aulos*, 69; which characters, sing in, 108-9, 112, 118-19, 122; *Oresteia*, 172, 190-4; *Agamemnon*, 115, 187 n.43; *Choephoroe*, 109; *Eumenides* 40, 49, 52, 67, 115, 191-3, 306-7; *Bassarai*, 254; *Myrmidons*, 254; *Persians*, 52, 96-7, 100, 117, 118-19, 122; *Seven Against Thebes*, 50; *Suppliants*, 50, 52, 118-19
Alexander of Pherae, 116

Alexander, the Great, 351
Aliki, Thasos, 360
Alkibiades, 234, 351; and *aulos*, 59, 82, 87-91
Alkman, 43, 131
amazons, 195
ambassadors, 9, 158
amendments, to decrees, 342, 344, 346, 351, 352-3, 354
Amphiktyony, 349
Anacreon, 24
anapaests, 106, 115-16, 139, 147
Anaximenes, *Ars Rhetorica*, 209-11
Andocides, (i) *On the Mysteries* 228-9; (iv) Against Alkibiades, 325
andreia, 267-70, 275-7
apate, see deceit
Apatouria, 329 n.29
Apemantos, of Thasos, 352
Apollo, and *aulos* 88, 93; singing by, 111
Apollodorus, 221-6
apotheosis, 313-14
Apulia, vases from 39-41, 55
Archelaos, king of Macedon, 351; *see also* Euripides, *Archelaos*
archives, at Athens, 346
Areopagos, 307-8, 346 n.13, 357; *see also* Aischylos, *Eumenides*
Aristides Quintilianus, 113
Aristogeiton, 251, 254
Aristophanes, 8, 12; and Athenian politics, 176; on sophists, 214; *Acharnians*, 9, 75, 79, 217, 230, 359; *Birds*, 172, 181, 191, 313-18; *Clouds*, 110, 237 n.20, 239 n.25; *Ecclesiazousai*, 167-97; *Frogs*, 50, 84, 99, 109-10, 112, 114, 170 n.13, 233, 234; *Knights*, 7, 230; *Lysistrata*, 46, 171 n.14, 177-8, 186, 190 n.53; *Pelargoi*, 255; *Ploutos*, 182, 195 n.62; *Thesmophoriazousai*, 99, 119, 171 n.14, 177-8, 186; *Wasps*, 85 n.102, 99, 106, 250, 359

410

Index

Aristotle, 231; on playing *aulos*, 82; on prose lacking *schema*, 5; on rhetoric, 216, 218; *Poetics*, 99–100, 104, 113, 128, 141; *Politics*, 92, 93–4, 109, 110–11, 185, 243 n.43; *Problems*, 96, 100, 103, 107; *Rhetoric*, 104, 120, 165 n.33, 207 n.16, 218, 219 n.53, 227, 235, 279 n.43
Aristoxenus, 104–5
Arrephoria, 335
artichokes, effect of eating, 114
assembly, at Athens, as site of performance, 1–3, 6, 239, 241, 244–8, 284, 304; parodied, 169–70, 184, 186–8, 194; language of decrees of, 341–58
Assyria, 296
astynomoi, regulating *aulētrides*, 84
Athena, and Marsyas, 59–69; and *aulos*, 88, 94; old temple of at Athens, 321; Nike, 344, 348–9; *see also* Parthenon
Athenaios, 269; on *auloi*, 62–3, 66, 86–7
Athenian Empire, 8, 133, 301; and tragedy, 121–2
athletics, 2, 5, 78, 278, 321, 355–7, 363, 367, 369
athlothetai, 355
audience, politics of membership of, 5–9
Augustine, *City of God*, 182, 193
aulētai, costume and status, 72–4, 79, 81, 82–5, 88, 90, 94; foreign origin, 58–9, 64, 78–80, 88–9; leading choros, 106
aulos, 26–7, 29, 210; at Athens, 58–95; invention, 60–1; description of, 69–70; and *tekhnē*, 67, 69; iconographic significance of, 76; 80; and sexuality, 70, 72, 83–5; Mariandynian, 117
Austin, J. L., and performance studies, 13–14

Babylonia, 296
Bacchylides, 43, 131
Bachofen, J., 189
Bakhtin, Mikhail, 11–12, 152, 289
barbarians, singing, 117–21
beards, 169–70, 186
beauty, 359–61, 367, 369
Benveniste, E., 126
body, of citizen, 24, 26–7, 64–5, 241–8, 288, 294
Brasidas, 318
Brauron, 334–5
Brauronia, 232
burial, public at Athens 21, 25, 80, 159
Butler, Judith, 14–15, 168–9

calendars, sacred, 20, 328–9, 331–2, 335, 337, 339; *see also* festivals

carnival, Bakhtin on, 11
cavalry, 301
Chalkis, 344
chorēgoi, legal regulation of, 243
choros, 21, 23, 27, 28, 38; of melic poetry, 127–8, 130, 131, 151–3; of dithyramb, 64, 68–9, 70, 75–6; of drama, 75–8, 96; role of in tragedy, 96, 125–53; contrasting with author, 150–1; contrasting with protagonist, 130, 134–5; describing action, 129, 142–3, 146, 148, 149; displaying emotions, 129, 141, 144, 147, 148; involving audience, 130, 137, 140, 147, 149; movements of, 295; self-reference of, 130–1, 135–7; use of performative language by, 126–7, 133, 135, 139–40, 141–4, 148–9, 153
citizen, rights and duties of 6–7; appropriate behaviour of, 241–56
citizenship, defined by performance, 1–8, 21–2, 25–6
city, essential features of, 34–5
Clement of Alexandria, 359
Cleon, 7, 235, 247
Codros Painter, 362
comedy, spread of, 34 n.2; travesty of epic in, 232; and democracy 167–97; *see also* Aristophanes
competition, *see agōn*, festivals
contests, *see agōn*
corruption, as political charge, 201–2
Council, 336; formulation of decrees by, 341–58
courage, *see andreia*
courting, of boys, 1; at symposium, 24; *see also* homosexuality; *kalos* inscriptions
Crary, Jonathan, on vision, 17–18
Crassus, 114
cross-dressing, 167–97, 310
crowns, 352–3, 355–6
curses, 206, 341

Damon, 92, 113, 275
dance, 178–9, 295, 321
dancing, 300; of choros, 135–6
deceit, and oratory, 28, 201–30, 280
decrees, language of, 331–58
Delia, 311
Delium, 270
Delphi, 67, 133–4, 136–7, 182, 302, 349, 357–8
Demades, comparing Athenians to *auloi*, 86
demes, 256, 300, 301, 325, 328–31, 336–40, 357; theatres in 36–7, 39, 155, 161, 164

Demeter, 333, 335; *see also* Eleusis
Demetrios Poliorketes, 318
democracy, development of, 10; and participation, 9; and elite behaviour, 23–4; and processions, 305–6; and theatre, 261–4; and tragedy, 34, 52–4; and comedy, 167–97; illuminated by performance, 1–2; modern, and spectacle, 16–17
Demosthenes, 8, 355; attacked by Aeschines, 22, 206–7, 210–16, 224; on Aeschines, 6, 154–60; on Meidias, 23; on Stephanos, 4, 220–6; (5) *On the Peace* 161–2; (18) *On the Crown*, 154–6, 158–9, 210, 256 n.89, 340; (19) *False Embassy*, 155, 157–8, 160–3, 213, 225, 229, 256 n.88; (20) *Against Leptines*, 350 n.20; (21) *Against Meidias*, 208–9; (22) *Against Androtion*, 245 n.49; (25) *Against Aristogeiton I*, 220–1; (35) *Against Lakritos*, 215; (37) *Against Pantainetos*, 225; (40) *Against Boeotus II*, 226–7; (45) *Against Stephanus I*, 220–6; (59) *Against Neaira*, 323 n.6; *see also* Aischines
desire, and *kalos* inscriptions, 360–1, 373–4; *see also* gaze; philosophy
dialogue, Platonic, 26, 28; performance of, 257–89
Diasia, 326, 329, 331
Dinarchos, 212, 340
dining rooms, 326–7, 363 n.19
Dionysia, Great, 8, 22–3, 26, 37, 47, 64, 72, 73, 75, 164, 299, 335, 354; rural 36–7, 39, 329 n.29
Dionysios of Syracuse, 35
Dionysos, 310–12; and *aulos*, 67–8; *see also* Dionysia
Dipolieia, 328
dithyramb, 61, 63–8, 70, 100
dokimasia, 246–8, 349
Douris (painter), 233 n.5
Douris (historian), on Alkibiades and *aulos*, 88–9
Draco, 242
drama, spread of 26, 27, 28, 33–57, 164
dress, in comedy, 27; *see also* cross-dressing
drunkenness, 160

eating, and the voice, 114
education, 155–6, 242–3, 246, 259, 267–72, 277–80; *see also* music
egalitarianism, of *Ekklesiazousai*, 174–7, 188
Egypt, 35, 296

eisphora, 352, 357
Eleusinion, 300
Eleusis, 334–5
enktesis, 352, 356
ephebes, 268–9, 361
Ephialtes, 346 n.13
epic poetry, travestied in comedy, 232; *see also* Homer, Homeric epic
epideixis, 2–4, 8, 21; 56, 168, 279, 283, 285–6
Epikerdes of Cyrene, 355
epiphany, divine, 313, 315–16
equality, fantasy of sexual equality, 174–5, 178
Erchia, 328, 330, 336 n.49, 338–9
Eteoboutadai, 301
Euergides Painter, 363
eukosmia, 245–6, 248, 255
Euripides, 67, 84–5; in *Thesmophoriazousai*, 178, 186; which characters sing in, 108–10, 112–19, 121; popularity of songs of, 99; plays with and without allusion to Athens, 49; and Macedonia, 41 n.26, 42, 101; in Syracuse, 42, 44, 52; in Thessaly, 42, 44–6, 48; and scenes on vases, 40–1; misogyny in, 100; *Alkestis* 45, 114, 254; *Andromache*, 45, 50, 105, 112, 121 n.119; *Andromeda*, 99, 102–3, 113; *Antiope*, 41, 51, 105; *Archelaos*, 42, 43; *Bacchae*, 44, 100, 114, 309–12; *Cyclops*, 111; *Electra*, 110, 114–15; *Erechtheus*, 49, 117; *Hekabe*, 44, 49, 100, 109, 119–20; *Helen*, 49, 50, 114, 117; *Herakleidai*, 41, 49; *Herakles*, 51; *Hippolytos*, 49, 50, 106, 112, 117–18, 121, 131, 141–9, 152, 271; *Hypsipyle*, 110 n.72, 113–14; *Ion*, 49, 50, 109; *IA*, 100, 116; *IT*, 49, 40, 117; *Medea*, 5, 49, 50, 106, 116; *Melanippe Desmotis*, 100; *Orestes*, 50, 100, 109, 112, 117, 118–19; *Phoenix*, 256; *Phoinissai*, 51, 112; *Rhesus*, 97, 108, 111; *Suppliants*, 49, 50, 52, 113; *Troades*, 44, 49, 109, 113, 116
Evagoras, of Salamis, 355
execution, public, 257
Exekias, 362
expression, facial, 4

female voice, in drama, 16
festivals, frequency of at Athens, 8, 20; performance at, 1–2; spectators at, 6; and participation, 9; competitive, 21–2, 321, 355–6; dramatic, 27; and dancing, 136; and processions, 294–5, 298, 303, 305; panhellenic, 53; *see also* Panathenaia
Foucault, Michel 16–17

Index

François vase, 362
Freud, Sigmund, and theatre, 14
funeral orations, at Athens, 9, 21, 235, 262
funerals, 294; *aulos* at, 58, 80; *see also* burial, public
funerary monuments, 187

gaze, Lacanian model of, 14; and desire, 257–61, 263; 285–7; of citizens 4–6, 220–2, 262–9, 276–7, 285, 294
gender, as performative, 14–15, 168–70; as staged, 18; stability of, 169–170
gene, 333, 336, 338–9
glossai, Homeric, 236–41, 249–56; of laws, 239–48
Goffmann, Erving, and performance studies, 13–14
gossip, 222 n.63, 227
grain, gift of to Athens, 352–3
gymnasium, 1, 3, 23–4, 26, 34–5, 258, 261, 263, 265, 266, 268, 284–5, 288, 359, 361, 365

Hagnon, 318
Harmodios, 251; 254
Hekabe, 303; *see also* Euripides, *Hekabe*
Heraclitus, 233
Herakleides, of Klazomenai, 351–2
Herakleides, of Salamis, 352–3
Herakles, 41, 45–6, 315; Attic festival of, 323
herald, 118, 156, 158, 313, 355
herm, 369
Hermai, 300
hero-cult, 45, 49
Herodotos, 3, 37, 79, 150, 296, 317
Hesiod, 2, 165, 180, 184, 234 n.8, 314; *Works and Days*, 250
Hibeh Papyrus, 113
hieropoioi, 326
Hipparchos, 304
Hippias, 304–5
Homer, 2, 67–8, 72, 165, 180; universalizing value of, 56; as *paideia* of the Greeks, 232–6; cited by orators, 26, 28, 231–2, 235–41, 249–56; performance of 22–3, 47; identified with democratic festivals, 232; *Iliad*, 24, 116, 220 n.54, 237–9, 250, 252–4, 303, 324; *Odyssey*, 324
Homeric epic, 121
Homeric Hymn to Apollo, 111, 311
homosexuality, 258, 285–7, 241–4, 247, 251–5, 359–73; and politics, 169, 178
honorific inscriptions, 342, 347–57
hoplites, and *aulos*, 80–1

horses, race, 355
hubris, 2, 244, 258
Hymettos, sanctuary of Zeus, 361
hymn, cletic, 133
Hypereides, 229, 255

Ilion, 325
initiatory cults, 155–6
inscription, of time and space, 331; *see also* calendars, sacred
inscriptions, language of, 28–9; relationship to performance, 341–58
Ioulis, 356
Isokrates, 9; on teachers of athletics, 5; (4) *Panegyrikos*, 233; (7) *Areopagiticus*, 326; (12) *Panathenaicus*, 266, 277–84; (17) *Trapezeticus*, 6

Jacobson, R., 127
Juba II, of Mauretania, 114

Kalami, Thasos, 360
Kallias of Sphettos, 354
Kallikrates, 344
kalos inscriptions, 28, 359–73
Karpathos, 348
katapugon, 361
katharsis, 14, 127 n.7, 128, 152
Kekrops, age of, 181–4, 189–93, 195–6
Kelly, Thomas, 341n.
Kerameikos, 300, 325, 365
Kithairon, 312
kithara, 61, 78, 84, 246 n.52; *see also* lyre
Kleisthenes, 336–8
Kleophrades Painter, 367
knowledge, and perception, 7–8
kolakretai, 348
koryphaios, 131, 134, 135 n.18, 139–40, 141–4, 148, 153
kottabos, 373
kouroi, 369
Kourotrophos, 334
Kritias, 82, 86, 213, 258–61, 271
Kronia, at Athens, 180, 182
Kronos, age of, 180–2, 184, 189

labour, to sound of *aulos*, 81
Lacan, Jacques, 14
lament, ritual, 113
language, of men different from that of women, 168
law suits, frequency of at Athens, 8
law-courts, 25, 284; organisation of, 177; fantasy abolition of, 174; citation of Homer in, 26, 28, 231–2, 235–41, 249–

law-courts (cont.)
  56; in *Eumenides*, 194–4; and status negotiation, 219
lawgivers, *see* Solon, Draco
laws, need to gloss, 239–48
Lenaia, 22–3, 35, 75
Leontinoi, 346 n.14
Leptines, 356
Lesbians, and music, 84
lesbiazein, sense of, 84–5, 109
Leukon, 350 n.20, 355–6
libations, 322
Linear B, 296
Little Master Cups, 363, 371
liturgies, 6, 22
locality, references to: in melic and lyric poetry, 42–3; in tragedy, 44–52; 133, 138
Lykourgos, *Against Leokrates*, 240 n.26, 250 n.66, 254 n.79
Lykomidai, 334
lyre, 76, 84, 87, 92, 105; *see also kithara*
lyric poetry, importance of singing it, 98
Lysander, 115
Lysias, (10) *Against Theomnestos*, 239; (30) *Against Nikomakhos*, 332

Maas, Paul, on song in tragedy, 108–12
Macedon, 351; performance of tragedy in, 36, 42, 44, 51, 101, 164
mageiroi, 325, 327, 331
Magnesia, on the Maiandros, 327
manhood, contests of, 2
manteis, 325
Marathon, 235
marriage, invention of, 183, 190; fantasy abolition of, 172, 176–7, 184
Marsyas, 59–69, 72, 90–1, 88, 93
masculinity, and citizen 258, 266; and political activity, 169–71, 178, 186, 191, 196; social performance of, 23
masks, 76–8, 121, 125, 129, 130, 152, 187 n.44; function of in tragedy, 55 n.57
masturbation, 363 n.22
meat, availability of 324, 326 n.16, 327–31, 333; division of in sacrifice, 322, 324, 326–31, 333
Megara, 357
Meidias, 22
Melanippides, *Marsyas*, 61, 63–7
Mentor, of Rhodes, 351
Mesogeioi, 323
Methone, 344–5
metics, 23, 300, 301, 306 n.60, 307–8, 324
military display, 3

military training, and gymnasium, 24; *see also ephebeia*
mimesis, 126 n.3, 128, 132, 149, 168, 264; Plato on, 92–3
modes of music, 92, 96
monody, 96–122
mother, status of, 188–90
mouth, of citizen, 58, 84–6, 158
Munychia, 334
museum, producing image of culture, 15
music, place of at Athens, 58–95, 149; competitions in, 22–3; and symposium, 24; in theatre, 261; and processions, 295, 301; expressing social distinctions, 96; modern reconstructions of ancient music, 97–8
Myron 60–2
mysteries, 228, 321, 334–5, 338
myth, as model for comedy, 27; on vases as evidence for tragedy, 40
Mytilene, 7, 360

Neapolis, 350–2
Nemea, 359, 360, 362
New Music 63, 119
Nikomachus (arithmetician), 104
Nikeratos, son of Nikias, 233–4, 252
Nikias, son of Nikeratos, 233, 267, 270, 272, 273–4
Nikomachos, 332

Olympia, 332
obscenity, 361; of Aristophanes, 177, 186–7
oikos, invention of, 183–4
Oiniades, of Palaiskiathos, 342, 345, 347, 350
Old Oligarch, 8, 20
Olympic games, 2, 24
omens, 322–3, 325
orator, cleverness in, 209–11, 214–18; sophistry of, 211–18; voice of, 26, 27, 28, 154–66, 224; body-language of, 247–8
oratory, at Athens, 154–66; 201–56; parodied in comedy, 168–9, self-reflexivity in, 206–7, 227–9, 231, 282
Orestes, at Delphi, 40
Orgas, Sacred, 357–8
orphans, 20, 302
Orpheus, 254
Oschophoria, 298

Paidikos' alabastra, 363
Panathenaia, 21–2, 24, 26, 63, 72, 78, 177, 232, 240 n.26, 269, 299–302, 304, 306,

Index

325, 328, 330, 331, 332–3, 335, 336 n.49, 355
Pandora, 180
panhellenism, 47, 51; and tragedy, 121
Parrhasius, 4
parrhesia, 272–3, 278
Parthenon, 21, 301 n.44, 321; sculptures of, 172, 182 n.36, 195–6, 324
Patroklos, 2, 251–4
Pausanias, 60, 302
Peisistratids, 232, 325
Peisistratos, 10, 317
performance art, 15
performance studies, review of, 11–20, 33
performance, value as a category, 1, 33; Bakhtin on politics of, 11–12; of drama, 16, 26–7, 33–57; scrutinized by comedy, 167–97
performers, see *technitai*
Pericles, 247, 267, 273; funeral speech of, 9, 21; building programme of, 25
Persia, 351
Persians, and *aulos*, 79
Phaidros of Sphettos, 354
Phanokritos, of Parion, 351–2
Phaselis, 343–4
Pheidias, 359
philia, 284–8
Philip II of Macedon, 37, 42, 111, 154–5, 161–4
philosophy, and desire, 258–64, 266, 284–8
philosophy, performance of, 28, 29
Philostratos, 86, 112 n.81
philotimia, 257–60, 267, 269–70, 274, 356
phorbeia, 70–2
phratry, 336, 338
Phrygia, and *aulos*, 61, 80, 92
Phrynichos (tragedian), 37, 118 n.109, 150
Phrynikhos (oligarch), 354–5
physiognomics, 4, 220–6, 229
Pindar, 43–4, 47, 48, 52, 68, 114, 131, 233, 254, 302 n.48, 315 n.94, 355
Piraeus, 25, 37, 257, 304, 337
Plato, 8, 231; and *theoria* 6, and gymnasium, 25; and performance of dialogue, 28, 257–89; on rhetoric, 216–17; on *philotheamones*, 7; on theatre, 38–9, 53, 55; on Homeric poems, 234; *Apology*, 234, 254 n.77, 265, 272, 276; *Charmides*, 258–61, 266, 267, 268, 271, 369; *Gorgias*, 237; *Laches*, 266–78, 284; *Laws*, 233, 261, 264, 269; *Lysis*, 262, 266, 268, 284–8; *Menexenos*, 262, 284, 346; *Phaedrus*, 217, 263, 355 n.25; *Protagoras*, 233, 235, 246 n.52; *Republic*, 92–3, 113, 171 n.15, 257, 261–3, 273 n.35; *Symposium*, 89–92, 253–5, 263; *Theaetetos*, 273 n.35
playwrights, non-Athenian, 35
pleasure, of viewing, 7
ploughing, 329
Plutarch, 114–15, 116; on *aulos*, 65, 72, 87–9
Plynteria, 335
Pnyx, 53, 347; see also assembly
poetry, popular debate about, 234; citation by orators, 235–6; see also Homer
poletai, 344, 348
Policoro (Herakleia), vases from, 41
Pollux, 158 n.16
pornography, 15
praise, 277–9, 283–5; economics of, 262; for beauty, 359–73; see also honorific inscriptions
Praxiergidai, 349
prayer, at sacrifice, 322, 325, 330, 341; in tragedy, 132–4, 141, 146; at assembly, 156
priest(ess), 326, 330, 338, 344, 348
processions (*pompai*), 21–2, 28, 177, 293–325, 333
proclamation, of honours, 354–6
proedria, 54, 353
Prometheus, 180–1
Pronomos, 39, 59, 89
property, fantasy abolition of, 172, 184
prostitution, male, 241–2, 244
Protogenes of Olbia, 354
proxeny, 347, 349, 351
Psellos, *On Tragedy*, 107 n.60
Pyanopsia, 329 n.29
Pylaia, 46
pyrrhike, 78, 269
Pythagoreans, on music, 104
Pythian games, 355
Python, 328

rhapsodes, 23, 233–4, 236, 367
Rhegion, 346 n.14
rhetoric, display of 3; formal study of, 3; theory of, 10; use of in law-courts, 25; and deception, 28; of anti-rhetoric, 201–20; see also orator, oratory
rites of passage, 12
rumour, 249–50; see also gossip

sacrifice, 22, 295, 303, 315, 316–17, 321–41; *aulos* at, 58, 79; fantasy abolition of, 176
Salamis, 235
Samians, 354

Sappho Painter, 371 n.36
Sappho, 24, 109, 314
satyr-plays, 65
satyrs, 82–3; at festivals, 21; and *aulos*, 59, 65, 71 n.56; *see also* Marsyas
schēma, 2, 4–5, 8, 168–9, 221–2, 224 n.69, 225, 247, 250
Schlegel, A. W., on choros, 125–7
sculpture, on temples, 21
Scythians, 359
Second Athenian Confederacy, 346–7
self, construction of, 9–10
servants, metre used by, 106; *see also* slaves
sexuality, comic view of female, 175, 179, 183–6
Sicily, drama in, 164
Sigeion, 349–50
silenoi, 90; *see also* satyrs
Simonides, 43, 52; on *phorbeia*, 72
singing, 23, 24, 110, 285, 295, 363; *see also* actors, song
siren, orator as, 154, 160, 163, 164
Sirens, 210, 215
Skambonidai, 328, 330
Skira, 298
slaves, 23, 177; playing *aulos*, 58, 75, 79, 81, 82–4, 88–9; singing, 160; in theatre, 53, 54; representation of in drama, 77; only sing in tragedy if freeborn, 109–10
Socrates, 4, 107, 113, 121, 182 n.36, 213, 216, 237–9, 257–77, 284–9; and *aulos*, 89–93
Solon, 297 n.23; and *theoria* 6; as performer, 10; recited by Aeschines, 158; as founder of festivals, 232; laws of, 232, 239–40, 242, 245–7, 255
song, in tragedy, 26, 27, 96–122
sophistry, overtones of, 211–18
sophists, 256
Sophokles, 315 n.94; as actor, 105; and Thessaly, 46, 48; on *aulos*, 71; which characters sing in, 108–9, 112, 117–18, 121; *Aias*, 49, 50, 117, 121; *Electra*, 115, 117; *OK*, 49, 50, 52, 112; *OT*, 132–40, 149, 109; *Philoktetes*, 46; *Trachiniai*, 46, 112, 118; *Thamyris*, 105
sophrosyne, 242, 245, 249, 259, 261
Sounion, 336 n.49
South Italy, drama in, 164
space, and procession, 297–8
Sparta, 266, 277–80, 283, 298
Spartokos, 355
spectacle, and democracy 6–8; *see also theoria*
spectator, ideal, 127–8, 130, 137, 140
Sri Lanka, 297

Stephanus, 221–6, 230
Stesichoros, 68
Stesimbrotos, 234
Stoa Poikile, 25, 359
Strato, king of Sidon, 351
surveillance, 16–17
symposium, as site of performance 1, 23–4, 26, 53, 253–5, 326, 363, 365–6, 370; *aulos* at, 58, 71 n.56, 82–4; Homeric poetry at, 233–4; singing at, 110–11, 115; democratization of, 84; material culture of, 28
Synoikia, 328, 332
synoikismos, 299, 328 n.26, 337
Syracuse, drama at, 35, 36, 42–3, 47, 51

technitai, 35, 36, 37, 38, 155, 158, 161, 164–5
Telestes, *Argo*, 66–8
Tetrapolis, Marathonian, 332, 336–7
Thasos, 350–2, 356, 360, 362
theatre, 22–3, 33; Renaissance, 16; and Greekness, 23; essential feature of city, 34–5; attendance at, 53; gender of audience, 38 and n.16, 53, 54, 171; as image of government, 168; and viewing, 294; culture of attacked by Plato, 261, 263–5, 289
theatres, spread of 36; scale of, 53–4
Thebes, 44, 47, 309–12; as setting for tragedies, 49, 50–1; and *aulos*, 59, 61, 74–5, 79, 80, 82, 87–8
Theodoros, 103–4
Theognidea, 229
Theognis, 233, 361
Theophrastos, *Characters*, 111–12, 326
theoria, 2, 5–8, 17, 168, 285, 310–11
theoric fund, 6
theoxenia, 327
Thera, 329 n.26, 359, 362
Thesmophoria, 173, 326, 334
Thespiai, 349
Thessaly, tragedy in, 42, 44–8, 50
Thirty Tyrants, 258, 304, 346 n.13, 352, 356
Thorikos, 328–31, 336 n.49, 339
Thrayboulos of Kalydon, 354–5
Thucydides, 56–7, 230, 276, 280, 318, 337, 345 n.12; on Cleon, 7, 214, 247; speeches of, 217
Timotheos, *Persians*, 119; *Scylla*, 100
tragedy, and Athenian identity, 33–4, 48–52, 121–2; and democracy, 52–4; outside Athens, 105; relationship to reality, 120; social class in, 96–7, 100; attractions of, 54–7; *auloi* of, 70; dialect

of, 52; indicators of status in, 96–7, 108–10; reperformance of in fifth century, 37
tribes, 22, 23, 64, 325–6, 332, 336, 343
tribute, paid to Athens, 8–9
triremes, *aulos* on, 58, 80–1
Turner, Victor, on rituals 12–14, 19
tyrannicides, 304; *see also* Harmodios, Aristogeiton
Tyrtaeus, marching songs of, 106

utopia, Aristophanic, 167–97

Varro, 182
vase-painting, evidence for drama, 38–9, 54; 55; evidence for sacrifice, 323
vases, inscriptions on, 359–73
Veblen, Thorsten, on leisure, 18
violence, over *aulētrides* 84; *see also hubris*
voice, of actors/orators, 154–66, 224
votive offerings, 303

walking, style of, 4, 221–3, 225
warfare, 24–5, 267–9

wedding, 53, 294, 314–16; *aulos* at, 58, 70
wine, competition to drink, 20
witchcraft, of orator, 211–13
witnesses, poets as, 249–50
women, as *aulos* players, 71 n.56, 79, 82–4, 88–90; of tragic choros, 127–8, 130, 132, 141–8; tragic monodies by, 112–16, 121; using anapaests, 115–16; and funerals, 80, 100; in processions, 324; and sacrifice, 322 n.5, 323, 333, 334–5; in theatre, 38 and n.16, 53, 54, 171; political conservatism of, 172–3, 179; political disempowerment of, 182–3, 189; sexual behaviour of, 175, 179, 183–6, 189–90; singing at symposia, 160; masquerading as men, 167–97

Xenophon, on Socrates, 4; *Hiero*, 7, 8; *Hipparch.*, 300; *Memorabilia*, 182, 237–9, 268; *Symposion*, 107, 111, 233

Zeus, portrayal of, 110–11; statue of at Olympia, 359

Lightning Source UK Ltd.
Milton Keynes UK
UKOW04f0150240717
305912UK00001B/28/P

9 780521 604314